ACCIDENT PRONENESS

*Research in the occurrence, causation, and
prevention of road accidents*

By

LYNETTE SHAW, B.Sc. (Rand)
Industrial Psychological Services, Johannesburg

and

HERBERT S. SICHEL, D.Sc. (Rand)
Operational Research Bureau, Johannesburg

With a Foreword by
H. J. EYSENCK

D1304093

PERGAMON PRESS
Oxford · New York · Toronto · Sydney
Braunschweig

Pergamon Press Ltd., Headington Hill Hall, Oxford

Pergamon Press Inc., Maxwell House, Fairview Park, Elmsford,
New York 10523

Pergamon of Canada Ltd., 207 Queen's Quay West, Toronto 1

Pergamon Press (Aust.) Pty. Ltd., 19a Boundary Street,
Rushcutters Bay, N.S.W. 2011, Australia

Vieweg & Sohn GmbH, Burgplatz 1, Braunschweig

First edition 1971

Library of Congress Catalog Card No. 73–105137

Printed in Hungary

08 006916 9

To

T. H. FRITH

Managing Director of Public Utility Transport Corporation,
and the Staff, Past and Present,
of Industrial Psychological Services
and the Operational Research Bureau

CONTENTS

**SECTION II NEW STATISTICAL TECHNIQUES FOR THE EVALUA-
TION OF THE CONCEPT OF ACCIDENT PRONENESS,
BY H. S. SICHEL**

FOREWORD

THIS is an important book, dealing with a topic of obvious social interest; but it is also relevant to many academic and theoretical issues and disputes. The concept of accident proneness has had a chequered career, from the early British work whose high scientific standard has been universally acknowledged, through a period when the concept was extended beyond the sound basis which had been laid, to a period of reaction when doubt was thrown on the very existence of such a notion. This book examines in detail the arguments brought forward by the proponents of both sides, and, more importantly, studies in detail the facts and figures quoted in support; this critical examination has been long overdue, and is carried out with such good sense, such absence of partisan bias, and such modesty that the conclusions are likely to be very widely accepted.

These conclusions, which point unmistakably to the existence of personality-related behaviour patterns which make people differentially prone to traffic accidents, are immeasurably strengthened by the long-continued experimental work in this field carried out by the authors; indeed, it is this experimental work which justifies the inclusion of their book in this series. Most, if not all, of the preceding studies have been statistical in nature, making use of existing data often collected for other purposes; these studies have almost universally suffered from certain weaknesses which even the most expert statistical treatment cannot cure—inaccuracies of recording, marked selectivity of data, wide differences in exposure, accident-generated interference with future driving (through death, disqualification, prison, etc.), and many others enumerated by the authors. Here, almost for the first time, we have an account of experimental procedures in which all these troublesome variables have been properly controlled, and where in addition independent variables have been manipulated to produce changes—predictable and in fact predicted changes—in the dependent variable, in this case the number of accidents observed. It is gratifying to an experimentalist to see how much clearer the picture becomes when such control is introduced—even though there is no change in the general outline of the picture. To be able to exclude drivers on the basis of certain test scores, or to dismiss drivers on the basis of their accident records and then study the effect of this on the number of accidents, is far more informative than a mere statistical study involving much larger numbers of units, but in which there is no control whatever over their behaviour, exposure, or even continued existence!

The book makes it clear that much of the controversy about the existence of accident proneness has been purely semantic. For me to say that cheese is good while you say that it is bad may seem to provide grounds for controversy, but translate these statements into: I like cheese and you don't, and the two statements can be seen both to be true and logically independent. Much the same has happened in this field too. Accident proneness can be defined in many different ways, and to deny its existence at one level does not necessarily contradict someone else's affirmation at another level. Thus critics have often denied the existence of accident proneness in its widest meaning, i.e. that some individuals are more prone than others to *all* types of accidents, or in its most inclusive form, i.e. all or most accidents are due to a small group of people. Both statements are so obviously wrong that one suspects they are just men of straw, put up to gain a semantic victory by knocking them down. There is no reason to expect that the baby who inadvertently swallows poison is more prone than other babies to become a hit-and-run driver, or that a woman who accidentally gets burned when bending over the oven will run her car into a wall at 100 miles an hour. Nor is it necessary to specify that only accident-prone drivers have accidents, and are thus responsible for all accidents; a much more likely and widely accepted hypothesis would be that those personal qualities related to accident proneness are normally distributed in the population, with most people being neither particularly prone to accidents, nor particularly safe, but with a "tail" of very safe drivers on one side, and of very unsafe drivers on the other. Extreme claims have never been made by reputable investigators, to my knowledge, and their refutation is irrelevant to the main theme of this book.

The hypothesis here examined may be put in a wider and in a more specific manner. In its wide form it asserts that the general set of automobile drivers can be subdivided into sub-sets which, when equated for exposure to different amounts and kinds of traffic, show different patterns of accidents, either by number, or kind, or both. These sub-sets may be formed in many ways; it is widely known that drivers over 30 years are less likely to have accidents than drivers under 30, that men are more likely than women to have accidents, that working-class subjects are more likely than middle-class drivers to suffer in this way, and that highly trained drivers are less likely to do so than poorly trained ones. These findings have been replicated so often, and in so many countries, that few experts would doubt that they represented tangible evidence for the concept of accident proneness in the field of automobile driving.

A more specific hypothesis relates to the existence of another sub-set of drivers characterized by certain personality features which are supposed to make them more likely to drive in a dangerous manner likely to lead to accidents. It is this hypothesis which has been regarded with much suspicion lately, and there is no doubt that in this general form it is difficult to disprove—the possibility of disproof being, according to Popper, the essence of scientific theory. One of the main contributions of this book is that it succeeds in making this hypothesis more concrete, and adduces very strong evidence in favour of this more concrete hypothesis. Future work will be much facilitated by having a clearer statement and a more realistic framework for the testing of this personality theory of accident proneness.

The book suggests that much of the current disbelief in the value of the hypothesis of accident proneness is due to the behaviouristic tenet of the specificity of conduct. Thorndike long ago expressed this belief that "there are no broad, general traits of personality, no general and consistent forms of conduct which, if they existed, would make for consistency of behaviour and stability of personality, but only independent and specific stimulus–response bonds or habits", and many behaviourists (but by no means all) accept some such statement. There are many experimental reasons for regarding this belief as oversimplified and outdated; within the S–R framework, for instance, stimulus- and response-generalization afford well-recognized and widely studied bases for consistency and broadening of specific S–R bonds. But even on a simple Thorndikean specificity theory the concept of accident proneness cannot be dismissed so simply. Let us assume that there are 1000 simple S–R bonds or habits involved in safe driving, and let us also assume that the probability of each of these habits being in the direction of safety is 0·5. (The actual numerical values are quite arbitrary, of course, and so is the either/or nature of these hypothesized habits; any other assumptions would lead to the same conclusions.) Let us also assume that these habits are distributed randomly over the whole driving population (or else that they are weighted by age, sex, experience, etc.); the result will be some form of binomial distribution (either over the whole driving population, or within each sub-set according to age, sex, etc.) in which most people will have safe and unsafe habits pretty well balanced out, but where some people have a majority of safe habits, others a majority of unsafe habits. Extremes along this curve, therefore, would give us our accident-prone drivers at the one end, and our exceptionally safe drivers at the other. And as habits are presumed to be permanent (unless specially extinguished by appropriate experimental procedures) we would here have a good theoretical substratum for our notion of traffic accident proneness.

I am not suggesting that this is a true or even a reasonable account of the origin of accident proneness; I am merely saying that psychological presuppositions and theoretical beliefs in a "specificity" position do not contraindicate the findings reported in this book; these are just as compatible with a specificity theory as they are with a trait theory of personality. The point is an important one which to my knowledge has not been made before; it suggests that Thorndike was wrong in drawing the conclusions he did from his own postulates. However specific the habits, chance distribution will lead to concatenations of similar and related habits in some people in whom consistency and generality of conduct should then be observable.

The argument just presented suggests that it might be possible to identify some of these specific habits and link them with quite specific types of accident. An illustration of how this can be done is the important work of Paul Babarik on automobile accidents and driver reaction patterns (*J. Appl. Psychol.*, 1968, **52,** 49–54). It is well known that in spite of theoretical expectation, reaction time measurement has never shown much (if any) relation to accident proneness. Babarik argued that some drivers are run into from behind because they react slowly to visual stimuli (initiate responses late), but that once the reaction is begun it is carried out exceptionally fast; he called this the desynchronizing reaction pattern (DRP). He submitted a number of taxicab drivers to a laboratory test in which he measured both the time to react to a stimulus and also the speed of the resulting movement. Comparing the types of accidents of these drivers with their reaction-time patterns, he found very strong relations between a pattern of driving behaviour consisting of many accidents of the "run into from behind" type, and DRP behaviour on the laboratory apparatus. Such specific relations can easily get lost in too general an approach to the problem of accident proneness, and the study suggests the importance of quite specific hypotheses relating to quite specific types of accident. Such studies complement, but they do not replace, the wider implications of personal determinants of accident proneness; they do suggest, however, that specificity theories may still have something to teach us if they are understood in the proper spirit, and not used on *a priori* grounds to suppress other types of research.

The notion of accident proneness is often played down because it is alleged that it implies a kind of therapeutic nihilism—if people have accidents because of some fore-ordained fault within themselves, then nothing can be done about it. This book makes it clear that this is quite an erroneous notion; strict disciplinary action is shown to have a most salutary effect on most if not all drivers. If we think of accident proneness in terms of a normal curve of distribution, then we might conceive of the effects of tightening up discipline as shifting the whole curve towards a safer, less dangerous level of driving. Indeed, it is the belief that accidents are indeed completely "accidental", unrelated to human faults and basic personality traits, which encourages therapeutic nihilism, and which would result in a relaxing of the rigid discipline which alone can prevent the rapid increase in automobile accidents otherwise inevitable. British readers will remember the almost miraculous effect the introduction of the breathalyser test had on accident figures. There is little doubt that rigid rules, strictly enforced, have a most powerful effect on all but a handful of drivers—and these would soon be eliminated altogether through withdrawal of licences. The work here described furnishes us with a firm foundation on which to build up a proper system of rules and restraints for the accident-prone driver.

This book, then, is an important contribution to an important field. It is written, however, in a style which should make it understandable (and even enjoyable) to more than the psychological experts to whom it is addressed in the first place. A sprightly style should not disguise the fundamental scholarliness of the approach, but it will no doubt be appreciated by all those who are professionally concerned with traffic safety, or just interested, for one reason or another, in this field. Even statistical arguments can be made understandable (if not enjoyable!) by non-statisticians, particularly when related to logical considerations and flavoured with a commodity sometimes missing in writings on this subject, to wit, common sense. Occasional autobiographical remarks help to show the reader how certain steps in the development of the research programme were initiated, and add to the general interest of the account of what will widely be regarded as an outstanding experiment in accident causation and prevention.

H. J. EYSENCK, Ph.D., D.Sc.

Institute of Psychiatry
University of London

ACKNOWLEDGEMENTS

A BOOK of this nature, which endeavours to cover the history of the thinking on accident proneness in several continents, would never have been possible without the co-operation of research workers in many different countries. This co-operation has been so willingly given that I would like to take this opportunity to thank the many people who went out of their way to provide information—often at the cost of much time and trouble. I am particularly grateful to Aart van der Burgh of Utrecht and Wolfgang Böcher of Cologne, not only for providing statements of their personal views but for scouring Europe in search of material (and am only sorry that translation difficulties have prevented me from making use of all the material they provided); to Ron Coppin and Ray Peck of the California Department of Motor Vehicles for their personal contribution and their many constructive suggestions; to Sauli Hakkinen of Helsinki, Günter Schubert of Cologne, Garth Arbous and John Kerrich of Johannesburg for contributing statements of their personal views.

I would like to express my gratitude to the Shell Company of South Africa and the South African Road Safety Council whose research grants enabled me to travel extensively, to obtain a wider perspective on the accident problem, and to meet so many of the people working in this field.

I wish to thank Professor A. la Grange for translating a number of continental papers; Trudy van der Merwe, Librarian of the South African Road Safety Council, for all her help in looking up references and locating publications; and also the staff of the library of the National Institute for Personnel Research.

The original research findings described in this book are based on a practical accident prevention project which has been in operation for the last fifteen years. This project has been the work of a whole team of people, all of whom have contributed immeasurably to its success. As the organizer of this project I would like to say how grateful I am to T. H. Frith, Managing Director of Public Utility Transport Corporation and Industrial Psychological Services, for his unfailing support, even in the early days of trial and error; to Jack de Ridder who suggested and designed the first African TAT and the Social Relations Test, who got the whole psychological research project off the ground, and whose interest and encouragement have made the writing of this book possible; to my co-author Herbert Sichel, who designed the time-interval accident criterion and who has acted as statistical adviser throughout; to Isabel Haden-Smith, Elise Gerber, Elizabeth Kretzschmar, Marjorie Low, Elsa Jones, Audrey Cobden, Peter Frost, and Johan Kritzinger, who between them have analysed some 7000 projective test protocols; to Don Strauss, Pat McCarthy, Raymond Mtembu, John Masilela, Jacob Molopyane, Stephen Masilela, and Moira Hokoane, who have administered the various tests and kept the accident records, and who, with all the other members of the team, have helped to process the material for publication; to Daphne Scully, Pat van Vuuren, and Sheena Ritchie, who have typed the manuscript of this book and have given me so much personal assistance.

I am also very indebted to the following bodies: Public Utility Transport Corporation for permission to use the material from the PUTCO study; The South African Road Safety Council for permission to use material from their sponsored research project on personality tests; the Ministry of Health of West Germany, the British Road Research Laboratory, the National Safety Council, the Highway Research Board and the Public Health Service of the United States, and the Motor Vehicle Department of the State of California for their assistance and for granting permission to use their research publications.

I wish to acknowledge my indebtedness to the authors and publishers who have permitted the reproduction of tables and figures and long quotations. A list of copyright holders who have agreed to such reproduction is as follows:

Harper & Row; John Wiley; W. W. Norton; Chandler Publications; C. C. Thomas; Faber & Faber; Routledge & Kegan Paul; Tavistock Publications; Oxford University Press; Columbia University Press; T. C. Willett; Scientific Researches, Finland; Harvard School of Public Health; the U.S. Government Printing Office; World Touring and Automobile Association; Association for the Aid of Crippled Children; *The Proceedings of the 1966 International Road Safety Congress, Barcelona*; *The Proceedings of the Second Congress of the International Association for Accidents and Traffic Medicine, Stockholm, 1966*; *The Proceedings of the Highway Research Board*; *The Highway Research Board Bulletin*; *Traffic Digest and Review*; *Traffic Safety*; *Traffic Safety Research Review*; *The Journal of American Insurance*; *The Journal of General Psychology*; *The Journal of Psychology*; *The American Journal of Psychiatry*; *The Journal of the American Medical Association*; *The Journal of the Royal Statistical Association*; *The American Sociological Review*; *Zeitschrift für experimentelle und angewandte Psychologie*; *Nature*; *Punch*; and the *New York Times*.

In conclusion I would like to thank the many researchers whose work has contributed to this book. I am especially grateful to Dr. H. J. Eysenck for his personal as well as his editorial assistance and encouragement, and for consenting to write the Foreword.

SECTION I

THE VALIDITY AND USEFULNESS
OF THE CONCEPT OF ACCIDENT PRONENESS

by

LYNETTE SHAW, B.Sc.

CHAPTER 1

ACCIDENT PRONENESS—FACT AND FICTION

THE study of accident proneness has been very aptly described as an attempt to give scientific backing to a common-sense notion which most people accept almost without thinking.

The man in the street definitely subscribes to the idea that certain people are far more likely to have accidents than others—and he is quite emphatic on the subject of road accidents. He will laugh at you if you suggest that accidents (except perhaps his own) are a matter of chance, and that there is no great disparity between one driver and the next. He thinks there is all the world of difference, and at the drop of a hat he will tell you just what sort of people are the ones who are the bad accident risks. And although he will probably be far too specific, and far too inclined to air his own pet theories, nevertheless his views, compared with the views of the man in the next street, and the man in the street after that, will have one major factor in common, namely the belief that certain people are indeed more likely to have accidents than others; and that these people will continue to have accidents—unless they get killed or incapacitated in the process, or some change within themselves brings about an equally radical change in their usual driving behaviour.

And who is to say that the man in the street is wrong? Apparently not the officials who handle the traffic offenders among the driving public—or the insurance companies for that matter. They seem to argue on exactly the same lines; and the idea that some people are much more susceptible to accidents, and that this susceptibility can continue for long periods, seems to play a very prominent part in their thinking.

The insurance companies seem to think that a man's past accident record is an indication of the shape of things to come—hence their reluctance to go on insuring certain people. And the traffic officials seem to consider that there are indeed people who drive so badly, or so dangerously, that they are actual or potential accident cases, and therefore a danger to the community—hence points systems designed to pick up the people with repeated traffic violations or accidents and prevent them from driving.

Yet, strangely enough, the concept of an unequal propensity for accidents, or of accident proneness, does not receive anything like the same unanimous backing from the scientists. In fact it is a subject on which, even after fifty years of research, there is still a great deal of argument, controversy and disbelief. Every aspect of the concept is still being debated and argued: so much so that it would probably be difficult to find any other subject on which so many words have been written to so little effect.

What is more, there is no sign of this controversy dying down—on the contrary, there is every sign that opinions are getting more divided and the arguments growing more acrimonious.

3

However, when my co-author and I were first invited to contribute this present volume on the subject of accident proneness, I, for one, was unaware of just how divided the scientific thinking was really becoming. Having always regarded the concept of certain people being unduly prone to accidents as a most rational one, and having had these views confirmed by every aspect of our own very practical research in South Africa, I found it very difficult to believe that anyone could seriously doubt the accident proneness concept. Argue about the finer points? Yes. But deny that people differ in their susceptibility to accidents, and maintain that accidents are largely random occurrences? No, that I did not really believe. I felt that any doubts there were about the concept were only what one might call technical ones—a sort of scientific pedantry which demanded that all the t's be crossed and all the i's be dotted before the concept could be given official scientific approval. I therefore welcomed the opportunity to join once more in the discussion, and even entertained optimistic hopes that by putting up some new evidence in support of the concept I could speed up its scientific acceptance and approval.

However, in the meantime, several things have happened which have opened my eyes somewhat. During the last year or two there has been a decided swing of the pendulum of scientific opinion on the subject of accident proneness, and the accident literature, particularly in the United States and to a lesser but still noticeable extent in Britain and other countries like Germany, has developed a marked anti-proneness bias. Apart from the appearance of a number of very critical articles and statements in various journals, two full-scale books have been published, both of which have repeatedly and emphatically condemned the validity of the proneness concept. The first one, published in England, Cresswell and Froggatt's *The Causation of Bus Driver Accidents* (1963) was primarily a description of a particular research project carried out in Northern Ireland. Its appearance therefore was not so very significant. But the second volume, published in the United States, was something different altogether. This book, *Accident Research*, by Haddon, Suchman and Klein (1964) was a major publication of some 750 pages dealing with every aspect of the human element in accidents, and intended apparently as a textbook for accident researchers in all fields. The enthusiastic reception which was given to this book, with its strong anti-proneness bias, by bodies such as the American National Safety Council, is a definite indication of the growing tendency to absolve the driver from any great degree of responsibility and to maintain instead that accidents are largely unfortunate occurrences which can happen to anyone at any time.

Difficult as it is to believe that such an attitude can have developed, nevertheless I have found, from personal experience, that this is very much the case. Having spent five months travelling through Europe and the United States talking to accident researchers, I have discovered by first-hand experience just how deeply entrenched, in some quarters, is the opposition to the proneness concept.

I did not find this attitude to be prevalent in Europe—in fact in most of the continental countries the proneness concept is accepted without question. It is accepted, on the basis of logic, backed by observation, that certain people just do have worse accident records than others, and the research tendency is to examine these people, as individuals, in order to establish just why they are having these accidents and to see what can be done about it.

In other words, the research approach is largely a clinical one and therefore is not be-devilled by the problem of statistical reliability or validity.

It is particularly in the United States that opposition to the concept is so deep-rooted. Here the whole research approach has such a strong statistical bias that every contention must be tested by statistical procedures before it can be accepted. This means the group approach as against the individual one, and the acceptance of the concept only if group data can produce evidence to support it. The stated basis of the opposition to the accident-proneness concept is the contention that this evidence has not been forthcoming. In fact the opponents of the concept maintain that not only does the group statistical evidence lend very little support to the concept, but that in many instances the evidence actually refutes it.

However, even in the United States, which is certainly the stronghold of the group statistical approach, opinions are still rather divided. In fact they range all the way from acceptance of the concept, to a very limited and guarded acceptance, to outright denial. At the one end of the scale of opinion are the psychiatrists, and those psychologists whose approach is orientated more toward clinical or "generalist" psychology. These researchers still seem to subscribe to the proneness idea. Certainly they do not think that accidents happen indiscriminately to just anybody—and some of them go so far as to say that there are a great number of people who are such inherently bad risks that they should not be driving.

At the other end of the scale are a number of statisticians, supported by those psycho-logists whose orientation is toward the earlier forms of behaviourism and the strictly experimental approach—and particularly toward a peculiarly American psychological doctrine (which seems to have no name, unless one could call it "specifism") which denies both the consistency and individuality of behaviour. These researchers are, in turn, strongly opposed to the concept, and speak of "a folklore of accident proneness" and "the universal discredit into which the subject has fallen among scientists".

In between the two groups, though still rather inclined to the "anti" side, are a number of researchers whose attitude seems to be that there is no definite proof one way or the other, but that by and large there seems very little actual evidence (by which they mean statistical evidence) to commend the proneness concept. The following sort of statement is very representative of the thinking of this group:

"It has not been convincingly demonstrated that an appreciable number of people tend to have more accidents than others under conditions of equal exposure." [McFarland, 1962.]

And in a leading article which appeared in the *New York Times* on 20 December 1964, on the occasion of the publication of Haddon's *Accident Research*, Robert Darnton quotes the opinions of leading accident research workers in the United States as follows:

"The favorite concept of psychologists in the field during the nineteen-twenties was accident-proneness, an attempt to explain why some individuals have more accidents than others. Psychologists have almost abandoned the concept now, because they have been unable to find enduring psychological traits that differentiate these unfortunate persons from others. They tend to believe that most 'accident-prone' individuals are victims of the laws of probability."*

The trend is therefore very much toward denying the proneness concept.

However, strangely enough, even the strongest opponents of the "proneness" concept do still sometimes seem to find it necessary to give it limited recognition. Haddon's book is an example of this. The main trend is definitely critical, and he and his co-authors maintain that offering accident proneness as the *explanation* why some individuals have more accidents than others "is a point that has aroused first minor and now major protest". And in discussing the Cresswell and Froggatt book on bus accidents, the authors say:

"This is but the latest evidence that the burden of proof that there are 'accident-prone' individuals must rest with those who defend the concept, since this most definitive study fails to provide evidence that such individuals exist."

However, elsewhere in the same chapter, they say:

"For one cannot claim that no cases of accident proneness exist. At the present state of knowledge we must best conclude that accident proneness as an explanation for any major proportion of repeated accidents is unwarranted but that, as a clinical phenomenon limited to some individuals, it may have some validity."

This dual thinking, which is always somewhat reminiscent of the sort of legal plea which states: "The defendant maintains that he did not do it—but if he did, it was unintentional", seems to appear quite often in the American accident research literature. It seems part and parcel of a rather strange anomaly where, although the proneness concept is widely condemned, and there is constant repetition of the belief that accident-prone repeaters (if they exist at all) are responsible for only a fraction of the accidents, nevertheless a considerable (though lessening) amount of research time and research money is still being spent on trying to develop psychological tests which will distinguish between the people who have many accidents and the people who are accident-free—to say nothing of the almost nationwide operation of points systems, the main purpose of which is to pinpoint the bad accident risks.

To an outsider these contradictions between theory and practice, let alone theory and logic, are, to say the least of it, a little odd. In fact one cannot help feeling that the amount of attention which the practical traffic officials in the United States give to accident repeaters and to traffic violators (who are presumably regarded as potential accident offenders, else why prosecute them) should sow a few doubts in *somebody's* mind—for according to widely accepted scientific theory these people are virtually non-existent, and certainly do not represent any appreciable danger to the community.

In fact one cannot help feeling that the wide discrepancy which exists between the basic thinking underlying, on the one hand, some rather untried theories, and, on the other hand, some very well-tried practices, indicates that the fault may possibly lie with the theories—and with the statistical data on which they are based.

Is it not perhaps more than likely that the traffic officials are quite right in their thinking? That accidents are very often anything but random events and that there are indeed

* © 1964 by *The New York Times*. Reprinted by permission.

such beings as accident-prone drivers, but that they are not a class all of their own, distinct in their abnormality—in fact that there is a whole spectrum of accident proneness ranging from the accident-free right up to the chronic accident repeater? That it is the *principle* underlying proneness which matters, namely the principle not only of unequal involvement in accidents but of unequal accident *potential*? That it is not just the tip of the iceberg, the multiple serious-accident offenders, whom the traffic officials are worrying about, but a much larger section of the community who, for all sorts of reasons, such as lack of driving skill, or physical defects, or personality defects, or wrong attitudes, have a *dangerous amount of accident potential*; potential which, under conditions of strict supervision is likely to manifest itself only in occasional bad driving or the occasional accident, but which would show itself far more clearly if the supervision were less strict—as is indeed demonstrated in countries other than the United States, where the driving is not nearly so disciplined and the accident rates far higher?

Nor does it seem very likely that the traffic officials are worrying about people whose weaknesses or faults are merely transitory, or about a problem which is of minor significance. They appear to consider the problem to be a serious one, and the reasoning underlying their policy of enforcement is that people do indeed differ fundamentally in their potential for accidents, just as they differ in their potential for crime, and that there are a number of basic similarities between the prevention of one and the prevention of the other.

But if, as the traffic officials seem to think, there are indeed fundamental differences between people's accident potential, how is it that the statistical evidence (derived from figures on reported accident occurrence) on which so much of the theoretical research thinking is based, does not show this up? Is it not possible that the fault may lie with the statistical evidence? That the figures which are always quoted as evidence against the concept are so incomplete, or so selective, that they do not give a true representation of the picture? That the figures on big intrastate studies, for instance, represent only the accidents involving injuries or fatalities or major property damage, and not all of those either—again just the tip of the iceberg? Or that the figures on professional drivers relate only to the more successful drivers, the men with long and continuous service, and exclude all the unsuccessful ones among whom one would expect to find the worst accident records?

And is it not also possible that there are significant shortcomings in much of the evidence (let alone theory) on which the psychological opposition to the proneness concept is based; such as the many failures to find, by means of psychological tests, enduring traits which distinguish the accident repeater from the relatively accident-free? Is it not possible, to quote Eysenck (1965), that "many of the investigations which have failed to produce positive results have been characterized by a poor choice of tests, a poor choice of problems, a poor choice of statistical methods of investigation, and a poor control over relevant variables"?

Moreover it would appear that some of these doubts as to the validity of the evidence against the proneness concept are also present in the minds of even its most severe critics. Otherwise why should they bother to mention that it is easier to find evidence of "proneness" in situations where accidents are more frequent or where accident recording is more complete? Or that there is some justification for believing that there is a relationship between accidents and social maladjustment? One has the feeling that underneath the condemnation of the proneness concept, on the basis of insufficient scientific "evidence", lies a certain amount of bewilderment as to why, for instance, so many of the studies nivolving the personality of the accident offender come up with such similarr tends. One feels that, to say the least of it, there is still a vague suspicion in the minds of even some of the critics of accident proneness that there are indeed such beings as accident-prone drivers, displaying a whole range of proneness and influencing accident rates to all sorts of degrees, but that they are so well camouflaged by the statistical and psychological "evidence" that they do not show up.

If this is indeed the case it seems to place many accident researchers rather in the position of the leopard in Kipling's *Just So Stories* whose plaint was: "I can *smell* giraffe, I can *hear* giraffe, but I can't *see* giraffe." (Although it also seems more than likely that there are a number of researchers whose credo is: "For purely ideological reasons I would prefer *not* to see giraffe.")

However, be this as it may, it is still very important to establish in some detail how all this contradictory thinking has come about. Just why is it that there is so much controversy? Why is it that the accident-proneness concept is accepted by scientists on one side of the world and rejected by scientists on the other? Why is it that if the concept is eminently acceptable to some scientists, there is still so little statistical evidence to support it?

It seems to me that unless we can examine the point of view of both sides of the argument, sort out the contradictions, and provide some detailed answers to these questions, then further discussion on the subject is futile, and that the contribution which theoretical, psychological and statistical research can make to the pressing problem of road accidents will continue to be depressingly negligible. In fact it is eminently possible that an actual retrogression will take place—if it has not already started. For it seems as though the constant belittlement by so many important and influential writers on accident research of even the basic principle underlying the proneness concept, namely that certain people are inherently worse accident risks than others, is already beginning to play a part in influencing the trend of accident-prevention policy in a country like the United States. Here the emphasis on accident prevention is swinging very noticeably away from the driver and towards the vehicle. Whereas the driver used to be regarded as Scapegoat Number 1, he is gradually being allotted the role of the innocent victim of circumstance, while the vehicle is now being groomed for the role of the villain of the piece.

For the moment this may be all very well, for there is undoubtedly much room for improvement in the safety aspects of vehicle design. But the real danger would come if the pendulum were made to swing too far; if the weight of the counsel of the accident researchers resulted in any discrediting of enforcement or even withdrawal of financial support from measures designed to discipline drivers and clamp down on traffic offenders.

An outcome like this may not be as far-fetched as it sounds. Already there is a good deal of talk in American research writings about the very doubtful value of punitive measures. There is also a good deal of talk about the doubtful relationship between accidents and traffic violations—which have even been described in a recent statistical paper (Haight, 1964) as a "schedule of actions harmless in themselves, which are supposed to 'cause' accidents"! And in the same article in the *New York Times* quoted earlier, one of the leading members of the Accident Prevention Section of the United States Health Department is quoted as saying that "law enforcement is a doubtful technique for reducing road accidents".

If this development does indeed take place it may well prove to be a most costly and retrogressive step. For in the United States, where big cities and high traffic density should, by rights, have resulted in one of the highest accident rates in the world, it is largely the work, not only of the highway engineers and the traffic controllers, but of the practical officials who discipline and control the drivers, that appears to have brought down the country's accident rate and held it at a figure which is the lowest in the world per mileage driven.

No one disputes the fact that the accident problem is a complex one, but this has not stopped the practical men from making a very good job of tackling it. And in all fairness to them one must admit they have achieved what they have achieved with very little assistance from the theoretical driver researchers. It would be a most unfortunate state of affairs if theoretical thinking, based on evidence much of which is still open to dispute, should be allowed to curtail in any way the activities of the practical officials—activities which appear to have brought about a most far-reaching and beneficial change in the whole attitude of the American driving public. It would be even more unfortunate if this sort of reaction were to spread to other countries where the need for controlling the driver is much greater.

This is why I feel that someone ought to make a determined effort to sort out the confusion in scientific thinking. I have my doubts as to whether yet another book on the subject of accident proneness will have any marked effect on entrenched opinion. Yet I feel all the more that one should be written, particularly one which is specifically aimed at reconciling theory with practice. Hence this dual volume in which I have covered the general and psychological aspects while my co-author has covered the statistical aspect.

As we feel that we would like the book to be of some use to the practical traffic officials, as well as to the research workers, I have given my section a more practical orientation than is usually given in a publication of this kind. I have also tried to write it in less technical language than is usual in a scientific work. The personal studies on which many of my co-author's and my contentions are based have been carried out on a large scale, over a long period of time, and with strict scientific "methodology"; and our findings have scientific authenticity. These findings, and those of many other researchers, are presented with scientific exactitude in certain chapters of the book; but in others which deal with the general aspects of the concept of accident proneness the presentation is less formal. It is my hope that what these chapters may lose in the way of scientific "elegance" will be compensated for by practical usefulness.

I have no intention of making this book yet another review of the accident research literature as there are a number of very comprehensive ones already available. In dealing with the literature my sole aim will be to endeavour to trace the trends of thinking on accident proneness and the developments which have influenced present attitudes, to see whether it is possible to discover the underlying reasons for the disagreements and the contradictions.

But in addition I would also like to do something more constructive, namely to put forward, with ample supporting evidence, a more moderate and flexible version of the proneness concept than is usually presented—a version which, to my mind, could account for a lot of the anomalies and bridge a number of the gaps.

However, I must reiterate that this concept is intended to refer specifically to the question of road accidents—not industrial accidents, or home accidents, or childhood accidents. In the first place I do not claim to have any specialized knowledge in these fields. And secondly I do not for one moment believe that it is justifiable to generalize from accidents in one sphere to accidents in another, and it has always struck me as most illogical that anyone should have even contemplated doing so. Because, surely, there is no justification for generalizing from one set of data to another when the circumstances are so diverse that there is even a fundamental difference in what constitutes an *accident*? Nor can one compare *situations* which make different demands on people's capabilities, or which call into play such different psychological forces, or serve such different psychological needs.

Unfortunately, however, when it comes to tracing the development of the thinking on accident proneness it is quite impossible to separate the road accident research from the research on other types of accidents. It is all too hopelessly interwoven. Not only has the thinking in one sphere influenced the thinking in the other, but figures relating to one type of accident have constantly been used to support or repudiate arguments about a completely different type of accident. In fact anyone wishing to study the road-accident proneness literature will find references to figures pertaining to everything from industrial accidents among British munition workers, to shunting accidents among South African railwaymen, to poisoning accidents among four-year-old children, to horse kicks among Prussian cavalrymen—which no doubt accounts for at least some of the confusion!

CHAPTER 2

METHODS AND APPROACHES

THE scientific study of accident proneness dates back roughly fifty years, and during that time literally thousands of papers have been written on the subject. Anyone wishing to make a serious study of proneness would be well advised to examine a number of these papers and certainly to read the reviews of the accident literature which have appeared from time to time, all of which have comprehensive bibliographies. I have listed some of the better-known reviews below and have included a brief commentary to indicate the areas they cover.

1942 (Published in the U.S.A.). DE SILVA, H. R., *Why We Have Automobile Accidents*. A very practically orientated book dealing with all aspects of the human factor in road accidents and describing a number of investigations carried out by various State Motor Vehicle Departments. Although published in 1942 it is by no means out of date.

1951 (U.S.A.). THORNDIKE, R. L., *The Human Factor in Accidents*. This publication was prepared for the U.S. Air Force but also deals with road accidents. It is a very good general account of various aspects of the proneness concept.

1951 (South Africa). ARBOUS, A. G. and KERRICH, J. E., *Accident Statistics and the Concept of Accident Proneness*. This paper is orientated towards industrial accidents but also deals with road accidents and the whole proneness concept. It consists of two sections, a general and psychological section (Arbous) and a mathematical statistical section (Kerrich). It is a comprehensive paper and an extremely well written one and is essential reading for anyone wishing to understand the concept of proneness. It examines the requisites for scientific research; gives suggestions for new lines of research; and also contains a very lucid and impartial analysis of the pros and cons of the mechanics, the possibilities, and the limitations of the statistical and the clinical approach to accident research.

1955 (U.S.A.). MCFARLAND, R. A. and MOORE, R. C., *Human Variables in Motor Vehicle Accidents*. This book contains a section on accident proneness and research developments. It also contains a most concise and easy-to-understand description of the principles underlying the traditional statistical techniques used in accident research. A new edition of this book, giving an up-to-date assessment of the accident literature is currently being prepared.

1960 (Written in Holland and published in England). WALBEEHM, T. B., *The Accident-prone Driver*. This book deals with all aspects of the human element in road accidents and is particularly noteworthy for the fact that it is one of the few publications translated into English which gives an account of the continental research work on proneness—especially the clinical research.

1964 (U.S.A.). HADDON, W., SUCHMAN, E. A. and KLEIN, D., *Accident Research*. This book presents a comprehensive description and discussion on the human factor in accidents of all kinds. It contains a chapter on accident proneness which includes long excerpts from many of the early papers on the subject—papers which are often very difficult to obtain as they are now out of print.

1967 (W. Germany). HOFFMAN, H., *Ausgewählte Internationale Bibliographie 1952–1963 zur Verkehrsmedizin*. A very comprehensive list of some 5000 papers, grouped under the various aspects of medical, psychological, and statistical road accident research.

1968 (W. Germany). BÖCHER, W., *Verkehrsmedizin und Psychologie. Sonderdruck aus Handbuch der Verkehrsmedizin*. This is a condensed account of the psychological aspects of accident research, and, as it includes international findings, is well worth studying.

In addition to the above publications, most of which are rather technical, there is another book which has recently appeared in a paper-back Penguin edition, which should prove of interest to the general reader. It should be particularly useful to the layman in whom the sight of a complicated mathematical–statistical formula usually produces feelings of either frustration or despair, for it is written in ordinary everyday language and contains no scientific obscurities.

1965 (England). EYSENCK, H. J., *Fact and Fiction in Psychology*. The book contains a chapter on accident proneness and accident research which gives a well-illustrated account of the methods which have been used and the results which they have obtained.

This selection of publications (the perusal of which should keep anyone in reading matter for the next ten years) gives a pretty good coverage of the accident-proneness literature. Unfortunately the continental work is not well represented as even the *German Handbook of Traffic Medicine* gives only the briefest of descriptions of the findings in various fields. This is unfortunate as the German scientists have done a lot of work on the clinical investigation of accident offenders; work which is not very well known to the English-speaking world.

In fact it is a great pity that there is so much isolation in our accident research thinking and that there is not more international co-operation on what is essentially a world-wide problem. Unfortunately, language difficulties often present an almost insurmountable barrier, as I know to my personal cost from my travels round the world in connection with accident research. It is extremely difficult to convey or understand technicalities in a language which is not your own, and there were many times in my conversations with the German scientists (let alone the Finns and the Japanese) when both sides realized that they had reached a hopeless impasse and just resorted to smiling at one another and exchanging papers in the hope (often unfounded) that we would be able to find someone who could translate them for us.

However, my difficulties in this sphere are by no means unique. Language problems do indeed inhibit the free interchange of ideas between one country and another, which accounts for at least one of the reasons why the thinking on a subject such as accident proneness has developed along different lines in different parts of the world. Another reason seems to be a preference for a different research approach. (According to Wal-beehm: "In Western Europe there is a tendency towards a theoretical contemplative approach whereas the Americans base their conclusions mainly on the statistical investigation.") To my mind, however, there is probably a third reason for the development of these different ways of thinking, a factor observable to anyone who has travelled, namely that the problem itself changes from one country to another; not only are accident rates much lower in some places than others, but national characteristics are inclined to demonstrate themselves in different ways in the driving behaviour of different countries. In countries like America, England, and Holland, which are relatively "conforming" countries, where people take more kindly to being disciplined, the driving behaviour is much more uniform and there is less evidence of unbridled self-expression, and therefore of undisciplined and dangerous driving with its concomitant accident potential. As a result the general accident rate is lower and the contribution which the blatantly accident-prone drivers make to national accident statistics is a relatively small one. But in other parts of the world such as, to quote a few examples, Germany, Italy, Japan, Egypt, and the emergent African States, there is a far greater tendency to unbridled self-expression—with the result that the driving behaviour seen on the roads displays everything from fierce competitiveness, to an uninhibited display of "temperament", to a preference for suicide rather than dishonour, to a fatalistic disregard for earthly perils, to a spirit of exultant and carefree emancipation. As a result a far greater proportion of the drivers have a high accident involvement, and there is much more evidence of accident repeaters—and therefore a greater readiness to accept the idea of accident proneness.

For without convincing evidence no self-respecting scientist can confidently continue to uphold a concept, however much he may feel that it should, on the grounds of logic alone, be a plausible one. And there is no doubt that accident statistics like the American ones do not usually appear to provide such evidence.

This brings us to the question of just what reliable evidence, for or against the proneness concept, has come to light in the different countries of the world—and what part this evidence has played in developing the existing differences of opinion. However, before investigating this question in any detail it would be as well to give some consideration to the concept itself, to what it means, to the sort of evidence which is necessary to support it, and to the sort of scientific investigations that should be made to provide this evidence.

Starting with the concept. Unfortunately here we run into trouble right away, for the scientific literature contains a dozen and one different definitions. The term "accident proneness" is apparently so vague and indeterminate that each research worker feels free to interpret it in his or her own particular way. Some people give it a wide and flexible interpretation like "a tendency to accidents" or even a "tendency to unsafe acts". Other people, however, hedge it in with the most rigid restrictions and say that for a person to be considered accident-prone he must be susceptible to accidents "under all circumstances" or "at all times".

It seems therefore that if we are to find any common ground between the definitions of the various research workers we will have to consider the underlying basic principles only. The most basic principle, acceded by all investigators, is that the concept of accident proneness implies *that even when exposed to the same conditions some people are inherently more likely to have accidents than others*—or, in other words, *that people differ fundamentally in their innate propensity for accidents.*

Now this is all very well, and one may agree with it or disagree with it. But in order to study it scientifically and to prove that it has validity, let alone any practical usefulness, there are a number of factors which need to be investigated.

In the first place do some people really have more accidents than others? Are these differences too great to be attributable to chance?

Are these differences largely due to differences in how much they drive or where they drive, or are they also innate personal differences between people? If you expose a number of people for the same amount of time and to the same sort of hazards will there be any significant difference between their accident rates?

Are these differences lasting? Do the same people go on having more accidents than others over long periods of time? If so, for how long? Long enough for the differences to have any practical usefulness? Long enough to designate these people as "accident-prone"?

How big are the differences? When people are exposed to much the same risk is there a very marked difference between the people with a high accident rate and the people with a low accident rate? Is the difference large enough to be important?

Are these differences mathematically measurable? Is it possible to classify people according to the degree of their accident involvement? Are the differences between them big enough and stable enough to form the basis for a reliable accident criterion for any research project on accident proneness?

What contributions do "accident-prone" people make to the total accident picture? If these people were excluded what difference would it make? Would it lower accident rates? How much? Enough to justify their exclusion?

Are the same people prone to different kinds of road accidents? To major accidents as well as minor accidents? To personal injury accidents as well as property-damage accidents? Is there any relationship between *numbers* of accidents and *types* of accidents? Which is the better measure of accident proneness—number, type, or a combination of both? Or should there be separate measures for different kinds of accidents?

What personal characteristics are associated with accident proneness? What differences are there between the people who have many accidents and the people who have few or none? In what area do you find the factors associated with high accident involvement and low accident involvement? Intelligence? Aptitudes? Physical factors like health or eyesight? Psycho-physical factors like reaction time, or movement control, or anticipation? Psychological factors like character or attitudes? Social factors like home background, childhood history, criminal record? Or, for that matter, in what combination or combinations of these factors?

Are there any tests which can determine these factors? If so, how well do they work? How accurately can they distinguish between various levels of "accident proneness"?

Can they predict future accident involvement? How good are they at predicting numbers of accidents, or types of accidents? If you were to exclude the people who failed the tests what difference would it make? How much would it reduce the accident rate? Enough to justify using these tests?

What changes are likely to take place in a person's susceptibility to accidents? Are there many temporary changes? If so do these temporary fluctuations obscure the issue or are they themselves very largely an integral part of each person's behaviour pattern and therefore part of his innate susceptibility to accidents? In other words is it one of the hallmarks of the accident-free person that his driving pattern does not vary very much, i.e. that he can exercise sufficient control to ensure that his driving is not unduly affected by his personal ups and downs? And conversely is it one of the hallmarks of the accident-prone person that his driving behaviour is inconsistent and that his susceptibility to accidents can vary from day to day according to circumstances?

Are there changes in accident susceptibility which are not just temporary day-to-day fluctuations, but which last for longer periods? Changes such as one would expect to be associated with certain diseases, or with some serious personal crisis?

Are there also certain long-term changes which alter the whole trend of a person's accident pattern? For example as people are known to change both physically and psychologically during a lifetime—some aspects changing for the better, some for the worse—what effect does this have on their accident potential? Do they, for instance, become better risks as they mature and go off again as they get older? Do you find similar changes with similar age groups or are the changes very individual?

Just how individual a matter is "accident proneness"? Is there a lot of similarity between people when it comes to the causes of their susceptibility to accidents and the way in which this manifests itself? Or are no two cases exactly alike?

Are group psychological tests suitable for accident work? Can you effectively test people in groups? Can you assess people's accident potential on the basis of a particular psychological characteristic or characteristics? Or would it be better to assess each person individually, as a composite whole, assessing his good points in relation to his bad points and giving consideration to the integration of his whole physical and psychological make-up?

Are group statistical techniques suitable for accident data? Are they sufficiently sensitive? Would it be better to use techniques which are "person-centred", i.e. where the pattern of accident involvement of each person can be examined over a number of years, and where the possibility that different people have different trends will not be obscured by grouping everyone together?

In fact are the psychological and statistical tools usually used for accident research either suitable or adequate for the job? What would happen, for instance, if scientific investiga-tions indicated that proneness does exist and that it appears to be stable enough and important enough to matter, but that it still cannot be satisfactorily pinned down—that it is too complex to be accurately predicted by any simple psychological test and too multi-dimensional to be accurately measured by any simple statistical technique? What new tools and techniques could we devise?

These are some of the essential lines of investigation which one could expect scientists to follow if they wished to make a thorough investigation of the proneness concept. To determine how far these investigations have progressed it is necessary to examine the accident literature and see what sort of research projects have been carried out and what results they have achieved.

Obviously when it comes to finding answers to most of the questions posed above, the experimental approach is the only feasible one, as the clinical approach alone cannot supply objective proof on a large enough scale. Revealing as it may be to study each individual separately, one swallow does not make a summer, and for a concept to be widely accepted and to have any practical value there must be proof that it applies to a great number of people. The clinical approach needs to be supplemented by statistical evidence. It is not surprising therefore that most of the major studies, and certainly all the best known ones, make copious use of statistical procedures. In fact it is quite impossible to understand the trend of the research on accident proneness or to follow any of the literature without at least some basic knowledge of statistical procedures and how they work.

Before embarking on a study of this research it would therefore be just as well, for the benefit of the lay reader if for nobody else, to examine a few of the usual statistical and psychological approaches to accident research and consider their advantages and their disadvantages.

The Statistical Approach

It is no wonder that the layman so often feels lost when it comes to statistics, for usually no one has taken the trouble to explain to him that his concept of the subject is not the modern concept at all and that what he thinks of as "statistics"—namely rows of figures on things like birth rates or accident fatalities—are merely statistical "data", and very partial data at that.

The term "statistics" actually means the science of handling these figures in order to reach some sort of conclusion as to what they may mean—with the emphasis very often on the word "may". For despite the fact that the layman has so many times been told (the biggest culprits here being the Press) that "statistics have proved this" or "statistics have proved that", the real truth of the matter is that statistics cannot *prove* anything. The science of statistics cannot even prove that a particular hypothesis is true or not—it can only indicate the degree of likelihood of it being true. Arbous in his excellent evaluation of the statistical approach to the investigation of accident proneness (1951) is very emphatic on this particular aspect of the subject and seems to think that it is not only the layman who labours under this misconception. He says:

> "There is regrettably a tendency in many psychologists today to forget very conveniently or unconsciously about the assumptions underlying all mathematical and statistical 'proofs', and the fact that it is never possible in any science to prove a hypothesis. The result is that very often claims are overstated, tenuous relationships are magnified to causal relationships, and possibilities become certainties as one turns over the pages of the literature."

The reality of the situation is that the science of statistics relies so much on sampling and on the theory of probability that it is actually anything but an exact science; rather it is, as Wallis (1960) puts it, "a method of making wise decisions in the face of uncertainty".

Unfortunately, however, things do not always turn out quite so well, for the wisdom of these decisions depends very much on the quality of the work that goes before. As statistics is a rapidly developing science, and as the people who dabble in it are often not really qualified to do so, it can (and unfortunately does) quite often happen that badly chosen data or faulty statistical work result in some very unjustifiable conclusions being drawn and some very unwise decisions being made. For the same reason it can, and often does happen that one set of statistical "evidence" seems to contradict completely another set of statistical "evidence"—much to the bewilderment of the unfortunate layman who is painstakingly trying to find out what it is all about.

It is against this critical, but nevertheless realistic background that one must consider the various statistical approaches to the study of accident proneness.

Firstly, there are several areas in which the phenomenon of accident proneness can be statistically studied. Usually the investigations are made in one of two specific areas, either among the general motoring public or among professional drivers—and there are definite snags in both. With the general public the main snag is the fact that data are often so incomplete as to be almost valueless. Not only is there no way of telling whether one person's exposure is indeed comparable with another person's exposure, but even the recording of the accidents is hopelessly incomplete, as usually only the accidents involving fatalities or injuries or major property damage are ever entered in the official records. And there is reason to believe that even this recording is anything but complete. In dealing with professional drivers, on the other hand, though it is much easier to obtain fuller information on exposure and accidents, here the snag is that care must be taken in generalizing too much from the results obtained because the sample is not necessarily representative of the public as a whole. In the first place, professional drivers are usually only males, and males of a certain social and economic stratum of society at that. But more important still is the fact that the sort of professional drivers who are usually investigated are the long-service ones, who are often a highly selective group.

When it comes to the actual methods used for "proneness" investigations it would probably be as well to examine the most commonly used ones in some detail. Here one finds two main lines of approach—the group approach and the individual approach.

Starting with the group approach.

Firstly, one can examine the actual number of accidents sustained by a particular group of people over a particular period of time to see whether, in fact, certain people do have more than their fair share of these accidents. For although chance can easily result in unequal distributions, one needs to know whether something other than chance is also operating. (Eysenck in his *Fact and Fiction in Psychology* (1965) gives a very apt analogy. He says that there is nothing to *stop* lightning striking twice in the same place—but if it goes on striking one is entitled to inquire why!) Comparison with the well-known Poisson distribution, which is what one could reasonably expect from chance, will indicate whether any other factors are indeed operative. It will also reveal whether the usual sort of unequal distributions encountered in accident statistics (which result in the usual sort of finding such as, for instance, only 10% of the drivers being responsible for 45% of the accidents) has any significance or not. But it is very important for accident *prevention* to appreciate that if this comparison does reveal that the hypothetical 45% should have been only, say, 30% on the basis of chance alone, this finding cannot be ignored. There is currently such a strong reaction against the layman's belief that any unequal distribution is a sure sign of accident *proneness*, that the tendency is to ignore *all* the evidence provided by this sort of investigation—including the many cases where the contribution of multiple offenders is very significantly different from chance. This is tantamount to throwing the baby out with the bathwater, for it means ignoring a possibly very important source of trouble.

However, as a way of investigating proneness as such, this method has distinct limitations, and it is usually only regarded as the first step in any routine statistical investigation. Proneness is commonly taken to imply a consistent tendency to accidents. It is therefore necessary to establish not only whether certain people have an undue number of accidents during one period, but whether the same people continue to have them in a subsequent period. A better method of investigation is therefore to compare the number of accidents sustained by the same people in two successive time periods. If the characteristics which make certain people more "prone" to accidents than others are durable ones, then you would expect to find a significant correlation between the distribution of accidents in the two periods. In other words, one would expect to find that, *on the whole*, the people with no accidents in the first period would again have none in the second period, and so on up the scale to the multiple offender. The degree of this association can again be measured statistically by means of various correlation coefficients.

This sort of investigation is a very important one, as, if the proneness concept is to have any practical value, then it must not be just a flash in the pan; it must be operative over relatively long periods of time. It is therefore common practice to take a group of people and tabulate their accident records for a period of time which can be anything from ten months to ten years, and then divide the period into two parts and correlate the number of accidents which each person has in the first part with the number he has in the second. In fairness, however, to the concept, it must be pointed out that there are several very valid reasons why this method is unlikely to produce high correlation coefficients, let alone perfect ones. In the first place, however durable the accident-predisposing characteristics may be, and however powerful their influence on behaviour, the element of chance is still operative and is therefore likely to obscure the issue. The number of accidents which each person incurs over a given period of time is likely to be a mixture of *person-caused* and *chance-caused* accidents, and it is difficult, if not impossible, to separate them, or to know what effect the chance-caused ones are having on the correlation coefficient.

Another difficulty encountered with this method is the choice of the two periods. If the periods are very short, then the influence of the chance-centred accidents often obscures the whole issue. If, on the other hand, the periods chosen are long ones, then it is inevitable that the evidence of proneness (in the form of a high correlation) will be reduced because a certain amount of *person-centred* variation will occur. Many of the characteristics which could predispose a person towards accidents are liable to a certain amount of change over a long period of time; for example health can deteriorate, young people can grow older and develop different attitudes, older people can grow older still and lose some of their physical capabilities; and people of all ages can be subjected to some form of discipline which puts a curb on their accident-producing behaviour. What is more, it is even possible that each person will change in a rather individual way. It is also possible that the very fact of having been involved in an accident might have different effects on different people, like making some people less reckless and therefore less susceptible, and other people more nervous and therefore more susceptible. It could easily happen therefore that in a group of people several of these factors could be operative at the same time, causing some people's accident records to improve while others deteriorated—a contingency which would naturally lower any group coefficient of correlation.

In choosing the most suitable period for group observations a statistician is therefore confronted with a Hobson's Choice. If he lengthens the period of study in order to neutralize the effects of chance variation, he increases the individual variations due to the time factor (and also limits the normality of his group because of factors which will be discussed later). If, in order to avoid these pitfalls, he shortens the time periods, he limits the number of accident events and therefore increases the effects of variation due to the chance factor.

In addition, in conducting this sort of investigation, there are a number of practical as well as technical snags. It is, for example, extremely difficult to find a group of people who are not only exposed for the full period of time, but also exposed to exactly the same hazards. It is virtually impossible to find such a group among the general motoring public; for even if one gets a group who are licensed over the whole period there is no reliable way of establishing just how much driving they actually did, where they did it, or even whether they were in the country or State during the whole period. As a result it is most unsatisfactory, and can even be rather misleading to use a group of ordinary motorists for such an investigation, as the lack of adequate controls makes it impossible to know how the results should be interpreted. It is therefore much more common to find this sort of study carried out on professional drivers. But even here there are some very great snags, the biggest of which has been mentioned before, but should be mentioned again as it is so often overlooked, namely that in order to obtain a group which is exposed for a worthwhile period of time, it is necessary to exclude all the new drivers and also the short-service, discharged drivers and use only the long-service men. This can defeat the whole purpose of the study, for as transport operators seldom keep drivers with bad accident records for any length of time, the groups which are studied are usually most unrepresentative, self-selected groups—one of the reasons for the self-selection being a relative lack of anything resembling accident proneness!

As a final straw there are also a number of technical snags in an investigation of this kind, such as the fact that the usual method of calculating a coefficient of correlation, the Pearson product-moment method, is only mathematically meaningful with normal distributions—which are hardly ever encountered in accident work. In fact r coefficients are so difficult to interpret, and give so little indication of the *practical* implications of the amount of correlation observed, that they are now regarded by many statisticians—though unfortunately not by psychologists—as an outmoded statistical tool. (In the statistical section of this book my co-author deals with this question very fully.)

It is not surprising therefore that one of the most common ways of testing for accident proneness, namely taking groups of people and using simple statistical techniques to correlate the accidents of one period with the accidents of a subsequent period, seldom comes up with any startlingly high coefficients of correlation.

Another method of investigating proneness over two periods of time is to concentrate on the multiple accident offenders and see (1) what proportion of the repeaters of the first period are again repeaters in the second period, (2) if the repeaters of the first period had been taken off driving, how many people would have been correctly penalized and how many falsely penalized, and (3) whether the removal of the repeaters of the first period would have made any appreciable reduction to the actual number of accidents of the second period. This is a very important line of investigation, for again if the proneness concept is to have any practical value, then prone people should continue to be prone and the detection and elimination of the worst offenders should significantly lower accident rates. Unfortunately, however, when it comes to carrying out such an investigation, statisticians immediately encounter all the difficulties outlined above and a few extra ones in addition.

When the studies are carried out on the general public, the usual difficulties arise concerning the controlling of exposure and risk, and it can easily occur that a multiple offender of the first period has a very much better record in the second period simply because he is driving less (possibly due to his licence being suspended or revoked because of his accidents!) or is driving in easier traffic conditions. Nevertheless, despite these anomalies, there is a good deal of support for this sort of investigation for the very simple reason that a study along these lines is regarded as a mock-up of the actual problem which confronts the traffic departments, i.e. whether in fact repeaters do go on repeating, and whether, when it comes to actual practice, there is any justification, or anything to be gained by penalizing people because they have already been involved in a number of accidents. However, the chief danger of this sort of study lies in the fact that enthusiasm for its apparent down-to-earth factuality (as well as the large scale on which it can be carried out) can lead to an uncritical acceptance of what may possibly be very misleading results.

For example, one of the biggest studies of this kind ever carried out (which will be described in detail later) involved a random sample of some 29,500 drivers licensed over two successive three-year periods, and came up with the startling result that removing the " repeaters" of the first period would have only reduced the total number of accidents *of the second period* by 3·7%. The utter paucity of evidence of any continued accident repeating in such a large sample of drivers could be regarded as a very potent argument against the whole proneness concept, and has indeed been used as such on many occasions. The danger of this line of thinking lies in the fact that with each quoting (often unfortunately out of context) the basic limitations of a study of this kind tend to be forgotten—limitations which require very serious consideration before the results can be presumed to have any wider or general application. For inherent in the data on which this particular study was based were certain factors (all of which were clearly stated *at the time* by its investigators) which could have had a very significant effect on the final figures—especially those dealing with the multiple offenders. For instance, in the first place, only certain of the accidents were recorded, namely the accidents involving fatalities, injuries, or major property damage (and even this recording was not guaranteed to be complete). In the second place, the American state where this study was carried out had a strict driver-enforcement policy. In view of even these factors (let alone the factor of incomplete reporting) the small number of the repeaters and repeater-repeaters in this particular sample is possibly not quite so startling—if for no other reason than the fact that it would be surprising, in any sample, to find large numbers of drivers being involved in repeated serious accidents over a period of six years without being either killed or injured, or without some severe punitive enforcement action being taken against them. For it would appear that removing the anomalies usually found in this sort of study promptly alters the picture, as can be seen by two investigations of professional drivers which will also be fully described later. In these studies, although a number of restrictive influences were still operative, at least the accidents were fully recorded and the exposure risk properly controlled, with the result that removing the repeaters of the first period was shown to reduce the accidents of the second period by far more than 3·7%.

Undoubtedly group studies are so fraught with pitfalls, and so much a battleground for statistical skirmishing, that the results are very difficult to assess.

Nevertheless, despite all the snags, it would be a great mistake to write off these group methods as impractical, or to ignore the results of the studies which have embodied them. For, if the concept of accident proneness is to have any practical significance, then these differences should be not only sufficiently enduring but also sufficiently potent to be evident, even if somewhat restricted or camouflaged. Among professional drivers there should be some evidence of innate differences even if the group is restricted to long-service drivers, for it is a rarity for transport operators to be in the position where they can be so "choosey" that they can dispense with the services of every man who has accidents. Usually the best that can be achieved is to build up a hard core of long-service drivers who are, by comparison with the ones who are jettisoned, *relatively* accident-free. If there is such a phenomenon as a continuum of accident proneness then these men should represent the better end of the continuum, and although the differences between them cannot be expected to be as obvious as they would be in an unrestricted group where no process of self-selection was operating, these differences should nevertheless be apparent.

Even among the general public, where not only does an element of self-selection operate (in the form of injury or death or of the withdrawing of driving licences from blatant accident offenders), but also the whole position is further confused by lack of uniformity of exposure risk, certain basic trends should still be evident. Here again if there is such a thing as a continuum of innate accident proneness, there should still be evidence of it, however muted down that evidence may be. This sort of group statistical study is therefore very desirable, as long as the results are not considered out of context, but against the background of the restrictions and limitations placed upon them by the particular data on which they are based.

Another statistical method of investigating the accident-proneness phenomenon is what one might call the person-centred method. Here, instead of considering a group of people in terms of some rather crude measurement like the number of accidents incurred over a particular period of time, each individual record is assessed in terms of a more sensitive measuring device such as the number of days or miles driven between each progressive accident. A method such as this has some very satisfactory features, for it has no new disadvantages and some very decided new advantages. The practical difficulties encountered in this approach, such as maintaining uniformity of hazard, are inherent in all statistical work on proneness. But on the credit side there are some very important gains over the group approach.

(1) It is now possible to test the proneness hypothesis *within each individual*.
(2) It is possible to assess each driver separately and at a relatively early stage, and to grade him, as soon as his record has stabilized itself, according to a standard such as the average of the time-intervals or mileage-intervals between his accidents.
(3) It is therefore possible to compare drivers of different exposure length and to obtain a much more representative sample, as it is no longer necessary to exclude all the short-service discharged drivers—the men who usually have the worst accident records.
(4) It is possible to investigate whole new areas of the proneness concept, areas such as individual trends of improvement or deterioration brought about by factors such as age, experience, punishment, illness, domestic worries, etc.

Of all the statistical approaches to the proneness concept this method is definitely the most satisfactory, but it can only be used to proper advantage where the information about each driver's accidents and driving conditions is both full and accurate.

So much for the mechanics of the statistical approach to accident proneness. A digression like this may seem unnecessarily elementary to any accident research worker, but my personal feeling is that it is one worth making all the same—not only for the sake of the lay reader but also because sometimes it does no harm to indulge in what the Americans call "getting back to basics". Sometimes it is not only the layman who is mesmerized by the size of a correlation coefficient, or misled by the outcome of a statistical study; often the researcher himself succumbs to the hypnotic effect of figures and appears to overlook the many factors which could be clouding the issue and influencing the results—a process which Arbous calls "letting statistics do our thinking for us". And sometimes, although the research worker himself may be very much aware of the complexity of the problem, he certainly does not give this impression in his writing, and presents a set of figures as though they were drops of pure, distilled truth—to the lasting bewilderment of anyone who has insufficient statistical knowledge to question his assumptions.

Unfortunately such statistical "misunderstandings" have been responsible for much of the confusion in the thinking associated with accident proneness, and have also exercised a pronounced influence on the development of the thinking on the subject. Some of the earlier ones were undoubtedly responsible for the over-enthusiasm of the 1930's and the 1940's, and it seems more than likely that some of the later ones have been responsible for the exaggerated swing of the pendulum to the scepticism and disbelief of the 1960's.

It seems to me that an honest look at the limitations and the inherent difficulties of the statistical approach provides a good background of realism against which to examine the developments of these trends and to study the research literature.

The Psychological Approach

By highlighting the statistical approach and its pitfalls, I am certainly not implying that the psychological approach is immune from these. Far from it. Anomalies abound here by the dozen. But many of these are still statistical in origin, as experimental psychologists make copious (and, alas! often very ill-informed) use of statistical techniques, in order to substantiate their findings. In fact the reason why some completely *illogical* psychological findings on accidents have been accepted by the extreme methodologists is because they have been hallowed by what appears to be statistical "proof". And the reason why a great many very *logical* psychological findings, although they fully support one another, have been condemned is because the supporting statistical evidence was said to be "inconclusive".

Altogether, it would appear that the psychological findings on accident proneness are equally difficult to substantiate, the main reason being the difficulty of obtaining a reliable criterion against which to assess their validity.

It will be appreciated, of course, that there are as many ways in which a psychologist can investigate a phenomenon like accident proneness as there are causes for accidents. But fortunately it is possible to group them into several broad lines of approach.

The first of these is comparing groups of drivers with high or low accident rates to see whether they differ with respect to certain psychological or sociological factors (e.g. intelligence, reaction time, aggression, personality type, age, home background, criminal record, etc.). Here again the main difficulty is to ensure that the criterion of high or low accident rate is reliable, which immediately plunges one back into the same sort of problems as were found in the statistical approach, especially those connected with obtaining accurate data and overcoming the problem of equal exposure in terms of quantity and risk. Very often it is virtually impossible to overcome these problems, especially with the general motoring public, and here the best that can be done is to choose the two groups in such a way that the differences in their accident rates are so marked that they can be presumed to override the other factors. But the difficulties in this approach are not all statistical; many such studies are doomed to failure even before they begin because of a poor choice of tests or discriminating factors. Accident involvement obviously has multiple and complex causes and it is therefore unreasonable to expect any one simple factor to discriminate between *groups* of people. But when the choice of tests or discriminating factors is more realistic, it is noticeable how often this group comparison approach has yielded good results despite the somewhat crude way in which the groups have had to be categorized, and how often significant differences have been found between such high and low accident groups. This seems to indicate that psychological research does not necessarily have to be hog-tied by the requirements of statistical methodology. Desirable as it may be to have a criterion which embodies all the necessary statistical controls, the fact that such a criterion is often virtually impossible to obtain does not mean that psychological research must come to a full stop. For the consistent trend of so many of these high and low accident groups studied seems to indicate that there are a number of personal characteristics which differentiate between "unsafe" drivers and "safe" drivers, characteristics deserving of further detailed study.

One way in which researchers try to overcome the difficulty of getting a more sensitive and reliable criterion is, of course, to use professional drivers, where it is sometimes possible to fully control the exposure element. But the use of such subjects immediately brings other difficulties in its wake because this means that in order to establish a reliable accident criterion it is necessary to use long-service employees. This means again a very selective population, for the ones with the really unsatisfactory records have probably already been winnowed out—and who knows whether their accidents were not related to the very factors which the investigator is trying to investigate! Unless he can use a person-centred statistical method like the time-intervals between accidents, a method which will enable him to compare drivers with different lengths of exposure, the use of professional drivers is definitely likely to water down the degree to which the subjects demonstrate any particularly undesirable characteristics. Nevertheless, as mentioned before, because most transport operators cannot afford to discharge every unsatisfactory driver, a good deal of variation still seems to exist, and a great deal can be learned. In fact it has been shown that with a good battery of tests and a well-worked-out accident criterion it is possible to use the whole group of drivers instead of just the worst and the best, and to investigate a whole continuum of accident involvement.

A different psychological approach is the individual case study where each accident is investigated in detail. This sort of study can be most revealing and can produce a wealth of information about the circumstances leading up to the accident. But the snag here is that often so much detailed information emerges that it becomes almost impossible to see the wood for the trees, and to determine where the true cause or causes of the accident may lie. For example, an accident may turn out to have antecedent history which appears to represent a chain of events like this: the driver was injured in a single-car accident; he was injured because the car turned over; the car turned over because it skidded; the skidding was caused by a wet road surface on a curve taken at speed; the driver was speeding because he was late for an appointment; the lateness was due to a breakfast-time quarrel with his wife; the quarrel was over the size of the household bills, and his wife's "extravagance"; the reason why he considered his wife extravagant was that, unlike himself, she had no regard whatever for security; the reason why he valued security was that he himself had come from a broken home and had known what poverty was like; the reason for his miserable childhood was that his father drank; etc. and etc.

One of the difficulties here is to decide whether the actual accident was in fact the direct outcome of this apparently sequential chain of events, or whether it was the result of a specific situation, i.e. a situation in which sheer chance had resulted in a most dangerous combination of circumstances. But there are other difficulties, too. Even supposing the accident was the end result of this chain of events, how far back should one go to establish the fundamental cause? Was it faulty driving judgement? Or the driver allowing his personal concerns to cloud his judgement or impair his concentration? Were his personal troubles caused by his childhood environment?

Unfortunately, however, there are other dangers as well, one of them being that a vital link in this seemingly logical chain of events may be wrong, and that it is in fact a red herring provided either consciously or unconsciously by one of the informants. The fundamental reason for the quarrel, for example, might have been quite different, namely that the husband came home drunk the night before—and did in fact have many of the character-istics of his despised father; or the speeding may have been more a matter of bad temper than hurrying because he was late—and the bad temper may have been a chronic personal failing.

Altogether it seems that one of the main dangers of these individual case histories is that they produce such a plethora of information that people are inclined to overlook the fact that quantity does not make up for quality, or accuracy, nor does it necessarily make for clarity. Undoubtedly every accident has a complicated pre-history—a fact which seems to lend support to the theory that most accidents are fortuitous events happening to quite ordinary people. But, on the other hand, if it can be shown that many of the people who become involved in accidents have certain characteristics *in common*, this in turn would indicate that such fortuitous happenings may not be so fortuitous at all; and that the unfor-tunate circumstances which precipitate accidents may in many cases be man-made—and not by such ordinary people either. But it is very difficult to make any decision on these points by means of case studies, as it is so difficult to disentangle the complicated strands of the evidence which they produce. These sort of studies are therefore usually regarded as being more productive on the engineering side than the psychological side of accident research.

Another psychological approach is to study individual accident repeaters to see whether there is any pattern in their accidents. Here, if the causal sequence does reveal some sort of similarity in most of the accidents sustained by an individual, at least it might be possible to pick out some salient feature which could be said to be an accident-precipitating charac-teristic of the driver himself.

Another psychological method for assessing accident proneness is to see whether it is possible to predict *future* accident involvement by means of some test or battery of tests. This very exacting method has unfortunately seldom been used—or at any rate seldom scientifically evaluated. There are a number of programmes in operation for the selection of professional drivers, but the only one of which I am personally aware where a pre-diction of each man's *future* accident involvement, made at the time of testing, has been compared with a statistical evaluation of his subsequent accident record, is a South African study reported later in this book.

Naturally, for a study like this, it is necessary to overcome all the statistical difficulties in connection with the reliability of the accident criterion. But if it is possible to establish all the necessary controls, such a study will yield a great deal of information about the per-sonal characteristics of various types of accident offenders. And if the study were to suc-ceed, i.e. the predictions of future accident involvement made on the basis of the tests were later borne out in practice, then a study like this would provide very strong evidence of the validity and the usefulness of the concept of accident proneness. For it would be impossible to predict *future* accident involvement with any accuracy, especially the *degree of future accident involvement over a period of time*, unless there were indeed valid and last-ing differences between people's susceptibility to accidents. For here you would be assess-ing each individual's accident *potential* as against the *actuality* of his subsequent accident record, and if, under controlled conditions, these turned out to be closely related, then accident proneness must be a reality—and one with important implications.

The ideal way to carry out such a study is to mount a three-stage programme. The first step is to establish an accurate and reliable accident criterion, which means overcoming all the difficulties of full accident reporting, equating exposure with regard to both quantity and quality, and determining by statistical tests that the accident criterion is a stable one. Unless these difficulties can be overcome, the scientific validity of the programme cannot by truly assessed. Fortunately it appears that even this last difficult hurdle can be overcome, especially if one uses a sensitive measure of assessing each man's record, such as mileage—or time-intervals between successive accidents.

The second stage is to develop a testing method based on knowledge derived from various sources, and to try it out (i.e. validate it) by applying it to a group of drivers whose past accident records are known, and can be statistically assessed. If the test battery succeeds in differentiating between these men (i.e. if the test scores correlate with the accident criterion of past accidents) then one can proceed. If not, it will need to be modified and re-validated until it does correlate.

Ideally the next stage is to apply the test battery to a group of drivers who have not as yet been exposed to the particular driving conditions under which the study is being carried out, and to then allow *all* these people, irrespective of their test results, to drive and build up subsequent accident records against which to validate the predictions made on the basis of the test battery. At this stage, however, it is more than likely that the proving programme will depart from the theoretical ideal. This sort of study is really only possible with professional drivers, for unless the subjects are going to drive on prescribed routes and remain on those routes, it is virtually impossible to equate exposure. But once you use professional drivers, then the decision as to whether these men are actually going to be allowed to drive (at any rate for the particular transport organization concerned) is yours. If you have any faith at all in your testing methods—and you would not have proceeded to this stage if you had not—then it would take a very dedicated scientist—and one without any social conscience at that—to deliberately allow a man to handle one of the company vehicles with what amounted to foreknowledge that he might not only endanger his own life but the lives of other people. Under practical reality conditions, the third stage of such a study is therefore likely to be restricted to selecting only those subjects who pass the tests. This will naturally restrict the range of the subjects used for the cross-validation process and, if the tests are any good, will also result in the restriction of the range of accident involvement on the accident criterion. It will therefore be more difficult to evaluate the results by any method such as an ordinary product-moment correlation technique between test prediction and accident criterion, as both predictors and scores on the criterion will be skewed to the good side of the accident continuum. Fortunately, however, there are other statistical methods of assessing these results.

But it could so happen that practical circumstances, such as an acute driver shortage, could result in the lowering of acceptance standards or the temporary cessation of the psychological selection. This would remove the decision as to who should or should not be allowed to drive from the hands of the scientific investigators. Such an occurrence could (and in the case of the South African study actually did) result in the theoretical ideal being realized, where a follow-up could be obtained of a whole range of test predictions and a whole range of subsequent accident involvement.

It should be noted, however, that any psychological driver selection scheme can still be a valuable source of information, even if circumstances do not permit a detailed scientific follow-up of the results. If a particular selection programme achieves its desired practical purpose and results in a significant reduction in the total accident rate, then it must be working on the right lines, and its findings should not be ignored because they cannot be validated with statistical refinement. Strict methodology is very desirable, but it need not be made the be-all and end-all of scientific investigation.

One way and another the many technical difficulties encountered should not (as they have been reputed to do) deter psychologists from working in the accident field, even if very often their findings can only be interpreted in a general way. The more of these findings there are, and the more they complement one another, the more sure one can be that they are reflecting a psychological reality—even if supporting statistical evidence is as yet hard to come by.

Actually, when one considers all the technical difficulties connected with research on accident proneness, it is surprising and encouraging that so much progress has in fact been made.

CHAPTER 3

BEGINNINGS OF EMPIRICAL RESEARCH

IN REVIEWING the extensive literature on accident proneness, I must reiterate that my main purpose is to try and trace how the current divergent thinking on the concept itself could have developed. The early accident literature has, in any case, already been very comprehensively covered by a number of writers, and Walbeehm has brought the record up to the end of the 1950's. The only studies which will receive any detailed attention are those which have proved to be particularly controversial, or later ones which are as yet not very well known. Occasionally I have anticipated history and inserted some later findings on some particular subjects, the purpose being to give the reader a wider background against which to assess some particularly controversial study. For the reasons why the findings of some studies were at the time regarded as either acceptable or unacceptable were not necessarily just a question of blind faith or blind prejudice; they might have been accepted because they were regarded as logical, or rejected because they were regarded as illogical— and many people may have felt it was only just a matter of time before further evidence would appear which would clarify this particular problem. I therefore felt that it might enliven this account of the history of accident research if the reader were given an idea of subsequent developments on some of the more controversial issues.

The earliest studies on accident proneness were German ones, but few of them are still remembered, except perhaps Bortkiewicz' study on horsekicks among Prussian cavalrymen—which still bobs up occasionally in the literature—and Marbe's work on the Law of Recurrence, which is well known on the Continent. But it seems that the truly systematic study of the personal element in accidents began in England just on fifty years ago.

The first major projects were concerned with industrial accidents, but they nevertheless laid the foundations for the statistical study of accident involvement in any sphere. And, as they are quoted and discussed and argued about in just about every publication that has ever been written on accident proneness, it is essential to have a look at them and see what all the talk has been about.

The first project, that of Greenwood, Woods and Yule (1919, 1920), dealt with minor-injury accidents sustained by women workers in munition factories, and was designed to serve the very utilitarian purpose of cutting down lost time and thereby boosting the production of shells for the First World War. The primary concern of the Industrial Fatigue Board, which instigated the research, was not so much the cause of individual accidents, but the question of finding the quickest and most effective ways of bringing about an all-over reduction in the accident rate. To do this they needed to know where the accidents occurred and to whom; whether the accidents were mainly associated with certain operations or with certain people, or whether they were so randomly distributed among the workers that they could be considered a function of chance.

The approach to the problem was therefore a purely statistical one, and Greenwood and his co-workers set about a most detailed and methodical investigation of all the possible contingencies—an investigation which revealed that although chance obviously did play a part, nevertheless a higher than usual accident rate was associated not only with certain occupations but also with certain people. Any attack on the accident problem in these munition factories would therefore have to be at least a three-pronged attack:

(1) A general one aimed at reducing the accident rate among all the workers by measures such as improved working conditions or safety education.
(2) One aimed at reducing specific hazards—by measures such as modifying dangerous equipment or devising new safety guards.
(3) One aimed at reducing the number of accidents caused by unduly susceptible people —by measures such as discipline, or retraining, or removal to another kind of job, or research into what caused people to be multiple-accident offenders.

As this sort of three-pronged attack is exactly what many of the world's present-day accident researchers—to say nothing of virtually all the industrial safety officials and traffic officials— now advocate as the best way to tackle the accident problem, it would appear that after fifty years we have merely "come out by that same door wherein we went"; though the intervening years have certainly witnessed some very heated arguments on the relative importance of the three prongs.

The way in which Greenwood and his team reached their conclusions was by means of a thorough statistical analysis of the accident records of several factories. Firstly, they established the importance of specific hazards by showing that certain departments and certain operations had consistently higher accident rates than others. They then uncovered another possible source of trouble, indicated by the fact that even among workers carrying out *much the same operation* there was still a very noticeable difference between the accident rates of *individual people*. To investigate what lay behind these differences they first used the basic statistical procedure of examining the distribution of the accidents incurred by several groups of workers over single periods of time and comparing these with the sort of distributions which could be expected if three different factors were operative: (1) a chance distribution, (2) a distribution based on unequal liability, and (3) a biased distribution where the occurrence of the first accident could have altered the probability of having another accident. In nearly every case the best statistical "fit" was obtained with the theoretical model, the negative binomial model, calculated on an assumption of unequal initial liability.

To confirm that this was the most likely explanation for the differing accident rates, Greenwood *et al.* carried out a series of further investigations, chief of which was the correlation of the accidents incurred by the same individuals in successive time periods. In two small groups of women workers, engaged on heavy lathe operation and profiling, the authors were able to obtain accident information over two successive three-month periods. They were also able to obtain sufficient information to ensure that exposure was homogeneous for each group; that all subjects had at least eight months' prior experience; and that there was no undue absenteeism. Correlation between the accidents sustained in the two three-monthly periods produced coefficients of 0·69 and 0·72 (for two small groups of lathe operators) and coefficients of 0·53 and 0·37 (for two similar groups of profiling operators)—the larger coefficients being associated with the more hazardous occupation and a high accident rate.

Even with this additional evidence, Greenwood and his team were still very cautious. They were prepared to state, and to demonstrate with figures, that "these results indicate that varying individual susceptibility to 'accidents' is an extremely important factor in determining the distribution; so important that given the experience of one period it might be practicable to foretell with reasonable accuracy the average allotment of accidents amongst the individuals in a subsequent period"; but they nevertheless qualified this statement by adding that before assessing the practical value of any of these findings, "we must be a little clearer as to what one ought to mean by this phrase 'individual susceptibility' ".

A higher than average susceptibility to accidents might perhaps be associated with higher output, or poor health, or undue susceptibility to fatigue, or age, or even an unequal tendency to report accidents. "Consequently we have sheltering under the term 'individual susceptibility' a motley host of factors which would be very difficult indeed to separate and measure." However, having investigated as many of these factors as possible, they concluded that, at least in their particular data, none of these factors appeared to be having any significant effect—though it was obvious that a great deal more investigation would be needed before any definite conclusions could be reached. Greenwood *et al.* then went on to say: "But so far as our present knowledge goes, it seems that the genesis of multiple accidents under uniform external conditions is an affair of personality and not determined by any obvious extrinsic factor such as a greater or lesser speed of work." This statement has been pounced upon by a number of later critics and described as "unjustified", "a highly questionable conclusion", "a diagnosis of exclusion". But, prefaced as it was by the words, "as far as our present knowledge goes, it seems", this rather tentative remark does not appear to warrant such condemnation.

The next major study (Newbold, 1926) was also a very good one. This study, again an industrial statistical one, was designed as a background for a more detailed psychological one to be carried out later by Farmer and Chambers (1939); and Newbold's main purpose was to carry on with Greenwood's work to see what use could be made of the sort of accident records which were kept in the normal course of work by a well-run factory. Her contention was that although accidents must have many causes, the trends of these mass statistics would probably prove very revealing.

The study was carried out on a very big scale, covering nearly 9000 workers in factories manufacturing products of all sorts from motor-cars to optical instruments, chocolates, and cardboard boxes—the choice of firms and departments being guided by opportunity for many small accidents, homogeneity of work done, and strict reporting of all trivial accidents. Carrying out the same type of investigations as Greenwood *et al.*, Newbold substantiated many of their findings. She found different accident rates associated with different hazards and also with different people. She found that differences in accident rates were significantly at variance with chance, that they were indicative of initial unequal liability, and also that they appeared to have a degree of stability. Correlating the accidents of eleven groups of workers over two successive periods of time (ranging from five months up to two years) she obtained significant coefficients ranging from 0·20 up to 0·62—the only two groups which failed to yield significant correlations being those which had such a low accident rate that there was little opportunity for variation between individual workers. She then set about an even more thorough investigation than Greenwood of any factors which could be influencing these correlations and concluded, (1) that the possibility of their being merely a reflection of a tendency for some people to be more eager to report accidents than others was offset by the fact that the most positive results had been obtained in a factory where reporting was complete, and where strict penalties were imposed for not reporting even the most trivial accidents, and (2) that in her particular sample there were definite indications that youth, inexperience, and possibly even poor health were associated with accident occurrence, and that there was also the possibility that some of the differences between people could be due to slight but unavoidable differences in exposure risks. But, nevertheless, she concluded that an element of individual susceptibility was definitely present and that "the consistency of this tendency to accidents is shown by the association found between (1) accidents in two different periods, (2) accidents of one kind and accidents of another type, (3) accidents in the factory and accidents at home". This latter statement has been severely criticized as being based on inadequate data, i.e. correlations of 0·2 and 0·3 for small groups and the possibility in some cases of a "tendency to report"—but it must be noted that it is not a statement of *fact*. Newbold is only talking of the *consistency of a tendency*.

In summing up her report, Newbold said that she felt that mass accident statistics could serve a very useful purpose in pinpointing the sources of trouble in individual factories. She also submitted a very practical suggestion. Presenting tables as a guide to assessing the situation, she suggested that if a high accident rate was found in a department where the accidents were distributed among the workers in a normal chance distribution, this would indicate that the work itself must be unduly dangerous. On the other hand, if a high accident rate was found to be associated with a very different-from-chance distribution, then "very little observation in the workshop by anyone thoroughly familiar with the work, or perhaps an experimental interchange of occupations or machines among workers, would soon decide whether the cause was mainly personal or mechanical, and so point if necessary to the remedy". Her final conclusion was, however, that for any detailed study of accident liability the statistical approach had distinct limitations, and she advocated individual case studies and the use of experimental psychology.

Although both these studies are very old and are concerned solely with industrial accidents, they do show very clearly that the early research on the proneness concept got off to a very good start. Not only were these studies very realistic and down-to-earth, but they also displayed a most methodical, as well as open-minded approach. Neither Greenwood *et al.* nor Newbold can be blamed for the misdeeds of people who later not only repeatedly quoted them out of context, but rephrased their statements until they were quite unrecognizable—a process which still seems to be going on today. For this kind of distortion is certainly not confined to the over-enthusiastic promulgators of the concept of accident proneness who followed in the wake of these early researchers—it is just as prevalent among its present-day detractors. Whereas in the early days people were apparently inclined to magnify both the actual findings of the early investigators and their importance to the accident situation, the present tendency is to minimize them; to omit any mention of the significant statistical findings and to overlook, as entirely inconsequential, the positive evidence which these studies *did* produce. It is currently the vogue to write papers which are hypercritical of every aspect of the concept of accident proneness, and to preface these papers (or books), with the briefest of brief histories of accident-proneness research. In these so-called "histories" (for they are often inaccurate as well as inadequate) two tendencies are very apparent, (1) to maintain that exaggerated reports of the findings and conclusions of the early investigators resulted in the development of an "illusion" or "myth" of accident proneness, and (2) to imply that this was most unfortunate, as neither the findings nor the conclusions were of any significance, or for that matter had any real basis in fact—as is shown by the "failure" of nearly fifty years of protracted research to produce any convincing corroborative evidence.

According to most of the recent "histories" of accident-proneness research one would imagine that the only substantive evidence of unequal liability provided by Greenwood *et al.* and Newbold was that they found the distribution of accidents in a single period of time differed from a Poisson one and resembled that of the negative binomial—a finding which they maintained was due to innate unequal liability, *without ever determining what other factors, such as unequal exposure to risk, could produce this same distribution.* The facts are otherwise. These investigators did everything possible to obtain homogeneous exposure; they investigated a number of other factors which could be creating inequalities of risk and showed that even when these factors were controlled, significant evidence of individual differences in accident liability still existed. They never restricted their investigations to only one period; they correlated the accidents of successive periods and the positive coefficients obtained were highly significant (significant coefficients which are seldom mentioned in the more recent "potted" histories)—in fact they went to a great deal of trouble to check their premises. The conclusions which they drew were ultra-conservative and fully justified by their data. And, despite anything that recent critics may say to the contrary, they have not been conclusively contradicted by the findings of any later research—in fact, if anything they have been substantiated.

Far from these early studies fostering unjustifiable beliefs or holding out false hopes, as many of the present-day critics are apt to maintain, what these early studies did in fact do—and do well—was to lay a sound foundation on which to build subsequent research. As to just what sort of superstructure could be built on these foundations, and what this superstructure could be interpreted as representing (either by the builder or the beholder) has turned out to be very much a matter of personal choice. All Greenwood and Newbold did was to lay the foundations; they certainly cannot be blamed for what happened afterwards. But it is ironical to note that even those critics who maintain that all the wrong sort of superstructures have indeed been built, and all the wrong sort of ideas propagated thereby, seem to think that they can still praise the quality (i.e. methodology) of the foundations without accepting any of the factual material of which they were constructed. Even Greenwood's findings on the distribution of accidents *in one period* do not deserve the scorn with which they are so often treated. Since those early days a great many people have unwisely used a distribution of accidents in one single period (as often as not without the proper controls over factors like exposure or risk) to "prove" the existence of accident proneness. But at the same time it should be noted that every study where it has been possible to impose strict controls has come up with distributions which are very, very different from chance; and that these distributions do seem to be one indication of unequal liability. Goodness knows there are few enough of these controlled studies, but that is because of the very real practical difficulties involved in imposing such controls. But, let it be noted, no controlled study has *contradicted* the findings of Greenwood and Newbold. In the same way a number of studies have come up with positive correlations between the accidents in consecutive periods. Sometimes these correlations could be due to extraneous factors, because again influences like exposure to risk have not been controlled. But here, too, where the controls have been satisfactorily imposed, the positive correlations remain—possibly muted down by the selectivity of the groups used, possibly camouflaged by the concurrent effect of chance—but always *there*, and more conspicuously there with full recording and higher accident rates.

What is more, it seems that if a good superstructure is built on the sound foundations laid by the early investigators, it will, like Hakkinen's study (1958), stand up to a good deal of critical bombardment, not only because it exhibits the same good *methodology*, but because it makes use of the same good *logical material*. Good statistical work needs to be generated by good logic and not by hypothetical assumptions, and a recent study, that of Cresswell and Froggatt (1963), which employed all the methodology of the earlier studies plus an additional intricate network of statistical "expertise", nevertheless displayed no lasting powers at all; it crumbled under the impact of one critical assessment by the president of the Royal Statistical Society (Irwin, 1964). This is not to imply that the logic of the early studies of Greenwood and Newbold was good logic because it favoured the concept of unequal liability, and that that of Cresswell and Froggatt was poor logic because it did not. The logic of the early investigators was good because it started with the *evidence*, and used that evidence to reach some logical and moderately stated conclusions: it did not start with a premise and then try to justify it by quasi-logical (as well as quasi-statistical) "acrobatics". To use one of Arbous' pungently descriptive phrases, it was logic which built from the ground floor upwards and not from the roof downwards.

Another thing to be said for the authors of these early studies was that like many of the authors of major studies to follow, they displayed a most moderate and open-minded approach—which is more than can be said for many of their critics. In fact it is ironical to see how often the very thoroughness of a study and the carefully worded manner in which all the pros and cons of the evidence are presented, have promptly been used to discredit that evidence. The *modus operandi* of a researcher like Greenwood or Newbold was to say: "Here are all the factors which might be affecting the issue; but it nevertheless seems that unequal liability to accidents does play a part—though just how important a part is something which needs further investigation." In contrast, the *modus operandi* of so many of the present-day critics is to say: "Obviously unequal liability to accidents plays little, if any part; just look at all the other factors mentioned by even the early investigators, and see how tentatively they stated their conclusions."

This line of argument has been used against virtually every scientifically presented

study which could be said to support the concept of unequal liability—as can be seen
from the actual excerpts from the currently fashionable type of critiques which I have
given in later chapters. I therefore feel that it is only fair, right here at the beginning of the
history of this sort of controversy, to point out once again to anyone unfamiliar with
the restrictions of scientific writing that there is an unwritten law that scientific studies
should be presented with ultra-conservatism. When a scientific author prefaces his conclusions with phrases like "it seems" or "the evidence suggests", this is merely a reflection
of the fact that he is adhering to this unwritten law—it does not mean that he is hopelessly unsure of his facts!

This scientific restraint is, however, anything but evident in the present-day critiques,
for this is the sort of arrant nonsense which is now being written about what was, in
reality, just some very good methodical research for which the authors made no extravagant claims.

"Within the short space of twenty years, a mountain of research, publicity, psycho-
analysis, police action, politics and folklore, had been balanced on the point of a
pin—the pin being an alleged superiority of the Negative Binomial distribution over
the Poisson distribution in accounting for mass accident data, and a possible explanation for this fact. In 1941, Dr. J. O. Irwin, in a presentation to the Royal Statistical
Society, knocked the pin away, and the pieces of the mountain are still falling about
our ears. The mathematical demonstration of Dr. Irwin showed simply that the Negative Binomial distribution could be obtained under at least two other hypotheses just
as well as under the hypothesis of accident proneness. ...

"One must hope that no new will-o'-the-wisp will lead our judgement so far astray
as accident proneness has done." [Haight, 1964.]

By contrast the opinion of Greenwood himself on these developments is refreshingly
sane. Writing in 1949, thirty years after the appearance of his first publication, he says:

"An eminent psychologist has written: 'When during the last war two statisticians
had their curiosity aroused by some accident figures in munition works, history was
made.' Dr. May Smith did not mean that these two statisticians were the first to
remark that some people had clumsier fingers and (or) less alert brains than others,
a fact no doubt commented on by the overlookers in manufactories of flint arrows in
the old Stone Age; she meant that they were the first, so far as present known, to propose an arithmetically simple test which could perhaps reveal the presence of some
human characteristic, later to be christened Accident Proneness. ... This simple test
interested psychologists and suggested to them the possibility of detecting persons
prone to accidents *before* they had had any accidents."

This paper was probably Major Greenwood's last completed work. It was submitted
for publication in *Biometrics* on the day of his death, 5 October 1949. Elsewhere
Greenwood had described himself as "not an expert on the subject of accident proneness,
but merely belonging to that diminishing class of citizen in this country who are not experts or authorities on anything whatever, but were merely inquisitive people". He must
have retained this inquiring interest in scientific matters right up to the end, for he died

suddenly at the age of 63 while attending a scientific meeting. Far from blaming him for promulgating any misleading "myth", accident research, which surely owes him a very great debt, can always be grateful that he was "one of those inquisitive people". Certainly his name has become well enough known in research circles, for there is hardly a paper written which does not start with a reference to his work (and it seems that his innocently submitted negative binomial distribution is still the main target of many an attack on the whole concept of accident proneness).

For the moment, however, the publications under consideration are not those of the critics of unequal liability. These only came later. Most of the earlier publications did in fact favour the concept, and I hope that in reviewing them I, who am quite frankly very much in favour of the concept, will be able to review them impartially and on their merits. I hope to criticize where I feel that criticism is justified, and to bestow praise where I feel that praise is due. But I also hope to do something which I feel is conspicuous by its absence in many of the recent reviews of the accident literature, namely to point out that there are *two* sides to every argument—and that a predilection for accepting only such evidence as happens to coincide with one's own particular psychological doctrine is not necessarily a sound basis for scientific judgement.

For, if one is going to judge a study by scientific standards, there is no doubt whatever that some of the studies which followed those of Greenwood and Newbold cannot stand up to impartial scientific scrutiny. Even if the studies themselves can qualify, the manner of the presentation of their conclusions can not.

Such, unfortunately, is the case with the series of studies carried out by Farmer and Chambers between 1926 and 1939. The studies themselves were meticulously, if somewhat misguidedly carried out, and the text is not only conservatively presented but also contains a wealth of information on all sorts of factors concerned with accident causation. The studies themselves are well worth reading, though they are difficult to obtain as they were not published in the usual statistical or psychological journals, but in reports of the Industrial Health Board, reports which are now very hard to get. One of them, fortunately the 1939 one on road accidents, is partially presented in Haddon's *Accident Research*.

The main defect of these studies lies in the fact that, this time, the conclusions erred markedly in the direction of over-statement, and contained few of the reservations given in the text. As the legitimate way to convey the gist of a scientific report is to repeat the final conclusions presented by the authors themselves, it is little wonder that these writers have been accused of misrepresentation. To accuse Farmer and Chambers (let alone Greenwood and Newbold), of fostering a "myth" or a "folklore" of accident proneness, as later writers have done, is a matter of opinion: but no one can deny the fact that the conclusions stated in Farmer's and Chambers' reports did in fact present an exaggerated and unjustified picture of the scientific evidence so far obtained in substantiation of the concept of accident proneness.

It was also unfortunate that these inaccuracies should have accompanied the entry of psychology into the field of accident research, for Farmer's and Chambers' work was a continuation of Newbold's statistical study, and the purpose was to find psychological tests which could pinpoint accident offenders. To do this Farmer and Chambers needed first of all stable accident criteria against which to measure the effectiveness of their tests—in other words they needed groups of workers, such as some of Greenwood's and Newbold's groups, where the exposure risk was controlled and the accident rate was high enough to highlight the differences between people, and where, as a result, one could expect a high correlation between the accidents of successive periods. Without this there was no chance whatever of the project succeeding for, again to quote Arbous: "Surely if the efficiency with which a criterion can predict itself is only of the order of 0·3, then it is a fond hope to expect that any test, which can only measure part of the criterion, will have a predicting efficiency as great as or greater than 0·3."

In the early stages of the project the investigators seemed fully aware of this fact and themselves said that "unless individual susceptibility to accidents is a stable quality manifesting itself during all periods of exposure, we cannot expect a very definite relation between psychological tests and accident rate". Yet, despite the fact that in the groups of people chosen for testing the highest correlation obtained was 0·44, and in most cases ranged between 0·18 and 0·33, Farmer and Chambers proceeded to carry out a series of extensive testing programmes, using all sorts of workers from dock workers to bus drivers, and applying all sorts of tests from paper-and-pencil intelligence tests to what they described as "aesthetokinetic" tests, namely instrumented tests like a dotting test, a reaction time test, and a pursuit meter. Unfortunately, between a rather random choice of tests and an unreliable criterion, the results were inevitable. In none of the groups tested was any really significant relationship found between the test scores and the accident criterion. The nearest approach to success was in the last project (London bus drivers, 1939) where, for at least the aesthetokinetic tests, although the coefficient was only 0·18 for 128 subjects, the investigators pointed out that there was a significant difference between the accident rates of the best scorers on the tests and the worst scorers; and that, for instance, excluding the worst scorers on the tests would have lowered the accident rate—a process, which, on the face of it, appeared rather impractical as it involved eliminating 25% of the men in order to reduce the accidents by 20%.

It seems a pity that so much effort should have been devoted to a project which was so obviously doomed to failure. For Farmer and Chambers undoubtedly did put a great deal of work into the project, and the many reports are well worth reading for the sake of the subsidiary findings which are very interesting, and also for the sake of some of their perceptive thinking. One particular example which has now become widely known is the use of the phrase "accident proneness", to define in a very rational manner the *personal* element in accident involvement. In this connection they say:

"The fact that one of the factors connected with accident liability has been found to be a peculiarity of the individual allows us to differentiate between 'accident proneness' and 'accident liability'. 'Accident proneness' is a narrower term than 'accident liability' and means a personal idiosyncrasy predisposing the individual who possesses it in a marked degree to a relatively high accident rate. 'Accident liability' includes all the factors determining accident rate: 'accident proneness' refers only to those that are personal."

Unfortunately, however, the contribution Farmer and Chambers made to the general thinking on accident liability was offset by the damage they did in perpetuating a number of misconceptions in the summaries of their reports. Despite all the difficulties they encountered in obtaining a stable criterion, and despite their failure to obtain any convincing results with their tests, their final reports contained such unjustified statements as:

"Accident proneness is no longer a theory but an established fact."

"Accident proneness among motor vehicle drivers is an important factor in the causation of accidents."

"Accident proneness was shown to manifest itself in all kinds of accidents and throughout all conditions of exposure."

What is more, the authors implied that the psychological tests used in the projects could successfully detect offenders and reduce accident rates. Statements such as these were undoubtedly very misleading, as none of the tests used did in fact produce any really significant results.

Nevertheless it is interesting to see a view expressed much later by Greenwood at a meeting of the Royal Statistical Society where Smeed (1949) was reading a paper on accident proneness. Greenwood's contribution to the discussion is reported as follows:

"He believed in proneness, and thought Mr. Farmer and his colleagues had done admirable work, but that we had not yet found practical tests which correlated so highly with what our ancestors called temperament that a satisfactory elimination of potentially dangerous drivers, which did not inflict hardship on individuals, was possible. But when we remembered the enormous increase of efficiency in tests of the cognitive side of human nature since the beginning of this century, it was surely not utopian to expect equally great improvements in our measures of the conative side of man."

Just what effect the studies of Farmer and Chambers had on the thinking on accident proneness is hard to say, but most of the writers on the subject are inclined to blame them for much of the over-optimism and loose thinking which followed. Haddon *et al.* are very critical of their work. Adelstein (1952), though much more favourably inclined to the proneness concept than Haddon and his co-authors, says: "Once the announcement of the 'accident-proneness' discovery was made, it was seized upon as the open sesame to all accident problems and a host of workers in the field began to use the idea without reference to the original work." And, though it seems most unfair to put all the blame on Farmer and Chambers, there is no doubt that whereas most of the earlier researchers seemed to have both feet firmly planted on the ground, by the early 1940's such a pleasurable degree of levitation had been achieved that for many years the thinking on accident proneness floated around on a balmy cloud of euphoria, blissfully unconcerned with the gravitational pull of reality. Scores of papers were written, few of them of any great consequence. They were written about traffic accidents, about industrial accidents, and children's accidents, nobody being very particular about where they were occurring as long as they could write a thesis about them. Research on accident proneness became the vogue, with few people bothering to make any further serious attempts to find out whether it really existed, and if so what contribution it made to the total accident picture. Though it is difficult to find specific examples in the scientific literature, possibly because most of the papers of that time have sunk into a merciful oblivion, it seems that the laymen of the period, particularly in the United States, managed to get the idea from somewhere that a small group of people were responsible for the majority of the accidents—and that it naturally followed that the detection and elimination of this small group would immediately solve the accident problem. Just how prevalent was this line of thinking, is impossible to gauge. It is even difficult to imagine how such an exaggerated idea could have gained wide acceptance, or for that matter that it actually did. But many of the later writers definitely maintain that this is so. Be this as it may, the atmosphere of euphoria was unmistakable. Possibly at least some of the blame can be laid at Farmer's and Chambers' door, but I for one am more than a little sceptical that any research work emanating from outside the United States could have such a very marked effect on American thinking. It might trigger off a spate of research *in* the United States—and certainly this spate did occur. But it would require *local* publicity to be given to *local* research before the idea could have gained general acceptance. This is particularly the case when one considers that Farmer's and Chambers' research was carried out over the period 1926–39, during which time a great many American papers were published on the subject of accident proneness.

One thing is quite certain, however, and that is that in no other country does one find widespread evidence of the sort of belief which apparently gained currency in America, that a handful of accident-prone people must be responsible for the majority of the accidents. But exactly how this came about is something which is, and probably always will be, just anybody's guess.

CHAPTER 4

DEVELOPMENT OF PRE-WAR RESEARCH

ONE of the earliest American publications to deal with the subject of accident proneness was Viteles' book *Industrial Psychology* (1932). This publication definitely could not be accused of fostering any mistaken ideas about "proneness" or any illusions about it being a simple phenomenon. In fact everything that Viteles said should have acted as a warning to future investigators that it was a complete waste of time to go on looking for any single factor which could be a major cause of accidents.

At the time that Viteles was writing, most of the urban transportation was by means of trams (or, as Viteles calls them, "electric streetcars"). He gives a most interesting (and alas, not all that outmoded) description of the various testing programmes which had been designed for the selection of these motormen, on the Continent as well as in the United States. He also mentions several places in which these testing programmes had achieved good results.

In the Greater Berlin Tramway Company an experimental battery of tests was set up in 1919 to deal with the problem of placing men returning at the conclusion of the First World War. This programme had been operating for many years since that time, and was being used on a large scale for the selection of motormen. Besides tests of technical intelligence and judgement, the battery included tests for day-vision, night- and colour-vision, steadiness of hand, and reaction to shock. The tests, says Viteles, proved to have reliability and validity. As far as accident reduction was concerned, he quotes the relative accident occurrence among two experimental groups:

Group A–50 motormen tested before selection, and:
Group B–50 motormen taken on without testing.
In the first year group B had 50% more accidents than group A.
In the second year group B had 40% more accidents than group A.

Another example which Viteles gives is the work of Lahy in Paris on bus and tram drivers. This programme was also accompanied by the following beneficial results:

The percentage of drivers discharged for incompetence either during or subsequent to training was reduced from 20% to 3·4%.
Drivers selected by means of the tests were responsible for 16·5% fewer accidents than their non-tested predecessors.

The selection programme reported by Lahy included tests for reaction time, motor suggestibility, immediate memory, perception of speed, distribution of attention, emotionality, etc. In this connection I remember only too well how, when our own PUTCO unit was installing its first programme of psychomotor tests, we wrote to the Régie Autonome des Transports Parisiens asking if they could let us have any details of this programme. They immediately sent us a mimeographed book with full details and photographs of all their tests, which proved most helpful, and for which we have always been sincerely grateful. But I also remember only too clearly the admiration with which we regarded one of the tests, the Paris-style test for distractability and emotionality. This consisted of a cinema screen surrounded by various lights and buzzers to which the subject had to react in a prescribed fashion while watching a series of films, including one very passionate love scene!

Some of the most interesting projects described by Viteles were the ones with which he was personally connected, such as the project on the Milwaukee Electric Railway and the Boston Elevated. Here, one might add, his personal concern went to the length of carrying out a complete analysis of the job of driving an electric streetcar, an analysis which included his going through the whole training course and operating a streetcar on all the different routes and under all sorts of conditions. So unusual is this approach, as indeed is the thinking adopted in all these programmes (and so seldom are they mentioned in the modern accident literature), that they are worth describing in some detail.*

Viteles starts by saying:

"The enormous cost of accidents to the Transportation Industry is largely responsible for the initiative which has been taken by this industry in applying psychological methods in the reduction of accidents. The manufacturing industries have largely contented themselves with the traditional methods of the safety engineer. A number of progressive companies operating street railways, motor buses, and taxi cabs have supplemented these by a scientific analysis of personal factors in accidents and by psychological techniques for detecting and rehabilitating accident-prone operators of motor vehicles. . . .

"The . . . study of accidents in the manufacturing industry has been largely confined to a statistical study of factors influencing accident susceptibility. Such statistical studies are of unquestionable significance in arriving at a knowledge of the causes of accidents, and in the development of a program for reducing accidents in industry. However, they suffer from serious limitations as practical aids in the reduction of accidents.

"In the first place the statistical approach is oriented from the viewpoint of discovering relations existing in a group of individuals, and not from the point of view of the adjustment of the single individual who has become involved in or is susceptible to accidents. It contributes little in the way of techniques or methods which may be useful in the adjustment of the individual worker who sustains accidents. The discovery, for example, that the proportion of younger men involved in accidents is greater than that of older men; that there is a correlation between minor illnesses and minor accidents; that there is a difference of 48 per cent in accident rate between those scoring above and

* Reprinted from Morris S. Viteles, *Industrial Psychology*, 1932. Copyright 1932 by W. W. Norton and Company Inc., New York. Copyright renewed by Morris S. Viteles. Reprinted with the permission of the publisher.

those scoring below the average on tests of psychomotor and other traits; etc., is of extremely great interest and importance. However, such facts are insufficient, in themselves, in helping one who has already become involved in an accident and in preventing further accidents on his part. The statistical approach limits itself to the accumulation of facts, but provides no procedure for applying these facts in the further study and adjustment of the individual worker.

"The function of the statistical approach and of statistical investigations in preventing accidents attributable to the human factor may be described as that of investigating *group* tendencies. In contrast with this is the *clinical approach*—the functions of which are to determine the relationship existing among a number of factors which have played or may play a part in the case of the individual who becomes involved in accidents, and to develop a program for the prevention of additional accidents on his part.

"Another limitation of the statistical viewpoint in accident prevention is its emphasis upon isolated aspects of individual personality, in contrast with the concern, in the clinical approach, for the *total personality* of the accident-prone individual. The point of orientation, in the statistical analysis, is not the individual who, in the final analysis, is the one susceptible to and suffering from accidents, but isolated sectors of individual make-up such as age, experience, reaction time, perseverance, accuracy of response, etc. It is assumed that the individual is a sort of mosaic, and that the sum of the single stones in this mosaic constitutes the whole. It is undoubtedly true that a detailed examination of each stone tells much about the *structure* of a mosaic, but the contribution of each to the value of the whole flows from the *integration* of the various parts, and can only be fully determined through an examination of the whole and of the inter-relationships among the parts in the whole.

"The aim of the clinical approach is to examine the whole individual, and from an examination of the whole to arrive at a knowledge of the significance of the various aspects of his personality—the relative importance of each sector of his personality in a given situation. The application of the clinical approach in the analysis of accident causes involves a complete study of the individual involved in accidents. As indicated in the discussion of the clinical method in the chapter on 'Psychological Foundations of Industrial Psychology', it makes the individual the point of departure, and provides for a thorough examination of every factor—physical, mental, social, and economic, and of those extraneous to the individual—which may have played a part in the accident in which he has been involved. From such a clinical analysis it is possible not only to assemble complete data on the causes of the accident, and to provide for the adjustment of the individual, but also to arrive at sound principles for the prevention of accidents in industry.

"In the transportation industry there is an increasing tendency to view the occurrence of accidents as an individual problem. Just as a physician diagnoses and treats a chronic ailment to effect a cure, so those employees who are repeatedly involved in accidents or are *accident-prone* are being studied and treated individually in the belief that many of them may be adjusted properly and become assets rather than liabilities. Case study methods, while reducing accident frequency among the small group of high-accident men, tend at the same time to encourage the entire group of employees to improve their records by breaking down the age-worn theory that accidents are a matter of 'hard luck' and that they cannot be prevented.

"The diagnosis of accident-proneness is being followed by specialized treatment based on an exact knowledge of the factors which are responsible for the accident record in the case of the particular individual. Treatment takes the form, not of mass education, or the more drastic measure of termination, but most frequently that of systematic instruction designed to efface such faulty habits of operation as may be responsible for the accident record. In other cases, medical treatment, discipline, encouragement, and supervisory follow-up may be employed in rehabilitating the accident-prone employee. This treatment is differential in character. It recognizes that there are many different causes of accidents and that they may be combined in different patterns in different individuals.

"The knowledge of the factors which play a part in the case of a single individual is obtained by an experimental study of the individual. This includes psychological examination, close observation of operation details, a review of his relationship with supervisory officers and fellow-workers, and possibly a detailed study of the home circumstances.

"On the basis of these facts, the program most suitable for that individual is laid out. In some cases, the causes for the bad accident record cannot be eradicated and, in these instances, discharge or transfer must be resorted to as a means of preventing further accidents on the part of such an operator. Perhaps, however, the most significant of the very many findings obtained from such an approach is the fact that termination or transfer need be resorted to in relatively few cases. So, for example, in the case of 54 men studied in one accident clinic, in a period of a year, only 3 men were recommended for discharge. The point of view of the accident clinic is that the dismissal or even transfer of a so-called 'accident-repeater' can be justified economically and socially only when it has been fully and reliably determined that it is impossible to correct the individual characteristics and habits which make him accident-prone.

"Where selection tests are being used a large proportion of those who are fundamentally unsuited for motor vehicle operation are being refused employment. The selective process of work itself results in the elimination of others who are totally unsuited for this work. Those who remain tend to be a somewhat selected group whose accident record is largely due to factors other than native capacity, such as faulty habits of operation, faulty attitudes, medical defects, etc., subject to correction when their exact nature is uncovered."

Viteles then illustrates this approach by describing the methods employed, and the results obtained in the study of accident-prone motormen in the Cleveland Railway Company (which, despite the name, operated mainly "electric streetcars"). One of the divisions of the company, Woodhill Station, had experienced a steady increase in accidents in 1927 in contrast to the other divisions. It was therefore chosen as the venue for an experimental study. A group of fifty motormen with the poorest accident records over the previous year were singled out for special attention. This group comprised some 30% of the total strength. Each man was individually studied, consideration being given to the following items:

Observation involving a careful examination of all his actions under normal operating conditions.

Analysis of previous and current years' accident record.

A personal interview.

A decision as to the primary causes of his "accident proneness".

Preparation of a report recommending specific treatment.

Treatment and later follow-up.

Viteles then quotes an actual case study. This man was 29 years of age, and had had two years' exposure. He had already had thirty-nine accidents, including operational accidents such as another vehicle striking the rear-end of his car, a vehicle cutting on to the track, side-rubs, and passenger accidents such as boarding or alighting accidents, or passengers falling in the car.

"DESCRIPTION OF FINDINGS ON CASE NO. 28

"Observations of Operation

"This motorman gives one the impression of being a conscientious worker; he attends strictly to business and seems to be alert constantly. When he is carrying a heavy load he puts all of his effort on the job, as though determined to do his utmost to get over the road in time.

"The subject clearly displays impulsive characteristics; he wants to keep going and is impatient to get off after making a stop. His stops and starts are much too fast, causing a standing load to lose its balance. Moreover, he frequently fails to close his door before starting. Twice within a few days he was observed starting his car while a passenger was still on the step. He has also formed a habit of opening his door before bringing the car to a stop.

"Attention, judgement of speed and distance, reaction and attitude appear to be beyond reproach. The causative factors of accidents in this case are almost solely faulty starting and stopping habits. This is substantiated by the fact that 35% of all his accidents are falls, boarding, in car, and alighting. Moreover, five of the twelve vehicle collisions in which he became involved during 1928 are 'vehicle striking the rear of car', also attributable to sudden stops.

"Personal Interview

"The subject is somewhat nervously constructed; his speech is rapid and his gestures and movements are impulsive at times. As observations of his work disclosed, he is inclined to be impatient; to make hasty decisions and then later to regret having made them. His attitude toward his work is excellent. He appears conscientious and is determined to make good. He seemed very much concerned about his high accident record, stating that he was glad to know all the facts and that he would do his best to correct the starting and stopping habits he had formed, none of which he denied.

"Mentality, health and family conditions are normal in every respect.

"Treatment

"That he be reinstructed weekly on the platform, and that his case be reviewed within two months' time."

Viteles then went on to say that the most significant finding of the Cleveland study was that in no two cases were the causes of accident proneness exactly similar. In most cases, several causes existed, although in each case one of these was found to be of primary importance. Physical difficulties were found to be of primary importance in only 12% of the cases (defective vision, organic disease, high blood pressure, and senility). This finding, he felt, was particularly important in view of the tendency of industrial medical men to place the responsibility for any maladjustment in industry upon physical difficulties. Actually in 22% of the cases an improper mental attitude or personality maladjustment was found to be the primary factor. The largest group of accident-prone men included those whose accident records were due primarily to operating defects—66% of the men exhibiting failure to recognize potential hazards, faulty judgement of speed and distance, improper distribution of attention, etc. The corrective treatment for each case was dependent on the driver's particular defects, and, as a result of this treatment, the accident rates of the motormen treated were reduced by 42·7%. Woodhill Station showed the largest accident reduction on the system for the period of the study, in contrast to the steady increase which it had shown in the two previous years.

Similar programmes carried out by himself and Bingham in the Milwaukee Railway and Light Company and the Boston Elevated Railway Company also achieved very considerable reductions in accident rates and accident costs, and clearly pointed to the economic value of applying psychological methods to accident reduction.

His book contains a wealth of interesting information and, old as it is, remains eminently worth reading. In fact, when one compares Viteles' broad-minded but down-to-earth approach with some of the present-day rather tunnel-visioned theorizing, one wonders yet again how it is that accident research has succeeded in going backwards while research in other fields is making such spectacular progress. For the conclusions he voiced thirty-six years ago have never been disproved, and his system for the individual diagnosis and treatment of accident proneness is still regarded in practical circles as the most effective one. Many of the tests and accident prevention programmes he described were stringently criticized later by critics such as Johnson (1946), saying that they had no proved validity. But what these critics fail to appreciate is that a number of these programmes for weeding out or treating accident offenders, have in fact brought down the accident rates of the transport organizations in which they have been used. This cannot always be explained away as a "Hawthorne" phenomenon, i.e. the result of someone taking an interest in the employees. For very often these programmes have resulted in not only the "clinical" treatment of accident offenders, but in a number of these accident offenders being discharged (which hardly falls under the heading of benevolent interest). Nor can these results be attributed solely to chance. Chance does not consistently operate in only one direction. No transport operator can reduce the accident rates of *specific accident offenders* for any length of time unless, while taking notice of them, he is able to pinpoint the reason for their undue susceptibility to accidents and then take some remedial action.

Nor is he going to reduce *overall accident rates* by firing drivers and hiring others to re-place them unless the quality of the hired is better than that of the fired.

All in all it would seem that the tendency, a tendency which has grown stronger and stronger in recent years, to decry the validity of the sort of practical work described by Viteles, because the results cannot always be presented with statistical "methodology" is perhaps just a little too glib—and too theoretical.

In assessing the practical possibilities of his work on the reclamation of "accident-prone" drivers, one must of course, bear in mind the conditions existing at the time. Not only was the traffic control in the 1920's much less effective than now, but even the vehi-cles were very much more difficult to drive. In his case study, he describes the task of a motorman in a sentence which speaks for itself: "When he is carrying a heavy load, he puts all his effort on the job, as though determined to do his utmost to get over the road in time." Under these sort of conditions it is not surprising that the accident rates of the motormen were so high. Nor is it surprising that he found that the main faults in 66% of the accident-prone men were operational faults which could be remedied by individual re-training. Under more modern conditions it is now possible to produce quite a high standard of proficiency during the course of a good, initial training programme. The faults which still remain are, however, much more difficult to overcome. A somewhat similar experiment in South Africa, with the PUTCO drivers, has shown that only in the case of long-service men who suddenly deteriorate has such an intensive reclamation policy been found to be a paying proposition. Re-training has, on occasion, had its effect, but by and large it has been found that many accident-prone drivers are, for some years at least, too inherently accident-prone to be reclaimable. As Tillman said in 1949, many drivers need to change their whole personality and their whole way of life before they can be consider-ed to be safe drivers. In a transport organization this process takes too long, and in the meantime is too expensive—and dangerous—to be a practical proposition. But, nevertheless, in the course of this particular fifteen-year practical project, everything that Viteles said about the individuality of susceptibility to accidents, has been borne out over and over again.

Nor, when one considers the realism with which he approached the whole question, can it ever be said that he created any false illusions about accident proneness. Never at any time did he claim that a handful of accident-prone drivers were responsible for the majority of the accidents. On the contrary, to achieve the results he did it was often necessary to take remedial action with as many as 30% of the total group.

A much less justified, but probably far more publicized source of encouragement for the harbouring of exaggerated ideas about the all-importance of accident proneness seems to have been the Connecticut study (Cobb, 1939), the reports on which appeared in 1938 and 1939. This is ironical, really, for nowadays some of the figures contained in the study are repeatedly used to decry the usefulness of the whole concept.

Cobb's study was a report on a very extensive programme carried out by the Bureau of Public Roads, on behalf of the U.S. Government—a study on which some of the lead-ing researchers of America were engaged. It was in two parts: (1) a statistical analysis of the accident records of 29,531 drivers from the general motoring public of Connecti-cut, and (2) a psychological programme involving giving a number of tests to 3663 similar drivers. (This latter programme produced no significant results and will therefore not be described.)

The statistical report cites as the background for the study the findings of previous research undertaken by the National Research Council. This research concerned, *inter alia*, the accident records of transport companies. Here, where every accident however trivial was recorded, it appeared that drivers who had an undue share of accidents of all kinds also had an undue share of serious accidents. And (although in no case was there any control over exposure risk) it also appeared that there were significant differences between the accident rates of various groups of drivers, and that these *group* differences were relatively stable ones.

In the light of these findings Cobb opens his preface to the study by saying:

"It is known from experience in the general field of safety work and from the studies of records of drivers in fleets used in industry that certain persons are prone to have mishaps while driving motor vehicles. But definite information as to the proportion of such persons in the general driving public and the extent to which they are involved in the total accidents has heretofore been lacking.

"In order to discover the facts of this situation and in the hope that they will give some indication of effective measures to combat the rising tide of motor vehicle casualties, the accident records of 29,531 drivers in Connecticut were investigated for the 6-year period 1931–36 inclusive. These drivers were selected in such a way that they constituted a random sample of the Connecticut drivers during that period and hence their experience should be typical of the whole driving population of that State, which is probably similar in make-up and experience to the driving population of other States."

Connecticut was chosen because the reporting of accidents was reputed to be better here than in other States, the belief being that practically all the fatal and injury accidents, and possibly half the major property damage accidents (damage in excess of $25) were reported. A second reason why Connecticut was chosen was that enforcement in that State was very strict.

The sample study consisted of drivers who were licensed during the whole of the six-year period. The first investigation was the currently popular one of comparing the accidents sustained over the whole six-year period with a Poisson distribution, a comparison which showed that the distribution was very significantly different from chance. The distribution was distinctly J-shaped, i.e. it had more people with no accidents and a longer "tail" of people with multiple accidents than a chance-expected one. This tail (two or more accidents) Cobb pointed out, only constituted 4% of the population but was responsible for 36% of the accidents. On the basis of this investigation, Cobb concluded:

"This showed the presence in the population of two groups toward which accident preventative measures should be directed: the large intermediate class, the members of which are not necessarily accident prone, but which has the bulk of accidents: and the comparatively small high-accident group composed of drivers who have accidents out of all proportion to their number."

Designating the latter group as "accident-prone", Cobb went on to say that their accidents "must be attributed to predisposing characteristics of the individual or of the conditions under which they do their driving".

The second investigation was to determine whether the future performance of accident repeaters could be predicted. To do this the accident records were split into two three-year periods. Tables were set out giving, *inter alia*, the correlation between the number of accidents sustained by each driver in the two periods. This distribution is set out in Table 4.1. Correlation of the accidents in the two periods yielded a coefficient of 0·11. A comparison of the average accident rates of the drivers who had 0, 1, 2, 3, and 4 accidents in the first period with the *average* accident rate of the same drivers in the second period gave the results shown in Table 4.1.

TABLE 4.1. ACCIDENTS RATES IN
TWO SUCCESSIVE PERIODS (AFTER
COBB, 1938)

Accident groups 1931–3 (accidents per driver)	Same group 1934–6 (accidents per driver)
0	0·101
1	0·199
2	0·300
3	0·484
4	0·700

From these data Cobb concluded (though he did say that it might be necessary to find some way of predicting the future involvement of individuals), "Once a group has been established as being predominantly accident-free or accident-liable, its future history as a group can be predicted with astonishing accuracy from its past performance."

The next step was a study of the relationship between age and accident involvement. This study revealed that the young drivers in the Connecticut population (and in other populations studied) had nearly twice their proportionate share of accidents, and that their record was particularly bad with respect to fatal accidents. It also revealed that they had two to three times their share of licence suspension for speeding.

Summing this up, Cobb says:*

"These are the facts: three definite groups in the driving population having different effects upon the traffic situation are recognized: (1) the great bulk of the drivers whose individual accident expectancy is slight but whose numbers are so vast that they roll up an appalling casualty total: (2) the high-accident or accident-prone group, small in number but mighty in deed: (3) youthful drivers, whose mishaps far outrun their proportion in the driving population.

* Reprinted by permission of the National Research Council.

"How best in the light of the facts developed by this investigation to direct remedial measures to these three classes of drivers is a matter for thorough consideration and to some extent for further research. However, a few pertinent and perhaps obvious thoughts can be set down at once.

"To lower the accident-rate level for the vast number of drivers in group one, who have no salient traffic characteristics, every resource must be applied which will make the roads and vehicles safe for reasonable use and will induce in the driving public better habits and safer practices. Here is a task for the united efforts of engineers, law-enforcement agencies and educators. Many phases of this united purpose are in need of further research and study.

"It has been shown that through the keeping and study of adequate accident records, administrative authorities can identify from past performance the group of high-accident drivers which must contain the accident-prone individuals who have distinguished themselves in the period examined. As time goes on, new additions will constantly be made. Questions for future study and research are: (1) How to separate in this group those who are truly repeaters or accident-prone from those who have merely been unlucky? (2) What preventative measures to take after segregation is accomplished?

"In the case of the youthful accident-prone class, it is not known whether the trouble is due to inexperience, lack of judgement, or poor training.

"... Far better than detecting accident-prone drivers from their records after they had done much damage, would be to examine prospective drivers and determine in some way whether or not they might be expected to have this propensity."

It is very difficult in a short review to do justice to any of these big studies, or even to choose quotations which will correctly portray the author's meaning. The best one can do is to try and convey the general tone of the report. And there seems little doubt that the tone of the Connecticut study was sufficiently positive and optimistic as to give quite a boost to the uncritical popularity of the proneness concept—but here again not anything like sufficient for anyone to ever get the idea that the accident-prone drivers could be held responsible for the *majority* of the accidents. In fact Cobb several times definitely stated otherwise. Anyone who wished to put this interpretation on the phrase "the high-accident or accident-prone group, small in number but mighty in deed" would need to lift this phrase completely out of context. They would also need to ignore every table of figures. The most that Cobb ever claimed for his so-called accident-prone drivers (with two or more accidents in six years) was that they were responsible for 36% of the total number of accidents. But there was nevertheless little justification for statements such as: "Once a group has been established as being predominantly accident-free or accident-liable, its future history as a group can be predicted with astonishing accuracy from its past performance." And, where his report was very misleading was in ever applying the term "accident-prone" to *any* of his accident repeaters, let alone this particular group, for two accidents in six years, even if they were serious accidents, can hardly be called "statistical proneness".

In any case, the study really contained no valid evidence applicable to the concept of accident proneness. If proneness is taken to mean the person-centred element in accident susceptibility, then it is not only undesirable but unjustified to use the word in a statistical study like the Connecticut study, where there was no way of controlling exposure. For one can hardly talk of proneness *in the statistical sense* when there is no way of telling how much of the discrepancy between the accident rates of *different people* is due to differences in the mileage they cover and/or the conditions under which they drive; or when there is no way of telling how much of the variation in the accident rate of the *same person from one period to another* is due to similar changes in exposure and risk. In addition the incompleteness of the accident recording, and the fact that increasingly strict enforcement was all the time bringing various pressures to bear, still further complicated the issue. It is an unfortunate fact, but one which must be accepted, that a study of this nature is anything but ideal material for a scientific statistical investigation of the proneness concept. Although Cobb and his associates appear to have appreciated many of the limitations of their data this did not, unfortunately, stop them from generalizing from their findings in such a way as to create an impression for which there was very little scientific foundation. This impression was undoubtedly enhanced by the size of the sample, most of the people who read the report at the time being apparently too overawed by the sheer number of drivers studied to stop and think that having 29,531 subjects in a study is of very little value when the data pertaining to those subjects are incomplete (a phenomenon which still occurs today and causes some of the figures emanating from this study to be quoted almost reverentially).

The general popularity of the study was shown by the fact that a very critical article (Forbes, 1939) which appeared shortly afterwards in the *Journal of General Psychology* seemed to attract very little attention. It is hard to find any references to it in the literature of the time and it is only in recent years that it has been resurrected and has become very much a talking point.

Forbes' contention was that the Connecticut study, far from proving the magnitude of the contribution made by the "accident-prone" driver to the general accident picture, had instead demonstrated that this contribution was negligible, and that the bulk of the accidents were caused by the "normal" driver. Reproducing the figures of the 3×3 year Connecticut study, he proceeded to calculate what effect eliminating the people who were "accident-prone" in the first period would have had in reducing the total number of accidents of the second period—and came up with the rather startling findings that:

(1) Only 398 ($1 \cdot 3\%$) of the 29,531 drivers could be called "prone" on the basis of their performance in the first period (two or more accidents).
(2) Of these 398 only 23 were still "prone" in the second period.
(3) Eliminating this $1 \cdot 3\%$ who were "prone" in the first period would only have reduced the total number of accidents of the second period by $3 \cdot 7\%$.

From this he concluded:

"The 'normal' driver constituted $98 \cdot 7$ per cent of the driver group studied and caused $96 \cdot 3$ per cent of the accidents which interfered with the efficiency of traffic within that State. This situation differs very markedly from previous interpretations of accident records analyzed by the total time period only [Cobb and other studies] in which accident-prone drivers or repeaters were apparently responsible for from 10 to 15 per cent of the accidents.

"It thus becomes obvious that for the purposes of traffic design and control we are more interested in the ordinary driver than the accident-prone driver. Although the selection and elimination of the small group which may be truly accident-prone is desirable, nevertheless, in order to attack the bulk of the accident problem and the problem of providing highways and traffic facilities which are efficient, we must consider essentially the ability of the majority of 'normal motorists'. This applies to all attacks on the problem whether engineering, education or enforcement."

Forbes' paper, with its attempt to debunk a popular concept, was certainly a change from the current run of publications of the time. But in another way it was still rather typical of its time in that it went in for shock figures and sweeping statements for which there was insufficient justification. His revelation that the accident-prone driver was only responsible for 3·7% of the accidents, as against the 10–50% quoted in the Cobb study, was rather in the line of a sales gimmick. For this sort of wide discrepancy is bound to occur when every investigator has his own standard of what constitutes "proneness". Although Forbes was arguing that proneness was more a matter of continuous involvement than merely numbers of accidents sustained, nevertheless, in doing so, he set very high comparative standards. In the different studies quoted by Cobb, drivers were considered to be on the more dangerous end of a continuum of proneness if their rate was anything from three to eight times that of *the average for the group they represented*. Forbes, on the other hand, divided the Connecticut drivers into two distinct groups: the "prone" and the "normal", the arbitrary cut-off for the prone being an accident rate sixteen times that of the average—a fact which makes his findings a little less spectacular.

Nor, for that matter, was Forbes, who concentrated on the accidents of the second triennium, really justified in generalizing from a sample of drivers—all with at least three years' exposure and experience and all with valid licences—to the general driving public with its annual crop of newly licensed youngsters and its quota of the sort of people who get themselves killed or injured, or removed from the driving register because of their bad driving.

He himself apparently later developed a few doubts as to the validity of his conclusions, and is reported to have said (in his *Handbook of Applied Psychology*, 1950, which is now unfortunately out of print) that he was not sure of the correct method of determining the relative importance of those drivers who are accident-prone over a prolonged period. However, despite a tendency for sweeping statements, he definitely appears to have had a good deal of right on his side, for it was apparently high time that somebody poured a little cold water on the fervid enthusiasm which was developing for regarding the ultra-prone driver as the major cause of accidents. But whether it was because his paper was not publicized in the way the Connecticut study was, or because his arguments were considered illogical, or merely unpopular, it appears that at the time nobody took very much notice of his views, and his was just a voice crying in the wilderness. Such a cursory dismissal of his findings was clearly unjustified. For despite the limitations of the Connecticut data, Forbes' paper should have rung a bell of warning that when it comes to serious reported accidents the person who has repeated accidents (if he survives to drive again) may, *if the records are correct*, contribute a much smaller proportion of the total tally than he was at that time believed to contribute. (This finding may of course be more applicable to the United States with its strict enforcement policies than to other countries where relatively little action is taken against traffic and accident offenders.) Forbes' reports should, in fact, have brought home the point that, as far as the individual is concerned, the number of past accidents which do happen to get reported to State Motor Vehicle Departments, is not a good indicator of reported accidents to come—an observation borne out by the later studies of the California Motor Vehicle Department (Coppin, 1964–7) which show that the number of *recorded* accidents is actually a very poor predictor of future reported accidents; that violations are a better predictor; and that a loaded regression equation, based on accidents, mileage, violations, and biographical data is the best predictor of all—though still woefully inadequate in the case of *individuals*, except to pinpoint cases which would merit further detailed personal investigation. Here, however, as Coppin and his co-workers themselves point out, there is no knowing (a) what proportion of the accidents which should be reported do in fact get reported, and (b) what effect disciplinary warnings or disciplinary action may have in influencing a driver's behaviour. For there is always the possibility that the man who has come to the notice of a Motor Vehicle Department, in connection with one or more serious accidents or traffic violations, may moderate his behaviour for some little time thereafter. Another possibility is that such action may also make a driving offender extra keen to pay out for a property-damage accident, rather than have it entered in his file. And Ross, in his paper "Traffic law violations: a folk crime" (1960), says:

"The work of courts and violations bureaus, in the attempted control of traffic infractions, is aided by the technique of police 'warnings' without arrests. In certain notorious situations the stopping of a motorist by a policeman has become a situation of informal trial, with a 'fine' in the form of a bribe collected by the policeman. The ethics of the situation aside, large scale bribery of police functions to relieve the strains on the legitimate processing system caused by volume of cases."

Altogether it would appear that a number of factors may be affecting, and possibly even distorting the picture of accident occurrence, as presented by the records of Motor Vehicle Departments—especially in States where the enforcement policy carries any severe penalties. What the position was like in Connecticut, way back in the 1930's, is difficult to say. But the Cobb report does mention that Connecticut was chosen as the venue for this study because it was necessary to select a State "in which the authorities are reasonably and consistently diligent about enforcement". He also says: "For a comprehensive and valid study of accident records, therefore, it seemed well to select some State in which the records have been kept accurately over a long period." The accuracy of the *way* the records are kept is not in question. But it seems eminently possible that the *completeness* of these records is subject to some doubt. Cobb himself says that he thinks most of the fatal and injury accidents were reported, but probably only half the property-damage ones. Other writers later estimated that possibly only about one-fifth of the total number of "reportable" accidents actually do get reported.

I must admit that when I first saw the figures of the Connecticut study I looked at them in amazement, a reaction shared by many of the continental researchers and traffic officials. All of us were astonished, not only at the small number of "repeaters", but also at what seemed to us to be the incredibly low average accident rate of 0·04 accidents per driver per annum. Unfortunately I have been unable to find any other country which could produce a similar analysis of accident experience among members of the general motoring public. But some of the figures from the analysis of the PUTCO data on South African bus drivers (described in Chapter 15) certainly reveals a different picture. Whatever the period studied and whatever the traffic conditions, the accident rate, even for only the serious accidents, was found to be *eight* to *ten* times that of the Connecticut study (the definition of a serious accident being comparable, i.e. an accident involving fatality, injury, or property damage in excess of $75—an even higher cost cut-off, but probably not so different from the Connecticut one in view of the fact that the PUTCO studies related to the 1950's when repair costs were much higher). Table 4.2 shows the comparison of Forbes' figures with those derived from the PUTCO study.

TABLE 4.2. COMPARISON OF FORBES' RE-ANALYSIS OF THE CONNECTICUT DATA (AFTER FORBES, TABLE 1, 1939) WITH SIMILAR DATA FROM A POPULATION OF SOUTH AFRICAN BUS DRIVERS

The Effect of Removing the Repeaters of One Three-year Period upon the Total Accident Rate of a Subsequent Three-year Period

	Accident rate in FIRST period	Number of drivers	No. of accidents accruing to these drivers in the SECOND period	Percentage of drivers with two or more accidents in the FIRST period	Percentage of accidents in the SECOND period which would be eliminated
CONNECTICUT 1931–6 (Forbes figures)	0	26,259	2660		
	1	2874	572		
	2	357	107	1·2	3·1
	3	31	15	0·1	0·4
	4	10	7	0·03	0·2
	TOTAL	29,531	3,361	1·3	3·7
SOUTH AFRICA 1954–9 (PUTCO figures)	0	52	47		
	1	44	45		
	2	26	27	18·3	17·5
	3	16	27	11·3	17·5
	4	3	4	2·1	2·6
	5				
	6	1	4	0·7	2·6
	TOTAL	142	154	32·4	40·2

From these tables the following information can be derived:

If a driver is considered to be a "repeater" (because he has X accidents in the FIRST period—then removing these drivers would have reduced the accidents of the FIRST and the SECOND period as follows:

$X = 2$ or more.

Connecticut	First period	22·7%	Second period	3·7%
PUTCO	First period	72·8%	Second period	40·2%

$X = 3$ or more.

Connecticut	First period	3·6%	Second period	0·6%
PUTCO	First period	40·7%	Second period	22·7%

$X = 4$ or more.

Connecticut	First period	1·1%	Second period	0·2%
PUTCO	First period	11·1%	Second period	5·2%

One can expect the accident rate of professional drivers exposed for eight hours each day to be higher than that of the general public—but not as wide a discrepancy as this.

In any case the most pertinent finding of all is that in the PUTCO data, out of 142 drivers:

46 had two or more serious accidents in the first three-year period.

19 of these 46 continued to repeat and had two or more serious accidents in the second three-year period.

This means 19 repeater-repeaters out of a minute group of 142, as against 23 repeater-repeaters out of a group of 29,531 in the Connecticut study! If nothing else does, then this finding alone should cast some doubt on the accuracy of the Connecticut reporting. And once the accuracy of this reporting is open to question then the suitability of such data for any study on the validity or the importance of accident proneness becomes very much open to question.

In fact, Forbes may be very far off the mark in talking of 98·7% of the drivers being just *normal* drivers for whom accident prevention should be directed towards providing highway and traffic facilities which are consistent with their *normal* ability. No one would deny that such an engineering approach is vitally important. But is the proportion of accident-prone drivers in fact so negligible, and are their contributions to the accident problem so insignificant that, as Forbes implies, enforcement policies have too small a target to be of any importance? The PUTCO data and many of Coppin's later findings, especially those on chronic traffic offenders, suggest otherwise.

Actually, it is ironical to note that one of the reasons given for the failure of the second half of the Connecticut project, the psychological testing of some 4000 Connecticut drivers, was the unreliability of the accident criterion *because of the incompleteness of the Connecticut accident records.* Case and Stewart (1956) talking of the low correlations between the attitude tests used in this study and the accident criterion say: "These low relationships (which are about as high as any obtained by the other so-called driver tests) are explained in part on the basis of the impossibility of being able to know the real extent of accidents as related to the group."

However, at the time that Forbes published his paper no one seemed to challenge his findings for the simple reason that they appear to have passed almost unnoticed—and to have remained so for another twenty years. But somewhere round the beginning of the sixties, when a section of American research opinion began to get very critical of the concept of accident proneness, his paper was suddenly rediscovered, and since then has been repeatedly used to demonstrate the fallacy of the whole idea. This is why I thought it best to introduce here some figures from another driving population, so that the reader would at least have some frame of reference against which to make his own assessment of a study which later exerted such a pronounced influence on research thinking, and which may yet have far-reaching effects on practical policy with regard to enforcement.

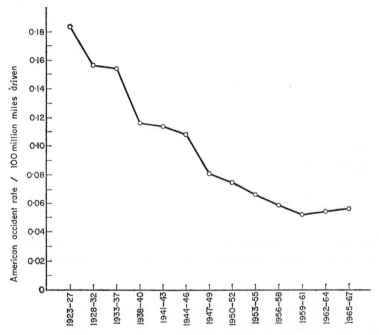

FIG. 4.1. America's accident rate per 100 million miles driven. (Information derived from *Traffic Accident Facts* 1968, United States National Safety Council)

No doubt there were several reasons why Forbes' study created so little impression at the time. His findings would not have been popular in research circles as accident proneness was currently very much the vogue. But his findings might also have been disregarded in practical circles because they were considered to be merely a theoretical opinion, and probably an illogical one at that. At that time America's accident rate was nearly double what it is today (Fig. 4.1) and the practical officials were obviously very concerned indeed with the problem of traffic offenders and the number of accidents in which they were involved. A research finding purporting to show that the high-risk driver was of no importance in the accident situation would probably have had a rather cool reception in practical circles.

This was very evident from the tone of a book which appeared in 1942, and was immediately very well received, De Silva's *Why We Have Automobile Accidents*. De Silva's whole approach was a very practical one, and most of his knowledge was obtained from officials connected with the Motor Vehicle Departments. His thinking on the driver is clearly expressed in his Introduction:

"Though our present roads have not been designed primarily from the safety point of view, they can be driven with impunity. The automobile, also, in most respects a safe piece of machinery, can be used with a minimum of damage. It is the driver to whom we must impute responsibility for the hazards presented by these instruments. Left gloriously free, free to follow his own inclinations, be they good or bad, he has been driving much as he pleased, and year by year he has managed to kill and injure his fellow men by the hundreds of thousands. Why? Because of wilful human faults—selfishness, lack of appreciation of his responsibilities to others, carelessness, wastefulness; because of lack of driving skill, because of unwillingness to conform to reasonable driving regulations. The driver is in need of a thorough overhauling. In place of his present casual education and lax control we need efficient and co-ordinated enforcement of suitable driver laws and regulations by all the State Motor Vehicle Departments.

"It would be difficult to find another field of such practical importance to millions as the improvement and control of the habits of those using our highways, in which so little systematic research has been attempted, so few needed facts gathered, so little analysis made of them, and so little accomplished. And yet real progress in accident reduction demands organized fact collecting, analysis, planning, and practical application of findings no less than does advancement in other fields. We need to obtain complete and accurate data about the occurrence of automobile accidents in each State, to analyze and assemble this information in easily understandable form, and, by the study of such factors as scientific research, to determine the most effective and economical means of reducing accidents in different localities."

De Silva felt that there were several causes for the apparent neglect of the road accident problem in the United States; a multitude of groundless opinions about the causes of accidents resulting in unsound proposals for solving the accident problem; the aura of publicity which surrounded the safety organizations and which made the public feel that something was being achieved; and both a conscious and unconscious resistance on the part of the public. The public, he felt, resisted encroachment on their freedom to drive automobiles as they wished, and would not relinquish their individual rights unless they were convinced that doing so was necessary for the national welfare. And convincing them was going to be very difficult, not only because they did not seem to want to be convinced, but because most people seemed to have a sort of mental block as far as accidents were concerned.*

"Human beings normally possess the tendency of all organisms to struggle for survival, not against it. Thus no one in his right senses tries to be killed or injured while driving. Yet each year hundreds of thousands of Americans are physically incapacitated to a greater or less extent in highway accidents. Nobody in his right mind presumably likes to smash up his car. Yet annually the loss in wrecked cars runs into millions of

* From H. R. De Silva, *Why We Have Automobile Accidents*, by courtesy of John Wiley, New York.

dollars. In the case of these continuously repeated accidents, something must be perverting our normal human behavior. What is it?

"One factor may be our human tendency to forget the unpleasant. Drivers and pedestrians alike tend to repress the distasteful remembrances of automobile accidents they have seen, or in which they have taken part. This repression removes from their minds the inhibiting, restraining influences which memory would exert over their actions and allows them to conduct themselves as though their foolhardy behavior would have no untoward results. This habit of repression seems to carry over into our community, state and national attitude towards accidents, and to lead us to sidestep our common responsibility for dealing with the problem. We pass a few laws, we encourage occasional face-saving safety campaigns, but we never really come face-to-face with the adversary."

One of the problems which De Silva felt must be dealt with was the problem of the driver, and this he said he proposed to make the main issue of his book, which is full of interesting information, most of it derived from the findings of various State Motor Vehicle Departments. It would be quite impossible to review the book here, but a couple of unusual observations are well worth mentioning. He devotes one chapter to what he calls "safety-mindedness". Skill, he says, is not enough, and in testing drivers he himself had often encountered numbers of people who had been able to drive safely over many years, even though their driving skill was well below average. The outstanding characteristics of these motorists were the possession of an insight into their deficiencies and a willingness to restrict their driving so as to make up for their weaknesses. On the other hand, he had often encountered drivers whose skill was well above average but whose safety records were most undesirable. He therefore considered that an all-important feature in accident susceptibility was the attitude which led a driver either to keep out of accidents or to almost court them. These attitudes he defined as:

"*Safety-mindedness*, a complex state of mind involving a recognition of the inherent hazards in driving and their relation to the lives of those who use the roads. Among its basic constituents are caution and consideration for the lives, property and comfort of others. Other traits that contribute to safety-mindedness are foresight, emotional stability, mental balance, and a desire to understand one's limitations as a driver with a view to surmounting them."

Some of his most interesting remarks concern what he calls the "less safety-minded types in our population":

"Twenty years ago the use of the automobile was limited to the upper economic classes of our society. Now with the improvement in our national standard of living and the increasing popularity of the motor car, one out of approximately three persons in the country has become a driver. Instead of the million drivers of 1919, we now have 40 million. [The 1968 figure was approximately 120 million!]

"This tremendous increase in the proportion of our population driving cars has naturally resulted in larger and larger numbers of our less fit citizens taking up driving. Although cheap automotive transportation has been a boon in many ways to the average American it has put behind the wheels of cars a large number of individuals who are not up to par physically, mentally, or emotionally and who consequently cannot be expected to possess all the characteristics necessary for safe driving.

"Safety-mindedness is a reflection not only of specific driving knowledge and experience but also of one's attitude toward life and one's fellow man. We all have certain responsibilities as members of our respective communities. Our ratings as desirable or undesirable citizens depend to a considerable extent on the way we fulfil these duties, or expressed differently, on our degree of social responsibility. Since safety-mindedness is based partly upon the very qualities that determine whether we are assets or liabilities to society, it follows that safety-mindedness is correlated with our status as citizens. Decent behavior on the highway may be in part a reflection of one's general respectability.

"Although some of our basic traits are inborn, the ability and willingness to adjust ourselves to society depend to a large extent upon our environment and training, or what is commonly referred to as our 'background'. The personal qualities which determine our degree of social adjustment naturally are influenced by and vary with our social status and the standards of social behavior it presupposes.

"Individuals who have been brought up in favorable surroundings where they have had the opportunity to learn how to behave as co-operative members of the community, to obey the laws, to earn a living honestly, and to respect the rights of others, acquire a normal sense of social responsibility, whereas individuals who have grown up in unfavorable surroundings where considerations of self-survival are all-important and education and the civic virtues neglected, frequently fail to acquire a normal sense of social obligation. This, in turn, makes difficult the development of a safety-minded attitude when they become drivers.

"The relationship between undesirable social phenomena and bad driving has not been much studied because bad driving has always been regarded as a problem to be solved principally by improvements in the roads and cars, or by general propaganda and safety education in the schools.

"Experts in various fields have testified that there is a very considerable causal relationship between living conditions in substandard areas in cities, and disease and crime. Crowding, defective sanitary facilities, improper ventilation, and inadequate heating do not make for physical well-being, nor in turn, for moral health.

"Studies in a number of cities throughout the country confirm the connection between squalid living conditions and delinquency. In Jacksonville, Florida, it was found that 32% of all major crimes and 42% of all sex crimes were committed in a slum section embracing less than 1·8% of the city's area. In Cleveland, Ohio, and Philadelphia, Pennsylvania, the rate of juvenile delinquency was found to be three times as high in the underprivileged areas as it was in the rest of the city. In Hartford, Connecticut, and Birmingham, Alabama, it was twice as high. In a tenement area in Chicago, more than 25% of all the boys between the ages of ten and seventeen passed through the juvenile court in one year. In Detroit, according to studies there are fifteen times as many criminals in slum areas as in normal residential districts.

"Two important elements of safety-mindedness—responsibility and consideration for others—need development through education and good example. Slum conditions do not facilitate their growth. The struggle there for the bare necessities of existence and for even a tiny portion of luxury makes the rule of life 'everyone for himself', a principle which by its very nature excludes consideration for others and responsibility towards society in general. Persons who have had to contend with so many adverse factors, especially if they have little mental and ethical capacity, find it hard to adjust themselves to society, and, accordingly, to the other drivers on the highway.

"A traffic survey in Saint Paul, Minnesota, in 1937–1939 revealed that the proportion of licensed drivers in accidents is much higher in some districts than in others, and that the census tracts having the highest proportion of the drivers in accidents were located in poorer portions of the city surrounding the downtown business section, where the residents were generally of the lower-income group. In these high-accident districts one out of every 12 or 13 drivers was involved in an accident during the year, as compared to an average of one out of 21 drivers for the city as a whole. The lowest rate of accident participation was for drivers residing in residential areas on the outskirts of the city where people of the higher-income groups reside. Only one out of 30 to 35 drivers in these better residential areas was involved in an accident."

De Silva then gives a number of figures and graphs illustrating his point and ends up by saying that these studies open up a new vista of problems which deserve further investigation. A lot would need to be found out about the age, sex, race, educational status, etc., of the people involved in the accidents, and also about the year, model, type, and condition of the vehicles involved. It would also be valuable "to have a group of the worst offenders from good to poor districts report to be interviewed and subjected to a battery of medical and psychological tests in an effort to discover underlying factors which might have predisposed them to accidents, and to detect differences in human deficiencies contributing to accidents among different classes of citizens". However, here he inserts a word of warning and says: "An attempt should also be made to check what part, if any, of the good record of citizens in the better districts can be attributed to their ability to pay for their mistakes, and to keep information about their accidents from the Press and from public records."

Other problem drivers described by De Silva were the non-owner group who, in several studies, had been shown to have a disproportionate number of accidents. Another group was the foreign-born and illiterate driver, often illiterate because of mental inferiority. Another group of problem drivers was the emotionally unstable or mentally diseased driver:

"Several investigations conducted of violator- and accident-drivers reveal the presence in their midst of a surprisingly large number of emotionally unstable and mentally diseased drivers.

"Mental instability frequently goes hand in hand with inefficient co-ordination of muscles and bodily movements. An unbalanced emotional system may show itself outwardly in jerky or uncertain actions. No matter how slight such movements may be or how harmless in other situations, they may have serious consequences when they occur in a driver traveling at high speeds.

"Emotional instability may occur in any class of citizen, although its manifestations may vary in different social groups. Emotionally unstable people from the slums are apt to show this defect in acts of aggression on the road, whereas those from the better sections are more likely to err in the direction of timidity and uncertainty. To those whose lives have always consisted of insecurity, the risks of the road mean less than they do to conservative persons from the middle and upper classes, whose more sheltered life has given them a different conception of personal danger."

De Silva then went on to describe all the different factors which can cause the *relatively* normal driver to have accidents—and particularly more than his share of accidents, such as lack of skill or faulty attitudes or temporary indisposition. He says, however, that the whole question of the human factor in accidents was one where research had as yet only just skimmed the surface.

On the whole he was very critical of the progress of accident research—especially on the human factor. His feeling was that this was a sphere where knowledge was badly needed in order to alleviate a very serious social problem, and that worth-while knowledge was not forthcoming. This was a rather different attitude from that displayed by many of the more dilettante researchers of the time. To them, accident research appeared to be just an interesting new field for experimental psychology, and the 1940's witnessed the appearance of a spate of papers, most of them American, describing a little study here and a little study there, everybody thinking up a test of some sort and trying to correlate it with an accident criterion of some sort—with complete disregard for the warnings of the earlier researchers (let alone the dictates of common sense) that the causes of accidents were far too complex for any one simple test to have any chance of success.

Johnson (1946) in a very critical review of the situation reached by that time, had some very scathing remarks to make about the quality of the research of the period. He was particularly scathing about the claims made to date on behalf of tests and procedures predicting accident susceptibility. In a very few instances, he said, was any evidence submitted of the reliability of these procedures, let alone their validity. He also maintained (with a massive list of references to back his claim) that people were constantly advocating the use of tests with very low predictive accuracy in situations for which they were totally unsuitable. As he said, a test with a correlation of 0·3 or 0·4 with an accident criterion might be all very well for the use of transport operators, who happened to have plenty of labour available, and who could afford to turn away a lot of likely material in order to get a couple of good drivers, but they were totally unsuitable for making a decision about *an individual* in a connection like the issue or withdrawal of a driving licence.

In his enthusiasm for counteracting the harm which many of these unjustified claims were doing to accident research, Johnson was, however, inclined to carry the debunking process a bit too far. (Though his achievement of covering 226 references in the space of one paper seems to have been regarded with a certain amount of envy by later critics!) In the process he included among his references of unjustified claims or inconclusive results just about every study which had ever been carried out, including the very good work of the early researchers, and the very factual practical achievements of people like Bingham and Viteles. But there was, nevertheless, a good deal of justification for much that he said, for the 1940's, though they seemed to represent the apogee of the popularity of the concept of accident proneness, also represented the nadir of the quality of that research—particularly the theoretical psychological research.

Fortunately, however, for the welfare of the general driving public, at any rate in the United States, the quality of the practical work of the traffic officials seemed to be getting progressively better and, even in the research field, most of the better work of the forties seemed to emanate from the American State Motor Vehicle Departments. An increasing amount of attention was being given to the accident problem and particularly to the driver, and more and more States were instituting systems for driver control such as more stringent licensing regulations and procedures like points systems for the disciplining of traffic offenders. In this connection it is interesting to note that belief in one of the basic tenets of accident proneness, namely the existence of significant differences between people's accident potential, obviously dictated a lot of their thinking. This does, however, always appear to have been the case among the people whose job it is to actually deal with the accident problem at close quarters and on a practical day-to-day level.

CHAPTER 5

EARLY POST-WAR RESEARCH

THE shift from intense enthusiasm to a more balanced reflection began to appear at the end of the forties and lasted through the fifties and into the early sixties. This period is certainly a very cosmopolitan one as the publications which appeared to have had the most marked effect on the thinking of the time were contributed by researchers from a number of different countries: Tillmann and Hobbs (Canada); Adelstein, and then Kerrich and Arbous (South Africa); Thorndike and McFarland (U.S.A); Hakkinen (Finland). To my mind it is also the most rational of the periods, and its publications are a pleasure to review.

The first of these, Tillmann and Hobbs' psychological study, "The accident-prone automobile driver" (1949) was a refreshing change from many of its predecessors in this field. Not only was the whole approach to the problem a more rational one, but in addition, unlike so many of the lesser psychological studies which had been ultra-theoretical, it also came up with ideas which could be of immediate practical value.

Tillmann's contention, for which he has now become famous, is that *a man drives as he lives*; and that a bad civil record is therefore a useful indication of an inherently bad accident risk. He based his findings on two very original studies. In the first one, on taxi-drivers, Tillmann spent three months with the drivers, riding in their cars, talking to them while they were waiting for calls, observing their driving habits and the condition of their cars, watching how they handled their passengers and how they got on with the other drivers. At the same time, in the course of seemingly casual conversation, he obtained a picture of their childhood, home and social background, a picture which he supplemented with information from police records and the records of the juvenile courts and social agencies.

Separating the drivers on the basis of their accident records (as recorded by the taxi company, the State, and the insurance companies) into high-, medium-, and low-accident groups, he compared twenty high-accident drivers with twenty low-accident drivers and drew up a profile of the sort of people found in each group. He sums up his findings on the drivers with a high accident rate as follows:

"It has been demonstrated that the high accident taxi driver most frequently comes from a home marked by parental divorce and instability. During childhood his life is marked by evidence of instability and disrespect for organized authority. As a result he has often encountered difficulty with the school authority and frequently has been before the Juvenile Court. In adulthood his occupation record is marked by frequent short-term employment and his connections with any firm are frequently terminated by the employer. He has a police record apart from traffic violations much more frequently than those within the low accident group. His personal life is marked by the same evidence of social disregard as noted in the other aspects of his life. For this reason he is frequently known to various social agencies such as the Children's Aid Societies, the Family Service Bureau, and the Public Health Department. He is an individual who places all emphasis on material values and who acts only with thought for immediate satisfaction without any concern for tomorrow. His driving is marked by the same tendency of aggressiveness, impulsiveness, and lack of thought for others and the disrespect for authority that was noted in his personal life."

A condensation of Tillmann's account of the taxi drivers with a low accident frequency is as follows. They most frequently came from a home marked by stability and a low parental divorce rate. During childhood their lives were marked by only mild instability of the non-aggressive type: and some of the most frequently found tendencies were fear of fights and extensive shyness. In school there was no history of truancy. Job records were mostly stable with long periods of employment. As individuals they tended to be quiet and conservative, especially in company and, in sharp contrast to the high-accident group, they displayed a marked interest in hobbies such as gardening, sport, and church organizations. If they drank at all it was moderately. Family relationships were good, and any promiscuity was associated with worry about their misdemeanours. They adjusted well to discipline and seemed concerned over the welfare of others and about planning their own future. On the whole, they were quiet, reserved people with whom it was difficult to make rapport, and while driving they often refused to talk. Their driving was marked by the same characteristics which appeared in their personal lives; they tended to be courteous to other drivers and aware that others on the road might do the wrong thing. In contrast to the high-accident group, they were courteous to passengers and their cars were usually clean and conservative in appearance.

As a cross-validation on these findings Tillmann then carried out a study on members of the general public. The Ontario Department of Highways supplied the names of 96 male drivers who, over a fifteen-year period, had a record of four or more accidents (reportable accidents involving fatality, injury, or property damage in excess of $ 50) and 100 drivers of a comparable age group with no accidents recorded against them. To remove the element of subjective judgement which was present in the first study, these people were not interviewed at all. Instead a purely objective approach was adopted. All the names were submitted to the juvenile court and the adult court, to the public health agencies and venereal disease clinics, and to social service agencies such as the Family Service Bureau and the Children's Aid Society. In addition the names were checked by the local credit bureau. These checks revealed that 66% of the high-accident group were known to one agency, or were known to more than one. Of the accident-free drivers only 9% were known to any of the agencies, and in no instance was a person known to more than one.

Summing up the findings of the second study, Tillmann says:

"Thus it would appear that social maladjustment of various types is to be found quite as frequently among the general driving population with a high-accident record as among the high-accident taxi drivers, and that one is justified in feeling that the same pattern exists in both groups.... It would appear that the driving habits, and the high accident record, are simply one manifestation of a method of living that has been demonstrated in their personal lives. Truly it may be said that a man drives as he lives. If his personal life is marked by caution, tolerance, foresight, and consideration for others, then he will drive in the same manner. If his personal life is devoid of these desirable characteristics then his driving will be characterized by aggressiveness, and over a long period of time he will have a much higher accident rate than his more stable companion."

Long excerpts from this paper are given in Haddon's *Accident Research*, but the book omits one passage at the end which I think is of particular importance as it represents a new departure in research thinking:

"(a) DRIVER SELECTION BY COMMERCIAL ORGANIZATIONS

"A great deal of time and effort has been applied to the problem of selecting drivers for commercial organizations. The method most frequently applied is a group of psychophysical tests such as reaction time to specific stimuli, tests for coordination, etc. However, we could find no evidence in the literature that would suggest that these tests can differentiate the high from the low accident driver. It would seem to us that the use of these tests is based on a simple, but fundamental error. They appear to test something that is related to driver skill. They could help in picking a good from a poor driver. However, this is something entirely different from safe driving. In our study of the high accident drivers we encountered many drivers that could be considered as highly skilled in the handling of an automobile but they were not safe drivers. Safe driving would appear to be more dependent on judgement, caution, and consideration of the possible errors of others, than upon reaction time and binocular vision. In accident proneness the defect is above, not below, the basal ganglia. Therefore, we would feel that some effort in driver selection should be directed to determining the type of individual that is being employed. The various factors described in this paper should be checked for each potential employee. This does not require special psychiatric training. Any intelligent personnel manager should be able to take the superficial type of life history that is capable of differentiating the mild psychopath from the well-adjusted stable individual. A simple enquiry covering the field of the family background, childhood characteristics, school and work adjustment, and interests will readily demonstrate the type of person that is being considered. Additional information should be available through the various social and law enforcement agencies of the type that we have obtained for the general driving population, and can serve as a confirmation of the interview. This information should make it easy to identify the accident-prone driver in advance and to see that he is directed to some type of occupation where he is of less danger to himself and to others than he is behind the wheel of a truck.

"(b) GENERAL DRIVING POPULATION

"An accident-prone individual can be easily identified by the record of his accidents. If one waits long enough and keeps an accurate record of accidents it becomes clear, after a number of years, that certain individuals have a sufficiently high accident record to make it unsafe for them to continue driving. During this period, however, many innocent persons may be maimed or killed. When a person has had one, two, or three accidents within a relatively short period of time would it not appear much more reasonable that he be called in for interview and that a history of the type we have described be taken, and that the various social and law enforcement agencies be contacted to determine if he fits the pattern that we have attempted to describe in this paper? If he does, we feel that one would be justified in revoking this man's license at a much earlier stage than would appear to be possible by simply considering the accident record alone. If this man were to apply for reinstatement of his license, then we feel that he must bring forward evidence that he has changed his general pattern of living before this license should be returned to him. Certainly this would seem much more reasonable than simply to revoke a license for a specific period of time on the assumption that something magical must take place during this period, whereby he will have learned his lesson and he will now become a safe driver. It is not a matter of learning a lesson, but rather it is a matter of basic inherent personality characteristics that must change before the man would be a safe driver. This suggestion will probably appear rather drastic. We do feel that at the present time there would be a great deal of difficulty in instituting such a programme. Undoubtedly it will be passed by as being ivory-tower type of thinking. We must wait until society is convinced that accidents are not always chance happenings, and that sometimes they reflect the basic personality of the individual."

This study probably created a greater impact than any before or since. It is certainly the most quoted, which in itself is a very great compliment. Naturally, like every other study, it has its critics. But these critics are usually the people with a strong statistical bias, and those who appear to be very antipathetic to the whole proneness concept. The main criticism is levelled at the accident criteria, on the grounds that these were calculated without regard to differences in exposure. However, Tillmann was quite aware of this and mentioned it several times, saying that because of these unavoidable difficulties he had selected only the two extremes of the criterion for study, and was only presenting a general picture of the sort of people who had many accidents recorded against them, and the people who had none. And, let it not be forgotten, Tillmann *did* find significant differences between the groups.

Haddon *et al.* (1964) were highly critical of this study, describing it as "theoretically inconclusive" and "typical of much of the research on accident proneness". Another of their comments was: "It provides no evidence that the social and psychological differences found between the high-accident and low-accident groups represent stable, inherent personality factors. It demonstrates that people who have accidents differ from those who do not, but one can conclude very little from this about the nature of the accident-causation process."

Somehow one has the feeling that this sort of criticism is more likely to enhance the reputation of Tillmann's work than to detract from it, particularly among the practical officials whose daily job it is to differentiate between "people who have accidents and people who do not". Certainly, among the practical people, this study appears to have had a very great appeal. It also seems unlikely that they shared Haddon's doubts that the social and psychological differences which Tillmann found between the high- and low-accident groups represented "stable, inherent personality factors". (They certainly would not do so today, as anyone will vouch for who has seen the assessors in the Motor Vehicle Departments of some of the big American cities time and time again refusing to restore a suspended licence with words which are an echo of Tillmann's: "Until your civilian and police record show that you are acting more like a responsible citizen, we cannot trust you with a driver's license.")

From the research point of view it is interesting to note that Tillmann's study has not become dated or invalidated in nearly twenty years—in fact different aspects of its findings have been corroborated again and again by subsequent studies, some of them using the same sort of approach, others using a quite different one, but all coming up with results which confirm the relationship between road accidents and personal and social maladjustment.

The first of these corroborative studies was one carried out by the Harvard School of Public Health (McFarland, 1954). Using truck drivers, where it was easier to establish some control over exposure, McFarland and his associates followed Tillmann's same line of investigation with 59 accident-free drivers (with no accidents of any kind over a twelve month period) and 88 accident-repeaters (with three or more responsible accidents over the same period). They found that there was a marked trend for the accident-repeaters to follow the pattern of Tillmann's groups. They had more driving offences, not only on the job but in their previous driving; they had more private accidents, more traffic violations, particularly serious ones such as speeding; their names appeared more often in court records associated with offences such as assault, rape, non-support, fathering an illegitimate child, theft, carrying a concealed weapon, drunkenness, and drug-addiction. Also a much larger proportion of these repeaters were found to be known to the social services agencies, and to have childhood histories of emotional disturbance and unsatisfactory home life. The investigators used these findings to develop a tentative scoring system for predicting the accident potential of newly engaged transport drivers. The system involved examining the previous records of these men and giving different weights to various motoring and civil offences. This system was tried out on a cross-validation sample of twenty currently employed truck drivers, and was found to distinguish between the repeaters and the accident-free with an accuracy of 85% ($p = 0.06$). McFarland concludes the report on this project by saying that, "the point of view that 'a man drives as he lives' stands out as the most promising basis for studying the accident-repeater and for differentiating between accident-free and accident-repeater drivers. This point of view can be restated in the form that the best way to predict future behavior is to evaluate what the individual has done in the past." The findings of this study not only confirmed Tillmann's findings but also illustrated another interesting factor, namely that the same sort of characteristics differentiated between accident offenders and non-offenders, even when the definition of what constituted an offender was very different. For in McFarland's group an offender was someone with *three or more accidents of any kind during one year*. In Tillmann's second group an offender was someone who had incurred *four or more serious accidents over fifteen years*.

Reverting, however, to the chronological sequence of the important publications of the time, the study which followed Tillmann's sociological one was of a very different nature. This was Adelstein's paper on accidents among shunters on the South African Railways. This was the first major statistical study on proneness since the famous early ones of Greenwood and Newbold and showed the same qualities of thoroughness and impartiality.

Adelstein, in this study, undoubtedly contributed towards a better understanding of the whole proneness concept, particularly in the portions of his report dealing with the more general aspects of the subject. Unfortunately the data on which the actual statistical shunter study was based were too restricted to provide very much new information. Here again Adelstein, who was using the conventional method of studying groups of people over a number of years, was confronted by the inevitable statistical difficulty that the people who had the high accident rates did not stay on the job long enough to qualify for the study groups. The stayers, being the ones who could be included, were therefore a very selective and homogeneous group—so selective in fact that out of 1442 shunters for whom records were available, only 182 could be used in a five-year study and 122 in an eleven-year study. Adelstein himself was very much aware of this and says: "It has been emphasized that as the period of observation lengthens the group under observation becomes more selected and the selection may be associated with the very factor which we are studying." In addition, with accident rates which were low even for the whole population, and very much lower for the surviving groups, there was little scope for individual variation. Even in the early days of accident research, Farmer and Chambers had discovered that if accident rates are low the proneness element is very much camouflaged by the chance element, and had suggested that it would always be difficult to produce any convincing *statistical* evidence of proneness with accident rates which were lower than three accidents per man per year. Adelstein's accident rates being much lower than this, it is very difficult to interpret the real significance of his results. Investigating three different types of accidents, Adelstein found that in both the injuries at work ($\bar{x}$ = mean accident rate p.a. = 0·26) and the injuries at home ($\bar{x}$ = 0·07) the correlations between subsequent periods were very low and it took exposures of up to eleven years to produce significant ones. Only in the property damage accidents ($\bar{x}$ = 0·87) was there any very real evidence of proneness. Here, not only the split-half correlation (0·355 for 157 subjects) but even the year-to-year correlations were significant.

Unfortunately, however, the limitations of the data must also have affected the findings of another investigation which Adelstein conducted, some of the findings of which have been quoted over and over again. This was an investigation to see whether removing the worst offenders of one year would have reduced the total accident rate in subsequent years. The conclusion he reached on the basis of his data was that this was not the case, as there was, in fact, no significant difference between the *subsequent* accident rates of the men who would have been removed and the remainder. (See Table 5.1.)

TABLE 5.1. THE EFFECT OF REMOVING THE SHUNTERS WITH THE HIGHEST ACCIDENT RATE
AFTER THE FIRST YEAR (FROM ADELSTEIN, 1952)

	The accident rates for the shunters who joined in 1944 and shunted for 3 years		
	1st year	2nd year	3rd year
Mean accident rate for 104 men	0·557	0·355	0·317
After removing 10 men with highest rate in 1st year, i.e. 94 remaining men	0·393	0·361	0·329

	The accident rates for the shunters who joined in 1943 and shunted for 4 years			
	1st year	2nd year	3rd year	4th year
Mean accident rate for 86 men	0·639	0·360	0·360	0·348
After removing 13 men with highest rate in 1st year, i.e. 73 remaining men	0·383	0·315	0·315	0·342

A study like this would have been very significant if the material had been more suitable. For this, after all, is the crux of the practical implication of the proneness concept. But, as it was, Adelstein chose to investigate only the seldom-occurring major injury-at-work type of accident, and also used a method which, with his particular data, was almost guaranteed to be self-defeating. For he investigated the *initial* years of exposure of two long-service groups, and selected for removal those who had two or more accidents *during their first year*. Considering that he himself had carefully pointed out how much evidence there was

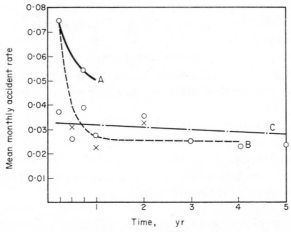

FIG. 5.1. Accident rate of three groups of shunters to show the effect of selection and experience (Adelstein, 1952).

A, men who began after 1 January, 1943 and left before 1948: 165–261 men.
B, men who began after 1 January, 1943 and who did not leave before 1948: 182 men.
C, Men who began between 1937 and 1943 and who did not leave before 1948: 181 men

of learning with experience among these shunters, particularly in the first year, and had even illustrated this with a very revealing graph (Fig. 5.1), it is surprising that he did not appreciate the effect this would have on his figures.

The learning factor should have been particularly evident to him in these two groups where the average accident rate of the first year is more than one and a half times that of the subsequent years. But strangely enough, he does not mention this at all in his brief paragraph on this investigation, where his conclusions are the same as those expressed in the summary:

> "When those men who have most accidents in their first year of exposure are compared during the next three years with the remaining men, it is found that the mean rates do not differ significantly."

Nor does Adelstein mention that the distribution of the accidents of the first year was such that, in itself, it gave no evidence of which were the "prone" drivers, (e.g. the 1943 group: 45 with 0; 28 with 1; 12 with 2; and 1 with 3 accidents). It can be seen that the "tail" of the distribution is a very short one and, as was pointed out by Whitfield in the discussion which followed the presentation of Adelstein's paper before the Royal Statistical Society, the accident rate per man for the first year was 0·639 and the variance was 0·579, and, as a result, there was no evidence on which to pick out the most accident-prone men. As Whitfield said: "By analogy, this was rather like using a fractionating column for five minutes and subsequently finding no change in the composition of the liquid underneath."

The inadvisability of drawing any far-reaching conclusions from this particular investigation of Adelstein's is demonstrated by the conflicting results obtained in a later study. In pp. 291–7 of this book the reader will find that similar exercises have been carried out using different groups of South African bus drivers exposed for a full six years. Here, where the accident rate is higher (using total accidents) and the turnover not anything like as great, a completely different picture emerges. Even removing the drivers with the highest accident rates during *their first year of driving* significantly lowers the accident rates of the subsequent years, as the drivers with the highest accident rate maintain a rate for the remaining five years which is almost double that of the remainder. And other analyses show that among experienced drivers a particularly high accident rate in *any one year* is significant. It would seem therefore that Adelstein's data were not really suitable for demonstrating this particular phenomenon.

But, nevertheless, the figures pertaining to this particular aspect of his study were used time and time again in later years to demonstrate the fallacy of the whole proneness concept: and this despite the fact that Adelstein, in the summary of his paper, expresses himself *in favour* of the concept (provided it is not stretched too far) and says that there is support for it in his own data. At the end of the summary he says:

> "The statistical techniques are applied to various groups of shunters and the following conclusion suggested: In regard to injury—during the first year of experience chance factors are enough to explain the data. Those men who have been observed for five years show more evidence that proneness plays a part, and in those 122 men observed for eleven years there is stronger evidence of differing degrees of proneness. But the cor-

relation between different periods is small, and the factor of proneness, although apparently present, is probably of small practical importance—in comparison with chance factors which play a predominant part. In regard to mishaps which cause damage to property there is good evidence for proneness. In the case of home injuries there is also some evidence."

In the body of the text Adelstein made some very interesting general observations. "The concept of accident proneness", he said, "is extremely useful if not stretched beyond the observed facts." For example, judging by the low correlations obtained between one type of accident and another, he did not feel that proneness operated under all circumstances. On the contrary it was much more likely that it only operated in regard to a specific type of event in a specific environment; and therefore it might alter in an individual in accordance with his changes of activity. He said he disagreed emphatically with the trend of thinking which had led to "an uncritical acceptance of the erroneous idea that each person has a fixed degree of 'accident-proneness' in all situations". "Even in specific circumstances", he said, "the situation is being over-simplified and this has resulted in a tendency to neglect the other factors underlying accidents, factors which are not fixed as accident proneness is assumed to be, and are amenable to improvement." Youthfulness and lack of experience, he suggested, were examples of factors which would influence the early years of exposure and later diminish.

He also suggested that possibly different character traits could be associated with accidents which involved injury to the person himself, as against accidents which merely involved damage to property belonging to other people; that the character traits associated with the latter type of accident were probably less deep-rooted and therefore more likely to be influenced by such factors as discipline or the growth of a sense of social responsibility; in fact that one might expect that the tendency to injure oneself and to injure others could be entirely different aspects of personality, and that to damage property could be still a third aspect.

He also made some very interesting comments on the question which so beset the early investigators, namely the question of whether the occurrence of one accident would make the possibility of another accident more likely or less likely; e.g. did it make the victim more cautious and therefore *less* liable to another accident—or more nervous and therefore *more* liable? On this subject he very sensibly suggested that "it is possible that some accident data consists of mixtures of various trends, some with 'proneness', some with learning, some with nervousness and some who change from one to the other".

This sort of flexible thinking was certainly a great change from some of the one-track reasoning which had become so common in the accident literature. It is only a pity that the material for the main statistical study was so circumscribed. In view of the indiscriminate use which was later made of Adelstein's actual figures it is also a pity that more workers in the accident field did not appreciate these facts, and particularly the dangers of generalizing from one field of accident research into another. It seems very unlikely that Adelstein, who was very emphatic about the dangers of this sort of generalization, would have approved of such an indiscriminate use of data which he himself said had distinct limitations. Unfortunately, as has happened with other excellent studies, his broader conclusions have been largely forgotten, and usually only a single set of his figures lives on, in one out-of-context quoting after another—figures which, it seems, are probably only a reflection of a particular situation.

Not only was Adelstein's paper very interesting, but so, too, was the discussion which followed, one particularly interesting contribution being that of Chambers. For here we get the current viewpoint of one of the founders of research on accident proneness—his viewpoint in 1951, fifteen years after his first paper was published:

"I am grateful to Dr. Adelstein for stressing the fact that the connotation of the term 'accident proneness' has been changed since Farmer and I first defined it, and in so far as his criticisms are directed against the popular use of the term I am in full agreement with him. However, when he attempts to explain away the quite large body of work done by our predecessors and ourselves I am much less happy. The fact that his findings do not altogether agree with Newbold's and ours does not necessarily mean that we are wrong and he is right. For example, he claims that the factor of accident proneness, even when it is present, plays only a small part in the occurrence of accidents, and from this he concludes that accident proneness is of small practical importance. Now we agree with his claim—we have never suggested otherwise—but we cannot agree with his conclusion. If only, say, 5% of accidents could be prevented by eliminating certain highly prone individuals, surely this would be worth doing? Dr. Adelstein's own figures about the cost of accidents and the loss of man-days of work indicate as much. It does not seem to be a very sound argument to say that because chance factors play a predominantly large part, other small factors should be neglected, particularly as Dr. Adelstein does not indicate how these chance factors may be prevented from operating. Perhaps my chief criticism of Dr. Adelstein's painstaking paper is that, imposing as it appears at first sight, his body of data is really not large, and it is drawn from a selected and rather unusual field of observation. Although from the records of 11 years he has quite a large number of accidents to deal with, the actual accident rate is small, . . . only one-fifth of an accident per man per year. This does not give much scope for the admittedly small factor of accident proneness to manifest itself except over a lengthy period of observation. In our report on accident proneness among motor drivers, Farmer and I indicated that usually we could not demonstrate the operation of accident proneness when the annual average accident rate was less than 3 and the period of exposure less than 4 years. Further, the type of accident sustained by shunters tends to be rather serious in nature. It may well be, therefore, that having incurred one accident a person tends to exercise more care and so tends to avoid future accidents. In other words, through experience a person may become less accident prone. Dr. Adelstein does in fact suggest that this may be the case. The opposite tendency, that of a person being rendered "nervous" by having incurred an accident and so becoming more accident prone, might also obtain. If both tendencies are present, it is most unlikely that a mathematical model could be fitted to the data unless some other information, such as that obtainable by psychological testing, were available in order to segregate the two types of individual. In point of fact, only 122 of the shunters survived the whole 11 years of observation, and several arguments are based on the records of these men. Surely it is a legitimate deduction to say that if these persons could survive 11 years in a very hazardous occupation they must have a very low degree of accident proneness? Even so, their records do indicate the operation of proneness to some extent. At the foot of Table 3 Dr. Adelstein states that 9 shunters died and 211 were permanently disabled. This is a total of 220 persons out of a population of 1,442, or almost one sixth. Dr. Adelstein does not appear to envisage the possibility that these 220 persons might include the most highly accident-prone individuals in the group, and that their disablement prevented their proneness from manifesting itself. . . . In summary, I should say that while Dr. Adelstein's conclusions may be justified as regards his own data, they do not necessarily invalidate the conclusions of other workers using different types of data."

One way and another these two studies, Tillmann's and Adelstein's, showed that a new trend was developing in accident research. Tillmann, instead of investigating only minor artifacts of the make-up of the driver, like his intelligence or his reaction time, had adopted a new line of psychological approach by investigating whether the broad picture of his everyday behaviour could indicate his accident potential. Now Adelstein, by departing from a narrow and rigid statistical concept of proneness and suggesting a much more flexible one, was breaking new statistical ground—if not in the techniques he used, at least in the scope of his thinking.

The continuation of this trend of broader thinking was very evident from the realistic but constructive tone of a number of critical reviews of the proneness concept which appeared about this time, especially those of Arbous and Kerrich (1951), Thorndike (1951), and McFarland and Moore (1955).

The attitude of all these writers was very similar to Adelstein's, namely that the concept of accident proneness could be extremely useful if not stretched beyond the known facts. They all agreed with him that there was no scientific justification for what Arbous called "that figment of the imagination, 'The Accident-prone Percy', who is prone to accidents of any kind, at home, at work, on the highways"; in fact, they appeared to feel that an individual's liability to accidents in one set of circumstances would give little indication of his liability in another. And most of them were very critical of the vogue for let's-get-on-the-bandwagon kind of research which had resulted in so much nebulous thinking—in suppositions being glorified into certainties, and in proneness receiving so much attention that other important aspects of the accident situation were possibly being neglected.

They were all keen to see the term "accident proneness" dropped from the scientific vocabulary because it was so vague and because everyone interpreted it so differently. Because of the confusion over the meaning of the term, McFarland suggested that it might be better to use a less prejudiced term, such as "accident repeater" until there was more definite knowledge about exactly what "proneness" implied. Arbous was even more emphatic, saying: "It is a difficult matter to define what is meant by the term and evolve a sensible measure of whatever it indicates." And Kerrich, after saying that both the phrase and the concept were still open to different interpretations and so uncomfortably nebulous that he himself much preferred not to use the term at all, went on to say: "To some readers this may seem to run contrary to certain trends in psychological literature, but the authors confess that they find the fashion of talking about nebulous entities which cannot be clearly defined nor adequately measured both wearisome and sterile." Most of the authors expressed their dissatisfaction with the vagueness of the thinking on the subject and their disappointment in the lack of progress towards any real knowledge. They all accepted (McFarland more guardedly than the others) that it was very likely that people did differ in their propensity for accidents, but that not much actual scientific proof of this had so far materialized—probably because the existing techniques, both statistical and psychological, were inadequate for dealing with anything quite as complex and multi-dimensional as accident liability had turned out to be.

This particular aspect of these very good publications is particularly interesting, for, reading between the lines, one can detect the first signs of the parting of the ways of the thinking on accident proneness—a parting which later led to the present very divergent schools of thought, with one school still believing in the concept (but losing faith in the power of the old techniques to demonstrate it properly and looking for better ones) and the second school losing faith in the concept itself. Thorndike, Arbous, and Kerrich appear to be forerunners of the first camp, McFarland of the second.

Thorndike's attitude was the most optimistic of them all. Although he was obviously very aware of how difficult it was to prove, by existing statistical methods, that people differed in their propensity for accidents, and particularly that these differences were durable ones, he nevertheless indicated that he himself felt that many of these difficulties could be overcome. What is more, the whole tone of his monograph implied that he considered the likelihood of some people having a greater accident potential than others to be a very important factor in the whole accident situation. In saying this he gave no indication that he was singling out the multiple offenders as the main culprits, but rather that he was thinking in terms of a whole range of degrees of proneness. He stressed the multiplicity of accident causation and submitted a mathematical equation representing the probability of an accident occurring as a function of a number of different factors—these factors including a whole range of elements, in the driver, the vehicle, and the external circumstances which could combine to make the total setting of an accident.

All in all it was a very good and very comprehensive monograph, dealing not only with the statistical but the psychological aspects of accident causation. And no doubt the generally optimistic tone must have lent encouragement to acceptance of the proneness concept.

In contrast the monograph of Arbous and Kerrich, "Accident statistics and the concept of accident-proneness" (1951), which appeared very shortly afterwards, was far more critical of the progress made to date, especially in the statistical field. But at the same time the attitude adopted by the two authors was both realistic and constructive. Though neither of these authors has, unfortunately, remained active in the accident research field, they have always retained their interest in this research. Some of their thinking on the subject has changed since the days when they presented this account, which they both stress was an account of the position *as it was in 1951*. I therefore asked them whether they would care to contribute a statement setting out their present views. They kindly agreed to do so and these statements are given in Chapter 13 of this volume. In view of the way in which what one can only call "assorted snippets" taken from their paper have been used, especially by later critics of the concept of accident proneness, the reader should find these statements very interesting.

The monograph consisted of two parts, a general one (Arbous) and a mathematical one (Kerrich). To deal with Arbous' section first.

This monograph, though it was mainly orientated towards industrial accidents, was a most comprehensive analysis of the whole concept of proneness to accidents of any kind, and it undoubtedly contributed greatly to the clarity of the thinking so typical of this period. It is referred to so often in the literature that it is worth quoting at some length. Arbous' views on the current state of progress in the study of accident proneness were very perceptive. After discussing the weaknesses inherent in the usual statistical approach to the problem and saying that because of these weaknesses most of the research findings to date must be reviewed with extreme caution, he said:

"The evidence so far available does not enable one to make categorical statements in regard to accident proneness, either one way or the other; and as long as we choose to deceive ourselves that they do, just so long will we stagnate in our abysmal ignorance of the real factors involved in the personal liability to accidents. This does not mean that accident proneness does not exist, but that so far we have not succeeded in defining it, assessing its dimensions and constituent elements, nor evolved a technique for putting it to practical use."

He went on to suggest that "what is needed is obviously more fundamental research and perhaps a completely new way of looking at the old problem".

Here he made several suggestions. Firstly, he suggested that what was needed was a more sensitive measure of susceptibility to accidents, in other words a more sensitive accident criterion; that, for instance, using as a criterion only such "events" as those involving injury, death, or major property damage could be very misleading, for such a criterion was not necessarily a true reflection of propensity for accidents—the measure here being the *outcome* (which could be purely fortuitous) and not the precipitating action. He suggested that because the addition of minor accidents improved reliability, if near-accidents could also be included one might have not only a more reliable but also a more sensitive criterion. (As was indeed subsequently shown in later studies such as Coppin's work in California (1967) where a combination of traffic violations and reportable accidents proved to have greater stability than reportable accidents alone.) He suggested that another of the reasons for the failure of the statistical approach to provide useful evidence of proneness was because of inherent weaknesses in the techniques themselves. Firstly, the figures which constituted the data were usually misrepresentations of the actual position as they excluded the people with short exposure, who were usually those with a high accident rate and the very people in whom the researcher was interested (as was subsequently shown by the work of Sichel (1965) in South Africa where a new time-interval technique, which made it possible to include nearly all the short-service drivers, produced a criterion with a high reliability). Secondly, he suggested that the techniques were seldom appropriate to the data for which they were used and added a very strong rider, saying: "It is essential to avoid the folly of applying statistical procedures, knowing at the same time that they cannot be justified on mathematical grounds. Self-deceit of this type has never produced any results worth having."

He suggested that most of the techniques were far too elementary; that they relied on a simple, one-cause-one-effect relationship; and that what was needed was some new technique of analysis which would enable researchers to "disentangle the skeins of a confused and intricate pattern of events". Continuing with the theme, he said:

"Furthermore, our attempts to oversimplify the accident-causing situation by seeking to subdivide it into 'personal causes' and 'environmental causes' tends to lead us nowhere. Greenwood and Woods in their original report recognized that individual susceptibility sheltered a motley host of motives and factors which will be very difficult indeed to separate and measure. Surely the essence of accident causation is the rather intricate interrelationship which exists between the individual and the environment and the influence of one cannot be appreciated without considering its interaction with the other, and to attempt to separate the two is about as profitable as attempting to unravel the respective influences in the heredity v. environment controversy. Full comprehension of these interrelationships and their statement in universal 'laws' will possibly only be achieved when we have evolved statistical techniques which will facilitate three- and four-dimensional thinking on these matters. Existing methods of analysis tend to make the problem too simple—too dependent on the direct cause-and-effect relationship."

Arbous summed up this argument very neatly by saying:

"The above comments do not constitute a denial of the usefulness of statistical procedures in investigations of this type, nor is it suggested that the research worker can ever dispense with them altogether. The conclusions indicate rather the limitations of these techniques, and emphasize the fact that statistics can never do your thinking for you."

After describing the equally discouraging failure of many of the psychological programmes to find any particular characteristics associated with accident proneness, Arbous did, however, end his monograph on a much more optimistic note by saying that one might well be very despondent about the whole state of affairs were it not for the encouraging fact that a rather different "clinical" approach, even if it did not lend itself to statistical analysis, did at least appear to offer a way of reducing accidents. "And surely", he said, "this is the ultimate objective of all this work?" He then described the particular type of "clinical" approach used by Slocombe and Brakeman (quoted in full earlier in the previous chapter). Here, because it was found that there were so many different causes for accidents, each accident offender was treated as a separate entity and given individual treatment based on the particular combination of physical, mental, social, or economic factors which, in his particular case, were found to be associated with his abnormally high accident rate. Commenting on how successful this approach had proved to be in the case of the Cleveland and Milwaukee Railways, Arbous ended his report by saying that in this method of diagnosing and treating the "accident-prone", it should be noted that the term "accident proneness" was now no longer being used in the original sense.

"It is now defined on the basis of a *clinical* and not a *statistical* diagnosis and, as such, is largely a term of convenience, rather than of precise mathematical definition. This loss of precision is perhaps more than compensated for by the advantages of a new approach which places special emphasis on the individual and recognises the great variety of the individual differences."

This final paragraph is one of the few instances in this very well-written monograph where Arbous has possibly not made his meaning very clear. He says that in this new approach accident proneness is now being defined "on the basis of a *clinical* and not a *statistical* diagnosis". By "clinical" he merely means "individual", i.e. that the diagnosis is an individual rather than a group statistical one. For each "accident-prone" offender was initially singled out for treatment on the basis of the *number of accidents he had incurred*, and in the studies he is describing such drivers constituted up to 30% of the total. But even if the meaning of this particular paragraph is not absolutely clear, there seems little justification for interpreting it the way that Haddon *et al.* (1964) did—namely that Arbous had suggested the "possibly valid limitation of the concept to clinical cases". Nor (as can be seen from their later statements) do either Arbous or Kerrich consider that there is any justification for the sort of belief expressed by these authors who, describing the monograph as one of the most decisive critiques of the accident-proneness concept, say: "There are some who believe that this analysis should have sounded the death knell for the accident proneness approach." In fact, they appear to resent the way in which time and again their paper has been used to discredit the whole concept.

For Kerrich was equally constructive in his approach and his much-quoted reference to "nebulous entities" was a criticism of the woolly thinking engendered by the multitudinous definitions of the *term* "accident proneness", not of the use of the *concept* to account for differences in innate liability to accidents. Far from it in fact, as would be clear to anyone who really studied his section of the monograph. In this section he examined the mathematical theory underlying the statistical methods commonly used for the investigation of these personal differences, such as the distribution of accidents in one period or the correlation of accidents in subsequent periods. Although, by means of more recent statistical knowledge, he was able to suggest various modifications of the mathematical treatment given by the early workers, his main contention was that these methods were inadequate. Referring to the mathematical theory underlying all the traditional statistical methods, Kerrich says:

"In a sense, this theory will always be useful. People will on occasion collect accident statistics over a period of time and need to describe them, by means of these or similar theories.

"In a sense this theory misses the mark altogether. It deals with people who have been under observation for the whole of a period of time and says nothing about the misfits who try a job and soon leave it. Now one of the fundamental problems that faces the industrial psychologist is how to spot the misfit, preferably before he begins a job, and the above theory will do little or nothing to help him here."

The concluding remarks of his monograph are ironical, particularly in view of the manner in which both he and Arbous have been selectively quoted ever since their monograph was published:

"Considerable pains have been taken to discuss the physical significance of the mathematical formulae developed, for the benefit of the non-mathematician, and great stress has been laid on the tentative nature of the conclusions arrived at in practical cases. This is of course flogging a dead horse. All of the writers quoted advanced their hypotheses tentatively and hedged them about with warnings and advice. This has not prevented other writers from beginning an article with: 'As so and so has shown...'."

Altogether it would appear that this very good monograph is yet another example of the old adage that "beauty is in the eye of the beholder". For since it was written it seems to have been acclaimed by a number of people for a number of very different reasons—reasons ranging all the way from an enthusiastic desire to support the concept of accident proneness to a desire to loudly and long ring its death knell.

Also very well written, well received and much quoted, were the contributions of McFarland *et al.*, which began to appear very shortly afterwards. These were the work of a number of investigators associated with the Harvard School of Public Health. They dealt mostly with original research on relatively unexplored areas of safety procedures in connection with professional drivers; matters like the health of the driver, his capabilities, the effect on these capabilities of factors like fatigue or alcohol or smoking or even badly designed vehicles. They dealt with the accident rates of transport drivers, with procedures for recording accidents and near-accidents, and with methods for selecting drivers. Altogether four very good reports along these lines were published, the best known of which was McFarland and Moseley's *Human Factors in Highway Transport Safety* (1954).

A fifth volume which became even better known soon followed, McFarland and Moore's *Human Variables in Motor Vehicle Accidents* (1955). This summarized many of the findings of the other reports and also reviewed the accident research and the literature to date. It was a very full review and it dealt with every aspect of the human element in road accident causation, paying particular attention to questions like the relationship between accidents and factors such as intelligence, psychomotor functions, physical fitness, personality, temperament, attitudes, and social background. It also included over 1000 references for further study. Although the original publication is now well over ten years old it is still a valuable reference work for students. The new up-dated version which is being prepared at the moment will be even more valuable.

It is this *Human Variables* report which contains most of the discussion on the concept of accident proneness. In a way the views expressed here are rather confusing—possibly due to the dual authorship. On the one hand, the text implies at least a tacit acceptance that there are important differences in the characteristics displayed by people with high or low accident rates. (This was indeed one of the findings of one of McFarland's own original research projects, reported in *Human Factors*, the study of the sociological background of the truck drivers, which led him to state that comparing accident-free and accident-repeater drivers by means of poor social adjustment had provided a highly discriminating procedure.) And yet, on the other hand, McFarland displays a strange reluctance to accept the implications of even his own findings, namely that if the characteristics which differentiate accident offenders are durable ones (like social and personal maladjustment) then the differences between the accident *potential* of these people must be durable, too.

Likewise in the *text* the authors indicate that research in an important field is being hampered by technical difficulties—but in the *summary* the attitude is quite different and the implications are that the research is not really worth doing and that too much attention is being paid to a relatively unimportant aspect of the accident problem. I will quote most of the summary of the chapter on accident proneness in full, as, despite the inconsistencies it contains, the effect it had on subsequent thinking is shown by the number of times that easily recognizable phrases, sentences, or whole paragraphs of this summary appear in the publications of later writers. In fact it seems to have been the source of information for a number of people whose lack of first-hand knowledge on accident research has, unfortunately, not prevented them from writing prolifically on the subject.*

"Much work has been done in an effort to substantiate the theory that certain individuals have an inherent predisposition to accidents. The voluminous statistical evidence, however, may be questioned, since it is based on doubtful assumptions and is derived by unacceptable methods. The general approaches are by way of simple percentages, by curve-fitting, and by correlation, all of which are subject to grave objections in this context. At present the evidence is limited to the fact that in some groups, something having to do with the individuals involved may have been influential in determining which ones had the accidents.

"Some of the mathematical research necessary to meet the objections to the statistical approach has been undertaken. Research is also being directed toward developing statistical methods capable of following trends and tendencies in individuals in such a manner as to reveal the fundamental mechanisms in accident causation. When the relationships between characteristics of drivers and their accidents have been studied, a number of personal qualities have been found to be slightly related to accident frequencies. The correlations have been low, however, and useless as a basis for predicting the accident tendencies of individual drivers.

"Intensive clinical examination of individuals suffering injuries led to the view that many accidents are unconsciously motivated, and are deemed to serve certain personal needs. According to this view, the personality of accident repeaters takes a characteristic form. Studies orientated from this standpoint in the vehicular accident field have given rise to the view that accidents are but one expression of faulty adjustment to the demands of life. As applied to driving, the concept implies that "a man drives as he lives". Comparing accident-free and accident-repeater drivers by means of objective indices of poor social adjustment has provided a highly discriminating procedure. This approach seems promising as a practical method in detecting those individuals likely to have multiple or repeated accidents.

"Since accident proneness, as originally conceived, seems to be a much more re-

* Reproduced by courtesy of the author.

stricted phenomenon than previously held, studies based on this concept have resulted
in little basic knowledge about accidents. It has been proposed that a less prejudiced
term such as accident-repeater be used. The study of those persons who have had
repeated accidents and an analysis of all the circumstances involved, is more likely to
result in basic knowledge about how and why accidents occur than are the attempts
to prove differences in susceptibility."

A superficial comparison between these views and those expressed by Arbous and
Kerrich, for instance, seems to indicate that the disparity is one of tone rather than
content. But the last paragraph shows that there were indeed differences in the fundamental thinking of the two teams of investigators. One of the most important of these
was a way of thinking about proneness which later became much more pronounced
among the American researchers. This was to think of it as a dichotomy—either a person
was prone or he was not. The only people who could therefore be regarded as "prone"
were the multiple accident repeaters, and therefore the importance of the contribution
which proneness made to the total accident situation must be judged by the size of the
contribution of this particular group. The assumption made by Thorndike and Arbous
and Kerrich, on the other hand, was that proneness, if it existed at all, must be a continuum; and that the importance of the concept would therefore lie in the possibility that
quite a large proportion of the community possessed a higher than average potential
for accidents—a potential which, if not lessened or controlled, could constitute a very
real danger to the community.

I may be incorrect in my interpretation of the underlying trend of this report, in regarding it as an indication of the shape of things to come, and of the parting of the ways of
the thinking on proneness. But it is an interesting speculation and one which, to my mind,
is confirmed by some of McFarland's later thinking, as exemplified by a later statement of his, quoted in the May 1961 issue of *Traffic Safety*. Here the trend is more
obvious:

"Taken at face value, the results from the statistical approach suggest that the phenomenon of accident proneness... is of considerably less importance in the total accident
picture than originally held.

"The usual findings have been that the accident distributions for various groups
differ only slightly, or not at all, from the distributions which would be expected from
chance alone. Moreover, it has not been convincingly demonstrated that an appreciable
number of people tend to have more accidents than others under conditions of equal
exposure. There is also insufficient evidence that the same persons tend to have repeated
accidents in successive time periods to be able to predict future accident occurrence on
the basis of the past history of accidents in individuals."

McFarland's name is a prominent one in accident research, and publications emanating
from the Accident Prevention Section of the Harvard School of Public Health are regarded as having a pronounced influence on opinions in the accident sphere. The somewhat
disbelieving tone of the 1955 publication must therefore have had its effect and, in view
of the marked swing of opinion in the United States since that time, it will be very inter-

esting to see what line is taken on the question of "proneness" and its importance to the accident problem in the new edition of *Human Variables*, which is now in the course of preparation. In my personal discussions with the two principal authors, Professor McFarland and Dr. Moore, I found that they were very aware of the conflicting points of view represented by the present anti-proneness climate of American research thought, and the evidence of studies emanating from other countries which strongly support the concept.

Another publication which appeared at this time and is very often referred to in the literature on road accidents, was Schulzinger's book *The Accident Syndrome* (1956). On closer study this work does not seem to be anything like as antagonistic to the basic concept of proneness as later quotations from it made it appear. Nor, for that matter, did it concern drivers; for although it has been quoted many times in connection with motor-vehicle accidents, with impressive statistics like "a study which took 18 years and involved 35,000 cases", these cases were just personal injury cases treated in Schulzinger's private medical practice—injuries received under all sorts of circumstances, by people of all ages ranging, as he said, from infancy to senility. Only a few of these injuries involved motor-vehicles and then only if the injured person happened to be one of his patients.

The findings of Schulzinger's book, which was a very good one, were therefore only applicable to road accidents inasmuch as he mentioned, in passing, certain characteristics which he noticed to be associated with drivers involved in these accidents—such as youthfulness, irresponsibility, or personal and social maladjustment. The conclusions he drew on the general subject of "proneness", especially proneness *to accidental injury*, were, however, very interesting. In the first place he considered that only some 10–20% of so-called "accidents" in which his patients were involved, were in fact "accidental", and he referred to "the remaining eighty per cent to ninety per cent of accidental injuries or accidents without injury in which unerringly may be traced the role of the victim in provoking his own misfortune". "Irresponsible and maladjusted individuals", he said, "have a significantly higher incidence of accidents, especially repeated ones, than responsible or normally adjusted individuals." And again: "Susceptibility to accidents, like susceptibility to illness, appears to be a problem of general morbidity. Individuals may be said to vary in their degree of susceptibility (or proneness) to accidents, rather than in the presence or absence of proneness."

Viewed against its proper background, the final summary of Schulzinger's views on proneness *to accidental injury* among *people of all ages*, makes a lot of sense. It is only a pity that this summary has so often been quoted either piecemeal or completely out of context:*

"The currently accepted theory that most accidents are sustained by a small fixed group of 'accident-prone' individuals is open to question. On the basis of clinical experience and studies, the author suggests that most accidents are due to relatively infrequent solitary experiences of large numbers of individuals. The total number of accidents suffered by those who injure themselves year after year, over a period of three

* From Schulzinger, M. S., *The Accident Syndrome*, 1956. Courtesy of Charles C. Thomas, Publisher, Springfield, Illinois.

or more years, is relatively small. The frequently observed unequal distribution of
accidents appears, among other things, to be due to unequal liability to accidents on
the basis of age and sex, to transient or prolonged states of physical, physiological or
psychological stress, to chronic 'accident proneness' and to chance. The evidence indicates that if the period of observation is sufficiently long, the 'small group of persons
who are responsible for most of the accidents' is essentially a shifting group of individuals with new persons constantly falling in and out of the group. It seems to be more
nearly correct to speak of varying degrees of 'accident proneness' rather than of the
presence or absence of proneness."

No, useful as some of Schulzinger's statements later turned out to be, his book can hardly
be described as the vanguard of any concerted attack on the idea of accident proneness
per se. He was talking only of accidents where people injured themselves and his criticisms seem to have been mainly directed against what he called *the currently accepted
theory that most accidents are sustained by a small fixed group of "accident-prone" people.*

But just where had this strange theory come from? Who had started it and who were
the many people who were currently supposed to hold it? Certainly these were not the
researchers who had carried out any of the big studies. They had never talked of a few
prone people doing all the damage. On the contrary, like the practical traffic officials,
they seemed to think that the importance of proneness to the accident situation lay in
the fact that, in various degrees, it affected so *many* people. Then where had it come from?
Like the story of the mysterious trainload of Russians "with snow on their boots",
reputed to have been seen by so many people in England during the First World War,
nobody seems to know. One possible source, however, seems to be behaviourist psychology and its off-shoots. In Chapter 10 of this present volume I have gone into this question
fully, endeavouring to assess the influence of this particular doctrine, and the effect which
its widespread acceptance in the United States must have exerted on the development
of America's thinking on the whole subject of accident proneness.

CHAPTER 6

FINLAND'S CONTRIBUTION

THE first European study to embody the American statistical approach was Hakkinen's *Traffic Accidents and Driver Characteristics* (1958). This monograph was an account of a most detailed investigation into the value of certain psychological tests for detecting various levels of accident proneness. The subjects were a group of Finnish bus drivers and tram drivers, and the study contained all the requisites of a first-class original research project. Not only did Hakkinen apply a wide range of tests, including some very ingenious ones, but he also established a reliable accident criterion against which he validated these tests with great statistical refinement. In addition, as a result of the first part of the study, he assembled a test battery incorporating elements of the most productive of the tests and carried out a series of cross-validation studies. In fact the only aspect of this investigation which departed from the ideal was that the tests were mainly used diagnostically, i.e. they were mainly used to detect offenders with *current* and *past* accident records, and were only once used for the prediction of future accident involvement and then with a very short follow-up period. But in personal discussions with Dr. Hakkinen he told me that the tests have now been used continuously since 1958 for the selection of professional drivers, with apparently very satisfactory results. Pressure of work has, however, unfortunately prevented him from carrying out the time-consuming work necessary to revalidate them and establish yet again their scientific validity in this particular connection.

I can personally vouch for the thoroughness of this testing. During my visit to Finland in 1965, Hakkinen's staff put me through the instrumented part of the test battery—a piece of practical research which I would have been quite happy to take on trust, as I was more than a little travel-weary at the time. However, between the enthusiasm of the Finnish testers and the insurmountable difficulties of the language question, there was no way of escaping from this particular form of inquisition once I had embarked on it. But my personal sufferings on these very exacting (and, I regret to state, very revealing) tests were a minor price to pay for the privilege of seeing Finland's Institute of Technology in operation. For this was something I had wanted to do ever since Hakkinen's monograph was published in 1958. Like many other workers in the accident field, I had been greatly impressed with his report and had considered this particular project to be quite one of the best original studies on accident liability ever to appear. Here at last was a study on accident proneness and its causes which not only displayed psychological and statistical expertise, but also one in which, for once, these qualities were not wasted because of an unreliable criterion. The fact that Hakkinen avoided this pitfall was by no means fortuitous. Maybe he was lucky in that he was able to find a venue for his work where the accidents were meticulously recorded, and where the subjects displayed such a wide range of liability. But it takes more than luck to perceive the possibilities of such a situation and to exploit them to the full by leaving no aspect of the situation unexplored and no loophole for ambiguity in the results; it requires perspicacity and an infinite capacity for taking pains.

The first area in which Hakkinen displayed these qualities was in the statistical investigation of his accident criterion. The bugbear of nearly all the previous investigations on proneness, especially those on road accidents, had been the problem of exposure in terms of time and hazard; for unless these could be equated there was no way of establishing to what extent differences in accident involvement were reflections of innate personal differences, or merely reflections of the conditions under which the different individuals did their driving. Hakkinen tackled the problem very effectively. The time question was easily overcome as the drivers all worked the same number of shifts per day. The hazard angle was more difficult. Investigation of the various routes on which they drove showed that the accident index for these routes varied between 0·7 and 2·7 accidents per man per year—with 86·5% of the driving being done on routes with an accident index which varied between 1·1 and 1·7. As there was a constant interchange of drivers on these routes, the variations in the index showed that the hazards were significantly different. It was possible, however, that the very fact that this constant interchange *did* occur would negate these differences as far as the individual drivers were concerned. To investigate this Hakkinen took various groups of bus and tram drivers and worked out the "loaded" accident rates for each individual, loading the amount of time that he had spent on each route by the accident index for that route. He then correlated these rates with the unloaded rates based on the actual number of accidents each man had sustained. These correlations produced coefficients in the 0·95 range; from which he deduced that the interchange of drivers was indeed achieving the effect of equating the hazard risk, especially over long periods of exposure.

The second problem which had confronted previous investigators had been the unreliability or lack of constancy of their accident criterion. In many cases this had been due to the fact that only certain accidents were recorded, resulting in a very low accident rate, which in turn meant that personal differences were being obscured by the chance element. In Hakkinen's material virtually every accident had been recorded and the rate was high enough to overcome this difficulty. This was particularly the case when accidents of every kind were included, irrespective of outcome, or cause, or degree of blameworthiness; and after a full investigation of all the possibilities, Hakkinen made this his criterion.

The reliability of his criterion was tested on five different groups of bus drivers and tram drivers with exposure ranging from two to six years. Correlating the accidents in two successive periods produced coefficients, most of which were significant at the 0·001 level. A summary of these results is given in Table 6.1.

As an additional check on constancy an investigation was made of groups of drivers with low or high accident rates during the first half of their exposure, to see whether a significant difference was maintained in the second half. This showed:

Group A (101 bus drivers exposed for six years)

Average accident rate in the second three years of
those drivers with few accidents (0–3) in the first three years   0·65

Average accident rate in the second three years of
those drivers with many accidents (4–12) in the first three years   1·79

(Differences significant at the 0·02 level.)

Group T (363 tram drivers exposed for four years)

Average accident rate in the second two years of
those drivers with few accidents (0–1) in the first two years   0·24

Average accident rate in the second two years of
those drivers with many accidents (2–9) in the first two years   1·81

(Differences significant at the 0·001 level.)

TABLE 6.1. CORRELATION BETWEEN ACCIDENTS IN TWO SUCCESSIVE TIME PERIODS

(Information derived from pages 30, 38 and 39 of *Driver Characteristics*, Hakkinen, 1958.)

Length of period	Tram drivers		Bus drivers	
	r	As corrected by Spearman Brown formula	*r*	As corrected by Spearman Brown formula
1/1 years	0·233 (N = 363)	0·378	0·361 (N = 322)	0·530
2/2 years	0·470 (N = 363)	0·639	0·454 (N = 141)	0·624
3/3 years 1, 2, 3/4, 5, 6 1, 3, 5/2, 4, 6	— —	— —	0·355 0·373 (N = 101)	0·524 0·543
4/4 years 1–4/5–8 1, 3, 5, 7/2, 4, 6, 8	0·674 0·726 (N = 44)	0·805 0·841	0·577 0·678 (N = 52)	0·732 0·808

Encouraged by these results, Hakkinen felt that a sufficiently reliable criterion could be established for two experimental groups of bus drivers and tram drivers. If he could find subjects with eight years' exposure, so much the better, as the split-half coefficients of reliability would probably increase as the exposure lengthened. If he could also contrive to include in this sample some of the people with the very high or very low accident rates, then this might improve the reliability of his *project* criterion still better. (This would of course only be the case if there was indeed evidence of constancy and if the subjects maintained their low- or high-accident records throughout their exposure.) A criterion like this would also have the advantage of being a better yardstick against which to assess the discriminating powers of the psychological tests to be used in the project.

To arrive at the experimental groups for testing, Hakkinen therefore took samples from each of the good/fair/poor/bad levels on the accident criterion, and tried to ensure that these samples were roughly equated on age and experience. He also eliminated those drivers who were too old for psychological testing, and those with bad medical histories or defective vision. He was left with 140 subjects from whom the two experimental groups (52 bus drivers and 44 tram drivers) were assembled by calling for volunteers.

The accident records of these subjects provided a very reliable accident criterion with split-half correlations of: first four years/second four years, bus drivers $r = 0.577$; tram drivers $r = 0.674$; odd years/even years, bus drivers $r = 0.678$; tram drivers $r = 0.726$; all coefficients being significant at the 0.001 level.

Comparison of the means for the split-half periods showed that the bus drivers with *good* accident records in the first period averaged 0.46 accidents in the second period—as against the 1.76 for the *bad* group. A similar comparison for the tram drivers yielded an average of 0.50 as against 2.45; both sets of differences being significant at the 0.001 level.

Having established a reliable criterion for the experimental groups, Hakkinen could then proceed with the application of his test battery. The distribution of the accident coefficients for the two groups is given in Table 6.2 and shows that the accident rate ranges from zero up to nearly four accidents per annum. As this means a range of 0–31 accidents over the eight-year period, the spread is much greater than that found in most studies.

He used a very big battery of tests, including some unusual ones which he described as psychomotor personality tests.

The test battery covered the following areas:

1. *Intelligence and mechanical aptitude.* Paper and pencil tests with the emphasis on reasoning and space perception.

2. *Simple motor speed and co-ordination.* Reaction-time and two-hand co-ordination.

3. *Choice reaction-time and a driving apparatus test.* These consisted of:

   (a) *The clock test.* Testing for factors such as span of attention, anticipation and correct timing.
   (b) *The driving apparatus test.* A test where the pace was set and the testee had to keep a stylus on a moving path, a task requiring him to maintain his concentration and co-ordination despite disturbances and increasing difficulties.
   (c) *The expectancy reaction test.* Designed to test whether the speed of motor performance was relatively higher than the speed of perception (i.e. whether the person acted before he really knew what sort of action was required).

4. *Psychomotor personality function.* In this connection Hakkinen says " a psychomotor test is regarded as a personality test if the principal aim of the experiment is to draw conclusions concerning the characterological attributes of the subject on the basis of motor performances, of muscle movements and muscle tensions." They consisted of:

TABLE 6.2. DISTRIBUTION OF THE ACCIDENT COEFFICIENT (NUMBER OF ACCIDENTS PER ANNUM) FOR THE EXPERIMENTAL GROUPS TESTED (FROM HAKKINEN, 1958)

Tram drivers $N = 44$	Accident rate per annum	Bus drivers $N = 52$
1	0·00	
	0·01–0·10	
1	0·11–0·20	111
	0·21–0·30	11
11	0·31–0·40	11111
111	0·41–0·50	111
11	0·51–0·60	1
11	0·61–0·70	11111
11111	0·71–0·80	111
1	0·81 0·90	1111
	0·91–1·00	111
	1·01–1·10	
1	1·11–1·20	1111
1	1·21–1·30	1
1	1·31–1·40	11
1	1·41–1·50	11
1	1·51–1·60	1
	1·61–1·70	1
111	1·71–1·80	111
11	1·81–1·90	11
11	1·91–2·00	1
	2·01–2·10	1
11	2·11–2·20	11
11	2·21–2·30	
1	2·31–2·40	
1	2·41–2·50	
11	2·51–2·60	1
1	2·61–2·70	1
	2·71–2·80	
1	2·81–2·90	
1	2·91–3·00	
1	3·01–3·10	
1	3·11–3·20	
	3·21–3·30	
	3·31–3·50	1
1	3·51–3·70	
1	3·71–3·90	

(a) *The ambiguous situation test.* This was a test based on Davis' Skilled Response Test. The graphic record of movement which the subject made with a pointer in response to certain clear or ambiguous stimuli, was studied for the way in which he organized his activities—for hastiness, indecisiveness, lack of movement control, etc., and also for evidence of neurotic traits which were thought to exert an impairing and paralysing influence on his performance in stress situations.

(b) *Myokinetic psychodiagnosis or Mira test*. Where the subject had to retrace certain simple patterns by drawing with a pencil without being able to see what he was drawing. The rationale behind this test was that certain personality traits were reputed to be associated with certain types of deviation from the original pattern.

(c) *The bodysway test*. Testing for suggestibility, and through this for lability and neuroticism.

5. *Questionnaires and interview variables*.

(a) *The personality inventory*. Derived from the inventory of Murray and that of Eysenck, testing for factors such as neuroticism, emotionality, calmness, self-assertiveness, aggression, etc.

(b) *The traffic questionnaire*. Designed to test the subject's attitudes towards traffic rules and regulations and towards accidents.

(c) *Other interview variables*, such as biographical data and ratings on (1) clear and frank *v*. vague, uncertain and concealed answers, and (2) calmness *v*. nervousness.

It took Hakkinen and his assistants nearly two years to apply this large test battery, as the subjects could only be tested when they could be spared from their duties. It took four years to process the results statistically and to prepare the report for publication—which gives some idea of the magnitude of this research project. It also indicates why it is quite impossible, in a short summary like this, to do justice to a 198-page report and to present the results in any detail.

The test results were analysed in a variety of ways. Every test was marked for a number of different variables, and these scores were subjected to just about every known statistical procedure, from reliability tests, to intercorrelation between the variables themselves and the accident criterion, and to a factor analysis of these correlations. Only a few of the more interesting results can be given here.

The two groups of bus drivers and tram drivers showed no very significant differences in test performances or in the correlations of these performances with the criterion. This demonstrated a very important point, namely that the characteristics associated with accidents were similar in the two groups although the actual driving operations they performed were very different. As a result of this investigation it was possible to combine the two groups and treat them as one.

The factor analysis showed that the tests were covering six major areas: *attention, involuntary control of motor function, stability of behaviour, co-ordination, simple reaction-time*, and *intelligence*.

The factor which had the highest loading on the accident criterion was the *attention* factor; namely the ability, when confronted with a sudden stimulus, to quickly choose and perform the correct response.

Second highest was *involuntary control of motor functions*; with the accidents being associated with lack of control in the form of hastiness, distractability, and motor restlessness. This factor was found to be different from the *attention* factor as the responses were involuntary and apparently beyond the subjects' control—whereas in the *attention* factor the responses were conscious and represented a deliberate attempt to achieve a certain goal.

Also with a relatively high loading on the criterion was the factor of *stability and adaptability of behaviour*; accidents being associated with the negative aspect, namely insecurity, tension, and neuroticism.

The *co-ordination* factor was loaded to a lesser extent. This was eye-hand co-ordination and required a certain amount of anticipation and also the ability to respond to changes in speed and distance.

The remaining two factors, *simple reaction-time* and *intelligence*, showed no association with the accident criterion.

The multiple correlation of test variables showed that ten of them had a high predictive value. Combining these ten into a test battery produced a multiple correlation with the accident criterion of 0·64. Confining the battery to only the five best test variables produced almost as high a coefficient, namely 0·59. Splitting the subjects into two groups and using only the younger group improved the position, and the five-test battery produced a multiple coefficient of 0·72. These coefficients were very high and showed the test battery to have considerable potential. In the general discussion of his findings Hakkinen mentions that the most important test variables correlated better with the criterion than with each other; from which he deduces "that accident proneness is composed of a number of factors, quite different from and uncorrelated with each other".

He comments on the fact that no relationship was found between accidents and intelligence. This agreed with the findings of many previous studies but, as Hakkinen points out, he feels that in his study this finding was largely a reflection of the fact that his group was a preselected one. In an unselected group he feels there would be a minimum cut-off on the intelligence scale, below which a person would be a bad accident risk. In the same way he feels that it is unrealistic to expect any linear relationships to exist between accidents and factors like health or vision, and that here again it is best to use a minimum cut-off.

He also comments on the fact that in his study none of the factors of the personality inventory showed any correlation with the criterion; whereas in studies like Tillmann's and McFarland's a strong association had appeared between accidents and factors indicating personal and social maladjustment. Here again he feels this was more a reflection of the selectivity of his group than of anything else. The very fact that his subjects had been continuously employed for eight years or more by the same firm, and in a responsible job, showed that they belonged to the more stable element in the community, where antisocial or psychopathic behaviour were very unlikely.

In the selection programme which he designed on the basis of this study, Hakkinen therefore still included tests for intelligence and simple reaction-time, medical and optical examinations, and interviews to determine previous job records and social and home background. Most of the original tests have now been modified so as to incorporate the important functions of the original tests in a shorter battery. The equipment has also been modernized, most of the recording being now electronic.

In his final summary Hakkinen gives his version of the profile of a safe and unsafe driver. These are very interesting, especially when compared with the profiles given earlier by Tillmann, and later by Conger, Malfetti, and Shaw. Each shows the orientation of the particular investigator and the angle from which he or she approached the problem. Whereas Tillmann's approach is sociological, Conger's, Malfetti's, and Shaw's characterological and behavioural, in Hakkinen's study the emphasis is on psychomotor functioning. But despite his very different approach, his conclusions are remarkably compatible with those of the other investigators.*

"One possible way of summing up the results achieved in the present study is to try to give a concise description of the safe and, correspondingly, of the accident-prone type of driver. The intention cannot possibly be, of course, to imply that all the traits mentioned should be present in every safe or accident-prone driver, respectively, but to try to examine the average driver type characteristic of each of the two groups. One may suppose that the safe driver type is a more unambiguous and uniform concept than is the accident-prone type. The safe group consists of those who satisfy certain empirically established minimum requirements, whereas the representatives of the accident-prone driver may fail to meet these requirements in respect of any of the traits or trait combinations concerned. A discussion of the sub-types of different kinds was not one of the objectives of this study, neither would the material in hand have been adequate for such a purpose.

"A safe driver may be described as follows. He possesses good ability of attention, which forms together with well controlled motor behaviour an integral whole. He need not necessarily be remarkably intelligent or fast in his reactions, but he rather represents the average level of drivers in these traits. Relative slowness of a certain kind, but at the same time adaptability and determination as well as control of motor behaviour, at all times, are typical of his performances. The trait mentioned last shows itself not only in voluntary reactions, but is typical of the driver in all situations and in every respect so that it can be considered to reflect a stable character in a general sense, independent of motor behaviour. His performances remain essentially unaffected when the situation grows more difficult or when distracting factors occur, even though he tries to be still more alert and active in order to achieve as good a total result as possible. In general, his behaviour is rated as stable and calm. In this respect he is not an outstanding individual, however, and it is with regard to this very trait that a driver who is good in the sense of merit rating deviates from the safe type of driver. One may assume that a safe driver feels a need for frank and straightforward knowledge and control of himself, reflected in a tendency to give a higher number of positive answers to the questions concerned with neuroticism than is given by the accident drivers. As a consequence of this his behaviour may also appear less natural and spontaneous than the behaviour of the drivers rated as the best by their superiors. His inward and outward control helps him to master himself as well as his vehicle so as to adjust his driving operations to his driving skill, his abilities, and the external conditions in every situation.

"The drivers who incur accidents naturally form, in most respects, the opposite of

* Reprinted with the permission of the author.

the above type and there is no need to repeat the above description as a whole. Let it only be pointed out, by way of additional illustration, that in certain extreme cases their poor ability of attention may arise from their lack of intelligence or from excessive slowness. It more frequently happens, however, that an adequate performance is impeded by hastiness and 'motor over-sensitivity' as well as by an inherent lack of control of the motor behaviour, which may or may not be a consequence of the first two features. Hastiness may reveal itself, for instance, as a mode of reacting, the typical feature of which is that a certain stimulus only serves to signalize that something is to be done; whereas the nature of the ensuing reaction is decisively dependent on what is the easiest or most customary motor performance in the situation concerned. Excessive tension, not always controllable, may cause a narrowing down of the perception and performance. This may show itself, for example, in the form of missed signals in the choice reaction tests. A subject's failure to respond to an entirely clear and perceptible stimulus may sometimes be so astounding that the examiner may gain the impression that at times the subject is not in possession of normal vision. When the situation becomes more difficult, a decline in activeness takes place or even a complete withdrawal from the situation. A further change in the performance accompanying an increase in the degree of difficulty of the situation is that the motor disturbances indicating the lack of an inherent control of motor functions become more frequent. A symptom of poor fitness for the occupation is also the fact that the duties of a driver are felt difficult and exhausting."

Apart from the valuable information which it revealed on the connection between psychomotor functioning and accident involvement, Hakkinen's study provided very strong confirmation of the whole concept of accident proneness. His statistical material provided positive evidence of proneness over long periods of time; and this was supported by the psychological aspect where durable psychological characteristics were found to correlate significantly with a reliable accident criterion.

Hakkinen, a firm believer in the basic tenets of the proneness concept, expressed some very interesting views on the subject. Right at the outset he said that he considered the concept to be a very reasonable one, and that he did not altogether agree with Arbous and Kerrich, when they said that accident proneness had not yet been demonstrated; and certainly not with views which he said had recently been put forward "that the concept of accident proneness was entirely devoid of empirical foundation". He agreed that the results of statistical studies on accident proneness had not been very convincing, but felt this was mainly because of fundamental weaknesses in the studies, or because of the technical difficulties involved. However, he maintained that the trends of the results of even the statistical studies were largely in favour of the concept, and that the part played by psychological factors could not be denied.

Unlike some other writers he did not maintain that the psychological factors associated with accident proneness were restricted to the field of personality alone. He stressed the fact that other factors contributed to the picture (his own tests, for instance, had a large ability component). In fact he referred to "the personal factors, the totality of which are called accident proneness, which affect accident rates".

He disagreed strongly with any suggestion taht proneness could be expected to apply to all circumstances—that, for instance, a person should be equally prone to both industrial and traffic accidents. He says: "It has been frequently suggested that accident proneness is a separate, unique psychological quality, which either exists and manifests itself in all investigations, or does not exist at all. This mode of thinking, based on assumptions of one-dimensionality and constancy, has proved fallacious in all fields of differential psychology."

Within a particular context, such as road accidents, Hakkinen felt that people displayed a whole range of accident proneness; and that, like any other manifestation of a complex network of causes, proneness could not be expected to be a rigidly constant factor. Certain elements of it *must* be expected to change with time. He said that the individual psychological and physiological factors which contributed to the phenomenon of accident proneness could be divided into three groups: constant factors; factors which change slowly with time, such as age and driving experience; and fluctuating temporary factors like illness or fatigue of short duration, or temporary states of depression or excitement. His concept of true accident proneness embraced the first two, the constant and the slowly changing, only the fluctuating temporary factors being excluded. But he went on to say that some factors which might appear to belong in the temporary group often do, in fact, exhibit a certain amount of constancy and affect some people more than others, in which case they must then be considered to belong to either of the previous groups; and the longer the period of exposure the more of them would fall into these categories.

He said that the problem of studying accident proneness, especially by statistical means, was very greatly complicated by the factors which change slowly with time. If, for instance, the group was composed of drivers of different ages and differing amounts of experience, then the effect of the constant factors could easily be overshadowed by the changing ones; and that the whole picture could be further complicated by the fact that some of the changes might go in one direction and some in another. Only if the material was well controlled in respect of the changing factors could the effect of truly constant factors be clearly demonstrated. (In his own material, for instance, he got much clearer results when he was able to split the data into age groups.)

In fact he declared himself as a strong supporter of the basic concept of accident proneness—namely that there were definite, innate differences between people's propensity for accidents, and that these differences were evident over long periods of time. His concept of proneness was, however, a flexible one which allowed for the fact that there was a whole range of proneness; for the fact that a person's degree, or level of proneness could easily change in time; and for the fact that the underlying causes of proneness differed from one individual to another. Altogether his whole approach to the problem was a very sophisticated one—backed by very sophisticated evidence.

Just what effect this study had on the research thinking on accident proneness is very hard to say. Hakkinen's name appears over and over again in the bibliographies of papers on accidents, but the actual references in these papers are usually short ones. He is usually quoted in connection with some specific factor like age, or experience, or a particular psychomotor function. The only times I personally have seen him extensively or even appreciatively quoted in connection with his contribution to scientific knowledge on the whole concept of unequal liability is by Walbeehm (1960), Eysenck (1965), Shaw (1965), and Van der Burgh (1969)—all publications emanating from outside the United States. His contribution to the scientific knowledge of accident proneness appears to have been very largely ignored by the Americans—with the exception of Coppin (1964–7). Haddon *et al.* (1964) in their 743-page book on accident research do not even mention Hakkinen's name. And certainly the positive evidence he produced in support of the concept did not seem to have had any effect whatever on the development, particularly in American research circles, of the current strong anti-proneness bias.

I think, myself, that there are several reasons for this. One is that the study was such a comprehensive one and the report (a translation from the Finnish) was so detailed that relatively few people seem to have studied it properly. The second reason is that it appeared at a time when opinions were beginning to become sharply divided. The third, and to my mind the most important reason, was that a review of Hakkinen's book which was published in England (Smeed, 1960) contained a number of criticisms which appear to have created an aura of doubt in many people's minds about the validity of Hakkinen's findings. Certainly Smeed's opinions have been quoted by a number of people who obviously have not taken the trouble to study the original report.

In view of this it would be as well to quote in full the most pertinent parts of Smeed's review (1960) and to determine whether his criticisms were in fact justified. Smeed's most pungent criticism is concerned with the reliability of Hakkinen's criterion, and especially with the effects on this reliability of factors such as age, experience, and different kinds of exposure. He says that Hakkinen, unlike many other investigators, was fully aware of the difficulties which these factors presented, but suggests they were not conclusively dealt with in the treatment of the data.

Talking of the question of exposure he says :*

"Hakkinen states that during the time period under consideration most of the drivers had been operating on many different routes and that this is bound to cancel out part of the effects of the possible non-homogeneity of the routes. He nevertheless examined the accident rates on the different routes and found that they varied between 0·7 and 2·7 accidents per driver per annum. However, he states 86·5 per cent of the driving was on routes where the accident rates per driver varied between 1·1 and 1·7, and the influence of the differences between the routes could not, therefore, have been decisive. This is, however, an opinion on a topic on which exact analysis is required. Hakkinen then states that in order to clear up the matter, he computed an expected number of accidents for each driver by adding the products of the time the driver had been operating on each route and the known accident rates of these routes in a manner previously attempted by Whitfield. He then divided the actual number of accidents by the expected number of accidents and correlated the resulting ratios for two successive periods. Unfortunately, Hakkinen does not give the detailed results of this most useful analysis. He merely states that the resulting correlations were of the same order as the original ones and did not differ significantly from them. He goes on to say that this is best seen from the correlation between directly evaluated accident rates and those calculated by adjusting the

* Reproduced with the permission of *Nature*.

accident rates per driver by the accident rates of the various routes on which they drive. He then obtained correlations of the order 0·95. The correlation is high, and Hakkinen therefore concluded that the differences between the routes could not have affected the results. I think that the argument is plausible, but that a more satisfying analysis is desirable. It is a pity that, in a book of 198 pages, more of the original data were not given so as to enable the reader to carry out some analyses himself."

Using Hakkinen's correlation coefficients between the number of accidents in two successive four-year time periods, Smeed then calculates, by means of a statistical formula, that some of Hakkinen's bus drivers must have had an accident rate more than three times that of others and says: "If, therefore, Hakkinen's results are correct they seem to be of considerable practical importance." (He could have established this more accurately if he had looked at table 28 of Hakkinen's report, which I have reproduced earlier on, where the accident rates of the experimental group are, in fact, set out in detail and show an even wider spread.)

After briefly describing some of the results of Hakkinen's tests he says:

"He claims that he may have discovered some psychological factors, particularly those of 'motor hastiness and distractability', which give rise to accident proneness and which have not been ascertained with equal clarity in previous similar studies.

"Some of the methods used in the analysis are, however, not satisfactory. Hakkinen well realizes that many of his results would be upset if there were material differences in age between the various groups of drivers with high and low rate of accident. Instead, however, of discovering the likely effects of the age differences that exist on the accident rates and test scores, Hakkinen calculated the statistical significance of the differences between the mean ages of the various groups of drivers. But this is irrelevant. If all the low-accident group were born on one day and the high-accident group one week later, the differences in mean age calculated would have been statistically significant but the effect on the analysis nil. If, however, two groups of 4 drivers were taken, one group consisting of 3 drivers aged 30 and 1 aged 45, while the other group consisted of 1 driver aged 30 and 3 aged 45, the differences in age—as calculated—would not have been statistically significant, but the effect on the analysis great. The fact that the analysis is clearly not satisfactory in one respect leads one to doubt it in others. For example, the report gives means and correlation coefficients and results of tests on their significance but, since results for individual persons are not given, it is not possible to check that the tests have been carried out correctly and used in conditions where they apply, that is to say, when the correlation is not due to one or two outlying individual points. The author does, however, make it clear that he realizes some of these difficulties.

"There can be little doubt that Hakkinen has carried out one of the most important investigations on accident proneness yet made. It would, however, be useful to re-examine his results."

Smeed glosses over the fact that Hakkinen did not merely rely on comparison of group averages to establish his results; he correlated each of the scores of each individual with the criterion—and "one or two outlying points" on a correlation surface cannot produce a coefficient of the order of 0·64—which was the result of the final multiple correlation (not when you have a continuous distribution on the criterion). Also, how *does* he expect the full data for this sort of factor analysis to be included in a report? Neither does he mention in connection with the age factor that Hakkinen had gone into the whole question in previous papers; or that he did in fact carry out a test/criterion correlation with the younger half of his subjects which showed that his results would, in all probability, have been even *better* if he had been able to split the group still further without making the numbers too small for statistical significance. This sort of omission from a critical review hardly entitles the author to say: "The fact that the analysis is clearly not satisfactory in one respect leads one to doubt it in others." (In any case a most damaging remark for which there was no justification.)

Criticism of this kind will obviously have different effects on different people. Some people will consider it quite in order. Others will consider the general tone to be so pedantic that it will merely make their hackles rise. But nevertheless the danger of this kind of criticism is that it can be used or quoted, either piecemeal or out of context. An example of this is Cresswell and Froggatt (1964) who do just this—only they add a little pedantry of their own.

"Hakkinen's approach was to calculate the number of accidents per driver year on each route, and, finding that over 85 per cent of the driving was over routes on which the accident rate varied between 1·1 and 1·7 accidents per driver year, he concluded: 'Thus the influence of the difference between the lines could not have been very decisive, even if the drivers would have driven mostly on only one line or on lines with equal risks, which, however, was not the case.' Smeed (1960) rightly questioned this assumption. Hakkinen proceeded to calculate a risk index for each driver based on the number of accidents, the 'accident coefficient' of the line (route), and the length of time driven on the line, a method similar in principle to that employed by Whitfield (1954) with colliery workers. To carry this reasoning to its logical conclusion would have involved the application of similar indices calculated for time of day, day of week, and other measurables influencing exposure to the risk of accident."

Admittedly a study of the calibre of Hakkinen's can stand up to a lot of pinprick attacks like this. But at the same time it is a pity that detailed comment on it should so often be left to its detractors. This is one reason why I have devoted so much space to reviewing it. It came out too late for most of the big reviews of the accident literature and therefore is not anything like as well known as some of its predecessors. But a second reason why I feel it is so worthy of attention is that I feel it is quite one of the best studies on accident liability ever to be published—and one of the very few to have such a good criterion that a very high degree of reliance can be placed on its findings.

CHAPTER 7

YOUTH AND THE AUTOMOBILE IN AMERICA

RETURNING now to the United States for a consideration of research developments there during the late fifties and early sixties. In reviewing the major publications of the time, one can see that the whole approach to the question of accident proneness was still one of open-minded inquiry. Despite a certain amount of despondency over the lack of statistical evidence to support the concept (especially in American statistics) there seemed to be a general feeling that there was a lot of psychological truth behind the proneness concept, and that it was important to go on exploring the psychological factors associated with accident involvement.

Conger's study (1957, 1959) was one of the most important of the period. Apart from the fact that his work is always noted for its thoroughness and for the impartiality with which he presents his results, certain aspects of his 1959 study are worthy of a detailed description because this was the first combination of the clinical and the experimental approach—clinical in the sense that a full clinical examination was given to each subject, but experimental in the sense that the results were assessed by means of a statistical analysis.

The report on this study is reproduced in Haddon's *Accident Research*, so I will only describe the project briefly here.

Conger felt that despite the technical difficulties which beset projects on accident proneness, the weight of the scientific evidence nevertheless suggested that significant differences did exist between the accident repeaters and the accident free. And he persisted with this belief despite the fact that an earlier project (1957) had produced few significant results. Here a group of 264 subjects were tested on a wide variety of psychological and psychophysical tests and the results were compared with a criterion of high-, middle-, and low-accident involvement. Most of the measures failed to discriminate consistently, for while a number of tests appeared promising initially, they failed to survive a cross-validation. Only one test proved consistently stable, namely a measure of the individual's value system. In sample after sample this test made it possible to differentiate between high- and low-accident samples with an accuracy of some 73%. On three scales of a modified Allport–Vernon–Lindzey assessment of values, the high-accident subjects were found to be consistently less orientated towards religious values and consistently more orientated towards aesthetic and theoretical values than the non-accident group.

However, as Conger felt that this result was very difficult to interpret, he decided that further investigations should be made to establish just what personality functions were producing these significantly different values. So, taking the extremes as being more likely to produce statistically significant results, he proceeded to carry out an intensive investigation of ten of the high- and ten of the non-accident subjects. High-accident subjects were defined as individuals who had two or more accidents for which they were officially held responsible in the past $4\frac{1}{2}$ years, at least one of which occurred within the year immediately preceding the testing. Non-accident subjects were defined as individuals who had no record of accidents, according to either official records or the individual's subjective report, during the same period.

The intensive investigation included:

A psychiatric interview.
A battery of clinical psychological tests including the TAT, Rorschach, and the Sacks Sentence Completion test.
A number of objective tests such as intelligence tests, the MMPI, the Kuder Preference test.
Tests for respiration, muscle tension, GSR, etc.

Of these methods the most productive of all, and the one which correlated best with the criterion was the battery of clinical psychological tests; and here the best results were obtained by using an evaluation made on the basis of the battery as a whole, rather than by using individual items from any particular test. The validation was done in two ways:

(1) By classifying the subjects into high- and low-accident groups. This was done by presenting the judges with a pen-picture of two personality types hypothesized to represent a composite "accident individual" and the other a composite "non-accident individual". (Results significant at the 10% level.)

(2) By rating the subjects on thirteen factors hypothesized to be related to accident frequency and severity on the basis of the findings of previous researchers. (Result: six factors were found to be significant—most of them at the 1% level.)

Conger's summing up of these findings is:

"In comparison with nonaccident subjects, the accident subjects showed a statistically significant tendency (1) to have less capacity for managing or controlling hostility; (2) to be either excessively self-centred and indifferent to the rights of others or excessively sociocentric (i.e. characterized by an 'over-determined' awareness of, interest in, and respect for the rights and feelings of others); (3) to be either excessively preoccupied with fantasy satisfactions or extremely 'stimulus-bound'; (4) to be more fearful of loss of love and support (and, by inference, more angry and resentful toward persons viewed as depriving); and (5) to be generally less able to tolerate tension without discharging it immediately. In addition, the accident subjects tended to be categorized more frequently as consistently or occasionally belligerent or covertly hostile, and less frequently as only appropriately assertive, or unassertive. While not statistically significant, there were tendencies for the nonaccident subjects to be rated as more conventional and generally better adjusted. There were no differences between accident and nonaccident subjects in ratings of reality orientation, castration anxiety, or friendship patterns."

As Conger points out, however, the findings were only based on twenty subjects and no cross-validation was carried out (which, as he says, should certainly be done before all the results could be accepted without reservation). He adds, however, that it would be most unlikely that so many significant differences would be obtained by chance alone. (A later study carried out in South Africa (Shaw, 1965) did in fact confirm his general findings.)

The study, naturally, has its critics, the weakest point being, of course, the criterion, as there was no way to check differences in exposure or even to be absolutely sure of the accuracy of the accident recording. This is possibly one of the reasons why the second part of the programme, where only the extremes were used, was more productive. But in view of the perpetual controversy as to what constitutes an accident repeater or true accident offender, it is interesting to note how many significant differences were found between the groups with only two accidents in $4\frac{1}{2}$ years, and those with none.

Conger was, however, fully aware of the weaknesses in his study and made it abundantly clear that he regarded his material as unsuitable for trying to prove anything, or for reaching any definite conclusions; but that he and his colleagues were using it merely "to obtain a broader knowledge of the characteristics of accident and non-accident subjects". Strangely enough, although Conger obviously regarded the findings of the clinical study to be the most important, the subsequent accident literature usually only mentions the results of the Allport–Vernon–Lindzey values test—despite the fact that Conger himself says that without further investigation it was impossible to interpret the psychological meaning of these findings. This is probably due to the preference displayed by so many American psychologists for the test-item as opposed to the clinical approach.

One very intriguing aspect of this study was the fact that the final results of the clinical study agreed so closely with the composite pen-pictures of the hypothetical high-accident and non-accident personality types, which were drawn up before the project even began. Admittedly these types had been largely based on the findings of previous researchers, but Conger's team had used its own judgement to omit certain features and include others—a judgement which was vindicated by the end results.

The project also showed that personality testing could possibly be a successful way of identifying bad accident risks, but that the difficulty was going to be to find any easy way of doing this. Once again the objective tests such as personality inventories or temperament scales had shown little promise (possibly because they are easier to fake); even psychiatric interviews carried out by trained clinicians had also failed. In fact the only successful method had been to carry out a clinical psychological investigation by means of a battery of projective tests, and make the assessment on the basis of the total personality pattern which they revealed.

Conger's two hypothesized personality types are interesting, especially when compared with those of Tillmann. In one case the approach was a psychological one; in the other a sociological one. But it is quite easy to see how a person with more than his fair share of the characteristics outlined by Conger, could develop the sort of social record which Tillmann described as being typical of the high-accident offender.

"*The high-accident type.* While there may be a fair amount of individual variation on specific characteristics, in general [this type of] person tends to be rather unconventional in his opinions and values and sometimes in his overt behavior. He is inclined to be rather self-orientated, to have difficulty in relating easily and warmly to other people, and to be somewhat unaware of or insensitive to their rights and feelings. He may in some cases feel that other people are difficult to understand. He often has feelings of dissatisfaction about his everyday life and is likely not to have clearly defined goals in life or consistent, practical methods for attaining such goals as he does have. He is apt to have difficulty in controlling his hostility, which may often be excessive, and consequently may at times be inclined toward over-determined 'acting-out' behavior, either at the level of overt physical belligerence or at the level of verbal aggression—in the form of sarcasm, carping complaints, or destructive comments. He is likely at times to exercise poor judgement in his evaluation of his environment or in choosing courses of action. In some cases, he may appear overly preoccupied with his own fantasy world and relatively cut-off from social relationships with others. If psychopathology exists in this type of individual it appears most likely to take the form of impulsive, hostilely-toned acting-out behavior, poor reality testing, emotional lability, impaired intellectual functioning, a highly personalized, idiosyncratic fantasy, withdrawal from interpersonal relationships, or excessive immaturity.

"*The low-accident type.* This type of person tends to be rather conventional in his values, attitudes and behavior. In general he seems to gain satisfaction for his needs from his everyday life and to have a fairly clear notion of the goals he wants to attain in life and of how to pursue them. He tends generally to have respect for the rights and opinions of other people, and in turn to be pretty well accepted by others. While he may be normally assertive in defending his own rights, he is seldom extremely demanding, domineering, or combative. In some cases, he may actually be somewhat less assertive than an adequate defense of his own rights would require. Such underlying hostility as he may have tends to be pretty well controlled and is seldom expressed in an obvious 'acting-out' fashion. If psychopathology is present in this type, it is most likely to take the forms of denial, overly strong needs for conformity, castration anxiety and fear of aggression from others, and overly strong needs to please or placate others."

Besides Conger's big four-year project, a number of other psychological studies were carried out in the late fifties. In most of them the techniques used were not very original, and no cross-validation studies performed. In many of them there were distinct weaknesses in the criterion, such as taking the subject's own word for the number of accidents in which he had been involved. But nevertheless the better-controlled ones continued to reveal personality characteristics which significantly differentiated the high-accident from the low-accident groups—characteristics which all had a certain consistency. These gradually helped to fill in the gaps left by the big studies, and to give a more rounded picture of the sort of character traits and behaviour patterns associated with the accident offenders and the people who were relatively accident-free.

A number of the studies of the period were concerned with young drivers, their disproportionately high accident rate being very much a matter for concern.

Rommel (1959) made a study of high school students in Pennsylvania. On the basis of a Driver Attitude Inventory and a test of emotional and personal adjustment, he conclud-

ed that youthful drivers having accidents tended to score high, and those free of accidents tended to score low, with regard to several attitudes:

An attitude toward driving as activity which relieves psychic tension.

An attitude toward driving as a form of behavior by which youthfulness may be
compensated for and the role of an adult may be assumed.

An attitude toward driving as a form of behavior in which confidence in one's ability
may be manifested.

An attitude toward driving which does not consider speed as an element of danger
or, if it is considered dangerous, an attitude manifesting desire for danger.

An attitude toward driving which places greater emphasis on the power of a vehicle
than on its style or utility.

On the personality tests he found that accident-incurring youths showed more disregard
of social mores, more defiance of authority, and more of a tendency to excessive activity
and enthusiasm.

On the basis of items in the various scales of this test, he concluded that persons who
had the following tendencies were more likely to manifest behaviour which resulted in
accidents:

A desire to leave home.

An urge to do something harmful or shocking.

A tendency to be influenced by people about them.

Association with peers to whom parents object.

A desire to frighten other individuals for the fun of it.

A tendency to become readily impatient with people.

A tendency to be somewhat suspicious of over-friendly people.

A possibility of having been in trouble with the law.

So great was the concern over the teenager accident problem that McFarland was asked
to prepare a paper on the subject for the 1960 White House Conference on Children and
Youth. This paper, "Youth and the automobile" (McFarland and Moore, 1960) was
widely circulated and became very well known, and most of it is reproduced in Haddon's
Accident Research.

McFarland and Moore started by saying that the wide use of motor-vehicles was one
of the outstanding characteristics of modern life and that they would therefore attempt
to review the role of the automobile in the cultural and behavioural patterns of young
people.*

"The automobile and the emotional needs and cultural patterns of youth: Automobiles, besides providing transportation and mobility, often seem to serve additional
individual needs or motivations of their owners or operators. As a symbol of economic
and social worth, the automobile has long provided its manufacturers with a promotio-
nal approach based on the inner needs of prospective purchasers. A vicarious sense of
power in the operation of a motor vehicle has also been cited as an important satisfaction in the lives of many who are denied outlet for such yearnings in other areas of
their lives.

* Reproduced by permission of the authors and Columbia University Press.

"The symbolic value of the automobile may be of particular importance for the adolescent and young adult. To many it is said to represent freedom and escape, both real and symbolic, from parental control and supervision. Moreover, the automobile has become an important factor in adolescent culture. For example, in many groups it is an accepted pattern that in order to date a girl, a boy must be able to provide a car for transportation; she may not go in a cab or allow herself and her date to be driven by parents. To many boys the car itself becomes a dominant motivating force. Having acquired a car for transportation, socialization, and dating, they become so involved in its care and upkeep that they have little time or interest remaining for activities of which the car is not the focus.

" One psychiatrist (Conger, 1960) has expressed the view that driving an automobile is one aspect of contemporary life which makes it possible for persons to express hostility, discourtesy, and emotional conflict without much fear of reprisal, and often with complete anonymity. In poor driving he sees a common factor of revolt, expressed in a variety of adjustments used by the young driver (as well as others) to relieve him of ordinary restraints and to deny authority. Thus, an aggressive person may show his revolt by such behavior as cutting in, stealing the right of way, or horn blasting. A youth who is oversensitive to the actions of others may react with 'getting even' behavior, finding an excuse for racing and speeding or employing obstructionist tactics toward other drivers. Or to prove his maturity and his mastery of the situation, the uncertain and insecure youth may race around, stop with a screech, and overcompensate with show-off kinds of driving.

"Other writers have pointed out that the youthful driver may often use the automobile to 'act out' the tensions and latent aggressions which arise from the increasing amount of social control which the teen-ager faces, not only in regard to driving but in many other areas of his life.

"Thus, the desire for status, for escaping special situations, for isolation, for working off tensions, and the like, all may affect the individual's behavior as a driver.

"*The role of the automobile among 'hot-rodders':* Perhaps the clearest analysis of the ends which the automobile may serve among youth has been made in regard to the so-called 'hot-rodder'. In one study, carried out by psychiatrists (Neavles and Winokur, 1957) the distinguishing features of 30 young 'hot-rod' drivers were summarized as follows:

1. Physical characteristics: the majority are physically advanced and strong.
2. Background: their early history shows evidence of emotional deprivation with an ambivalent relationship to the mother. Most of the boys come from middle-class homes.
3. Interests: interest in automobiles develops at an early age. At 14 years of age they want to drive a car. They do not participate in competitive sports, and they dislike reading and literature. Their verbal ability is low compared to their mechanical ability.
4. Personality dynamics: they have aggressive temperaments which were probably manifested quite early in life. Rorschach responses and dream material indicate

that they have oral-sadistic fantasies (a lion is going to eat me). There is also evidence of severe compulsive early training. They usually manifest two alternating moods: a mood of boredom and a mood of stimulation that is attained on wild rides. Neither of these moods, however, is extreme enough to be classified as either depression or hypomania.

5. Perception of the automobile: the cases reveal that the automobile can become part of the body image, with the ego expanding to include the car. This gives the driver a feeling of megalomaniacal power and invulnerability. The present increasing tendency to give the car a nonfeminine name is an indication of the expansion of body image.

6. Accident experience: these drivers tend to be involved in few accidents. Although a self-destruction element can be seen in their behavior, the vitality, urge to live, and skill of the drivers pull them through. The 'near miss' is the important thrilling event."

The difference between the American teenage driving problem and that of many other countries is brought home by McFarland's remark: "The view is commonly held that, among boys especially, the desire to get a driver's license and to own a car is probably the most powerful anti-intellectual force that our schools meet." One study, carried out in a California High School (Allstate Insurance Company, 1960), offered some support for these views, namely that among the boys who frequently drove to school the drop-out rate was about four times higher than in the non-driving group; absenteeism was nearly twice as great; average grades were lower; and more courses were failed. With regard to delinquency:

"Various juvenile and adult courts as well as enforcement officers, have pointed out that a large majority of those who are 15 to 18 years of age come to their attention either directly or indirectly as the result of the ownership or use of the motor vehicle. For example, offenses peculiar to the automobile, such as the stealing of gasoline to keep the car on the road, are said to be very common.

"One probation officer has stated, in relation to the social problems that arise out of adolescent driving:

'For many, the "clubhouse on wheels" is a medium for holding a party, to get out from under the control of parents, for having dangerous "drag" races, conducting gang meetings, committing a crime, or assaulting a girl. The list of problems resulting from driving is a long one: loss of control and supervision by a parent, increased temptations in the area of morals and liquor, giving up of school to work in order to operate and maintain that idol the car, hoodlumism and bumming, pseudo-sophistication and materialistic attitudes, and a false sense of values.' "

McFarland went on to say that one of the most serious problems with regard to youth and the automobile was the disproportionately high loss of life and the great number of injuries sustained. Nearly one-quarter of the traffic deaths of the United States in 1957 were persons between the age of 15 and 24. The high death rate in these age groups was of special importance because they cut short the most productive years of life. On the basis of life expectancy rates it could, for instance, be estimated that the youthful traffic fatalities of 1957 cost the country 800,000 of the total of 1,440,000 life-years lost that year. Not only did youth suffer heavily in death and injury from motor accidents, but also it would appear that youthful drivers, as a group, were more frequently involved in accidents, and showed higher accident rates than would be expected on the basis of their numbers in the driving population. Here it was difficult to assess the relative contribution of the young female drivers as their exposure was no doubt different from that of the young males. But it would appear that the girl drivers were more conforming and also probably more closely supervised by their parents. (Coppin's later studies (1965–7) indicated that the sex difference was a fundamental one.)

Research had shown that a disproportionate number of teenage drivers were involved in certain kinds of accidents such as single-car accidents, particularly those which involved running off the roadway, overturning in the roadway, and colliding with fixed objects. Several studies had shown that the two age groups which had the most disproportionate number of these accidents were those under 20, followed by the 21–25 range. Analysis of the characteristics of the drivers in these accidents indicated that the susceptibility of the younger group could be due to inexperience, as features commonly found in these accidents were poor or slippery road surface, narrow roads, or absence of centre-line markings. "A study of personal injury accidents in Great Britain (Garwood and Jeffcoate, 1955), also supported the view that inexperience is the major factor in teenage accidents . . . errors which sharply differentiated the younger drivers from the others included over-taking, losing control, swerving, skidding, and inexperience with type of vehicle in use at the time. Teen-age drivers were also responsible for significantly more accidents resulting from 'being asleep' or 'fatigue'. In a number of studies it had been shown that excessive speed was the major characteristic of teenage driving accidents."

Data on the frequency or severity of violations by youthful drivers were inconsistent. The issues were confused by differences in attitudes on the part of law-enforcement officers toward youthful or toward adult driver offenders, differences in reporting practices, and differences in the severity of penalties in various parts of the country which could produce variations in the deterrents to violation. An example of the difficulties encountered was the interpretation of the findings of a study on the detection of speeders by radar where only 2% of the speeders were found to be drivers under 18. "The two interpretations suggested are that the young drivers may be responsible for fewer speed violations or, as has been suggested, that young drivers may be more alert to the presence of police and may do their speeding when and where they are less likely to be apprehended." There was also some suggestion that among youthful offenders there was a group, comprising up to about one-third of all youthful offenders, who were repeatedly apprehended for violations.

On the question of attempts to interpret the high accident rates of youthful drivers, McFarland's discussion is very interesting:

"It is well known that the best scores on tests of physiological functions, sensory abilities, psychomotor coordination skills and mental ability are made by young adults.

Reaction times, for example, are shortest, night vision and glare resistance are best, and the ability to learn coordinated skills are highest in the late teens and early twenties. Thus, evidence that accident rates among young drivers are disproportionately high presents the paradox that the driver is most susceptible to accidents at the time of his greatest potential operating skill. Hence 'youthfulness' rather than age *per se* has been cited as the important factor. The factors underlying this 'youthfulness' have usually been interpreted as inexperience, various factors of immaturity, and attitudes particularly characteristic of youth.

"Since increasing age and increasing experience go hand in hand, it is almost impossible to separate the experience factor from the other concurrent changes which may be occurring on the basis of age, and hence to assess accurately the influence of inexperience on the safety record of young drivers. It is well known that in industry accidents are characteristically most frequent during the early phases of learning a new job or skill and decrease with increasing time on the job. It would be reasonable to assume that the same situation would prevail on the highway. Certainly, in the process of learning to drive, there are many accident-potential situations which are never encountered, and practice in handling such situations is not gained except during the course of acquiring further experience. One writer has pointed out that the judgement of traffic situations is perhaps the most important factor in whether or not an accident occurs and that developing this judgement depends on actual experience on the road. This writer has also commented that the young driver may often operate with insufficient margin of safety simply because his experience has not yet been sufficient to enable him to appreciate completely the speeds with which emergency situations develop and his own limitations in regard to the time relationships and physical forces involved."

McFarland and Moore then discuss the applicability of the psychological research findings to the question of the youthful driver. Here they say the most promising results are those concerning personality, adjustment, and attitudes, and that there is an urgent need for further research in this area.

The authors then discuss driver training and driver "education" and the various programmes and procedures which had been developed in an attempt to reduce accidents and particularly to improve the driving and the safety records of the teenagers and young adults. Here they say that not much is known about the effectiveness of the various programmes, except that of actual driver *training*. But they quote one study where 4000 young and adult violators were interviewed on the basis of their poor driving records and the conclusion reached was that "in general, when pre-examination records were not heavily weighted by the more serious offenses, educative and persuasive procedures were more effective than more drastic actions. If pre-examination records were extremely poor, no type of action seemed to be more effective than any other."

Readers of this very good paper by McFarland and Moore may not agree with the rather permissive attitude which the authors display toward the driving behaviour of the younger age group (and which is often in sharp contrast with the tone of many of the studies they quote). They might, for instance, want to point out that the fact that the accidents of young drivers which are associated with speeding on roads with poor surfaces, or no centremarking line, are not necessarily merely an indication of inexperience—they could in fact reflect sheer recklessness and foolhardiness. Here it seems that they would have the support of the practical traffic officials, for it is very evident that of all the studies referred to in this paper, those whose conclusions are most critical and outspoken are usually the work of bodies such as State Motor Vehicle Departments. This ambivalence is often found among American writers on youthful accidents, for they seem to be pulled between, on the one hand, the factual evidence of the amount of damage done by American youth, and, on the other hand, by the very prevalent American attitude towards youth, an attitude of permissive indulgence.

McFarland and Moore's paper can in fact be interpreted any way one wishes, and has in fact been quoted many times for very different purposes—particularly to support or belittle the importance of accident proneness. The supporters of the concept seem to consider that it contains evidence of personal characteristics which would make a great many young drivers very accident-prone; characteristics which would be operative over periods of time which are quite long enough to matter. Those who are opposed to the concept either stress the impermanence of youthful characteristics or maintain that the paper supports the contention that the high accident rate of youth is largely a matter of inexperience or insufficient education on safety attitudes. The influence which this widely circulated paper exerted on the development of current thinking on the subject of accident proneness was, therefore, in all probability, very largely determined by the personal orientation of the reader.

A later study on teenage drivers, not covered by McFarland's review of the publications on the subject, was Beamish and Malfetti's "Comparison of youthful violators and non-violators in the 16–19 year age group" (1962). Here, although the criterion was traffic violations and not accidents, the findings followed the same pattern as those of previous accident studies, especially on young drivers.

The tests used were a personal history form and a battery of psychological tests consisting of the Guilford–Zimmerman Temperament Survey, the Minnesota Counselling Inventory, the Otis Self-administering Higher Examination, and the Siebrecht Attitude Scale. The subjects consisted of two groups of 16–19-year-old male adolescents: 84 young male violators who had been referred to a juvenile court for two or more traffic violations; and a control group of 186 non-violators matched with respect to age, education, miles driven annually, and principal use made of the car.

The conclusion reached by the investigators was:

"That the deviant behavior of the Violator Group can be attributed at least in part to a measurable set of psychological characteristics: (a) by accepted standards, they do not give proper thought to the implications of their behavior for themselves and others; (b) they tend to be in disagreement or conflict with others, including those closest to them, and perceive themselves as held down and imposed upon; (c) they are rebellious and selfish; (d) their hypersensitiveness, lack of self-confidence, and feelings of personal unworthiness may lead them to over-compensate with erratic and ill-considered action resulting in traffic violations; (e) their parents are relatively in-active in the community, indicating in the children a lessened sense of civic responsibility."

The investigators then went on to show that there were shades of differences within this group, and that some of them were probably more amenable to corrective action than others. All the violator group were made to attend the Cleveland Driver Improvement School, where they were given a course designed to change their attitude toward traffic and safety. A year later a comparison of their official driving records indicated that 75% of them had shown improvement—whereas 25% had shown no improvement despite the course and despite the fact that they were growing older. Referring back to the original test results, the investigators found:

"The violator who appears to benefit from the type of remedial training provided by the Cleveland Driver Improvement School: (a) enjoys a variety of social contacts and activities and is interested in having friends and making conversation; (b) tends to have greater respect for other people than his non-remediable counterpart; (c) gives more thought to the implications of his actions for himself and others; (d) is more observant of himself and others; (e) is more aware of the necessity for cooperation; (f) tends to be more energetic and has strong drive, and is enthusiastic and quick in action. His reflectiveness and social consciousness may result in direct and positive response to corrective education rather than in an empty rationalization of his behavior. He tries to change an anti-social characteristic when its existence is pointed out.

"The remediable violator rates his parents as being more politically active in the community. It can be inferred, therefore, that he may place greater stress upon civic-mindedness in his own life. Further, his home seems to have more 'holding power' on him than that of the non-remediable violator."

There has been criticism of the way in which post-training improvement was determined; but the trends are obvious and the conclusions very compatible with the findings of other studies.

Another study prompted by the high accident rate among young servicemen was Barmack's and Payne's very good study "Private injury-producing motor vehicle accidents among airmen", published in two main papers (1961a, b), both of which are fortunately reproduced in various sections of Haddon's *Accident Research*.

The study was confined to private vehicle (as against on-the-job) injury-producing, lost-time accidents—where either the driver or a military passenger was injured. There were several reasons for choosing these particular accidents:

(a) Practical concern in military circles over the undue loss of manpower time caused by these accidents.

(b) The supposition that such injury-producing accidents were associated with different personality characteristics from those which might be associated with property-damage or on-the-job accidents; and that combining these different kinds of accidents might obscure the issue.

(c) Research interest as to whether the sort of personal characteristics associated with this particular type of accident would conform to the trend of research findings on accident repeaters. The particular research findings for consideration were:

"That accident repetition reflects a pattern of inadequate adjustment which does not fit into existing psychiatric diagnostic categories. The accident repeater has been described as the product of a broken home, socially immature and impulsively resentful toward authority, with escapist and/or self-destructive tendencies."

To qualify as accident cases the subjects need only have been involved in one injury-producing accident over an eighteen-month period, and the fact that they did indeed show much the same trend of characteristics as the repeaters in previous studies is therefore very interesting.

The subjects came from 239 drivers who had been involved in an injury-producing accident. Some of them had been involved in motor-cycle accidents; some had been moved to other stations or were in remote hospitals; some were too critically injured for examination; and as many as 19% had been killed in the accidents, which gives some idea of the seriousness of this kind of accident. The number available for the car-accident study was 138 and the mode of investigation was a very comprehensive semi-structured personal interview. For comparative purposes a group of 100 drivers (with no reported accident of any kind over a period of a year) was used as a control group.

The first significant finding was that two-thirds of the drivers admitted to pre-accident drinking. Nor was this drinking an isolated event—in fact the incidence of drinking and driving in the accident group was found to be twelve times that of the control group. As a result of this finding the investigators decided to pay particular attention to the nature of this drinking and to the role which it played in the men's lives. The accident group was divided into two: (1) a drinking-accident group (89) who admitted to having had at least two alcoholic drinks in the four hours preceding the accident, and (2) a non-drinking accident group (49) who said they had only one, or no alcoholic drinks in the same period. A third group consisted of the no-accident controls. The authors were careful to point out that their sample must not be taken as being representative of the general public. These were all young males (average age 23–24), and conditions of service naturally excluded extreme cases such as known alcoholics and psychiatric cases. The findings should not therefore be considered in terms of actual figures; their importance lay in the significant trends they displayed. Some of the most important of these trends are evident in Table 7.1.

The various categories of personal characteristics in Table 7.1 are deserving of further comment.

Problem drinking

As mentioned before, the sample contains no "alcoholics" (defined here as persons confined to institutions for alcoholics). Problem drinkers in this study were persons with one or more convictions for offences involving drinking. These problem drinkers, though only 34% of the drinking-accident group, were nevertheless more prevalent in this group than in the others. The authors feel this finding throws some doubt on a contention which

TABLE 7.1. PERCENTAGE INCIDENCE OF VARIOUS PERSONAL CHARACTERISTICS FOUND IN THREE GROUPS OF YOUNG AIRMEN. (INFORMATION EXTRACTED FROM BARMACK AND PAYNE, 1961a)

Personal characteristics investigated	Drinking accident group (89) (%)	Non-drinking accident group (49) (%)	Control group (100) (%)
Problem drinkers	34	10	9
Parent(s) problem drinkers	8	2	1
Traumatic family background	39	16	28
Reports of previous civil and military infractions	88	74	50
Single or married, but living apart from their wives	74	61	42
Average number of previous accidents admitted	0·92	0·82	0·92
Percentage with two or more previous accidents	21%	22%	20%
Percentage with no previous accidents	47%	47%	44%

had been put forward that traffic accidents associated with drinking were largely a problem of alcoholism. (Much, of course, depends here on the definition of alcoholism; in other studies the definition is sometimes extended to include some of Barmack's and Payne's problem-drinkers. But the point is nevertheless well made because the accidents of this group were certainly not associated with alcoholism in its usually accepted sense.)

Traumatic family background (including problem drinking parents)

This group includes subjects who were separated from one or both parents before the age of 13 for reasons of parental death, desertion, separation, divorce, imprisonment, or commitment to a mental hospital; or whose parents were problem drinkers (in this case drinking to the extent of requiring intervention from an outside agency). The authors put forward some very interesting hypotheses concerning the effects which these traumatic family backgrounds could have exerted. Discussing the question of the relevance of the findings to a study like that of Tillmann, associating accident repetition with the history of a broken home, they say: "The question may be raised as to how much this association owes to the intervention of alcohol as a palliative for the feelings of loneliness, rejection, resentment, etc., generated by the broken home experience." (I personally think other factors might have been added here, such as lack of parental discipline and the influence of heredity as well as environment.) One clue, they say, is the fact that, although the other groups contained a number of subjects from broken homes, a much higher proportion of the drinking-accident group came from "socially stigmatized" homes where the parents had been convicted of a felony, or hospitalized for mental illness, or had committed suicide, or were problem drinkers. The authors suggest that another clue to the quality of the home life of this group lies in the fact that problem drinking parents may generate a variety of family disturbances, of which drinking by the offspring may be one expression; or that such parents could set an example of using alcohol to deal with tensions or other unpleasant feelings. On the whole, they feel that this group probably had more to contend with in childhood. They do, however, point out that individuals vary in their ability to cope with traumatic childhood experiences, and studies have shown that a great many people do manage to rise above these difficulties.

Reports of previous civil and military infractions

These included one or more infractions such as civil gaol incarceration, moving vehicle violations, minor military infractions, and court martial. Here the trends showed that the drinking accident group had not only a greater percentage of offenders, but also a higher number of infractions per man. This, the authors feel, indicates that the group displayed greater conflict with authority not only in their driving but in other spheres of life.

Single, or married and living apart from their wives

Here the authors feel that the data suggest that not only the drinking accident group but the whole accident group divides itself into two sub-groups:

(1) The single men who could be drinking for pleasure or to demonstrate such factors as independence or masculinity.
(2) Married men living apart from their wives and who could be drinking "in response to a recent source of unhappiness". (I suppose it takes a woman to suggest to these male authors that this might be putting the cart before the horse, and that the subjects' drinking, or their personal characteristics, could perhaps have been the *cause* of their domestic sorrows!)

Average number of previous accidents admitted

Here the authors point out the striking similarity of the accident histories of the three groups prior to the accident under consideration. This is a very interesting finding. Self-admitted accident histories are notoriously unreliable, but the very fact that the subjects admitted (under promise of anonymity) to drinking and to previous law infractions, indicates that there would be no particular reason why they should suppress information on previous accidents.

Table 7.2 shows that the previous history of all three groups is, indeed, very similar. And yet both accident groups who, let us for argument's sake say were singled out by chance to have one injury-producing accident (for half of them their *first* accident), were actually found to *differ significantly from their fellows on a number of personal characteristics*. It seems, therefore, that because of these characteristics they had a higher accident *potential*. This has important implications for the consideration of accident proneness in terms of this sort of potential for a serious accident in addition to the usual statistical basis of accident repeating. A balanced accident prevention policy is not directed solely against the repeaters; it is directed against the prevention of accidents, whether they be the driver's first accident or his tenth—particularly against the sort of injury-producing accident dealt with in this study—let alone the 19% of the original ones which proved fatal. A driver needs only to have one serious accident for the damage to be great and the effects far-reaching. It is therefore just as important to be able to detect someone with this potential as it is to detect repeaters—and the study seems to indicate that the two types of offender (which must in any case overlap) have a number of characteristics in common.

There is also the question of the implication which this finding has in connection with the interpretation of State accident rates. Set out in Table 7.2 are the details of the previous accident histories of the group.

TABLE 7.2. ACCIDENT HISTORY BEFORE THE CURRENT ACCIDENT. (INFORMATION EXTRACTED FROM BARMACK AND PAYNE, 1961a)

No. of previous accidents	Drinking accident group %	Non-drinking accident group %	Control group %
0	47·2	46·9	44·0
1	31·4	30·6	36·0
2	14·6	16·3	12·0
3	3·4	6·1	4·0
4 or more	3·4	0·0	4·0
Average	0·92	0·82	0·92

Looking at Table 7.2 one is struck by the fact that there was no indication whatever in the figures that either of the accident groups had any greater accident *potential* than the control group and yet, to state the case again, (a) they did have a serious accident, and (b) a significantly large number of them displayed certain personal characteristics which were not found to anything like the same extent in the control group. A finding like this casts some doubt on the justification for splitting a population of drivers like the Connecticut drivers into *repeaters* (1·3%) and *normal* drivers, as Forbes did in 1939: or, as is the current tendency, to consider that the whole driving public consists of a small group who are possibly "accident-prone" while the rest are *normal* drivers. On the contrary it seems very probable that among the so-called *normal* drivers are an appreciable number of people whose personal potential for accidents is anything but normal. This may seem to some people to be belabouring a point which is so self-evident that it does not need belabouring. It is, for example, very unlikely that any practical traffic official would believe that only 1% of the population had any unusual accident potential. But the point apparently needs to be stressed because of the way in which Forbes' figures were later so repeatedly used as proof of the negligible role played by unequal liability to accidents in the total accident situation.

Barmack and Payne themselves carefully pointed out that no definite conclusions could be drawn from their study, which was restricted to one class of accident among one class of subjects. But the very fact that its findings do dovetail into the pattern of the findings of so many other studies makes them seem very plausible.

Before leaving this study there are a few minor, but interesting points made by the authors which are worth considering. In comparing the characteristics of the accident group with those which were usually associated with repeaters, the authors were only looking for those particular characteristics which could be revealed by a comprehensive interview. Their original frame of reference was that accident repeaters often display inadequate (but not psychotic) maladjustment; are the product of broken homes; are socially immature; are impulsively resentful toward authority; and display escapist and/or self-destructive tendencies. The authors did in fact find that the accident groups were over-represented in all of these characteristics with the exception of the self-destructive tendency. (Up to that time this tendency had usually been referred to in studies dealing with extreme groups, namely multiple accident and traffic offenders who had been regarded by the courts or the traffic officials as cases which should be referred for psychiatric examination. But two studies, Porterfield (1960) and Morton (1968), have indicated that this type of suicidal " accident" is perhaps not as rare as one might think. Nevertheless, Barmack and Payne's contentions were valid for their particular population.)

"While evidence for the operation of a variety of unconscious processes was obtained, the interview protocols do not support the view that the aim of these processes was necessarily to achieve a self-aggressive, destructive end. Rather in many instances their aim appears to be tension discharge inappropriate to the reality requirements of the road. However, the possibility remains that the shift from active to passive psychic processes may be itself an expression of a destructive aim."

The paper also contains a number of interesting discussions on the deleterious effects of alcohol on judgement and perception.

One final point is a conclusion drawn by the authors which does not seem to be altogether justified. This was:

"There are other implications from the findings of the present study. The data suggest that some part, or all, of the relationship between biographical data or personality measures and accidents, reported in other studies, owes its existence to drinking as an intervening variable. The validity and importance of previously reported findings are not in question. Rather, the position is taken that, if the nature of the processes that lead to accidents is to be understood, it is important to clarify the interrelations between psychic trauma, drinking, and accidents."

No one would deny the important role played by alcohol, particularly in the accidents of the general motoring public. But the statement given above concerning the findings of previous studies is obviously incorrect. Most of the studies on the personality of accident offenders had been carried out on professional drivers (Slocombe and Brakeman, train drivers and bus drivers; Tillmann, taxi drivers; McFarland, truck drivers; Hakkinen, bus drivers, etc.). These studies had all involved accident repeating among a class of driver where, if there is any suspicion of drinking–driving, the man is usually immediately discharged. Undoubtedly alcohol does increase the likelihood of accidents, and also very often their seriousness. But it seems that there are still significant differences between people's accident potential without the intervention of alcohol—though in many cases the addition of alcohol would no doubt serve to magnify these differences. It is a pity that Barmack and Payne missed this point. For the slight over-emphasis which they themselves placed on the role of alcohol has, it seems, prevented a number of people from realizing the importance of their other findings, and has encouraged the viewpoint that these two papers, good as they were, were merely studies on accidents as related to alcohol.

Barmack and Payne published a follow-up of this study of injury-producing accidents during the same year: "The Lackland accident counter-measure experiment" (1961b). In this paper the authors describe how an experimental programme of accident counter-measures was put into practice on one particular airfield for a period of a year and how it reduced the occurrence of this type of accident.

As the relatively strong association between problem drinking (and abnormal family background) with accident occurrence seemed to indicate that safety propaganda or appeals for better behaviour would not be effective, a stronger counter-measure was devised. This was designed to undercut the prevailing image that "tanking up and taking off in a car" was an act of personal courage and daring, or at least a tolerable pecadillo. Instead the idea was to hold this up as an example of "sick" behaviour. To force home this point any airman who became involved in a lost-time injury accident was tagged for special attention, which included a thorough review of his value to the Service by his squadron commander. This review could lead to a recommendation for discharge or to his being referred to the base psychiatrist (whose role in this case was to be more severe and threatening than usual). In addition a good deal of rather down-to-earth publicity

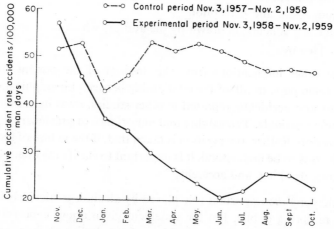

FIG. 7.1. Cumulative accident rate during the experimental and control years of the Lackland accident counter-measure experiment. (Barmack and Payne, 1961b)

material was put out dealing with factual articles on social drinking, alcohol and accidents, interviews with accident victims, and articles stressing that the tendency of some young people to take risks on the road was really an indication of "abnormal" behaviour or "emotionally disturbed" behaviour—the sort of behaviour which on Lackland Base would be referred to a psychiatrist.

At the end of the experimental year the accident rate was compared with that of the previous year. The authors point out that no proper comparison is possible without some index of exposure—which, for a large population operating private motor vehicles, was naturally impossible to obtain. As a compromise they used a rate based on the number of accidents per 100,000 man-days, a procedure which at any rate adjusted for variations in manpower and days in the month. Figure 7.1 shows the cumulative averages of the accident rate during the two years.

Apparently it took over three months for the effects of the counter-measures to become apparent. This is attributed by the authors to two possible causes:

(1) It takes a little time for the majority of the population to become aware of such counter-measures; or
(2) Information about the counter-measures spreads rapidly but has no effect until concrete action has been taken with specific cases.

Various tests were carried out which indicated that the decrease in the accident rate was in itself significant, particularly in relation to trends on other air bases and the divergent trend in the accident rate of the motoring public, which *increased* during the year.

The authors point out that one other factor could have affected the accident rate and that was that shortly after the initiation of the counter-measures a new provost marshal was appointed. He had not been present at the staff meeting in which it was requested that no major changes in operating procedures be initiated, and he did in fact expand the number and the activities of on-base patrols. This intensified campaign continued until the end of June, and possibly contaminated the results. The authors therefore state that: "It can be said that the program worked and worked very well in reducing lost-time injury accidents. But it is not known which attribute or combination of attributes contributed to its effectiveness. Further research on these components is clearly indicated."

One interesting point, which the authors do not mention, but which must have occurred to many of the people who read this report, is the similarity between the counter-measures and a strictly enforced points demerit system. Undoubtedly in some ways the counter-measures were more severe, in that notice was taken of one accident instead of waiting for the accumulation of a certain number of accidents and/or violations. But the basic principle on which the counter-measures operated was very similar, in that the procedure was to single out each offender for attention, attention which might have unpleasant repercussions. There are many officials, both in the Motor Vehicle Departments of those American States which operate a points system, and in countries such as Germany, who feel that it is this process which has such a salutary effect—not only on the persons singled out, but on others. It seems that we all like the anonymity of being just one of the herd—particularly the herd on the right side of the law. It could be argued that this process might only work with the more conventional law-abiding section of the community.

Probably, up to a point, it does, and this is in fact regarded as one of the reasons for the rather unexpected effectiveness of the ostensibly ineffectual first stage of any points system, namely the first polite warning letter. What then of the people who are not so easily influenced or affected? For example, Barmack and Payne's previous study had shown that in their population of young airmen, the people who seemed most likely to have a serious accident were people who had already been singled out by some act or some circumstance—and who had apparently not been deterred from further undesirable actions like drinking–driving or dangerous driving. There was no reason to assume that such people were not represented on the Lackland Base. Could it not be expected therefore that they would be impervious to any further singling-out process? Perhaps some of them were; but the very fact that the accident rate was *halved* indicated that many of them were not. One or more aspects of the counter-measure programme, or some factor operative during the experimental year, must have had a very salutary effect. Without further research there is no saying which. But my guess (and guess it must be) is that at least two of the counter-measures were effective:

(1) The fact that an injury-accident would trigger off an *official* investigation into the whole question of the man's *value to the Service*. This could have acted as a stronger deterrent than any threatened State action, where it was probably popular knowledge that even losing a driving licence was usually only a temporary measure—and one which possibly carried little or no stigma with their young friends and associates.

(2) The fact that being branded as "abnormal" or "emotionally disturbed", or "in need of psychiatric treatment", did carry a stigma with these same friends and associates.

At the same time one might hazard another guess, a rather discouraging one, namely that any increased fear of the consequences of their actions did not include any unduly increased fear of being injured or killed. People, and young people particularly, are, it seems, often more afraid of making fools of themselves than of dying. And one way of making a fool of oneself is to depart from socially accepted norms of behaviour. Change the norms of a group and you can often change the behaviour pattern of that group. It seems to me quite possible that this is what occurred with this particular group (just as—such is my personal contention—has possibly happened, over the years, with at least the adult members of the American driving public).

Altogether it is a very great pity that this study was not continued for a further year, as was originally planned. It would have been extremely interesting to see whether the accident rate would have reverted again, and if so how quickly, once the counter-measures were stopped—especially as it was so arranged that the end of the counter-measure period was specifically announced by the Base Commander and publicized in the base newspaper. Unfortunately support for the project terminated before this could be accomplished, which is a sad loss to research as it would take a great deal of time, effort, and expense to mount such an excellent study again.

It is difficult to assess just what effect this study had on the development of the thinking on accident proneness. Like McFarland's "Youth and the automobile" (1960), it seems that much depended on the personal orientation of the reader. A number of people seemed to see the wider implications of the findings and thought of them as adding more knowledge, not only on the question of why people have accidents, but why some people are *more* likely to have accidents than their fellows. But others appeared to feel that the two were virtually synonymous, and that Barmack and Payne's study merely showed that young people can have an isolated accident because they drink, and that some young people are more likely to have an isolated accident because they drink more, or they drive after drinking. The factors leading up to the accident-producing situations and the question of individual differences in these factors was completely overlooked. The problem was regarded as a *group* one—the problem of the young driver; the lack of experience of youth; the attitudes of youth; and the effect of alcohol on both. Little or no account was taken of the *individuality* of youth.

CHAPTER 8

RESEARCH ON ADULT DRIVERS

THOUGH most of the bigger studies of the late fifties and early sixties were concerned with young drivers, the period also witnessed the publication of some very interesting studies on widely divergent aspects of the accident problem. One of these was Porterfield's "Traffic fatalities, suicide and homicide" (1960)—also fortunately reproduced in Haddon's *Accident Research*.

Porterfield opened his paper by saying:

"The objective of this study is to test the prediction that rates of death caused by motor vehicle accidents, if appropriately compared with rates of suicide and homicide by matched population groups, could prove to be similarly distributed, or positively correlated with the combined rates of the latter. This prediction is based on the postulate that a significant number of drivers of death-dealing cars, as well as their victims, have attitudes similar to those who become involved in suicide and homicide. . . .

"Some influences on rates of death caused by traffic accidents may be other than lack of driver education, driver fatigue, deficiencies of roads or of machines, or the fact that the driver 'took one for the road'. And some of these influences may have deep roots in driver attitudes which cannot be separated from a given type of personality.

"For example, it may be predicted that drivers who have little regard for their own lives or the lives of others, or both ('other things equal') will have higher rates of accidents than drivers who place a high value on human life. As a corollary, if the populations of some areas have a higher ratio of persons who do not value life than have other areas, it may be predicted that the former populations will experience more motor vehicle fatalities than the latter. . . . Is this prediction supported by ascertainable facts?"

Porterfield then went on to compare age-adjusted fatality rates from motor-vehicle accidents with rates of suicide and homicide (both for white males and females) using the thirty-nine Metropolitan areas of the United States with the highest and the lowest homicide–suicide rates. (The reason he gives for combining the suicide and homicide rates is that some populations more readily express frustration through suicide and others through violence toward other people: both tendencies therefore need to be included.) The comparison showed that the suicide–homicide rate was significantly related to the accident fatality rate, both for males and females—the relation for the males being higher. He then went on to make a very interesting observation: "Since men preponderate among drivers, and women more often occupy the adjacent 'suicide seat', it is pertinent to com-

114

pare *male* suicide–homicide rates with *female* auto death rates." This comparison, he says, produced a higher coefficient than either male–male or female–female comparisons and showed that there might indeed be some connection, though more investigation was obviously necessary. (Anyone who has sat helplessly in the so-called "suicide seat" while the driver dices with death would, I am sure, be quite prepared to accept this idea. In fact the title "murder seat" might be far more appropriate. At least one has some say in one's own suicide!)

Porterfield then examined the question of whether there was any connection between accident rates, suicide–homicide rates, and crime rates. He took two indices of traffic fatalities among white males, per mileage driven, and per population, and compared these with a suicide–homicide index *for white males*, and with a *total* major crime rate (murder, burglary, aggravated assault, robbery, larceny and theft). This time the figures were for various States, those with the highest and the lowest *accident rate*. These figures are so interesting and give rise to so much speculation as to what lies behind them, that they are reproduced in Table 8.1. (For example, is Nevada's accident rate as fantastically high as its suicide and crime rate because some unlucky gamblers are so cleaned out that they cannot even buy a gun? Or are all these rates a statistical mirage, created by the antics of the visitors being measured in relation to Nevada's small indigenous population?)

Porterfield sums up the conclusions of this interesting and unusual paper as follows:

"The prediction that rates of death caused by motor vehicle accidents are positively correlated to suicide–homicide rates is suppported by comparisons of the data. No doubt other factors contribute to the observed positive relationships. But it was the *driver attitude rationale* that led to the comparison of given variables; not such other factors as differences in social structure, mobility, composition of population, and social controls. Whatever factors play a part in the positive correlation of suicide–homicide, other crimes, and accident death rates, there is no reason to doubt that aggressive, hazardous driving is likely to be characteristic of persons similar to those who have suicidal, or homicidal, or both tendencies—and *vice versa*.

"The Metropolitan data (1949–1951) and the data for the States (1954–1956) leave little room for doubt. They suggest, however, the need for further research which will incorporate case studies of accident prone drivers, and which will seek information about attitudes of drivers and riders, and about their family, class, educational and vocational background. It might be enlightening, for example, to take a census of a sample of wrecked-car cemeteries and to study the 'life-histories' of automobiles and their owners. But sociologists have shown little interest in traffic behavior. If this comparison of suicide–homicide rates, with rates of death from traffic accidents, stimulates further research, it will have served an important purpose."

Dealing with the opposite end of the scale of social behaviour was another Columbia study, this time on the characteristics of the very good driver, Malfetti and Fine's "Characteristics of safe drivers—a pilot study" (1962). This was based on a study of six subjects who had received the National Safety Council's Safe Driving Award for twenty or more years of driving without a preventable accident. The subjects were chosen from the 9095 drivers from business, transport, and governmental fleets, who received their twenty-or-

TABLE 8.1. INDICES OF TRAFFIC FATALITIES, SUICIDE–HOMICIDE, AND MAJOR CRIMES KNOWN
TO THE POLICE. COMPARISON BY STATES. 1954–6. (From Porterfield, 1960)

States	Index of traffic deaths		Index of suicide– homicide among white males	Index of major crimes among the total population
	Among the population (per mileage driven)	Among the white males per 100,000 population		
New Mexico	155	156	86	114
Arizona	151	154	133	176
South Carolina	148	142	107	115
Nevada	145	180	236	188
Alabama	140	148	121	142
Kentucky	140	125	114	174
Wyoming	128	182	146	70
Idaho	128	147	110	70
Louisiana	126	115	86	135
Georgia	122	143	126	164
Montana	122	149	144	91
Arkansas	120	123	67	113
United States	100	100	100	100
Colorado	88	114	131	121
Minnesota	86	94	85	60
New York	83	63	74	88
Nebraska	82	112	97	62
Washington	77	86	129	91
Pennsylvania	75	80	86	75
Maine	69	87	113	43
New Hampshire	68	85	100	27
Rhode Island	60	45	54	54
New Jersey	58	63	72	64
Massachusetts	57	52	61	50
Connecticut	52	64	88	49

more-year safe driving awards in 1959. They were selected on the basis of availability for examination and the excellence of their records in relation to exposure and hazard. Each one had no violations recorded against him *in his entire driving career*, and each one drove a very high annual mileage.

The group was therefore a highly selective one. With such exceptional records, and being on the whole older men in their late fifties who had chosen to spend their lives doing full-time driving, they were not considered as truly representative of the ordinary " safe " driver among the general motoring public. In fact it was expected that they would show a certain number of distinguishing characteristics. But nevertheless it was felt that the study could give some insight into characteristics associated with safe driving and give a lead as to techniques suitable for the selection and training of professional drivers. The National Safety Council also felt that the study could provide some positive propaganda "to counteract somewhat the 'homicidal maniac' image people must have of drivers as a result of publicity given to violators and accidents".

The examination consisted of twelve hours of medical, psychological, knowledge, and driving-performance tests, administered by people who were all specialists in their respective fields. Because, as Malfetti puts it, of "mounting evidence that the basic personality of a driver was an important influence", the psychological tests included a number of personality tests, the Rorschach, the TAT, the Sentence Completion Test, and an experimental Semantic Differential Test designed by the Columbia unit, and a personal interview.

Some of the findings that emerged from the study were rather unusual and, it seems, rather unexpected. In fact the driving performance tests were the only ones where the findings were entirely as per expectation, and therefore presented no difficulties in connection with the general publication of the results.

These showed that all the subjects displayed a uniformly high standard of driving, especially characterized by courtesy, caution (but not over-caution), and an unusually good ability to position the vehicle for every manoeuvre and to anticipate hazards in the making. In fact, when later in the project the two drivers adjudged best on all counts were given a further gruelling twelve-hour driving test, it became even more evident that the safe driver seems to have the ability to organize instantly all of the factors in a complex driving situation so that he acts appropriately and correctly through simple reflex. Malfetti goes on to say that this high speed "computer mechanism" may be one of the important differences between a safe, average, or unsafe driver.

The results of the knowledge tests were much harder to handle. Strangely enough the subjects were found to be not very knowledgeable; in fact they scored average to low on laws, regulations, and the mechanical aspect of their vehicles. However, the investigators noticed that the subjects did appear to use what knowledge they possessed to a greater extent than do most drivers—a finding which led them to say:

"The groups' basically average achievement on knowledge tests tends to confirm the prominence of psychological dimensions in safe driving. Degree and correctness of knowledge concerning laws, regulations, mechanics and operating procedures for driving seem important primarily in terms of the manner in which this information is put to use. Rather than knowing specifically what the law requires, for example, these individuals are governed by a pervasive sense of caution tempered by previous experience."

On the medical examination they were found to be no better physically than the average for their age. They were average and below average in terms of suggested standards for medical fitness to drive, and in terms of some of the physical standards currently used in licensing. In most cases, however, they were aware of their physical deficiencies and, in view of their good records, had apparently learned to compensate for these in the driving task. This led the investigators to conclude that although it was obviously necessary to have minimum standards of physical fitness, vision, etc., nevertheless intensified concentration, caution, and ability to reach a quick decision, apparently can more than compensate for some physical deficiencies.

In the sphere of biographical data, intelligence, and personality, the findings showed these men to be rather a group apart.

"All subjects operate in at least the average range of intelligence. In general, they are non-aggressive individuals with a high level of impulse control. They are loyal, dependable, sober, saving, cautious husbands and fathers as well as dependable, loyal, hard-working employees. A high degree of security in social and vocational environments seems more important to them than competitive, aggressive strivings. This is reflected further in a tendency to plan conservatively and well for financial commitments, retirements and other phases of their own and their family's future. In doing so, they invest in safety and security to the exclusion of other potential gratifications. In addition, all share a strong preference for an 'outdoor' job—that is, one which does not require formal, long-term and close relationships with others.

"As a group they seem to be somewhat compulsive about safe driving. Their ratio of aspiration to achievement has been consistently maintained by moderating aspiration. They are highly sensitive to the opinions of others and to the mores of society. While they are sensitive to external threat, they try to avoid, deflect and deny such threat before it evokes anti-social feelings or impulses. This is particularly true of threats which might normally arouse anger, so that, for example, they do not seem irritated by the bad manners and poor driving skill of others. Even if a hostile threat 'gets through' to these men, they are still more likely to experience anxiety than anger which leads to counter-action. They are willing to 'give in' and not retaliate in kind. Impulsivity or rebelliousness are totally foreign in their patterns of adjustment. Their behavior seems to be modeled after a parent who was non-aggressive. In the light of these factors, their social behavior is probably stable, even though the evidence suggests that a high percentage of these men underwent extremely stressful childhood experiences."

It is apparent from the report that the investigators found a number of these findings rather puzzling. This is not surprising, really, in view of the fact that the subjects were such exceptionally safe drivers. The personality dynamics which motivate people to an extreme form of behaviour in any sphere are bound to be rather unusual, and later research on a much larger number of subjects (Shaw, 1965) certainly confirmed that ultra-safe drivers often display very strange personality patterns and also quite a high degree of neuroticism.

One can therefore appreciate not only the bewilderment which these findings must have caused to the investigators, but also the dilemma in which it must have placed them. A lot of public attention had been focused on the project, especially on the final contest between the two winners; and the National Safety Council was very eager to publish the findings of the scientific investigation as it was sure these findings would have good propaganda value. This must have placed the investigators in a very awkward spot, for it would hardly be good safety publicity if they announced, for instance, that some of these much publicized safe drivers were real "oddballs", and rather neurotic ones at that!

As it was, Malfetti handled the situation very deftly. His delineation of the personality "profile" of these drivers, and his discussion on the difficult question of whether his findings were applicable to the general motoring public, was a masterly piece of writing.

In this discussion he comments, among other things, on the amount of repression revealed in the personality tests—and in the biographical data and the men's actual driving performance. He says:

"In one sense, the characteristics which seem to make a driver safe are not those which necessarily bring that person to greatest personal or social fulfilment. Would we wish, therefore, to train people, even if we could, to possess these traits for the limited purposes of safe driving? Perhaps we should concentrate on techniques for changing portions of personality characteristics which are specific to driving—like competitiveness in traffic situations as opposed to competitiveness in life situations. Group discussion-decision is thought to have good potential in this regard."

(My personal feelings on this point, based on experience of disciplinary measures with professional drivers, is that a strict enforcement probably achieves this very desirable result with an appreciable section of the driving public.)

Malfetti goes on to say:

" There is also the clear implication that safe driving may be one desirable by-product of a particular mode of adapting to extremely stressful early experiences—much as unsafe driving seems to be an undesirable by-product of another mode of adapting to the same type of experience. What leads to these extremes, and prediction of the direction these kinds of adjustment will take, are important problems for future research."

He also suggests:

"Another tentative conclusion is that given a choice between projective psychological test data and a personal history, the latter may be more predictive of driver behavior. Or, to put it another way, knowledge about habits and patterns of living which has the closest relevance to the action required in driving might be more predictive than knowledge of underlying dynamics."

Our own later study in South Africa has rather reversed this order, showing how well projective tests can predict driving behaviour and how very much more practical they can be for professional drivers in view of the difficulty in obtaining correct biographical data. With the general driving public, where projective tests would be very difficult to use, if not legally impracticable, biographical data might be one of the few sources of information, and it is comforting to know that it holds out hopes of success—a confirmation of Tillmann's early findings. But I can fully appreciate the difficulties of the investigators in this particular project. The ultra-ultra-safe driver is probably the most difficult person to predict by means of any psychological tests, even projective ones, as often it is very hard to know whether this sort of person is going to be a very good or a very bad risk. For although a certain amount of anxiety and repression and neuroticism is apparently a good thing for making a person a safe risk, just a bit too much immediately seems to tip the balance and make him a very unsafe risk. The practical experience of my own unit has shown that it is often very difficult indeed to predict in which category such people are going to fall. Malfetti was therefore using projective tests at the extreme and most difficult end of the accident continuum; for as it progresses down the line the diagnosis becomes much easier. The average good driver seems to be quite an ordinary fellow, and when it comes to some of the really bad risks—as, for example, the immature, or exhibitionistic, or actively aggressive, or psychopathic person, or hopelessly maladjusted person—it is relatively easy to detect them by means of projective tests, as was shown by the work of Conger (1959).

Malfetti's study was, certainly, a very good one, representative of the high standard of research which has always been associated with the Columbia unit, and also very representative of the open-minded thinking of the period.

An investigation in another rather different field was the study on accident occurrence among African and Coloured bus drivers in South Africa (Shaw and Sichel, 1961). This was the first of three papers (which were all published in the United States) describing a research programme which had been operating since 1953 in a transport organization. This was essentially practical research, and the reports were, in fact, accounts of methods devised by the Company's own psychological unit and its statistical consultant to monitor trends in the general accident rate, to assess each driver's accident potential, to winnow out the bad risks, and to select better driver material by means of psychological tests. Some of the methods were, however, unusual, particularly the extensive use made of the projective personality tests for selecting new drivers and the development of a new person-centred method for assessing accident proneness based on the time-intervals between successive accidents. The practical use of the new statistical method was the subject of the first paper to be published, "The reduction of accidents in a transport company by the determination of the accident liability of individual drivers" (1961). The second and third papers did not appear until 1965. These were a statistical paper (Sichel) dealing with the mathematical rationale underlying the new time-interval method, and a psychological paper (Shaw) describing several validations of these tests and their successful use for the prediction of future accident involvement. This paper also described in some detail the findings on the relationship between personality and accident involvement.

None of these papers included any detailed statistical substantiation of the actual concept of accident proneness (especially by the conventional methods) for the very reason that my co-author and I did not, at the time, consider that this was necessary. Like Jacobs (1961), we felt that carrying out elaborate exercises to "prove" the validity of the proneness concept was of academic interest only, and that no one who had ever had any practical dealings with accident records would be likely to dispute that it existed. In any case we felt that it should be obvious that the elaborate practical programme described in these reports could never have succeeded unless the concept of proneness was a reality. For the whole programme was based on the fundamental belief that people differ very greatly in their susceptibility to accidents, that these differences are lasting ones, and that these differences can be predicted by means of suitable tests. And, as the programme had obviously succeeded, our feeling was that any further "proof" of the existence of accident proneness was redundant.

The easiest way to cover this first report is to quote from it quite extensively. This, I might add, is not being done because I think its appearance was such a significant event in the history of the thinking on accident proneness, but because it will save a good deal of repetition in later chapters where the study is used for a detailed analysis of the whole concept of accident proneness.*

"THE GENERAL BACKGROUND OF THE RESEARCH PROJECT ON ROAD ACCIDENTS

"The company in which the investigation was carried out, Public Utility Transport Corp. (PUTCO), is a company supplying most of the bus transport for the nonwhite communities of the South African cities of Johannesburg and Pretoria.

* Reproduced in a condensed form by courtesy of the U.S. National Safety Council.

"The drivers are all non-whites—mainly Bantu, with a small admixture of Coloreds and Indians.* These drivers operate diesel-powered buses, most of which are large 85-passenger-carrying single-decker vehicles. Most of the driving is done in heavy city traffic and between them the drivers travel 11 million miles a year.

"The cities of Johannesburg and Pretoria have the unenviable record of having one of the highest accident rates in the Western World (the death rate per vehicle registered in Johannesburg is reported as being four times that of New York). A variety of causes, ranging from dense traffic in narrow streets to a polyglot population with a fast pace of living, all contribute to this high accident rate. When one adds to this the conditions prevailing in the rapidly-expanding and often overpopulated Bantu townships on the outskirts of these cities, it will be appreciated that a company operating Bantu transport is bound to have its bus fleet involved in a considerable number of accidents.

"What may be termed an operational headache is, however, a statistician's opportunity and the records of a company functioning under conditions such as these provide ideal material for an investigation on accident occurrence.

"The company has been operating since 1945 but this particular investigation has been limited to the years of 1951 to 1960 inclusive. It covers the analysis of the accident records of 898 bus drivers employed by PUTCO during this time.

"These records are kept in very great detail. Each driver has an individual accident file containing comprehensive forms which are filled in for each accident in which he is involved. These forms give, inter alia, the driver's account of the accident, statements taken from witnesses, the findings of the official investigating the accident and details of causation. They also contain an assessment of the seriousness of the accident and the degree of culpability which can be attributed to the driver. In addition, records are kept of any unusual time off driving, such as annual leave, sick leave, absenteeism, etc., so that it is possible to calculate actual driving exposure.

"In addition, this exposure is standardized. Although traffic conditions differ in the various divisions of the company, it is possible to assess the effects of these differences. Within each division the conditions are the same for each driver. The buses are the same and each man drives an eight-hour shift. The shifts are changed from time to time so that over a period each driver is exposed to the same traffic risks.

"All the drivers are trained to a high degree of driving proficiency and regular inspections are made to ensure that this is maintained.

"The age of each driver is known and information is available as to whether he had driving experience before joining the company. They are all literate and the minimum educational level is Standard 5 (post elementary school).

"All the drivers are given regular medical and optical examinations and are required to meet high standards of physical fitness, vision and hearing.

"Every incident, however trivial, in which the company's vehicles are concerned is regarded as an "accident" and is recorded on the file of the driver concerned. Over the 10 years covered by the investigation, the 898 drivers were involved in 7,452 "accidents."

* The South African Information Service defines Bantu as the generic term for Negro tribes, Colored as persons with a mixture of white and non-white blood lines, and Indians as descendants of immigrants from India.

"Because of the difficulty of finding good bus driver material amongst the African population, the company has often been unable to discharge unsatisfactory drivers. This has provided unusual evidence of repeated accident occurrence over periods of long exposure.

"With this wealth of material it was possible to carry out a very comprehensive investigation on road accident occurrence, the general outline of which is given here.

"THE RESEARCH PROJECT

"The investigation followed two main lines:

(1) The analysis of the total accident statistics of the company;

(2) The analysis of the accident records of each individual driver."

1. The Analysis of the Accident Statistics

This portion of the report described the method devised for preparing control charts to record the accident rates (number of accidents per 10,000 miles driven) for the company as a whole and each separate division. This section is not germane to the subject of individual accident liability but some of the findings which emerged are of general interest. The charts proved very useful for management control as they revealed factors such as the competency of local management and changes in management, the effects of special measures such as new driver-selection methods, and the effects of local events such as civil disturbances. On one occasion, for instance, a sudden and suspicious change in a divisional control chart soon revealed that a local official was falsifying the accident returns. On another occasion, the removal of a popular divisional superintendent was immediately followed by a significant rise in the accident rate which took more than a year to revert to its old level. On yet another occasion, rising operating costs brought about an unavoidable increase in the bus fares, which resulted in a boycott of the company's buses. This boycott lasted for three economically crippling months and resulted in a big retrenchment of staff. The unrest and feelings of insecurity which this produced caused an immediate increase in the accident rate, which lasted for many months after the boycott had ended. A similar but not quite so pronounced phenomenon marked the Sharpeville civil disturbance in 1960. (These occurrences are depicted in Fig. 15.1 given later, which reflects the company's accident rate right up to 1968, and all the factors which have affected it.)

"The Analysis of the Accident Records of Each Individual Driver

"At an early stage in the research project it was decided to undertake a detailed study of the individual accident records of the company's drivers. The main objects of this study were:

(1) To establish whether individual drivers did have individual accident patterns.

(2) To establish a reliable method of classifying the company's drivers on the basis of their accident records.

(3) To determine whether it was possible to predict a driver's future accident record on the basis of his past record.

(4) To establish an accident criterion against which to measure the success of new driver selection methods.

(5) To apply the findings of the investigation for the purpose of reducing the company's accident rate.

"(Note: It is gratifying to note that as a result of this investigation all these objects have been achieved.)

"Basically, the investigation boiled down to a practical research project on the much-debated question of 'accident proneness.' The approach to the problem of accident proneness by means of the study of individual records was a somewhat unusual one. Previous studies on proneness have largely concerned themselves with the study of groups of drivers, and attempts have been made to establish whether predictions of future behavior could be made on this basis. These studies have yielded rather poor results. In the opinion of the present writers, this is largely because of the 'blanketing' effect of any group technique, where predictions for the behavior of any one individual are made on the basis of the pattern of a group of which he happens to be a member.

"The individual approach was therefore regarded as being more likely to yield good results. Another and more important consideration was, however, the fact that the research project was essentially a practical one and in practice it is the individual that counts, particularly in the operation of a transport company. In such a company the composite accident rate is the summation of the performance of its individual drivers, and managerial policy cannot hope to be effective unless it has a means of assessing each driver on his own particular merits.

"For this reason the research project resolved itself into an attempt to establish a reliable method of evaluating accident liability in individual drivers.

"The Research Project on Individual Drivers

"The first objective of the study was to investigate such features as:

"What was the important feature of a man's accidents—was it the frequency, or the severity, or the degree of blameworthiness, or the outcome in terms of property damage, injury or death? Was there any meaningful pattern in an individual's accidents or were they merely occurrences dictated by chance? What was the effect of experience or long exposure? Did the drivers improve over the years?

"To achieve this study the individual records of all drivers employed by the company since 1951 were assembled and analyzed in detail.

"The question of severity was considered first. Although some interesting trends were disclosed, in that several drivers appeared to have more than their fair share of 'major' accidents (accidents where the costs exceeded £100), this approach did not yield any very helpful results. This was not regarded as surprising, considering the fact that the outcome of an accident in terms of costs, or in terms of injuries or death, is often purely fortuitous.

"The question of the blameworthiness of the driver was then considered. Every accident sustained by every driver over a period of five years was assessed by experienced officials of the company's accident bureau and was graded on a five point scale: 100% to blame, 75%, 50%, 25% and 0%. It soon became apparent, however, that this approach, although laudably comprehensive, would not prove very practicable either. In over 50% of the accidents the accident bureau officials rated the company's drivers as entirely blameless. On the face of it, this appeared to be extremely improbable and further investigation confirmed this fact.

"In the first place, it was found that often the only evidence available was the driver's own statement—a statement which naturally presented his case in the most favorable light. In the second place, the assessors, who happened to be the men most competent to do the assessment, happened also to be the officials who handled all the accident claims—with the result that they were in all probability conditioned into thinking with a definite bias in favor of the company's interests!

"It appeared therefore that a rating system such as this, although intended for the objective allocation of driving blame, was in fact merely a reflection of such functions as the assessor's way of thinking, or the driver's ability to present a good case for himself. Subsequent attempts to arrive at a true assessment of blameworthiness were equally disappointing and, in the end, the whole approach of differentiating between one accident and another had to be condemned for statistical purposes as being too subjective, or too dependent on chance or on the reliability of the evidence available.

"It was therefore decided that though all relevant information concerning accidents was of interest and of administrative value, the only reliable unit for statistical purposes was the number or rather the frequency (meaning the pattern of the occurrence) of an individual's accidents, and the research program was therefore directed towards an intensive study of this factor.

"Fortunately it was later established that by limiting the investigation to this one aspect very little was being lost. It was later proved that the frequency of an individual's accidents is not only a reliable statistical measure, but also a highly significant one. Whatever the result of an accident and whatever the degree of the driver's blameworthiness, the fact that he is involved in a situation resulting in an accident is apparently very significant and the frequency with which he is involved is even more so."

There are certain occasions, however, when there is objective proof that a particular driver is completely blameless and his involvement so fortuitous that it would be illogical to debit him with the accident. Examples of this type of occurrence are (1) bus stationary for some time in an authorized parking zone, (2) accidents due to a mechanical defect in the bus, (3) very occasional incidents such as when a vehicle driven by a drunken driver has crashed out of control into the bus, (4) passenger-injury accidents (omitted because of the uncontrollable and generally foolhardy behaviour of many of the passengers).

However, to check the validity of the argument for omitting such accidents a statistical check was made which showed that their distribution among the drivers was a Poisson one and therefore largely chance-directed.

An accident "build-up" sheet was then drawn up for each individual driver. This showed:

(a) The time-intervals (t) between successive accidents in terms of actual driving days (i.e. driving time less leave, etc.), the first interval being that between the start of exposure and the first accident.

(b) The logarithm of these time-intervals.

(c) The cumulative average of these intervals ($\bar{t}$).

Each driver's record was then transferred on to an individual control chart with the abscissa recording a point for each successive accident and the ordinate the logarithms of the time-intervals. (Logarithms were used partly to condense the spread and partly in order to apply a control grid, as is explained in the later statistical section of the book.)

"Specimens of these time-interval control charts for individual drivers will be given later in the text. In reading them, the following features are of importance:

"(1) The significant factor is not the number of accidents (for this may be dependent on short or long total exposure); it is the time interval (t), i.e. the height of each point on the ordinate.

"(2) A good record (Fig. 8.1) is one where the points are mostly above the line indicating the median for that division.

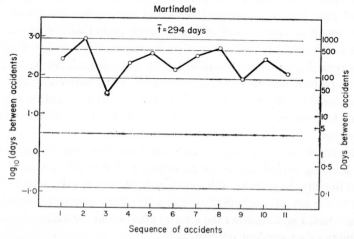

FIG. 8.1. The control chart of a driver with a good record and most of the points above the median line and only 11 accidents in nine years (an average of 20,000 miles of driving between accidents)

"(3) A bad record (Fig. 8.2) is one where the points are mostly below the median line for that division.

"(4) An upward trend indicates a lengthening of the time intervals, i.e. an improvement.

"(5) A downward trend indicates a shortening of the time intervals, i.e. a deterioration.

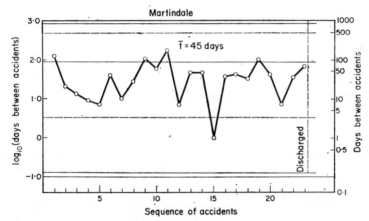

FIG. 8.2. A bad record with most of the points below the median line and 23 accidents in three years (an average of 3,000 miles of driving between accidents)

"A study of the accident graphs and the build-up sheets of all the drivers produced the following valuable information:

"(a) In many of the drivers, particularly the relatively inexperienced ones, a definite learning period of up to six months was clearly discernible. During this learning period, a new driver usually had several accidents at relatively short intervals.

"(b) At the end of the learning period a pronounced improvement was noticeable, the time intervals became longer and each driver developed an individual accident 'pattern.' The cut-off of the learning period was so obvious that it was possible to exclude this period when evaluating his true accident liability. Fig. 8.3 shows a typical learning period followed by a stable accident pattern.

"(c) This pattern was remarkably consistent, so consistent, in fact, that it was apparent, even to the eye, that the time intervals (t) were not dictated by chance but that they played around a stable level. This level was different for each individual driver.

"(d) The graphs were so easy to read that it was possible, by eye alone, to mark off the learning period and make an estimate of that driver's individual level of accident liability. In practice, this rough estimate was usually a very close approximation to the actual mathematical mean ($\bar{t}$) of the intervals calculated from his build-up sheet. Fig. 8.4 shows the control chart of an individual driver illustrating the stability of an accident pattern.

"(e) Significant learning periods were only found among the men who had turned out later to be good accident risks.

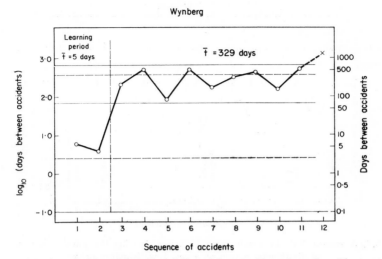

FIG. 8.3. A typical learning period followed by a stable and good accident pattern

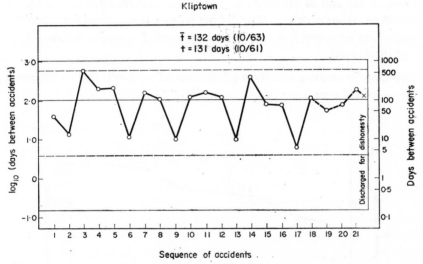

FIG. 8.4. The control chart of an "average" driver illustrating the stability of an accident pattern

"(f) In the case of the bad risks, 'accident proneness' was definitely exhibited. These drivers had started with short time intervals between accidents and, even after the period when learning should have ceased, had continued to show no real improvement. Fig. 8.2 is a typical case of a bad record extending over three years with no real improvement. In many of these instances the driver had eventually been discharged but not before he had been involved in a number of accidents. Fig. 8.5 shows the record of a driver who, over a period of 10 years, had been involved in one major and 44 minor accidents. Disciplinary action was always followed by a period of improvement, but in each case this was only temporary.

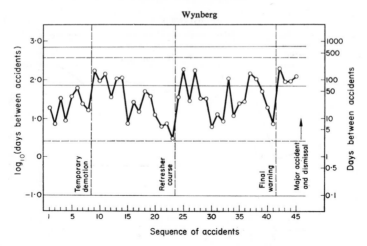

FIG. 8.5. A record with 45 accidents in 10 years showing the purely temporary effect of disciplinary action on a very unsatisfactory driver

Towards the end of his career he was given a severe reprimand and told that he would be taken off driving if he did not reform. He then had fewer accidents which made him overconfident and he finally caused a major accident for which he was discharged.

"(g) Only in an unexpectedly small number of cases was there evidence of gradual improvement over a period of years (Fig. 8.6).

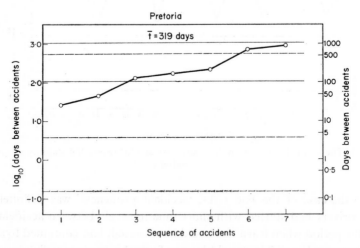

FIG. 8.6. Record of a driver showing steady improvement over a period of six years

[*Note* (December 1968): Extensive experience with these control charts has shown that the proportion of drivers who improve steadily over the years is greater than was originally thought. This has been particularly noticeable among the younger drivers selected by means of personality tests. Even some of the worst test failures have been found to later show some improvement, but here the process is so slow that it is too expensive to be tolerated by a transport company unless it is so short of drivers that it has no alternative.]

"(h) In the majority of the cases, once the initial quick learning period was over and the driver had attained his own individual level, he remained there and only very minor variations occurred in the pattern of his graph or in the cumulative average of the time interval between his accidents, as shown in his build-up sheet.

"(i) Where a significant variation did occur in the pattern, indicating marked deterioration, this could usually be correlated with some definite cause such as ill health, domestic or other worries or his taking to drink. Fig. 8.7 shows the deterioration in the record of a driver after his wife had run away (with his life's savings).

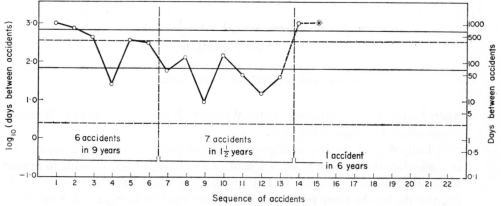

FIG. 8.7. The record of a good driver showing a significant deterioration caused by domestic worries

[*Note* (December 1968): The company's welfare department, which is apt to adopt a very realistic attitude to staff problems, ultimately solved this dilemma by the simple expedient of getting back what was left of the savings and letting the wife go. As a matter of general interest the subsequent accident history of this driver is indicated in dotted lines.]

"(j) A very interesting phenomenon was demonstrated in the control charts of men who had been transferred from one division to another and who had to adapt themselves to driving under different conditions. In each case the transfer was accompanied by a change in the level of the pattern of time intervals between accidents; but here again the individuality of each driver's specific accident potential was clearly demonstrated. In most cases the change in level was purely relative, e.g. a driver with a good $\bar{t}$ (average time interval) transferred from an easy division to a more difficult one would have shorter time intervals but the new level of his $\bar{t}$ on the control chart would still be above the level of the median $\bar{t}$ for the new division. In other cases, however, the control chart of a transferred driver would reveal either a significant improvement showing that this particular individual functioned better in this new division than in the old, or a significant deterioration showing that he was unable to cope with the new conditions. Fig. 8.8 shows the significant fall in the level of the time intervals between accidents of a driver transferred from the Pretoria Division, where traffic conditions are relatively easy and

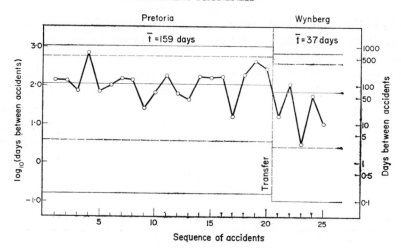

FIG. 8.8. Control chart showing the effect of an inter-divisional transfer on a driver unable to cope with more difficult traffic conditions

where his $\bar{t}$ was very satisfactory, to the Wynberg Division where, even by Wynberg standards, it was dangerously low.

"(k) Fully 90% of the drivers displayed accident patterns that were so consistent in themselves that, on the basis of a man's past history, it was possible to predict what his future record would be like (predictions which have been borne out in practice during the three years since the system was first inaugurated).* Of the remaining 10%, most of the changes in accident pattern had occurred because of some definite explainable circumstance. There were, however, a small percentage of the drivers whose records showed no particular pattern and fluctuated in a manner that made predictions of future behaviour very difficult. Later experience proved, however, that the very fact that these people did fluctuate meant that they were not good risks. In many cases it was found that these men were drinkers.

"(l) Major or serious accidents were found to occur mostly in the records of the drivers with the short time intervals. Over a period of six years, during which time only 20% of the drivers displayed patterns of short time intervals, 60% of the serious accidents (accidents stemming from reckless and dangerous driving) were caused by drivers in this category.

"(m) The effects of age were clearly demonstrated by factors such as:

"(1) The greater incidence of bad records and unduly expensive learning-periods amongst the young drivers. (One young driver of 19 who had slipped in by falsifying his age had a learning period of two years.)

"(2) Obvious deterioration among certain of the older drivers after the age of 50. "These factors were so evident that the company's regulations were altered; the age of admission for drivers was gradually raised from 21 to 26 and stricter checks were kept on the records of all the older men.

* Note: (December 1968) and confirmed by a further seven years of practical experience with this system.

"It was, however, found that there was an appreciable difference between the accident liability of individual drivers of the same age.

"These observations were made on the study of the individual records of 898 drivers. They were later confirmed by an exhaustive statistical analysis of all the available data. (Details of this analysis will be given in the statistical paper by Sichel.) [Published 1965.]

"The most significant aspect of the whole investigation was the proof it provided of the individuality of each driver's accident liability, and of the fact that this liability was so consistent that it was possible to predict what sort of an accident risk a man was likely to be in the future on the basis of his past behavior.

"THE PRACTICAL APPLICATION OF THIS PART OF THE RESEARCH PROJECT

"As one of the primary objects of the whole research project had been to find a sensitive and reliable method of assessing the accident liability of individual drivers, the success of the research study had important practical implications. It was possible now to maintain visual accident records of all the company's drivers and also to devise a method of grading them into various accident categories for the purpose of managerial control. Using the means and the range of the $\bar{\imath}$s of the current drivers, it was possible to set separate standards for the traffic conditions prevailing in each division and a system was devised for classifying the drivers into five categories in such a way that the relative meaning of each category was the same for each division.

"The following table shows the limits of the $\bar{\imath}$s set for each division in order to obtain five accident categories:

Categories	Range of $\bar{\imath}$/s (Average number of days between accidents)			
	Wynberg	Pretoria	Martindale	Kliptown
A Excellent	200 & ov.	300 & ov.	260 & ov.	300 & ov.
B Good	125–199	175–299	150–249	175–299
C Satisfactory	75–124	125–174	100–149	125–174
D Poor	50– 74	74–124	50– 99	75–124
E Bad	0– 49	0– 74	0– 49	0– 74

"It will be noticed that the spread of $\bar{\imath}$s is narrowest in Wynberg where the traffic conditions are very difficult and widest in the Pretoria and Kliptown divisions where operating conditions are much easier.

"Having established a basis for a classification system, consideration was given to the most productive ways in which this could be used."

A system of company "Accident Ratings" was devised where each driver was classified into one of five categories: A *excellent*, B *good*, C *fair*, D *poor*, and E *bad*, and these were published every six months and circulated to central and divisional management. The classification was based on the man's current $\bar{t}$ and comments were added on any significant trends which might be developing—such as an improvement or deterioration or a tendency to serious accidents. The system took a lot of work to establish, but has been found very easy to maintain. It has also proved a very valuable aid for driver management.

"RESULTS OF THE PRACTICAL IMPLEMENTATION OF THE ACCIDENT RESEARCH PROJECT

"In assessing the improvement or deterioration in the general accident position of a transport company there are so many factors which might have a bearing on the situation, and which should be taken into consideration, that it is virtually impossible to determine how much credit or blame can be attributed to any particular one. There are, for instance, such factors as alterations in managerial control, changes in the standard of training, or intensified accident prevention campaigns. There is also the important question that if certain measures lead to the pinpointing of bad drivers and their consequent dismissal, these men have to be replaced by new drivers, and that the quality of these new men will have a marked effect on the general accident position.

"In point of fact, as stated before, the accident research project outlined in this paper has run concurrently with a major research project on the selection of new driver intake by means of psychological tests. In the course of this psychological project, several new and somewhat revolutionary procedures have been developed, particularly the use of personality tests such as the Thematic Apperception Test for driver selection. The use of personality tests for driver selection was based on psychological investigations which established the important part played by personality and temperament in accident causation, and also by the succesful statistical validation of a specially designed African T.A.T. as an accident predictor. This investigation, the various personality and temperament tests used, and also the results of selecting African bus drivers by this means, will be described in the third paper to be written by the present authors.

"Whatever the contributory reasons, the fact remains that a marked improvement has occurred in the accident position of the company since this particular accident investigation was put into operation.

"In the Johannesburg area alone, where greater traffic density has been accompanied by an increase of 25% in the accident rate of the motoring public over the last eight years, the company's accident rate has shown a contrasting decrease of 38%.

"The following facts concerning the percentages of drivers in the various accident categories are also of interest:

"The standards for the new categories were originally set in 1956 on the basis of all the drivers on strength at the time. These standards placed 75% of the current drivers in the C (satisfactory) or better categories, a reasonable working basis.

"However, before the new classification system could be put into routine operation, a good deal of statistical verification was still necessary and it was nearly two years before the first Accident Ratings were published for official use. During that time no significant change had taken place and the percentage of drivers in the satisfactory and better categories was found to be 78%.

"Publication of the new Accident Ratings did not have much immediate effect; in fact they were met with the sort of suspicion that is so often accorded by branch management to head office innovations. However, the opposition died down when it became obvious how accurate the classification system was and how well it could predict each driver's future behavior. When the passing of time showed that a man who had been classified as an 'A' category driver continued to be relatively accident free while an 'E' category driver continued to be accident-prone, the practical value of the system was recognized. The bad accident risks were eliminated and replaced by men of a better calibre, scientifically selected. The result is that three years later, instead of the original 75%, the company now has 93% of its drivers in the satisfactory accident categories.

"It is apparent, therefore, that a marked improvement has occurred in the company's accident position, particularly over the last few years. Whatever the contributory reasons for this state of affairs, there is no doubt that the new systems of recording the company's accident position and of evaluating its individual drivers has proved very successful.

"DISCUSSION

"...These findings have significant implications for companies employing professional drivers. They highlight the individuality of accident liability and the need for keeping individual records and for recording each driver as an individual entity.

"They indicate also that a man's past record of accident liability is a very good guide to his future behavior. In practice this means that because a man with a good past record is unlikely to deteriorate, his services are valuable and his good record should receive due recognition. But, more important still, it means that the man whose past record has been very unsatisfactory is unlikely to improve; punishing him will have little effect and retraining him means throwing good money after bad. The only practical way of ensuring that he does not have accidents is to prevent him from driving.

"The findings indicate too, that it is possible to detect a bad accident risk among professional drivers at a relatively early stage. The number of accidents (relative to exposure) in which a driver is involved has been shown to be so significant that any new driver who becomes too frequently involved in accidents, however trivial, should be regarded as highly suspect. Although allowance must be made for a learning period, nevertheless any new driver whose 'teething stage' appears to be unduly long or expensive is in all probability not worth keeping.

"On the other hand, any sudden deterioration on the part of a good driver is also very significant and can often be remedied by individual attention. It should not be regarded merely as a run of 'bad luck'; it is probably symptomatic of personal or domestic problems, or ill health, or psychological disorder, or dissatisfaction with his working conditions.

"When it comes to the question of employing professional drivers whose previous records are unknown, or of selecting inexperienced men for training as professional drivers, selection methods based on tests of intelligence and innate skill are unlikely to give any real indication of future accident liability. Accident liability appears to be something so innate in the individual that it is reasonable to presume that it is dictated by the interplay of those functions that make him an individual and distinguish him from other individuals. The only selection precedures, therefore, which are likely to prove successful are those which are comprehensive enough to assess his physical capabilities in relation to such psychological functions as emotional stability, outlook, personality, and temperament.

"With regard to the application of the findings of this investigation to the general motoring public, the present writers appreciate only too well the obvious practical difficulties involved, but feel nevertheless that they do provide food for thought in the planning of safety campaigns. They are particularly relevant to the subject of the issuing or retention of driving licenses, for it would appear that the findings provide even further proof of the fact that certain people are such inherently bad accident risks that they should not be allowed to drive.

"However, at present it is usually difficult to stop them from doing so. The case of the transport company in which this investigation was carried out is an illustration in point. This particular company was able to identify the bad accident risks among its drivers and to make a substantial reduction in its own accident rate by refusing to employ these men. But it could take no action whatever about preventing these men from driving elsewhere. Most of them are, in fact, driving privately or for some other firm and are continuing to be a danger to the community.

"Individual action is not enough. Action on the part of a higher authority is needed."

The reactions to the American publication of this report were mixed. My co-author and I received a number of very pleasant letters from various bodies in the United States concerned with the more practical aspects of the accident problem, such as transport operators and insurance companies. But American research circles were virtually silent and have remained so. The only reference to the report in the research literature was one brief sentence. Discussing the question of the increasing emphasis placed by modern research on *describing* accident occurrence without investigating the underlying causes, Haddon *et al.* (1964) said: "A paper by Shaw and Sichel, for example, claims the successful identification for uniform exposure of individual accident rate patterns, derived without substantial attention to the activity of specific 'causes'. Other examples, easily identified by their complete or substantial avoidance of the term 'cause' or 'causation' are to be found in the chapters that follow."

In Europe, however, the reception was more favourable. There it was accepted as an interesting contribution to accident research; and from England it elicited the invitation to contribute the present volume to this International Series of Monographs in Experimental Psychology.

CHAPTER 9

EUROPEAN RESEARCH

IT WOULD be interesting to see what developments were taking place in Europe during this time.

The studies reported here were published at various times during the fifties and early sixties but I felt there was no need to intersperse them between the American studies of that period, in strict chronological order, for so tenuous is the contact between America and Europe in the matter of accident research that continental thinking seems to have had little or no effect on developments within the United States. The European countries always appear to have been aware of developments in American research, but the contrary is not the case. In fact it is seldom that any continental publication is ever mentioned in the American literature—except perhaps that of Hakkinen, and then only in passing.

Hakkinen's study was, however, accorded a very different reception in Europe. There it was immediately recognized as very good psychological research, which provided valuable information about the causes of accident proneness. The fact that at the same time it provided valid statistical evidence regarding the concept itself was not regarded by many people as being important. The Europeans are not anything like as statistically minded as the Americans, and they are prepared to accept what they consider to be a reasonable concept on its merits, with or without the backing of figures: and to them the concept of proneness, particularly with regard to road accidents, has always been a most reasonable one. They are prepared to accept that people do indeed differ in their susceptibility to accidents over long periods of time, and also that the proportion of people in the community who are potentially bad risks is quite large enough to deserve attention. It is interesting therefore to see on what premises they base this belief. It is also interesting to have a look at an area of accident research which is seldom mentioned in the accident literature, particularly the literature of the United States.

The only way in which one can describe European thinking on road accidents is in the most general terms—to describe the general climate of opinion rather than specific views. For, dangerous as it may be to generalize about the fifty States which comprise the United States of America, to try and make a single entity out of the Continent of Europe would be ridiculous. Even apart from national differences in outlook, there is so much variation in the accident rates of the various countries that the problem itself assumes different proportions in different parts of the Continent. But, strangely enough, despite all this there is a certain degree of unanimity in the attitude adopted by the European countries towards the concept of proneness.

In the European countries the concept of accident proneness is regarded as being acceptable provided it is not defined in too narrow or rigid a way. To them "proneness"—or whatever the local equivalent word or phrase may be—means, generally speaking, a "tendency towards accidents", a tendency which most people possess to a greater or lesser degree. It is not something which is confined to one section of the community, and most certainly not to one particular type of person. On the contrary, the Europeans think that people exhibit various shades or degrees of proneness, and for a wide variety or reasons —or combinations of reasons. They think that the factors which under lie this tendency to accidents operate more often and more readily in highly "prone" people than in people who are less "prone"; they think most of these factors are quite powerful enough and stable enough to differentiate between the people who are good risks or bad risks; and they think action should be taken against the bad risks. But, on the other hand, they do not think of proneness to accidents as something inevitable and unalterable; they think, for example, that in many people the tendency can be immediately affected by measures like effective discipline, and ultimately affected by a process like growing up, or a shift in national attitudes towards anti-social driving behaviour.

And because, to the continentals, proneness means an undue tendency to accidents, they feel that you cannot limit it down to only those factors which are almost impervious to change. If you do you are only dealing with part of the tendency and only some of the factors which differentiate one person from another. The Europeans seem to feel that people can be a danger to the community and cause a lot of damage without being "prone" throughout prolonged periods of time. They are therefore quite prepared to accept the idea of a type of proneness which changes in time and also to accept the idea of short-term "proneness". In fact they think of the whole concept more in terms of its usefulness than in terms of any statistical definition, and they feel its usefulness is very much curtailed by restricting it to the very-long-time offenders. They maintain for instance that a man who has had a number of accidents within a short period of time because of defective eyesight is definitely "prone" as long as he *continues to be likely to have accidents*—even if later you can stop this tendency by making him wear spectacles. And they regard young people with a high accident rate as being most definitely "prone", even though this high accident rate may not last for a "prolonged period".

And because, on the whole, the European countries do not have the same regard for the experimental-statistical approach to a problem, European accident literature is singularly devoid of the kind of "proving" study so common in America. In fact the only big European studies which appear to have been conducted along strictly experimental lines, with statistical procedures applied at every stage, are Hakkinen's big study (1958) on the Finnish bus drivers and Schubert's very recent German study (1967).

In other words the European concept of proneness is a very flexible one; so flexible that it would be difficult to fit it to any statistical model, except a person-centred one. But, by and large, this does not worry them. Their approach is a "logical" one and they are inclined to think America's preoccupation with figures and statistics is overdone; that all these elaborate and often self-defeating efforts to establish statistical "proof" of proneness are interesting but not very important, and really only tend to obscure what should be a reasonably clear and logical issue.

At least this is how the Europeans appeared to think in the fifties and how a great many people whom I have personally spoken to in Europe still think today. But, creeping in is a noticeable trend to "think American", to quote American findings, and to begin to doubt the whole proneness concept because American research says there is no conclusive evidence to support it.

Some of these doubts began to appear in the late fifties—although at that stage it was more a question of bewilderment than doubt. For how could it be possible that so little empirical evidence was coming forward in support of an "undue tendency to accidents" when this was a phenomenon which was apparent to the naked eye? So, being very much aware that proneness was one of the cornerstones of their driver-enforcement programmes and insurance programmes, first Holland and later Germany decided that it was time a local investigation was made on the whole subject.

The result of Holland's decision was a study, commissioned by the Royal Netherlands Touring Club in 1958, and carried out by T. B. Walbeehm of the Netherlands Post and Telecommunication Services, in collaboration with Professor H. W. Ouweleen of Rotterdam University and a number of prominent people including medical officers and senior officials connected with the Roads Department, the Licensing Officer, and the Traffic Police. The report on this investigation was therefore a reflection of both research and practical opinion in Holland.

In the introduction to this report which appeared as a book, *The Accident-prone Driver* (Walbeehm, 1960), an official of the Royal Netherlands Touring Club set out some of the conflicting opinions current at the time.*

"A much discussed category of road users is that of the 'accident-prone individuals', those who repeatedly have accidents, or at least are more than normally often involved in them. Statistical data are then brought forward and it is strongly urged by some that this category be traced and eliminated from traffic in order to decrease the number of accidents by, for instance, 25%. On the other hand, the existence of a distinct group of 'accident-prone individuals' is denied by others, and it is maintained that the results of the investigations are interpreted wrongly or are too specific to be generally valid, or, in other words, that the accident-prone individual cannot (yet) be identified."

The first part of Walbeehm's book was therefore devoted to a valiant, but understandably rather unsuccessful attempt to reconcile these conflicting views. In fact his book illustrates very clearly the dilemma in which many European writers are placed when they try to reconcile their very flexible approach to the concept of proneness with the much more rigid, statistically orientated approach adopted by many of the American writers.

Walbeehm attributed some of the contradictions between the thinking on the two sides of the Atlantic to the fact that "the American pattern of traffic is usually entirely different from the European one". Others he felt were due to the fact that it was so seldom possible to produce positive statistical evidence of proneness because of the practical and technical difficulties involved. But despite the differences of opinion, he nevertheless felt that on the basis of all the available evidence it must be concluded that accident proneness did exist, though it was difficult to quantify its importance to the total accident problem. In reaching his conclusions he paid special attention to Hakkinen's study, which he describes as "being of particular importance", and "having a special place in the developmental history of the statistical approach to accident proneness".

* Reproduced by courtesy of the World Touring Association.

He sums up his chapter on the statistical approach as follows:

"By means of the statistical methods which have been developed in the course of years it has been possible to prove with a reasonable degree of certainty that there are individual differences in accident-proneness over a prolonged period. Thus factors in the personality structure which remain operative over prolonged periods play a part in the susceptibility to cause accidents.

"However, the practical question of what percentage of drivers are accident-prone over a prolonged period to such a degree that they should be forbidden to participate in traffic on the road, is a matter of policy to which scientists can give no answer.

"The share of this group of drivers in the total number of accidents on the road has not yet been fixed accurately. However, it is clear that this share is smaller than it was formerly assumed to be, in particular on the basis of the results of the percentage method. Considered from a statistical point of view, the various forms of accident-proneness (the relatively constant, the variable, and the incidental) make the problem of "accident-proneness" more complicated than it was originally supposed to be. The definitions of these various forms are still based mainly on global practical discriminations An extensive field of investigation has still to be explored here. The great practical difficulties involved in these investigations have already been pointed out."

Walbeehm, like most continentals, does not appear to be at all happy with the limitations imposed on the proneness concept by statistical requirements. In another part of this chapter he says:

"Another objection, which is sometimes raised against the statistical method discussed up to now, is of quite a different nature. It is not so much a question of raising a fundamental objection as of laying stress on the fact that these methods can only give information on a very special and limited aspect of the problem of 'accident-proneness'. In actual fact the methods described hitherto all aim at demonstrating accident-proneness which is constant over prolonged periods. A variable accident-proneness which is only present during a relatively short period or even only incidentally during an extremely short period, is not sufficiently recognised by means of these statistical methods."

It should be noted that Walbeehm's concept of accident proneness differs somewhat from that of Hakkinen. Whereas Walbeehm calls all forms of an undue tendency to accidents "proneness", including the incidental temporary forms, Hakkinen's concept embraces only the constant ones and the ones which change slowly with time. The difference is even more marked between Walbeehm's concept and that of many of the American research workers who think of proneness as applying only to prolonged periods of time and then only to the restricted group with a very high accident rate. But it seems that even the Americans themselves are not consistent in their definitions, for in American research literature the term "accident-prone" is often used in connection with people whose accident records have only been examined over a period of one or two years, and who therefore might fit any of the categories, constant, changing over time, or purely temporary. It is no wonder therefore that so much confusion has developed.

Apart from Walbeehm's very interesting attempt to reconcile all the contradictory thinking prevalent even in the late fifties, *The Accident-prone Driver* is very well worth reading, and it is possible that copies can still be obtained from the publishers of the English version, The World Touring and Automobile Organization, London. It is not written with the detailed precision and clarity of thinking of Hakkinen's book, but then the orientation is quite different. It is just a general dissertation and a review of the literature. And, although there are times when it is inclined to develop into a rather hotch-potch of quotations from various writers, some of them merely opinions and not always well-informed opinions at that, it does, nevertheless, give a very good overall view of the whole subject of proneness among drivers of motor-vehicles, especially as seen by the Europeans, and of the factors which contribute to it. Certain portions of the book are particularly good. The chapter on the statistical approaches usually employed in accident research is clear and simply set out. The chapters on the role played in accident causation by alcohol, by visual defects, by various medical conditions, by mental disorders, and even by such strange phenomena as radiation are extremely interesting. And an unusual and very informative aspect of the book is the information it gives on the findings of the various European traffic institutes on the relatively large contribution made to the European accident problem, not only by the drinking driver, but also by people suffering from severe physical as well as mental disorders.

A lot of Germany's work, for instance, on accident offenders has been done in the medical field. This has been the direct outcome of the establishment, since the war, one in each of the main Federal Areas of West Germany, of institutions designed to look after all aspects of industrial and road safety, each of which contains a Medical Psychological Institute. These institutes are expected to carry out some research, but their main purpose is the examination of those of the traffic offenders, or new licensees, who are considered by people like the licensing officers or traffic officials to be doubtful risks as drivers.

At the present moment it is probably correct to say that, with a few exceptions (such as the institutes in Stuttgart, Munich, and Cologne), the main emphasis of these examinations is still on an actual road driving test and the medical examination. The psychological aspect of the examination is mostly confined to testing intelligence and a few selected functions such as reaction time and concentration.

Only occasionally is the psychological examination a clinical one which includes depth testing of personality functions. The medical aspect definitely does predominate over the psychological. If this is the case now, then it must have been even more so in the fifties when psychology was still trying to recover from the almost total eclipse which it suffered during the Nazi regime. It is not surprising, therefore, to find that a lot of the West German publications, which emanate from these institutes, have a strong medical bias.

Walbeehm gives some interesting figures published by Grossjohann (1953) of the Medical Psychological Institute for Traffic Safety at Stuttgart. Grossjohann says that by means of a thorough medico-psychological investigation, important data can be obtained as to whether an accident-offender should be allowed to go on driving. Provided the accident was not due to a traffic engineering fault or a technical defect in the vehicle, such an examination can usually determine whether the accident in which the offender was involved can be ascribed to a "temporary deficiency" in the driver or to one of longer duration. He quotes the following figures.

Since the establishment of the institute, of the traffic offenders examined:

54% had been considered *fit* to drive as they had satisfied the standard set;
20% had been considered *conditionally fit*;
26% had been considered *unfit*.

Again subdividing the last two categories the *conditionally fit* and the *unfit*.

Among those who were considered to be *conditionally fit*:

41% suffered from increased working of the endocrine glands;
25% appeared to be handicapped physically;
26% appeared to be disturbed in their adjustment to traffic, as a result of a neurotic condition or a characterological deficiency;
4% showed a decrease in achievement due to an organic cerebral dysfunction;
4% were found to be lacking in intelligence.

Among those who were considered to be *unfit*:

31% were, as regards reaction speed, considerably handicapped by serious organic or mental defects;
26% suffered from nervous irritability to such a degree that it must be considered impossible for them to have complete mastery of present relationships in road traffic;
17% suffered from characterological defects or from neurotic conditions in such a measure that it was not considered justifiable to let them participate in road traffic;
8% showed senility phenomena which made the driving of motor vehicles impossible;
7% were mentally disturbed;
5% were mentally defective;
4% were suffering from serious internal diseases;
2% were subject to epileptic fits.

These figures are very interesting but, in considering the proportions, one must appreciate that these offenders had been specifically *sent* to the institute for examination, and were therefore a selective group, being no doubt the people with the most blatant defects. Nevertheless, the fact that nearly half of these offenders were considered to be unfit or only conditionally fit to drive, is very revealing. So, too, is this combination of medical and psychological deficiencies, a combination which is not only interesting but, unfortunately, also rather unusual.

A very original study to emerge from the Stuttgart Institute was on the relationship between accidents and bioclimatological factors.

"In later years a great deal of attention has been given to the different phenomena of air electricity, and especially to the influences of the long-wave high-frequency radiation. At present it is rather generally assumed that it is this very radiation that must be considered as an indicator of biotropically operative atmospheric processes. On the basis of explanations given by Zinc & Kühnke (1956) it must not be considered impossible that these high-frequency radiations influence the biological processes to a very great extent."

He then gives some figures attributed to R. Reiter (1953) which relate accident rates to different strengths of this high frequency radiation. Reiter uses the average accident rate as a base, and shows the way in which this rate varies according to the type of weather.

During periods when there is no high frequency radiation the accident
    rate decreases by   18%

During periods of normal radiation it varies as follows:
    During Föhn wind it increases   0%
    During fine days with a great deal of sunshine it increases   5%
    During fog or mist it increases   8%
    During rain or snow it increases   16%
    During periods of strong radiation it increases   30%

There is no indication of what length of time these figures cover, but the idea is a very interesting one. Anyone wishing to know more about it could probably study the papers read at the International Bioclimatological Congress, the first of its kind, which was held in Vienna in 1957 under the auspices of the International Society for Bioclimatology and Biometeorology.

Walbeehm's book (of which this is only the briefest sketch, as it deals with every aspect of accident research from age to human engineering) brings the account of the continental literature on accident proneness up to 1960. Since that date, judging by the bibliographies, hundreds of publications have appeared which have a bearing on the subject. But although I have received a number of them, the difficulty (and expense) of finding someone to translate them has been insuperable—particularly the German ones, as technical German is so complicated that even my German-speaking friends have had to admit that they are completely baffled. I therefore have to apologize to the many continental researchers whose work is not included in this book and refer the reader who is better linguistically qualified than I am to bibliographies such as those of Schubert (1965) and Hoffmann (1967), and Böcher's section of the *German Handbook of Traffic Medicine* (1968).

However, Professor A. J. le Grange, ex-Director of Research for the South African Road Safety Council, has kindly translated for me two very interesting papers by Grunert. These papers are excellent examples of the clinical approach to the study of accident proneness adopted by many of the German psychologists (and, I might add, scorned by others).

In these papers Grunert (1961a, b) describes what he calls "the accident disposition" of various kinds of driver, wherein he feels lies the "germ" of the accidents in which they become involved. He bases his views on the findings of other German psychologists such as Munsch, Sievers, and Schultz, and also on his personal experience with accident cases in the Medical Psychological Institute of Bavaria. Taking the two papers together, the following is a very general outline of Grunert's ideas. (If the wording is at times a little awkward, this is because Professor le Grange and I have tried to keep as close as possible to the ideas expressed in the original German version.)

He starts by saying that he does not agree with what he calls the "minority theory" on accident proneness, i.e. that most accidents are caused by a minority of people, the so-called "evil seven"—the only people who, according to this theory can be termed "accident-prone", and whose accidents are largely regarded as being "the result of unavoidable fate". He feels that at least as far as traffic accidents are concerned, there appears to be no scientific proof for this theory whatsoever. On the contrary, the facts indicate that *everyone* is accident-prone to a greater or lesser extent; the degree to which this is displayed by a particular person in a particular situation being primarily determined by a combination of his own structural personality characteristics and the specific situation. In other words, what a person would do, or neglect to do in a given situation is actually determined *in the first place* by the amount of accident potential he possesses—his "disposition" to accidents. An accident cannot therefore be regarded as resulting from a deficiency or a failure of one or more disparate organic or psychological functions; rather is it a failure of the co-ordinated psychological functions of the personality *as a whole*. Grunert seems to feel that this is one of the reasons why such poor results have been achieved by trying to trace the causation of accidents to defects in intelligence, or the ability to comprehend, or to the ability to concentrate, or to manual skill, speed of reaction, etc. For, as he says, even when it can definitely be stated that the accident was due to lack of concentration, the question still remains: to what was this lack of concentration due?

Grunert feels that when it comes to the actual accident, the point of departure, the "germ" of the accident, lies in the fact that most accidents are preceded by an inner psychological conflict in the person, i.e. when different motives or drives are acting in opposite directions or are actively, antagonistically opposed to one another. The external circumstances only play a secondary role in causing the accident, though it often appears as if it were an unavoidable fate due to the external environment. This state of conflict can be found to run like a red thread through the whole of that person's biography, and finds its culminating point at the time of the accident. But the manner in which such a conflict is built up, the form in which it appears, and the kind of solution sought, are almost entirely dependent on the fundamental structure as well as the regulating forces of the total personality.

This is why the element of accident proneness which is present in nearly everyone is suppressed in some people, whereas in others it develops into an actual disposition to accidents, i.e. the narrowing of consciousness, plus faulty perception of reality, as well as aggression and motor impulses. People differ regarding the strength of their conflicts and the level of their frustration tolerance. The tolerance is high in those people with a stable and more balanced "self-feeling". These people are able to keep the development of a disposition to accidents to a minimum.

In the less well-balanced person, the conflict is usually the result of a threat to his self-esteem, i.e. it stems from the vulnerability of that self-esteem, and his consequent failure to maintain the balance of his personality structure. When the level of frustration tolerance is low, too much psychic energy is diverted to the conflict, with the result that too little energy is available for effectively carrying out the action required by the situation, *as perceived*. For perception as well as behaviour is disturbed.

The wrong behaviour in the accident-producing situation may be seen as an attempt to find some outlet for the tension produced by the conflict. It is therefore not a true solution to the conflict, rather it is a short-circuit, or way of evading it altogether.

Grunert then develops the theory that in the psychological make-up of most people we find definite structural characteristics which are the result of not only his heredity but his environment. These characteristics may be described in terms of the well-known personality structures used in psychopathology, viz. the schizophrenic, the depressive, the compulsive, and the hysteric. But he stresses the fact that in the sense in which he is using these structures they are *not* to be regarded as abnormal or psychoneurotic. They are just useful patterns on which to classify the basic personality traits of *normal* people. Nor, he says, are these types usually found in their pure form. Most people are a mixture of all four, but usually with a predominant inclination towards one type or the other. Nor, he says, should it be presumed that because these particular structures form the background of known types of neuroses, that neurotic disturbance necessarily brings about an increased tendency to accidents. On the contrary, he feels that there are many neurotics who are completely safe drivers because of a compensation mechanism which makes up for the defect caused by the neurosis.

The following are short sketches of the four main structures, with special reference to the typical road behaviour of each.

1. The Schizoid Personality

The main characteristic of this structure is the tenuous contact the person has with the outside world. Genetically seen, it is a personality which cannot succeed in directing psychic energy sufficiently away from the self towards the environment. He remains enclosed as if he were in a "glass cage". He lives in an unrealistic world of his own and reacts to the outside world with distrust, scepticism, and even hostility.

As a car driver, the schizoid is divorced from the outside world more strongly than other drivers. He has little contact with what happens around him in the street. The vehicle is, to him, a foreign body (glass cage) with which he cannot identify. He handles it in a rough fashion, presses unnecessarily hard on the hooter, drives with fits and starts and jerks, without a thought to the finer technical properties of the vehicle. His progress is never smooth but goes with sudden spurts of varying fast and slow movements. He seems, to other road users, to be reckless, inconsiderate, and dangerous.

In spite of his peculiarities the schizoid is nevertheless alert and intelligent. He perceives carefully, although his perception is mostly selective and sectional by nature and his attention is not evenly distributed.

The schizoid is inclined to find fault with other road users and will rather blame others than look for faults in himself. Real or imagined faults in others apparently hurt him a lot and can even be taken up as insults eliciting aggressive actions on his part. He sees the other man as an obstacle or an opponent more often than as a well-meaning friend.

The maladjustment of the schizoid is due to his strengthened egocentricity and his hostile withdrawal from the world. The accident *germ* in his personality structure is situated in his inability to perceive reality in its true form. When internal tensions start, perhaps as a result of the technical demands made on him as a driver, he can easily lose his self-control, become aggressive, and do wrong things.

2. The Predominantly Depressive Personality

This structure develops as a result of deprivation in early childhood and primary needs which have never been satisfied.

The main characteristic of this personality is a strong tendency to depression, and a passive acceptance of rather than active resistance towards the environment. His reactions are slow and hesitant rather than spontaneous and hasty. From the driver's point of view, his most favourable characteristics are his carefulness and his avoidance of risks.

Characteristics which expose him, as a driver, to danger are the fact that he tends to react too slowly where quick action is demanded, and the fact that he is passive where he should be active; also that he is unobservant and lost in dreams in situations which demand alertness.

On the other hand, there are also factors in his structure which are favourable for his safety on the road; among others his anxious, insecure attitude to the world which enables him to anticipate and avoid dangers. It protects him from the danger of being taken unawares. He would rather wait than react with violence in dangerous situations.

As a result of his anxiety he will anticipate all possible dangers and will therefore never be startled by unexpected events. If it should happen that he lands in an unexpected danger situation, he will never be so shocked that he loses self-control.

The attitude of the depressive personality towards his environment expresses itself in an overwhelmingly strong tendency to adapt and to submit; and the stronger his anxiety and tension situations become, the stronger his desire to adapt and submit. It often happens that he adapts himself to circumstances merely because he has not the courage to demand what is rightfully due to him.

When the depressive tendency becomes acute, the attitude to the environment can so deteriorate that he falls into a state of neglect. He becomes careless of his car, indifferent to traffic rules, indifferent to punishment, and fatalistic. Fortunately, Grunert says, it is a fact that few depressives fall into such a pathological situation. Many of them are first-class and safe drivers of public vehicles.

The accident *germ* on the personality structure of these people is situated in the fact that their mental depression and the heavy spiritual burdens they carry can sometimes lead to aggressive actions directed towards themselves. In such circumstances they can develop an irresponsible attitude—a "come what may, what do I care?" attitude.

There are good grounds for the belief that some road accidents are nothing else but suicide or suicidal attempts by depressive people who lose control over their aggressive tendencies, which then become aimed at themselves.

3. The Compulsive Personality

The main characteristic of this personality is his compulsiveness. This is the person who is subject to compulsive actions and he shows a lack of spontaneity and is always pedantically correct and dead-sure of himself. As a result of a strongly developed super-ego, he shows repressed aggressive tendencies, heightened tension, and submissiveness to authority.

He does his best to be businesslike in all his actions. He lives according to the rules laid down by others, and expects everyone else to do the same.

As a driver he takes it for granted that all provisions, rules and laws are to be obeyed to the letter. In driving his car he is always mechanically correct but inelastic and rigid. He is a slavish follower of regulations for which he has a higher regard than for a flexible and meaningful adaptation to the demands of specific situations. Live or die, the regulation must be observed.

The compulsive person finds it difficult to adapt to different situations. He likes the straight and narrow path and is irritated by unusual occurrences. He drives carefully and always makes sure that his road is on all sides open and safe. His attention is higher and it seems that he is always on the lookout for possible irregularities on the part of other motorists. Such irregularities he sees as a direct insult to himself.

In the handling of his vehicle, he is stereotyped, inelastic, and unimpulsive. In his attitude to his fellow road-users he is tolerant as long as they obey strictly the rule of the road, but if anyone disobeys a law he immediately becomes angry, aggressive, and even insulting; if he believes he is right it does not matter if the whole world is against him, he will defend himself without listening to other points of view.

The accident *germ* in the structure of the compulsive personality is situated in his rigid, inflexible attitude in unusual situations, and his way of standing up for his rights to such a degree that it can lead to aggressive behaviour. As a result of his inability to anticipate unexpected situations, his shock reaction is so great that he becomes confused and muddled in his movements. He can then be involved in an accident without precisely knowing what happened.

4. The Hysteroid Personality

The chief characteristic of this person is that he lives in a world of false assumptions, a pseudo-world. His contact with reality is superficial and false. His super-ego is poorly developed and he has a lack of confidence in measures of law and order. He has little self-feeling and likes to imagine himself in the role of others.

The hysteroid is a fast and skilful driver, but he can be reckless and dangerous. He can grasp a situation quickly but his insight is often careless and superficial. In his excessive self-confidence he is liable to over-estimate himself and will easily disregard traffic rules. He likes to tease the officers of the law and to see how far he can go without being caught.

Although skilful, he is an unreliable driver. Other road users feel they cannot depend on him and he is regarded as impulsive and reckless. He will, out of pure impatience, refuse to remain in his lane, break out and race past and stop at forbidden places, etc.

To the hysteroid the car is a means of expressing his need for self-assertiveness. He drives in order to show himself off. He wants to be seen and admired. He does not think of a small collision with another car as an accident; it is a bagatelle, a meaningless occurrence.

He is inclined to close his eyes to unpleasant situations and tries to avoid responsibility. As a result of his natural skills he usually manages to avoid dangerous situations, but if it does happen that he is involved in an accident, due to his lack of anticipation, he takes it very badly. His feeling of infallibility is shaken badly.

The hysteroid always reacts to his fellow man in a competitive way with, however, the underlying assumption that he is better than they are.

The accident *germ* in his personality structure is situated in the fact that his need for self-assertion may gain the upper hand at the wrong time, and that he will then try to do dangerous things of which he is not capable. Further, he is inclined to take traffic rules lightly, to behave impulsively, and to over-estimate his own capabilities. This can easily lead him to take unnecessary risks.

Grunert then illustrates his theory by giving several case studies where he traces the development of the whole accident-producing situation and relates it to a particular conflict in the driver's life, then relates this conflict to his general personality structure as revealed by his usual behaviour pattern. The main conclusions which he reaches are:

(1) Road accidents are predominantly due to human shortcomings, and the causes of these shortcomings are not situated in the mere disregard of traffic rules and laws but in the fact that the human personality is so constructed that in certain circumstances it is overstrained and cannot function.

(2) Different basic personality structures bring about different degrees of accident proneness and expose different people in different ways to road risks. But at the same time it must be remembered that there are certain factors in each personality structure which function favourably in the direction of accident avoidance and safe road behaviour.

It is possible that some people would object to this paper on the basis of the classification of people into four main types. But, as Grunert takes pains to point out, this classification is not a cut-and-dried one, as most people are a mixture of all four types—with perhaps one more dominant that the others. The interest in this paper lies in its deep perception—and in the fact that although it is based largely on individual case studies, and interpreted largely in terms of the author's psychological knowledge and experience, its findings are in no way at variance with the findings of many of the larger controlled experimental studies. It is, for instance, quite easy to recognize some of the traits displayed by Malfetti's ultra-safe drivers in Grunert's "predominantly depressive" type, and some of Tillmann's unsafe taxi drivers in the hysteric and schizoid types. It is particularly interesting in view of later research developments such as the work of the British Road Research Laboratory (Quenault, 1967–8) on the classification of drivers into four types on the basis of their *actual driver behaviour*. Quenault calls his types the "Safe, Injudicious, Dissociated Active and Dissociated Passive." And although these types are naturally not synonymous with Grunert's, nevertheless many of the driving characteristics which Grunert has described here have also been observed by Quenault in the course of a systematic road test—as can be seen from Chapter 17 where I have described the RRL project in some detail.

It is also very interesting to compare Grunert's four types of personality structure (and their inferred driving behaviour) with the findings of the factor analysis of personality characteristics found in South African bus drivers (Chapters 16 and 17). Here it was found that the accident-associated characteristics grouped themselves into two main higher-order units of personality, extroversion, and emotional instability—and that a high degree of either, and particularly of both, was a potent accident predictor. When one considers that the accident "germ" in each of the four personality structures as seen by Grunert lies in these same factors or combination of factors, the connection between Grunert's study and later findings in a very different field is interesting indeed.

But to my mind one of the most interesting features of Grunert's study is the intricate description he gives of the sort of driving behaviour which could be expected from certain kinds of personalities. There is so much information available on the *sort* of people who have accidents and so little on *why* they have them, that this unusual study is very welcome. Admittedly it could be said that this is not information, it is only speculation; and I can just imagine the treatment which a study like Grunert's would receive at the hands of the present-day almost professional critics of accident research. If they can tear Tillmann's study to shreds, as they have done, then Grunert's study, with only a few case studies by way of "evidence", would suffer an even worse fate.

But is all this criticism justified? Just how far is this worship of the twin gods Methodology and Computer getting us in the study of something as complex as the interaction of man and his environment? It certainly is not providing *all* the answers. Human behaviour cannot be described solely in terms of figures: there are aspects which can only be described in words—words based on deductive reasoning and sound psychological knowledge. And to my way of thinking it is quite unjustified to condemn the logico-deductive approach in the way it is so often condemned—and also to condemn out of hand the element of subjectivity it must inevitably contain. For how else, except by embodying an element of subjective judgment, is one going to infer the behaviour of a complex individual in whom certain characteristics will, for instance, be conducive to safe driving and others to dangerous driving? The theoretical methodologists will no doubt merely say that such "unscientific" inferences are quite valueless (although one wonders how they are going to account for the practical success which we in South Africa have had using just such a subjective approach to infer driving behaviour from information supplied by a test like the TAT—and where we have been able to predict the *future* accident involvement of 1139 subjects with an accuracy of $r = 0.66$. But no doubt they will find *some* way to query the validity of this result!) No, it would seem that this sort of condemnation is very much overdone, and that to overlook a study like Grunert's just because it is not carried out on lines of strict experimental methodology, is to overlook some very valuable leads as to the causes of accidents.

This is only a very brief description of research developments in Europe during the fifties and early sixties, being little more than a few examples of different lines of approach. In any case it was not a very productive period as most of Europe was still struggling to recover from the war, and there was very little opportunity or money for research. For the same reason car ownership was not on a scale anything like that of the United States, and the whole accident problem was taking longer to develop.

But now it has developed: between a tremendous upsurge in the number of vehicles and between the weather, the narrow streets, and the road behaviour of the drivers (giving vent in a big way not only to national characteristics but to what seems to be a sort of displaced reaction against all the deprivations and restrictions of the last twenty years), Europe now really does have an accident problem—and one that is getting worse every day.

It was therefore only comparatively recently that the European researchers really re-entered the field of accident research. In doing so they naturally tried to take advantage of the research which had been carried out in the interim in less-disturbed parts of the world, and here, it seems, immediately ran into trouble. For it is difficult enough for anyone whose home language is English to try and reconcile the positive trend of the research findings which I have outlined in the last six chapters, with the negative trend of the publications which began to emerge in the sixties—and which I will review in subsequent chapters. For someone battling with a foreign language it must be quite impossible. This no doubt accounts for much of the confusion and dissension which is now beginning to appear in European research circles: with some writers still protesting their belief in proneness; others following the "new" American way of thinking and saying that the concept has never been proved; and still others adopting a middle-of-the-road attitude which is such a mixture of a continental-psychological YES and an American-statistical NO that it illustrates only too well the confused state into which European opinion is drifting. But as it is very difficult indeed for an outsider to accurately assess this opinion, especially in these controversial times, I feel that this is best left to the Europeans themselves.

I have therefore asked four people who are prominent figures in European research circles whether they would care to let me have a brief outline of their personal views on the question of accident proneness and on developments within their own countries. These four people, Dr. Wolfgang Böcher and Dr. Günter Schubert from Germany, Dr. Sauli Hakkinen from Finland, and Dr. Aart Van der Burgh from Holland, have all kindly consented to do so and their very interesting statements are to be found in Chapter 13.

CHAPTER 10

THE PENDULUM STARTS TO SWING

THE beginning of the 1960's seems a good point at which to pause and review the situation.

The research of the last decade had certainly made a significant contribution to the knowledge on the human element in road accidents. The different approaches adopted in the various studies and the fact that they had used such different groups of subjects, belonging to different age groups, different social strata, often even different parts of the world, made it that much more valuable.

In fact, by the early sixties quite a clear picture was beginning to emerge of the sort of people who were most likely to be involved in motor accidents. It was a complex picture but also a very rational one. For it showed that there was nothing mysterious about the people who were unduly "prone" to accidents—or unduly susceptible, or predisposed to accidents, or whatever one might care to call them. On the contrary, they were very much the kind of people you would expect to find involved in accidents if you were working on the basis of common sense alone. They were, for instance, the untrained and inexperienced people, the very unintelligent people, the people with limited ability and poor psycho-motor control—in other words the sort of people whose mental, physical, and psycho-physical defects, or whose inexperience, could render them unable to cope with the complexities of driving, and therefore more vulnerable to its hazards.

But in addition, clearly emerging from the research findings, was a picture of a very different class of accident offender. These were the people whose faults were ones of personality, and whose accidents were more a matter of commission than omission in that they themselves probably created most of the driving hazards which were their undoing. These were, for example, the immature youngsters, the socially irresponsible people, the selfish or aggressive people, the impulsive people with poor self-control, and even the well-meaning but unduly rigid or nervous or indecisive or neurotic people.

It appeared therefore that a number of very different characteristics, or combinations of characteristics, were to be found associated with high accident rates, and, what is more, that these would not all operate for the same length of time. Some of them, like the characteristics associated with immaturity, would obviously improve with time, and people could therefore be expected to remain bad accident risks only for as long as these particular characteristics persisted. Conversely, people who had been good risks could slowly deteriorate because of the gradual onset of ageing, or neuroticism, or alcoholism. In fact it had been suggested that the factors which made people more susceptible to accidents could be grouped into three main groups; those which remained virtually unaltered over long periods of time, those which changed slowly with time, and those which were

149

purely temporary in nature (remembering always that many factors which might appear to be temporary, like temporary fits of elation or depression, were often more prevalent in some people than in others, and so really belonged among the more constant factors). It had also been pointed out that these changes in accident liability were very individual ones and that the pattern of development which took place in a person's susceptibility to accidents was almost as individual and as distinctive as a fingerprint.

What then was meant by "accident proneness"? How durable was it and how long must a person be unduly susceptible to accidents before he could be labelled "prone"?

Unfortunately there was still no standard definition of proneness and each researcher could still define it in his own way. However, many researchers felt that this was not very important and that it was in fact inadvisable to try and define in too rigidly. But there was still a pronounced tendency, especially in the United States, for other researchers to insist on a rigid definition, and to say that a person could only be called "prone" if he displayed a *constant* tendency to accidents.

But what did this actually mean? Constant for how long? Two years? Four years? Six years? Eight years? Presumably not a lifetime anyway, as very few human beings (except perhaps some psychotic or mentally retarded people) could be expected to display the same characteristics, in the same way, and in the same strength, from adolescence to senility. But where then did one draw the line and say *this* constitutes proneness and *this* does not?

Hakkinen had found evidence of involuntary psychomotor malfunctioning in bus drivers with bad accident records dating back eight years. Tillmann had found evidence of social malfunctioning in members of the ordinary driving public with bad accident records which dated back fifteen years. Apparently therefore some of the factors which made people more liable to accidents could be operative over very long periods of time.

But how about the more changeable factors? If it took someone six years to grow up and become a responsible road-citizen, shouldn't he too be considered "prone"? And how about the person who improved after only three years but had managed during those three years to do a great deal of damage?

Despite the demand in some quarters for a rigid definition of accident proneness, the feeling of many research workers, particularly those most actively engaged in the field, was that there was no way of putting a finite time limit on "proneness"; and that the only thing which really mattered was the practical usefulness of the concept, i.e. whether the tendency lasted long enough for the person to be a danger to the community. If science was going to be pedantic about its definition of proneness, and if the search for factors which could cause people to have accidents was going to be limited to only those factors which were operative for some arbitrary period like, say, ten years (let alone a lifetime), then it was going to leave unexplored many vitally important areas.

By the beginning of the sixties, therefore, considerable changes had occurred in research thinking on accident proneness. Obviously it was a far more complex matter than originally envisaged—so complex in fact that it seemed unlikely that it could be properly measured by the usual group statistical techniques. But encouraging research developments had shown that even these difficulties could possibly be overcome. It appeared that a statistical method of assessing each individual separately, by means of mileage or time-intervals between accidents, could overcome many of the problems encountered in the old group methods.

Another feature about this new, more complex concept of accident proneness was that, despite its complexity, it was still a very logical one. It was in no way incompatible with common sense—in fact it was far more compatible than any rigid concept. It was also very compatible with the sort of practical thinking which had resulted in the demand, by practical traffic officials, for measures such as better road-engineering, better driver training, stricter licensing standards, more stringent law enforcement, and even more sensible and effective safety propaganda.

However, by the beginning of the sixties, accident research had achieved rather more than merely to confirm the need for such common-sense practical measures. It had started to uncover whole areas of knowledge which could be used to improve and to supplement these measures—knowledge of the fundamental dynamics of accident-generating behaviour. Some of this knowledge was in the field of capabilities, being information about the sort of mental and physical and psychophysical limitations and deficiencies which could impair driving efficiency and make accidents more likely. Some of it was in the field of human development and concerned factors, some of them amenable to training and education, some of them to discipline, which could be responsible for the high accident rates usually associated with youth. Some of it was in the field of basic personality, and concerned traits much deeper than those related only to immaturity, traits which could generate accident-producing behaviour of much longer duration. Some of it was in the field of social factors—localized factors such as slum conditions, or broken homes, or unhappy home environments, which could facilitate accident-producing behaviour among sectional groups of the community or among specific individuals—or much more widespread factors, such as national characteristics or attitudes, which could affect accident rates over large sections of the world's population. In most of these areas research had already produced much valuable information. In others, information was still sketchy, but vistas of knowledge had been opened up indicating promising lines of research for the future.

One of the most interesting and provocative of the findings was that road accidents were apparently often yet another manifestation of a person's inability or failure to adjust to the demands of life. As such they apparently had features in common with other manifestations of maladaptive behaviour: with scholastic failure, with truancy, with a limited earning capacity, with unemployment, with delinquency, with sex problems, with marital difficulties, with crime, with drinking or alcoholism, with nervous disorders, with senility, and with various forms of psychosis. Some of the road-accident problem was therefore closely associated with other social problems. However, though alleviation of environmental conditions could possibly benefit the accident problem to a certain degree, most of the accident research findings had indicated that the personality traits associated with accident involvement were so deep-seated, so reflective of each individual's personality make-up and consequent style of life, that changing his environment would not necessarily make the accident offender change his driving behaviour.

A second provocative finding was the degree to which proneness must permeate the whole accident problem. Despite the paucity of statistical evidence (Hakkinen's study being the only one which, to date, had produced really substantive statistical evidence of the wide "spread" of proneness), nevertheless the accumulated psychological evidence had indicated that people were anything but equal in their liability to road accidents and that "proneness" was certainly not confined to a small section of the community. Much of this evidence was admittedly "coarse" evidence, as in only a few studies had it been possible to compare people who had been graded on any kind of scale as to the degree of their accident involvement. Most of the studies had merely compared people who had been involved in several accidents with those who had been accident-free. But the people who, in these comparative studies, had been classified as the accident "offenders", usually constituted a fairly sizeable proportion of the total group studied—sometimes up to a third of the total number. And time and again this sizeable group of offenders had been found to differ from the accident-free group on a number of deep-seated and important psychological characteristics. In addition the groups studied had represented all sorts of different facets of the community, bus drivers, truck drivers, taxi drivers, military personnel, and members—young and old—of the general motoring public. The people from these groups who had been designated for comparative purposes as accident "offenders" were therefore in no way extreme cases representing some abnormal element in the community. They were the sort of people who could be found in any population of drivers; many of them being, in fact, the sort of people whom the practical traffic officials were obviously endeavouring to single out by discriminatory measures such as points systems.

What then was the position regarding the general scientific acceptance of accident proneness, as such, at the beginning of the 1960's? All the more recent scientific evidence had been in favour of the concept. All the more recent psychological studies had shown that there were important differences between the people who had an undue number of accidents and those who did not. And, although statistical evidence was still scarce, the authors of two major studies had recently come out strongly in favour of the concept—one study (Hakkinen, 1958) giving detailed statistical evidence, the other study (Shaw and Sichel, 1961, 1965), as yet only partly published, indicating strong support for this evidence. In both cases the authors had maintained that under conditions of equalized risk it was possible to demonstrate that people differed significantly and *over long periods of time* in the degree of their accident involvement.

Even on the question of finding suitable tests for detecting potential accident offenders, much progress had been made. True, no simple testing method had been evolved, but then everything that had been learned about the complexities of accident causation had confirmed that it was unrealistic to expect any such simple solution. But there were, nevertheless, very encouraging indications that more complex tests like projective personality tests or a battery of psychomotor personality tests could do a good job of predicting. No doubt formidable practical difficulties would have to be overcome before one could use such tests on the general motoring public, but in the meantime several possibilities could be explored. Firstly, tests like these could probably be used for the selection of professional drivers. Secondly, they might be used on that section of the general public whose accident or violation records had already placed them on the suspect list. And thirdly, the knowledge gained from the findings of these tests could give valuable leads for developing differential rather than standardized methods for *treating* such offenders.

By the beginning of the sixties it seemed, therefore, that there was only one direction in which the research on accident proneness could move, and that was forward; forward to find out more about the extent to which people differed in their propensity for accidents and the reasons why they differed; and forward to utilize this knowledge as part of a multi-pronged practical attack on the road-accident problem.

But, strangely enough, this is not what happened at all. Starting in the United States, and gradually spreading to other parts of the world, a most unexpected reactionary trend set in. A series of publications began to emerge, each more critical and nihilistic than the last, first querying and then denouncing all the more positive and progressive findings of the earlier research. The harmonious research atmosphere of the fifties disintegrated into open disagreement, and two completely divergent schools of thought began to emerge. As the sixties progressed, so the gap widened, till now, at the present moment, a most confusing state of affairs exists where different countries hold widely different views, and where scientific opinion on accident proneness ranges all the way from outrightly denying the validity of the concept, to unequivocally accepting it and maintaining that proneness (and all its implications) is one of the vitally important factors in the whole road-accident situation.

These radical differences of opinion appear to centre round disagreement on three main issues: disagreement about what does or does not constitute "proneness"; disagreement about what does or does not constitute valid statistical evidence for or against it; and even disagreement about the psychological acceptability of the very idea of proneness.

In reality the three issues are closely linked, the psychological one being in all probability the kingpin. A statement like this requires some clarification—especially as the American literature of the sixties gives the impression that proneness has been rejected because of lack of statistical proof. But there seems little doubt that the other issues are subsidiary, and that the American psychologists are the real motive power behind the anti-proneness movement. The only puzzle is why it has taken so long for their opposition to the concept to come out into the open.

For one must remember that a high proportion of America's psychologists are still inclined to behaviourism, or some "congenial" psychological discipline, such as the specificity of behaviour. The very idea that any innate characteristic, like a deep-seated personality trait, could make one person consistently more liable to accidents than another, would therefore be anathema to them. (Allport (1952) says: "The acceptance of specificity was made easier because of its congeniality to behaviorism, the theory recently prevailing in the American psychological ethos, with its reflex pathways and conditioned response, its objectivity, its simplicity, and practicality.") According to Allport, this theory is "virtually unknown in the psychological theories of other lands". But it has been so popular in America since the early 1920's that most of the current American psychologists must have been trained in the "specifist" tradition. Its popularity is now said to be on the wane. But even if it is perhaps losing ground on the broad psychological front, it apparently still has its devoted adherents among the accident researchers (particularly the more theoretical critics of this research). In fact it now seems to have the upper hand and to be exerting an influence which is so powerful that it has extended beyond the realm of pure research and is having a decisive effect on the whole federal accident prevention policy.

As this influence may have far-reaching effects, it would be just as well to examine the premises on which it is based. The effect which an almost exclusively American-held psychological theory has on accident-prevention policies within America is interesting, but it is really the concern of the United States alone. However, the indirect influence which such a theory may exert on the policies of other countries is of much more general concern—especially when these other countries are possibly unaware of what is really happening.

For it certainly would appear from the current trend of the world's accident literature that people outside the United States believe that some new important development has made America change its mind about the whole question of accident proneness. They feel that the American researchers must have found some very convincing evidence *against* accident proneness and, as a result, have now come to the conclusion that this very nice idea must have been an illusion. To revert back to the analogy I used in the beginning of this book of Kipling and his leopard; people outside the United States now believe that the contention of the whole of America's research community is: "We thought we *heard* giraffe, we even thought we *smelt* giraffe, but we're very much afraid we were mistaken for, try as we may—and we really have tried very hard indeed—we just cannot *see* giraffe." However what people outside of America may not realize is that the realities of the situation are otherwise. American opinion is not by any means unanimous on the subject, and there are still very many eminent researchers in the United States who, it seems, can see giraffe quite clearly, and what is more, seem to think he is rather a big animal. The voice which the outside world is hearing is the voice of only a certain section of the American research community; and what this section is actually saying is something quite different, namely: "*You* may think you can hear giraffe; *you* may think you can smell giraffe, *you* may even think you can see giraffe, but you are obviously mistaken because, according to *our* psychological theory, THERE AIN'T NO SUCH ANIMAL."

However, as the confident tone in which these pronouncements are made is often more apparent than the reasoning which underlies them, it seems very necessary, before proceeding any further, to investigate this particular psychological theory so that people in countries other than the United States are in a better position to decide for themselves whether or not they need go along with the "new" American thinking. And, in doing so, it might also be just as well to jettison the usual scientific circumspection in favour of a good, down-to-earth, outspoken discussion.

What then is the scientific doctrine of "specifism", and how does it differ from the more "generalist" doctrines subscribed to by most of the rest of the psychological world? This is a very complex subject; and this is no place to enter into too detailed a discussion of the many arguments which underlie the marked difference of opinion on the dynamics of behaviour which are held by psychologists on the two sides of the Atlantic—or of the lack of psychological rapprochement which this has brought about. Both Allport (1952), and more recently Eysenck (1960) discuss these arguments in detail. All one can do here is to deal with those aspects which most affect accident research.

The fundamental difference, as far as driving is concerned, is that "generalist" psychologists believe that people possess certain inherent personality dispositions or traits which predispose them to behave, under all sorts of different circumstances, in a manner which is relatively consistent, because it is a manner characteristic of the persons themselves.

The "specifist psychologists" (to coin a phrase) maintain that human behaviour is not consistent. They maintain that it has very little pattern; on the contrary, it is just a collection of thousands and thousands of little habits, each learned in some specific situation. "There are no broad, general traits of personality, no general and consistent forms of conduct which, if they existed, would make for consistency of behaviour and stability of personality, but only independent and specific stimulus–response bonds or habits." Any consistency which behaviour may display is only because certain situations have "identical elements" in common, and because a person has learned, by a process of conditioned responses, to associate them and to react to them in the same way. But, according to Symonds (1928), "This generalization of conduct does not extend as far as most people suppose, with the result that conduct of the large masses of people remains unorganized, a rather loose bundle of unrelated and dissociated habits." In fact as Eysenck (1964) says (describing this theory in one of his critical reviews) the specifists believe: "All actions which are performed by a person are specific, and separately learned, and do not combine in such a way as to make possible the postulation of traits or types, thus making it unnecessary to postulate any such notion as personality at all." People are not therefore *motivated* by traits such as honesty; they are only honest *in specific situations where they have learned to be honest*. To quote Symonds again: "Banks need not know whether or not a man is honest—they need to know whether he is an honest teller."

Applying what seems to psychologists outside the United States to be this rather strange theory to the question of road accidents and the driving situation, this means that people will, for example, only be careful *in those situations where they have learned (or been taught) to be careful*—hence the insistence in America on driver "education" where teenagers can be taught "safety" and made "safety-minded"—a process which aims at making the be-careful habit habitual, and at "developing in the young person those attitudes which will permit him to operate a motor vehicle in all safety to himself and to others for the remainder of his life".

Pursuance of the doctrine of the specificity of behaviour is equally evident in the cult of general "conduct education" which is so prevalent in American schools, where the purpose is to instil *habits* (such as habits of trustworthiness or citizenship) into youth by means of projects involving all the various situations in which these habits may be required. Charters, in the *Teaching of Ideals* (1927) gives eleven pages of fine print listing the various situations in which children should be conditioned *not to be dishonest*—everything from borrowing and not returning money, to not keeping promises, to not making untrue defamatory statements about other people, to disobeying signs which say "keep off the grass" just because nobody is looking. Payne, in his Magna Carta on driver education, *Education in Accident Prevention* (1919), makes the purpose of this new kind of education based on "modern psychological theory" quite clear:

"We have come to regard education purely with reference to its effect on some form of behavior of the individual. We no longer look upon the function of education as being that of giving information about arithmetic, geography and the like, but as a means of securing to the individual the right sort of social action, and of developing in the individual the right kind of feelings, attitudes, points of view and ideals. We look upon the various subjects in the curriculum as means to these ends."

"Non-specifists" outside the United States seem to disagree with this. (There are apparently also a number of psychologists and educationalists (such as Tenney, 1962) within the United States who disagree very strongly and say that it "robs children of the power of individual thought and of their intellectual health and vigor"—without even the recompense of achieving any of its "lofty aims".)

However, leaving the moral side of the argument to those whom it may concern and retreating to more neutral territory, the generalist dynamic psychologists maintain that there is no need for all this, if only for the reason that the basic premise on which this educational system is based, namely the theory of specificity, is psychologically unsound. People do not have to be taught just what to do in every situation. And, what is more, they are not always going to do just what *you* want them to do—they are very often going to do what *they* want to do, which is follow, wherever possible, their own personal dispositions and inclinations and behave like individuals, for better or for worse. They say that people *are* individuals and they *behave* like individuals and that this behaviour is directed by something far more complex and far more dynamic and organized than a series of automatic habits; it is directed not only by their personal experience but by their personal character, temperament, intellect, heredity, and neuro-endocrine endowment—in other words, by their own individual personality. And, because an individual's personality is not constantly changing, neither will his behaviour be constantly changing. It will not be just a "loose bundle of unrelated and dissociated habits"; although there will be evidence of a certain amount of adaptation to specific situations, his behaviour will have a meaningful pattern, a pattern directed by his dominant predispositions—in other words by his dominant traits. They say that, as often as not, it is the traits *which create the habits*; that a person is careful in various situations not because someone has had to teach him to be careful in all these situations, but because his particular personality make-up, as well as his experience, *predispose* him to behave carefully.

They say that the specifists do not make anything like sufficient allowance for individual differences—presumably because they do not believe in these differences. But whether one believes in them or not, the fact remains that you can apply exactly the same conditioning (e.g. discipline) to different people and get completely different results!

They also maintain that the "specifists" place far too much emphasis on the environment and the situation, and seem to feel that it is the environment which makes the man. The generalists say that man is not totally at the mercy of the environment, to which he must always learn to adapt: on the contrary, man is capable of creating his own environment—especially his immediate environment; e.g. of creating his own slum conditions or the accident hazards with which he has to contend. The generalists also place a good deal of emphasis on personal characteristics acquired through heredity—whereas the more extreme specifists are prepared to discount the hereditary element altogether.

In other words, the generalist psychologists disagree with the sort of contentions put forward by the specifist psychologists—such as that put forward by Percival M. Symonds (while he still believed in specifism): "A widespread misconception of conduct is that it is an expression of traits... which cause one to act in certain ways." The generalists say that it is not a misconception at all: on the contrary, conduct appears to be quite clearly related to personality traits; and the more basic and fundamental the trait the more consistent the behaviour in that respect.

Nor do the generalists think that it is logical to adopt (as the specifists do) an all-or-nothing approach and say that because only a few people are, for instance, always honest, or always dishonest, and the majority are sometimes honest and sometimes not, that very few people can be said to display this "postulated" trait of honesty. As Eysenck points out, you might just as well demand that the concept of intelligence be applied only to those who can answer every question in a test, or to those who can answer none. Generalists say that a trait is still a trait no matter what its strength, and that this all-or-nothing approach is illogical: that the only realistic way to think of a trait, like for instance aggression, is in terms of a continuum, with intermediate degrees of aggression: to think of it as a characteristic which we all possess, but which is more pronounced and more easily aroused in some people than in others.

In fact, the generalist psychologists maintain that the whole theory of the specificity (and therefore the inconsistency) of behaviour is full of *non sequiturs*: that it is not only improbable but highly impracticable: and that the specifists are always having to indulge in a series of mental gymnastics in order to fit the realities of life to a highly theoretical doctrine. It is no wonder therefore, as Allport points out, that they do not extend many of their theoretical ideas into the realm of their daily living. He says that even the specifists appear to rely very much in their everyday lives on the manifest consistency of human behaviour—otherwise they would never even know how to approach the "boss" for a rise, or which guests to invite together for dinner!

> "If we become intentionally naive, and ask whether any specifist in daily life can believe and be guided by his theory, we discover swiftly that he cannot. To be in keeping with his own doctrine, he would never be entitled to apply descriptive adjectives to persons. He could not say that his friend is trustworthy, affable or humorous; that his child is high-strung, dominant or sociable; that his wife is kind or tactful. In the midst of an argument for specificity, in a passage commenting on the filling out of questionnaires, one author makes the fatally contradictory observation, 'The truthful person finds it very difficult to be untruthful'—a statement, of course, not of specific habits but of traits." [Allport, 1952.]

Allport also maintains that no one can for long live or think according to the sparse concept of specificity, and that it is only when he enters his laboratory or classroom that a specifist "is likely to leave common sense behind him, and embrace a scientific theory".

Unfortunately, however, although he himself may not live with it or by it, it would appear that a devout theorist can sometimes propound his theory so diligently and so convincingly that it can have far-reaching effects on other people's lives. Dressed up in technical language, a theory can so impress the layman that he no longer stops to think of its *a priori* improbability. Instead, bowing to what he considers to be "authoritative scientific opinion", he can allow himself to be talked into a policy decision which puts into effect a *nationwide* laboratory experiment. One wonders sometimes what a person like Percival Symonds (who later changed his views so drastically, and abjured specifism in favour of dynamic trait psychology) thought in later life when he saw the theoretical doctrine he had preached so eloquently in his youth, mushroom into a nationwide programme of "conduct" education—possibly at the expense of general erudition and independent thought. One does not need to speculate as to the apprehension with which the practical traffic officers, who deal at first hand with the road accidents and traffic offences of the American teenagers, view the expansion of driver *education*—at the expense of driver *training and the development of practical driving skills*: or their amazement and alarm over the current trend in accident prevention policy, which, because "authoritative scientific opinion" has declared that accident proneness "has no empirical foundation", is apparently now being geared to the principle of don't-blame-the-driver-blame-everything-else.

However, to revert to the current antagonistic attitude of the American specifist psychologists towards the concept of accident proneness, the most interesting point is not *why* they should be antagonistic, but why it has taken them so long to declare their opposition and launch a concerted attack.

The antagonism is easily understood, for just about every aspect of the concept would be unacceptable to any right-thinking specifist. In the first place, the concept implies a definite consistency of behaviour; a tendency to accidents which is operative over relatively long periods of time. In the second place, it implies the existence of certain definable traits (such as aggressiveness or irresponsibility) which would predispose people to accidents. And in the third place (if one is to believe many of the accident research findings) it implies that the behaviour caused by these traits is not specific to the driving situation but is evident in many other aspects of their everyday lives.

Undoubtedly the real puzzle is why, when American psychology has been specifist-orientated since the twenties, the attack on proneness took so long to eventuate. One can only presume that while the uncritical popularity of the concept was in its hey-day, while the layman at least might have been optimistically looking to it to solve the whole accident problem, that the specifist psychologists lacked the courage of what ought to have been their convictions, said nothing, and just tried to stay in the stream and come to terms with this popular belief as best they could. About the only way in which this could be done would be to attempt to explain the phenomenon, and particularly the most popular and best-known research findings, in terms which could, at a stretch, be reconciled with specifistic theory, i.e. in terms of inadequate training, or bad habits, or undesirable environmental pressures. The high accident rate of youth need not therefore be due to the personal characteristics usually associated with immaturity; it could be due to inexperience with the hazards of traffic—or insufficient conditioning in the instillation of safe habits—or incorrect attitudes (an "attitude" being something which was permissible in specifistic theory as it could be explained as a *physiological* condition of the nerve synapses brought about by habit and resulting in a "readiness for response"). Similarly, Tillmann's well-known research findings that *a man drives as he lives* need not be interpreted as evidence of dynamic personality traits producing a characteristic "style of life"; the fact that accident offenders were very often known to a number of social agencies such as debt collectors, or juvenile and adult courts, or home investigators, could, if necessary, be interpreted as the effect of the pressures of a bad social environment. And McFarland's apparent corroboration of Tillmann's findings, namely that truck drivers with high accident rates even had *previous* records of traffic violations, could similarly be explained as *habitual* behaviour resulting in subsequent accidents.

But in order to avoid any implications of generality or consistency in accident-producing conduct it was, above all, necessary to explain that these findings really only applied to *extreme cases of accident repeating* (irrespective of the fact that Tillmann's so-called "extreme" cases, for instance, were people with four or more reported accidents in fifteen years). It was also necessary to adopt the same sort of all-or-nothing approach to proneness as had been applied to the "so-called traits", and to say that proneness was a phenomenon only applicable to certain people: it was a dichotomy—either you were "prone" or you were not—and the only people who qualified to be called "prone" were the extreme cases. The specifists could then say: "There are some people who are *always* having accidents (the very few "prone" ones): there are others who *never* have accidents (e.g. Malfetti's Safety Award winners); but the majority of people only have accidents sometimes (*on specific occasions*) and they are the NORMAL people."

Just how anyone could get into the ALWAYS or NEVER categories was something which the specifists never seem to have got round to explaining. Presumably the environment is exceptionally hard (or easy) on some people, or else some people condition to bad (or good) habits remarkably easily—apparently, however, without the aid of any predisposing characteristics. Anyway, the obvious thing to do was to take no chances and introduce driver "education" to condition everybody for safety, just in case.

Also left unexplained was the reasoning which led the specifists to insist that accidents in all spheres of life must be lumped together. Or that all accident-prone people must display the same characteristics (or even characteristic)—they must represent a "psychological entity"—they must display a "global personality trait". The psychological (or even logical) basis for these particular contentions is something which has remained known only to the specifists themselves.

And most definitely also left unexplained was the contention that for accident proneness to have any validity, let alone utility, it was necessary to establish that the majority of the accidents were caused by a small fixed group of accident-prone people (i.e. the extreme repeaters): and if this was not shown to be true then the concept was obviously of very limited value. However, the fact that this all-or-nothing, one-type-or-none, forever-or-never concept of proneness was most unrealistic does not seem to have worried the specifist psychologists at all. In fact it seems possible that this was partly a sort of tactical manoeuvre. For the more unrealistic the concept, the more difficult it would be for the opposition to substantiate it, and the easier it would be for the specifists to shoot it down if and when the opportunity arose.

The developments of the fifties and early sixties must therefore have been most unwelcome. For instead of accident research running aground on the rock of this rigid and unrealistic and therefore unprovable idea of proneness, researchers from all over the world proceeded to disregard it completely and to develop, and substantiate, a much more flexible and realistic version of the concept—a version which was now totally incompatible with specifistic theory. There were only two ways in which those who still remained devout specifists could deal with these developments: either disprove them or ignore them. Very wisely, considering their lack of ammunition, they apparently decided to do the latter. Even when the hypercritical reviews of the sixties began to appear, not one of these reviews so much as mentioned the new way of thinking. The criticisms, muted at first but growing stronger later, were all against the old rigid, and seemingly self-created concept. This was a significant phenomenon. For the logical—and scientifically acceptable—procedure would have been at least to take cognisance of recent research developments and argue accordingly. But instead the critics of the sixties chose to argue that because proneness (as defined by their own all-or-nothing concept) was still unsubstantiated, it was therefore untrue; that it was time the proneness "myth" was replaced by more realistic (specifistic) thinking, such as accidents being events just which happen to "normal" people because some transient weakness makes them liable to misfortune on *specific* occasions, e.g. a quotation from *Accident Research* (Haddon *et al.*, 1964): "In fact, rejecting the concept of accident proneness, with its implication of a global personality trait, forces one to search for many different psychological factors and their significance in given environmental circumstances."

At first the attack seemed to be a rather indirect one where the critics of proneness began to slowly discredit the whole idea without looking as though they were discrediting it at all—in fact by giving the impression that they were being rather broadminded about the entire issue. This was achieved by periodically examining the subject with apparent detachment and impartiality, finding some of the evidence in favour of the concept to be "interesting" but "scientifically inconclusive", ignoring other evidence which was more difficult to handle, and ending up by appearing to be a little sad and disillusioned about the whole thing. With the aid of the magical word "statistics", this process was apparently quite effective. Such continuous scientific scepticism gradually had its effect and caused a number of erstwhile supporters to begin to doubt the wisdom of supporting a concept which they were repeatedly told had "no empirical foundation". So one by one they withdrew their support, and the pendulum of American opinion on proneness began to swing. There being no longer any real need for hesitancy, the specifists were then able to go straight into the attack and, after setting fire to the grotesque scarecrow version of the concept which they themselves had created, were able to announce with righteous indignation that the American public had been sadly misled on the question of accident proneness and that they hoped such a thing would never happen again.

The most intriguing aspect of this whole development was undoubtedly the feat of logical acrobatics by which the specifists seemed to be able to use the sheer illogicality of their own self-devised concept of proneness in order to hold up to ridicule the whole idea. Somehow or other they managed to convey the impression that this was the sort of scientific "ballyhoo" that the supporters of the concept were trying to put across, and from which they, the specifists, were protecting the public by means of diligent scientific scrutiny. A typical critique, written by a specifist at any time during the sixties would, in fact, go rather like this: (the wording would vary according to individual preference, and according to the time at which it was written—in the early sixties a certain amount of diplomacy would be used, but as time went by diplomacy would be replaced by an attitude of rather scornful derision).

TYPICAL CRITIQUE OF THE 60'S (With additional arguments indicated in brackets.)

"Accident proneness is generally conceived as a constant, unchanging tendency to accidents [accidents of any kind, road accidents, industrial accidents, childhood accidents—the wider the field the better]. If proneness exists at all [which is unlikely] it must therefore be due to a stable and enduring *personality* characteristic [as yet unidentified]. The accident-prone person must therefore be a definable single type, a psychological entity [also as yet unidentified].

"Accident *proneness* must not be confused with accident *repetitiveness*, which is purely a descriptive term applicable to those who have repeated accidents. Such people are known to exist but they are probably either (a) people who are consistently subjected to excessive exposure and/or hazards or (b) just 'extreme' cases [which, if necessary, can be airily dismissed as 'psychiatric cases']. Statistics have however proved that accident repeaters are few in number and contribute only a very small percentage of the total accidents. [Quotation here from Forbes' figures on the 1938 Connecticut study.]

"Accident proneness [again if it exists] is apparently therefore of little importance in the general accident picture, and the claims made by its supporters that a handful of accident-prone people are responsible for the majority of accidents are unjustified. [Ignoring the fact that no major scientific study supporting the concept has ever made any such claim.]

"There is very little empirical proof that accident proneness really does exist or, for that matter, that accidents are predictable. Statistics have shown that accidents in one period are poor predictors of accidents in another period. [Omitting here any mention of the high correlation which Hakkinen, with full accident reporting, obtained between accidents in successive periods—or else referring to the fact that Smeed was very critical of Hakkinen's findings.] Traffic violations sometimes appear to be slightly better predictors. [No explanation for this apparent anomaly need be given—unless it is explained in terms of undesirable 'habits'.] But even here the findings are usually statistically inconclusive.

"There is also very little psychological evidence to substantiate the existence of proneness. Psychological tests have proved to be poor predictors of accidents and the correlations between these tests and accident criteria are 'uniformly low'—certainly too low to be of any practical use. [Omitting that (1) no test can be expected to correlate highly with an 'unreliable' criterion, and (2) that Hakkinen, who did have a reliable criterion, obtained a very high multiple coefficient between his *battery* of psychological tests and his criterion. In fact, let's face it, if possible omitting any mention whatever of positive research findings.]

"Altogether the results of psychological studies, particularly those aimed at identifying personality characteristics associated with accident pronenes, are very disappointing. The most they appear to do is to demonstrate that there are differences between the people who have accidents and the people who do not [indicating if necessary that this is a rather unscientific thing to do]; or that driving *habits* may possibly reflect an individual's general behavioral attributes. But this seems to have very little to do with accidents *per se* and certainly does not test accident proneness as a psychological hypothesis. [A cryptic remark best left unexplained.]

"The lists of characteristics which are claimed ['claimed' is a useful word; it is technically correct but manages to convey the impression that these claims are not necessarily justified] to be associated with accident repeaters are very contradictory—so contradictory in fact that they could not possibly represent a single psychological entity, or even a global personality trait. [As specifists do not believe in the existence of 'types' or 'traits' this process of throwing up a clay pigeon and then shooting it down serves the double purpose of vindicating the specificity theory and, at the same time, ridiculing the proneness one.] In any case these characteristics have usually been found only in *extreme* groups of accident offenders.

"The findings of the psychological studies [most of which are in any case poorly designed and controlled] are in fact so inconclusive that one is driven [always use 'driven'] to the conclusion that the concept of proneness is as yet unsubstantiated. Perhaps there is no such thing as an accident-prone *person*? There are only isolated accident-prone *characteristics* which could be present in any one at any time [and only result in accidents on *specific* occasions when the individual encounters a *specific* situation].

"All in all it seems a great pity that so much research time and money should have been devoted to such an unprofitable exercise. Would it not be better to stop this chase after an illusive and probably non-existent will-o'-the-wisp like accident proneness, and instead spend the public's money on identifying and modifying those specific elements in the environment which cause the unfortunate NORMAL driver to have specific accidents?"

There is, of course, another version of this argument—but this is only used when the writer feels that there is no need for diplomacy at all. In this version all he does is to put up an even more exaggerated version of the concept, such as accident proneness implying a tendency to accidents "of all kinds under all circumstances and at all times"—or that the public is being asked to believe that accident proneness is an "immutable load to which the unfortunate possessor is chained as inexorably as Ixion to his wheel". After this, all that is necessary is to say in a dignified fashion that such ideas are "scientifically unacceptable".

Such are the arguments of the specifists with regard to accident proneness. I make no apology for what may appear to be a very exaggerated and biased description, for every one of these arguments has been used at some time by the adherents of this doctrine. This can be verified from a study of the actual publications of the sixties, the tone of which has in recent years become progressively more "specifistic". At the present moment a state has been reached where a member of the Research Division of the United States National Safety Council can confidently say (Vilardo, 1967):

"It is interesting to note that in the 1966 hearings on traffic safety, not only did the Congressional Committee avoid the term 'accident-proneness', but the emphasis of the committee was placed on the vehicle, not the driver. It would seem this Committee was reflecting the current viewpoint of the accident prevention community which no longer subscribes to the concept of accident-proneness. It is now felt that while certain characteristics make one more liable for an accident, these are not necessarily inherent in the personality of the individual but may be present at any given moment in time. Thus no-one is 'accident-prone' all the time, but perhaps all are 'accident-prone' on occasions. Instead of accident-prone individuals there exist accident-prone characteristics which are present in all persons and in all environments at certain moments in time."

If, however, this development had been confined to America, it would be of purely local importance. Psychological theories have come and gone before now, and it is quite on the cards that the popularity of this particular one may decline among the American accident researchers as it is reputed to be doing in more general American psychological circles. This could conceivably bring about a noticeable change in the trend of the scientific thinking of the United States on the question of accident proneness. But in the meantime, such is the influence of American accident research that the repercussions of this thinking have spread to other parts of the world—probably, as I said before, without these other countries appreciating just how or why this thinking has developed. The enthusiastic acceptance of orthodox behaviourism, and the "congenial" theory of the specificity of behaviour, being virtually confined to the United States, it seems more than likely that the extent of their impact on accident research has not been appreciated outside the United States—especially as the arguments used against proneness are seldom if ever psychological ones. Had this been appreciated it would undoubtedly have inspired some spirited controversial argument from psychologists in places like Europe, where this particular psychological doctrine has been accorded very short shrift. As it is, no one has even commented on this aspect of the trend of developments. Instead, America's growing opposition to the concept of proneness is presumed to be based purely on factual, statistical findings and is therefore regarded as something which must be taken seriously.

To my mind this is what has led to the air of growing bewilderment which is now to be found not only among research workers but among the people whose job it is to implement measures for accident control. In those countries where accident rates are still high (and this goes for most of the countries of the world today) people appear to be torn between the evidence of their own eyes and "informed scientific American research opinion". Their eyes tell them in no uncertain way that a large proportion of the accidents in their own countries are caused by the reckless, or dangerous, or inconsiderate driving of a sizeable section of the community—and that, on the basis of common sense alone, these people could well be described as being "accident-prone". But, on the other hand, if one is to believe American research opinion, this cannot be so. American researchers are always saying that, when it comes to accident causation, so-called common sense is notoriously unreliable. As they are "prone" to saying: "After all, in Columbus' day the common-sense view was that the world was flat!" (See Fig. 10.1.)

The Americans, it seems, maintain that there is "no empirical foundation" for the belief that some people are inherently more likely to be involved in accidents than others, and that accident proneness is "an exploded myth". The vast majority of accidents are, in fact, caused by NORMAL people. Accidents are therefore everybody's fault (or nobody's)

"Hello earth . . . look, I'm not quite certain how to put this . . ."

FIG. 10.1. Reproduced by permission © *Punch*, England

and if the accident problem is to be solved, or even ameliorated, it must be tackled on this basis. In other words, it must be tackled on a *scientific* basis and not on the basis of some bit of folklore like accident proneness. Just what that basis should be, and just how one is supposed to go about solving or even easing the problem, is something which is apparently still a little vague. But it appears that the Americans strongly advocate a "systems approach".

A lot of people outside America are very impressed with all this, particularly with the idea of a "systems approach"—though many of them are not at all sure just what this means but are a little afraid to say so. They are also (unfortunately) by now more than a little afraid to resist the weight of all this confidently worded "scientific opinion". The result is that fewer and fewer people today—especially those associated with accident research—are prepared to get up on their hind legs and say that they flatly disagree with all this: that there is as much if not more scientific evidence in favour of proneness as there is against it, especially if you define it in a realistic way: that it is all very well being so scathing about "common sense", but people in glass houses should not throw stones: that it is bad enough to be condemned as a medieval myth-worshipper for believing that a person who is known for his dangerous driving (and who has already had at least one major accident) is an inherently bad accident risk—but when, in place of this common-sense thinking you are presented with a "scientific" theory which says that this driver is just a *normal* driver, and that any accident he may have is merely the result of some temporary accident-prone *characteristic* quite fortuitously meeting up with a lurking accident-prone *situation*, and this meeting resulting in a little accident-prone *act* ... well, *that* is carrying condemnation of common sense a bit too far!

However, it seems that very few people are prepared to voice any such militant sentiments, possibly because they do not fully understand what all this talk about putting the blame on the environment instead of on the driver is about. All the more reason therefore to examine the accident literature of the sixties to see if it is possible to trace how the moderate and rational thinking of the fifties has become so unrecognizable in the course of a few short years; why the progress of research on the human factors in accidents, which was going ahead so purposefully and successfully during that decade, should suddenly receive such a set-back; and why, in fact, such a concerted effort is now being made to halt that progress and turn the clock back to what really amounts to an attitude of nobody-really-knows-what-causes-accidents, an attitude reminiscent of the days before the First World War.

The very fact that scientists in other fields, who seem capable of pooling their resources instead of spending their time tearing other people's constructive ideas to pieces, have been able to land a man on the moon, makes the position with regard to accident research that much more depressing and that much more in need of a thorough soul-searching examination. For, after all, it is not only the progress of research that is being impeded—or even only the research clock which is being turned back. The implications are more serious. It seems that the move is towards undermining the authority of the officials who deal at first hand with the practical realities of the accident situation. Perhaps an extract from a letter written to the editor of the *Research Review* of *Traffic Safety* by the Manager at that time of the Motor Transportation Department of the United States National Safety Council (Imhoff, 1963) will illustrate my point. The letter was written after the publication in the *Research Review* of an article disputing the effectiveness of a well-known practical driver *training* system.

"To the editor:

"Three cheers for Dr. Goldstein for his article 'Whither Accident Research?' in the March 1963 issue of *Traffic Safety*. And particularly for one of his parting observations concerning the 'need for communication between the researchers and the program people.' We could not agree more.

"Program people, among them fleet safety directors, must cope with the vehicle accident problem on a day-to-day basis and keep management and the drivers sold on the idea that their safety programs make sense. These people have more problems than an umbrella has rain drops in a storm, and deserve better of the research fraternity who should be trying to diminish their problems instead of adding to them, and who should be giving them new and better tools to work with instead of breaking up what few imperfect tools they have.

"There seems to be a trend in accident research today to shoot down the old and honorable concepts that have been the mainstay of successful accident prevention programs for many years."

It seems that I am not alone in my misgivings!

CHAPTER 11

ERA OF DOUBT

IN TRYING to trace the recent drastic changes in the thinking on accident proneness, I shall have, perforce, to quote copiously from the publications which have helped to bring about these changes. The reader may find these extracts very repetitive but, believe me, it is no fault of mine that so many of these papers say the same thing, often in the same words. It would have made my task infinitely easier if I had just condensed the next two chapters into one small section by saying that A said something, then B repeated it with a few variations on the theme, and then C did likewise. But firstly I doubt whether anyone would have believed me; and, secondly, I think it is important to show how a drastic change of attitude has been brought about, not by new evidence but by the sheer weight of repetitive statement of what really amounts to little more than an opinion, and what is more, an opinion based on unrepresentative and very out-of-date research findings. I think it is also important to show that there is a distinct element of doubt as to whether even those research findings which have been used as supportive evidence have been correctly portrayed. This I could never do without verbatim quoting.

The text will, I hope, be enlivened by some spirited argument. This, I must admit, will be not so much intentional as unavoidable. When one has spent the last fifteen years, as I have done, in an operative driver-selection unit, dealing at first hand with drivers and their accident records, one is apt to get a little impatient with people whose arguments are based on theory alone—especially when one has enough research experience to be able to see the flaws even in the theory. I therefore make no further apology for the length of the next two chapters. I feel that if one is going to try and combat the cumulative effect of paper after paper of critical comment, then I see no way of doing it except to reproduce long excerpts from these papers, all in one place, so that the reader himself can assess whether they in turn are able to stand up to critical evaluation.

It is often difficult to know how a movement began, particularly when it has no designated High Priest, (unless, in this case, one bestows the title on J. B. Watson!). But, as far as it is possible for an outsider to judge, it seems that the organized drive to discredit the theory of accident proneness originated round about 1960 in a group of American psychologists from the Eastern States and was associated with a well-known body, the Association for the Aid of Crippled Children. It may not have actually originated there, but it seems that it was there it developed from a talking-point into a writing-point, and emerged in a number of published papers.

This very active Association had at that time subsidiary study groups, one of which, the New York City study group, in 1960 sponsored the preparation by Suchman and

Scherzer of a report on research in childhood accidents. This report appeared just ahead of a big conference which had been called by the AACC to investigate behavioural approaches to accident research, and had obviously been read by several of the speakers at this conference. It therefore seems a fairly logical point at which to start; for, even if it was not the first strong critique of the proneness concept, at least it seems to have been the first to receive serious consideration.

Suchman's report, *Current Research in Childhood Accidents* (1960), was ostensibly designed to deal with research as it applied to children's accidents, as in fact most of it does. But in the first section dealing with conceptual approaches to the accident problem and containing his discussion on accident proneness, it seems he is talking of accidents of any kind, in any field. I say "seems" because very few of the American psychological writers on accidents (particularly the theoretical writers) appear to think that there is any need to differentiate between them, or to doubt whether findings which apply to children's accidents, can in fact be applied to miscellaneous adult accidents, industrial accidents, and road accidents.

This is a point worth examining in more detail, for it has far-reaching consequences. There are a number of people who feel that this is unjustified and that it also obscures the whole issue. Apart from the sheer illogicality of thinking that the same research findings could apply to events in the life of people ranging from infancy to senility, there are research findings which show that there are, for instance, significant differences between accidents involving property damage and accidents involving personal injury. There are also a number of considerations (such as the symbolic meaning of a car and driving) which would differentiate road accidents from, for example, industrial accidents. In fact there seems to be no justification for lumping together accidents occurring to such different age groups and in situations which make such different demands on people's abilities or invoke such different psychological forces. Much of the confusion on the personal factors in accidents, and particularly on accident proneness, seems to stem from this practice (a practice which in itself seems to be yet another by-product of specifist psychological thinking). The spread of the anti-proneness, anti-unequal-liability movement, as displayed by the publications of the sixties, clearly shows the influence of this factor: for what was said in the earliest papers in a discussion on children's accidents, was said in such general terms that it could be later quoted—and actually was quoted—over and over again in entirely different contexts. In fact, if one really examines the snowballing development of the current attitude towards the role of the driver in *road accidents* one will find that right at the core of the snowball are findings on the accident behaviour of *pre-school children!*

However, it is obvious that this confusion of concepts would only upset someone who is not a believer in pure habit-psychology and the specificity of these habits. To the critics of proneness (whose psychological leanings are often very apparent in their writings) it is apparently of no consequence whatever that this confusion between different types of accidents exists. In virtually all the critical papers on proneness no distinction is made, and one will suddenly find that an argument based on accidental poisoning in three-year-olds is being used to support a contention on speeding accidents among adult motorists.

To return, however, to the paper by Suchman and Scherzer. It is a long paper and the authors start the first section by expressing their disapproval of the accident research already carried out (again whether this refers to children's accidents or accidents in general is very difficult to establish, but it is apparently the latter). Accident research, they say, is "characterized by many unconnected studies of a host of disparate factors that are variously related to accidents". This lack of any systematic formulation is very undesirable, and therefore a conceptual analysis of accidents and the accident situation is very necessary. (Sometimes one wonders how the critics of accident research reconcile their condemnation of the slow rate of progress with the fact that they are always demanding that everyone should start at the beginning again.) The authors, however, do start at the beginning with all the various definitions of what constitutes an "accident", and from there proceed to outline various research approaches which have been used, such as accident proneness and the "newer" approaches, e.g. the decision-making approach, and systems analysis. They are obviously very much in favour of the last two and dead against the first.

As these "newer" approaches are so often referred to in the critical reviews of the sixties I think it is important that we take this opportunity to find out what they are about. According to Suchman and Scherzer, recent developments in social psychology have shown that many events which were thought to be chance-determined (probably only by psychologists!) are really subject to individual and social control. "Perhaps the most recent noteworthy attempts to conceptualize the accident phenomenon from an organized behavioristic point of view is the analysis of human behavior in so-called 'chance' situations in terms of individual risk-taking and decision-making."

They then go on to give an interesting discussion on risk-taking derived mostly from writers such as Cohen and Hensel (1956). However, the picture they paint of this risk-taking behaviour is one which is so difficult to reconcile with a disbelief in unequal liability that it is most intriguing. The *quality* of an individual's decision-making and risk-taking depends, they say, on how closely his estimate of the situation fits reality. This in turn will depend on his training and experience; on his norms, values, and ability; on his personality and background—"with the personality aspect fundamental". The way in which a person *assesses* a risk may be conscious or subconscious, normal or pathological. Moreover it is likely to be influenced by physical, psychological, social, and cultural factors. A description like this would seem, to most people, to indicate that the writers regarded decision-making and risk-taking as being such a reflection of each person's inherent individual make-up that one could expect a certain consistency of behaviour (and therefore "proneness")—but apparently not.

Suchman and Scherzer seem to feel that this approach has great potential. They think it is a fruitful way of interpreting accidents; that we can seek both the *cause and the prevention* of accidents among those factors which make for high risk, bad decisions, and unsafe environments:

> "In terms of *research*, the problem becomes one of determining for all environments the degree of risk-taking involved and the decision-making process whereby the individual determines just how much risk to take."

And in order to *predict* the occurrence of accidents:

"We need to know (1) the accident potential of the environment, (2) the awareness on the part of the individual of this accident potential, (3) the motivating forces toward the prevention of an accident, (4) the behavior of the individual in terms of his risk-taking."

As an account of a theoretical approach this is very interesting, but the first thing that any practical person would ask is just *how* anyone is going to *do* all this? How, for instance, do you accurately and methodologically measure the accident potential of the environment? Or the motivating forces of the individual?

In reality the only hope of success you might have with this risk-taking approach would be if there *was* some consistency in risk-taking behaviour—in which case you could assess risk-taking as part of the person's general behaviour pattern by means of some comprehensive battery of tests. But if, on the contrary, it is true that people's behaviour is not consistent, then it would appear that this method still offers very little hope for predicting accidents. And certainly if, as Suchman maintains in a subsequent paper (1961), accidents are "events falling at one end of a continuum of unpredictable and uncontrollable behavior", then it would seem that the authors' optimism about the fruitfulness of the decision-making and risk-taking approach is somewhat unjustified.

Suchman and Scherzer's attitude to systems analysis as a method of attacking the accident problem is also favourable. An accident, they say, is a complex interaction between human beings and their environment, involving a sequence of events and a multiplicity of casual factors. By viewing the accident as a single operation in which all factors must be interrelated rather than divorced from one another, one may be able to simulate the accident sequence in such a way as to be able to analyse the relative importance of the various factors.

Quoting from the 1958 conference sponsored by the President's Committee for Traffic Safety, they say that a "system approach" to road accidents would involve the following processes. First one would need to develop an *index* of "normal" driving behaviour for any specific situation. It could then be presumed that the actual behaviour of various drivers—or the same drivers at different periods of time—would sometimes pass outside the "normal" range; and when this happened, either a near-accident or a real accident would occur. "It seems desirable to have a quantitive study of a continuum ranging from safe to disastrous patterns of behavior in which observational and experimental findings would be given an appropriate theoretical base."

I *think* what is meant by this last part is that the situation could then be re-created on a simulator—and studied in detail. But how, for example, is one going to create the indices of normal behaviour? And how is one going to ensure that people would drive on a simulator as they would in a real life situation? I see problems ahead. And even if I am wrong in my interpretation and the study is to be done in real life situations, then how are all these examples of unsafe behaviour going to help solve the problem? I don't want to sound too iconoclastic, but I think the traffic officials could actually supply most of this information at a fragment of the cost. For this reason I feel that there is still something to be said for being able to single out the *individual* who is more likely to indulge in this sort of behaviour. But apparently my views on this question are not shared by Suchman and Scherzer, as is shown by their attitude toward approaching the accident problem via accident proneness.

As this was probably one of the earliest strong attacks on the concept, and as it was later used as a suitable introduction for the chapter on accident proneness in Haddon Suchman and Klein's widely known book, *Accident Research*, I think this section should be quoted in full so that we can see the line of argument which has been adopted. I have here and there included a few personal remarks in square brackets, where I feel that comment on certain lines of argument is badly needed.*

"One idea prevalent in accident research is that a high frequency of accidents incurred by certain individuals may be explained in terms of some abnormal personality characteristic of those involved. There is a great deal of confusion and unprofitable debate about this concept of accident proneness. It is our contention that accident proneness does deserve a limited place in accident research but not the central position it is now given by many research workers.

"The concept of accident proneness arose out of the observation that certain adults and children seemed to have more accidents than others. The term implies the existence of a particular personality type which is predisposed toward having repeated accidents. [It is interesting to note that researchers who are in favour of the concept of proneness do not consider that it implies only a personality function; in fact they connect high accident involvement with a *number* of personal factors. Even when they stress the importance of the personality element, they are adamant in their contention that a number of different personality traits are involved, traits which differ from individual to individual. The strange contention that the accident-prone person must represent a 'particular personality type' appears to be restricted to those who oppose the concept.] This predisposition is regarded as a psychological abnormality due to some underlying neurotic or psychopathic condition. [Surely a very exaggerated description?] For example, as summarized in the *Proceedings of the First Conference on Home Accident Prevention*, 'the accidents, then, might well be unmotivated, and the defect a developmental one in the ego-control mechanisms.'

"Certainly a psychiatric point of view justifies the hypothesizing of a neurotic tendency on the part of some adults and children to inflict self-injury through deliberate accidents. Such clinical cases have been reported by various psychiatrists. However, can one use such clinical evidence to justify the use of accident proneness to explain all, or even most, of the cases of individuals who have a high frequency of accidents? [No. Nor can one justify making the whole concept of accident proneness synonymous with this particular limited, psychoanalytical interpretation of the genesis of personal-injury accidents.]

"There are several reasons why this extension of a legitimate psychiatric concept is unwarranted. These reasons are statistical, methodological, and theoretical.

"The existing evidence has serious statistical shortcomings. Since chance plays a part in many accidents, we would expect to find that during any given period a certain pro-

* Reproduced by permission of the Association for the Aid of Crippled Children.

portion of the population would suffer an inordinately high number of accidents *by chance alone*. [Virtually every investigation has shown that the distribution of accidents in any given period is significantly *different* from chance.] The concept of accident proneness is based on the assumption that the membership of this group, in terms of individuals, remains unchanged with the passage of time. Actually, as Schulzinger observes, 'The evidence indicates that if the period is sufficiently long, the small group of persons who are responsible for most of the accidents is essentially a shifting group of individuals with new persons constantly falling in and out of the group.' [Schulzinger was actually talking about personal injury accidents sustained by members of a *shifting population*—patients who came to him over an 18-year period, and who, as he says, ranged from 'infancy to senility'. Hakkinen's figures had shown that if the group and the exposure was controlled, a very different picture emerged.] Moreover, statistical correlations between present and future accidents are often low; the mathematical models and techniques utilized to establish these relationships are subject to severe criticism by responsible theoreticians; observable injury or damage are not necessarily adequate indicators of the occurrence of accidents; and the multitude of possible intervening factors requires statistical controls which are not generally applied. [These are very valid arguments, but they require more detailed presentation. It can be pointed out, for example, that the criticism of the 'responsible theoreticians' does not by any means imply that the correlations obtained when proper statistical controls are imposed on the data are *overestimates* of the position. In fact, for a number of very valid reasons, it is felt that these correlations are, in fact, usually *underestimates* of the stability of accident occurrence (Cobb, 1938; Thorndike, 1951; Arbous and Kerrich, 1951; Jacobs, 1961, Coppin, 1965). The 'criticism' as such is really levied against using correlation techniques of any kind when the data are too restricted, or too inaccurate, or too uncontrolled, or too non-normally distributed to warrant such statistical treatment—or against the limitations of the techniques themselves for dealing with a multi-dimensional problem.]

"After considering accident proneness from a theoretical and mathematical point of view, McFarland concludes that the scanty evidence which remains after critical review may hardly be taken as adequately supporting the concept.

"From a statistical point of view the problem of prediction becomes extremely important as proof or disproof of the concept of accident proneness. To what extent can we predict that individuals with a high frequency of accidents in the past will continue to have more than their share of accidents in the future? Very few studies have attempted to do this. [No, a number of studies had already done this. In fact, whenever possible.]

. . .

[For some reason, the following paragraph, and only this paragraph, which rather bears out what I said earlier about predictive correlation coefficients being underestimates, was omitted when the whole of this section of Suchman's paper was reproduced in *Accident Research*.]

"As Arbous points out, this is extremely difficult because of the selective nature of accidents."

" 'The cases which are self-eliminated and cannot be included in correlation because of incompleteness of exposure, are usually those who have accidents and are precisely the ones we are interested in. A mathematical model should be built, and tested if possible, to allow for this factor. Without this allowance, it is possible that r is estimated on a restricted range *viz.*: those cases who happen to survive the respective exposure periods, which may be long. (Arbous and Kerrich, 1951).'

. . .

"Methodologically, too, there are a number of inadequacies in the current research on accident proneness. Perhaps most important is the failure to control an environmental exposure or risk. Certain individuals are more likely to be exposed to hazardous occupations or environments and thus to incur more accidents. Comparisons, therefore, must attempt to equate individuals on exposure before comparing them on accident frequency. [Where exposure was equated, as in Hakkinen's study, significant differences between individuals were apparent.] Unless we take this differential exposure into account, we are likely to attribute to personality characteristics what is in fact attributable to the environments that attract such personalities. [A strange stress on the environment. Even if, say, a 'dangerous' environment attracts high-risk-taking people, surely it is the high-risk-taking *behaviour* of these people which is the important element and which is going to step up the accident rate?]

"There also appears to be some confusion between the concept of predisposing factors and accident proneness. Because certain groups of individuals (i.e. young males) are apt to have more accidents than others, we cannot say that individuals who belong to these groups are accident-prone. There are a great many social factors which contribute to a differential rate of accidents among subgroups of the population, and these factors have to be taken into account in explaining why some groups have more accidents than others. [An argument which I, personally, find rather difficult to follow, but which does seem to represent a sociological viewpoint not shared by many other researchers and which runs contrary to nearly every research finding.]

"Finally, from a theoretical point of view, there is some reason to doubt the existence of any identifiable personality type that could be labeled as the accident-prone personality. Dietrich is not fully convinced of the accident proneness concept because the accident repeater has not been successfully identified as a psychological entity. In fact, most studies have shown highly contradictory results concerning the traits of 'the accident-prone personality.' For example, in some cases this may be an overly timid individual, whereas in others this type of individual is more likely to be aggressive. Unless the accident-prone individual can be identified and described as a meaningful type [note the stress on one meaningful type] it would seem to be more useful to identify those separate personality characteristics that are more or less associated with repeated accidents.

"This analysis presents only some of the reasons why the concept of accident proneness must be viewed with caution. Certainly the evidence in its support is not conclusive. It seems likely that greater progress will be made in accident research through concentration upon the specific causes of repeated accidents and through restricting the concept of accident proneness to the limited number of psychiatric cases in the total population of accident repeaters."

This last paragraph is reminiscent of an earlier paper by Kerr (1957) who also appeared to feel that accident-prone people were psychiatric cases—only he went a little further. In this paper, talking about industrial accidents, and following a rather shaky mathematical line of argument, he reached the point where he felt justified in saying that much less than 15% of the variance in accident rates was due to accident proneness.

> "It is interesting [he said] that an earlier study of automobile drivers by Forbes arrived independently at the similar conclusion, that the accident repeater contributes not more than three or four per cent to the accident problem. . . . Relevant, also, is the fact that Hunt, Wittson and Burton computed the psychiatric discharge rate at Naval induction stations and subsequently during World War Two to vary between four and nine per cent."

When one considers that these "psychiatric" discharges include every case from psychosis to homosexuality, the postulated connection of these two sets of figures seems perhaps a little far-fetched.

Returning, however, to Suchman's report. This report was apparently made available shortly before the conference of the Association for the Aid of Crippled Children held in October 1960, and is mentioned by several of the speakers. This was a big conference, and a number of people—not necessarily associated with accident research but all authorities in their various fields—were invited to present papers. These papers were later published in book form under the title *Behavioral Approaches to Accident Research* (AACC, 1961) The papers covered a wide range of topics, being mostly theoretical discussions on various approaches to the study and prevention of children's accidents. Several of them did, however, refer to the question of accident proneness, usually on a broad and general basis. I therefore propose to limit discussion of these papers to this particular aspect.

Reading through the papers one is immediately struck by (1) the number of different ways in which accident proneness is defined, and (2) the wide divergence of views on the validity and the usefulness of the concept. This latter divergence was particularly apparent between the attitude displayed by the first speaker, Jacobs, and those who followed.

Jacobs, speaking on "Conceptual and methodological problems in accident research", adopted the kind of attitude which had characterized so many of the writers of the previous decade, namely an *a priori* acceptance of the *idea* as such, leading to an exploration of its usefulness for determining the causes of accidents. In sharp contrast was the attitude of other speakers who maintained that overconcentration on the idea of proneness has hindered the whole progress of accident research. In this they were merely echoing what McFarland had said way back in 1955; but whereas McFarland's criticism had been largely directed against the *extent* to which proneness affected the accident situation, the emphasis in most of the papers at this 1960 conference was on the *right* of the supporters of the concept to say that it influenced the situation *at all*. As such their criticism was far more fundamental and, though they expressed it largely in terms of "not proven", the wording in which it was phrased gave a clear indication that their opposition to the idea was basically ideological.

Jacobs devotes his paper to the very real difficulties which confront the accident re-searcher looking for counter-measures which are effective and at the same time "socially, politically and economically practicable". He says that a great number of practical preventative measures were already in operation, especially against the sort of accidents which have obvious causes. But to tackle the remaining ones, for which causes and remedies are not anything like as obvious, represents a challenge to accident research—a challenge (1) to identify the more subtle causes, and (2) to find preventative techniques which do not already exist. (I think, myself, he could have added (3) to prevent already successful counter-measures from being undermined on theoretical grounds!)

Contrary to popular belief, he says, much research effort has gone into the treatment of these problems over the last fifty years, yet despite all this it is difficult to point to more than a handful of findings which have led to the development and application of useful counter-measures. The question is why? Jacobs then begins to outline some of the "whys". Dealing with obvious first-hand knowledge of the sort of problem encountered in accident research (obtaining meaningful accident recording, defining and measuring exposure, etc.), he finally comes to the question of investigating the accident potential, not only of *situations* but of *people*. Here he mentions, in passing, the question of accident proneness.

"One of the problems that will be recognized as falling within this class is that of test-ing the hypothesis of accident proneness, and, perhaps more interestingly, of identifying the personal characteristics associated with proneness. In fact, much of the accident research performed by behavioral scientists during the past fifty years has tended to concentrate on the almost trivial problem of demonstrating the existence of accident proneness—e.g., testing the hypothesis that different individuals have different pro-pensities to have accidents. This problem could easily be dismissed as one of minor aca-demic interest. Accidents are, after all, the result of behavioral activities and, since in-dividuals possess unique patterns of behavior, it can be argued easily that the existence of individual differences in accident propensity does not require demonstration beyond that which has already been established for the existence of individual behavioral differences in general.

"This issue is actually only a very small part of a much more important research question which has never been answered satisfactorily. This is the question of inferring the structure of individual accident processes along with the population distribution of the characteristics of these processes. If this can be done, then the subsequent problem becomes one of relating characteristics of individual accident processes to other charac-teristics of the individual. Presumably at this point it should become possible to develop hypotheses of causal relationships between individual characteristics and individual accident proneness."

This problem, he says, presents very great methodological difficulties. Here he outlines several difficulties often described in the accident literature, but also others which are very often overlooked by people who have never undertaken any research—e.g. the fact that the accident potential of an individual could vary according to the type of accident and using the total number of accidents as a criterion might confuse the issue. But trying to solve this difficulty would, says Jacobs, bring other difficulties in its wake, for trying to achieve homogeneity by means of narrower classification reduces individual expectation to the point where the effects of chance represent such a large part of the variance between individuals that it is futile to investigate the significance of the differences between them or to use these differences as a criterion against which to measure any personal differences.

He then goes on to the statistical difficulties encountered, particularly those involved in correlating an accident predictor with an accident criterion and, *inter alia*, points out that because of the markedly skewed distributions so often found in accident data, the usual interpretation given to the product-moment correlation coefficient *r* in accident research is invalid—and presents a statistical rationale for his contention that "for samples of the kind frequently reported in the literature, the estimated degree of association would be about one-third of that which might actually exist".

It is not an easy paper to read, but for anyone embarking on the analysis of complex accident material it is a very worth-while one. Its whole approach is factual and realistic and constructive. Seen against the background of many of the publications of the fifties, this paper would not appear so remarkable. But seen in contrast to most of the papers that followed in this particular conference, it is immediately obvious that Jacobs was swimming alone against the communal stream in his attitude to accident proneness, and also that his down-to-earth realism was rather out of place in a conference notable for its hyper-critical, ultratheoretical approach to the whole question of accident research. Admittedly the purpose of the conference was to obtain the views of a number of people whose approach would naturally be rather theoretical as they had little or no direct contact with this research. But it is interesting to note, all the same, that one of the speakers who was allocated the task of summing up the findings of the conference felt it necessary to comment on the fact that a number of the psychological papers had asserted that there had already been too many studies which led nowhere, and what was needed was more theory. He suggested instead that what in fact was needed was some more good studies on which to base some fruitful theorizing!

The paper which followed Jacobs' was one by Suchman, "A conceptual analysis of the accident phenomenon". I am going to restrict comment on the paper to the sections dealing with the various behavioural approaches to accident research, where again as an example of one of them he mentions accident proneness. This time he dismisses it in one short paragraph, again confusing the findings of the general scientific literature on proneness with his own limited version of the concept:

"One model that we do not feel has proved productive in the past, despite its widespread use, is that of 'accident proneness'. There are very good reasons for disregarding this model on theoretical, methodological, and mathematical grounds. We agree with Arbous and McFarland that this approach is quite inadequate. We cannot take the time in the present paper to review the evidence for and against this concept. Suffice it to say that we do not believe that the complex behavioral phenomenon of accidents can be explained adequately in terms of a single personality type which seeks out accidents through some neurotic motivation. Such people undoubtedly do exist, but they account for only a small minority of accidents."

He then mentions again the approach via decision-making and risk-taking and the systems approach. Regarding the latter he says:

> "Probably the most ambitious model for the analysis of accidents as part of a series of events, has been developed in relation to research on automobile accidents. A project under way at Harvard, for example, involves the use of inter-disciplinary teams of physicians, lawyers, engineers, and behavioral scientists who proceed to the scene of a traffic accident as soon as possible and attempt to make an on-the-spot evaluation. . . . It is too early to evaluate the results of this approach, but this kind of systems model is a far cry from the simple classification of host, agent, and environmental factors associated with traditional epidemiological research on accidents."

I feel that Suchman might not have been so enthusiastic about this kind of systems model if he had been able to foresee that one of the chief findings of this particular study—possibly influenced by a certain amount of subjective apperception on the part of one of the behavioural scientists involved—was going to be that a pronounced suicidal element was discernible in the causal sequence of events which precipitated many of the accidents. This particular study did in fact emphasize the danger that even "systems approaches" can contain a large subjective element—a source of error which was not as apparent in a later study undertaken elsewhere (Baker, 1961) where the emphasis was more on the engineering aspects, one of the reasons being that the organizers had great difficulty in getting the various psychologists and sociologists allocated to the team to turn up in time at the scene of the accident!

To continue, however, with the comments of the various conference speakers on the subject of accident proneness.

MacIver then followed with a very well-written paper, "Safety and human behavior". This paper is interesting not only because it gives the views of an American psychiatrist on the accident problem, but because it also demonstrates the bewilderment of a rational thinker not directly connected with accident research when he is asked to accept some of the peculiar ideas on accident proneness obviously current in America.

MacIver's paper deals with accidents in general, and I will therefore only comment on those parts applicable to road accidents. He says that much preventative work had already been done, especially in the field of primary prevention, but much remained to be done in preventing those accidents where it is the *human being* who has to impose the controls *on himself*. But even here, he says, there are signs of a spread of interest because of the enormous toll which accidents are taking; and he feels that soon one of the most important activities of health departments will have to be accident research and accident prevention.

The human factor, he says, is very important. But, he says:

> "There is currently a tendency to equate the psychological determinants of accidents with psychopathology. It must be kept in mind, however, that psychological determinants include many healthy behavior patterns—healthy, that is, except in the particular context of the accident occurrence. Further, behavior patterns not in themselves unhealthy may be to an extent imposed on the individual by social pressure and no doubt determine many accidents.

"Drinking, for instance, plays an important part in our social relationships; and all sorts of habits, customs, and norms carry definable accident potential. Education is needed not only to change people's attitudes, but to change social opinion. For example, there will have to a be change in the present lack of social stigma attached to driving after drinking."

He goes on to say that undoubtedly some (but not all) of the psychological determinants are psychopathological ones. And here he mentions the question of accident proneness—or rather what he obviously believes to be the current views on the subject.

"Of all the human factors, one especially has received a great deal of attention: the possibility that certain individuals are predisposed to accidents because of their mental makeup and in fact have more accidents than the average person. This theory of accident proneness has been accepted as absolutely proved by many individuals in safety, psychiatry, and psychology. To state the theory again, accident proneness carries the implication that many accidents occur because of a particular kind of mental abnormality, and that accidents are concentrated in a minority of the population with this abnormality. This minority is said to be accident prone. It is further said that 20 per cent of the population have 80 per cent of the accidents. In point of fact, there is only the smallest element of truth in this reasoning. For the most part it is fallacious, and the term 'accident proneness' should be dropped. To paraphrase Thomas Huxley, the concept of accident proneness is a beautiful theory killed by a number of ugly facts."

What MacIver apparently does not appreciate is that a "beautiful theory" is perhaps being killed by a number of ugly misrepresentations! For, obviously believing implicitly that the supporters of accident proneness contend that *the majority of accidents occur to a small minority of mentally abnormal people*, he carefully proceeds to give reasons why such a contention is unwarranted. He points out the fallacy of the idea that 80% of the accidents occur to 20% of the people and deals, one by one, with a number of points which were fully appreciated and covered by even the earliest accident researchers—such as an unequal distribution of accidents being caused by chance or unequal exposure. Even the contention that accident proneness is caused by "mental abnormality" is, he says, an unjustified claim:

"Our conclusion is as follows. The bare fact that an individual has one or more accidents over a given period of time does not necessarily mean that he is accident prone—that is, that he had the accident because he was emotionally disturbed. Until this is realized, we shall be misdirecting much of our efforts toward accident prevention. A far better term is 'accident susceptibility'. This takes into account *all* the factors which tend to predispose an individual to accidents (or protect him from them). The chance of having an accident is largely built into the particular environments in which we happen to carry out our daily activities. Within the limitations of a given environment, there are, of course, individual differences in personal adjustment, emotional and otherwise, as determined by the efficiency of operation of all the human factors which have been mentioned."

He then goes on to illustrate these individual differences. Though, he says, many accidents occur when people are temporarily upset, there are those who are so seriously disturbed emotionally that they may have more likelihood of getting involved in accidents than the average individual. Perhaps 10–15% of any population have very serious emotional problems, and no job which carries minimum accident potential should be opened to them. In addition, everyone is beset at times with aggressive and destructive impulses, but these are under much better control in some individuals than in others— though the control can be weakened by certain drugs. Individual physical differences are also very often obvious.

Unfortunately, he says, difficulties will be encountered in determining which psychological or emotional characteristics will distinguish the accident-prone person.

"Regretfully, we must lay to rest any oversimplified black-and-white concept of the accident-prone individual. Unfortunately, we have not been able to isolate him with any consistency. Neither are there usable yardsticks of accident proneness or measures of the degree of stability of this quality. The truth of the matter is that the potential for having accidents is spread widely throughout the population. . . . This is not to suggest that the investigation of temporary and enduring normal and abnormal emotional patterns is not warranted. There is wide agreement among psychiatrists that men and women are equipped with aggressive drives, mostly benign—indeed helpful—but also frequently destructive to the individual and those around him.

"To understand these healthy and unhealthy emotional patterns—how they operate, in whom, and under what circumstances—should be the aim. The approach to safety should be twofold. The environment should be neutralized for hazards as far as possible. Then, from the human point of view, some notion of the degree of accident susceptibility of particular groups and, so far as is possible, of individuals should be arrived at. Prevention programs should be instituted on the basis of all available findings."

MacIver then goes on to a very interesting section on the significance of accidents as symptoms of some sort of disorder within the individual or within the community, and of accidents as related to socio-economic classes or different cultures. He ends on a much more optimistic note than most of the papers, saying that many accidents are, in fact, predictable, and that people can be educated to less dangerous behaviour because "human nature is extremely plastic and modifiable". (Like many Americans, he is possibly not aware of just how disciplined American drivers already are in comparison with most other countries.)

The pity about this very well-written and interesting paper is that it illustrates so clearly how misinformed people are on the subject of accident proneness. MacIver seems to be unaware of any of the major research findings on personal accident liability carried out over the last thirty years. And, what is more, his objections to the concept are such that he is fighting a non-existent foe, as *not one* of the authors of the big studies has *ever* suggested that the majority of accidents are caused by a small minority of "unbalanced" people. For even the reports of Greenwood, Woods, Yule, and Newbold, let alone Tillmann, Malfetti, Conger, and Hakkinen—all of whom had published before 1960— would have shown him that proneness to accidents was most certainly not regarded by these prominent researchers as being confined to the mentally abnormal but was, in fact, regarded as stemming from factors such as the very inequalities which he himself had mentioned; and that, far from its supporters maintaining that it was the major cause of accidents, they merely maintained that it was one of many causes—but nevertheless an important one. In fact, it would appear that MacIver would have been quite at home with the real research thinking on the subject. It was some weird "scarecrow" version of the concept that he found so unacceptable.

But the interesting point is where *do* people like MacIver, who are relative strangers to accident research, encounter these weird ideas? As he could never have found them in the writings of the major researchers, it seems that he must have found them in some so-called review of the literature. Undoubtedly there has always been a certain amount of misunderstanding on the subject of accident proneness: but what is unpardonable rather than unfortunate is that this sort of misunderstanding (or misdirection) still carries on, and is in fact being perpetuated by people who are not strangers to accident research, and who *are* aware of the findings of that research—but apparently feel justified in ignoring them.

The rest of the papers given at this conference were devoted mostly to children's accidents and, although the question of proneness was occasionally mentioned (never with any enthusiasm and always associated with some misconception), I think enough extracts have already been given to indicate the prevailing attitudes and the sort of incomplete information which was perpetuating these attitudes. It appears that the wide circulation given to these papers, and to Suchman and Scherzer's earlier one, perpetuated them even more. For many of the statements made at this congress were quoted thereafter. MacIver's apparent disbelief in "accident proneness" was later quoted by Suchman, and Suchman was several times quoted by later writers such as Goldstein and McFarland—and so it progressed, in ever-widening circles.

Dealing now with the next of the critiques to appear: Goldstein's paper "Where we are in accident research" (1961b), which was read to the Accident Prevention Research Study Section of the United States Public Health Service. This time the subject was restricted to road accidents, and although Goldstein never so much as mentioned the phrase accident proneness, his whole paper is devoted to disproving its tenets and to stressing that accidents are more or less random events associated with characteristics which are only temporary in nature.

Goldstein is obviously a keen exponent of experimental methodology, and supports his arguments with large quantities of correlation coefficients. He is also equally obviously a believer in the specificity of behaviour. It is interesting, therefore, to see how he develops his arguments, for this is one of the few critiques of the period in which the reasoning is explained in any detail and where one gets an insight into how a "specifist" psychologist interprets the actual findings of accident research. But before dealing with the paper itself, it would be as well to sketch in its background.

In June 1961 Goldstein (1961a) brought out his now well-known publication *Research on Human Variables in Safe Motor Vehicle Operation: A Correlation Summary of Predictor Variables and Criterion Measures*. The main purpose of this summary was to present the findings of the research studies carried out prior to 1958 in terms of easily understood figure abstracts—in other words to tabulate the results, usually in the form of the statistical correlations obtained between the accident criterion used in each study, and the various human factor variables studied, such as driving behaviour, intelligence, vision, personality factors, or attitudes. In addition, the tables indicated the *statistical* significance of these coefficients.

For a number of years now this summary has served as a handy reference table for accident research, and it has been widely circulated and quoted. Recently several similar summaries have been brought out in Germany (Schubert, 1965, 1967; and Section 12 of the German Handbook of Psychology, 1967). Despite the apparent usefulness of this sort of document it should be noted that there are actually a number of people who are opposed to this kind of approach and who feel that summaries of this kind probably do more harm than good to the cause of accident research. Their contention is that you take all the valuable "meat" out of a study by doing this: that you cannot reduce research findings down to just a few figures; and that it is actually very misleading to do so. Figures, they say, have a dangerously mesmeric effect, and a list of correlation coefficients which people can (and somehow automatically do) compare for size can give a very misleading picture of the relative importance of various factors in the accident situation (as, for example, the false picture given by the low correlation coefficients obtained between accidents and vision: a relationship which should never be measured in this fashion). Figures also have a hallowing effect. A relationship expressed as a figure seems, to many people, to assume the mantle of truth—even if the relationship is a completely spurious one as between, for instance, an inadequate test and an unreliable criterion. But, more important still, they feel that many people do not realize that a correlation coefficient, even with an indication of its statistical significance, simply cannot be accepted on its merits: *it is necessary to know its antecedents before one can even begin to interpret it.*

A number of researchers feel that a summary, like the Washington Correlation Summary, is therefore virtually meaningless unless the reader is familiar with the studies themselves—and, if he is, then he does not need it. It is also dangerous, the danger being that the people who *are* going to use summaries are the very ones who are least qualified to do so, either because they cannot understand the original studies or, as so often happens, because they cannot obtain them or appreciate their implications as they are written in a foreign language. But unfortunately the figures are not: their language is international. This I know from personal experience as many times during discussions with research workers in Europe I have seen Goldstein's summary whipped out of a drawer and consulted as though it were as factual as a ready-reckoner. No, I for one do not like correlation summaries, and my personal view is that, necessary as statistics are for the advancement of experimental psychology, it is very important to see that they are not elevated to such a position of importance that the tail starts to wag the dog!

This I feel seems to have been very much the case in Goldstein's (1961b) paper "Where we are in accident research" in which, basing his whole argument on the figures from this summary, and going from one low coefficient to another, he succeeded in painting a picture of the current state of this research which I feel was as misleading as it was gloomy.

The burden of the paper was that the figures revealed a number of very sobering facts about accident research: that although there seemed to be a *few* signs that some human factors *might* have something to do with accidents, the evidence was inconclusive and only really seemed to apply to the extreme cases: that nobody had found any one factor which caused accidents and therefore nobody had found any way of predicting accidents: that really, when you came to think of it, this was not surprising, as accident occurrence was apparently not a stable characteristic in individual drivers—so what hope was there of being able to predict accident occurrence anyway?

Goldstein's paper was in fact one of the first of the rather sad, disillusioned critiques which later became such a feature of the sixties. As such, the mechanics of his arguments are definitely worth examining, for they are very interesting.

To start with it is as well to remember that the date was 1961, and though Goldstein opens his paper by saying that he believes he is acquainted with the most important experimetal work published since the summary closed (mid-1957) and will refer to it under each heading, there is no mention whatever of Hakkinen's major psychological and statistical study—by then very well known throughout the world. This omission could possibly have occurred because Smeed's criticism had aroused some doubts about Hakkinen's criterion. But this explanation seems doubtful as the criteria used in most of the studies quoted had never been subjected to any statistical analysis whatever; and in fact several pages of the summary had been devoted to a study of attitudes by Goldstein and Mosel (1958) where the subjects were the authors' friends and acquaintances and where the accident and violation criteria were based solely on the say-so of the individuals themselves! Possibly, at the time, Goldstein did not know about Hakkinen's work— but then he has never mentioned it in any of his subsequent papers either.

The inclusion of Hakkinen's study would have had interesting repercussions as his coefficients would have looked like giants among the pygmies in relation to many of those quoted, and would have necessitated a very different line of argument. For Hakkinen's results would have shown that accidents *had* been found to be a stable characteristic of individuals when exposure was controlled and the accidents fully recorded; and they would also have shown that accidents can be *very satisfactorily* predicted (for the lesser offenders as well as the extremes) by a well-thought-out battery of tests. However, as it so happened, Hakkinen's study was not included—so one must examine the progression of Goldstein's arguments on the basis of the evidence as given.

Starting with the question of the inconsistency of accident involvement, Goldstein refers to what he calls the "best available data", the Connecticut study (1938) where the correlation between the accidents of 29,531 drivers in two successive three-year periods was only 0·11. Pointing out that it is very difficult to interpret this coefficient because of the non-normal distribution of the data (but not mentioning the complete lack of control of exposure), he says that possibly the best way to interpret these figures is in terms of Forbes' 1939 re-analysis—which, he says, is "extremely enlightening and should be extremely sobering". Quoting from the text (with a few relevant comments, as Goldstein's mathematical logic is sometimes a little difficult to follow):*

"Forbes' analysis shows that if all drivers with accidents in the first triennium were removed from the distribution for the second triennium, 79% of the accidents remain:

* Reproduced by permission of the author.

you would have removed 21%. Remember, this is if everyone who had one accident or more in three years is eliminated from driving, you would eliminate 21% of the accidents! We could hardly call a person with one accident in three years a repeater. You would also have tremendous legal difficulties in removing such a driver from driving.

"Let's take it one step further: if only those with *two* or more accidents in the first three-year period are removed from the second three-year period, 96% remain. You would have removed only 4%. Now this presumes perfect identification; notice, that is, it means we have the criterion scores, the actual accident reports. If we are involved in identifying such drivers by means of tests which *predict* accident records, we have indeed a far less effective procedure.

"Now I must hasten to say that we are all very much aware that accident records do not tell the whole story. I think it is fair to say that something like only 1/4th or 1/5th of the accidents which actually happen get into the records. This is a familiar story. My point is, if this is so, let's multiply the figures 4% by 5; so, if we then remove everybody with 2 or more accidents in a three-year period we will remove 20%; 80% of the accidents will remain. [An unfortunate mathematical *non sequitur* from a writer who repeatedly insists that proficiency in mathematical statistics is essential for a proper understanding of accident research.]

"I don't know who would be willing to call a driver an accident repeater if he has 2 accidents in 3 years and I don't know how you would make it stick. [By Goldstein's mathematical logic, where apparently—though I may be wrong—only drivers with reported accidents have unreported ones as well, these two-reported-accident types must in reality have had some incomputable number of accidents, which Goldstein may have thought of as 10, but which would have to be *more* to account for the 20%!] I don't think we need take this another step and say let's make it three accidents [15 or more?] in a three-year period. I think the point is made poignantly. To me this is an extremely sobering bit of data and is rather devastating to the expectation that we can make much of a dent in the accident problem by identifying (predicting) and removing the accident repeaters. Not that they don't exist, but they don't account for much in the total picture. [A pity about that mythical 20%, it really would have made quite a dent!] It would appear that *most* accidents on record are *first* accidents on record. It would appear that it is not the few with extremely deviant behavior which account for the major portion of the problem, but the extremely many who behave in ways that are condoned, that constitute the traffic accident problem." [A somewhat sweeping generalization which overlooks incomplete reporting, lesser degrees of "deviancy" and also the whole question of enforcement and its effects.]

Goldstein then runs through the other studies in the summary where accidents are compared for two succeeding periods, and points out that although the correlation is usually higher for bus drivers than for general drivers, even these are not high, certainly not high enough to form a reliable criterion. From these coefficients he concludes that "this low 'reliability' of the criterion of accidents limits the degree to which any other measure or combination of measures can possibly correlate with accident rates"—a conclusion which, if true, should have precluded the necessity for the rest of the paper which dealt with the relationship between these unreliable criteria and a number of human factors *in terms of the correlation coefficients obtained*. However, he does go on, feeling that perhaps there are some human variables related to accidents "which we might manipulate by means of training or therapy or redesign of signals or controls, or something that we haven't thought of yet". The following is a brief summary of his comments.

Violations. Not much evidence available here. There seems to be a slight relationship but, because many of the violations recorded would probably have gone unnoticed by the police had they not been associated with an accident, these correlations are "almost certainly over-estimates of the degree to which accidents occur to drivers who violate the law but do not happen to conformers". [A statistical nicety, but it would appear that these particular violations actually precipitated the accidents.] However, he says, in one particular study the position seems to be rather different. McFarland and Moseley found a significant relationship between prior, and therefore unrelated, violations and on-the-job accidents. This he feels is an extremely interesting study relating "habitual behaviour" with subsequent accidents. He feels we need a great deal more information in this area.

Talking of factors which can be measured by actual tests, he says that, to start with, it must be appreciated that no single factor accounts for much in the accident picture— accidents are generated by a multiplicity of factors. However, it would be as well to look at some of the studies done of these factors.

Vision, he says, should not really be treated by means of correlation coefficients, but in passing he nevertheless stops to remark: "Just a moment on the nine visual acuity measures in a study by Cobb on 2 to 3 thousand drivers. The correlations as computed ran from a high of ·065 to ·028! No comment!"

Going on to the psychomotor functions. Reaction time? Sensory perceptual tests? Psychomotor apparatus tests? Not much here. [Shades of Hakkinen!] Cognitive measures? This section can be summarized by saying that "there is a little something to be said for knowing something or having the ability to learn something".

Moving on to what he describes as "a class of variables which has in recent years occasioned a good deal of discussion and also a good deal of research, namely, the personal, emotional, attitudinal realm". Not much to be said for the first two except that the results of some studies are contradictory. Attitudes? Several significant findings here; but the best results seem to be obtained when the accidents and violations on record are supplemented with accidents and violations revealed in interviews—a "dangerous" thing to do, but "under proper conditions" very useful. [One is tempted to ask here just what are "proper conditions"?]

Now to "perhaps the most interesting and fruitful, and exciting class of variables, namely, background, sociological types of variables'. Tillmann and Hobbs, he says, showed a remarkable difference between the accident-repeater group and accident-free group with respect to the percentage of drivers known unfavourably to the local social service agencies. This finding was supported in another group of 100 accident-free drivers as against 96 accident repeaters. The work of McFarland and Mosely on 59 accident-repeater versus 88 accident-free truck drivers was pretty much in support of Tillmann's findings.

"It seems that extreme accident repeaters do indeed present a behavior pattern that is characterized by social irresponsibility, perhaps even social hostility. I think it should be no surprise that people who are troubled and disturbed behave like people who are troubled and disturbed, and if we were selecting drivers for a bus company or a freight company or a taxi company, we would do well to pay attention to background factors to screen out such people. But as indicated earlier it appears that such people do not account, by any means, for a major portion of the total traffic accident problem. Accidents are generated by a wide range of human beings."

[Just why the large number of accident offenders in these studies should be *extreme accident repeaters* or *troubled and disturbed* people is a little difficult to see.]

"Turning now", says Goldstein, "to a variable on which the research has been *quite consistent*." Young drivers below 25 and older drivers beyond 65 have consistently been found to have worse accident records than the other age groups—particularly the youthful drivers. The youthful driver does, in study after study, turn out to have more accidents. This is often contrasted with the fact that physiologically he is at the peak of his health and efficiency. One study reports that this is not due to inexperience, but another study in Great Britain indicates that inexperience does play an important role.

Education? Education may help here. Evidence is conflicting about the high-school driver education. More research is needed.

Alcohol? The research findings show that alcohol has a deleterious effect on behaviour at a much lower concentration than is generally realized. And alcohol plays a greater role in fatal accidents than is generally known—probably somewhere between 30% to 50% of traffic fatalities.

Goldstein then sums up (the italics are mine):

"Traffic engineers have indeed made important, substantial, and demonstrable contributions to safe and efficient travel and transportation. I am sure they will continue to do so. But unless they take control of the vehicle entirely out of the hands of the human being, and that is currently being worked on, it seems to me that there is little that engineering can do about drinking driving, or irresponsible driving, or stupid driving, or blind driving, or impassioned, aggressive driving. They have done remarkably well in minimizing the hazards, making it easy to drive safely. But I think it is clear that in addition to minimizing the hazards inherent in the roadway and in the vehicle, we have to minimize the hazards inherent in the human being. *From what has been said here, that accidents in one period are not highly predictive of accidents in a subsequent period, and various measurements of human characteristics are not highly predictive of accidents, and even the relationships that have been found might easily be explained away as due to differences in exposure to hazard rather than to the human factor, it might be concluded that human characteristics play no role in accident involvement. I would hasten to say that we must distinguish at this point between relatively fixed or stable characteristics of human beings and variable characteristics; that is, it seems important to study the characteristics of people that vary with time, place and situation and are subject to influence by experience. In all the 'reliability' studies the effect of time on learning and maturation and skill, foul up our data.* In addition to the traditional three E's of traffic safety, namely, Engineering, Education, and Enforcement, we might add the three A's which need attention, namely, Age, Alcohol, and Attitudes."

This paper of Goldstein's has been dealt with at some length because, as mentioned before, it is one of the few critiques of the sixties in which the reasoning leading up to the final conclusions is given in any detail. Perhaps, being one of the earliest, it was considered necessary to give this reasoning. In most of the later critiques (including Goldstein's later ones) conclusions like these were merely stated as facts.

It is interesting the way Goldstein never mentions the phrase "accident proneness"; in fact, he carefully avoids it. However, his antipathy to the basic principles of the concept is very apparent—as is his own particular psychological orientation. Studies indicating any consistency in accident involvement, or studies indicating that accidents are associated with stable human characteristics, are glossed over, or described as inconclusive, or unfortunately not mentioned at all. (Not only is Hakkinen's statistical and psychological study omitted, but also Conger *et al.*'s clinical study (1959) on accident offenders.) Where positive findings are mentioned they are interpreted as being applicable only to that specifist dumping-ground, the "extreme cases", or in terms of rationalizations which are acceptable to specifistic theory. Consistent behaviour is interpreted in terms of a few "extreme cases", or "habitual" behaviour; findings on attitudes are acceptable, possibly because attitudes are regarded as a purely physiological phenomenon; sociological findings are tolerated because the environment can be blamed instead of the man; and the high accident rate of youth is regarded as a very welcome finding because it can be associated with inexperience and therefore interpreted as a need for more "conduct" education.

But although the psychological orientation of the paper is interesting, more interesting still is the type of deductive reasoning used, for this is very germane to the validity of the conclusions drawn. This deductive reasoning has a peculiar sort of double-take quality as it constantly employs the kind of argument which denies the existence of the cake, and yet at the same time permits one to eat it. Arguments such as these. Correlation coefficients derived from non-normal distributions cannot really be interpreted—but you can nevertheless use them as the whole basis of your thesis. Accident data are obviously incomplete —but the distribution of such accidents as *are* reported can be used to prove that accident occurrence is not consistent. The criteria used in most studies are "unreliable" and therefore you cannot expect any predictor tests to correlate highly with them—yet you can nevertheless use the low level of correlation obtained to prove that these predictors are incapable of predicting. Accidents are obviously not caused by any single factor but by a combination of factors—yet you can use the cumulative effect of a number of low correlations between *single* factors and accidents to show that accidents are not associated with stable human characteristics. When you do find a significant relationship between a *combination* of factors and an accident criterion, then you can say this finding applies only to "extreme cases". As a sort of extra insurance policy you can say that accident repeaters must be people who are "troubled and disturbed"—but at the same time you can say that they are probably only people with greater or more hazardous driving exposure. And, ignoring the fact that even all the so-called *negative* evidence you have been quoting has a consistently *positive* trend, you can say there is nothing to indicate that there is any pattern or stability about the characteristics associated with accidents—so they must be transitory ones, ones which vary with time, place, and situation, and which are subject to influence by experience (presumably our old friends "the loose bundles of dissociated habits"). Never in any of the arguments is it apparently necessary to consider that if the general trend of the facts does not fit your premises, there may indeed be something slightly wrong with your premises; or for that matter that if your premises were more reasonable there would be no need for these pretzel-like arguments. No, the logic, as such, seems to be purely destructive. There seems to be no need whatever to defend your contentions, let alone substantiate them with any definite proof. All you need to do is to explode your opponent's contentions (or what you maintain to be his contentions) with a loud bang, and then quickly hop into the resultant vacuum.

Unfortunately, in his later papers, Goldstein never produced any more of these interesting logical exercises. He merely repeated the conclusions of his first paper again and again, each time with more conviction and confidence. For the next two critiques to appear in the sixties were also Goldstein's. "Human variables in traffic accidents" (1962) was a digest of the 1961 paper. Most of the explanatory comments are missing, but he quotes the same sets of figures (even the ones about multiplying the 4 *per cent* by 5 to estimate the effects of full reporting). But it is noticeable that the conclusions were getting more definite—and the outlook for finding any solution to the accident problem more gloomy.

> "Drivers with extremely poor attitudes of aggressiveness, social irresponsibility, and/or who are highly unstable, have more accidents than those who are responsible, stable and less aggressive than average; nor do these account for but a slight portion of the accident total."

And:

> "It might be argued that, as far as human variables are concerned, accidents are largely a function of age, alcohol and attitudes. The more basic behavioral variables underlying these '3 A's' seem to deserve concentrated attention on the part of psychologists, sociologists, physiologists, and, perhaps, anthropologists as well. Or perhaps the engineers should be encouraged to remove the driving task from the hands of the driver."

"Whither accident research" (1963) again indicates that the "whither" is not in the direction of solving any practical problems (though, never let it be forgotten, he did end up by saying that there was a need for "communication between the researchers and the program people"). But the detailed instructions which he gives for the direction of research are all towards what Allport, in his very well known book, *Personality* (1952), describes as "the thickets of specificity and the aimless cause of the doctrine of identical elements". Goldstein, after stating his now familiar credo that nothing is associated with anything, and nothing predicts anything, says:

> "The fact that accident involvement is not a stable characteristic of individual drivers, and is therefore only slightly predictable on the basis of other stable characteristics of individuals, does not mean that accidents are not attributable to people and to transient

or momentary behavioral failures. I think there is evidence to show that much depends on the interaction between individuals, vehicles, the roadway environment, and the societal situation in which we move and live and have our being (the driving situation). Although visual acuity as such—depth perception, etc.—do not relate importantly to accident involvement, this does not mean that perception of hazards, which is a function of training, knowledge, judgement, attitude, alertness, etc., is not involved. As a matter of fact, some of the most successful measures in this entire problem area have been via traffic engineering, which has provided aids to perception and decision-making by means of street markings, 'channelization', better signals, proper timing of signals, better signs—more legible at greater distances and better placed with anticipated turns and intersections being indicated beforehand. The kinds of studies which appear to be fruitful are those directed at the interaction variables; those aimed at providing drivers with information they need in time for decision-making; and providing them with the necessary prior preparation in the first place."

There is something vaguely familiar about the last part of this statement. Is it possible that Goldstein is referring merely to the traffic control measures designed by the traffic engineers? If so, perhaps the accident position is not as gloomy as he makes out, for it seems that with the aid of such people (and despite the efforts of the accident-research critics), there may be some hope for the accident problem after all!

Moving now to a different type of commentary and to a different venue, namely the Harvard School of Public Health and McFarland's "The epidemiology of motor vehicle accidents" (1962). As McFarland's incidental papers are usually summaries of the accident literature, it is not surprising that, in the portion dealing with accident proneness, he echoes several of the previous critiques.

By 1962 McFarland's views on accident proneness had become decidedly more critical than in his earlier *Human Variables* (1955). But something which I personally find rather puzzling in this new paper is the number of rather strange contradictions which it contains. This I think is probably the result of McFarland trying to combine his own views with those of the people he is quoting. For although he seems much more convinced (on *statistical* grounds) that proneness does not last, yet at the same time he obviously attributes accidents to deep-seated *psychological* factors in the personal make-up of the driver, which must surely be operative over long periods of time. The following extract illustrates the tenor of McFarland's views in 1962:

"One concept which has been very prominent is that certain persons suffer accidents repeatedly on the basis of their inherent and persistent behavior tendencies and that the identification and treatment of such individuals would prevent many accidents. However, thus far, these tendencies have not been precisely defined or identified by research. Moreover, the statistical evidence is quite convincing that the influence of a proneness factor, where it can be detected in the accidents occurring within large groups, is quite limited. Furthermore, the small group of accident repeaters is a constantly shifting one over a period of time, persons dropping out of the group and new persons coming in continually (Schulzinger, 1956)....

"There is also some doubt, even in psychiatric circles, that there exists an identifiable type which could be labelled an accident-prone personality. Studies in this area have shown highly contradictory results concerning the traits comprising the postulated personality syndrome (Suchman, 1960).

"It is questionable whether the accident proneness concept could explain an appreciable number of the cases of high frequency of accidents. Proneness would be but one of many factors influencing the frequency. Some persons are accident repeaters on the basis of chance alone; others have more accidents than their fellows because they are more frequently exposed to risk. It would be more profitable in accident research to concentrate on the specific causes of repeated accidents and to try to identify those specific personality characteristics that are associated with repeated accidents for which the individual is primarily responsible."

The last argument in this extract seems to me to be self-contradictory. If there are "*specific personality characteristics that are associated with repeated accidents for which the individual is primarily responsible*"—then isn't this proneness? According even to McFarland's own original definition, proneness, if it exists, is due to a person's own inherent and persistent *response tendencies*. If, for example, one's own response tendencies are to "repeatedly make mistakes"—then wouldn't this be proneness? I am afraid this is one line of argument that I simply cannot follow, for the examples which McFarland then gives of specific characteristics which are believed to be associated with repeated accidents (and whose investigation he feels would be more profitable than the investigation of proneness) all seem to me to be ones which could very easily come under the heading of "inherent and persistent response tendencies".

The first of these is the "repeated mistakes" kind:

"A promising concept is that frequent accidents in an individual represent one manifestation of a poor adjustment in meeting the social and personal demands of life. That is, if a person repeatedly makes mistakes in meeting his personal and social obligations, he is also likely to make errors in other activities while at work, at play, or driving. This concept implies that a man works or drives as he lives. Objective support has been given to this concept." [Here McFarland cites several studies including his own 1954 study on the truck drivers.]

Another of these characteristics is attitudes. It seems quite logical, he thinks, that risk-taking behaviour would be influenced by wrong attitudes towards speed, or traffic regulations, or social and legal restraints: and that the relative anonymity afforded by the driving situation would enhance the sort of behaviour which in other contexts would be considered anti-social. He also mentions with approval several studies on the personal values and also the psychodynamics of the driver—all factors which would be anything but temporary. In fact he obviously believes in the importance of studying the characteristics which he mentions—but just why studying these characteristics should be different from studying *accident proneness* is something which I, personally, cannot understand. But, then, I do not see the "repeater" argument either. In 1955 McFarland decided that it was best to call people with lots of accidents "repeaters' because they did not seem to have any distinctive *psychological* characteristics. But now they appear to have the psychological characteristics but still cannot be called "prone". This seems to me to be psychological hair-splitting.

And just what is the *statistical* difference between the repeater or someone who is accident prone? Presumably a *repeater* is someone who has two or three accidents (usually serious ones) and a *prone* person is someone who goes on and on repeating this sort of accident—that is if he lives to tell the tale. It would appear therefore that proneness in a statistical sense must only apply to the very extreme cases, the lucky survivors of *multiple serious accidents*. This must be what McFarland means for him to say: "Moreover, the statistical evidence is quite convincing that the influence of a proneness factor, where it can be detected in the accidents occurring within large groups, is quite limited."

But one of the important points at issue is, does someone from Europe, for instance, who reads such statements made by a well-known American writer know this? Does he know that in America only the very extreme cases are called "prone"? No, because *his* whole concept of accident proneness is quite different. To him it is a relative matter, not a dichotomy, and people can display all sorts of degrees of proneness.

And if you ask a European whether he believes in accident proneness, ten to one he will say yes—unless he has already been influenced by American opinion. But the thing is that he *is* being influenced—and very often by a whole lot of misconceptions, of which this is one. For he is taking the American pronouncements at face value. To him a statement like that of McFarland's means that the Americans have found that *individual differences* between drivers count for next to nothing in the total accident situation. Now this may be exactly what is meant by psychologists with a strong inclination to behaviourism and allied doctrines like specifism, but I very much doubt that it is what McFarland means, as he cannot have changed his whole philosophy since he and Moore wrote *Human Variables*.

But, nevertheless, this is just what Europe *thinks* he means—as can be seen from the next paper to be published, where Norman (U.K. 1962) incorporated McFarland's "views" into a report for a meeting of the World Health Organization, who then reprinted it and distributed it all over Europe.

Unfortunately, as well as possibly not quite understanding McFarland's views, Norman added yet another complication by incorrectly reporting the findings of Hakkinen. I do not for one moment think that this was his fault as, being a medical practitioner, he undoubtedly obtained his information from outside sources. But, as these inaccuracies are being perpetuated by being re-quoted in his name, I think he would be the first to wish to see them corrected—especially those concerning Hakkinen.

Norman starts his report by repeating McFarland's views which he interprets as being that great prominence has been given to the idea that some people are accident-prone—but that the validity of this idea, let alone its utility, does not appear to be borne out by research findings. As *corroborative* evidence of this, he cites what he apparently thinks are the actual findings of Hakkinen's study!

"The present position of knowledge is that statistical evidence does not indicate clearly whether there are individuals who have a consistently higher accident liability than average. It is possible that, since such differences in accident liability have not become evident after considerable study, they are not likely to be large, even if further research should demonstrate their existence.... Hakkinen (1958) in a study of bus drivers in Helsinki, found that individual drivers had an accident liability which remained constant in two successive four-year periods; the differences between individuals were not great. This work has been criticized by Smeed (1960) on the grounds that some of the methods used in the analysis are not satisfactory. Hakkinen was unable to find a reliable method of identifying drivers with high accident rates by means of laboratory tests; it is important to distinguish between knowing that such people exist and being able to identify them."

Unfortunately this is a very inaccurate description of Hakkinen's findings, with the big differences in the accident rates of his drivers, his highly predictive test battery, and his very convincing results.

In view of Norman's misconceptions and the inaccuracy of his information it is no wonder that a sort of puzzled note runs through his final summary of this section of his report. For this again seems to illustrate the dilemma in which someone outside the theoretical accident research field finds himself when confronted by two apparently irreconcilable lines of reasoning, his own common-sense thinking and seemingly irrefutable scientific "evidence".

"Whatever may be the truth about accident-proneness, it is certain that some drivers have repeated accidents while others have fewer than average. In the present state of knowledge it is probably best to use the term 'accident repeater' and to define such a person as one who has more than a given number of road traffic accidents in a given time. Action may then be taken to examine the records of the driver concerned and if necessary the driver himself. The improvement or elimination of accident repeaters would obviously be effective in reducing the number of accidents, but if the repeater condition is temporary, a new crop of accident repeaters might be found in successive time periods. It is possible that a small group of 'problem' drivers exists, but such a group has not yet been clearly identified."

If by now the reader is more than a little confused, then all I can say is that he has my deepest sympathy. It took me much painstaking effort to try and disentangle the web of who said what first, and who influenced whom—and I probably still haven't got it right. But I do not think that the minor details matter at all. All that does matter is that the foregoing extracts illustrate very clearly that up to this stage *not one single scrap of new evidence had been added since the movement for discrediting the idea of accident proneness started:* it was just the same old line of argument going round in circles and suffering a few sea changes in the process. Somehow I find it reminiscent of the tale of the author who sold the film rights of his book to Hollywood and was most indignant when he saw the premiere. So, with much sarcasm, he said to the producer: "Fine story you have here—do you mind if I use it for a book?" "Not at all," replied the producer, "as long as I can have the film rights."

CHAPTER 12

ERA OF DISBELIEF

THE next publication, this time from Belfast, Northern Ireland, and this time, at last, an original study, was a very comprehensive one, Cresswell and Froggatt's book *The Causation of Bus Driver Accidents* (1963). On the dust cover the publishers give an account of the scope of the book, which summarizes the authors' views and conclusions:*

"The term 'accident proneness' is widely used although few understand its precise meaning. It was coined by psychological research workers in 1926, and since then its concept—that certain individuals are always more likely to sustain an accident than others, even though exposed to equal risk—has seldom been seriously challenged.

"The present book, which contains the results of an exhaustive investigation into the road accidents incurred by bus and trolley-bus drivers in Northern Ireland over a period of four years, presents an alternative hypothesis which is considered to be more realistic in the context of road accidents. In this new model of accident causation every driver is assumed subject to 'spells' during which he is more liable to accident. The authors speculate that a 'spell' may be associated with temporary factors, such as domestic worries or ill-health, which can be imagined to lead to impaired efficiency. This model, unlike the theory of accident proneness, also allows for the occurrence of accidents primarily due to other road users. This is important because a driver is not always to blame for every accident in which he is involved.

"After subjecting the data to statistical analysis and conducting clinical examinations of certain drivers, the writers conclude that the validity of the concept of accident proneness is more than doubtful."

Opinions on the value of this study are somewhat divided. Haddon *et al.*'s *Accident Research* (1964) describes it as follows:

"Their work, moreover, reports the results of a highly sophisticated analysis of the accidents of a large population of bus drivers. On the basis of this analysis they conclude that their data do not support the contention that there were comparatively many, if indeed any drivers in the population who were 'accident prone'.

"This is but the latest evidence that the burden of proof that there are 'accident-prone' individuals must rest with those who defend the concept, since this most definitive study fails to provide evidence that such individuals exist."

A somewhat different opinion is expressed by the President of the Royal Statistical Society of England when he reviewed this book in the journal of that association (Irwin, 1964):

* From Creswell, W. L. and Froggatt, P., *The Causation of Bus Accidents*, 1963, Published by Oxford University Press for the Nuffield Provincial Hospitals Trust.

"As far as I know, this is the first text book devoted almost entirely to the personal factor in accidents. It may gain wide currency. For this reason it seems necessary to point out its less as well as its more satisfactory features. If it reaches a second edition it is hoped that any errors will be corrected, even at the cost of considerable re-writing."

Irwin then proceeds to show that the statistical evidence in Cresswell and Froggatt's study is as much, if not more, in favour of the concept of proneness than against it!

Other research workers with whom I have discussed this work not only agree with Irwin but feel that the actual study does not warrant very serious consideration because there are fundamental flaws in the data on which it is based. My co-author and I have to admit that we are in agreement with these latter opinions. In fact I, personally, am prepared to go further and say that this study is a classic example of what happens when, as Arbous says, people let their statistics do their thinking for them.

As a matter of fact, while reading this book I have several times had the feeling that the authors themselves do not take it very seriously either; that it is all, perhaps, one big Irish hoax, and that Cresswell and Froggatt are taking the whole self-involved psychological accident research world for a glorious ride. I have a mental picture of them sitting somewhere in Belfast, chuckling at the thought of all the accident psychologists, confronted with pages and pages of mathematical hieroglyphics representing the statistical rationale of the "spell" theory and, like the courtiers in Hans Andersen's story, *The Emperor's Clothes*, looking wise and enigmatic, and making profound remarks like: "sophisticated ... methodological ... elegant ... definitive". However, much as I would like to believe this, I really do not think it can be true. The authors did mention, tucked away near the end of the book, that the project was only "planned as a piece of purely academic research", but it still cannot be a satirical hoax for the main findings were later re-published in the *British Journal of Industrial Medicine* (Froggatt and Smiley, 1964). It seems, therefore, that we must endeavour to take them seriously too.

For the "spell" theory, as postulated by Cresswell and Froggatt as an explanation of how accidents occur, is in reality rather more bizarre than was indicated by the summary on the dust cover. Nobody would cavil at the idea that there are times when people are "below par" and that accidents might be more likely at these times. (Though there might be some who wish that it was not necessary for some drivers to behave as though they were permanently *above* par!) But certainly most people would have considerable difficulty in swallowing a theory which postulates that everyone has *exactly* the same chance of having a "spell", as spells are "rare" and "occur only by chance". But if they have difficulty in swallowing this theory, let them be grateful. They were almost asked to swallow an alternative theory (also with seventeen pages of statistical justification) which maintained that *every* accident must occur during a "spell" and that no accident could occur outside a "spell". Fortunately, however, although this theory had a nice statistical "fit"—often better in fact than the other one—even the authors apparently thought better of trying to substantiate this academic mirage and abandoned it.

But not so with the *pièce de résistance* of the theory. "Now perhaps a reason can be advanced for the conspicuous failure of the attempts to isolate the 'accident-prone' by psychological tests, in that when examined after the period of exposure to the risk of accident, the spell may have 'worn off'." (I am sorry to keep reverting to Hakkinen's study, but in view of his conspicuous *success* one wonders whether there is not perhaps something odd about those Finnish drivers. How come they got spell-bound so often and for so long? It must be something to do with the long winter nights.)

It seems a pity to have to leave these realms of fantasy and leprechaun-logic and get down to examining the factual evidence which caused Cresswell and Froggatt to jettison the theory of accident proneness in favour of their quaint "spell" theory. But even here we do not seem to be on very solid ground. For these reasons—as set out in the beginning of the book—constitute one of the shortest and sharpest accounts of the Rise and Fall of the Proneness Empire ever seen. (Even Irwin, in his very circumspect critical review, describes this history as "somewhat biased and occasionally incorrect in matters of fact"!) At the end of the book, the writers go over the whole history again in greater detail, and I think it would be as well to refer to both versions so as not to miss any of what a well-known American comedian would call the "darlin' bits".

According to Cresswell and Froggatt, accidents were first considered to be manifestations of some unpropitious deity (Latin quotation from Virgil). Later they were thought to be a matter of chance (French quotation from Poisson). Still later, during the First World War, Greenwood, Woods, and Yule suggested that human characteristics *might* play a role in accident causation. To explain this observation Farmer and Chambers introduced the idea of "accident proneness", namely that people are not equally likely to incur an accident even if exposed to equal risks. This personal accident proneness was considered by Farmer and Chambers to be relatively stable "in the sense that people who had a larger number of accidents than their fellows in one period tended to have more accidents in a subsequent period". As a result of statements such as these (say Cresswell and Froggatt, waxing lyrical if not logical), "few could cavil at the widespread acceptance of accident proneness as an immutable load to which the unfortunate possessor is chained as inexorably as Ixion to his wheel".

Such widespread acceptance of a theory just because it was plausible was, however, later shown to be most unjustified. Even up to the present day the proneness thesis has not been proved to be valid. Not that people have not tried to prove this—even by being tempted into drawing conclusions which their data hardly justify—like Wong and Hobbs in 1949, who studied some workers for two four-week periods and concluded that "accident tendency was a lifelong characteristic and that it appears to invade all aspects of life". People have even tried to introduce the most radical views on the subject, like Jones who said that accidents were caused by a person's "unconscious" interfering with his driving; or Adler who said that would-be suicides might consider being involved in accidents as a substitute for suicide.

But, despite these efforts, no proof of accident proneness as such was forthcoming. Even apart from this lack of scientific proof, say Cresswell and Froggatt, it would have been nice, from a practical point of view, if accident-prone people could have been identified. But no effective test or battery of tests was found; nor was any proof obtained that any particular characteristic, "from corporal dexterity to the psyche", was significantly correlated with accident experience; nor was it possible to show that removing the so-called "accident-prone" actually reduced accidents. (Extract from Adelstein's figures.)

And yet, for some unknown reason, some researchers seem to have gone on believing in proneness; believing that there are *a priori* differences between people with high or low accident rates. When you consider that "protracted" research has not demonstrated these differences more clearly, it seems "most disquieting that so many investigators have assumed that such differences must exist, if only they could be identified".

But even if these investigators are right (say Cresswell and Froggatt, apparently suddenly losing confidence and getting a mite hysterical), even supposing that such differences *do* exist: even supposing that *accident proneness* exists as a measurable and stable entity, then at least someone ought to set some temporal limits for it. "For example does it originate in adolescence, in childhood, or at birth; does it terminate at retirement or is it carried to the grave? On this and other basic properties, its promulgators are silent." (I know one "promulgator" who is silent: that one's got me beaten!)

However, continue Cresswell and Froggatt, stepping delicately over the recumbent forms of their adversaries, even though the concept of accident proneness as a human characteristic becomes less credible the more it is examined, certain facts remain. Accidents do indeed seem to be distributed in a manner which is not compatible with chance, and there usually does seem to be a *slight* correlation between accidents in one period and accidents in another. Some explanation other than proneness must exist. But to find this explanation, some new approach, some radically new approach, must be adopted.

Hence the "spell" theory. This theory can account for all the statistical facts: accidents in any one period are unevenly distributed because some people are in "spells" during this period and others are not: small positive correlations can be expected between the accidents of consecutive periods because "sufficient 'spells' can be imagined to straddle the junction between the consecutive periods and hence produce a small correlation". (Page 71 in case anyone does not believe that this quotation is correct.)

Working up to a grand climax, Cresswell and Froggatt say that one way and another their own theory, based on the concept of a human being as a creature of alternating efficiency and subject to "spells", appears to be a far more likely explanation of accident occurrence than the proneness one. Not only is it statistically acceptable, but it is also a far more reasonable hypothesis than proneness "which assigns to each driver the animus of a marionette", and is "hung like the albatross around each person's neck". (Apparently no one is expected to cavil at the implications of the "spell" theory, which seems to assign to each driver the animus of a Zombie!)

Such is the outline of the history, according to Cresswell and Froggatt, of the downfall of the accident-proneness concept and the rise of a new star in the North. In all fairness one must admit that what this history lacks in general accuracy is at least partially made up for by the picturesqueness of the prose. One is tempted to wonder whether, if the reputedly "cold and materialistic" North of Ireland can produce something of this calibre, what could not a writer from the "fey" Gaelic South produce if only he put his mind to it!

The authors, however, appear to be quite satisfied and, convinced now of the righteousness of their cause, proceed with the analysis of their own data. These data, to my mind, fail to justify the need for any complex statistical analysis whatever as they do not meet the primary requisite for a study on the personal factor in accident occurence, namely equality of exposure to risk. But as there may be people who dispute this view, let us deal with the study from two angles; what I have to say about the basic data, and what Irwin has to say on the validity of the conclusion drawn from that data.

For their data the authors rely on the total number of accidents recorded by six groups of bus and trolley-bus drivers employed by the two transit authorities who between them, supply the public transport for the whole of Northern Ireland. All the drivers used in the study had been exposed for the four consecutive years 1952–5. Because of the effects of age and experience the groups were restricted by excluding all the young or inexperienced drivers and those nearing retirement. The authors do not give any details of how this was done, but it seems as though any driver who at the beginning of the exposure period had less than three years' driving experience and was under 30 or over 50 years of age, was excluded. I may be wrong, but the authors give no details of how these important restrictions of the data were made—or of the relative homogeneity which this would produce.

The remaining drivers were allocated to six separate groups, each group representing drivers operating on a constellation of routes whose accident rates were regarded by the authors as providing adequate homogeneity of risk. On this question of eliminating any inequality of risk, Irwin says; "The authors have, of course, taken all possible steps to allow for this sort of inequality before analysing the data." Although I grant that they have taken some of the possible steps, nevertheless my considered opinion, backed by a great deal of practical experience of this particular problem, is that these steps were not anything like *adequate* to eliminate gross inequalities of exposure to risk. It even appears that the authors themselves are not anything like as confident on this point as they might wish to be.

TABLE 12.1. ACCIDENT RATES FOR THE AREAS COVERED BY THE BELFAST CORPORATION TRANSPORT AND THE ULSTER TRANSPORT AUTHORITY (DERIVED FROM CRESSWELL AND FROGGATT, 1963)

Group	Accident rate for period 1954–5
Belfast bus areas	32·6–74·5
Belfast trolley-bus areas	42·5–85·0
Derry city	51·0
Newry and Portadown	38·9–39·6
Ballymena (town and dist.)	13·0–16·1
Ulster areas (small towns and rural routes)	18·5–33·7

The routes driven by the drivers covered the whole of Northern Ireland and therefore involved everything from city driving to small-town and country driving. This is mirrored in the six groups chosen for the study. Each of these groups represented a number of different routes with differing accident rates. What information is available on these rates is given in Table 12.1 where I have regrouped the data from the various tables given in Cresswell and Froggatt. It will be seen that these rates differ very substantially. (The rate is per million miles driven.)

The authors say it is reasonable to presume that, as in most public transport authorities, there was sufficient interchange between duties to equalize the effects of driving on various days of the week, day versus night driving, peak traffic periods versus valley periods. This is a reasonable assumption, especially over a four-year period. But on the important matter of interchange between routes they were unable to obtain any information as duty rosters were only available for the last of the four years. All the authors can say is that it is *assumed* that drivers sampled all driving conditions equally, or that it was *postulated* "that the duty changes within each group were so frequent and so varied that they precluded any driver from contributing unduly to the accident rate of a route by reason of consistently driving on it". (A strange argument to use when the purpose of the study was to demonstrate the fallacy of unequal liability.) On this point I maintain that even without duty rosters there were certain checks which the authors could have made from the accident registers alone which would have enabled them to test some of these assumptions, (1) to make a list of the accidents on several *routes* so as to see whether the accidents were debited to a *whole lot of different drivers* or whether certain names appeared rather too often, and (2) to check the records of a number of *individual drivers* to ascertain the locale of their accidents, so as to see whether they had incurred them *on a number of different routes or on the same route*. But no such checks were in fact made. The interchange between routes was therefore merely postulated.

As an alternative it was suggested that the differences between the accident rates of the various routes in each group were not sufficiently great as to present any inequality of risk. In this I disagree so strongly that I think it would be best to examine some of the figures. Let us take the group Belfast City bus drivers. The areas in which they operated (which were themselves aggregates of routes) ranged in accident rate from 32·6 to 74·5 (plus a special route of 94·1 to which any driver could apparently be allocated). To establish whether the chance of a driver incurring an accident varied significantly between areas, the authors carried out a statistical analysis of variance (after transforming the accident rates to their square roots). This produced a variance ratio which the authors say was not significant at the 5% level. From this they concluded that *the chance of a driver incurring an accident was reckoned to be independent of the route over which he drove.* As a statistical procedure this may have its merits, and the authors say that it is usually used when the variable is likely to be unstable under repeated sampling. Analysis of variance or no analysis of variance I maintain, however, that there is not a single operator of public transport who would concede that differences like these represent equality of risk—they could not or else they would not produce such different rates. The authors themselves saw fit to be very critical of Hakkinen on this point and said that Smeed had "rightly questioned" his assumption that differences in the accident rates of routes was unimportant for his particular subjects. (In Hakkinen's case, the range in accident indices was only from 1·1 to 1·7 and he was able to demonstrate satisfactorily that the interchange between routes was sufficiently frequent to negate these differences). There are also a number of other complications such as there being no information available as to if or when the drivers were transferred from trams to buses; or the extreme unlikelihood, on the grounds of domicile alone, of constant interchange between drivers operating the country routes and routes in the bigger cities.

It seems that Cresswell and Froggatt are therefore on very weak ground. In fact, the authors themselves seem to be aware of the shortcomings of their data. For instance, on p. 47 they say: "With the Belfast groupings the accident rates varied considerably . . . suggesting a true heterogeneity to accident risk between some routes, but the data were insufficient to establish this as a fact." My contention is, however, that doubts of this nature do not entitle the authors to say on the *very next page*: "It seems reasonably certain that, as far as can be ascertained, all drivers within each grouping selected were indeed equally exposed to the risk of incurring an accident": or to omit *any mention whatever* of the possibility of inequality of exposure in their final conclusions where they make the unequivocal statement that their data provided little if any evidence of accident proneness.

However, let us grant that some people would disagree with me on this (though I very much doubt whether anyone with practical experience of transport operation would do so). So let us examine what Irwin has to say on the methods used in this analysis, and the validity of the conclusions reached—*even if the basic data are considered to be adequate.*

Irwin commences his detailed critical review of this study by examining the various analyses carried out by Cresswell and Froggatt, the one to which they devoted the most attention being the very much outmoded curve-fitting one of starting with the distribution of accidents in various time periods and testing for goodness of fit. The four distributions used were the Poisson (representing pure chance), the negative binomial (which could, they say, represent proneness), their "Long Distribution" ("spells" but no accidents outside "spells"), and their "Short Distribution" ("spells" plus chance-engendered accidents). This evidence is such that even Cresswell and Froggatt consider it somewhat ambiguous; but they nevertheless conclude that their Long Distribution and Short Distribution offered the most likely explanation of the facts, with the final preference going to the Short Distribution.

Irwin starts his critique of this analysis by demonstrating the fallacies both in the approach and in the conclusions drawn. Discussing the various definitions of accident proneness he says:

"However, in spite of all ambiguities, it would be most surprising if individuals did not vary innately in their tendency to accidents when exposed to the same risk. All living creatures exhibit some biological variation, in any character we like to examine. No one would doubt that there was a tendency for some men to be taller than others in adult life. But if their 'expected' statures were not too different, environmental circumstances in childhood or adolescence might well reverse the expected result.

"There is, in fact, a great deal of circumstantial evidence to suggest that the personal factor exists, though it may be relatively small compared with other factors. It does not follow that this can be definitely proven or disproven by the construction of mathematical models which lead to theoretical accident distributions. In fact, so far, the reverse seems to be the case. It is necessary to look rather more closely at the history and theory of the matter."

Irwin then examines the statistical theory underlying the four theoretical distributions and shows that Cresswell and Froggatt's Long Distribution could equally well arise if the number of accidents in each "spell" was *generated by proneness*. As the Short Distribution merely represents the addition of a certain number of chance-directed accidents, then this "*could also be interpreted as adding a general random risk to the 'proneness' mentioned*".

He then examines the performance of the four distributions in fitting the data. Here Cresswell and Froggatt had fitted the Poisson, negative binomial, Long and Short Distributions to eighteen sets of data. In general, says Irwin, the negative binomial, Long and Short Distributions all give a satisfactory fit (in fact, so does the Poisson in several groups, especially those where the number of subjects was small). "There is clearly nothing to choose between the fit of the Long Distribution and the negative binomial, and the Short Distribution seems to be rather worse than the Long." (The Short Distribution was the one representing Cresswell's and Froggatt's main hypothesis.)

Irwin then takes the argument a little further. We have seen, he says, that the Long and Short Distributions are capable of either a "spell" or a proneness interpretation. Examining the distribution of accidents in one period will not enable us to discriminate between them, but examining the distribution of two successive periods will. This, he says, is something which the authors should have realized.

"If their 'spell' hypothesis were true, the distribution in two different exposure periods should be completely independent. Thus the correlation coefficients between the accidents sustained by the same individuals in the two periods should be zero. This is contradicted by the data in Chapter 6. There are small but significant *positive* correlations; these have often been reported in the literature."

Irwin does not mention this, but in reality the authors made very heavy weather over these particular correlations, which ranged from 0·237 ($n = 708$) to 0·420 ($n = 79$). In various different parts of the book the correlations were attributed to:

(1) A certain number of "spells" straddling the two periods.
(2) A departure from the ideal in equality of risk.
(3) A departure from the ideal in controlling for age and experience.
(4) The presence of "a small group of accident-prone drivers, which (if it exists) is likely to be one whose numbers change as time goes on".
(5) The fact that the coefficient might be present now but would probably diminish with time, i.e. with an increasing gap between time periods. The words they use are: "The suspicion (and it can be no more) is that the value of the correlation coefficient does in fact decrease through time."

This latter explanation alone would, they feel, mitigate against the need to regard these positive coefficients as evidence of proneness. As Irwin points out, such a diminution of the correlation coefficient would be quite commensurate with proneness, "as any correlation due to the personal factors would tend to get more and more diluted by increasing changes in environmental conditions of a non-systematic nature, affecting different subjects differently and thus increasing the chance component".

Having dealt with the section devoted to correlation coefficients, Irwin then turns to Chapter 7, which deals with "repeaters" (here defined as drivers with one or more short time-intervals between accidents). He again reworks the relevant statistical theory and states that: "The authors draw the conclusion that the study of repeaters favours the 'random' hypothesis, and this is quite unwarranted. . . . If anything, this would tell in favour of, rather than against the proneness hypothesis."

Is it necessary to go on? I do not think so. As Irwin says: "Where simple statistical methods have been employed—for example, in studying the effects of age and experience and in the clinical study—the work is at its best, the inferences drawn are nearly always correct. Even here, occasionally, statistical techniques have been wrongly applied."

But it is on these very statistical procedures, especially the less simple ones, that the authors have relied to support their conclusion that there are not many, if any accident-prone drivers among the drivers they studied, and that, in fact, the concept of accident proneness was considered to be of doubtful validity. And these are the conclusions which are being perpetuated by re-quoting. Had these conclusions been reached solely on the basis of essays into advanced statistical theory, such errors might be understandable, if not pardonable. Statistical accident research requires considerable specialized knowledge. But what I personally feel is not pardonable at all is that the authors themselves were aware that their conclusions were not really justified. Right throughout the book one can see that they were aware of flaws in both their data and their reasoning. They knew that there were doubts that the groups were exposed to equal risk; they knew that there were doubts as to which hypothesis best fitted their own data, proneness or their "spell" theory; they knew that many of the reasons for deciding in favour of the latter were very shaky. They knew, in fact, that all they were doing was carrying out an academic exercise to see whether a new theory could be made to look as plausible as an old one. Their conclusions should therefore have been equally tentative and should have gone no further than saying that, on the basis of their own particular data, no definite conclusions could be reached. But instead, all the doubts they felt were hidden in the text and their conclusions were clear cut. For this reason I think that Irwin is too benign in his criticism of the book—though he does say that if it reaches a second edition he hopes that any errors will be corrected, even at the cost of considerable re-writing. What he does not appreciate, I think, is the damage that it can do in the meantime. Perhaps because he himself can see the statistical flaws so clearly, he feels that others will also see them. In this he is obviously wrong. In the first place many people, even accident research workers, lack the statistical knowledge; and, secondly, it seems that even the people who write about books on accident research do not necessarily read them properly. Take, for instance, Haddon et al. (1964). They are quite prepared to give wide circulation to *only the conclusions* of this book (which do not in fact fit the text) despite their own strongly expressed views that the constant repetition of *only the conclusions* of the early writers, "favoured the development of a folklore of accident proneness". It seems therefore that a book like that of Cresswell and Froggatt has its definite dangers. For it looks as though the current condemnation of accident proneness is being just as effectively perpetuated.

Before leaving the subject of Cresswell and Froggatt's book I think one must mention the aspect of their study which the authors call the "clinical" aspect, namely the individual examination of drivers with consistently good or consistently bad accident records. As justification for this study, the authors say;

"Few of the... bus drivers when observed over a period of four years, appeared consistently each year in the group with the worst accident experience. None-the-less the practical importance of identifying (if possible) drivers who were more likely than their colleagues to appear in such a group, at any time, justified searching for some characteristic, biological or otherwise, which might correlate with accident experience."

Many studies, they say, suggest that such differences exist, but on examining these studies it seems that in many cases either the data, or the techniques used, are not altogether acceptable. To support this, Cresswell and Froggatt describe, again with a rather obvious bias, a number of these studies and their results—with, as usual, the noticeable exception of the results achieved by Hakkinen. All Hakkinen's *negative* findings are described in detail, e.g. vision tests, personality inventory, intelligence tests, etc.; but the main battery of psychomotor personality tests and the high correlation between this battery and the accident criterion receives no attention at all. Cresswell and Froggatt say, in passing, that Hakkinen reported *some* differences between the performance of *some* of his group on *some* of his tests, but not others—which is undoubtedly the understatement of the year!

However, despite all the so-called negative evidence, Cresswell and Froggatt apparently decided that they had better investigate their own material to see whether any significant differences emerged between drivers with consistently high or consistently low accident rates. The subjects for this clinical study were chosen with great care and ingenuity, every high-accident "case" being matched by a carefully selected low-accident control. But, yet again, it seems that all this statistical expertise and care was wasted because of the hopeless inadequacy and unsuitability of the investigations made.

The clinical study consisted of an investigation of (a) biological functions, and (b) biographical data. The former consisted of tests for vision, phenotype, androgyny, and personality. The only significant results were that accident offenders among the Belfast *trolley-bus* drivers (not the bus drivers) were found to be significantly more androgynous. (The term "androgyny" is not clearly defined by the authors but is defined in the psychological dictionaries as " a tendency for the male body to resemble that of a female, and vice versa".)

Chronic accident *repeaters* (those with pairs of accidents with short time intervals between them) were *definitely* less fat and *possibly* less well-adjusted than the remainder.

On the matter of personality, the personality inventory showed that those designated as "possibly maladjusted" were more numerous among the *low-accident control group*, than among the accident offenders.

For some reason the authors decided that none of these rather strange results should be unequivocally accepted—the usual explanation being the unreliability of the tests.

The biographical-data project was done by interview. Sixty drivers were categorized, after interview, as either high-accident or low-accident types—"the interviewer using as criteria the general impact of the man's personality, background, opinions, 'interview behaviour', and 'clarity of answers'. Those who impressed as possessing qualities of the 'accident personality', as conceived by some previous writers were graded as accident 'cases'." The results of this exercise were that *62% of the drivers were classified incorrectly.*

Again, the authors do not claim that these results have any particular significance—except to say rather cryptically that the findings "have obvious implications". Instead they offer the twice-damning explanation: "This could suggest that the inexperienced interviewer should be cautious in predicting a driver's accident experience, whether previous or future, on impression at interview."

Despite the somewhat obvious shortcomings of this "clinical" study, and despite the fact that the authors appear to repudiate most of the findings, they nevertheless feel justified in saying that the clinical study supports their main contentions. These they sum up as being:

(1) That there were comparatively few, if any accident-prone drivers amongst the group which they had investigated.
(2) That the observed differences in the accident rates of these men must be due to their being "subjected to a greater number of environmental circumstances likely to produce distraction or disinterest". (A rather vaguely expressed conclusion, but presumably meant to imply that the drivers' faults were not in themselves but in their "spells".)

However, despite the stringent criticisms which I and others have levied against the Cresswell and Froggatt study, no one would contest that the appearance in the anti-proneness literature of an *original study* was a very welcome change. One may criticize the methods used or deny the justification for the conclusions reached. One may lament that so much meticulous work should be carried out on such unsuitable material. But the fact remains that it was original work. In fact, of all the ultra-critical publications of the time it was the only one where the authors set out to back their contentions with new data. As such, its appearance was a landmark. It is interesting to note, however, that this study (unless one counts Forbes' brief statistical reanalysis of the Connecticut data) is the only original study ever carried out where the authors do not lend support to the basic tenets of accident proneness. It is also interesting to note that in this one and only study the psychological author (Froggatt) would probably not *wish* to support the concept, purely on ideological grounds. In his later paper (1964) he talks of accident proneness as being "largely discordant with contemporary theories of human activity". So here again it appears that the primary opposition was an ideological one.

Returning to the United States, we again find evidence of the activities of the same group of psychologists connected with the Association for the Aid of Crippled Children. This time the New York study group had proposed, instead of a conference like that reported earlier, the preparation of a sponsored book on the behavioural aspects of accident research—a proposal which eventually led to the publication in 1964 of Haddon *et al.*'s *Accident Research* which has since been very widely circulated.

This was a major publication of some 750 pages, the purpose of which was "to bring together in a single volume significant studies in accident research and to embed these studies as examples in a text dealing with the methodology of accident research". The book will always remain a most valuable contribution to that research, for it contains a number of excellent studies which many workers in the field have wanted to read and been unable to obtain. It also contains some enlightening critical comment on these studies. As the authors point out, some of the criticisms may appear to be "unnecessarily harsh". But this, they feel, is justified, as their purpose is "not to denigrate good work by carping, but rather to demonstrate how an exciting and original approach can be invalidated or seriously damaged by inattention to basic principles of research methodology".

No doubt there are a number of readers of the book who feel that too strong an insistence on methodology has its drawbacks as well as its advantages. There are certain aspects of accident research which just do not lend themselves to the experimental methodological approach. In addition, methodology has its dangers, particularly in accident research where the available statistical techniques on which it has, perforce, to place such great reliance, are often woefully inadequate—even when the researchers know how to use them. Cresswell and Froggatt's study is a classic case in point. The authors of *Accident Research* were very impressed with this methodological study and were lavish in their praise. But, because they apparently had insufficient first-hand experience with accident rates in public transport to detect the flaws in the basic data and insufficient advanced statistical knowledge to detect the flaws in the statistical treatment of the data, they were unable to see that the praise they were bestowing might not be justified. Methodology, as such, is not enough: and to elevate it to the position of a *sine qua non* for research, without at the same time pointing out its dangers, is not necessarily the right way to direct the footsteps of those "newcomers to accident research" for whom the book is apparently mainly intended.

It would appear that Kaplan, who has made an intensive study of research methods, would agree with me on this. For in his book *Conduct of Inquiry* (1964, p. 406) he says:*

"Many behavioral scientists, I am afraid, look to methodology as a source of salvation: their expectation is that if only they are willing and obedient, though their sins are like scarlet, they shall be as white as snow. Methodology is not turned to only as and when specific methodological difficulties arise in the course of particular inquiries; it is made all-encompassing, a faith in which the tormented inquirer can hope to be reborn to a new life. If there are such illusions, it has been my purpose to be disillusioning. . . . There are behavioral scientists who, in their desperate search for scientific status, give the impression that they don't much care what they do if only they do it right: substance gives way to form. And here the vicious circle is engendered; when the outcome is seen to be empty, this is taken as pointing all the more to the need for a better methodology. The work of the behavioral scientist might well become methodologically sounder, if only he did not try so hard to be scientific!"

Certainly, in *Accident Research*, those studies which do not contain large quantities of statistics usually come in for a good deal of criticism—though much seems to depend on whether the study deals with an aspect of research of which the authors approve.

As the authors have deemed it necessary to be at times unduly "harsh" in their criticisms of certain studies they will, I feel, not take it amiss if their presentation of these studies also comes in for some rather harsh criticism.

My first criticism is that the book is a hotchpotch of studies on accidents incurred by

* From Kaplan, A., *Conduct of Inquiry*, 1964, published by Chandler Publishing Co., San Francisco, © Chandler Publishing Co. Reprinted by permission.

people of all ages and under all circumstances; and that the subject of accidents is discussed as though it were one homogeneous field. I feel this is not only unjustifiable, but merely makes the existing confusion more confounded.

A second criticism—and this is a much more serious one—is the cavalier way in which certain of the studies have been treated. I maintain that good work *has* been denigrated, not only by carping criticism, but by derogatory criticism, which is a very different matter—especially with studies which have been meticulously carried out and very conservatively presented.

My third criticism is the most serious of all, namely that I feel the matrix of comment in which the authors have embedded the studies is not one of impartial evaluation, but in many cases has a most pronounced personal bias. I feel that everyone is entitled to their own opinion, but I also doubt very much whether they are entitled to let that opinion intrude so blatantly into a book *which is intended as an instructional manual*. This is particularly the case with the section which concerns us most here, the section on accident proneness. In other parts of the book the authors have found it necessary to be critical, but in many cases constructive. The attitude has been: this is an interesting approach—let us see the different ways in which it has been tackled. In the section on accident proneness, however, the attitude is completely different. Here it is not a matter of considering the merits of an approach, it is a matter of denouncing an idea. The total unacceptability of the concept (to the *authors*) is stated right at the beginning of the chapter, and persists throughout.*

"What is meant by accident proneness? First we have to distinguish between accident repetitiveness and accident proneness. The former simply refers to the descriptive fact that some individuals have more accidents than others, a distribution statistic that is true for a great many other social, psychological, and medical phenomena. There can be no quarreling with this statistical truth, but this is not what is meant by accident proneness, although a large number of studies proceed as if this were the case. Rather, accident proneness is offered as the *explanation* of why this distribution occurs, and it is this point that has aroused first minor, and now major, protest. As a theoretical explanation of repeated accidents on the part of the individual, accident proneness is a *psychological* abstraction and, as such, it is assumed to refer to the existence of an enduring or stable personality characteristic that predisposes an individual toward having accidents.

"The critical words in this definition are the adjectives *enduring* and *stable*. Various researchers have attempted to identify such stable personality characteristics and have listed many unvalidated, negative personality traits, foremost among which are aggressiveness, impulsiveness, maladjustment, antagonism toward authority, immaturity, inconsiderateness, and hostility. Dunbar (1939), one of the prominent exponents of the accident proneness concept, so described the accident-prone individual, as did Tillmann and Hobbs in a study discussed later in this chapter.

"It should be obvious to the reader that so indiscriminate a listing of personality traits could hardly be expected to define a *single* type of individual. The list of distin-

* From Haddon, W., Suchman, E. A., and Klein, D., *Accident Research*, 1964, published by Harper & Row. By courtesy of the publishers, authors, and the Association for the Aid of Crippled Children.

guishing characteristics changes from study to study; the results concerning any single characteristic are inconsistent; and, in general, the correlations between personality characteristics and, hence, their predictive value, are extremely low. (Thorndike, 1951; McFarland, 1955; Goldstein, 1961.) The bulk of evidence indicates that there is no such thing as a single type of 'safe' or 'unsafe' individual. Rather, each individual has a *range of behavior*, any portion of which may be safe or unsafe, depending on the environmental hazards to which he is exposed. Thus, instead of a single type of accident-prone individual, there may be many reasons why some individuals may incur more accidents than others.

"For example, individuals may vary considerably: (1) in their exposure to hazards; (2) in their sensory, neural, and motor functioning; (3) in their capacity for correctly recognising and making judgements concerning hazards; (4) in their experience and training; and (5) in the extent to which they are exposed to pertinent social and other environmental stresses. In addition, individual variations in susceptibility to trauma... may bias the data when accidents are defined in terms of the occurrence of given degrees of structural damage or personal injury. Finally, because individual variations in accident rates may result completely from chance, it is never adequate to show merely that a small fraction of similarly exposed individuals accounts for a disproportionate share of accidents. Rather, it is necessary to demonstrate that the disproportion observed is greater than that which would be commonly expected on the basis of chance alone. This has been overlooked by many, if not most, of those who have concerned themselves with accident proneness.

"From this list it should be clear that accident proneness—as a psychological concept—must be viewed as only one possible explanation for individual variations in accident rates. This is not to deny the occasional usefulness of the concept but to indicate that there are other explanations which must always be considered."

Reading this, I found I was in complete disagreement with (among other things) the statement made by the authors: "The bulk of the research indicates that each person has a *range of behavior*, any portion of which may be safe or unsafe, depending on the environmental hazards to which he is exposed." On the contrary, I know of no research study which even mentions such a conclusion. This seems to me to be a purely behaviouristic (or "specifistic") interpretation of the fact that a number of different characteristics have been found to be associated with accidents. The portion of the text which follows this sentence: "Thus, instead of a single type of accident-prone individual . . . ", also appears to be just a statement of the authors' personal views; and as the meaning does not seem very clear, not wishing to misinterpret them, I wrote to the authors asking for further information. Mr. Klein was good enough to reply on behalf of his co-authors:

"Essentially we believe that attempts to identify accident-prone individuals are less fruitful than attempts to identify those characteristics in the individual and in the environment that are likely to precipitate accidents. Perhaps an example will make this clear. If a state of frustration (either general or highly specific) leads to accident-inducing behavior in certain environments, it is true that within those environments those individuals who are chronically or continuously in a state of frustration are likely to have more accidents than those who are not. But we believe that there are more people who have accidents in these environments because of temporary and transitory frustration and that hence it is more useful to identify the significant variable (frustration) than to identify the 'accident-prone' individual who has repeated accidents because he is constantly frustrated. In short, more accidents are attributable to temporary characteristics in 'normal' people than to stable characteristics in 'accident-prone' people.

"There is no question that there are innate differences among people in neural and motor functioning (as a consequence of minimal brain damage, to cite only one example), but we believe that these differences do not account for more than a small minority of accidents. As for differences in the capacity for recognizing and judging hazard, this depends so strongly on the immediate environment and the current psychological state of the individual that any generalization would be questionable indeed.

"We have not found, in your work or in the work of others, convincing documentation on accident-proneness as a stable characteristic of individuals or that repeated accidents are not largely attributed to differences in exposure."

The most important feature of this statement of the authors' views is contained in the last paragraph. It appears that the authors' objection to the concept of accident proneness is a fundamental one, in that they have "not found . . . convincing documentation on accident-proneness as a stable characteristic of individuals *or that repeated accidents are not largely attributed to differences in exposure*".

To proceed, then, with the chapter, which continues by saying "The concept of accident proneness has been criticized on statistical, methodological and theoretical grounds. Some of these criticisms are summarized in the following report." They then reproduce that portion of Suchman and Scherzer's book *Current Research in Childhood Accidents* (1960) which I have earlier quoted in full, the gist of which is as follows: that there is no adequate proof of the validity of the concept of accident proneness (which is defined as an extension of a psychiatric concept that some people inflict self-injury through deliberate accidents): that unless the accident-prone individual can be identified as a "meaningful type", a "psychological entity", then it would be better for accident research "to concentrate on the specific causes of repeated accidents and to restrict the concept of accident proneness to the limited number of psychiatric cases in the total population of accident repeaters". None of the authors express any disagreement with the views given in this article, and the chapter proceeds as follows:

"The foregoing discussion should suffice to indicate that we are dealing here with a greatly misunderstood concept. In view of this, and in view of its considerable influence on accident research, we are reproducing below three of the early reports dealing with the subject. We do this not only for historic purposes but also because the first two remained the best work by far that had been done on the problem until the recent work of Cresswell and Froggatt. . . .

"We begin with the classic paper in the field. As so often happens with new concepts, its originators state their case with greater moderation than their disciples. Greenwood and Woods did not describe some workers as 'prone' to accidents but developed the thesis that a small minority of individuals have greater numbers of accidents than would be expected on the basis of chance alone. This theoretical formulation led others to undertake hundreds of such studies and hence served as the basis for much of the research on accident proneness."

The bulk of the rest of the chapter is taken up with long excerpts from some of the well-known studies of Greenwood and Woods, Newbold, Farmer and Chambers, Tillmann, the dissertation of Arbous and Kerrich, and a paper on children's accidents by Krall. Unfortunately the main emphasis is on the very early and now outdated studies: and although there must be many people who appreciate the opportunity to see these excellent papers, to my mind it is a great pity that none of the recent studies were included. In fact, I think that their omission, particularly the omission of studies like those of Conger, Malfetti, and particularly that of Hakkinen, is a very serious omission indeed. The most recent of the studies on accidents other than children's accidents is Tillmann's, which was published in 1949; Arbous and Kerrich published their critique in 1951. This leaves a gap of *thirteen years* during which research on accident proneness had been anything but stagnant. To my mind it seems very misleading that a book published in 1964 should take no cognizance of that research. Even if the authors had only wished to illustrate the methodology of various approaches to the investigation of accident proneness, it seems that it would have been more representative (as well as more informative) to reproduce portions of Hakkinen's study rather than *three* papers published as long ago as 1919, 1926, and 1939! Hakkinen's study is one of the most comprehensive, as well as one of the most methodologically sound studies ever carried out. Even if these other studies had not been reproduced in this chapter (Conger's study is in fact reproduced elsewhere in the book), at least their findings should have been mentioned. The chapter should not have been written as though they never existed and as though research on accident proneness had virtually foundered on the rock of Arbous' and Kerrich's critique in 1951.

However, to return to the text of the chapter, the commentary in which the three earliest studies are embedded reveals such an odd interpretation of these works that one wonders at times whether the authors have, in fact, read the actual reports. After all, it is one thing to attempt to demolish the research work of fifty years by means of a somewhat fanciful history, like Cresswell and Froggatt's; it is still feasible if a little more difficult when your weapons are correlation coefficients, as in Goldstein's paper; but to present some very good *actual studies* and then expect the reader to ignore the *evidence which they contain*, seems strange indeed. And yet this is exactly what the authors do.

In the first place they seem to find that it is quite in order to praise the methodology of these early studies without having to accept any of the evidence they produce of stable differences between people's liability to accidents. And in the second place, they seem to feel it is necessary to interpret any attempt at investigating these stable differences by means of any kind of test (whether it be an intelligence test, a pursuit meter, or a dotting test) as a failure to establish that accident proneness has anything to do with *personality*.

"Like that of Greenwood and Woods, Newbold's report embodies qualities often lacking in current research, the detailed attention paid to exposure factors . . . [etc.] shows a mastery of scientific methodology that might well be emulated today. As we shall note later, the weakness of these early researchers lies not in their methodology or their statistical treatment, but in their theoretical interpretation of the findings as indicative of a stable personality characteristic called accident proneness by later workers."

And again:

"Nonetheless only their conclusions are considered and quoted by many concerned with accident research. This has favoured the development of a folklore of accident proneness, which does not correspond closely to the evidence on which it is said to be based. As more and more personality tests were used in subsequent research, the contradictory and confusing findings that resulted brought the accident proneness concept advanced by Farmer and Chambers into disrepute among informed research workers, but not among the public."

(If any reader of *Accident Research* has cause to wonder why, throughout this particular chapter, the authors appear to see a "personality" bogeyman behind every accident proneness bush, he is reminded that this would be a very natural reaction from anyone whose particular psychological orientation is as apparent as that of the psychological members of the authorship trio.)

It seems to be with a certain amount of relief that the authors then turn from the actual studies to the paper of Arbous and Kerrich (1951). But here, too, some very strange interpretations occur. Describing it as "one of the most decisive critiques of the accident-proneness concept", they say:

"Although there are some who believe this analysis should have sounded the death knell for the accident proneness approach, a more reasoned evaluation would consider it a warning against the indiscriminate use of this concept to explain all cases of repeated accidents. For one cannot claim, on the basis of current evidence, that no cases of accident proneness exist. At the present stage of knowledge, we might best conclude that accident proneness as an explanation for any major proportion of repeated accidents is unwarranted but that, as a clinical phenomenon limited to some individuals, it may have some validity. . . .

"Although there is good reason for skepticism about accident proneness on a statistical basis, the concept may nevertheless have utility for the clinical differentiation of an extreme type of individual who, for psychological reasons, may seek self-harm through incurring an accident. Arbous previously made this point about the possibly valid limitation of the concept to clinical cases."

I think anyone reading this commentary after reading the actual paper would just scratch his head in bewilderment. However, I have pointed out some of the discrepancies in my earlier review of Arbous' work, and both Arbous and Kerrich take up the cudgels themselves in their personal statements in Chapter 13. It would appear that the interpretation which the authors of *Accident Research* have given to this very good and very clear monograph, bears little resemblance to the original.

Haddon *et al.* then introduce yet another different aspect of the accident situation, namely the study of accident injury among children, and quote in full the very good paper,

"Personality characteristics of accident repeating children" by Krall (1953). This study is concerned with the investigation of certain personality characteristics of accident-repeating children and consists of a clinical examination of a group of repeaters as compared with a control group who were accident-free. Krall's conclusions contain some very interesting findings on the accident-repeater children, especially their aggressive tendencies, their poor control, their lack of realism, and the fact that their home background appeared to be less satisfactory than that of the accident-free children.

This study is rather severely criticized, being described as "lacking in methodological rigour", and displaying the type of shortcomings "which characterize the bulk of the clinically-orientated accident proneness literature".

The authors then turn to Tillmann's study "The accident-prone automobile driver" (1949). Here they apparently feel it is necessary to criticize the study strongly before they even introduce it.

"This widely quoted study is typical of much of the research on accident proneness. Its authors studied groups of Canadian taxi drivers with high and low accident rates in terms of a number of social and psychological characteristics. They considered the differences in personality structure as being indicative of accident proneness. On this basis, they claimed that the accident-prone individual is characterized by marked intolerance and aggression toward authority, dating back to early childhood. In comparison with a group of 100 accident-free individuals, a group of 96 drivers with a record of four or more accidents was found to contain more individuals known to social and law-enforcement agencies. From these results, the authors conclude that 'a man drives as he lives'.

"Although this study illustrates interestingly that automobile driving habits reflect an individual's general behavioral attributes, it does not really test accident proneness as a psychological hypothesis. It provides no evidence that the social and psychological differences found between the high- and low-accident groups represent stable, inherent, personality factors. It demonstrates that people who have accidents differ from those who do not, but one can conclude very little from this about the nature of the accident-proneness process."

Most of Tillmann's study is then reproduced, after which the stringent and somewhat inaccurate criticism continues: "theoretically inconclusive . . . methodologically inadequate", etc. Even the detailed personal evidence which Tillmann obtained from the social agencies, as well as from actually working with his taxi-driver group for three solid months, is dismissed as "a personality measure of unknown validity and reliability".

The authors then continue with a brief reference to the only study on accident proneness with which they apparently can find no fault, that of Cresswell and Froggatt, and which they feel, "provides the most nearly definitive review of the accident-proneness concept and literature published to date. It should be consulted by all those concerned with accidents from any point of view." Referring to the fact that in "this highly sophisticated analysis" the authors found no evidence of accident proneness, they conclude: "This is but the latest evidence that the burden of proof that there are 'accident-prone' individuals must rest with those who defend the concept, since this most definitive study fails to provide evidence that such individuals exist." The authors then present their final summing up:

"The foregoing studies indicate that accident proneness is a psychological abstraction based upon a statistical frequency. As often happens when a statistical distribution is given theoretical significance, the concept quickly assumed much more meaning than was originally intended. The unacceptability of the concept of accident proneness in a technical sense should not, however, be taken to mean that personal factors do not play an important role in accidents. In fact, rejecting the concept of accident proneness, with its implication of a global personality trait, forces one to search for many different psychological factors and their significance in given environmental circumstances."

There are, indeed, some strange and rather unfortunate features about this particular chapter of *Accident Research*. In view of its hypercritical tone, its omissions and inaccuracies are most regrettable. But, in my opinion, more regrettable still is the fact that the authors have chosen to convert one whole chapter of a book which is ostensibly a teaching manual into a platform for their own personal views. Surely the more logical, and more scientifically acceptable method would have been to present the arguments on both sides of this complex and controversial subject and let the reader do a little thinking for himself? Possibly the authors feel that by presenting studies containing "so-called" evidence in favour of the concept, and then questioning, if not refuting the validity of the findings of these studies, they *are* making people think. If so, it seems that they may yet succeed in this aim. For the obvious contrast between the open-minded, eclectic, and realistic tone of these studies and the dogmatic, parochial, and ultra-theoretical tone of the text in which they are embedded is sufficient to make anybody think—but not necessarily along the desired lines. In fact, the final results of this thinking could easily be that the attitude displayed in the actual *studies* is: "*Here is an important problem: it is obviously a many-sided one: but as accidents happen to people or are caused by people, then investigating these people, by any method we can, should help.*" In contrast, the attitude displayed in the *text* may appear to be: "*Here is a theoretical premise, a hypothesis: we maintain that it is right, therefore everyone else's hypothesis must be wrong. By the way, what was that problem you were talking about?*"

For, except for the excellent papers which it contains, where *does* this chapter of *Accident Research* get us on the urgent question of how to reduce accidents? It is, in fact, the ultra-theoretical atmosphere of the whole chapter which I find to be one of the most disturbing features. If you *have* to teach researchers how to research, then would it not be an idea to teach them to keep in some sort of touch with reality? To teach them that they are supposed to be working towards the practical aim of doing something with the accident situation *as it is in real life*, and not as it may appear in some fantasy of "elegant" research?

It seems, however, that the authors are occasionally aware of this fault. For in another section of Suchman's (1960) paper, he made the following rather revealing statement in describing the various methods which could be used for undertaking accident research (the italics are mine):

"But we must not lose sight of the fact that we want this knowledge for the purpose of reducing accidents. In the final analysis, the validity of our basic research will depend upon our success in translating this knowledge into prevention programs. In doing basic research on the behavioral science aspect of public health, *there is always the danger that one may forget* that the ultimate objective of such research is not so much to advance our knowledge of human behavior as it is to apply such knowledge to the public health problem which originally gave rise to our concern. Research and the application of knowledge gained from it must proceed hand in hand."

Personally I find it rather alarming that researchers need to be taught how to research, let alone not to forget that research should have some practical application. But it seems rather sadly apparent that some people think they do. This being so, then I think a little further word of warning for future "newcomers to accident research" might be in order.

If you are going to follow the line of reasoning advocated by this "new" thinking on accident causation, then presumably research will have to be carried out to substantiate the assumptions made by writers such as the authors of *Accident Research*. Assumptions such as: " . . . in fact, rejecting the concept of accident proneness, with its implications of a global personality trait, forces one to search for many different psychological factors and their significance in given environmental circumstances." Or " . . . attempts to identify accident-prone individuals are less fruitful than attempts to identify those characteristics in the individual and in the environment that are likely to precipitate accidents."

For let it be noted that these hypotheses *still have to be experimentally substantiated.* At the moment they are merely what the authors, in criticizing Greenwood, themselves rather scathingly call "a diagnosis of exclusion". But—and here comes the rub—the path of such validation (to be carried out presumably under conditions of strict experimental methodology) is going to be a thorny one indeed. *For any given environment*, these characteristics will have to be investigated, one by one. Don't ask me how, but they will; with *identical environments* now instead of *comparable exposure*; with subjects, let us say, of known frustration tolerance; with subjects matched (according to the authors' own demands) for all sorts of variables such as sex, age, and sociological background; with the criterion containing enough accidents to make it reliable; etc. And even if it is possible to achieve this, then what information will the study yield—statistically speaking, of course, since we are apparently not interested in any other type of information? Frustration, for example. This cannot be the only factor involved in accidents: there must be many. So what will a study on frustration yield? If you are lucky, one *small* positive correlation coefficient—like all the other *small* positive coefficients which have been so summarily dismissed before. And even if in *this* particular instance this small coefficient is regarded as having some meaning, then how is it going to be interpreted? That an element of frustration is present at some specific place or under specific traffic conditions? But *is* such a conclusion justified? Remember that a finding being commensurate with common sense means nothing at all: so there is no reason to think that your conclusion is going to be considered *scientifically* acceptable just because asking the "cop" on the corner would have produced the same answer.

And if you are going to ensure that your "research and the application of knowledge gained from this research should proceed hand-in-hand", then how are you going to apply your findings? Remove the frustration from the environment? Try passing on this new pearl of wisdom to the traffic engineers and see what happens. As the innkeeper said to Don Quixote:

> But oh, when you do,
> What will happen to you,
> Thank God I won't be there to see!*

Or are you going to tackle the drivers? Condition all of them to be less frustrated? Ah, now perhaps here is something you could get your teeth into. More conduct education, perhaps, or more driver education? But then the effectiveness of *this* will still have to be experimentally and methodologically validated. So there you go again.

No, I feel that budding researchers (and budding critics, too, as it is now apparently becoming the fashion to preface even an original study with criticism of all previous studies) are also entitled to the warning that people who live in glass houses should not throw stones. If you are going to condemn every assumption of anyone whose views are different from yours, and criticize every aspect of every study which they have painstakingly carried out, then you must appreciate that your own unborn research projects, and your own "inconclusive findings" may possibly meet with a similar fate. It is no good feeling that you are safe because you are on the majority bandwagon. There will come a time —and I predict that it is not too far off—when a number of people who have devoted years of work to an effort to contribute to the world's knowledge on accident causation will suddenly decide that if accident research is going to be turned into a shooting match, with all the shooting coming from one side, then they are going to get in on the fight too—and *you*, O budding researcher, are going to be right in the firing line!

However, I hope—and I think—that these warnings are not really necessary. I think that the research workers who actually contribute most to practical, applicable knowledge, and whose point of view will win out in the end, are those who research for a purpose. They research because they believe in what they are doing; they are not just looking for a grant, or trying to get another degree, or keeping up a quota of publications. I think there will always be such people, and that they will not need to be taught how to research. They will bark their shins and learn their lessons in the hard school of reality—but this will not stop them. They will carry on because the problem they are working on, like the accident problem, is a very real one.

However, to get away from my own personal viewpoint (which I must add has only intruded here because I get so impatient with perpetual negativistic theoretical criticism) and to return to a more general assessment of the book, *Accident Research*, as apart from the chapter on accident proneness.

The book itself is a very important contribution to research on road accidents as well as to research in other accident fields. It contains many excellent studies and, where the approach is less biased than in the proneness chapter, the commentary in which they are embedded, though extremely critical, is still informative. Probably it is the triple authorship which results in the commentary in different sections displaying not only marked

* From the stage production *Man of la Mancha*, play by Dale Wasserman, lyrics by Joe Darion.

differences in tone, but also such divergent and often almost contradictory attitudes and points of view. It is certainly very difficult to reconcile the views expressed in the accident proneness chapter (which virtually denounces the idea that accidents can be associated with any enduring personal characteristics) with many of the statements made in other parts of the book. In fact, throughout the book there is evidence that there are significant differences in the approach which the three authors adopt to the question of accident research—certain of them having a much broader and more eclectic approach than others.*

To continue, however, with the various publications which influenced the development of the current thinking on the thorny question of accident proneness. There were others besides the ones mentioned here, like Haight's "Accident proneness, the history of an idea" (1964) where his contention was that the idea was now meeting the just fate of a once-popular myth. (He talks of the "universal discredit into which the subject has fallen among scientists".) Here the attack was a statistical one. But as Haight was still belabouring such outmoded debating points as the negative binomial distribution, his arguments do not warrant any detailed examination. His psychological knowledge is unfortunately equally out of date, for the last publications he mentions are those of Adelstein and Arbous and Kerrich, odd snatches of which he quotes with great relish and very little concern for context. The work of the traffic officials comes in for equal censure. The policy of prosecuting people for traffic violations is, he feels, unjustified, such infringements being "actions, harmless in themselves, which are supposed to 'cause' accidents". He thinks the connection between them is anything but clear "although as much effort has been made to prove this as was made to prove accident proneness". Nor does he feel that there is any justification for singling out people on the basis of their accident records. "Even if those persons with an accident liability 100 times the average were segregated, it would hardly be justified to deny them the right to drive."

On the face of it, one should not take a publication like this seriously—except that although Haight is a Californian, his paper was published in Italy, thereby spreading the belief that "the Americans no longer believe in accident proneness". And the addition of his name to the growing list of references in bibliographies of people who have "disproved the validity of the concept" shows that somewhere, someone is taking his pronouncements at face value. And, what is more, the constant repetition of this sort of paper, deriding (on so-called scientific grounds) the idea that the driver is in any way to blame for the accident situation, constitutes one of the greatest dangers to the efforts of the practical traffic officials.

Such are the best known of the critical reviews of the sixties. When you are thoroughly *au fait* with your subject and aware of all the major research projects which have been carried out, you can immediately see the obvious flaws in the arguments put forward in these now fashionable critiques. But apparently in order to do this (judging by the effect these publications have had and the influence they have exerted) you really do need to know your subject and to be prepared to study the full reports on these research

* Haddon, for instance, has recently said (Oct. 1968, *Traff. Dig. Rev.* **16** (10), 14): "It seems that the same people who through their carelessness and irresponsibility cause serious crashes and those who commit overt, deliberate acts of violence quite often have the same characteristics, and society must try to find out what these common denominators are. I think that we can and should bring our research resources to bear on this most serious problem, and that we can someday hope to get useful results."

projects in the original. Obligatory as this should be for critics of accident research, the layman, or even the lay official, cannot be expected to do this—he has neither the time, nor the opportunity, nor the necessary background scientific knowledge. And he is the person who, without full knowledge of the facts, is apparently the one who is being influenced. The most obvious example of this is, of course, the trend in American accident-prevention policy. A recent article by Goen (1968) which appeared in *Traffic Safety* was entitled, "Is the driver traffic's 'forgotten man'?" Goen says that two years after the foundation of the new National Highway Safety Bureau it is obvious that no new safety measures involving the driver are even contemplated. He feels there are several reasons for this which can be inferred from prevailing opinions in the traffic-safety literature, from the research projects of the National Highway Safety Bureau, and from the speeches of people in the Department of Transport. One is a reaction to the "blame the driver" philosophy which is reputed to have, for too long, distracted attention from other more necessary measures. Haddon, for instance, "has recently pointed out the fallacy in assuming that because drivers cause most accidents, countermeasures emphasizing the driver should have priority".

"The second reason is based on the currently prevailing opinion in the traffic safety community that the 'accident proneness' concept is not valid. The concept, previously widely believed, was that a small group of accident-repeater drivers was responsible for most accidents, or at least a large proportion of them. This notion has been supposedly demonstrated to be untrue in the following way. If all drivers involved in accidents in one year were removed from driving, the number of accidents the following year would be reduced only slightly. Although the point is valid, it is not sufficient to rule out the hypothesis that high-risk drivers can be identified and that changing the driving behavior of this group, or preventing them from driving, could effect a large reduction in accidents and fatalities. Unfortunately, Dr. Robert Brenner, the deputy director of the Highway Safety Bureau, has indicated lack of interest in measures dealing with high-risk drivers on the basis that the accident proneness concept has been discredited."

Although Goen, for one, obviously disagrees strongly with the prevailing attitude, the trend of America's current safety literature undoubtedly shows that the driver is, for the moment at any rate, most definitely "traffic's forgotten man".

But the trend is spreading to other countries as well, a concrete example being an official document which has recently been published in Holland under the auspices of the Ministry of Transport—a document which has already aroused scientific protest in that country. This document, *Bÿdragen voor de Nota Verkeersveiligheid* (1965), is a comprehensive report on traffic safety, and the particular section with which we are concerned is based on a subsidiary report supplied by the SWOV (the Netherlands Road Safety Research Foundation) which acts as official scientific adviser to the Minister in this sphere. A translation of the relevant excerpts is as follows:

"Statistical research on the matter of accident proneness has not indicated that this susceptibility can be ascribed to *permanent* characteristics in the driver. For the most part the explanation seems to lie in *temporary* characteristics (age, lack of experience, etc.), in the traffic environment, and in chance.

"The percentage of the total accidents in which persons with a high measure of accident proneness (due to permanent personal characteristics) is involved, is slight. The exclusion of this small group of accident-prone persons (a group which can only be identified with difficulty and which constantly changes) would do little to affect traffic safety throughout the country." (References: Goldstein, 1961a and b; McFarland, 1955; Ouweleen, 1964; Thorndike, 1951; Hakkinen, 1958; Walbeehm, 1960; Forbes, 1939.)

Note: Both Hakkinen and Ouweleen have been amazed that they should be quoted *in support* of such a statement. Ouweleen says that he does not even know to what paper the 1964 reference applies, as there was no such publication.

And, in a later part of the report:

"Moulding of traffic users must be orientated more toward actions than toward conscious attitude. . . .

"Research in other countries has indicated that there is little or no correlation between the attitudes of road users and the incidence of accidents. (Goldstein, 1961a and b; Schubert, 1965.) [One feels that both these authors, too, might be a little surprised at these particular references.]

"The characteristics of the individual, as a road user, which are relevant to traffic safety can be divided into temporary aspects such as age, alcohol, nutrition, and fatigue, and to permanent aspects such as acuity of vision and reaction time."

The publication of this report immediately called forth a protest from Van der Burgh who, in a document sent to the Minister of Transport and later (1969) published in *Psychologie* said that the *Nota Verkeersveiligheid* was very misleading, as it was based on information which was not only incorrect in certain places, but also very out of date: the findings of researchers such as Goldstein and Schubert had been wrongly interpreted: the valuable work of earlier researchers such as Tillmann and Hobbs, Malfetti, Lauer, McGuire, Bernard, Steffen, etc. had been overlooked: and findings from the important work done by recent researchers such as Hakkinen, Shaw, and Sichel had been completely omitted. Inclusion of these findings would have forced the authors of the *Nota* to change their thinking. Criticism of scientific research, said Van der Burgh, should display the same regard for accuracy and impartiality as is to be found in the research itself. It should not contain as many errors and omissions as this report did. Nor should policy decisions be based on such an unscientific presentation of the facts.

Apart from Holland, West Germany, too, is being affected. There, despite the fact that the accident situation is considered to be sufficiently serious for each federal area to have its own Medical-Psychological Institute for the examination of traffic offenders, I am told, by traffic psychologists there, that there is an increasing tendency to "think American", to discourage research on the psychology of the driver, and to turn the spotlight of public attention off the driver and on to the highway and the vehicle.

And this is happening in other places, too. I know that on my travels round the world in connection with accident prevention I was constantly meeting people who said: "Well, none of the American research findings seem to support accident proneness." And comments like this can be found over and again in lay journals and newspapers. But, strangely enough, these remarks are often embedded in articles dealing with the need for enforcing speed limits or disciplining unruly drivers—apparently because the people in countries with high accident rates cannot believe that anyone could seriously mean that there is no difference between one driver and another, and that the accident situation is largely the work of the NORMAL driver. For here the irony of the whole situation seems to be that the weight of "American research opinion" is being turned against itself. For apparently the way the layman chooses to interpret this opinion is to say: "Look, the Americans have now proved that it is quite untrue that anyone is just mysteriously 'prone' to accidents through no fault of his own. So let's get after all those reckless and dangerous drivers who can be seen on our roads and who are involved in so many of the accidents and do something about *them*."

Which all points yet again to the depressing amount of muddle and confusion which surrounds the whole question of accident proneness—but also perhaps suggests the not-so-depressing thought that those countries most in need of effective practical accident prevention policies may not be too drastically side-tracked from implementing these policies by America's "new" theoretical thinking on the subject. Not only does it seem probable that that much-despised commodity, common sense, will continue to prevail in practical circles, but also that the "new" thinking is not necessarily going to prevail in scientific circles either. There is obviously going to be a good deal of opposition, not only to the validity of this new way of thinking but to the manner in which it has been brought about. For the objections which Van der Burgh voiced on the way in which the findings of accident research have been presented and interpreted in Holland, are equally applicable to the publications reproduced in the last two chapters. Criticism of research findings is quite in order. The very fact that a research worker is prepared to publish his findings in a scientific journal shows that he is also prepared to submit them for inspection and open discussion. But Van der Burgh is quite right in saying that such criticism of scientific research should maintain the same high standard of accuracy and open-mindedness as is demanded of the original researcher. And it stands little chance of ultimate survival if it does not do so. No wholesale condemnation of a scientific concept can for long be considered as valid if it relies only on a selective (and possibly inaccurate) quoting of research findings. It must present the other side of the argument too—and be able to contest it. Conviction comes from strength—not from weakness.

As matters stood at the end of 1964, the case for declaring the concept of accident proneness to be either totally invalid, or at best of very limited utility, was a palpably weak one. In my opinion it still is, as in the intervening years no attempt has been made to take cognizance of any of the research findings supporting the concept and its usefulness. But I am fully prepared to concede the fact that since that date new evidence has come to light which, dependent on the interpretation put on it, could be said to give some substance to the arguments of the detractors of the concept. Up to the end of 1964 the detractors were relying mainly on negative criticism, the only positively stated evidence from actual research studies being that derived from Cresswell and Froggatt, and Forbes' re-analysis of the Connecticut data. The intervening years have, however, seen the publication of the reports of the Research and Statistics Section of the California Motor Vehicle Department (Coppin *et al.*, 1965–7). This analysis again shows that there is little statistical evidence of accident repeating to be found in an American State's records of serious accidents. As such it could be interpreted as confirmation that the theoretical detractors of proneness were right in their thinking all the time. But my contention is that this particular interpretation is very much open to question. In fact, in later chapters I propose to put forward a no doubt contentious but to my mind valid line of argument (and back it with a similar statistical analysis of the records of a South African transport company) that the findings of Coppin's study, regarded *in toto*, are in no way incompatible with the concept of accident proneness. In fact I propose to argue that they can be interpreted as the *end result* of a most beneficial policy of driver control based on the very principle of unequal liability to accidents which forms the cornerstone of the whole accident proneness theory.

This is something which I have discussed at length with Coppin and his associates. We have discussed all the reasons why his California study and our South African study come up with such different figures, and yet at the same time the conclusions which the two research units reach on the basis of these figures can be *conceptually* compatible. In fact I believe it is going to come as a surprise to many of the people who might expect (and possibly even hope for) open disagreement between the views of the two research units to find how very compatible these views are.

But even if a pleasant measure of agreement can be achieved between research workers (which in itself is nothing unusual), let it not be forgotten that the stand taken by the theoretical opponents of the concept of accident proneness, particularly in the United States, has not changed one iota. No major critiques of the concept have been published since 1964—it being apparently now accepted that there is no need for further argument, and that all that needs to be said has already been said. The new way of theoretical scientific thinking on accident proneness is currently firmly entrenched. But in the light of the rather strange way in which this thinking has come about, the reader might find it interesting to see the up-to-date views of some of the most prominent research workers in the field, the men whose publications, whether they have been quoted, misquoted, or ignored, have formed such an integral part of the history of the accident proneness controversy.

CHAPTER 13

CURRENT VIEWS ON ACCIDENT PRONENESS

Present Thinking on Accident Proneness

SAULI HAKKINEN

Institute of Occupational Health, Helsinki, Finland

My concept of accident proneness has not changed much from that which I expressed in my book *Traffic Accidents and Driver Characteristics*. I cannot fully understand any discussion of the topic "Does accident proneness exist or not?" What happens if we allow a group of blind or feeble-minded persons to drive a car—after adequate training—and ignore all accidents they have so long as they keep themselves alive?

I think we do find differences in accident figures between this kind of groups and a normal driver group. Something we must consider, in my opinion, is just what possibilities there are for situations where accident proneness can express itself in a society where we try to protect people in all possible ways. Even the occurrence of one accident—by changing conditions, or possibilities, or attitudes, or many other things—makes the question of accident proneness a very difficult one. This may be easier to comprehend in the case of industrial accidents. It is not surprising that, for instance, there are not many accident-prone persons working with a pressing-machine. It is enough for a worker to lose one finger: he does not want to lose all fingers eventually only for the purpose of verifying the existence of accident proneness for scientists.

The continuous selection caused by the above-mentioned and many other factors affects the difficulty of the research of accident proneness. When considering these problems it is easy to understand why poorly planned studies, made by people not familiar with the theoretical and statistical aspects of accident research, have created a situation where "no accident proneness exists". In many studies the simple and "mystic" idea of accident proneness has been the starting point of the research without the researchers having any understanding of the whole set of criterion problems. I think that greatly detailed and well-planned studies are now necessary to simplify the unclear situation and conception of accident proneness. As we know, the most difficult question is the reliability of the criterion. Therefore it seems necessary to find other criterion variables, which correlate with accidents but which are more frequent and which are not confused with emotional and other predicting factors. Critical incidents, near accidents, observations of driving habits, and developed merit rating systems are some possible methods for criterion research.

The present strong underestimation of accident proneness (or individual differences in general) may be a reaction to earlier phases, when all traffic psychology meant studies of accident proneness only. The enormous increase in road traffic and the general opinion that very few restrictions should be made in the licensing of drivers, have moved the focus of attention from individual differences to general human factors, such as driver behaviour, ergonomic factors, and system developments. But the ignoring of stable, changing, and temporary individual liabilities means a very strong narrowing of the psychological aspects. The statement "No accident proneness exists" is a typical school statement. Earlier it was usual in psychology to have such a rigid reaction to questions not fully understood. Nowadays it seems unwise and unrealistic. We need more flexible and operational thinking in all fields—and also when dealing with the concept of accident proneness.

Epilogue to an Earlier Publication on Accident Proneness

A. GARTH ARBOUS

*African Explosives and Chemical Industries, Johannesburg, South Africa**

I feel very honoured to have received a request from the authors of this work to make some comment on recent developments in the field since the publication of our paper in 1951. It is regretted that illness has prevented me from making full use of this request, but I still remain grateful for the opportunity accorded me to indicate my continued interest in this subject and my concern for the development of new thinking in the future.

My first and immediate concern has been to note the manner in which our original article has been used and interpreted by subsequent research workers. I can only see looming ahead the danger that through unwitting misrepresentation, or quotation out of context, a false impression of the real message which we wished to contribute at the time will be perpetuated in the literature on the subject; and I can see there is a danger of history repeating itself, as when the world was so misled in the years after Greenwood and Woods, and Greenwood and Yule, first published their very conservative account of their work.

I can therefore only make a strong appeal to the future research worker not to rely on quoted excerpts or indirect interpretations when he wishes to understand our contribution in 1951. The serious seeker after truth in this area should go back and read, and study, and read again, our original work before drawing conclusions or using it to plan further advances, so that the clock is not put back again, and some subsequent person will not once more have the duty to perform which Professor Kerrich and I tried to perform in 1951. I feel there is a serious danger in this regard. This is particularly noticeable in the tendency displayed by some authors (whose objectivity could be questioned even though their intentions be laudable and honourable) to use our publication as proof for existence, or conversely non-existence, of the human phenomenon of "accident proneness" (or personal liability or whatever you want to call it) in identical environments. In

---

* It is with great regret that we have to announce the death of Mr. Arbous shortly after this statement was written. On behalf of the many research workers who have benefited by the perceptive thinking displayed in his 1951 monograph we would like to express our appreciation of his contribution to accident research.

fact no attempt was made by us, and we left the case unproven. This the objective and careful student will see clearly in our writings. For example, on page 373 it is stated: "The evidence so far available does not enable one to make categorical statements in regard to accident-proneness, either one way or the other; and as long as we choose to deceive ourselves that they do, just so long will we stagnate in our abysmal ignorance of the real factors involved in the personal liability to accidents."

It is implicit, of course, in our discussion that anyone who is familiar with the laws of statistical probability would be extremely rash to *deny categorically* that in this one single attribute (i.e. proneness) the theory of individual differences does not apply and that "all men are equal", when this is not the case in all other measurable aspects of man, e.g. brain capacity, height, weight, eye colour, etc. What we said at the time was that so far nobody had succeeded in defining precisely what was meant by this term nor in measuring it in any way which could be of use to the accident-prevention practitioner. We concluded that the sort of statistical approach which regards the individual as a plum in a statistical pudding, or a tally stroke in a frequency distribution, is a barren approach; and all we could do at the time was to suggest that more profitable results might be achieved by regarding the *individual* as the field of study, and by collecting over a period of time mass information *on individuals*, and by using these data as the statistical variables.

For this reason I personally would regard the work done by Sichel and Shaw as being the most significant breakthrough in this field that has occurred in the last quarter century; it is in fact the scientifically planned follow-up of what we could only hint at in our work in 1951. For example, on p. 373: "What is needed is obviously more fundamental research and perhaps a completely new way of looking at the old problem." Or, again, on p. 364: "The personal factor in proneness (which differentiates between individuals) should be more properly based on intra-personal study of individuals' accident records." And p. 386 where I quoted Viteles:

"The aim of the clinical approach is to examine the whole individual and from an examination of the whole to arrive at a knowledge of the significance of the various aspects of his personality—the relative importance of each sector of his personality in a given situation. The application of the clinical approach in the analysis of accident causes involves a complete study of the individual involved in accidents—it makes the individual the point of departure, and provides for a thorough examination of every factor—physical, mental, social, and economic, and of those extraneous to the individual—which may have played a part in the accident in which he has been involved."

And also p. 390 where Viteles was quoting Bingham: "In dealing with each motor-man, or each truck driver, or each automobilist, he is recognised not as one of the mass, but as a distinct personality, unique."

In this sense the work of Shaw and Sichel can be regarded as a happy marriage between the *clinical* and *statistical* approaches, a combination which has produced such profitable results.

Comments on Accident Theory

JOHN E. KERRICH

Department of Statistics, University of Witwatersrand, Johannesburg, South Africa

I am an applied statistician, and during the past forty years have employed such statistical knowledge as I possess in a wide variety of practical problems. Round about 1951 I was inveigled into writing the mathematical background to a monograph on "Accident tsatistics and the concept of accident proneness". The aim of this work was to examine the mathematical theory currently used for analysing accident statistics.

In the course of this monograph my co-author and I had occasion to make some rather pungent remarks on the thinking at that time on the subject of accident proneness (remarks which seem to have been quite often quoted out of context), the reason being that frequently, when reading the literature, we had found an annoying lack of appreciation of the complexity of any accident situation.

One of these glib and misleading simplifications which was popular at the time can be stated as follows: "Many of the accidents occur to a few of the employees. If we discharge the few who are obviously accident-prone then in future the accident rate will be greatly reduced."

Another confusing simplification was the tendency to rely on simple but rather meaningless measures for assessing accident records. The one commonly used was: α = average number of accidents per individual per unit time (accident rate for short).

α might *appear* to be an arithmetically simple measure of the accident situation among certain people in a certain environment during a certain time period. But it is extremely difficult to pin down exactly what it *does* measure because it can be affected by so many things. For instance, in a factory the installation of new machinery in the middle of the time period under consideration might change the accident situation consistently during the second half. Or a safety campaign during that period might educate the workers to have consistently fewer accidents for some considerable portion of that period, and so on. In addition, the possibility exists that one worker is *innately and consistently* more capable of avoiding accidents in this environment than is another worker. Another possibility is that some workers may be able to *learn by experience* to become consistently more capable of avoiding accidents then they used to be, and so on and on. Superimposed on all this there is a mishmash of haphazard happenings that momentarily might help accidents to occur or to be avoided. Their effects on the accident situation are commonly termed chance effects.

What a muddle!

α is very much an average measure—and because of all the uncontrollable factors it is often a somewhat meaningless measure of overall accident *liability* rather than of accident *proneness*. This was one of the reasons which led me at the time to say: "Bluntly, no *absolute* measure of accident proneness exists. Thus the concept of accident proneness remains uncomfortably nebulous . . . and the authors confess that they find the fashion of talking about nebulous entities which cannot be clearly defined or adequately measured both wearisome and sterile."

Another criticism I made was levelled at the standard mathematical theory used at that time for analysing accident statistics.

"In a sense this theory will always be useful. People will on occasion collect accident statistics over a period of time and need to describe them, by means of these or similar theories.

"In a sense this theory misses the mark altogether. It deals with people who have been under observation for the whole period of time and says nothing about the misfits who try a job and soon leave it. Now, one of the fundamental problems that faces the industrial psychologists is how to spot the misfit, preferably before he begins a job, and the above theory will do little or nothing to help him here."

Since 1951 I have done no work on accident statistics. Now, in 1969, I am suddenly asked to comment on what has been happening in the field of accident research in the interim. I neither dare nor care to comment in detail. But I would like to remark briefly on some work that seems to me to flow on from the conclusion quoted above.

This new work deals with the accident situation associated with a bus company in South Africa which has divisions in several parts of the country. A bus driver working in a particular division has a route assigned to him and remains on it day after day. When the bus he is driving is involved in an accident, the circumstances of that accident are carefully assessed by responsible officials. I have personal knowledge of and considerable admiration for the manner in which these accident records are compiled and evaluated.

The analysis of these records is to a great extent based on methods described by Sichel (1965). His basic measure is *driving days between each person's successive accidents*. Contrast this with the standard measure m = number of accidents per unit time for each person. Given a driver's record $t_1, t_2, \ldots, t_n$ of time-intervals between successive accidents, his $m_1, m_2, \ldots$, can easily be obtained for successive time units. But the converse is not true. Irreplaceable information has been lost if records are kept in terms of m instead of in terms of t. *In this sense t is an immediate improvement on anything used and described in my original paper.*

His basic model for the distribution of t for any particular driver is the "pure chance" distribution whose probability density is

$$\gamma(t) = \frac{1}{\theta} e^{-t/\theta}, \qquad (0 < t \leqslant \infty). \tag{1}$$

$\bar{t}$ = average driving time between accidents for a particular driver seems to be a natural and simple measure of that driver's response to the accident situation. (Technically, $\bar{t}$ is the maximum likelihood estimate of θ.)

For a practical study of the behaviour of individual drivers it was found convenient to work with the transformed variable

$$x = \log_e t,$$

because the scatter of observed values of x, as measured by

$$\text{var}(x) = \frac{\pi^2}{6}$$

is independent of θ.

Sichel shows that for two drivers whose records extended over four years and over seven years respectively, the "pure chance" distribution of t held reasonably well (each with a different value of θ). This gives one some confidence in accepting the distribution mentioned as a reasonable first approximation. No one in his senses would expect it to be absolutely correct.

He also gives values of $\bar{t}$ (the average time-intervals) and their associated confidence intervals for ten drivers who were stationed in the same division. Here again is interesting evidence which strongly suggests that different drivers can have consistently different accident records.

Finally, the psychologist may find himself on more familiar ground when examining the split-half reliability test illustrated in Sichel's fig. 4, with its correlation coefficient of $r=0.62$.

All in all there seems to be very sound evidence for concluding that among drivers who work on the same route, some are consistently "better" drivers than others, and that $\bar{t}$ is a simple and sensitive measure of an individual's behaviour.

Turning next to an article written by Shaw and Sichel (1961). Here the theory evolved by Sichel was put into practice for evaluating the accident records of individual drivers. I found the control charts for the various drivers interesting and illuminating. Figure 4 in this paper also shows how during the years 1951–61 the accident rate of the company as a whole had dropped considerably in spite of adverse factors such as increased traffic.

Here, then, is a situation where accident statistics have been collected over a period of time and described. For this situation the methods of description used are, in my opinion, in advance of methods described by me in 1951, and have led to useful results.

In the meantime, under the direction of Shaw, a great deal of work had been carried out on devising a personality test that could be given to applicants for the job of bus driver. A description of some of this work appeared in an article (Shaw, 1965) and will no doubt be described further in this present volume. However, here is a set of data obtained quite recently by means of the psychological and statistical methods developed in this particular study (Table 13.1).

TABLE 13.1

Class of test ratings	Class of driver				Total
	D_1	D_2	D_3	D_4	
T_1	112	23	9	2	146
T_2	80	133	46	28	287
T_3	28	107	201	133	469
T_4	4	21	68	144	237
					1139

Here 1139 of these drivers have been divided into sixteen categories, as shown, according to:

(a) type of driver they have proved to be consistently during several years' employment.
    (D_1 denotes *good*; D_2 *fair*; D_3 *poor*; D_4 *bad*.)
(b) Type of test rating each driver was given *before* being employed.

From personal knowledge I am very reasonably satisfied that the company has officials on its staff who are agreed upon the standards required to assign a driver to a particular category, can keep these standards reasonably constant, and are capable of teaching others to recognize and maintain these standards. Call this basic assumption A_1. Granted this assumption, surely the next step is to consider the observations in a particular row, for example T_1? The observations in this row refer to people who *after* they were placed in test class T_1 worked as drivers under remarkably uniform conditions for quite a long time. In course of time, further groups of applicants will repeat this particular process. It is suggested that any such group is a "random sample" from a reasonably well defined "population" (associated solely with test class T_1). Repeat the argument for the other three classes. Call all this basic assumption A_2. Granted assumptions A_1 and A_2, then the observations in each row in Table 13.1 are a random sample from a different multinomial distribution and we proceed to estimate the *conditional* probabilities $P(D_jT_1)$, $P(D_jT_2)$ etc., by standard methods (Hald, 1967). The results are given in Table 13.2 in the form of upper and lower limits to 95% confidence intervals for the values of $P(D_jT_i)$, etc.

TABLE 13.2. 1139 BUS DRIVERS
Limits to 95% confidence intervals for $P(D_j/T_i)$

Class of test ratings		Class of driver			
		D_1	D_2	D_3	D_4
T_1	lower limit	·698	·111	·040	·004
	upper limit	·836	·230	·118	·049
T_2	lower limit	·227	·406	·128	·069
	upper limit	·331	·521	·210	·141
T_3	lower limit	·046	·190	·384	·243
	upper limit	·088	·266	·473	·324
T_4	lower limit	·007	·061	·229	·545
	upper limit	·046	·137	·344	·670

Thus in the next large group of applicants who fall into test class T_1 one can expect that between 70% and 84% of them will become good drivers, while from a similar group who fall into test class T_4 one can only expect between 1% and 5% good drivers.

This company has considerable difficulty in recruiting drivers and cannot always pick and choose. But surely here is a test that gives them valuable knowledge before ever the applicants start to drive. Admittedly, the analysis in Table 13.2 is somewhat crude, but it shows that if a group of applicants contains a high proportion of men in groups T_1 and T_2, the company can expect a high proportion of consistently capable drivers. If it has to take on men in groups T_3 and T_4 then at least it knows in advance that it must expect trouble.

Here then, at least in this situation, is an answer to my comment that "one of the fundamental problems that faces the industrial psychologists, is how to spot the misfit, preferably before he begins a job".

I congratulate Shaw and Sichel on the measure of success that they have achieved.

Other methods of analysing Table 13.1 exist, such as:

(a) Calculating some type of coefficient of contingency.

(b) Attaching scales to tests and to subsequent performance and calculating Pearson's coefficient of correlation r.

(a) and (b) can be criticized on the grounds that they are based on the rather doubtful assumption (A_3) that the data *as a whole* in Table 13.1 are a random sample from some fixed population. Furthermore, even if A_3 is valid, exactly how is the ONE descriptive constant mentioned in (a) or (b) to be interpreted physically? (I have stressed this point before and will stress it again on every suitable occasion.) The analysis used here avoids A_3, proceeds directly to extract information that will be of practical use, and describes a complicated situation fairly clearly by means of a suitable *number of descriptive constants*.

As an applied statistician I emphasize the practical value of the work done by Shaw and Sichel in that it *describes* and *predicts* and will continue to do so no matter what *explanations* may be suggested as to why it does so.

It appears to me that there is a strong trend in modern accident research (Haddon *et al.*, 1964) to insist always on explanations as to the causes of accidents. I agree that this is an extremely worth-while ambition and should be vigorously pursued even if it proves to be an extremely tricky business, more so than in chemistry, physics, or medicine, for example. But if this modern trend creates an atmosphere in which we frown on work which results in the actual prediction and prevention of accidents, no matter why, then it seems to me that we are throwing out the baby with the bath-water. If we do wish to prevent accidents, then surely any method that actually does so should be acclaimed even if it is not properly "understood". However, I gather that people consider that psychological tests such as Shaw's tests *do* offer very useful explanations of why accidents happen, in terms of personality traits. But I am not a psychologist and this is outside my ambit.

Finally, in my monograph in 1951, I concluded by saying that although *all* the scientific writers whom I had quoted in this monograph had advanced their hypotheses tentatively and hedged them about with warnings and advice, this had apparently not prevented other writers from beginning an article with: "As so and so has shown ..." and on occasion going on blithely to absurd conclusions. As this tendency seems to have carried on in the intervening years, I would like to say, here and now, that if any reader of these present comments, assuming that anyone does read them, begins his next paper with: "As Kerrich proved in 1970 ...", I solemnly promise him that I, or my heirs and assigns, will prosecute him for libel!

Driver Research in West Germany

DR. GÜNTER SCHUBERT

Arbeitsgruppe für Audio-visuelle Information, Cologne, West Germany

The driver plays a very important role in the total accident picture, *but* psychological research and practice should concentrate on developing methods for educating the driver rather than on methods for his selection.

To prove my point I would like to quote some of our publications.

On the Subject of Driver Selection

"Zusammenstellung von bisherigen wissenschaftlichen Untersuchungen über Prädiktoren und Kriterien des sicheren Kraftfahrens" (Schubert, 1965).

A summary of the research done to date in different countries on predictors and criteria of safe driving shows:

> A connection between test scores (and other factors of human behaviour) and criteria of accident proneness has been proved by a number of tests.
>
> The correlations between accidents and various determinants of behaviour are diverse. The results obtained for any particular test seem to be more dependent on the choice of the sample—and the criterion—than on the test or method of examination used.
>
> The best way to demonstrate the connection between performance factors and criteria of safe driving seems to be by using a sample consisting of some particular class of driver.
>
> Significant results can only be expected with samples which reflect the entire driving population when the criterion covers a long period of observation.
>
> Owing to the great dependence of the results on the choice of both the sample and the criterion it is only with reservations that one can make statements regarding the importance of different factors for predicting driver performance.

Better results will probably be obtained by:

> Tests for attempts at orientation rather than tests of vision.
>
> Complex reaction tests (i.e. choice-reaction tests involving multiple actions) rather than simple reaction time tests: systematic investigation of curriculum vitae rather than personality questionnaires.
>
> Methods of investigation which are adapted to traffic conditions rather than tests which are generally applicable.

On the Subject of Driver Suitability

"Die Begutachtung der Fahrereignung" (Schneider and Schubert, 1967).

Research work reported in the accident literature on the validity of psychological tests for diagnosing driver suitability shows that significant correlations between test results and criteria of traffic performance were only found among certain sections of the tests.

It is certain that the low validity of the predictors is partly due to the unreliability of the criteria. Even if it were possible to measure the different variables accurately, there would be only a slight correlation with the criteria used in the above-mentioned research work. It is therefore impossible to deduce from the results obtained in this research that the tests are useless for predicting traffic performance. The question of the suitability of the tests remains open at the present, and for the near future.

Does this mean that for *individual* cases a psychological evaluation of driver suitability is neither possible nor worth while? Some theoreticians seem to think that this is the case. Drösler, for example, advises the traffic psychologists to find methods, other than character studies, to reduce the risk of making a wrong prediction. However, against this contention it can be stated that nobody is better equipped than an expert psychologist to try to limit the influence of estimations when determining driver suitability. Even if the low validity of any particular test still means that some of the "suitables" and some of the "unsuitables" obtain the same test scores, there are groups on either side of the "unclassified" area where the test results are quite reliable (or very reliable) indicators of suitability.

Is it possible, after certain presumptions, to make a prediction of the traffic performance of the "unclassified" group? The examination of the accuracy of a predictor test described above is based on *one* test only. However, when examining a particular person, an assessor does not use the result of only one test, but uses information from a number of sources. At the same time he only chooses those tests or items of information which have already proved to have some connection with driving performance—as it can be assumed that these will give better results than unproved ones.

It seems at least probable that better results will be obtained by using the more superior methods listed before—with the addition of traffic-adjusted personality tests rather than general personality questionnaires.

If there are a number of tests whose individual validity is low, the probability of making a correct diagnosis should be improved by means of the method of multiple correlation—and increases the greater the number of tests used and the smaller the amount of intercorrelation *between* these tests. The lower the validity of each test, the more (and if possible different) tests will have to be added in order to obtain a clear result. However, there is little definite proof up to now that continuing to add new tests or new methods of investigation results in a more accurate prognosis—except for Hakkinen's study where the tests were very carefully chosen. The unsatisfactory aspect of this line of approach (by way of multiple correlation) is that it relies exclusively on linear relationships—and such relationships are usually not consistent with theories of psychological research—particularly with regard to character.

On the Subject of the Education of the Driver

"Untersuchungsverfahren zur Begutachtung von Kraftfahrern" (Schubert and Spoerer, 1967).

Another field of research deals with an analysis of the sequence of road offences in "multiple offenders". A multiple offender is defined as a person receiving three or more penalties for road offences over two years, each offence being registered at the Central Traffic Office (Kraftfahrt-Bundesamt) and also reported to the local traffic authority. Information on 174 multiple offenders reported to the traffic authorities of the city of Cologne for the years 1964–5 were evaluated for this research.

The hypothesis presented for examination was:

> Multiple road offenders repeat similar offences more often than corresponds to the calculated expectation of an accident.

The following can be said about multiple road offenders:

> The offences are not independent of each other. More often than can be expected by chance, the succeeding offence is similar to the preceding one.

The following explanations of this fact can be given:

> Specific external traffic conditions lead to a repetition of similar offences.

Specific personal characteristics of the multiple offender lead to the repetition of similar offences.

"Untersuchung der verkehrsspezifischen Haltungen und Meinungen von Kraftfahrern
durch Fragebogen" (Schubert, 1967).

This research work dealt with the following problems:

(1) What are the connections between the specific traffic opinions and behaviour of drivers and their traffic performance?
(2) What are the connections between traffic opinions and traffic behaviour and behaviour in other ways of life?
(3) Is it possible to examine these connections through tests based on printed questionnaires, using a system of different answer selections?

The results of this research verify the hypothesis that opinions and behaviour developed
in traffic conditions are not an integral part of the structure of otherwise formed opinions
and aspects of personality. Driving is therefore a relatively independent and little integrated section of general behaviour.

The conclusions show that as far as traffic education is concerned, a strengthening of
the general human tendency towards safety and adjustment can hardly have any effect on
traffic performance. A direct influence on drivers' attitudes to traffic appears to promise
more success. According to this research the following opinions and attitudes of drivers
are proved to be harmful to safety and the regulation of road traffic:

The tendency to fast driving: e.g. the use of top speed; the pleasure of getting "more"
out of one's car than other drivers; the pleasure of cornering on screeching tyres;
the refusal to accept the fact that accidents are, in general, caused by too fast speeds.

The tendency to "pull away" at speed from other cars, e.g. at traffic lights; to always
want to be at the head of a line of cars; to weave between other cars; to change
lanes as much as possible so as to manoeuvre one's way through the traffic.

To be against speed limits in general: e.g. to plead against a general speed limit on
motorways and main roads; to support a raising of the speed limit in built-up areas;
to object to speed limits of 25 mph (40 km) or 20 mph (30 km) in residential areas.

To disagree with the highway code: e.g. to be of the opinion that there are too
many street signs about; to believe that the lifting of a number of traffic rules would
lower the accident rate; to think there are too many "no-overtaking" signs; to be
against police controls, especially speed traps and surprise checks; to have a dis-
agreeable feeling when stopped by the police; to be of the opinion that the police
should deal with traffic flow rather than be concerned with minor offences.

To be prejudiced against policemen and traffic court judges: to believe that policemen
are often unfriendly or prejudiced, that they overlook offences of drivers in big and
expensive cars, that they let themselves be bribed by pretty girls, and sometimes go
out on patrol intoxicated; as far as traffic court judges are concerned for drivers to
hold them to be generally superficial, to sometimes give wrong judgements and
usually not be drivers themselves.

To believe that traffic discipline is generally good and that the reason for accidents is
bad road conditions and not undisciplined drivers.

To be prejudiced against other road-users, especially pedestrians; to be frustrated by other road-users or traffic conditions, for example to become bad tempered in traffic jams; to repeat impolite remarks of other road-users in a similar manner; to reject defensive driving, for example by preferring fast highways to quiet side streets; never to be deterred from driving in bad weather, or on icy roads, or in fog; not to reduce speed when driving in rain; to believe it is necessary to be ruthless in modern traffic conditions and to believe that the attitude of other road-users forces one to be inconsiderate, for example to use one's headlights against oncoming traffic while overtaking in critical moments and to accelerate rather than give way.

To have little knowledge of how an accident occurs or what caused it to happen.

Not to be concerned so much with the safety and economy of one's car but rather to emphasize its comfort and appearance.

To have an unfavourable opinion of driving lessons and the driving test.

The results of this research work give rise to the belief that drivers who are firmly convinced of their opinions and attitudes will not change by themselves even with increasing driving practice.

Brief Summary of the Main Points of View in Present-day German Traffic Psychology

Wolfgang Böcher

Technischer Überwachungs-Verein Rheinland e.V. Medizinisch-Psychologisches Institut, Cologne, West Germany

The following are some of the views expressed by prominent researchers in the field of German traffic psychology.

Graf Hoyos: It cannot absolutely be denied that there are accident-prone people. However, it does not follow that accident-prone people:
(1) would necessarily be involved in many accidents;
(2) would be inclined to have accidents throughout their lives;
(3) would be inclined to get involved in accidents of all kinds.
An accident predisposition in the statistical sense cannot be proved and must be rejected.

Undeutsch: It is not possible to conclude solely on account of a high accident rate in one year that there is such a thing as accident proneness or an accident-prone personality. A great many accidents are, in any case, to be seen as warning signs that the driver should be investigated or pure chance events.

Mittenecker: To be sure, one can describe many accidents as being caused by accident proneness, but nevertheless the statement that most accidents are caused by a small number of highly accident-prone people cannot be accepted as proved nor even as probable.

It cannot be maintained in general that a tendency to accidents is strongly dependent on personality. The application of test methods for the individual prognosis of accident proneness is only possible in extreme cases. The few clearly indicated relationships between accidents and personality are mainly of general scientific and theoretical interest.

BÖCHER: German traffic psychologists seem to be predominantly of the opinion that accident proneness, *in the literal sense of being involved in many accidents*, seldom occurs, or cannot be proved by statistical means. However, on the other hand, it cannot be denied that there may exist an inclination of certain people for traffic accidents.

In my opinion the pure statistical considerations against the concept of accident proneness which have lately become very fashionable, are not convincing. It is not logical to say that because the apparently simple minority theory is a fallacy that the antithesis is true and there is no such thing as accident proneness.

There is even a logical error in the deductions made from the statistical considerations of chance. Accident figures are by no means the only data distributed according to a chance pattern—all psychological and biological data are distributed likewise. For instance physical size in a fairly large population would show the classic normal distribution. But if we derive the same conclusions as is done with the distribution of accidents, then we would conclude that a person's physical size was determined by chance alone and was not connected with the person as such. In contrast to this it can be proved that physical size can be determined by factors such as heredity, disease, deprivation during childhood, errors in upbringing, environmental influences, etc.

It seems to me that the concept of chance occurrence is used in an inappropriate sense both in the case of accident proneness and statistical analysis. In colloquial language an accident acquires a kind of metaphysical quality—something in the nature of a dispensation of God and not accessible to research. When, therefore, the question of chance is raised in traffic psychology, the picture of the ancient Nemesis is involuntarily brought to mind as a force hovering over the highway, sometimes grasping a motorist by the scruff of the neck and throwing him to the ground, and at other times allowing other motorists to escape without a scratch. Such a concept of chance is not only mathematically but also scientifically unsound.

Mathematical chance should be conceived in a narrower sense. Here a chance event is one in which:

(1) many independent factors are operating simultaneously, and
(2) with a certain degree of probability, any factor may either make its appearance or remain hidden.

Science in this sense does not acknowledge any inexplicable interconnections but only that there are phenomena which in the present state of knowledge cannot be explained but which would in principle be explicable in the future. Without any doubt, chance distributions are determined by the operation of numerous independent factors. What the nature of these factors are is not disclosed by pure figures.

To me it seems important that one should finally give up the erroneous idea still prevalent in certain circles that accidents are caused by a single factor and accept the fact that an accident is the point of intersection of many factors working together. In this respect it is not at all surprising that a person with certain deficiencies, or an abnormal personality structure, could have driven for many years or even decades free from accidents, and then, in the end, find that his hazardous way of driving can no longer be compensated for in the present lively system of modern street traffic.

The earlier hypothesis of a single, solitary determining accident disposition is in principle hopelessly out of date. In spite of this it is still presumed in many instances that accidents are homogeneous phenomena entirely determined by one single factor.

When, however, I choose as my fundamental statistical unit a multi-dimensional causal agency with a complex factorial structure (as it appears in the circumstances of the accident) and when I acknowledge that the weight of the single factors in a random sample of accidents would vary from case to case, then, if I were to correlate the accidents with the various factors, I would probably likewise obtain only chance values or near-chance values. In other words: the influence of chance in accident distribution is a repeated demonstration that factorial weight varies by chance from one accident to the other. From a qualitative statement regarding the nature of the factors involved, the material should be elevated to qualitative differentials.

In spite of this the following two statements are important:

(1) In exceptional cases, chance distributions, as such, also have a determinant which cannot be located merely by virtue of the numerous undifferentiated variables.

(2) According to many investigations the spread of the observed distributions appears to be larger than would be expected purely mathematically. Also in cases where a great many of the factors influencing the distributions are eliminated, there appears to be a basis for presuming the presence of individual accident proneness.

In addition it has been proved in practice that suitability for driving can be regarded as doubtful when in any one particular year more than two accidents occur. One would, however, hesitate to make a definite decision that the permit of an individual driver should be withheld by reason of these findings. But, on the other hand, one could very well regard high numbers of accidents or traffic offences as warning signs which indicate the necessity for a thorough psychological and medical examination of the road-user concerned.

Deficient and Constructive Human Factors in Road Traffic

AART VAN DER BURGH

Stichting Psychologisch Verkeerslaboratorium, Utrecht, Holland

I do not agree with many of the views stated by those present-day writers who criticize the psychological research on accident liability and say that the psychological testing of drivers is not necessary or is not even possible. In my opinion writings like these are very dangerous to road safety as they may make people believe that nothing can be done or that nothing needs to be done about the driver except to protect him from chance events.

This is not true. The work of many researchers has shown that drivers are not equal in their accident liability and that many of them are accident-liable because of their own shortcomings. These people can be identified if one knows what to look for, as has been proved by Finnish, South African, Swiss, and Dutch evaluations. In my own Institute we have found more and more in recent years that drivers who are sent to us for testing for-suitability as professional drivers are not suitable or safe. Many of the young drivers, although they have the skill to deal with the demands of modern traffic, have other danger-ous shortcomings, such as emotional instability, a tendency to over-estimate themselves, an extreme need for achievement, and lack of realism. Many of the older drivers show lack of adaptability, or a lessening of ability and confidence, or a tendency to ignore their decrease in driving suitability. Nevertheless, these same people either already have driving licences, or can easily succeed in obtaining such a licence, which permits them to drive freely on the streets and highways of the country as private motorists, thereby adding considerably to the dangers of road traffic.

The discoveries we have made in my Institute are the same as those of reputable re-searchers in many parts of the world, but it is becoming fashionable recently for people to overlook such psychological findings and to say that statistics have not proved that they are true or that they have a different meaning. The inconsistency or baselessness of their sayings must have escaped the notice of these critics.

Very often the present-day critics of accident liability or accident proneness use only a partial selection of the literature with the findings amplified by subjective interpretations and ideas founded on behaviouristic views and the conditioning concept. Their would-be psychological interpretation of safe driving is only an outward adjustment for self-protec-tion against the man-in-the-street—it bears no relation to the more essential possibilities of man like free choice, doing one's best, allowing for one's short-comings, or thinking ahead.

Accident liability is acknowledged but at the same time trifled with by referring to the study of Forbes (1939) and saying that this study proved that very few people were dan-gerously accident-liable, and that most accidents were events of chance. But a driver-population of about 30,000 having a mean of one accident in twenty-five years must be an exception—supposing it is consistent—in the motorized world, and cannot therefore be a representative sample. A study in Ohio (Lauer, 1960) with much higher accident rates already gives rise to other thoughts. Rather than saying that this proves that acci-dents, are events of chance, then this ought to stimulate investigation as to why in Connec-ticut accident-liability was so rare or so small—as it seems to have done with Forbes himself (1954). Thoughts about driving defensively and not giving an opportunity to chance then arise instead of thoughts about eliminating the dangers of chance for irre-sponsible drivers. Too much reference to chance Poisson distributions in accidents is misleading.

In my opinion the essential factor in man which contributes to survival, and therefore promotes safety, is positive choice by the driver himself as to the conduct with which he will succeed—an earnest and courageous perseverance to cope with those dangers in the environment which have not been eliminated, and also with those short-comings in him-self that occur.

Deficiencies in this factor mean that at times man is subject to chances he cannot con-trol, and does not control, and is thus accident-liable. Then—but only then—he becomes a candidate member of the Poisson population.

This Poisson population (the people to whom the so-called chance accidents happen) consists of people who are victims of their lack of initiative to take prevention into their own hands; for the Poisson process is an awaiting process in which chances for accidents are constantly occurring for people who reduce themselves to passive objects, dependent on good or bad luck.

The Poisson "chance" model as an explanation for accidents is only a limited, empty statistical model if it is not integrated with a constructive anthropological model of man. Without this it does not allow for responsibility; it does not offer any prospect of improvement; it excuses the driver at fault; it dishonours the driver whose success is not due to good luck. It can only account for accidents which happen during man's irresponsible periods on the roads, i.e. during such time as he is without sufficient self-protection and situation-control. People are to be pitied as long as they merely fit into such a Poisson model, but they earn respect if they regulate their conduct by responsibility and an appreciation of reality.

To prevent accidents we must realize that heavy demands are made on the majority of road users when the standard of the roads and the quality of the vehicle are too low. Therefore conditions should be made optimal; they should be adjusted to the capabilities of the average responsible road-user but not made too comfortable lest people forget the realities of chance mishap. And road-users should fulfil sufficiently high requirements of being trustworthy under the usual driving conditions. This calls for acceptable road equipment, the proper education and training of road-users, and preventative and repressive measures which, if necessary, will keep the unsafe drivers off the roads until they have become mature for responsible driving.

In short this is my philosophic starting point for a logically consistent way to promote road safety.

A Position Paper on Accident Proneness and Driver-oriented Safety Models

RAYMOND C. PECK and RONALD S. COPPIN

Research and Statistics Section, Department of Motor Vehicles, California, USA

Since its emergence over fifty years ago, the concept of "accident proneness" has played a capricious role as a model of accident behavior. Psychologically, emphasis has shifted from psychoanalytic and other monistic explanations of accident behavior to more multi-dimensional, probabilistic orientations. Paralleling these psychological explanations have been a number of treatise on the relationship between the mathematical properties of accident distributions and accident proneness, many of which have since been rejected as specious (Arbous and Kerrich, 1951; Sichel, 1965). Some writers have gone as far as to question the idea that person-centred variations in accident propensity even exist.

Historically, the phenomenon of traffic accidents has been confounded by (1) conceptual confusion regarding the relationship between mathematical distributions (Poisson, neg. binomial, etc.) and person-centred attributes, (2) speculative psychoanalytical interpretations of accident etiology, (3) semantic confusion, (4) inadequate research design and data, and (5) epistemologic pitfalls such as reification and circularity. The latter tendency is responsible for the unfortunate view that proneness is a discrete unitary entity or syndrome which people carry within them, like a disease. Either you have it or you do not.

In effect, the syndrome accident proneness is inferred from the consequences of behavior and then invoked as a causal explanation of the very behavior it describes. Even investigators adopting a more sophisticated paradigm often seem to assume that accident proneness is a discrete entity which affects certain people, rather than a probability continuum arising from a variety of often dissimilar causal sources. In reality, a multitude of "syndromes" and sub-populations may be involved in any population of "accident-prone" drivers. And to complicate matters even further, a substantial segment of any population of accident repeaters are quite likely to be included by chance. Thus the reification is often compounded. All accident repeaters are assumed to be truly "accident-liable" and to share a common underlying accident-etiology.

It has long been known that accident distributions can be statistically manipulated to show that a small percentage of drivers account for 100% of all accidents by shortening the time-interval of the accident frequency distribution. Do these accident subjects represent proof of the accident-prone concept? Hardly, since the size of this percentage is a function of the interval length; furthermore, the vast majority of the drivers who have accidents in one period will be accident-free in the next interval of time.

Regardless of how accidents are univariately distributed in a given population, the existence of accident proneness or differential accident liability is contingent upon the following statistical criterion: are the accident frequencies of a given group of drivers (equated on exposure) correlated with measurable person-centred variations among the subjects comprising the group? If so, one has evidence that the accident probability of each driver is not the same but that some drivers are more likely to be involved in accidents than others. With exposure controlled one must assume that the differential accident probabilities are a function of certain behavioral tendencies and patterns which influence the manner in which different subjects drive (i.e. react to the driving task and driving stimulus complex). These behavioral tendencies may be of a persisting nature, in which case the subjects will be accident-liable over a long period of time—perhaps a life-time. Or they may be of a transitory and/or situational nature, in which case the individual will be accident-liable for only a brief period. It is generally the persisting traits which investigators are most interested in, perhaps because they are more measurable and amenable to research investigation. Regardless of their causal role, transitory states are only meaningful to the extent that they are correlated with more enduring attributes of drivers, or persist over sufficiently long periods to permit replicable measurement. Otherwise, such variations can only function as random error variables in any prediction model of individual accident experience. The present authors and many others have presented strong statistical evidence that accident-prone drivers do exist—at least in relatively small numbers (Coppin, McBride and Peck, 1967; Hakkinen, 1958; Shaw and Sichel, 1961; Schuster, 1968; Schuster and Guilford, 1963; Burg, 1967; Campbell, 1958; Sichel, 1965; McGuire, 1956; Shaw, 1965).

There can, of course, be no absolute or completely general accident frequency criteria for designating a group "accident-liable". No matter what criteria are used, some of the subjects are really "safe" drivers who meet that criteria because of chance, while many others possessing accident traits will remain accident-free by chance. One can only minimize the role of chance by requiring that the group designated "accident-liable" have highly deviant accident records and that this statistical deviancy be evident over a long period of time.

In attempting to discredit the concept of accident proneness, many writers have alluded to the Poisson-like nature of accident distributions and the temporal unreliability of accidents (i.e. the accident population is a largely changing one over time). First of all, it must be pointed out that traffic accident data generally is not Poisson, more closely approximating a negative binomial; and that a Poisson distribution, in and of itself, does not prove randomness, just as a negative binomial does not prove proneness. As to the low degree of temporal stability shown by accident rates, it should be remembered that these "stability coefficients" are not valid measures of intrinsic reliability but are dependent upon a host of more-or-less incidental parameters: heterogeneity of driving population, length of temporal periods correlated, adequacy of accident reports, and exposure to accident contingencies (quality and quantity). One will find increasing evidence for accident proneness to the extent that (1) variability in driving skill within the population becomes larger, (2) the intervals of measurement become longer (within limits), (3) accident reporting becomes more thorough, (4) all subjects are exposed to a large number of accident contingencies, (5) exposure to accidents is constant over time. An important corollary to the first postulate is that evidence for accident proneness will decrease as the selective processes (drivers' licensing, etc.) become more stringent. The fourth postulate is also very important in any discussion of accident proneness, for it delimits both the manifestation of variations in driver behavior and the emergence of accident occurrences from that behavior. Obviously, then, any population whose total accident exposure consists of driving a few miles in light traffic and under ideal conditions will neither be involved in many accidents nor exhibit much variability on accidents, even though they may differ greatly in driving skill and other person-centred parameters. In addition, the within-subject accident occurrences over time will be almost entirely uncorrelated, since the rare accident occurrences would almost entirely be a function of chance external contingencies, and other non-replicable circumstances. However, if this same population were to drive in very dense traffic eight hours a day, 100,000 miles a year, they would accumulate a much greater number of accidents and exhibit much more variability on accident frequency; as a result, the accident experience of this population would become more highly correlated with person-centred variations among the population members. In addition, the accident experiences of the individuals would be more highly correlated over time, since the role of chance external contingencies has been lessened relative to persistent person-centred contingencies. By increasing the reliability and dimensionality of the drive task, it tends to become a more sensitive and discriminating test of individual difference among the population members, thereby providing more convincing evidence of accident proneness.

While the above considerations may be quite obvious to many readers, they are often not fully appreciated by many authorities when citing evidence as to the non-existence of accident proneness. It should be clear that it is meaningless to discuss accident proneness independent of the context in which the specific phenomena have occurred and the operations performed in measuring them.

The present authors take the approach that people do vary in accident liability, that the sources of this variability are multi-dimensional, and that the effects are probabilistic. In addition, some of the sources are transitory whereas others are more persistent, although even the latter vary within subjects over time and across context. There is little evidence of overlap between proneness and disease, and we do not feel it is fruitful to conceptualize accident proneness in diseased-organismic terms. It is quite possible, in fact, that persons with accident liabilities far below average are as "sick" or "sicker" than those with exceedingly high accident liabilities.

The optimum research paradigm from our standpoint is to view accidents and driving as a problem in systems analysis, in which the driver is one component and variable in a drive-task system. Such a model would permit one to talk not only of accident-liable drivers but also of accident-liable vehicles and accident-liable systems. In such a system, certain drivers may be prone to certain types of accidents and only under certain conditions. For example, a driver with poor glare recovery may only be predisposed to night accidents on open highways.

In discussing the contribution of the various system components, many investigators have alluded to the relatively small contribution of accident-repeaters to the overall problem, and have recommended altering other aspects of the system so that driver error is less likely to result in an accident. Such a position is neither a refutation of accident proneness nor does it rest on convincing evidence that the other system components are more important *sources of variability*. Part of this confusion has arisen from the use of unequal observational units in comparing the various system components. When evaluating the driver contribution, the individual driver becomes the observational unit, so that one is confronted with an individual prediction model. However, when evaluating external factors such as type of road, the observational unit is often a certain class of roadway or long highway, which is comprised of many individual roads or sections of roads. Under such circumstances, it is not too surprising that relationships between highway type and accident experience prove higher than driver relationships, since group criteria are much more stable and easier to predict. For example, the present authors have developed regression equations which, though predicting *individual* accident rates very poorly, would predict with high accuracy the accident means of *groups* of drivers from a knowledge of the age and prior violation record of the groups. To make the situations equivalent, the observational unit for environmental factors like highways should be *individual* homogeneous sections of highway, so that the model would have to predict the accident rates of specific sections of road. Actually, a more important and valid basis of giving priority to the non-driver system components is that they are easier to modify and completely controllable.

The present writers are of the opinion that a large source of variation in accident experience will continue to be chance in that individual accidents cannot be accurately predicted from measurable variations in persons, vehicles, or environments. This belief is predicated on the low probability of accident occurrences combined with the complex of interrelationships which determine such occurrences. This in no way should be construed as a refutation of the concept of accident proneness (i.e. differential accident probability among people). Rather, it merely means that the nature of the driving task in the United States is such that most drivers, even those of low skill or reckless predispositions, are unlikely to become involved in many traffic accidents throughout a lifetime. In addition, there are many possible counter-forces to a demonstration of accident proneness, such as selective attrition (e.g. accident fatalities) and accident-produced modifications in driving behavior ("burnt-fingers" paradigm).

Despite the many complexities inherent in person-centred liability models and research paradigms, differentials in proneness have been convincingly demonstrated by many investigators and these differences take on increasing significance under conditions of high exposure (e.g. professional drivers, etc.). The highly positive results obtained by Sichel and Shaw emphasize the inextricable relationship between the driving context (socio-ethnic factors, exposure, range of talent, etc.) and evidence for accident proneness. The latter author's results were obtained on South African commercial driver populations in which (1) the variation of talent among population members was apparently high due to non-stringent pre-selectivity, (2) the accident rate of the population exhibited wide variability, and (3) the population was exposed to many accident contingencies. In addition, socio-ethnic factors in other countries could have a dramatic influence on attitudes regarding risk-taking and driving. The present authors interpret such variations in findings as strong evidence against a generalized model of accident proneness. At the same time, we feel that even the less positive evidence for accident proneness in this country is sufficient to justify the construction of driver selection and driver improvement programs, on both scientific and humanitarian grounds.

In a very interesting recent paper, The nature and prediction of driver accident frequencies (*Accident Analyses and Prevention* (1970), **2,** 2) Peck, McBride and Coppin discuss in greater detail many of the issues raised in this statement and in the following chapter.

CHAPTER 14

THE CALIFORNIA DRIVER RECORD STUDY

IT WOULD seem that the supporters of accident proneness have not changed their views, and that even some of the people most often quoted for "exposing" the fallacy of the whole idea have, in fact, been rather misquoted.

But these completely independent statements, particularly the continental ones, also illustrate more vividly than anything I can say how much of the confusion on accident proneness has arisen because people are unwittingly talking about quite different concepts.

But they also show that there is very little disagreement, let alone dissension, between the major researchers in the field. In fact they seem to be quite willing to accept that anomalies are bound to arise in a subject as complex as this—but that there will always be a valid reason for these anomalies. It cannot happen in science that properly controlled research will come up with complete *contradictions*—it can only produce findings whose disparity stems from the source of the data or the particular methods used. It is not a question of one set of research findings being right and the other wrong. They can both be right; but they need to be interpreted in terms of their origins, and in a manner which is flexible enough to allow for the contingency that other data from other sources and processed by other methods might produce other results. This the researchers themselves seem perfectly able and willing to do. It is the theoreticians who are so inflexible in their outlook and who appear to be fostering the dissension.

I think therefore that the number one priority is to try and sort out the confusion. The continuation of a controversy like this can do irreparable harm not only to the repute of accident research but to the whole progress of accident prevention. So, before presenting any new evidence, let us go back to basics and see if we can quickly determine just which are the main issues at stake and the main points of disagreement.

There are, of course, differences in shades of opinion but, by and large, those who oppose the concept of accident proneness seem to maintain:

"That if it exists at all it is of very little importance in the total accident situation. There may be a very few truly chronic accident repeaters, but they form such a small proportion of the driving population that they do not deserve anything like the attention they have received.

"That most of the people who look as though they might be repeaters, and who have so mistakenly been called 'accident-prone' (because they have had a number of accidents) are not 'prone' at all. Their multiple accidents must have been largely dictated by chance, for in a subsequent period they will no longer be repeating and others will have taken their place.

"That apart from the fact that the contribution which the true repeaters make to the total accident picture is so small, there is no reliable way of singling them out beforehand from the rest of the group. You certainly cannot single them out on the basis of their accident records. You cannot do it on the basis of their violation records as the connection between traffic offences and accidents seems to be only slight, if it exists at all. Nor can you do it by means of psychological tests as no psychological factor has been proved to be closely related to accident involvement.

"That the existence of accident proneness has therefore never been established, and it is a fallacy to say that it is responsible for the majority of the accidents. On the contrary the vast majority of the accidents must be caused by some temporary lapse, some transitory weakness in people who are otherwise just normal drivers. This is the area where research time and money should be spent, not on pursuing some unimportant and unvalidated illusion like accident proneness."

In contrast to this, what do the supporters of the concept say? Actually they have never set out to argue their case in as definitive a manner as their antagonists. They are usually content to present their evidence and leave it at that. So let me present their case for them—in a manner similar to that of their critics. Very briefly, I think that the supporters of the concept would say:

"That although they believe that accidents have many complex interwoven causes, nevertheless they consider accident proneness to be a reality and an important one.

"That there are reliable ways of singling out the accident-prone.

"That it is not they, the supporters of the concept, who have been led astray by an illusion. It is the other way round. It is the 'so-called' evidence *against* the concept which is an illusion—the illusion being created because so much of the evidence has been inadequately presented or incorrectly construed."

These are the bare bones of the controversy and it seems, on the face of it, very unlikely that any worth-while conclusions will be reached if this militant attitude is maintained by either side. So, rather than argue the pros and cons in terms of "East is East and West is West and never the twain shall meet", let us examine the evidence, and particularly the more recent evidence, both for and against the validity and the usefulness of the concept in a spirit of realistic compromise.

I therefore propose to present the evidence of two recent major and seemingly contradictory studies, the California study and the PUTCO study, not individually but one in terms of the other—and both in terms of the findings of other pertinent studies either recent or of long standing. Perhaps, by doing this, some sense can be made of the confusion.

Both studies have been carried out on a very big scale over long periods of time, and both with strict methodology. The California study is important because it deals with the general public and therefore with the accident problem as a whole. But the very broadness of its scope imposes limitations on the absolute accuracy of the data and the detail in which it can be gathered. The PUTCO study, on the other hand, is concerned only with professional drivers, but is also important because of the detailed information available on those drivers. It is a study not only of trends, but in depth, and one in which it has been possible to investigate the causes of accidents as well as their occurrence. The two studies should therefore complement one another very well. *Quantitatively* one cannot generalize from the PUTCO data on professional bus drivers to the total accident problem of the California motoring public. But *qualitatively*, one can. Human beings are human beings, wherever or whatever they drive. And if it can be clearly demonstrated within one group that certain personal characteristics are closely related to accident occurrence, then there is every reason to presume that the same qualities will be operative in another group. No doubt they will be operative in different degrees, relative to the composition of the two groups, and also relative to the extent to which the people who comprise them are encouraged or discouraged from expressing these characteristics in accident-producing driving behaviour—either by the mores of locally accepted standards of the driving behaviour or the laxity or strength of some deterrent such as an enforcement policy. And where the PUTCO study can also be applicable to the California study is that as well as people being people, *individuals* are *individuals* the world over. They show a wide range of personal characteristics and a wide range of behaviour. Although quantitatively one cannot compare groups of South African bus drivers with a random sample of driving population of California, there must be many *individuals* in the bus-driver groups who have their counterparts in California—or for that matter in any other part of the world (particularly as the PUTCO study and its allied research projects deal with several racial groups, involving both White, Coloured, and Negro subjects).

There is even another way in which the two studies should complement one another. The California study was carried out in a country with a very low accident rate and where for many years the driving population had operated under the control of a strong system of enforcement. In South Africa the accident rate is still extremely high (the current fatality rate per mileage driven being *seven* times that of the United States). Although the PUTCO bus drivers have always been subjected to a great deal more discipline than the South African general driving public, they nevertheless operate within the context of the prevailing and often very unsatisfactory traffic conditions, and the prevailing (by United States standards) very undisciplined driving behaviour of the motoring public as a whole. Also the PUTCO study was carried out over a period of eighteen years during which (as a result of steadily implementing its findings) company discipline has become progressively more effective. Whereas the California study demonstrates the outcome of an established policy of driver control, the PUTCO study demonstrates every phase of a progressive effort to attain that control.

Surely then, in view of the tremendous scope of the two studies, it should be possible to use this wealth of material, backed by all the previous research, to clear up some of the confusion and to gain some worth-while knowledge on who has the accidents, why they have them, and how these accidents can be prevented or controlled?

Starting, then, with the California study carried out under the direction of Coppin of the Research and Statistics Section of the California Department of Motor Vehicles.* This was designed for the very practical purpose of gathering information which would assist

* The material from the California Studies is reproduced by courtesy of the Motor Vehicle Department and the authors.

the California MVD to assess the effectiveness of current programmes for driver control and improvement. It is covered by several main groups of reports. The chief of these is *The 1964 California Driver Record Study*, Parts 1–9 (1965–7) which is devoted to analysis of a completely random sample of 148,006 drivers representing some 2% of California's *eleven million licensed drivers*! One of the purposes of this analysis was to get a picture of the distribution of the total driving population in terms of sex, age, occupation, etc., so as to provide a "norm" against which to measure particular sub-groups such as teenage drivers, drivers involved in fatal accidents, or drivers singled out for action under the California points system. Another purpose was to use the records of these 148,006 drivers, which went back over a three-year period, in order to study a number of factors such as proneness to accidents or traffic violations, the relationship between violations and accidents, and the ability of one to predict the other. Future reports, still to come, will extend the study of this sample group for a further three years. As Coppin says, most of the basic work was done in order to show up those areas in which further detailed study was needed. Some of these areas have already been investigated, and the research, which is practical on-the-job research, is still in progress. (Various sections of the study have been carried out by different teams of investigators, who will be referred to under specific headings, but in discussing the general aspects of the California study it will be simpler to quote only Coppin's name.)

The *Driver Record Study* deals with three main indices of driving behaviour.

Accidents. Here the data are limited to those accidents contained in the departmental file, as represented by the following categories:

(1) All fatal and injury accidents.
(2) Property damage accidents investigated by the California Highway Patrol (CHP), or reported to them by the local police.
(3) All accidents reported by individuals in accordance with the Financial Responsibility Law. (Each driver involved in a property damage accident where the damage to the property of any one person is in excess of $100 is required to report the accident.)

Convictions. Full details of the various traffic offences are given in the text of the reports, but for most of the investigations only convictions for moving traffic violations were used.

Negligent Operator count. This is the particular points system used in California. One point is allotted for each accident for which the driver is deemed responsible by the MVD. One point is given for each traffic violation involving the safe operation of a motor vehicle. Convictions for reckless driving, drunken driving, hit-and-run driving, and driving while under licence suspension or revocation count double. A Negligent Operator is defined as one whose record shows a point count of 4 or more points in one year, 6 or more points in two years, and 8 or more points in three years.

As far as the accuracy of the departmental records is concerned, Coppin in his reports takes pains to point out that there is no guarantee that the accident reporting is complete (especially with PD accidents); and that the proportion of traffic violations detected and recorded, in relation to those which are actually committed, is completely unknown. (His personal feeling is that certain people would be more motivated to suppress information, especially on property damage accidents, than others, e.g. Negligent Operators, people with physical handicaps, etc.). However, as there is no possible way of knowing how accurate or complete the recording is, he says that in order to proceed with any statistical analysis of these records one has no option but to assume that there is a linear relationship between recorded and unrecorded events, i.e. those who have more violations *on their records* do in fact have *more unreported violations* and *more unreported* accidents. Unfortunately, one really cannot assume this at all because inevitably the "no-accidents" category would split up, (and once this had occurred it would, for instance, completely change the shape of the distributions and no doubt alter the size of the coefficients of correlation). One just has to admit it—the data are incomplete and in a manner which is quite unmeasurable.

Even apart from incomplete reporting, there are a number of other difficulties inherent in a study of this kind. The limitation of accident data to only the more serious accidents itself creates great statistical difficulties. It results in a very low accident rate, in much less obvious differences between individuals, in markedly skewed distributions, and in accentuating the influence of chance—especially as for practical reasons accidents are recorded on departmental file irrespective of the culpability of the driver. This latter factor may not be as important as it sounds, for several studies, such as Hakkinen (1958), Shaw and Sichel (1961), and Coppin (Jan. 1966), show that a record of all accidents irrespective of blame is, on the whole, a more sensitive discriminating measure than a record of only those where the driver is *officially* judged at fault. It seems that there is a factor of contributory negligence at work as people with an undue number of blameworthy accidents seem to have an undue number of *apparently* blameless ones as well. The most sensitive criterion would obviously be one which omitted the truly blameless accidents, but in practice it is often very difficult to determine exactly which these are. But, naturally, the lower the accident rate of the population under investigation the more the inclusion of the really blameless accidents would obscure the issue.

In addition, in data on the general driving public there is no control whatever over exposure, either in terms of time, or mileage, or traffic conditions. This factor makes it virtually impossible to produce any meaningful statistical comparison between one person and another, as there is no possible way of assessing the effects of these factors. Take mileage, for instance. Even if the subjects can give an estimate of the mileage they cover, it is hard to assess what this means. Undoubtedly a relatively high mileage increases the number of hazards encountered but, as can be seen from the accident records of drivers like the American transcontinental haulage drivers with their low accident rate, the relationship between mileage and accident rate is not a direct linear one and is obviously affected by other factors. Nor can one trust the estimates that people give. In Coppin's data he found a significant relationship between high mileage and high accident rates, but still could not be sure how much of this was due to the fact that Negligent Operators were suspected of grossly exaggerating their exposure, it being common knowledge that allowance is made for high mileage when deciding the severity of the action to be taken against them. With regard to the effect of traffic conditions, the PUTCO study shows that although more difficult traffic conditions naturally produce higher overall accident rates, nevertheless the *proportion* of these which are serious "reportable" accidents (reportable as defined by the fatality, injury, and PD standard used in the California study) differs according to traffic conditions. Heavy traffic conditions produce a higher number of total accidents, but a lower proportion of serious "reportable" ones. Less congested traffic conditions produce fewer total accidents and a higher proportion of "reportable" ones—probably due to the opportunity they offer for greater speeds. When one considers the diversity of the driving conditions in California, from country driving to congested city driving, to inter-city freeway driving, to city freeway driving (especially in a city like Los Angeles) the ensuing complications must be immense.

Another complicating factor is that only a certain amount of information is available on departmental files. Take, for instance, the problems involved in trying to assess the records of a group of drivers over a previous three-year period. If a driver has a current licence, it has to be presumed that he was driving during all that time. But in reality most licences only have to be renewed every four years, so during the period he could have died, or moved away, or driven for only part of the time because of injury, revocation, or suspension of his licence. This would mean curtailed exposure for a particularly important sub-group which could be expected to contain many of the people with higher than normal accident rates—the older age group, migratory labourers, students or military personnel, Negligent Operators, people killed or injured in accidents, etc.

Still another complication is the "suppressor effect" on negligent driving behaviour of knowing that disciplinary action could be taken; or even the possibility of actual disciplinary action—let alone the differential effects which both would have on different people. For example Coppin illustrates how both disciplinary action and involvement in accidents seems to have different immediate effects on males and females—being more apparent in the latter.

As Coppin repeatedly points out, all these conflicting factors are operative in his data, and make it essential that his figures are interpreted not in *absolute* terms, but in terms of general trends, and also in terms of all the many reservations with which he presents them. In fact his completely open-minded approach is conspicuous throughout his reports, as exemplified by the following extract from the *Control of the Negligent Operator* (1966):

> "In conclusion the authors feel that an explanation is in order for the numerous qualifications which have appeared throughout this report. The reader may have received the impression that more questions were raised than answered. It must be remembered, however, that research is not a panacea by which all problems are magically solved. It is merely a tool, which, if used in a certain way, can permit the forming of conclusions regarding specific events at a statistically determined level of confidence."

These factors would have such an influence on the California figures and so much bearing on how these figures should be interpreted that, despite their complexities, it is essential to try and evaluate them is some way. Much of what I am going to say now must therefore be regarded as supposition. But at any rate it can be informed supposition as it can be made in terms of Coppin's own suggestions, and also the findings of other relevant research.

Coppin's reports cover such a tremendous amount of ground that this discussion will unfortunately have to be limited to those findings which would appear to have exerted the greatest influence on current thinking: those findings which have in fact been interpreted as confirmation of the negligible role played by differential liability in the total accident picture.

The obvious starting point is therefore to examine the figures of the *California Driver Record Study* (Part 2, Coppin *et al.*, 1965) on the proportion of drivers with 0, 1, 2, 3, etc., accidents recorded against them over a three-year period; for there are many people who appear to think that one need look no further than these.

Coppin gives figures for the distribution of accidents among the sample group of 148,006 over the three years 1961–3. From these it is possible to estimate the proportion of the accidents in which each group was involved (Table 14.1).

TABLE 14.1

Drivers	No. of accidents	Responsible for % of total
122,592	0	0·0
21,349	1	70·5
3426	2	22·7
531	3	5·3
89	4	1·2
13	5	0·2
3	6	0·1
2	7	0·1
1	10	0·03

From this it would appear that the two-or-more accident "repeaters" do only constitute 2·8% of the sample—and as it is a very big random sample one is entitled to generalize from it to the whole California driving public.

It is the smallness of this proportion which is considered by many to be sufficient justification for saying that one need look no further, as the accident-repeaters are obviously too few and far between to matter. This, however, is possibly not in itself a good argument for a number of reasons:

(1) There are good grounds for believing that this 2·8% is not a true reflection of the position at any given moment.
(2) Even if it were a true reflection 2·8% still constitutes *a lot of people* with a *lot of accidents* (30% of the accidents of this period).
(3) It might not be justifiable to dismiss this 30% as the inevitable result of a chance distribution.
(4) The distribution does, in fact, appear to be anything but a chance one and, what is more, there is good reason to believe that the explanation as to why many of these people were involved in these accidents had very little to do with their being just victims of the law of probability.

Starting then with the size of the 2·8% proportion. With California's accident rate being very similar to the low rate of the United States in general, it is to be expected that only a small proportion of the population would have multiple serious accidents, for America's good highways, good traffic control, and generally orderly driving behaviour immediately strike any visitor from abroad. But, nevertheless, compared with the figures from a group of PUTCO drivers, this figure does seem suspiciously small. In the PUTCO group described in connection with Forbes' study, the proportion with two similarly defined "reportable" accidents in a three-year period was 32% of the group (responsible for 73% of the accidents!). There were also as many as 19 3×3 accident *repeaters* among a little group of 142 drivers, and only 23 among the huge group of 29,500 in the Connecticut study. One would expect a higher accident rate from these full-time bus drivers, but not a difference as startling as this. There must be other powerful influences, besides generally lower accident rates, operating in State records to create such wide discrepancies.

One of them is undoubtedly incomplete reporting, the effect of which cannot be assessed.

Another is the fact that whereas the PUTCO drivers were all males, Coppin's 2·8% applies to a mixed sample of males (87,000) and females (61,000) and there are considerable differences in their accident rates. In fact the males in Coppin's sample were (for various reasons) found to have a rate roughly twice that of the females and to be involved in two-thirds of the accidents. The distribution of accidents in the male portion of Coppin's group would probably give different results, which in fact it does (figures kindly supplied by Coppin) (Table 14·2).

TABLE 14.2

Drivers	No. of accidents	Responsible for % of total
68,216	0	0
15,168	1	67·3
2775	2	24·6
457	3	6·1
85	4	1·5
13	5	0·3
3	6	0·1
2	7	0·1
1	10	0·1

The two-accident offenders now constitute 3·8% of the drivers and are now responsible for 32% of the accidents, which means that the gap is closing, though hardly noticeably.

Another reason for the discrepancy could be action taken by the California MVD itself to *prevent this sort of repeating*—a warning or, in the worst cases, suspension or revocation of licence. The Department does not have to wait for a series of accidents before it acts. It is in fact empowered to pull in for re-examination or hearing anyone who has been involved in even one serious accident and to scrutinize the record of *every* driver involved in a fatal one. It would also take some form of action against all Negligent Operators, who, as Coppin's study shows, are people with a much higher than average accident potential, but one which is very often curbed as a result of departmental action.

Certainly something must happen to a number of the high-accident offenders either to curtail their exposure or remove them from the group. Coppin gives figures for three groups of people licensed during the individual years 1961–3 but not necessarily over the whole period. The groups are therefore larger than the one with 148,000, but nevertheless each of the yearly groups *does contain this group*. Here one can see that there were people in each year with two, three, or four accidents *in one year*. Whatever the purely statistical chances might be of this happening, I think there are very few practical traffic officials who would attribute people's high accident involvement, *or* their apparent miraculous improvement, purely to chance. Actually an analysis of the losses between 159,000 subjects included in the 1961 group, and the 148,000 whose California licences were still unexpired at the end of the three years and therefore entitled them to be included in the three-year group, shows a characteristic pattern of loss especially for the males.

In the 0 accident group	7·7% of the males and	5·8% of the females
1	7·0%	5·2%
2	11·0%	5·9%
3 or more	10·6%	0·0%

The most likely explanation for this seems to be that the losses (due to people not renewing their licences) consist largely of a mixture of:

(a) People with good records—mostly older people who are good risks or do very little actual driving.

(b) People who have very bad records where the loss could be due to death, injury, imprisonment, removal of licence, or the moving away from California of a number of young job seekers, students, or military personnel.

This supposition seems to be borne out by a subsidiary study of Coppin's (Oct. 1962) where questionnaires were sent out to 350 people who had been classified as Negligent Operators but whose records were found to be *completely* clear for three years after departmental action. Here it was found that:

17 people had died.

104 questionnaires were returned unclaimed.

64 were delivered but no replies were received.

165, only, were filled in and could be studied—and of these only 142 of the subjects had not been absent from the State.

This means that in a small, important group, anything up to half the people were probably not driving all the time—although there was nothing entered on their files to indicate that they should be excluded from any investigation of drivers with currently unexpired licences. (Interestingly enough, of the 17 people who had died within three years of action—plus 4 more who had died subsequently and before the inquiry took place—10 were by violent means, 6 of them being killed in auto accidents.)

Individually these various factors (except the incomplete reporting) would possibly only have a small effect, but collectively they might have a significance which would mean that the 2·8% is not a true reflection of either the size of the multiple offender class, or of its accident potential.

Nor does it seem that the actual number of accidents (30%) which were recorded against these people can be lightly dismissed.

In the first place it does not seem to be a vagary of chance. Coppin's comparison of the distribution of accidents within groups licensed for three years, or even only one year, shows them all to be significantly different from chance—though he reports that the significance was not great. But as the subjects are not equally exposed one cannot really assess his findings in this respect. However, here, one can get some information from other studies. When the exposure *is* controlled, as in Hakkinen's study and the PUTCO one, the significant differences from chance still persist. Something beside the law of probability is obviously operating to produce unusual distributions amongst professional drivers, and there is no reason to believe that it would not be operating to some degree in the California drivers also. (However, it is interesting to note here that in the PUTCO study the differences between observed and chance-expected distributions diminished steadily in progressive chronological groups as the company's disciplinary programme against accident and traffic offenders became more effective.)

In any case, isn't this traditional method of comparing accident distributions with Poisson ones (of necessity calculated from the same data) rather overdone? After all this is not a theoretical problem of the manner in which chance would be most likely to distribute exactly x balls in y pigeon-holes. There do not *have* to be x accidents at all. The number x is the total number of accidents incurred by a group of y people; and whether x is small or large must depend to a considerable extent *on the accident-producing behaviour of the people who constitute this group*. So one is already using as a comparison a distribution which could in fact be anything but chance-dictated.*

However, for the moment, this is a minor, and no doubt highly controversial point. For even such distributions of accidents as happen (or manage to get reported), usually turn out to be very different from chance, and therefore, at least in part, are presumably due to differences in the accident liability of the drivers themselves.

As to what causes these differences, Coppin has not yet published any specific reports on his multiple accident offenders as such, but there are several of his general reports where the information given is very pertinent; for he shows that groups which, on the whole, display *relatively* high accident rates do also display characteristics which are significantly different from the norms of the "average" population. A group of over 4000 Negligent Operators, being those contacted by the Department over a six-month period, had accident rates which, compared with the general driving population were:

4 times as great for the three years before action.
2·5 times as great for the three years after action.
2 times as great for the subsequent three years.

The group was over-represented with males (96·5% as against 52% in the general driving public), with people belonging to the labourer, or artisan, or professional driver class, people with criminal records, and people with a high count of previous traffic violations (this count being eleven times that of the general public for the three years prior to contact

---

* As in the PUTCO data on p. 277 where the distribution of accidents in the 1954–6 group was not significantly different from the Poisson—and yet this was the group with the highest accident rate of all.

by the Department). So it seems that there are a number of significant differences in this group.

Coppin's study clearly shows that people with a high accident rate tend to have more than the average number of traffic violations. This finding, namely the relationship between traffic offences, and accidents, is so important, and also is one which has been the subject of so much controversy, that it would be worth examining his findings on this question in some detail—especially as his studies are not only the most recent, but also the most comprehensive, and also the only ones where the findings for males and females are given separately. This relationship can be considered in two contexts:

(1) The concurrent relationship, i.e. where the violations and accidents occur *within the same period*; or
(2) The predictive relationship, where violations are considered in terms of how well they will *predict future accidents in a subsequent period*.

For the moment the first is our main consideration.

Coppin's data on concurrent accidents and citations cover the three-year period 1961–3 and again involve the records of the sample of 148,000 drivers. His findings are given in Part 4 of the *Driver Record Study* (Coppin, Lew and Peck, 1965). His data, he says, are limited to those violations and accidents recorded on departmental file, and one has to assume that these are highly correlated with the unrecorded ones. However, many citations for moving traffic offences are written after full investigation of a traffic accident. Thus one can safely assume that persons involved in accidents tend to have a greater likelihood of receiving traffic citations than those that are not involved in accidents. This "built-in" correlation he refers to as the "spurious" element. In establishing a true relationship between citations and accidents, he feels that one must remove this "spurious" element; otherwise a somewhat inflated picture of the relationship would result. (Coppin admits that this is a moot point, as these citations refer to negligent driving behaviour which was apparently considered by the investigating police as contributory to the accident. But in view of the many occasions when this "spurious" relationship has been regarded as the reason why any relationship exists *at all*, his conservative approach is a very wise one.) Figure 14.1 depicts the relationship between the accident and citation rates. Even if only the non-spurious citations are considered, Coppin points out that the accident rate (per 100 persons) of the nine-or-more-conviction group is slightly more than $6\frac{1}{2}$ times that of the no-citation group. If spurious convictions are used the ratios are slightly higher throughout. (The fluctuations in the higher categories are primarily attributable to small sample sizes.)

The accident/citation correlation coefficients are: 0·23 (non-spurious) and 0·27 (spurious).

Figure 14·2 depicts the relationship between accident rates and *non-spurious* citations for males and females separately. Here the correlations are 0·22 (males) and 0·16 (females) —all coefficients being significant beyond the 0·01 level. As Coppin points out there is a statistically significant sex difference in the relationship between accidents and citations:

"It may be inferred from this finding that violations are more highly related (linearly) to male accident frequency than to female accident frequency. The reader should not

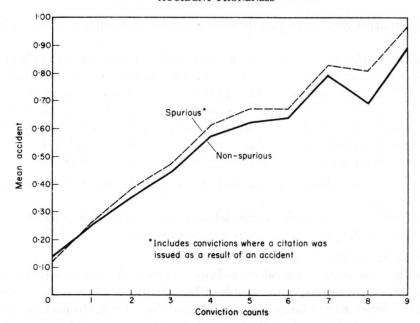

FIG. 14.1. Mean accidents (over three years) by spurious and non-spurious conviction counts. (Coppin, 1965)

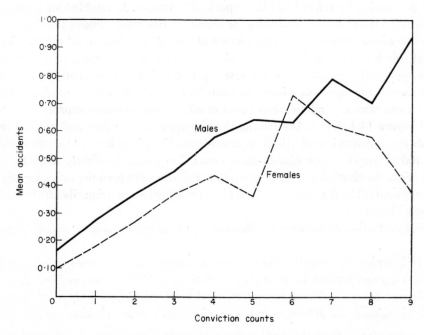

FIG. 14.2. Mean accidents (over three years) by non-spurious conviction counts and sex. (Coppin, 1965)

interpret the relationship between citations and accident frequency as necessarily being a causal one, since it is possible that all or part of the relationship between the two variables stems from the effect of other variables. (For example, exposure could possibly account for some of the correlation between citation and accident frequency.) This may be due to the fact that females generally drive under conditions different from those which males experience and are thus exposed to relatively different degrees and types of traffic hazards. Lastly, the female psychology with respect to driving may be different from that of males, thus resulting in more cautious, or more defensive driving behavior, even when external driving conditions are similar."

My personal feeling regarding the relationship between mileage and accidents/or violations, is that mileage would be more highly related to accidents than to violations. But Coppin is, nevertheless, right in his conservative approach and in pointing out the possible influence of the mileage factor. However, saying that "all or part" of the relationship between citations and accidents could be due to other factors besides a causal one, later turned out to be rather over-conservative. This can be seen from Table 14·3 below, which reveals a definite relationship between citations and *subsequent* accidents. As Coppin says in a later report (Nov. 1965) some sort of interrelationship must be expected because of the "accident-related elements" contained in the traffic citations. To quote him on this point: "By this the authors are referring to the fact that violations of traffic laws (reckless driving, speeding, etc.) are often cited as being precipitating factors in accident involvement. In fact, many traffic control laws were established in response to specific histories of accident experience."

This relationship was confirmed by a later study of Coppin's reported in Parts 8 and 9 of the *Driver Record Study* (Jan. and March 1967), and also by Harrington, one of the project members, in the *Research Review* of *Traffic Safety* (1968). Here, using two samples of some 43,000 males and 30,000 females licensed during 1961–3, a factor analysis was carried out on a number of possible accident predictors such as various traffic offences, age, marital status, etc.

In the *Driver Record Study* the most predictive of the variables were refined out by multiple regression analysis and formed into predictive mathematical formulae. Among the findings were, that for both males and females, the item of information which was by far the best predictor of *future* accident involvement was the actual *number* of traffic convictions (i.e. the number of separate occasions on which the driver had been caught and convicted for a moving traffic offence of any kind).

In Harrington's slightly different analysis of the same material eighteen variables were intercorrelated and reduced to five main factors, moving violations, non-moving violations, age, weight, and height. Only two of these correlated with accidents; age, slightly but significantly; and, very significantly, the moving violation factor. As Harrington says, the relatively close association between accidents and this factor is to be expected because the "moving violation factor is descriptive of actual driving behavior and the type of errors made by drivers".

The purely theoretical belief that there is little evidence to suggest a significant relationship between accidents and traffic offences does not seem to receive much support from

TABLE 14.3. PREDICTION OF ACCIDENTS FROM PRIOR CONVICTION
RECORD AMONG A GROUP OF CALIFORNIA DRIVERS (FIGURES SUP-
PLIED BY COPPIN)

One-year Accident Rates Based on Two-year Conviction Record

Number of convictions in 1961 and 1962	Accidents per 100 drivers in 1963	Times as many*	Number of drivers
TOTAL	6·3		148,000
0	4·6	1·00	101,127
1	7·9	1·72	29,000
2	10·7	2·33	9944
3	13·5	2·93	3991
4	16·8	3·65	1833
5	16·9	3·67	929
6	18·7	4·07	503
7	25·8	5·61	279
8 or more	20·3	4·41	394

Two-year Accident Rates Based on One-year Conviction Record

Number of convictions in 1961	Accidents per 100 drivers in 1962 and 1963	Times as many*	Number of drivers
TOTAL	13·5		148,000
0	11·2	1·00	118,555
1	19·8	1·77	21,689
2	27·9	2·49	5225
3	33·6	3·00	1536
4	43·3	3·86	563
5	42·6	3·80	235
6	37·3	3·33	93
7	75·6	6·75	41
8 or more	28·6	2·55	63

* This number represents the relative increase in accident rate
over the "0 countable citations" group.

Coppin's findings. This belief has always been based on the low correlation coefficients
obtained, but the inadequacy of the *r* coefficient to adequately portray a relationship when
the distributions are so tremendously skewed, is rather graphically revealed by Coppin's
two charts. This seems to be yet another occasion when a most irrational conclusion has
been drawn on the basis of this rather dangerous statistical technique.

   The contention that people with higher than usual accident rates display distinctive
characteristics is one which has received a very strong confirmation from other studies.
Time and again, among groups of very different subjects, major studies have come up
with this sort of finding. And though it is often held that the fact that different studies have

highlighted different characteristics has shown the evidence to be "contradictory", this again is not a very logical conclusion. The differences have occurred because different studies have used different approaches and investigated different areas, and the findings they have produced do in fact *supplement* one another very satisfactorily. Some of the major studies in this field are:

TILLMANN (1949) on Canadian taxi drivers and members of the general public where the characteristics were those of social maladjustment, and the criterion of a high accident offender was someone with four or more serious accidents over the previous fifteen years.

McFARLAND (1954) on United States truck drivers where the characteristics were social maladjustment plus traffic offences, and the criterion was three or more responsible accidents over a previous twelve-month period.

CONGER (1959) on United States airmen where the characteristics were personality defects, and an accident offender was someone with two or more responsible accidents over the previous four years.

HAKKINEN (1958) on Finnish bus drivers, where a battery of psychomotor personality tests (which included a large element of skill) were able to distinguish between drivers with a whole range of accident involvement, namely 0–30 accidents per man over the previous eight years: $N = 94$; $R = 0.64$.

The PUTCO study on South African bus drivers (full details of which will be found in the following two chapters) where a battery of projective personality tests was able to predict *future* accident involvement (irrespective of the length of exposure) in terms of the average number of "driving" days between accidents: $N = 1139$; $r = 0.66$.

There are even studies which show that groups of people involved in one single serious accident show characteristics which differentiate them from the accident-free:

BARMACK and PAYNE (1961a, b) where the subjects were young United States airmen, and where the characteristics were involvement in civil and military infractions, problem drinking, and problem home backgrounds; and the criterion of a high accident offender was someone who had survived a single accident (involving a fatality or serious injury) occurring over the previous eighteen months.

KAESTNER (1964), where the subjects were 904 United States drivers involved in a fatal accident over a two-year period, and this time included those who had been killed in the accidents. Here, compared with an accident-free control group, the characteristics of the fatal-accident group were: a preponderance of young drivers, especially males; a higher prior accident and conviction rate, particularly for certain types of convictions; and the tendency of drivers in their thirties and forties, or even older, to have convictions similar to the younger drivers and indicative of immaturity.

SELZER, ROGERS and KERN (1968), where information was obtained from the drivers held responsible for a fatal accident (if they survived) and also from their relatives, employers, and the State records, and compared with a control group of ninety-six drivers not involved in similar accidents, matched according to age, sex, and home county. The F (fatal accident) group showed highly significantly more paranoid thinking, suicidal tendencies and thoughts, and clinical depression. They were inclined to more violent behaviour, especially to being involved in fights and getting beaten up in them. Those of the F group who displayed the psychopathological symptoms had at least 50% more prior accidents of all kinds and twice as many previous serious accidents (where someone was killed or injured or the car totally demolished or overturned) than those without the symptoms. Nearly 20% of the F group had had violent quarrels, mostly with women (wives, girl-friends, barmaids, and female drinking companions) in the six hours preceding the accident. (Like Tillmann's group of male traffic violators brought in for therapy (1965) who were markedly paranoid and antagonistic to women, whom they blamed for most of their troubles, including their accidents.)

And Coppin's own subsidiary study (Jan. 1966) (Coppin and van Oldenbeek, 1966), where a group of 777 surviving drivers brought in for re-examination after an accident involving a fatality, were found to be significantly different from the driving population "norm", in that the group contained proportionately more males, more young drivers under 35, less people with auto-liability insurance; they were more often single, widowed, or divorced, or belonging to the labourer, unskilled, or semi-skilled category; they had worse violation records (but in this study there was no difference in their previous accident records—a finding similar to that of Barmack and Payne with the young airmen involved in one serious accident). Most of Coppin's findings —like Kaestner's—were accentuated for those of his drivers who were considered to be entirely responsible for the accidents in which they had been involved.

There seems to be ample research evidence to support the belief that multiple accidents (and even one serious accident) are unlikely to occur by chance; that the people who are involved in them usually display different characteristics from the lesser offenders; and that there are methods available which can even pick them out in advance. It seems, in fact, that there is ample scientific confirmation of the old adage that there is no smoke without fire—the practical man's interpretation of accident proneness in terms of accident *potential*, and also the practical principle on which driver enforcement policies are based.

It also seems that the statement made in 1939 by Cobb about the multiple accident offenders in the Connecticut study, "small in number but mighty in deed", was no exaggeration; and the fact of the California multiple-accident offenders being involved in 30% of the accidents of a three-year period was by no means a statistical vagary of chance. It seems, in the light of research findings, that the probabilities are that not only were they *involved* in their accidents but that they actually *caused* many of them, *because they were the sort of people who, during one period at least, were very unsatisfactory accident risks.*

However, so much, for the moment, for the consideration of Coppin's findings on the distribution of accidents in one period.

The evaluation of an accident risk in terms of whether or not he goes on repeating is an equally valid one; and again one of very great practical importance. For in a practical situation such as that found in an insurance company, a man's past accident record is often one of the few available yardsticks by which to assess his future accident potential. In State Motor Vehicle Departments where adequate records are kept, this can be augmented by data on traffic violations. Until Coppin's follow-up study of those of his 148,000 group who remained licensed for a *further* three years (1964–6) is published, the evidence from his studies is confined to an examination of his group over the *first* three years (1961–3) and the predicting power of one year against another, or two years against a third. In view of the short time-intervals used and the fact that the investigation was limited to only seldom-occurring serious accidents, it is not to be wondered at that the results were not, from a statistical point of view, very encouraging. It will be interesting to see what emerges from his 3×3 year follow-up study, though it will be surprising if, in view of all the forces operating to suppress further involvement in serious accidents, the results are very different from those of the earlier Connecticut study. However, as the rather disappointing findings of this year-by-year study have no doubt exerted consider-able influence on current American thinking, it should definitely be described here. This formed Part 6 of the CDR study, McBride, Peck and Coppin, Nov. 1965.)

The study involved not only accidents but traffic offences (for both males and females) because, as the authors say, the whole policy of withdrawing a licence on the basis of previous citations and/or accidents is based on certain assumptions regarding the rela-tionship between past and future performance on both counts. At the same time they wished to relate their findings to the question of accident proneness. As they put it:

"It has been commonly held that there is a relatively small portion of drivers who are consistently responsible for the majority of all accidents. However, there has been much controversy among safety experts about the accident proneness concept. In recent years it has been frequently pointed out that the contribution of accident re-peaters to the over-all accident picture is negligible and that accidents are only slightly related to persisting individual differences among people. [Forbes, 1939; Goldstein, 1963.]"*

However, in view of the fact that there was no control over exposure in their data, they felt that their study could not be used to evaluate the concept *per se* but only to assess overall liability in the form of continued repeating, whatever the underlying reasons.

Among the investigations they carried out was to examine the distributions for the three years 1961–3, both for accidents and citations. All were found to be significantly different from the Poisson ones, which indicated that a factor of "proneness" could be present, but the lack of control over exposure made it impossible to say that it definitely was present, let alone quantify it. However, the data indicated that the element of chance was more operative in accidents than in citations, and more operative in females than in males for both accidents and citations.

A second investigation was to see how the drivers with 0, 1, 2, etc., accidents or cita-tions had fared in the subsequent years. These results are set out in Tables 14.4 and 14.5.

Discussing these results the authors say that in terms of relative contribution it was readily apparent that both the accident and citation frequencies for the various groups were directly related to their 1961 frequencies. They then went on to explore this rela-

* A joint statement by Peck and Coppin on their current views on the whole question of accident proneness is given in Chapter 13.

TABLE 14.4. THE RELATIVE ACCIDENT RATES IN SUBSEQUENT YEARS (IN TERMS OF THE 1961 RATES) OF A GROUP OF CALIFORNIA DRIVERS (FROM COPPIN, NOV. 1965)

1961 accident frequency	Number* of drivers	1962	1963	1962 and 1963 combined
		Times as many†	Times as many†	Times as many†
MALES and FEMALES				
0	138,343	1·00	1·00	1·00
1	9072	1·81	1·70	1·76
2	547	2·37	2·43	2·40
3 or more	44	5·68	4·55	4·97
MALES				
0	79,595	1·00	1·00	1·00
1	6638	1·61	1·49	1·56
2	451	1·94	2·01	1·99
3 or more	42	4·60	3·76	4·09
FEMALES				
0	58,748	1·00	1·00	1·00
1	2434	1·69	1·89	1·79
2	96	2·74	3·03	2·86
3 or more	2	—	—	—

* Sample totals: males and females, 148,006; males, 86,726; females, 61,280.
† This number represents the relative increase in accident rate over the 0 accident group.

tionship by means of correlation techniques, the resulting coefficients being given in Table 14.6.

Discussing these coefficients the authors say that in every case the results are consistent with those presented descriptively in Tables 14.4 and 14.5.

"Although none of the obtained correlations are very high, the between-violation coefficients are several times higher than the between-accident coefficients, and the male correlations are higher than the female correlations. It is readily apparent from these results that citations can predict citations far better than accidents can predict accidents and that male driving performance (record) is more predictable than female driving performance. This should not be surprising in view of our earlier findings concerning the shape of the respective distributions in relation to the Poisson.

"These results provide much more evidence for the existence of 'violation-proneness' than for accident proneness. Concerning the latter, it would appear that the contribution of accident-prone subjects to the over-all California accident picture must be a very small one indeed. First of all, the correlations between accident frequencies among drivers in different intervals of time, though statistically significant, are very low and of little predictive utility."

It is interesting to note, they say, that combining a two-year record to predict a third-year record yielded a relatively higher coefficient than correlating one-year periods. This

TABLE 14.5. THE RELATIVE CITATION RATES IN SUBSEQUENT YEARS (IN TERMS OF THE 1961 RATES) OF A GROUP OF CALIFORNIA DRIVERS (FROM COPPIN, NOV. 1965)

1961 citation frequency	Number* of drivers	1962 Times as many†	1963 Times as many†	1962 and 1963 combined Times as many†
MALES and FEMALES				
0	120,569	1·00	1·00	1·00
1	21,045	2·40	2·21	2·31
2	4620	4·00	3·73	3·87
3	1227	5·80	5·08	5·46
4	370	6·42	5·44	5·95
5	99	6·66	6·27	6·32
6	44	10·25	7·58	8·99
7 or more	32	10·29	3·88	5·18
MALES				
0	65,777	1·00	1·00	1·00
1	15,406	2·04	1·90	1·98
2	3926	3·16	2·97	3·07
3	1112	4·40	3·98	4·20
4	340	5·00	4·15	4·60
5	95	5·02	4·70	4·75
6	41	7·57	5·98	6·83
7 or more	29	6·90	2·87	3·46
FEMALES				
0	54,792	1·00	1·00	1·00
1	5639	2·36	2·17	2·28
2	694	4·03	4·05	4·07
3	115	7·04	5·01	6·10
4	30	4·00	7·25	5·59
5	4	5·00	10·87	7·85
6	3	16·67	3·62	10·47
7 or more	3	33·33	7·25	17·45

* Sample totals: males and females, 148,006; males, 86,726; females, 61,280.
† This number represents the relative increase in accident rate over the 0 accident group.

is to be expected in view of the fact that "increasing the time interval allows for a more extensive sampling of the driving behavior, which, in turn, increases the degree of stability by reducing chance variations".

The authors then go on to a discussion of the various limitations inherent in their data and the effect they could be having on these results—particularly on the correlation coefficients—and here they mention all the points discussed earlier in this chapter. Because of the lack of control over exposure, the correlations obtained between time-intervals could in one sense be considered to be overestimates of stability. But, in another sense, because of a number of other factors (such as changes in highways and traffic conditions, incomplete reporting, curtailed exposure due to death, illness or migration from California,

TABLE 14.6. CORRELATIONS BETWEEN ACCIDENTS AND
CITATIONS AMONG A GROUP OF CALIFORNIA DRIVERS
(COPPIN, NOV. 1965)

Accident—Accident Correlations over Time*

Years correlated	Males	Females
1961 by 1962	0·054	0·028
1961 by 1963	0·036	0·041
1961, 1962 by 1963	0·060	0·041
1962 by 1963	0·050	0·028

Citation—Citation Correlations over Time*

Years correlated	Males	Females
1961 by 1962	0·252	0·142
1962 by 1963	0·239	0·153
1961 by 1963	0·217	0·137

Correlation between Citations and Accidents*

Conviction year	Accident year	Males	Females
1961	1961	0·116	0·072
1961	1962	0·089	0·066
1961	1963	0·075	0·048
1962	1962	0·115	0·073
1962	1963	0·083	0·057
1963	1963	0·100	0·069

* All correlations in these tables are significant at
beyond 0·01 level of confidence.

action by the MVD, or even the suppressor effect of the accidents themselves) they could alternatively be *underestimates*.

"Now that it has been reasoned that the obtained correlation coefficients are underestimates of the reliability of accidents and citations, the magnitude of the underestimates must be considered. Toward this end, Newbold and Cobb (Thorndike, 1951) have proposed a mathematical model which represents the maximum correlation of reliability which can be obtained between two sets of accident scores and an infallible set of predictive scores. Application of this formula to the accident and citation distributions produces a maximum reliability coefficient of 0·29 for accidents and 0·52 for citations. These reliabilities are considerably higher than the previous underestimates based on between-interval correlations and represent correlational ceilings. In other words, we can never expect a variable or set of variables, even accidents themselves, to correlate beyond 0·29 with a given year's accident frequencies; furthermore, since no set of measures can be infallible the realistic reliability ceiling must be considerably lower, falling somewhere between the obtained correlation of 0·06 and the Newbold–Cobb estimate of 0·29. The difference between the two correlations provides an indication of loss of predictability due to lack of control of exposure and person-centered variables over time. With such variables perfectly controlled, any remaining difference between the coefficients would be attributable to inherent unreliability (inconsistency) in the occurrence of reported accidents and citations."

They feel, however, that the maximum estimated reliability ceiling is too low to be of any great practical value.

Dealing with the contribution of accident-repeaters to the overall accident problem, they say: "It has been popular to suggest that the best solution to the traffic accident problem would be to remove the accident-repeater from our roads and highways." This, they feel, is not borne out by their data. Removing those with one or more accidents in 1961 (6·5%) would have reduced the accidents of 1962 by 11·4% and 1963 by 11·0%. Although this shows a continuation of a disproportionate contribution in accidents, they nevertheless point out that those not involved in accidents in 1961 still contributed almost 90% of the accidents of the two subsequent years. "It should be clear from this presentation alone", they say, "that the removal of accident-involved drivers from the driving population would not result in a drastic reduction of future accidents."

Extrapolating from some of their figures on accident-repeaters to the general population, they say that although the contribution of those with accidents in *both* 1961 and 1962 was twice that of those with none, removing them would have entailed removing 55,400 California drivers in order to reduce the total reported accidents of 1963 by 7300, of which 59 could be inferred to have involved a fatality.

Remarking on this, they say:

"It must be admitted that the above analysis is somewhat oversimplified since it assumes that the accident rate of the remaining drivers would not have been affected by gross removal of the accident repeaters, and also that accident fatalities are a random component within total reported accident frequencies. Since the accident repeater probably causes a disproportionate number of accidents in which he is not involved, the accident reduction, consequent to his removal, would be somewhat greater than the above figures indicate and, of course, the driving task of the remaining driving population would be less fraught with danger. Despite this inherent oversimplification, it should still be apparent that the removal of accident repeaters would not have appreciably reduced the accident rate of the remaining population of drivers, nor have effected a dramatic reduction in fatality."

McBride, Peck and Coppin conclude their report as follows:

"In addition to providing an abundance of data, this present effort has led to a more precise formulation of the problem and its subsequent exploration. It should be clear from the foregoing analysis that attempts to predict and control accidents through focusing attention on individual drivers can never produce dramatic results in the overall traffic safety problem. Based on the estimated reliability ceiling ($r = 0.29$) for accidents over a three year interval, it is impossible that any predictive battery or model can ever account for more than nine percent $(0.29)^2$ of the variability in accidents over a three year period. (Due to the greater frequency of accidents among Negligent Operators, the stability and reliability ceiling of the accident variables among the Negligent Operator population would be somewhat higher.) This, of course, drastically limits the total amount of accident control or reduction which can be achieved through driver improvement programs directed at the negligent driver and it is probably why it has been so difficult for such programs to demonstrate significant accident reducing effects. (Coppin, 1965.)

"This should not be construed as meaning that such programs should be discarded, for even a small reduction is worthwhile when the saving is in the form of human life. In addition, the existence of such programs probably has indirect effects on the accident problem by removing negligent drivers from the driving environment and by reinforcing the prescribed driving norms. It seems clear, then, that the task facing all administrators of driver improvement and driver licensing programs is the development of programs with a *maximum* potential of reducing citations and accidents. However, the present research has also demonstrated the need for improving the skills of (or reducing hazards for) the general driving population—not just the accident repeater or habitual violator."

In a later report by the same authors (Report No. 9, March 1967) the conclusions reached were a little more optimistic. Using regression equations to obtain the best combination of predictors they found that combinations of exposure factors such as mileage and local traffic density, plus person-centred factors such as total number of convictions, age, and marital status, yielded better predicting coefficients. (The reader is asked to refer to the actual report for details of this very complex investigation.) The most significant person-centred factors were those "indicative of how a driver drives", and these remained significant even when the exposure factors were held constant. From this the authors concluded that the study provided evidence "for at least a statistical concept of accident proneness, in that some people are more likely to be involved in accidents than others, even with exposure (as measured by annual mileage and traffic density) controlled". And again they said that the existence of such people justified research into improving the programmes for identifying, controlling, and rehabilitating them.

However, despite this more hopeful note, the authors are careful to point out that the small magnitude of prediction achieved, plus the relatively low optimum ceiling of prediction as computed by the Newbold–Cobb formula, indicated that the magnitude of the contribution of the accident-liable driver must still be a small one.

Both these studies are very informative and shed some much-needed light on State statistical records and the problems associated with the handling of these records.

I think, however, that in both studies the authors' final summing-up is unduly pessimistic, and that they have perhaps allowed themselves to get so depressed by the poor showing of their figures that they have at times forgotten their own reservations—with the result that they have arrived at some rather far-reaching conclusions which are *mathematically* justifiable in terms of absolute data, but not necessarily *logically* justifiable in view of the limitations of the data.

For a most important point which one must never lose sight of is that the population they are working with is *not* an undisturbed one. It is one in which action is constantly being taken against the very people in whom one is most interested—action which might mean a drastic curtailment of exposure and therefore of even the chance of a further accident. Only if it were a truly undisturbed population would one be able, for instance, to measure from the accidents of a subsequent period what *would have been the true effect if one had removed certain people*.But when the relatively small contribution which they actually made to the accidents of a subsequent period could have been due to the fact that for part of the time they were *already* removed, then fully removing them is naturally not going to produce dramatic effects. In addition, even if they were not actually removed by death, injury, or departmental action, it is pretty certain that some effort was made to improve their subsequent records. These points are clearly illustrated by Coppin's findings on the pre- and post-action records of a big group of Negligent Operators. Their pre-action accident rate was four times that of the general public, but their post-action rate, though still well above the norm for the population, was nevertheless roughly half of what is was *before action was taken*. Whatever the reasons for these differences in accident rate (and they could be anything from natural improvement, to the salutary effect of action, to the fact that their exposure was curtailed, or they died, or just moved away), the important thing is that this drop did occur, *and any figures relating to post-action exposure in a subsequent period must reflect this*.

I think, therefore, that it is unjustifiable to use the disappointing results of the *further* whittling down of accident rates which have *already* been whittled down as a measurement of how little these people actually contributed. I think what one ought to keep in mind is not what they *still* contributed but *what they could have contributed had no action been taken*. In similar 3×3 year statistical analyses (see Chapters 4 and 15) on professional drivers the groups are *limited to those people whose exposure was not curtailed*. And although this means exclusion, because of dismissal, of the worst risks, it is undoubtedly one of the reasons why these studies come up with such different results: in fact, why the offenders of the first period contribute such a relatively substantial portion of the accidents of the second period. In the figures on serious "reportable" accidents among the PUTCO drivers, given in Chapter 4 in connection with the Connecticut data, the contribution made by the repeaters (whether one defined them as two, three, or more accidents in the first three-year period) fell consistently to *half* in the second period. In the Connecticut data, with its 3×3 year analysis, it fell consistently to *one-seventh*.

Exactly the same line of logic applies to the conclusions drawn from applying the Newbold–Cobb formula to the California data—namely that with a low reliability ceiling such as $r = 0 \cdot 29$, no set of predictive indicators could ever correlate with the accident data beyond this level. So far so good, but one need not get too depressed about the potential of the predictors when much of the fault obviously lies with the criterion which, with its incomplete and uncontrolled and virtually tampered-with data, is unreliable in rather more senses than a statistical one. Undoubtedly no battery of predictors will ever correlate highly with this *unreliable kind of criterion*, which limits the *mathematical* success one can have, but not necessarily by any means the *practical* success—as, for instance, where judgement of future accident potential is based on something completely independent of all the mathematical imponderables, i.e. the judgement of officials in the Motor Vehicle Departments, experienced in dealing with traffic offenders, judgements which do in practice seem to be working very well. (The same applies to another practical situation, where the PUTCO battery of personality tests has correlated with a reliable criterion of future accident involvement with an *r* of 0·66.)

In the same way I feel one cannot generalize from a mathematical model, based on data which are of necessity rather shaky, to the whole accident situation: to say that because the Newbold–Cobb formula (derived from a distribution which Coppin himself says is affected by factors such as non-reporting) produces such a low ceiling, that this limits the total amount of accident control or reduction which can be achieved through driver improvement programmes directed at the negligent driver; and is probably why it has been so difficult for such programmes to demonstrate significant accident-reducing effects.

In some of the PUTCO data, where exposure was controlled and every accident recorded, the Newbold–Cobb formula could produce a much higher optimum ceiling of 55–57% (see Chapter 15)—although, here again, even these data have limitations because the population consists only of long-service drivers and excludes the much worse short-term ones. And the PUTCO figures also show how, left to their own devices, many repeaters most definitely went on repeating, but that when strong disciplinary action was taken many of them were capable of reforming; that a programme which was directed at doing something about those who did not or could not reform (i.e. discharging them and replacing them with psychological-test-selected drivers) *did reduce* the company's accident rate; that keeping on with this programme *kept the accident rate down*; and that being forced to let up on it again because of a shortage of drivers immediately *made the accident rate go up again*. So, focusing attention on negligent drivers and taking action against them can have a very marked effect.

But the extent of this effect will, of course, be dependent on the very practical consideration of what sort of action one is allowed by circumstances to take! One cannot "fire" drivers from the general public; one cannot even be sure that revoking their licences will stop them from driving; but it nevertheless seems from Coppin's Negligent Operator study alone that the activities of even the hard-core recidivist Negligent Operators are at least *curtailed* by the action which the MVD is taking. And, judging by the orderliness of so much of the American driving, this sort of big-brother-is-watching enforcement programme also seems to have a number of very salutary side effects.

My personal feeling is that it would be most unfortunate if, for theoretical reasons, these programmes were to fall into disrepute. It would also be a very great pity if Coppin's excellent studies, stemming as they do from a Motor Vehicle Department where his figures no doubt reflect many of the beneficial effects of a good enforcement policy, were used by others as a weapon for condemning that very policy. For this is what actually seems to be happening in the case of the reports of the Research and Statistics Division of the California Motor Vehicle Department; which reveals the irony of a situation where some very good research seems in danger of producing an unexpected boomerang effect; where figures reflecting the beneficial effect of a driver control policy are being used to show that there is no need for that policy—nor for that matter any need for this particular type of research. Because in addition to being regarded as a good reason for changing accident prevention policy, Coppin's figures are apparently now also being used as a reason for changing the direction (and the financing) of accident research. They are, in fact, being regarded as the final proof that all the wrong emphasis has up till now been put on this research, and priority given to all the wrong aspects. Accidents are apparently not anything for which the driver can really be blamed, they are just a matter of how much he drives and what hazards he encounters; or of how much he drinks, or of his youth and inexperience. He does not need discipline, he needs *help*. And this help can obviously only come through research in the right areas and carried out by people who are "properly" qualified to do it. In fact it has been suggested that research should not be left in the hands of "concerned but untrained laymen, such as motor vehicle administrators or legislators". Instead it needs to benefit from the "inter-disciplinary cross-fertilization that has produced such substantive methodological advances in other fields". In other words, a lot more money should be made available for research, but this time research on the "right" lines and by the "right" people. [It has even been said (Moynihan, 1962, at a meeting of the Association for the Aid of Crippled Children—strange how that name keeps bobbing up) that there is "the possibility, even the likelihood, that many of the 'persistent violators' of the traffic laws are innocent victims of the Poisson distribution whose misfortunes have been compounded by a statistically illiterate bureaucracy"!] Somehow it does not seem likely that the intention is for places like the Statistical Research Divisions of Motor Vehicle Departments (from one of which Coppin's excellent research has emanated) to get much of a place in the sun in this new affluent research society. Nor for that matter does it seem likely that in the enthusiasm for getting going on this new research the enthusiasts are likely to stop long enough to have a really good look at what underlies Coppin's figures. If they did they might realize there was a great deal more in them than meets the eye—as he himself has repeatedly pointed out.

For while these figures undoubtedly show that it would be possible, if somewhat difficult, to *lower America's present accident rate*—they also show that it would be as easy as falling off a log to *let it go up again*, as indeed it already appears to be doing. For these figures explain one of the reasons why, in a world of escalating accident rates, America has been able to maintain the lowest rate per mileage driven of any country in the world. They show that the attention given to the traffic offender by the "concerned but untrained" and "statistically illiterate" laymen has been fully justified: that the reason why there are so few chronic accident-repeaters seems to lie in the fact that their dangerous accident potential has long been realized by these laymen, and that they are doing as much as they are allowed to do to stop these offenders, or at least to halt them in their tracks: that the policy devised by lay legislators and carried out by laymen (including here the city and highway police who, by definition, must also rank as "scientifically" untrained) seems to have brought about in a lot of people a healthy respect for the highway law, and to have developed an attitude among the general driving public where irresponsible driving is frowned upon, and where action against such drivers is welcomed by the community at large—who, it appears, would prefer to see a stronger line of action being taken.

But unfortunately it seems rather doubtful whether, between the current unpopularity of the accident proneness concept and a veneration for "statistics", even if they are not fully understood, that the immediate tendency (in America anyway) will be to stop and think, let alone appreciate the value as well as the significance of the work of Coppin and his associates. For if all their work on the accident *potential* of the traffic violator, and the teenager driver, and the different sexes, and the different work classes, is going to be glossed over, then the greatest value of their work will be lost. Into the wastepaper basket will go nine-tenths of the California reports, where they will join all the other work carried out over the years by researchers from all over the world—research devoted to showing over and over again that the chronic, irredeemable accident repeater is not the only danger, and that there can be significant differences between the people who have even one serious accident and the people who do not.

The fact that I feel that one of the most important aspects of Coppin's excellent work is being grossly overlooked is one of the many reasons why I am glad that he and Peck have consented to give me a statement of their personal views for inclusion in this book. These views may come as a surprise to many people who have only heard their figures quoted. They will, however, come as no surprise to anyone who has studied the California reports. These show only too clearly the authors' appreciation of the fact that figures often hide as much as they reveal. They also show that they believe that there is no simple solution to the accident problem, and certainly not one which involves throwing away all the old, well-tried remedies and starting again with a nice clean slate. I feel therefore that Coppin and Peck would agree with me in saying that it would be a pity if, without serious thought, the following line of argument was used: *Studies like the California study and the Connecticut study are the only ones dealing with the general driving public and with the particular problems inherent in dealing with this public; therefore even if figures from these studies do not represent the complete picture, they are the only data available and the only reliable evidence on which major policy decisions can be made.* My feeling, here, is that it might be more dangerous to make radical changes in policy on the basis of an unanalytical acceptance of certain figures, derived from data whose origins are obscured by such complex and often unmeasurable factors, than it would be to leave unchanged policies based on "scientifically unvalidated" common sense.

A short discursive review like this is a very perfunctory way of dealing with a study of the magnitude of the California one. But it is all that is possible here. Fortunately, due to the generosity of the Californian authorities, the reports have been made available to government and research bodies in many parts of the world, where they have been very appreciatively received. Let us hope that they will inspire similar much-needed studies in other places. For what would one not give to see studies of this kind carried out in other parts of the world where accident rates are so much higher that many of the trends apparent in Coppin's work would no doubt be much more clearly defined! Unfortunately, although I have inquired all over the world, I have been unable to find any other place or country which can produce even a semblance of an analysis like this. Not on the general driving public anyway, and this is where the knowledge is needed, *particularly local knowledge to assess local priorities*. For this is another area where the danger of the present thinking on accident causation lies. It would be indeed ironical if any of the higher-accident-rate countries, seduced by the siren song of current American thinking on a subject like accident proneness, were to try and short-cut their own much-needed research and to overlook the different results which might emerge from their own data; if they were to base their decisions of priorities on the results of findings which might have little applicability to their own particular conditions, but which they have swallowed whole.

Unfortunately, it is quite on the cards that this is exactly what could happen. The people who most need the research could easily be the people to say there is no need for it. For one of the dangerous anomalies which arise so often in accident research is that the official bodies who are prepared to sponsor internal, practical, on-the-job research like this, are those who are most actively engaged in trying to prevent accidents, and whose efforts are reflected in their data. Statistical data from the Motor Vehicle Department of California might therefore be most inapplicable to many of the places where they are likely to be used.

It would appear, for instance, that there are a number of other places in America alone where the driver-control policies are much slacker and the accident rates considerably higher. (These higher rates, particularly in the South, can be seen from a study of any edition of *Accident Facts*, produced by the American National Safety Council.) It can also be seen from the views expressed by the American insurance companies. An editorial, "Let's stop pampering deadly drivers", which appeared in the May–June issue of the *Journal of American Insurance*, 1967, expresses very clearly the views of the American insurance companies:

"Such lapses in control of problem drivers are of compelling concern because of the disproportionate toll of death, injury and destruction caused by this sizeable minority. These drivers constitute much of the reason for rising auto insurance rates, isolated but significant policy cancellations and non-renewals, and high-risk auto insurance company insolvencies. Insurers find that in states which allow problem drivers to remain on the roads, there are much higher rates of accidents and claims. Alternatives for insurers are requests for higher rates or the tightening of underwriting practices to avoid problem drivers who are uninsurable risks. Even when pools for high-risk drivers are formed, these must generally be subsidized from premiums of good drivers. And the great majority of insurance companies' insolvencies are among companies organized to accommodate high-risk drivers, many of whom should be ruled off the road. . . .

"In addition to legal and procedural tightening, driver improvement systems must also be given the funds needed for larger and better qualified staffs. These systems must be given co-operation by the police and court agencies on whom they depend for records and enforcement. They must be backed by appeal procedures that bring home to motorists not only their right to question an unfair control measure, but their duty to accept needed correction.

"Ultimately, stemming the enormous toll inflicted by problem drivers depends upon citizens of the states and their highest officials; elected and appointed leaders must find the will to make licensing an effective tool for driver safety. They must carry out the laws to fully reform deadly drivers or restrain them from violating the public's right to safety."

CHAPTER 15

THE SOUTH AFRICAN BUS DRIVER STUDIES

IN THIS chapter I propose to present some of the statistical data available from the records of the PUTCO bus drivers. I wish to use these particular findings here rather than in the statistical section as the presentation is a very simple one, and I would like it to follow Coppin's study so that the two can be compared. The data are going to be presented according to the orthodox "group" methods, leaving the presentation of the time-interval method to my co-author in his statistical section.

I must admit that I have carried out this comprehensive group analysis with a certain amount of reluctance, reluctance enhanced by the vast amount of work it has entailed to process the records according to these methods. When my co-author and I first discussed the format of this book neither of us felt that there would be any need to indulge in this particular strenuous statistical exercise. We felt that Hakkinen's study had supplied all the evidence along these lines that was needed, and that the statistical presentation of our own data should be limited to the time-interval method, which is not only unusual but also works so well in practice. We felt that the major contribution which the PUTCO study could make was the information which this sensitive statistical tool had produced on the individuality of the patterns of accident behaviour.

But then, at the time, we felt that there was no need to enter into any discussion, let alone argument, about the validity or the usefulness of the concept of accident proneness, either! When you routinely handle the records of over a thousand individual drivers, accident proneness is just a common-or-garden reality that you have to cope with every day, and one on which your whole plan of action is based. For if it were not a reality, if there were no consistent differences between one driver and the next, then there would be no point in keeping individual accident records, or discharging the men with bad records, or maintaining an expensive psychological unit to select their successors. It would make no difference anyway. The only way to control the drivers of a transport company, and keep down the company's accident rate as a whole, would be to.... Frankly, we don't know. For even disciplinary control would collapse if accidents were to be regarded with a tolerant, to-err-is-human attitude.

So, blissfully unaware of how drastically opinion in some quarters was changing, we felt there was no need to begin at the beginning again and start proving what to us was merely the obvious. (Though we must admit we were a little mystified when, at the time our 1965 papers on the PUTCO study were accepted for publication in the United States, the editor of the National Safety Council's *Research Review* commented that these papers would "represent a basic challenge to our currently held opinion on accident proneness".)

But if we did not know then how markedly opinion in a place like America was changing, we certainly do now. And although we have not found it necessary to change our personal views, we have found it very necessary to change the format of the book. A volume on accident proneness—which is what we were asked to produce—was hardly likely to serve any useful purpose if it was written with intellectual blinkers and took no heed of developments in other countries. As a result the whole approach had to be changed, including the nice, easy presentation of the PUTCO data purely in terms of time-intervals—the form in which all the individual records are kept. The statistical data would obviously have to be examined much more fully and, what is more, by the old methods as well as the new; as otherwise it might be difficult to make any direct comparison between the PUTCO findings and those of other much-quoted studies.

So, to see what would come out of using these group methods, I have processed the voluminous PUTCO data, which go back to 1951, and reproduced not once, but repeatedly over different periods of time, replicas of the sort of investigations which have been featured in the four major statistical studies on accident proneness, i.e. Cobb and Forbes, Adelstein, Hakkinen, and Coppin—testing for stability, examining the effects of removing the high accident offenders, etc.

The result is a bewildering mass of figures from which the one finding which stands out more clearly than any other is that figures can prove anything or nothing, depending on how you interpret them.

It is therefore to illustrate this, as much as anything else, that I want to use this particular analysis, carried out according to the conventional group methods which, unfortunately, are those almost invariably used in accident proneness work. I do not particularly want to use it to examine either the validity of proneness or to measure to what extent it prevails—but rather to show how ill-suited these group statistical methods are for doing either. And I want to use it to show how dangerous it is to compare the findings of one group with another group, without taking into account the constitution of each group and the factors which are operative within it.

For the reader will see from this analysis of records which go back over seventeen years that it is possible to obtain groups which illustrate any number of the factors which can influence accident data. There are groups who were driving when the company's accident rate was high, and others who were driving when it was low—showing the difference in the findings when accident proneness was tolerated and when it was not. There are groups who were exposed to difficult traffic conditions and others exposed to much easier traffic conditions—showing how evidence of proneness can be magnified or diminished by such conditions. There are groups where it is possible to analyse each man's accidents in terms of total accidents however trivial, and also in terms of serious accidents only—showing how this sometimes, but not always, changes the main trend of the evidence. In fact there are so many groups in which so many different factors are operating that it is possible to show only too clearly how, in the records of even *one* transport company, evidence of proneness seems to wax and wane, depending upon what portion of the data you happen to choose.

I hope that by doing this that I can at least lay some of the statistical ghosts which have for so long haunted the work on accident proneness—and also explain some of the reasons why it has often been so difficult to establish either its validity or its importance by statistical means.

However, before setting out to do this, it would be as well to sketch in a little more of the background of the PUTCO study than was given in Chapter 8, so that the reader can better understand the various factors which have produced these particular data.

To begin with I ought to stress again that the whole project was, and still is, a purely practical one. It has, in fact, always been just a practical job of trying to improve the efficiency of a transport company, a job carried out by people who were either full-time employees of the company or had been appointed as specialist consultants. For many years the psychological unit was an integral part of the company. Its main task (aided by my co-author as a statistical consultant) was to develop better methods for the selection and control of the company's drivers, and every bit of research which was carried out was undertaken for that specific purpose. It was only much later that the status of the psychological unit was changed, and, in answer to requests for assistance from other bodies with driver problems, it was made into a consultant unit. This naturally extended the scope of its activities and explains why the unit has been able to use the testing methods developed in PUTCO for selecting drivers to drive any kind of vehicle—from a scooter to a big earthmover. It also explains why the unit's research activities have also expanded and how, for instance, it came about that it was able to undertake a controlled research project on accident prediction among White (Caucasian) bus drivers for the South African Road Safety Council, and why it is currently assisting the British Road Research Laboratory with a research project on driver behaviour. However, despite this general expansion of activities, the connection with the original transport company remains unchanged. Selecting the PUTCO drivers, following up on this selection, and the regular grading of all the drivers according to their accident records is still routine. Hence my familiarity with every aspect of this project which I have directed and actively participated in for the last fifteen years.

As previously explained, PUTCO (Public Utility Transport Corporation) is a company which supplies transport for the non-White communities of the South African cities of Johannesburg, Pretoria, and Durban. The drivers are all non-White, mainly Bantu (Negro) and some Coloureds. (For purposes of simplification the subjects will be referred to here by the rather arbitrary collective term "Africans".)

The current driving strength is just on 1000 full-time bus drivers. In the early days of its operation PUTCO, which was expanding from small beginnings, did not run its own training school and relied for its new recruits on already-licensed drivers. This system, however, proved most unsatisfactory as many of these men turned out to have little or no training and to be dangerous as well as rather inept and mechanically insensitive drivers. As a result the company was faced with most alarming maintenance costs and a very high accident rate—the 1951 rate being 2·43 accidents per 10,000 miles driven. Figure 15.1 gives the PUTCO accidents rate in six-monthly averages, showing the various factors which have affected the rate over the years 1951–68. This particular figure is not quite the same as that published in an earlier publication (Shaw, 1965) as it has been limited to the accident rate of the Transvaal province. In 1961 PUTCO opened a new and very large division in Durban (Natal) where the driving conditions on the main routes operated are

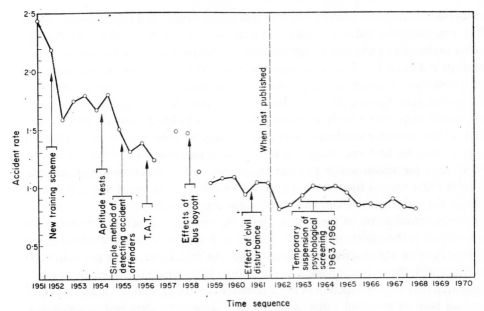

FIG. 15.1. The steady fall in the PUTCO accident rate associated with the use of personality tests for selection purposes, and the rise which occurred when the testing was temporarily suspended

rather different from the Transvaal conditions. To maintain continuity and a proper comparison, only the Transvaal accident rate is given here.

In an attempt to overcome these problems, the company decided to run its own driving school where it would re-train all the existing drivers and also re-train all the new drivers even if they had licences, and also when necessary train applicants with no previous driving experience. The policy of re-training the old drivers was found to relieve some of the maintenance problems and also to have a marked effect on the accident rate (which came down to 1·75 accidents per 10,000 miles). But the training of the unlicensed men proved to be very difficult, as only 40 per cent of these men (selected by interview) were found to have sufficient innate skill to make their training worth-while economically. After a time it became apparent that a better driver-selection system would have to be devised, and it was decided to experiment with the use of aptitude tests.

In 1953 when this experiment began, there was little information available about scientific driver-selection methods, and no information at all whether such methods would be suitable for African subjects. Two sets of tests were experimentally assembled, the first being a battery of psychometric tests for assessing intelligence and adaptability, the second a small battery of psychomotor tests for testing some of the basic driving skills.* This latter set of tests consisted of a test for two-hand co-ordination; a test for a simple reaction time, with and without distractions; a test for anticipation, concentration, and

* The intelligence and adaptability tests were designed by the South African Council for Scientific and Industrial Research for the grading of African mine workers. The psychomotor tests were copied by permission of Dr. D. P. du Toit, Director of Personnel for the Pretoria Municipality, who was using them for the selection of European (White) bus drivers.

distribution of attention. (Attempts were made to construct a test for estimation of relative speeds and distances, but it has still not been found possible to develop a reliable model.)

After preliminary experimental application, a tentative validation was carried out—on a sample of 102 drivers—of the adaptability tests and the three psychomotor tests against a rather makeshift criterion (driving proficiency as rated on a four-point scale by three independent supervisors). Although the criterion was rather vague in that none of the raters could state very clearly on what basis he was judging "driving proficiency", the results of this tentative validation were encouraging. So great was the practical need that the tests were put into immediate use for selection purposes—accompanied by comprehensive tests for vision and a medical examination. The experiment had started, and, during the first year of its operation over 1000 subjects were tested and 150 new drivers selected, the majority of whom had no previous driving experience.

With the introduction of the aptitude tests the driving instructors reported a distinct improvement in the quality of the new trainees, and the pass rate in the school rose in the first year from the old unsatisfactory figure of 40% to 70%. Later, as the unit acquired more experience with the tests, the pass rate rose to over 90%, where it has remained ever since. It appeared that the introduction of these relatively simple psychometric and psychomotor tests had been of practical value as far as the training problem was concerned. But it remained to be seen whether the new selection methods would have any effect on the other major driver problems of employee behaviour and accident liability.

As the tests could not be expected to predict future disciplinary records, all we could say on this score was that the chosen applicants had appeared pleasant and co-operative and that their behaviour in the driving school had been good. On the question of accident liability, however, the fact that during the testing (and during their training) these men had given evidence of considerable alertness and skill led us to assume that their future accident records would be at least reasonable. Unfortunately this assumption proved to be very wrong, for as soon as the new trainees went on to full-time driving the accidents started. Allowance was made at first for the fact that so many of them were inexperienced, but, as time went by and many of them had to be discharged not only for repeated minor accidents but for really serious ones as well, the fact emerged that although the new selection methods might have solved the training problem, they had in no way alleviated the accident problem. Investigations were made whether the quality of the training could be to blame, but repeated driving tests showed that the new men could handle their vehicles very well. From the point of view of mechanical sensitivity, and therefore of wear and tear on the buses, they were often better than many of the older and more experienced drivers (a fact borne out by the maintenance workshops). As a group they were apparently more skilful drivers than the company had ever had before. But this fact did not prevent them from having a most unsatisfactory number of accidents.

It will be appreciated that it takes a little while before the effects of any new selection programme can be accurately measured, for each new driver as he comes on must be allowed to build up an accident record. During this time we had introduced a simple method for evaluating the accident records of all the drivers in terms of the number of accidents per annum (a system which later developed into the method based on the time-intervals between accidents described in Chapter 8). This system had pinpointed many of the old drivers with bad records and had resulted in a weeding-out process intended to reduce the company's accident rate. Unfortunately, however, so high was the accident occurrence among the new aptitude-test-selected men that the accident rate began to increase rather than decrease; and it soon became apparent that the only way it could be controlled was by using the same process to weed out an alarmingly high proportion of the new drivers too. In fact a subsequent investigation showed that 45% of these men developed accident records which classified them as unsatisfactory according to the new time-interval accident criterion.

The underlying reason for this state of affairs was revealed by a second and much more detailed validation of the selection tests. This time the validation was a follow-up study carried out on the men selected by the aptitude tests, using their test scores at the time of selection and the time-interval accident criterion. This validation revealed three significant *negative* correlations which indicated, in general, that the better the scores on the tests the worse the accident record. The correlation coefficients were as follows:

(a) Accident criterion/scores on the intelligence and adaptability tests ($r = -0.33$).
(b) Criterion/scores on the reaction-time test ($r = -0.15$).
(c) Criterion/scores on the psychomotor tests ($r = -0.20$).

As these three testing measures were the backbone of the selection programme it was hardly to be wondered at that the result, in terms of accidents, was so unsatisfactory.

Fortunately, this further objective proof of the failure of the tests as accident predictors had already been anticipated. We were already acutely aware of two unpleasantly incompatible factors: (1) the necessity for continuing to use the existing tests in order to keep down training and vehicle maintenance costs, and (2) the fact that using these tests was only aggravating the accident situation. Even before the statistical validation was completed we therefore embarked upon an intensive investigation of the underlying causes of the accident problem.

This investigation showed that one of the most obvious causes was the unsatisfactory attitude of many of the new drivers towards their jobs, for their personal files were found to be studded with disciplinary offences such as carelessness, recklessness, insolence, drunkenness, and the most ingenious forms of dishonesty. The negative correlations between the tests and the accident criterion therefore merely confirmed that the intelligence and basic skill the subjects had displayed on the psychomotor and psychometric tests were being used for all the wrong purposes. It was found that a bad disciplinary record and a bad accident record very often went hand in hand. (In fact a subsequent investigation showed that 70% of the men with very bad disciplinary records also had very bad accident records.) This did not, however, account for all the cases of accident failure, for there were still a number of men whose employee behaviour was good, but whose accident records were, nevertheless, very unsatisfactory. Inquiry revealed the presence in these men of other factors which were possibly causing their accidents, factors such as nervous tension, indecisiveness, lack of poise and confidence, and even unduly strong primitive beliefs and superstitions.

This investigation made it very obvious that the existing testing programme was hopelessly inadequate, and that some test, or tests, would have to be found which would reveal not only undesirable character traits, but would also reveal factors such as maturity of outlook, motivation, attitudes, and personality integration. It was felt that the only techniques which could possibly provide such information were the projective tests, although the available accident research literature on the subject of projective techniques in accident work was not very encouraging. We nevertheless felt that a possible reason why these projective tests, particularly tests of the TAT kind, had not been used very much for pure accident research projects was because they did not lend themselves to the itemized statistical analysis of group results. The success of the TAT (Murray, 1938) in the clinical field did, however, indicate its value for the diagnosis of the individual. It was therefore possible that in this present project, which was essentially a practical assignment involving the selection or rejection of *individual* candidates, and not a theoretical research study, it could be very useful. In view of this it was decided to try out both the TAT and the Rorschach (Klopfer and Kelly, 1942). Experiments with the Rorschach showed that the African subjects did not respond very well to this test and that the administration took too long. The TAT, however, looked more promising, and an experimental African TAT, suitable for urbanized African subjects—and later described in a book, *The Personality of the Urban African in South Africa* (de Ridder, 1961)—was constructed. This experimental TAT was tried out on a number of subjects. Right from the start it appeared that it had considerable potential. Despite the limitations of the original model it was evident that it would detect the sort of attitudes and gross personality defects which would have an obvious bearing on driving behaviour. So great was the need for some method of eliminating the worst accident and disciplinary offenders that it was decided to put the test into immediate use for selection purposes and to attempt to refine it and validate it later.

This somewhat unscientific approach, dictated once again by practical necessity, did, however, pay dividends despite the fact that it brought new selection difficulties in its wake. For so many of the more intelligent subjects showed up badly on the TAT that the pass level of the performance tests had, perforce, to be appreciably lowered in order to obtain enough new drivers to meet the company's requirements. This lowering of the standard of skill called forth an immediate protest from the driving school, but as time went by the protest died down when it became apparent that the new type of trainee, though often more difficult to teach, was usually a much better employee and a better accident risk than his non-TAT-selected predecessor (a fact which was demonstrated when a follow-up study of the TAT-selected drivers revealed their superiority on all counts over the non-TAT-selected group). It appeared, therefore, that personality testing would probably overcome many of the problems of driver selection, so a second projective test (the PUTCO Social Relations Test, or SRT,) was designed to supplement the TAT. This test, which used a comic-strip technique instead of the static pictures of the TAT, turned out to be a most successful experiment, as between them the two projective tests gave us the sort of information on personality functions, attitudes, and social and interpersonal relationships that we needed. Needless to say, it took a couple of years of practical use to refine them and arrive at the most productive pictures and comic strips, but by 1958 they were working very well indeed.

The tests themselves will be more fully described later. All that concerns us here is the manner in which they are used. The predictions of accident potential are made on the basis of the findings of the TAT and SRT combined into one test. There is no detailed marking system based on individual characteristics. The analyst derives as full an assessment as possible from the stories written by each subject—a kind of mental picture of what sort of person he is and therefore of how he is likely to behave and how he is likely to react to the driving situation. The analyst then uses his or her personal judgement (augmented nowadays by the knowledge derived from hundreds of follow-up case studies of previous predictions) to assess each subject (1) as an accident risk, and (2) as an employee risk. This is done on a basic five-point scale: 1—*excellent*, 2—*good*, 3—*fair*, 4—*poor*, and 5—*bad*. The TAT cards and comic strips contain no pictures of driving situations—these having been discarded at an early stage as all they evoked from the subjects (who are fully aware that this is a selection test) were pious dissertations on the virtues of safe driving. The pictures reflect somewhat ambiguous situations which could occur in everyday life— the subject being free to interpret these situations in any manner he pleases.

While we were developing the early version of the TAT we turned our attention to the question of developing the time-interval method for assessing each driver's subsequent accident record, and also to developing a method of assessing his employee record. These gave us two criteria against which to measure the predictive accuracy of the tests and the general quality of the selection programme. The first major statistical follow-up study was not carried out until 1961, but the institution of the regular Accident Rating System (where each man's accident record is also assessed on a five-point scale) made it possible to keep a regular check on the progress of each individual driver. (The Accident Rating System was described in Chapter 8.)

The routine Accident Rating System went into full operation in 1958—just about the time that most of the wrinkles had been ironed out of the selection tests, and the ensuing four years witnessed a concentrated effort to use both the weeding-out and the selection systems to reduce the company's accident rate by improving the general standard of the drivers. Those of the existing drivers who consistently showed up badly on the Accident Ratings were gradually weeded out and replaced by men whose psychological testing now included the projective personality tests as well as the psychomotor tests. The results of this programme were very satisfactory and the accident rate went steadily down until by 1962 the rate for the Transvaal divisions had been brought down to 0·81 accidents per 10,000 miles driven.

However, by mid-1962 the company was growing so fast that it was becoming more and more difficult to get sufficient good quality applicants to fill the driver ranks—especially as industries springing up all over the country were offering much less arduous driving jobs. To try and cope with this situation the test unit lowered selection standards to rock bottom, even most of the *poor* test ratings being accepted. The result of this lowering of standards was immediately apparent and the company accident rate started to go up again. But even this emergency measure was not enough, and in 1963 it was decided that the only way the company could be brought up to full driving strength was to take on a whole batch of new drivers who already had Heavy Duty licences and who could therefore be quickly re-trained. These men would have to be accepted on the basis of a practical road driving test, almost irrespective of the results of their psychological tests—only the very worst risks being excluded. They were engaged on sufferance, it being made clear to them that their retention would be dependent on their behaviour; and they were even given special company coding numbers (the 6000's) so that the divisional managers could distinguish them and keep an extra watch on them. Alas, however, this was one of those temporary emergency measures which proved to be anything but temporary. So poor was the quality of these men and such bad accident (and disciplinary) risks did they turn out to be, that the company never seemed to be able to catch up with the turnover. It took three years before the *status quo* could be restored. By dint of repeatedly raising the wage scales to attract the better type of applicant, by 1966 the position was once again reached where the company was sufficiently up to strength for it to be able to revert again to the old policy of only taking on those new drivers who could pass the psychological tests—or squeeze through them under still lowered, but nevertheless reasonably discriminating standards.

The results of these unfortunate but nevertheless necessary developments were faithfully mirrored in the company accident rate which climbed steadily and for a period of eighteen months hovered round the old unsatisfactory level of 1·0. It would no doubt have gone higher still were it not for the fact that so many of these men were discharged, the company preferring the expense of training endless new licensed recruits, rather than tolerate too much continuous accident proneness—or for that matter continuous "dishonesty proneness". However, such was the driver shortage that many of them had to be kept on strength quite long enough to do a considerable amount of damage.

But I suppose it is an ill wind that blows nobody any good, for in the course of this struggle to keep the wheels rolling and supply public transport on an ever-increasing scale, a lot of people learned a lot of things. The practical officials, for instance, again learned, the hard way, the important practical implications of accident proneness; and also the value of the psychological testing programme, which in their heart of hearts, they had been inclined rather to mistrust and resent, regarding it as just one of these new-fangled head office notions (like the new computer). The fact that the accident rate had gone down while the psychological test programme was fully operative had been regarded by many as purely coincidental, just about everyone from middle management to the accident prevention officers, to the training school, to the route supervisors (not omitting, of course, the psychological unit) secretly thinking that the real credit was theirs—and everybody apparently rather waiting for just such an opportunity to prove it. As it so happened, however, the fact that despite intensified training and intensified supervision the accident rate promptly went up when the psychological screening was virtually abandoned, made a number of erstwhile sceptics accept (with I must say a very good grace) that there might be something in this "psychology racket" after all!

As far as the members of the psychological unit were concerned, this whole development gave them the opportunity to do a little more than try to resist the temptation to adopt a smug, I-told-you-so attitude. It gave them the opportunity to prove *to themselves* that the principles on which they had been working were the right ones. No one in their sane senses, dealing with the complexities of human nature, can always be sure of their judgements, however carefully and painstakingly made. Although the unit was selecting men for an arduous and very responsible job, the high failure rate on the selection tests had always worried them. Were they, in fact, turning away people who could have handled the job and whose accident potential was not nearly as bad as their selection tests, and particularly their personality tests, indicated?

But a management decision, based on the purely practical necessity of maintaining a vital transport service, presented them with the opportunity to see whether the test failures would in reality fail on the job. The latest validation of test predictions against future accident involvement (1967), has shown that by an overwhelming majority (86%) they did. (Details of these validations are given in Chapter 16.)

This, very briefly, is the history of the various developments within the transport company which have affected the accident rate over the last seventeen years. It provides the background against which the presentation of the statistical data should be viewed. For it explains not only why the company's accident rate has waxed and waned, but also why groups of drivers representing different periods of the company's development also represent different periods of company policy, and therefore provide very different statistical data—these data being largely dependent on the amount of driver control operative at the time.

Obviously a transport company operating under practical difficulties such as those outlined above provides ideal material for a statistical analysis of accident occurrence. It is only a pity that the very bad 6000-category group could not be used for this particular group analysis as the groups used are all six-year exposure ones. But the earlier groups provide evidence enough.

Another great advantage of the PUTCO data is the detail in which the records are kept—particularly the full recording and the guarantee of standardization of exposure. The sheer practical necessity for arriving at strictly comparable standards so that the drivers can all be routinely classified for *management purposes*, has resulted in dividing the company into a number of homogeneous "risk" areas as represented by different accident rates. And the fact that each driver's record is kept in terms of the number of actual driving days between accidents means, that in converting these records to the orthodox method of number of accidents per annum for group analysis purposes, each year of exposure can be standardized, being taken as 350 driving days (a convenient unit which allows for a factor like annual leave and relates the driving year to the calendar year).

The conventional group statistical analysis has been carried out on five groups of drivers, who were exposed for the six-year periods 1952–7, 1954–9, 1956–61, 1958–63, 1960–5. Each group has then been divided into two sub-groups, Difficult Traffic Conditions and Easy Traffic Conditions. Every driver remained on the same route throughout the six-year period and every driver was exposed for 6×350 actual "driving" days.

The split into difficult and easy traffic conditions was made by combining the two high accident rate Transvaal divisions of the company and the two low ones (the new Durban Division being omitted as it was not operative over the whole period). The relative accident rates are comparable for the various sub-groups under consideration, as shown by Table 15.1 which gives the average accident rates per annum of the various groups over the six-year periods (the figures in brackets being the number of subjects in each subgroup).

It is only in the last periods that the accident rates become sufficiently divergent (in

TABLE 15.1. AVERAGE ACCIDENT RATES PER ANNUM (OVER A SIX-YEAR PERIOD) FOR VARIOUS
GROUPS OF DRIVERS

Groups	Difficult traffic conditions		Easy traffic conditions	
	Division A	Division B	Division C	Division D
1952–7	2·34 (63)	2·34 (19)	1·23 (21)	1·43 (53)
1954–9	2·46 (60)	2·20 (20)	1·47 (35)	1·32 (47)
1956–61	1·98 (56)	2·07 (18)	1·34 (45)	1·18 (38)
1958–63	1·46 (46)	1·63 (16)	1·27 (44)	0·90 (35)
1960–5	1·43 (30)	1·63 (13)	1·18 (32)	0·83 (25)

view of the number of subjects used) for it to become questionable as to whether the divisions should have been combined. But, as any figures on these last groups have been used only to demonstrate general trends, the combination was retained. Using only one division here would have drastically reduced the number of subjects available. In any case, throughout the discussion that follows, the emphasis is on the 1952–7 and 1954–9 groups, as these were the periods when discipline was relatively slack, when more accident repeaters were retained, and consequently more evidence of continued accident proneness was evident.

The data for each sub-group have been subjected to virtually every kind of analysis found in the major statistical studies on accident proneness. And, so that the results can be more closely compared with the big American studies, a separate analysis has been made for certain of the sub-groups using the "serious" accidents only (involving death, injury, or property damage in excess of R50 in South African currency, i.e. the equivalent at the time of approximately £25 or $75). Unfortunately, it was only possible to do this laborious costing for two groups, 1954–9 and 1958–63. Much as one would have liked to use the high accident rate 1952–7 group where proneness to even serious accidents was very conspicuous in the data, the costing for the earlier years was obviously incomplete, so the 1954 group was chosen instead.

As these analyses of serious accidents are interspersed with the ones of total accidents, it would be advisable to discuss here some of the findings which emerged from the whole statistical study on the relationship between serious accidents and total accidents. It would also be as well to reiterate that all passenger-injury accidents (boarding, alighting, and falling in the bus) are omitted from the PUTCO data because of the irresponsible behaviour of many of the passengers. The accidents are all *collision* accidents, whether with a vehicle, fixed object, or a pedestrian. This makes it easier to compare the results with other studies, particularly those on the general public, where the proportion of such accidents must be infinitely smaller.

The first finding to emerge from the PUTCO data on the relationship between serious accidents and total accidents was that different traffic conditions produced different ratios, these being generally higher when traffic conditions were less congested. This is a perfectly logical finding and one which appears to be accentuated in the general public where the tendency is for more of the serious accidents to occur outside city boundaries.

However, in the PUTCO data the proportion of serious accidents to total accidents (as defined in the American studies) was found to differ from one division of the company to another—one of the complicating factors being that pedestrian casualities were higher on those routes which ran for any distance through sub-economic housing areas. It was decided, therefore, to limit the detailed analyses of the serious accidents to only one Difficult Traffic Conditions division in order to avoid this lack of homogeneity.

The second finding was again merely an empirical confirmation of common sense, namely that serious accidents were found to occur at rather different stages of the driving careers of different drivers, depending on their development and their personality make-up. The most prevalent pattern was that they occurred (a) during the "learning period" of promising but young and inexperienced drivers; (b) during the first few years of exposure, when learning in terms of frequency was over, but when young drivers had started to acquire too much self-confidence; (c) on rare occasions, after many years of driving, among the older, more positive drivers who, because of their experience and competence, were inclined to take chances; (d) at any time during the careers of drivers with generally unsatisfactory accident records.

To establish any true statistical relationship between serious and non-serious accidents is therefore very difficult using group techniques because of the conflicting trends. It is increasingly difficult among self-selected groups of long-service professional drivers for the very reason that as soon as any positive connection starts to appear the driver is usually discharged. In other words, a series of small accidents might be tolerated in a new driver but the addition of serious ones as well would be too much. Or the occasional more serious accident might be tolerated in an experienced driver, but he would have difficulty in talking himself out of a number of minor but avoidable accidents as well.

Because of this, among these PUTCO groups of long-service drivers, the degree of statistical correlation between serious and non-serious accidents was found to vary according to the amount of disciplinary control operative at the time; as can be seen from the higher coefficients obtained in the early years when discipline was slacker.

$$1954\text{--}9 \quad N = 60; \quad r = 0{\cdot}47$$

$$1958\text{--}63 \quad N = 46; \quad r = 0{\cdot}34$$

The more sensitive time-interval method is a much better tool for investigating this relationship—especially amongst the worst offenders—because here all the drivers can be used including the discharged ones. The investigation described in Chapter 8 revealed this very clearly. During the period 1958 through 1963, after the introduction of the Accident Rating System, the proportion of *all* the drivers employed by the company who were rated as *poor* or *bad* on the basis of *short time-intervals between accidents of any kind* was gradually whittled down from 25% of the total strength to 7%; yet during that same period these same drivers were involved in 60% of the accidents attributed by the company's investigators to *reckless and dangerous driving* (a more meaningful definition of a truly serious accident than that which has had to be used in the big American studies).

However, where long-service records can be very helpful (especially when discipline is slack) is that they can provide evidence that certain individuals do display lasting and dangerous proneness even to "serious" accidents as defined in the American studies. This will be demonstrated later.

For the moment let us see what emerges from processing the PUTCO data by means of all the different conventional group statistical techniques.

Distribution of Accidents over a Single Period of Time

Tables 15.2 and 15.3 show the distribution of total accidents over various three-year periods (and the comparison with the relevant Poisson distributions). Table 15.4 shows the distribution of serious accidents over two three-year periods.

TABLE 15.2. PERCENTAGE DISTRIBUTION OF ACCIDENTS (TOTAL ACCIDENTS) IN VARIOUS THREE-YEAR PERIODS (DIFFICULT TRAFFIC CONDITIONS)

Number of accidents	Percentage of drivers				
	1952–4	1954–6	1956–8	1958–60	1960–2
0	3		1	5	5
1	7	3	1	3	5
2	11	6	7	6	5
3	7	10	8	15	19
4	17	9	7	15	9
5	7	9	11	19	16
6	9	16	10	18	16
7	12	5	13	3	16
8	7	12	11	5	5
9	4	10	10	3	2
10	3	6	5	3	
11	6	1	5	3	
12	1	1	3	2	2
13	1	1	1		
14	1	3			
15	3	1	3		
16			1		
17			3		
18		1			
19		4			
20		1			
21					
22					
23		1			
24	1				
	100	100	100	100	100
N	82	80	74	62	43
Total accidents	564	596	529	309	209
Mean accident rate (3 yrs.)	6·88	7·45	7·15	4·98	4·86
Mean accidents rate p.a.	2·29	2·48	2·38	1·66	1·62
Significance level of difference from Poisson distribution	0·01	0·01	0·01	0·05	NS*

* Not significant.

TABLE 15.3. PERCENTAGE DISTRIBUTION OF ACCIDENTS (TOTAL ACCIDENTS) IN VARIOUS
THREE-YEAR PERIODS (EASY TRAFFIC CONDITIONS)

Number of accidents	Percentage of drivers				
	1952-4	1954–6	1956–8	1958–60	1960–2
0	7		1	3	9
1	9	7	8	14	14
2	7	14	18	15	18
3	13	17	12	22	21
4	20	12	21	16	16
5	12	17	11	11	3
6	7	12	12	6	5
7	14	10	4	5	9
8	4	6	8	5	5
9	4	5	1	3	
10			4		
11	3				
Total accidents	325	372	356	291	187
N	74	82	83	79	57
$\bar{x}$ (3 years)	4·39	4·54	4·29	3·68	3·28
$\bar{x}$ per annum	1·46	1·51	1·43	1·23	1·09
Significance level of difference from Poisson distribution	0·01	NS	0·05	0·05	0·01

It will be noted that the PUTCO accident rates are very much higher than in most studies, as can be seen from the comparison of these rates with other three-year groups, which have figured in well-known statistical investigations:*

PUTCO (bus drivers, all accidents)	1·09–2·48 p.a.
Hakkinen (bus drivers, all accidents)	1·21
Adelstein (railway shunters, personal injury accidents)	0·23
PUTCO (bus drivers, serious accidents)	0·35
Coppin (general drivers, serious accidents):	
Males	0·09
Females	0·04
Cobb (general drivers, serious accidents):	
Males and females	0·04

* The relatively high accident rates evident in some portions of the PUTCO data should not, however, be construed as representing some unique situation nor should the results of these analyses be regarded as inapplicable to other groups of drivers. The period of observation covered by these analyses is 1952–61, and over this period the company accident rate was brought down from 1·75 accidents per 10,000 miles driven to 0·82. This was achieved by better driver selection and control. But in a completely different public transport operation, operating in the same area and employing only White (Caucasian) drivers—but unable to adopt any stringent measures regarding the hiring or firing of their employees because of acute competition from industry—the similarly calculated accident rate for 1962 was 1·38—nearly double that of PUTCO.

TABLE 15.4. PERCENTAGE DISTRIBUTION OF SERIOUS ACCIDENTS IN
TWO THREE-YEAR PERIODS (DIFFICULT TRAFFIC CONDITIONS)

Number of accidents	Percentage of drivers	
	1954–6	1958–60
0	43	46
1	33	37
2	12	9
3	8	4
4	2	4
5	2	
	100	100
No. of drivers	60	46
Total accidents	58	39
Mean accident rate (3 years)	0·97	0·85
Mean accident rate p.a.	0·32	0·28
% age of total accidents	15	17
Significance level of difference from Poisson distribution	0·05	NS

Secondly, the groups each reflect a number of different factors:

(1) The different results associated with different traffic conditions.
(2) The different results when there is weak or strong driver control, i.e. the high accident rates in the PUTCO data before the Accident Rating System pinpointed the
bad drivers, and before better selection methods enabled the company to replace
them with better material.
(3) The way in which these factors are reflected in the comparison of the various distributions with the relevant Poisson ones.

The comparison of the observed/chance distributions is very interesting. In the Difficult
Traffic Conditions groups the accident rates (total accidents) are apparently sufficiently
high for the chance element not to obscure the individual element. Here it can be seen
that the difference between the observed and the chance (Poisson) distributions is significant at the 0·01 level for the early groups, diminishing to the 0·05 level, and finally to
non-significance in the last group. These changes faithfully reflect the changes in company
policy—better selection and a growing reluctance to retain the worst accident offenders.
They apparently also reflect the diminishing amount of accident proneness present (as can
be seen from Table 15.5 which shows that the amount of correlation between this three-
year period and the subsequent period diminished in the same way).

TABLE 15.5. THREE-BY-THREE-YEAR CORRELATIONS FOR FIVE GROUPS OF DRIVERS (ALL ACCIDENTS)

	Difficult traffic conditions			Easy traffic conditions		
	N	Mean accident rate p.a. over the six years	r	N	Mean accident rate p.a. over the six years	r
1952–4/1955–7	82	2·34	0·64***	74	1·37	0·31**
1954–6/1957–9	80	2·40	0·47***	82	1·38	0·38**
1956–8/1959–61	74	2·00	0·34**	83	1·27	0·37**
1958–60/1961–3	62	1·50	0·28*	79	1·11	0·22*
1960–2/1963–5	43	1·49	0·28	57	1·03	0·15

*** Significant at the 0·001 level.
 ** Significant at the 0·01 level.
  * Significant at the 0·05 level.

In the Easy Traffic Conditions groups the accident rates (total accidents) are much lower and the chance element (or some other factor) apparently obscures the issue in certain of the groups as far as distribution of accidents in one period is concerned. The correlation coefficients, on the other hand (Table 15.5), follow the same trend as in the Difficult Traffic Conditions groups, but at a generally lower level of significance.

In the serious accidents groups (Difficult Traffic Conditions only) the average accident rates are considerably lower, but the individual element seems to be strong enough for the distributions to follow the general trend of the correlation coefficients (which are of much the same magnitude as in the total accidents).

This simple analysis of the distribution of accidents during successive periods of time (reflecting different company attitudes with regard to the tolerance of accident proneness among its drivers) is therefore the first indication of how necessary it is to interpret the results of such analyses in terms of *the factors which produce the data*.

The Correlation Between Accident Occurrence in One Period and Another

Like virtually every statistical study this one has again produced confirmation that the longer the time-period the greater the evidence of stability. One group is therefore sufficient as an example. The group chosen is the one with the highest accident rate, namely the 1952–7 Difficult Conditions group as this will show the trends more clearly. Here the *identical* eighty-two drivers are used throughout, and the analysis is given in Table 15.6.

The consistency of these trends is by now so well established that one hopes that this is one finding which will now be unequivocally accepted, and that future investigators will be spared from having to subject their data to similar analyses. In fact the only finding of any new interest here is the apparent confirmation which the last two coefficients give to Coppin's theory on the suppressor effect of a high accident year on accident occurrence in the next year (plus, we feel, the *release* of the suppressor effect in the *following* year in the case

TABLE 15.6. CORRELATIONS OVER
GIVEN PERIODS FOR THE SAME
GROUP OF DRIVERS ($N = 82$)

Years of exposure	Correlation coefficients (r)
1, 2, 3/4, 5, 6	0·64***
1, 2/3, 4	0·46***
1 and 2/3	0·36**
1/3	0·31*
1/2	0·17

*** Indicates significance at the 0·001 level.
** Indicates significance at the 0·01 level.
* Indicates significance at the 0·05 level.

of chronic offenders). This can be seen from the fact that the 1st×3rd year correlation is higher than the 1st×2nd. In Coppin's data, this was applicable to females but not to males. Here it is applicable to males. But Coppin was dealing with serious accidents only, which would probably have a less traumatic effect on males. In the PUTCO group one must also remember that unless a bad year was followed by a marked improvement, the driver was often discharged and therefore eliminated from the group. This sort of oscillation in response to disciplinary action is, however, symptomatic of chronic accident proneness, as will be demonstrated later.

As a matter of interest, 43 of the 82 drivers in the PUTCO group were exposed for a further two years and the 4×4 correlation coefficient was 0·66. In fact with four groups, *where every driver exposed from 1952 for the period used* was included, the coefficients were as Table 15.7 shows

TABLE 15.7

Time periods	Difficult traffic conditions		Easy traffic conditions	
	N	r	N	r
4×4 years	43	0·66***	46	0·36*
3×3 years	82	0·64***	74	0·31**
2×2 years	99	0·49***	81	0·19
1×1 year	120	0·26**	102	0·24*

*** Indicates significance at the 0·001 level.
** Indicates significance at the 0·01 level.
* Indicates significance at the 0·05 level.

On another point of interest, the following correlations illustrate what happens when exposure is no longer controlled in terms of hazard as represented by different traffic conditions. These are all 3×3 year coefficients for the 1954–9 groups:

Difficult Traffic Conditions $N = 80$ $r = 0.47$

Easy Traffic Conditions $N = 82$ $r = 0.38$

Both together $N = 162$ $r = 0.56$

(An artificial coefficient produced by two clusters, one with a high average rate of 2·40 accidents per annum over six years and the other with a lower rate of 1·38)

Drivers excluded from the above groups because they changed during the six years from one set of traffic conditions to another. $N = 70$ $r = 0.25$

All together $N = 232$ $r = 0.44$

(A generally meaningless coefficient)

An essay on the obvious but nevertheless a reminder that there really is no way of interpreting a correlation coefficient unless the data are homogeneous enough to be comparable.

For our purposes, however, the main interest centres on the investigation of stability as represented by two consecutive 3×3 year periods, as these are the units used in the Connecticut study and which will be used in Coppin's follow-up (although in both these studies control over exposure will be absent). The correlation coefficients have therefore been calculated for all the PUTCO sub-groups to demonstrate again the effects of various factors such as differing traffic conditions and/or disciplinary control. The coefficients are given in Table 15.5 (p. 279). (The bivariate distributions for the two early periods 1952–7 and 1954–9 are given in Tables 15.8 and 15.9.)

Here the same trends as were seen in the distributions are evident. The only exception is the 1954–9 group (Difficult Traffic Conditions) where, although the average rate is higher, the coefficient is lower, mostly due to some enforced rapid learning among the survivors of the well-meant but rather disastrous experiment of using aptitude tests without personality tests. (See Table 15.1, p. 274.) But apart from this somewhat deviant group, the trends of the coefficients are inclined to follow the trends of the accident rates.

However, even these coefficients are rather misleading for they, too, represent conflicting influences. Just to take as an example the 1952–7 Difficult Traffic Conditions group for which the full bivariate distribution is given in Table 15.8. This is undoubtedly the group where the data are least affected by disciplinary control and therefore the one in which continuous proneness is most likely to be evident—as seems to be the case from the relatively high coefficient of 0·64. But even this group of drivers, all exposed to the same traffic conditions over the same period of time, is anything but homogeneous with regard to age and previous driving experience. The minute you start splitting the group on the basis of these factors the resultant divergent trends within the group—and their effect on the correlation coefficient—become evident. Let us split them up in the following manner (see bottom of next two pages beneath the tables):

TABLE 15.8. CORRELATION OF ACCIDENTS (TOTAL ACCIDENTS) BETWEEN TWO THREE-YEAR PERIODS (DIFFICULT TRAFFIC CONDITIONS)

Number of Accidents 1955–7

Number of Accidents 1952–54	0	1	2	3	4	5	6	7	8	9	10	11	12	13	14	15	16	17	18	Tot.
0																				0
1			1				1													2
2		1		1	3	1														6
3				2	2	3			1				1							9
4			1		3	1							1							6
5			1	1	2	2	1	2	2	1		1			1					14
6				2	2				2											6
7					3		1		2			1								7
8					3	2	1	1		1	1						1			10
9					1		1	1	1				1						1	6
10							1			1				1						3
11											1		1							2
12												4	1							5
13										1										1
14									1											1
15												1								1
16																		1	1	2
17																				
18																				
19																				
20																				
21																				
22																				
23																				
24																		1		1
Total	0	1	3	6	18	10	5	4	9	5	7	3	4		2		1	2	2	82

$r = 0.64$

A: <34 years old and <2 years' previous bus driving experience.

B: Mixed: either <34 but with >2 years' experience; or >34 but with <2 years' experience;

C: >34 and with >2 years' experience.

TABLE 15.9. CORRELATION OF ACCIDENTS (TOTAL ACCIDENTS) BETWEEN TWO THREE-YEAR
PERIODS (DIFFICULT TRAFFIC CONDITIONS)

Number of Accidents 1957–9

Number of Accidents 1954–56 (row labels down the left side)

	0	1	2	3	4	5	6	7	8	9	10	11	12	13	14	15	16	17	18	Tot.
0																				0
1						1				1										2
2			1	2		1		1												5
3				4	1	1	1						1							8
4			1	1	1		2			2										7
5				2	2		1		1	1										7
6			1			6	1	2		1				1				1		13
7				1			1	1				1								4
8			1		1		4	2			1									9
9			1	1	1	1		1	1		1	1								8
10							1			1	1	1		1						5
11										1										1
12													1							1
13						1														1
14						1				1										2
15										1										1
16																				
17																				
18																			1	1
19						1						1		1						3
20													1							1
21																				
22																				
23										1										1
			3	9	8	12	14	6	2	7	7	4	3	3				1	1	**80**

$r = 0.47$

This gives the results shown in Table 15.10.

And even this grading system could do with a good deal of further refinement! In a number of previous studies, subdividing the data along similar lines has invariably produced better results—but unfortunately there is a limit to the amount of subdividing one can do. There is also the complication that age and experience affect different people in different

TABLE 15.10. THE EFFECT ON THREE-BY-THREE-YEAR CORRELATION COEFFICIENTS OF SPLITTING THE GROUP ACCORDING TO AGE AND EXPERIENCE

Sub-group	N	No. of drivers whose accident rates, between the 1st and 2nd triennium			Correlation coefficient r
		Improved	Stayed the same	Deteriorated	
A: <34 and <2 years' experience	28	16	3	9	0·84
B: Mixed	31	15	3	13	0·39
C: >34 and >2 years' experience	23	5	2	16	0·82
TOTAL	82	36	8	38	0·64

ways. It would appear that, one way or another, in using virtually any group of drivers where factors like age and experience are of necessity inextricably mixed to produce a correlation coefficient, one often has no idea in the end of what that coefficient means. In the case of these particular data it is apparently an underestimate of the amount of correlation present—but how much of an underestimate is quite impossible to gauge.

It would also appear that of all the group statistical techniques used in accident research, the ubiquitous r coefficient is undoubtedly the most abused and most misinterpreted of all.

For impressive as some of the PUTCO coefficients (whatever they may mean) appear to be in comparison with other studies, it would be as well to remember that the "depressing" Connecticut 3×3 coefficient of $r = 0·11$, and Coppin's even smaller coefficients applicable to shorter periods, are, with their huge N's (29,000 and 148,000 subjects), all significant at the 0·01 level (though with no control over exposure it is now anybody's guess as to what they could mean). Unfortunately, people are very apt to judge a correlation coefficient by its sheer numerical size without any reference to the size of the group on which it is based.

The correlation coefficients for the serious accidents in the PUTCO data are of much the same order as for the total accidents, i.e. a fair degree of correlation is present when discipline is slack, and fades away when unsatisfactory drivers are more readily discharged. The following coefficients have been calculated using the *same* men, i.e. only the drivers from Division A who were used for the serious accident analysis (the 1954–9 distribution of serious accidents is illustrated in Table 15.11):

	Total accidents	Serious accidents
1954–9 difficult conditions $N = 60$	$r = 0·48$	$r = 0·47$
1958–63 difficult conditions $N = 46$	$r = 0·31$	$r = 0·34$

TABLE 15.11. CORRELATION OF ACCIDENTS (SERIOUS ACCIDENTS) BETWEEN TWO THREE-YEAR PERIODS (DIFFICULT TRAFFIC CONDITIONS)

Number of Accidents 1957-9

No. of accidents 1954–56	0	1	2	3	4	Tot.
0	9	16	1			26
1	5	7	5	2	1	20
2	3	3	1			7
3		1	3	1		5
4			1			1
5					1	1
	17	27	11	3	2	**60**

$r = 0.47$

The Stability of Accident Rates as Shown by Relative Rates in Subsequent Periods

Table 15.12 shows how the different classes of accident offenders of the first period fared in the second period.

TABLE 15.12. ACCIDENT RATES (TOTAL ACCIDENTS) IN TWO CONSECUTIVE THREE-YEAR PERIODS FOR FIVE GROUPS OF DRIVERS
Difficult Traffic Conditions

Accident rate in first period	Accident rate in the second three-year period				
	1952–7	1954–9	1956–61	1958–63	1960–5
N	82	80	74	62	43
0–2	3·6	5·6	2·6	2·9	2·5
3–5	6·0	5·6	4·6	3·9	4·1
6–8	6·3	6·6	5·0	4·4	4·9
9–11	10·0	7·8	5·0	5·0	4·0
12–14	9·7	8·2	7·7	6·0	2·0
15–17	15·0	10·0	6·2		
18–20		12·0			
21–24	17·0	10·0			
Accident rate p.a. over the whole six years	2·34	2·40	2·00	1·50	1·49

Easy Traffic Conditions

	1952–7	1954–9	1956–61	1958–63	1960–5
N	74	82	83	79	57
0–2	2·9	2·4	2·4	2·5	2·7
3–5	3·9	3·8	3·4	3·1	2·7
6–8	4·1	4·8	3·8	3·3	3·5
9–11	5·6	3·8	6·2	4·5	
Accident rate p.a. over the whole six years	1·37	1·38	1·27	1·11	1·03

Here again the evidence is quite dramatic for the slack discipline groups and diminishes rapidly under conditions of stricter control—where one even gets a curvilinear relationship because of the extra disciplinary action taken against the worst initial offenders (all of whom did, in fact, receive warnings, pay cuts, etc.).

But, dramatic as this evidence is, it is no different from that revealed by the big studies on the general public. In the Connecticut 3×3 year study, the relevant figures were:

Accident rate for first three-year period	Accident rate for second period relative to the 0 accident group (i.e. times as many as the 0 accident group)
0	1·0
1	2·0
2	3·0
3	4·8
4	6·9

And the California figures, even over a much shorter period, show that the 1961 male multiple offenders also had an accident rate in 1962 which was six times that of the accident-free group. But these figures are always disregarded because they are accompanied by such small r coefficients.

Cobb's and Coppin's findings on the subsequent activities of their first-period multiple offenders are in fact much *more* dramatic than the PUTCO findings when it comes to the

TABLE 15.13. ACCIDENT RATES (SERIOUS ACCIDENTS ONLY) IN TWO CONSECUTIVE THREE-YEAR PERIODS

Accident rates in the first period	Accident rates in the second period Difficult traffic conditions	
	1954–9	1958–63
$N =$	60	46
0	0·7	0·5
1	1·4	0·7
2	0·7	0·5
3	2·0	1·0
4	2·0	2·0
5		
6	4·0	
Mean accident rate for the 2nd period	0·34	0·25

serious injury, fatality, and property damage accidents. This is shown by Table 15.13. Again it is a pity that the 1952–7 PUTCO group could not be used as this group would no doubt have shown more pronounced trends. For it is obviously the fact that in professional driver groups the worst offenders (especially with regard to serious accidents) get discharged that is affecting the issue here—which only goes to show again that such findings among the public should not be ignored.

The Effect of Removing the Worst Accident Offenders on Subsequent Accident Rates

As pointed out in Chapter 14 on Coppin's study, this sort of investigation would be far more effective if one was not usually dealing with data from which the worst offenders had *already* been removed, and those who remained severely disciplined. In the case of professional drivers this obviously makes a tremendous difference. Figure 15.2 shows the accident rates of two long-service groups as compared with those who would have qualified for inclusion had they not been discharged.

The "stayers" were those drivers who were exposed for the full six-year periods 1954–9 and 1956–61 respectively (Difficult Traffic Conditions). The "leavers" were those who would have qualified for inclusion in the group *had they not been discharged before the end of the period*. In each case the accident rates for the leavers are the average rates (up to the time of discharge) of those discharged during their first, second, third, etc., year. The rate for the stayers is the average for those whose services were retained for the full period. In both periods it can be seen that the leavers had worse records than the stayers—as is only to be expected among professional drivers where the stayer always represents the survival of the fittest. Producing graphs like these would therefore seem to any transport operator to be merely going to a lot of trouble to depict the obvious.

But Fig. 15.2 also depicts another factor and that is the effect of the stepping up of disciplinary control. The 1954–9 group illustrates a period when discipline was relatively slack with the result that only the short-exposure leavers were markedly worse than the stayers. If a driver survived his first few years without being fired he was usually pretty firmly

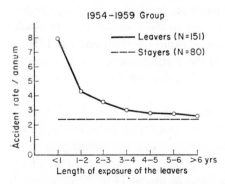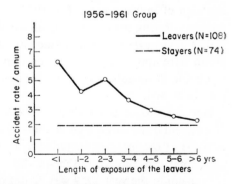

FIG. 15.2. The accident rates of two groups of long-service drivers exposed for periods of six years compared with those who would have qualified for inclusion in the groups had they not been discharged

entrenched, the supervisors being reluctant to part with an experienced man who at least knew the ropes. But in 1958 the Accident Rating System was introduced, and this apparently brought home to the supervisors just how bad the accident records of many of these experienced drivers were. This resulted in a general tightening up of disciplinary control and the weeding out of those men with consistently bad records irrespective of the length of their service. The effect of this is very evident in the 1956–61 group where the discrepancy between the leavers and the stayers is very much more marked, and the average accident rate of the stayers is lower than in the earlier group. Only the better men were now being retained—hence the diminishing evidence of accident proneness to be found in this and later chronological groups in every analysis carried out in this "group" statistical study!

But more interesting still is to observe the salutary effect which this policy of no longer tolerating proneness had on the *stayers*. Figure 15.3 shows the year-by-year accident rates of the two stayer groups plus the 1952–7 group, and demonstrates what can be

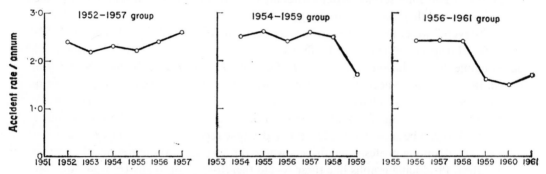

FIG. 15.3. The effect of the introduction of a new disciplinary measure on two groups of long-service drivers (measure introduced in August 1958)

achieved by a policy of "either you improve or you stop driving"—backed by concrete supporting evidence in the way of wholesale dismissals that this was no idle threat. The 1952–7 stayer group apparently coasted along merrily for the whole six years without any sign of improvement. The 1954–9 group did likewise, for five years, then the first Accident Rating list (classifying all the drivers according to their records on a five-point scale from *excellent* to *bad*), came out—and, hey presto! rapid reformation! The 1956–61 group were apparently also taking things easy until the Ratings came out, followed by wholesale dismissals, and this produced not only rapid reformation but lasting reformation as well.

Nor was this dramatic drop in the accident rate in two groups due to just a handful of men—and the same men at that. There is, of course, an overlap between the groups as some of the men are included in more than one group, using a different portion of their total exposure. But the number of men in the groups who showed marked improvement in the year 1959 was 32 out of 80 in one, and 29 out of 74 in the other—only 11 of them being overlappers. This means that 40% of the men in both groups reacted to this new disciplinary measure and proceeded to drive more carefully—which gives an indication of the salutary effect which a strict enforcement system must have on the driving behaviour of the general public!

However, to return to the traditional analysis of what the effect would have been of entirely removing the high accident repeaters of one triennium on the accident rates of the subsequent triennium. This has been carried out for all of the six-year groups. Despite the exclusion of all the high accident leavers from these groups, this analysis shows just how much damage could have been avoided if the dangerous amount of accident potential inherent in even those repeaters whose services were retained had been appreciated and they, too, had been discharged.

This is naturally particularly evident in the years before the new Accident Rating System highlighted just how much damage these men were doing.But the fact remains that in nearly every one of the groups the repeaters of the first triennium were also responsible for a very disproportionate percentage of the accidents in the second triennium. Tables 15.14

TABLE 15.14. THE EFFECTS OF REMOVING THE HIGH ACCIDENT OFFENDERS (TOTAL ACCIDENTS) OF THE FIRST THREE-YEAR PERIOD (DIFFICULT TRAFFIC CONDITIONS)

Definition of a high accident offender	Period starting	Percentage of total drivers	Percentage of accidents in which they were involved			Percentage improvement from one period to another
			First 3 years	Second 3 years	Total 6 years	
9 or more	1952	27	47	41	44	13
	1954	31	54	40	47	26
	1956	31	50	36	44	28
	1958	11	23	14	19	39
	1960	5	10	3	7	70
12 or more	1952	13	28	22	25	22
	1954	14	31	20	26	35
	1956	11	22	15	19	32
	1958	2	4	2	3	50
	1960	2	6	1	4	83
15 or more	1952	5	13	11	12	15
	1954	9	22	14	19	36
	1956	7	15	6	11	60
	1958	—	—	—	—	—
	1960	—	—	—	—	—

and 15.15 show the percentage of the drivers in each group who could be termed the dangerous repeaters of the first triennium and the percentages of the accidents in which they were involved during the first triennium, the second triennium, and total six-year period. These tables show very clearly how in the years when discipline was slack the multiple offenders of the first triennium did almost as much damage in the second triennium, and how, as discipline was stepped up, the amount of subsequent damage diminished. They also show how even the *rate* of improvement changed as a result of the disciplinary action, particularly among the worst offenders—the worse the offender of the first triennium the more he was expected to improve if he wanted to keep his job.

TABLE 15.15. The Effects of Removing the High Accident Offenders (Total Accidents) of the First Three-year Period (Easier Traffic Conditions)

Definition of a high accident offender	Period starting	Percentage of total drivers	Percentage of accidents in which they were involved			Percentage improvement from one period to another
			First 3 years	Second 3 years	Total 6 years	
6 or more	1952	31	53	36	45	32
	1954	33	52	41	47	21
	1956	29	49	36	44	27
	1958	19	37	22	31	41
	1960	19	41	24	33	41
9 or more	1952	12	15	10	13	33
	1954	5	10	5	7	50
	1956	5	11	9	10	18
	1958	—	—	—	—	—
	1960	—	—	—	—	—

To make this analysis more comparable with the Connecticut and California studies, a similar one has been done for the serious accidents only. The results are shown in Table 15.16.

TABLE 15.16. The Effects of Removing the High Accident Offenders (Serious Accidents Only) of the First Three-year Period (Difficult Traffic Conditions)

Definition of a high accident offender	Period starting	Percentage of total drivers	Percentage of accidents in which they were involved			Percentage improvement between one period and the next
			First 3 years	Second 3 years	Total 6 years	
2 or more	1954	23	66	32	48	51
	1958	17	56	27	43	53
3 or more	1954	12	41	24	32	42
	1958	9	36	20	29	44
4 or more	1954	3	16	9	12	41
	1958	4	21	13	17	35

Here again the trends are interesting, especially with regard to the *amount* of improvement shown. On the whole the amount of improvement between the first period and the second is greater than with the total accidents—which could be due to stronger disciplinary action being taken against the serious accident offenders, or to the more traumatic effects of the accidents themselves. Again, the improvement is more noticeable in the 1958–63 group than in the 1954–9 group, which seems to place the emphasis more on discipline than on the trauma factor. But here, with the serious accidents, the trend for the worst offenders to show greater improvement than the lesser offenders is reversed.

This reversal may, of course, be due to some unrevealed artifact of the data, but it nevertheless opens up an interesting line of conjecture. Are the personal characteristics which result in repeated *minor* accidents more amenable to disciplinary control than those which result in repeated *serious* ones? It is a very logical conjecture and one which will be explored in a later chapter on the personality make-up of various types of accident offenders. It is one which also ties in with Coppin's findings on his hardcore chronic Negligent Operators who continued to do at least some driving even when their licences were revoked, and continued to have a much higher than average rate of serious accidents despite curtailed exposure.

This analysis shows that it is possible to demonstrate, even among the professional drivers whose services are retained by a transport company, how important the practical implications of continued accident proneness can be. These figures are also very different from, for instance, the much-quoted finding from Forbes' analysis on the Connecticut figures, where removing those offenders with only *two* or more reportable accidents in the first period (1·3% of the drivers) would have resulted in a reduction of only 3·7% of the accidents of the second period. Undoubtedly, one of the main difficulties in carrying out any meaningful analysis of this kind among the general public lies in incomplete accident reporting and the fact that it is virtually impossible to determine from the records of a State Motor Vehicle Department whether the bad offenders of one period were fully exposed in the subsequent period, or for that matter whether they were exposed at all.

The Effect of Removing the Men with a High Accident Rate in Their First Year of Driving

This is another group statistical method which has been used to demonstrate the effect (or lack thereof) of removing the repeaters. It is the one employed by Adelstein (1952) in his study on railway shunters, and his figures in this connection are so often quoted that it should be worth while to compare them with similar analyses of the PUTCO data. Here again I have used early and late groups to illustrate the results of stricter driver control as well as using groups operating under different traffic conditions.

Adelstein set out to determine whether removing from the group those shunters with the highest accident rate *in their first year of exposure* would have resulted in any appreciable reduction to the total accident rate of subsequent years. The conclusion he reached on the basis of his data was that this was not really the case.

As was pointed out before in discussing Adelstein's study, this is not a very satisfactory way of investigating accident proneness among professional employees as it entails using only the better subjects whose services have been retained.

Consequently:

(1) Those with the very highest initial accident rate are probably the very ones who have *already* been winnowed out. In fact, very often, the only ones who are usually retained are those who start well or show quick improvement.

(2) Even amongst those remaining to constitute the groups, one can expect relatively higher accident rates *in the first year of exposure* due to the learning factor alone—complicated by the fact that some drivers have less previous experience than others.

(3) There are many inherently bad risks who are quite intelligent enough to do a "new broom" act. They behave themselves for the first year or so while under strict surveillance and only later reveal their true colours. In the same way it often happens that new drivers start quite well and later become over-confident, as demonstrated by Coppin in his study on teenage drivers (Feb. 1965).

Nevertheless, in a group where discipline is relatively slack (i.e. where accident proneness is condoned and accident-prone drivers are retained), even removing those men with the highest accident rate in their first year of exposure apparently has significant results as can be seen from the data on the difficult conditions group for the early period of 1952–7 (Table 15.17).

TABLE 15.17. THE EFFECT OF REMOVING THE MEN WITH THE HIGHEST ACCIDENT RATE IN THEIR FIRST YEAR OF DRIVING

Drivers who Started in 1952 and Were Exposed for Six Years (Difficult Traffic Conditions)

Number of accidents	Number of drivers	Total accidents for each group for each year							Average accident rate per annum over the next 5 years
		1st	2nd	3rd	4th	5th	6th	Total 2–6	
9	1	9	4	2	4	3	3	16	3·20 ⎤
8	2	16	7	13	3	14	10	47	4·70 ⎥ 3·84
6	1	6	3	4	3	4	2	16	3·20 ⎥
5	1	5	5	2	2	3	5	17	3·50 ⎦
4	2	8	6	1	3	7	2	19	1·90 ⎤ 2·33
3	4	12	8	12	10	12	9	51	2·55 ⎦
2	8	16	10	15	12	12	13	62	1·55 ⎤
1	3	3	12	12	5	6	8	43	2·87 ⎬ 1·80
0	1	0	0	2	1	0	0	3	·60 ⎦
Total	23	75	55	63	43	61	52	274	2·38

The Effects on the Yearly Mean Accident Rate of Removing the Five Drivers with the Highest Initial Accident Rates

Mean accident rate	No. of drivers	1st year	2nd year	3rd year	4th year	5th year	6th year	Yearly mean 2nd–6th year
The whole group	23	3·26	2·39	2·75	1·87	2·65	2·26	2·38
The remainder	18	2·17	2·00	2·33	1·72	2·06	1·78	1·98
The 5 offenders removed	5	7·20	3·80	4·20	2·40	4·80	4·00	3·84

Of the total group of 82 drivers there were 23 who started driving in 1952. Removing the five worst offenders (with five or more accidents in their first year of driving):

(1) would have significantly lowered the accident rate for *each succeeding year*: and
(2) would have meant removing 22% of the drivers and prevented 35% of the accidents of the succeeding five years (their rate being almost double that of the remainder).

The effects of removing even only the four very worst offenders would be significant and would mean removing 13% of the men and preventing 23% of the subsequent accidents.

These results are a little more encouraging than Adelstein's which, for interest's sake, are reproduced below.

Among his shunters the mean accident rates per annum for a group ($N = 86$) exposed for four years were:

	1st year	2nd year	3rd year	4th year
The whole group	0·639	0·360	0·360	0·348
Remainder after removing the 13 men with the highest accident rate in the first year (three accidents)	0·383	0·315	0·315	0·342

Those for a group ($N = 73$) exposed for three years:

	1st year	2nd year	3rd year
The whole group	0·557	0·355	0·317
The remainder after removing the ten men with the highest accident rate in the first year	0·393	0·361	0·329

Strangely enough the second set of findings is the only one which ever seems to get quoted!

In addition, despite the blanketing effect of group statistical techniques, which tend to obscure the different patterns of accident behaviour shown by different kinds of people, this particular analysis of the PUTCO data also reveals some interesting subsidiary findings, especially among the worst offenders.

Obviously, in any group of long-service men there are a number of bad starters who would have had to show some quick improvement or they would not have been retained. But the interesting factor is the way in which many of them revert again. The PUTCO figures show how often a year with a high accident rate is followed by a better year, and then the pattern reverts again. Individual control charts show this even better, but it can also be clearly seen from the accident rates of individual drivers given in Table 15.19. There is much talk in statistical circles about this oscillation being a phenomenon of chance (the "regression toward the mean" so often mentioned). But an examination of the personal files of the PUTCO drivers shows that these oscillations are, on the whole,

anything but chance-directed. In fact any sudden improvement is usually closely associated with disciplinary action. But the year-by-year accident rates of the worst offenders
given in Table 15.19 nevertheless illustrate the very temporary nature of this improvement. (The control chart of driver A is given in Fig. 8.5 (p. 128) of Chapter 8.) Among
professional drivers this means that it is usually a waste of time to try and reform the hard-
core offenders—it is better to dismiss them. Some of them might improve eventually,
but six years is too long and too expensive a period for a transport company to wait.
Among the general public this is the same sort of recidivism illustrated by Coppin among
his Negligent Operators. This good-year–bad-year oscillation phenomenon among the
worst offenders of the PUTCO drivers also adds additional confirmation to Coppin's
theory of the immediate, if temporary, suppressor effect of accident involvement—in his
case, no doubt, accentuated by curtailed exposure.

Another factor which this PUTCO group shows up is the "new broom" act, which is
particularly evident among some of the very good starters both in Tables 15.17 and
15.18.

A similar analysis has been carried out for the 1952–7 Easy Traffic Conditions group
(Table 15.18). Of the 74 men in this group, 17 started to drive in 1952. Here one can see
that the accident rate is much lower.

TABLE 15.18. THE EFFECT OF REMOVING THE MEN WITH THE HIGHEST ACCIDENT RATE IN THEIR
FIRST YEAR OF DRIVING

Drivers who Started in 1952 and Were Exposed for Six Years (Easy Traffic Conditions)

Number of accidents	Number of drivers	Total accidents for each group for each year							Average accident rate per annum over the next 5 years
		1st	2nd	3rd	4th	5th	6th	Total 2–6	
4	2	8	6	6	5	3	4	24	2·40
2	4	8	7	9	8	3	5	32	1·60
1	5	5	7	9	2	2	2	22	0·88
0	6	0	9	7	7	9	5	37	1·23
TOTAL	17	21	29	31	22	17	16	115	1·35

The Effects on the Yearly Mean Accident Rate of Removing the Two Drivers with the Highest Initial Accident Rates

Mean accident rate	No. of drivers	1st year	2nd year	3rd year	4th year	5th year	6th year	Yearly mean 2nd–6th years
The whole group	17	1·24	1·71	1·82	1·29	1·00	0·94	1·35
The remainder	15	0·86	1·53	1·67	1·13	0·93	0·80	1·21
The 2 offenders removed	2	4·00	3·00	3·00	2·50	1·50	2·00	2·40

In this group the suppressor effect is not so obvious—again possibly because the variation is not so great due to the lower accident rate, but also no doubt because patches of bad behaviour are not readily tolerated under easy driving conditions and usually result in dismissal.

But here, even with these lower accident rates, removing the worst offenders with four or more accidents *in their first year of exposure* would still have had significant results. Apart from the general year-by-year reduction of accidents, removing them would have entailed removing 12% of the drivers and would have prevented 21% of the accidents of the next five years (their rate again being virtually double that of the remainder).

The Significance of a High Accident Rate in Any Year
of a Driver's Career

Another interesting study which can be carried out with the 1952–7 group of drivers is to see whether a high accident rate *in any one year* has significance or not. Is is just a quirk of chance or is it usually symptomatic of genuine accident proneness?

Table 15.19 gives the year-by-year accident records of those drivers who had an undue number of accidents *in any one year*. Also, to show that their accident rates were not merely the result of youth or inexperience, both the ages and previous exposure as at 1952 are given.

This analysis shows:

Average accident rate per annum (*over the other five years*) for the group with seven or more accidents *in any one year* ($N = 11$)   3·64

Average accident rate per annum for the whole group ($N = 82$) *over the whole six years*   2·34

Average accident rate for the remainder ($N = 71$) *over the whole six years*   2·01

Even removing the offenders with a slightly lower accident rate in any one year has significant results:

Average accident rate per annum (over the other five years) for the group with six or more accidents *in any one year* ($N = 18$)   3·31

Average accident rate for the whole group ($N = 82$) *over the whole six years*   2·34

Average accident rate per annum for the remainder ($N = 64$) *over the whole six years*   1·87

It could perhaps be argued that using the "remainder group" as a comparison might not be justified, as removing the ones with a high accident rate in any year sets a "ceiling". Let us therefore adopt the conservative method of comparing the accident rate per annum of the group with an excessive number of accidents in any one year with the average annual rate of the group as a *whole*. This means including these same men and the contribution which their high accident years made to the total. If these years had been just a quirk of chance, then the accident rate of these men *over the other five years* should not differ

TABLE 15.19. THE SIGNIFICANCE OF A HIGH ACCIDENT RATE IN ANY YEAR OF A DRIVER'S RECORD (DIFFICULT TRAFFIC CONDITIONS 1952–7)*

Driver	Years of previous exposure at 1952	Age at 1952	No. of accidents in highest year	Number of accidents in each year						Total for six years	Total excluding the highest year	Average per annum for the remaining 5 years
				1	2	3	4	5	6			
A	0	22	12	8	4	12	2	10	5	41	29	5·80
B	7	45	11	6	3	7	11	5	1	33	22	4·40
C	0	25	9	9	4	2	4	3	3	25	16	3·20
D	0	36	8	8	3	1	1	4	5	22	14	2·80
E	1	42	8	5	0	0	3	3	8	19	11	2·20
F	6	38	8	5	2	2	5	5	8	27	19	3·80
G	6	46	8	4	4	8	7	5	6	34	26	5·20
H	2	30	8	4	3	1	6	8	2	24	16	3·20
I	2	29	8	1	5	6	1	1	8	22	14	2·80
J	1	29	7	2	5	3	3	4	7	24	17	3·40
K	0	34	7	1	5	6	4	0	7	23	16	3·20
L	0	32	6	6	3	4	3	4	2	22	16	3·20
M	1	49	6	5	5	1	2	4	6	23	17	3·40
N	6	40	6	4	2	6	5	3	2	22	16	3·20
O	3	34	6	4	0	0	5	1	6	16	10	2·00
P	2	42	6	4	1	6	4	3	3	20	14	2·80
Q	0	23	6	3	1	3	1	6	1	15	9	1·80
R	0	22	6	3	5	6	4	1	3	22	16	3·20

Average accident rate per annum over six years for the whole group ($N = 82$), 2·34.

from that of the total group. The very fact that highly significant differences do occur is surely pretty convincing evidence of the existence in this group of true accident proneness.

In fact, the only one of these men whose accident rate over the remaining five years was *below* the average for the remainder was case Q and there was a reason for this: he was one of the company's good drivers, but he was a boxer and his one bad period was due to the fact that he started suffering from double vision but would not admit to it at first as he thought he might lose his job. (He did not lose his job but was made to give up boxing!)

It would seem, therefore, that the old argument that removing the accident offenders of any one year fails to reduce subsequent accident rates is not borne out by the PUTCO data—no matter to what sort of analysis one submits it. Removing them from the PUTCO groups would have had very significant results—which is not the least bit surprising as it was the process of *continually* removing these high accident offenders and replacing them with better material which finally succeeded in reducing the company's total accident rate.

* In the 1960–5 group, where discipline was much stricter, the highest number of accidents in any one year was five.

In fact what it all boils down to is that these complicated analyses I have carried out here are only yet another attempt to substantiate *statistically* that same simple principle adhered to by every motor vehicle department, or transport company, or insurance company—the principle that *there is no smoke without fire*. If a driver has a dangerously high accident rate *now* there is every reason to believe that he could possess a dangerously high accident *potential* for the future. And the reason why these bodies have continued to adhere to this principle, despite the doubts cast upon it by some of the theoretical thinkers on the subject of accident proneness, is no doubt because ignoring it has been found *in practice* to have such disastrous results.

The PUTCO study is an obvious case in point. As long as this principle was overlooked, as in the 1952–7 groups, and no drastic action was taken against current high-accident offenders, most of them merely went on offending. It was only by recognizing the dangerous accident potential of these men and doing something to curb it that the total accident rate was reduced. But doing something meant refusing to retain the services of any offender who either would not or could not show marked improvement—which is why the later groups were found to contain fewer and fewer examples of continued accident proneness, and *ipso facto* why using exactly the same statistical techniques on these groups came up with progressively less and less evidence in support of the concept. Statistical procedures are not conjuring acts. If you are going to pull rabbits out of hats there must be some rabbits there to start with. And if you have used the principle of accident proneness to eliminate most of the accident-prone drivers from the groups you are studying, then you are not going to find overwhelming evidence of proneness!

This is one of the reasons why I have gone to the trouble of carrying out all these traditional statistical analyses on the PUTCO data. My object was not only to demonstrate that it is, after all, possible to produce statistical confirmation of continuous accident proneness, even by using these rather insensitive group techniques, but to demonstrate *why* it is that such methods often fail to produce this confirmation. The fault lies with the enforced choice of selective and unrepresentative data for these studies, not with the principle of accident proneness itself. To illustrate accident proneness properly by means of group techniques requires a group which has remained undisturbed for a long period of time—not one which represents the survival of the fittest and the best. And it is very seldom that such a group can be found for the simple reason that the official bodies who keep accurate accident records are almost invariably those who make use of the principle of accident proneness and take action against accident offenders, thereby disturbing their groups.

One of the reasons why Hakkinen's study produced good evidence of accident proneness was because selection and retention standards for the Helsinki bus and tram drivers were not as stringent over the period of his study as they are now (i.e. it was only as a *result* of his study that his rigorous selection system was introduced).

And undoubtedly one of the reasons for the lack of evidence in the big studies on the general public (apart from the incomplete reporting and the lack of controls) is that the groups used are those in which action is constantly being taken against the worst offenders—or groups in which the early offenders still count as a statistic although they may be no longer driving.

If this intricate analysis of the PUTCO data according to the conventional "group" statistical method has achieved nothing else, let us hope that it will at least have shed some light on the weaknesses of these techniques. Let us also hope that it will have highlighted the danger of using data on professional drivers, where the worst offenders are subjected to severe discipline (if they have not already been removed by discharge) on which to found an argument that such offenders do not exist, or at any rate do not count for much in the total accident picture.

Surely the obvious conclusion to be drawn from the PUTCO data is that *these accident offenders count for as much as they are allowed to count for*? For the more tolerance that was shown to this type of offender, even in long-service groups, the greater their contribution to the total accidents of the group—and, at the same time, the higher was the accident rate of the company as a whole. The less tolerance showed to them, the less they contributed to the total accident tally of the group and the lower was the accident rate of the company as a whole.

But it is also to be hoped that this analysis of the PUTCO data, especially that relating to the early years when the worst offenders were still being tolerated, will stop some of the controversy on the validity of the concept of proneness itself. For this analysis provides even stronger confirmation than Hakkinen's findings. It would be impossible for two controlled studies of this magnitude to produce such strong supporting evidence if accident proneness was not a scientific reality.

CHAPTER 16

PREDICTING ACCIDENT POTENTIAL

IF ACCIDENT proneness has been shown to be a scientific reality then at least we have answered the most basic of the research questions set out in the beginning of this book. But a very important one remains still unanswered: "Is it predictable?" Many of the studies described in the course of the book have shown that methods can be devised for differentiating between those people who *in the past* have been more prone to accidents than others, but the only study of which I am personally aware where such methods have been used to predict *future* proneness, and where the accuracy of these predictions has been scientifically evaluated, is the PUTCO one. I therefore propose to describe another aspect of this study, namely the use of projective tests of the TAT type for the practical selection of professional bus drivers in terms of their accident potential. But as personality is only one of the factors associated with accident potential—let alone driver efficiency— the best way to describe the successive validations of the personality tests would be against the background of the selection programme as a whole.

There is one rather important difference between a project involving routine practical driver selection and a pure research project, and that is the question of the prediction errors. Unlike a pure research project, where these errors are just tally-strokes in the wrong corner of a correlation table (which can if necessary be blamed on the theory of accident proneness and not on the testing method), in a practical situation these prediction errors are apt to come home to roost. And too many of them coming home to roost will mean the end of the testing programme and the end, no doubt, of some promising careers for those involved in it!

In fact there can be no more stringent test to which any accident-predicting system can be put than in a transport company—especially one keeping the sort of records which PUTCO has kept and where every driver's accident record is assessed every six months. Any system which can survive twelve years of this must therefore have some merit, and it is therefore worthy of a little detailed examination.

In a practical situation like this, each candidate presents the selectors with a separate problem. Here is an *individual*, not a member of a group—an individual who may have certain attributes that compensate for his failings and certain vices that counteract his virtues. In assessing him with regard to a factor as complex as his accident potential, it is therefore of little avail to consider him, characteristic by characteristic, in terms of group standards. For this will reveal little of how he himself integrates these characteristics, of how he uses his capabilities or adjusts to his limitations—in other words of how he, as an individual, is likely to function and behave. The selection procedures for the PUTCO drivers have therefore been designed as an attempt to do just this—to assess each man *as a functioning whole.*

Since 1956 the system has consisted of a four-stage process of elimination:

(1) The first stage is a short pre-screening interview, checking for basic requirements such as literacy and physical build (someone too small and light cannot stand up to the strain of handling a big bus, and being too tall has disadvantages as it often results in spinal trouble), and an examination of previous job record, which is required to be generally satisfactory—although previous driving experience is not necessary, the company still being prepared to train any man from scratch if he has the makings of a good driver.

(2) The next stage is the psychomotor testing programme. Here from ten to fifteen people are handled daily (for other organizations as well as the transport company) and the programme consists of quite a small battery of psychomotor tests. The psychometric tests used in the earlier days of the programme have been dropped as they were found to be redundant. The psychomotor battery still comprises the original tests (two-hand co-ordination, anticipation, distribution of attention, reaction time with and without distractions), but a stress test has been added which consists of a very successful improvisation where the candidate is required to repeat the two-hand co-ordination test under pressure, this time being interrupted by lights which he has to put out, and harassed by a gong which rings every time he gets into any kind of difficulty. (The unit has never had much research capital, so the policy has always been that necessity is the mother of invention!) The psychomotor battery has, however, recently been augmented by the addition of three tests which colleagues in Europe have kindly allowed us to copy. These are Hakkinen's Ambiguous Situation Test, and two tests which are used by Van der Burgh in Holland—a reaction-time test which also measures irregularities in reaction time, and a simple but ingenious test known as the Mouse Trap (though a large rat trap would be a more appropriate description) which tests for manipulative dexterity and at the same time embodies a good deal of frustration tolerance. These new tests are, however, still in the stage of being experimentally integrated into the battery.

A basic pass level has been set on each of the tests, but a battery score is no longer used. In this particular context we have found it better to use the psychomotor tests to assess each person *on his individual merits,* which, with the chronic shortage of good driver material, often means sacrificing some element of skill which can be compensated for by extra training. The testers are also taught to use their powers of observation to the full. For instance, any subject who really tries is allowed to proceed further unless he is obviously too lacking in psychomotor skill or is incapable of handling a complex situation without going to pieces. On the other hand, any subject who puts up a flamboyant performance rules himself out automatically. Experience has shown that if a subject has not got the sense to moderate his behaviour while under test, there is no point in going to the trouble of analysing his personality further, his chances of being a safe driver being virtually nil.

(3) The personality tests (consisting of a six-card TAT and the PUTCO comic strip SRT) form the third stage of the elimination process. These are written tests. At the beginning of each day's testing, every man is furnished with his own set of TAT cards and his comic-strip SRT booklet. The instructions are administered to the group as a whole and

each man then sits and writes his stories, being called upon at intervals to do the individual psychomotor tests. The whole testing programme takes a batch of subjects the best part of a day to complete—the personality tests being analysed on the following day. Only the protocols of those who survive the psychomotor screening are analysed unless there are vacancies for other less exacting jobs. The logic here is that even with the best will in the world, a driver with very poor psychomotor functioning is going to be a poor accident risk as well as a liability from the point of view of both training and vehicle maintenance costs.

(4) The fourth stage consists of the assessment of each of the "possibles" in terms of his combined tests findings, i.e. his abilities in relation to his total personality pattern—the acceptance standard being adjusted according to current demand. Successful candidates are then given a full medical examination and eye test. The medical officers are particularly on the alert for cardiac weaknesses, tuberculosis, liver troubles (which could be indicative of drinking), epilepsy, and hypertension (the company being prepared to treat these conditions, if controllable, in existing staff, but seldom in new applicants). The eye tests comprise acuity, muscular balance, stereoscopic vision, colour vision, range of vision, night vision, and recovery from glare. Anyone with visual defects is sent to an optician, and the company grants each driver an annual allowance for spectacles. Defects in night vision and adaptation to glare are treated with vitamin A to which they usually respond fairly quickly.

Every successful candidate, even if he has a Public Service licence, then goes through the full driver training course, the length of the course being dependent on his individual progress. A trainee driver with no previous driving experience can spend up to ten weeks in the driving school, gradually progressing from elementary vehicle handling right through to driving in heavy traffic, and is then supervised by an experienced co-driver during his first two weeks of actual route-driving with a full passenger load.

After that the routine system of driver management takes over. Spot checks are made on the driving proficiency of each new driver during his first year, and he gets re-training if necessary. The whole staff is given regular eye tests and six-monthly medical examinations, plus having their accident records graded every six months on the Accident Ratings. In addition, free medical services are available, and a large Welfare Department—staffed with trained social workers—looks after any personal problems which might arise.

With such a thorough selection, training, and driver management system it should be theoretically possible to have a staff which consists only of first-class drivers. But the interesting finding, here, is that despite all the training and supervision the standard of performance on the job of the finished product is anything but uniform and tends to follow very closely the five-point grading given to each new driver on the basis of his initial psychological test results. This is especially noticeable with regard to his accident record; and here the most interesting finding of all is the close relationship which has emerged between the assessment of each driver's future accident potential on the basis of the *personality tests alone* and his subsequent grading on the factually-based Accident Rating System. This is particularly noteworthy in view of the fact that the psychologists who analyse these projective tests never see or interview the subjects at all. In fact, in outlying divisions of the company the protocols are all posted to head office and analysed there.

This close relationship between the personality rating and the accident rating is therefore not merely attributable to the fact that only the best applicants are chosen. The unfortunate period of the 6000-category drivers mentioned in the last chapter (when virtually every available licensed driver who showed driving ability had to be accepted almost irrespective of his personality test results) demonstrated that the tests were every bit as effective in predicting the bad records as the good ones. They are, in fact, genuine predictors.

This means in effect that the degree of success achieved by the earlier test passes in the days when selection standards were relatively high was not only due to their innate skill or their training but to their satisfactory personality make-up as well. It also means that the degree of failure of the numerous test failures who were accepted during the driver shortage was largely due to the fact that no amount of innate skill or training was able to override their personality defects. And, most important of all, because of its far-reaching practical implications, this means that much of the pessimism about it being impossible to predict the accident behaviour *of the individual* is unfounded. With a comprehensive personality test which enables one to gain an insight into the total personality structure, it is indeed possible to predict with very satisfactory accuracy what sort of an accident risk a person is going to be in the future.

However, a statement like that requires some rather detailed confirmation. So before elaborating on the tests themselves, I think it would be as well to describe the four successive statistical validations to which they have been subjected.

These consisted of three validations within PUTCO, and one in a different context.

(1) *The first experimental validation* (1956). This was the only one where the tests were not used to predict *future* accident involvement. It was carried out merely to explore the value of the tests. The subjects were 163 current or ex-PUTCO drivers and the criterion was based on their *past* accident records.

(2) *The first follow-up study* (1961) where the subjects were 212 drivers selected on the basis of the tests, and the criterion was their *subsequent* accident records.

(3) *The second follow-up study* (1967) where the number of subjects was now 1139.

(4) *The fourth validation* was a separate controlled research programme carried out on behalf of the South African Road Safety Council. The purpose of this was to determine whether the tests would be equally effective on subjects with a different cultural background. The subjects were 115 White (Caucasian) bus drivers employed by a Transit Authority, and the criterion was based on each man's *subsequent* accident record as from the day he was tested.

The accident criterion for each of the validations was on a four-point scale equivalent to the test ratings *good, fair, poor*, and *bad*—a driver's allocation to a category being dependent on the average number of days between accidents, this average being assessed according to the standard for the route on which he operated. (If a man is transferred from one route to another, then his average is proportionately assessed.) The differences between the standards for the various routes was illustrated in Chapter 8. (The original rating scale included another category, *excellent*, and although this category is still used for classifying the company's best long-service drivers on the routine Accident Ratings, it has not been used for follow-up studies because the shorter exposure does not warrant such a refinement.)

In the two earlier validations the statistical unit used was $\bar{t}$ (the average of the time intervals up to his last recorded accident). In later ones, a new unit $\hat{t}$ was used, based on a slightly different method of calculating the average. The use of $\bar{t}$ entails using the man's exposure only up to his last accident. This in turn means sacrificing the period of exposure since that accident, which, with the better drivers, is often considerable. As this period of time *has* elapsed without his having an accident, it is legitimate exposure and should by rights be included. The new statistic, the $\hat{t}$ is therefore calculated as follows:

$$\hat{t} = \frac{\text{total exposure}}{n+1},$$

where n equals the number of accidents he has incurred.

This $\hat{t}$ is always an underestimate of what his average will be when the next accident occurs, and occasionally penalizes a driver with a very short unexpired period. But analysis has shown that on the whole it is a closer approximation then the $\bar{t}$. The statistical rationale for this change in method is fully explained later in the purely statistical section. But the issue is a minor one and only concerns us here because the $\bar{t}$ method was used in the earlier validations and is the one described in previous publications.

In all the validations each subject is exposed for a different length of time, but this does not matter because each driver is assessed individually as soon as his record has stabilized itself sufficiently for the $\bar{t}$ or $\hat{t}$ to be a reliable estimate.

When it has been necessary to use a "disciplinary" criterion, the following system of grading each man's record has been used:

A   *excellent*   A record containing virtually no disciplinary offences.
B   *good*   A record containing only a few minor offences over a relatively long exposure period.
C   *fair*   A record containing minor offences such as absenteeism, lateness, carelessness, and minor dishonesty, and a very occasional more serious offence such as speeding.
D   *poor*   A record containing more serious offences such as speeding and disobeying instructions, and also a record of chronic dishonesty in the collection of fares ("ticket offences").
E   *bad*   A record containing serious offences such as reckless driving, traffic offences, insolence, insubordination, assault, and drunkenness. Also all cases discharged for unsatisfactory employee behaviour.

This method of assessing a disciplinary record, though the best available, cannot be regarded as being really reliable. Whereas the recording of accidents is meticulously correct, the recording of disciplinary offences has been found to vary in different divisions of the company. In any case, an assessment like this is highly subjective. With these particular data it is also complicated by the fact that dishonesty in connection with fares is very often found amongst even the best drivers. The reason for this seems to be a sociological one. It appears that according to a black man's logic, taking money from a company run by a white man is not "stealing" (a line of reasoning which is now becoming rather apparent in American society as well). The PUTCO drivers are no exception to this way of thinking: so much so that they are inclined to gang up on any driver who does not "conform". (They have even been known to run a "kitty" financed from very illegitimate sources to subsidize any of their fellow drivers whose pay has been cut for ticket offences!) Assessing potential dishonesty by means of a TAT, or any other personality test, is therefore anything but easy. For this sort of pilfering carries very little social stigma within the cultural group, so it produces little feeling of internal guilt; and although much effort is expended in attempting to predict this form of dishonesty (because of the considerable loss of revenue that it entails), these efforts are naturally not always successful—which no doubt accounts for the fact that every validation of the tests has produced better results using an accident criterion than a disciplinary one. The findings on the disciplinary criterion are only included here because they were used in the first validation and because, despite the blurring effect of the "dishonesty" factor in these particular data, some very interesting relationships do emerge between the accident involvement of the drivers and their general behaviour as exemplified by their employee records. The first two validations have been described in an earlier publication (Shaw, 1965) so only the main findings and general points of interest will be given here.

1. The Experimental Validation

At the time the first validation was carried out, the whole project was still in its early experimental stage. Some of the pictures of the new African TAT were still rather unproductive, and the comic-strip SRT had not yet been designed. In addition the TAT was being tried out merely as a driver-selection tool. For instance we had not yet realized that the best working method would be to use the test findings to make two separate evaluations of each subject: (1) as an accident risk, and (2) as an employee risk. So the test rating was a general one, meant to represent the subject's over-all chance of success on the job. Later, as a result of this validation, we decided that the two separate prediction ratings were very necessary in order to cope with the sort of complications produced by accident-loaded factors like anxiety, or employee-loaded factors like dishonesty.

But most experimental of all was the method of assessing each individual's accident potential on the basis of his personality. That was 1956, and very little research had been published anywhere on this question. All the research literature we had been able to obtain had merely led us to two rather unhappy conclusions: (1) that no very successful method of predicting accidents by means of psychological tests had as yet been found, and (2) that we had better find one quickly if we as a unit were going to justify our existence—particularly in view of the disastrous activities of the men we had already selected on the basis of aptitude tests alone. We therefore decided that the only way we could tackle the problem of selecting a driver in terms of his personality was on a common-sense basis. So one Saturday morning we all got together and drew up a list of those failings which we felt would make for bad driving and employee behaviour.

This original list is as follows:

Imbalance	Aggression
Anti-social attitudes and values	Discontentedness

Carelessness	Lack of confidence
Immaturity	Anxiety
Irresponsibility	Lack of intelligence

Since then many accident-related factors have been isolated and amplified and the grouping of the various factors very much refined, but it is interesting to note that no fundamental changes have been made. Even after twelve years of using the tests, the method of assessing an accident risk still retains its basis of common sense—a basis which, incidentally, has not been refuted by subsequent research in many parts of the world, research which from time to time has highlighted the importance of many of the personality characteristics given in this simple experimental list.

The original purpose of this list was merely to act as a guide to the assessors, for right from the start we were aware of the fact that if we wished to predict how a driver was going to behave we would need to know much more about him than whether he possessed certain specific characteristics. We would need to know how these characteristics were integrated into his total personality pattern, to know his ambitions, his motivations, his conflicts, his fears—in fact what sort of a *person* he was. It seemed to us that a projective test like the TAT would be ideal for this purpose; but apart from the fact that it would be a criminal waste to go fragmenting the valuable information which it produced, such fragmentation would also serve no useful purpose on a practical assignment such as this. Here, again, this is a conclusion which has remained unchanged over the years. In fact the more experience we have acquired with accident prediction, the more convinced we have become that it is the *total* personality pattern that matters, and particularly the balance and integration of that pattern. If this is sound and the person functions on a fairly even keel, is well adjusted to his particular circumstances, and has learned to live with himself and his environment, then the prognosis of his accident potential is good. If there is a pronounced imbalance of any kind, if the personality is poorly integrated, if his adjustments are inadequate, or over-compensatory, or unrealistic, then the prognosis is bad.

However, we have never lost sight of the fact that, ideal as the projective tests have proved to be for predicting accident potential, there are almost insuperable difficulties in applying them on any large scale to the general public. Here some other testing method will obviously have to be found—possibly one based in some way on specific personality characteristics. This is why we developed the amplified marking sheet, and although it has seldom been used in the PUTCO project except for the training of new assessors, it was used for the South African Road Safety Council research project. Years later, in co-operation with Professor Eysenck, these carefully preserved data were subjected to a computerized factor analysis, the results of which have opened up the prospect of a new and promising line of research. For the moment, however, although the marking sheet was used in the course of the first validation, it would be best to defer any findings on specific characteristics to a later discussion on this subject.

The first validation is therefore described purely in terms of the results achieved by using a composite personality rating, as this is the way in which the assessment of accident potential has been done in practice over the last twelve years, and as this forms the bsait for each of the subsequent validations.

In each succeeding validation of the projective tests little use has been made of product-moment r coefficients. The combination of an abnormal distribution with an arbitrary four-point rating scale usually produces a correlation surface which does not lend itself to the use of this particular statistical technique. The r coefficients were therefore not even given in previous publications. But I will include them here if only to demonstrate some of the shortcomings of this technique. For although the three PUTCO validations all yielded very satisfactory results from the point of view of the practical usefulness of the tests, the r coefficients underwent spectacular changes from time to time, mostly because of skewed distributions and restrictions in range.

One of the most satisfactory ways of analysing this sort of data is to establish what percentage of the subjects rated as *good, fair, poor,* and *bad* actually turned out to have satisfactory accident records. This is after all the most important consideration from a purely practical point of view, as the test unit (and the management of the transport company) want to know what proportion of satisfactory drivers they can expect from each of the test ratings. If these expectancies do not conform to a realistic progression, then something is wrong. The ideal progression would be a success rate which would range from 90% to 100% at the 1 and 2 *(excellent* and *good)* levels of the test, down to 0–10% at the 5 *(bad)* level. In each successive validation one of the main objectives has therefore been to see how well this is being achieved.

In the first validation, because the test rating was a composite one, this had to be measured against a composite criterion, representing general success on the job. (This was made by combining each man's rating on the accident and disciplinary criteria with an arbitrary loading of two to one in favour of accidents—the latter being considered to be more serious and costly offences.) The subjects were chosen at random, their choice being largely dependent on which of the drivers could be spared from their duties, and the numbers were supplemented by using ex-drivers applying for re-engagement. The testing was done "blind" as the TAT analyst had no knowledge of the man's accident record. In any case these were still being assembled for processing on the time-interval system. The group comprised 163 subjects.

The first investigation was to see what proportion of those rated as 1—*excellent,* 2—*good,* or 3—*fair,* etc., were in reality "passes" or "failures" on the combined success-on-the-job criterion. Their test ratings were also compared with their classification on the accident and disciplinary criteria separately. (Classes A, B, and C on the accident or disciplinary criterion were considered to be above average, and therefore passes, D and E were below average and therefore failures, a suitable cut-off being established for the combined criteria.) The percentage of passes (or successes) among the subjects in each test rating is shown in Table 16.1.

Correlation of the test ratings with the actual criteria ratings yielded the following r coefficients (all significant at the 0·001 level):

TAT/Accident Rating	0·57
TAT/Disciplinary Rating	0·45
TAT/Combined Rating	0·61
Accident Rating/Disciplinary Rating	0·42

TABLE 16.1. THE EXPERIMENTAL VALIDATION OF THE TAT.
ACHIEVED PERCENTAGES OF SUCCESS AT EACH LEVEL OF THE
TEST

TAT rating	Number of subjects	Achieved percentages of success on the criteria		
		Accident criterion	Disciplinary criterion	Combined criterion
1 *Excellent*	3	100	100	100
2 *Good*	17	100	82	94
3 *Fair*	25	96	72	80
4 *Poor*	53	51	51	42
5 *Bad*	65	34	28	23

If one were to judge the results of this validation by the r coefficients alone, the results could be regarded as very satisfactory—particularly the correlation between the TAT and the combined criterion rating of general success on the job, as this is what the TAT was then aiming to measure.

But Table 16.1, giving the achieved percentages of success, nevertheless shows that the standard currently set on the tests was obviously far too strict for practical purposes, for it would exclude too many likely candidates if the tests were used for selection. Further investigation, on the accident side, disclosed that this over-strict rating was occurring mostly among the drivers operating in the easy traffic conditions areas. This pointed to the need for a deeper analysis, so we started to do then what we have done ever since, and that is to investigate each incorrect prediction separately—a process from which we have, over the years, learned a great deal about how to handle this very sensitive personality test. For instance, most of the wrong predictions in this early validation were cases who had been rated down on the test for slow thinking or inadequacy but who were apparently coping adequately with easy traffic conditions. Lesson No. 1 learned: allocate this type of driver to the easy routes where possible and if necessary give him separate accident prediction ratings, one for easy traffic conditions and one for difficult conditions.

Lesson No. 2 was that we would obviously have to lower the standards if we were ever to get enough drivers, so we reorientated our ideas and set ourselves a more realistic standard, our aim being to achieve the following approximate rates of success at each level of the test.

Rating 1 } *excellent* and *good* with a 90% prognosis of success.
Rating 2 } (Combined because there were so few rating 1's among the applicants.)
Rating 3   *fair*   with a 63% prognosis of success.
Rating 3.5 *borderline* with a 50% prognosis of success.
Rating 4   *poor*   with a 37% prognosis of success.
Rating 5   *bad*   with a 10% prognosis of success.

The *borderline* category (3.5) was deliberately inserted as a halfway mark between the *fair* and *poor* categories to allow for the consideration of those of the more innocuous 4—*poor* test ratings who could perhaps be accepted if necessary. Here the analysts were asked to give special consideration to those cases in which the personality pattern indicated that although the man's record would probably start in an unsatisfactory manner, there was nevertheless a chance of reasonably quick improvement (e.g. cases of immaturity with a hopeful prognosis, or lack of confidence which could improve with experience). Even if using such a rating scale would entail the selection of more men who were likely to turn out failures, it was obviously a practical necessity in order to avoid losing likely material. The intention was that the 1, 2, and 3 ratings could be considered at any time; the borderlines could be considered in time of shortage: and the ratings 4's and 5's would be excluded. But theory is one thing and practical reality is another. As rapid company expansion made it increasingly difficult to find sufficient good bus-driving material, over the next few years every *borderliner* had to be accepted and quite a number of the rating 4's. It was even necessary to accept a few rating 5's who were senior employees of the company and who had to be given a chance as drivers. Later still, the test standards had to be lowered even further, and finally, when the shortage got complete-ly out of hand, for over two years the tests were used to screen out only the very worst cases.

2. The First Follow-up Study

The next major statistical investigation was carried out at the end of 1961, this time on the results of the actual selection by means of the personality tests.

By this time 260 men had been selected. Some of the earlier ones had by then acquired up to five years' exposure, and 212 had been exposed long enough for it to be possible to classify them on the accident criterion. As up to that time the driver shortage was not too bad, the majority of the men were test passes.

This group contained every classifiable driver selected since the beginning of 1956, when the first experimental TAT was put into operation. It therefore reflected all the "growing pains" of the project. However, even despite this fact, the first follow-up study was very encouraging, giving as it did a clear demonstration of the value of the tests for practical driver selection.

The Comparison between Achieved and Expected
Successes on the Criteria

The first investigation carried out was to determine whether the tests had lived up to the rough expectancy scale set at the time of the first validation—namely whether the proportion of subjects who had turned out to be a success on the criteria would range from about 90% of the *good* test ratings down to only 10% of the *bad* ratings. Table 16.2 shows that as far as accident prediction was concerned, the tests were working very well (although there were not very many 4 and 5 test ratings by which to judge the predicting power of the lower levels).

The fact that 48% of those rated 4—*poor* on the tests had been successful, as against the expected 37%, was no reason for alarm. The expected 37% was meant to apply to all subjects rated *poor* on the tests, but naturally, even under pressure, we had accepted only the best of them. And it was interesting to see that none of the rating 5's had succeeded.

TABLE 16.2. THE FIRST FOLLOW-UP STUDY

Comparison between Expected and Achieved Percentages of Success
on the Accident Criterion at Each Level of the Personality Tests
(N = 212)

Test rating	N	Number who were successes on the accident criterion	Achieved percentages of success	Expected percentages of success
1 and 2 *Good*	51	44	86	90
3 *Fair*	78	53	68	63
3·5 *Borderline*	53	30	57	50
4 *Poor*	25	12	48	37
5 *Bad*	5	0	0	10

The results of the comparison between expected and achieved success on the disciplinary criterion are given in Table 16·3 which shows that the achieved percentages of success were not quite so satisfactory, particularly at the higher levels of the test. Possibly one of the reasons for this was that the criterion was too strict, particularly in view of the dishonesty factor and the fact that it had been too complicated to allow for any learning periods. (This accounts for the fact that the disciplinary group had more subjects than the accident group.) Nevertheless, the steady upward trend of achieved successes at each level of the test was encouraging.

TABLE 16.3. THE FIRST FOLLOW-UP STUDY

Comparison of Expected and Achieved Percentages of Success on
the Disciplinary Criterion at Each Level of the Test
(N = 224)

Test rating	N	Number who succeeded on the criterion	Achieved percentage of success	Expected percentage of success
1 and 2 *Good*	87	61	70	90
3 *Fair*	72	40	56	63
3·5 *Borderline*	40	20	50	50
4 *Poor*	18	5	22	37
5 *Bad*	7	1	14	10

Taking the pass/fail cut-off on both test and criterion as a definition of a *safe* and *unsafe* risk, a χ-square test yielded the following results (depending on whether the *borderliners* were considered to be "passes" or "fails"):

TAT/Accident Criterion $\chi^2 = 10·12$ or $13·53$
TAT/Disciplinary Criterion $\chi^2 = 15·03$ or $11·77$

All of these results are significant at the 0·01 level.

CORRELATION OF TEST PREDICTIONS WITH THE CRITERIA

Tables 16.4 and 16.5 show the full results of the testing in terms of the accident and disciplinary criteria.

TABLE 16.4. THE FIRST FOLLOW-UP STUDY

Personality Test Predictions vs. the Accident Criterion

$(N = 212)$

Category on the accident criterion	Test predictions					Total
	1 & 2 Good N	3 Fair N	3·5 Borderline N	4 Poor N	5 Bad N	
A and B *Good*	28	27	16	9	0	80
C *Fair*	16	26	14	3	0	59
D *Poor*	4	11	10	10	5	40
E *Bad*	3	14	13	3	0	33
TOTAL	51	78	53	25	5	212

TABLE 16.5. THE FIRST FOLLOW-UP STUDY

Personality Test Predictions vs. the Disciplinary Criterion

$(N = 224)$

Category on the disciplinary criterion	Test predictions					Total
	1 & 2 Good N	3 Fair N	3·5 Borderline N	4 Poor N	5 Bad N	
A and B *Good*	38	21	14	2	0	75
C *Fair*	23	19	6	2	1	51
D *Poor*	17	16	9	8	2	52
E *Bad*	9	16	11	6	4	46
TOTAL	87	72	40	18	7	224

As can be seen from these tables, the range of test ratings is so restricted that r coefficients would be virtually meaningless, and none were given when the results of this particular follow-up study were first published in 1965. However, as several people whom I later met in the United States had apparently gone to the trouble of working out these coefficients and argued that they showed the tests to be very ineffectual, I think this aspect should be mentioned here.

To calculate any coefficient one must do something about the 3·5—*borderline* ratings as they do not fit into the rating progression, being merely an interim step between the 3's and the 4's. The best one can do with them is to throw them in with the 3—*fair*, or the 4—*poor* groups—it would hardly matter which as their success rate on the criteria was, as expected, as borderline as their test ratings. Combining them either way produces:

TAT vs. Accident Criterion $\quad r = 0.24$ or 0.27
TAT vs. Disciplinary Criterion $\quad r = 0.31$ or 0.28

These coefficients (whatever they may mean) are certainly not impressive to look at, even if they are all significant at the 0.01 level. But fortunately in a practical situation one does not have to live or die by the sheer size of an r coefficient alone. Even by the time the complex statistical follow-up was completed, the routine follow-up of all individual drivers had revealed that most of the 3—*fair* and 3.5—*borderline* test ratings who had made a poor start were showing the sort of improvement which had been predicted for them when, at the time of selection, they had been judged to be reasonable long-term risks. And, most important of all, by 1962 the company accident rate had reached an all-time low—which was a clear indication that the process of weeding out the bad accident risks among the older drivers and replacing them by these new TAT-selected men was having the desired effect. (However, even an r coefficient will apparently yield to more balanced distributions, as is shown by the next follow-up study, which included large numbers of test failures taken on during the driving shortage. Here the r coefficient swung back to 0.66 for an N now grown to 1139—accompanied unfortunately by a marked increase in the company accident rate brought about by the spate of accidents in which the test failures were involved.)

Comparison with a Control Group

The generally better records of the TAT-selected men as compared with their predecessors was very apparent, but we nevertheless felt that it would be as well to carry out a detailed investigation to see in which respects they differed. A statistical comparison was therefore made between the follow-up group (TAT group) and a control group consisting of those drivers selected before the personality tests were introduced. Both groups had been given the same psychomotor tests and had received the same intensive training, the fundamental difference between the two groups being that the TAT group had also been required to pass the personality tests. (The TAT group therefore contains only the subject ($N = 182$) of the follow-up group who had been rated *borderline* or better, i.e. a "pass" on the personality tests.)

This comparison was very fully reported in the earlier 1965 publication; but as it is no longer of such importance in view of the confirmation given by later developments regarding the obviously beneficial effects of the tests, only the main findings will be given here.

Whereas 70% of the TAT group had succeeded on the accident criterion (75% if the borderliners were excluded and only the genuine passes were considered) the control group had achieved only a 55% success rate—even despite generally longer exposure and generally better psychomotor skills.

The TAT group passes were of a better calibre with longer time-intervals and more of the men in the *good* accident category.

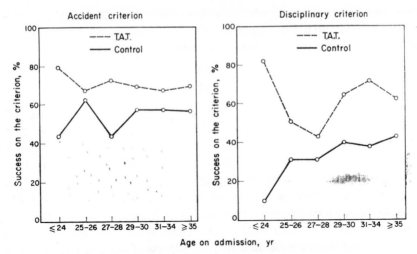

FIG. 16.1. Comparison according to age at admission of the success rates of the TAT-selected group vs. the non-TAT selected group

Age group by age group they had turned out to be better accident risks, and disciplinary risks, as can be seen from Fig. 16.1—the difference being particularly noticeable at the younger ages.

The TAT group's rate of involvement in serious accidents due to reckless and dangerous driving was considerably less than the control group, as can be seen from the figures of Table 16.6.

TABLE 16.6

	Control (%)	TAT (%)	Proportion
Percentage of drivers in each group involved in at least one serious accident due to reckless driving	25·2	13·0	±2:1
Percentage of drivers in each group involved in more than one serious accident due to reckless driving	3·4	1·1	±3:1
Percentage of drivers in each group involved in an accident due to driving under the influence of alcohol	3·2	0·5	±6:1

Although these results indicated the general superiority of the TAT group, the fact that 13% of this group were involved in accidents due to dangerous driving behaviour was still considered to be most unsatisfactory. A detailed investigation of these cases was

therefore carried out which showed that most of these offenders were *borderline* test ratings, and that in the more serious discrepancies the fault lay more with the testers—particularly the new trainee testers—than with the tests.

The proportion of the TAT group discharged for blatantly unsatisfactory services was
also much smaller than in the control group (Table 16.7).

TABLE 16.7

	Control (%)	TAT (%)
Discharged for ticket offences (dishonesty)	4	5
Discharged for generally very unsatisfactory service	10	6
Discharged for drinking	11	6
Discharged for accidents	15	5
Total percentage of men discharged as failures on the job	40	22

These figures are interesting in themselves, but an even more significant factor is that
whereas the TAT group has produced only one "delinquent"—a driver who was imprisoned for civil theft—among the control group were: one imprisoned for extortion and
theft; one imprisoned for armed robbery; two who had to be certified as mentally unbalanced; one suicide; one who was discharged for threatening a supervisor with a re-
volver; three who were discharged for assaulting and stabbing fellow employees; and
one who was sentenced to death for murder.

3. The Second Follow-up Study

The next major statistical follow-up was carried out at the end of 1967. The intervening years had been very difficult ones for the company as it had been necessary to take on
(and repeatedly discharge) large numbers of the special 6000-category drivers in an effort
to bring the driving strength up to the 1000 men needed to provide transport for new
housing areas as yet not serviced by the railways. Although these 6000-category drivers
were all tested on the personality tests, the need for drivers was so great that only the
worst could be screened out. Those screened out included a number who were found to
be alcoholics or near psychotics, which in itself is an alarming reflection of the need for
better countrywide driver control as all these men had *valid* heavy duty licences! In fact
the whole 1967 follow-up study is alarming, for it indicates only too clearly how many
totally unsuitable people must be in possession of a driver's licence—people whose dangerous potential could, it appears, be detected *in advance*, but whose right to hold a
licence is inviolate until somebody is killed or seriously injured—and even then the chances

are that very little action will be taken. For every prediction made about the 1139 subjects included in this study was made *before that man ever started to drive for the company*, and these predictions were made on a very detailed predictive rating scale.

Long before the second follow-up study was carried out, the test rating scale had been refined still further. Halfway ratings, 2·5, 3·5, and 4·5 had been introduced all down the scale, so as to make even finer distinctions, particularly at the lower levels of the test. Just as in better days a 3·5 rating had been introduced in order to pick out the better material from the 4—*poor* ratings, now a 4·5 rating was necessary to pick out the slightly better ones even from the 5—*bad* ratings. This was not done purely for selection purposes, since the test unit would never have voluntarily countenanced letting through anyone with a test rating as bad as this. But it was needed during the period of the 6000's so that the hard-pushed supervisors would know which of the very bad starters could possibly be retained a little longer, and which were such innately bad risks that they should be jettisoned at once.

Another refinement which we had made in the rating scale was the greater use of "improver" ratings. Although the analysts had always indicated in their test predictions if they thought that a man was likely to show any worth-while improvement within a reasonable period of time, the "improver" ratings were now extended as low down the scale as possible. However, despite drastically lowered standards, the only cases which were allowed improver ratings were those where we felt that the risks involved were not too great. We knew from the records of some of the very unsatisfactory drivers whom PUTCO had retained for long periods during the earlier days that many bad risks can improve, given enough time or subjected to enough discipline. But the amount of damage which these expensively slow learners had managed to do in the process had brought home to us that it was essential that no encouragement should be given for history to repeat itself. The men with the unsatisfactory personality patterns *must* be distinctly labelled as bad risks to be got rid of as soon as possible. (This is in fact our attitude to the whole question of accident proneness. We feel that only a relatively small proportion of any population consists of people who are hopelessly and incorrigibly ultra-accident-prone; but our belief is that a much larger proportion is so dangerously prone *right now and for some time to come*, that to allow them to drive is just asking for trouble.)

When the records were processed for the 1967 follow-up, allowance was made for these improver ratings.* As some of the earlier men had been exposed up to twelve years, it was considered desirable to equalize the length of exposure to a certain extent, so the follow-up period for the long-service drivers was limited to four years. In most instances the only difference which using the full exposure would have made was the difference between a man being *statistically* classifiable as *excellent* instead of merely *good*. There were only a few cases where any significant alteration in the $\hat{t}$ had occurred beyond the four-year period, and these were cases of sudden deterioration after many years of a good record—mainly due to drinking as the result of a change in the country's liquor laws. (And there isn't, I fear, a test made which could predict this!) To allow, however, for such *improvement* which had been predicted, those with improver ratings were put up a notch, or half a notch, depending on their exposure.* If their original ratings had

* 19% of the subjects were allowed "improver" ratings.

included no indication of improvement, these original ratings were retained irrespective of how long the man had actually been exposed.

Many of the TAT-selected drivers, even the short-term ones, had already attained a standard which seemed to place them in the A—*excellent* category on the accident criterion. But for follow-up purposes, this rating has always been merged with the B—*good* because of the statistical unreliability of classifying a man as A—*excellent* without very long exposure to allow for a number of long time-intervals.

The full bivariate distribution for the test predictions vs. the accident criterion is given in Table 16.8. The number of subjects in each test category is inclined to fluctuate due to the half-ratings, resulting in a rather uneven correlation surface. But even grouping the ratings into the main categories which they represent (Table 16.9) makes little difference to the final coefficients which are still significant at any level one might care to choose—a significance level with endless noughts before it being a little difficult to comprehend!

TABLE 16.8. SECOND FOLLOW-UP STUDY*

Correlation between the Predictions on the Personality Tests and the Accident Criterion

Category on the accident criterion	Test predictions							Total
	1+2	2·5	3	3·5	4	4·5	5	
1+2	112	8	72	16	12	3	1	224
3	23	10	123	68	39	18	3	284
4	9	4	42	56	145	52	16	324
5	2	0	28	35	98	98	46	307
TOTAL	146	22	265	175	294	171	66	1139

$r = 0·658$ (significant at almost any level).

Interesting as these coefficients may be, the more detailed analysis of the predicting power of the test at each of its rating levels is of greater practical importance. Table 16.10 gives the achieved as against expected percentages of success.

This shows the marked effect of greater experience with the use of the test itself and the deeper understanding which this whole practical project has produced on how to assess a person as an accident risk. The gradual progression from the 90% down to 10%, which we had originally set as a theoretical target, has been replaced by a marked differentiation between the test passes and the test failures. This does not mean that accident proneness as displayed by these men is indeed a dichotomy. On the contrary, they displayed every shade of a wide spectrum of proneness or it would not have been possible to classify them on a continuous accident criterion. What it means is that a sensitive

* A more sophisticated presentation of these data is given by Kerrich on p. 223.

TABLE 16.9. SECOND FOLLOW-UP STUDY

Correlation between the Grouped Predictions on the Personality Tests and the Accident Criterion

Category on the accident criterion	Test predictions				Total
	Good	*Fair*	*Poor*	*Bad*	
Good	112	80	28	4	224
Fair	23	133	107	21	284
Poor	9	46	201	68	324
Bad	2	28	133	144	307
TOTAL	146	287	469	237	1139

$r = 0.642$ (significant at almost any level).

TABLE 16.10 SECOND FOLLOW-UP STUDY

Comparison between Achieved and Expected Percentages of Success on the Accident Criterion at Each Level of the Test

Test category	Test rating	N	Number who were a success on the accident criterion	Achieved percentages of success	Expected percentages of success
Test passes	1 and 2 *Good*	146	135	92	90
	2·5 *Fairly good*	22	18	82	77
	3 *Fair*	265	195	74	63
Borderliners	3·5 *Border-line*	175	84	48	50
Test failures	4 *poor*	294	51	17	37
	4·5 *very poor*	171	21	12	23
	5 *bad*	66	4	6	10

test in the hands of an experienced assessor makes it possible to relegate people to three main categories in terms of their accident potential—those who are going to be satisfactory or better risks and who need not be worried about; those whose potential is so borderline that it is probably largely dependent on circumstance and the pressures they encounter but who should obviously be watched; and those who are going to be poor or worse risks and whose accident potential is very real and therefore often very dangerous.

This is demonstrated very clearly by a further analysis of Table 16.10 which shows:

Success rate of the personality test passes $(N = 433)$ 80%
Success rate of the personality test borderliners $(N = 175)$ 48%
Success rate of the personality test failures $(N = 531)$ 14%
A χ-square test on a dichotomous pass/fail basis yields $\chi^2 = 361 \cdot 73$ (which is again highly significant).

Another interesting feature of Tables 16.8 and 16.10 is the evidence which they produce of the ability of these tests to make fine distinctions as well as broad ones. The purpose

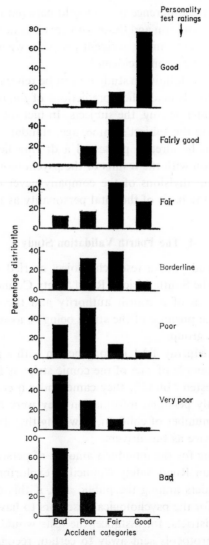

FIG. 16.2. The second follow-up study. How the subjects predicted to be *good, fairly good, fair, borderline, poor, very poor, bad* risks on the personality tests actually turned out on the accident criterion

of introducing half-ratings was to try and single out the slightly better risks from among the 3—*fair* and particularly the 4—*poor* and the 5—*bad* test categories—a purpose which they seem to have fulfilled admirably. In fact, Fig. 16.2, which shows the manner in which the subjects in each of the test categories were distributed on the accident criterion, is a very clear indication of the sensitivity of these projective personality tests. The way in which the distributions within each test rating consistently follow the sort of trend which one would hope to find—and the dramatic reversal of these trends as these ratings move down from *good* to *bad* is also a very clear indication of the influence which personality exerts on accident-producing behaviour and the power of these projective personality tests to predict this behaviour. For one must remember what this reversal in the trends means. There is all the difference in the world between the people who are classified as *good* on the accident criterion and those who are classified as *bad*. The *good* drivers, on average, have only about one minor accident per year, whereas most of the *bad* ones average less than fifty days between accidents!

In viewing the results of this follow-up study it must be reiterated that the psychologists who analysed the test protocols made their predictions of *future* accident potential without ever seeing, let alone interviewing, the subjects. In fact the only biographical details they had to guide them were the subject's name, age, standard of education, his marital status, and whether or not he already possessed a driving licence. Nor were the predictions made in conjunction with the results of the psychomotor tests—in fact many of the drivers from the distant divisions of the company never did these tests at all. The predictions were made on the basis of the total personality as revealed by the projective tests *alone*.

4. The Fourth Validation Study

The fourth validation study was a research project carried out by the same team of investigators on behalf of the South African Road Safety Council. The project was made possible by the co-operation of a transit authority and the subjects were 115 White (Caucasian) bus drivers, the purpose of the study being to assess the effectiveness of the tests on a different culture group.

The tests used were the Murray TAT in conjunction with a newly developed PUTCO International SRT. (An example of one of the comic strips is found in Fig. 17.1, p. 354.) Again the subjects were tested "blind"; they came under a code number and were not interviewed at all. The only personal information they were asked to supply was age, education, marital status, number of children, how long they had held a driving licence, and the length of their service as bus drivers.

This policy of only asking for the minimum amount of personal data was deliberately adopted. The South African Road Safety Council is exploring the possibility of using these tests on traffic offenders among the public and, if this ever does come about, it might prove very difficult for the psychological assessors to have any initial contact with the subjects. In outlying districts, for instance, the tests would have to be administered by a lay official and the protocols sent away to certain recognized clinical centres for analysis. Under these circumstances it would only be feasible for these lay officials to ask for such limited items of personal information as could be easily verified from central records. Personal information which could not be verified might be so untrue as to be not only valueless but also very misleading. (In this study, which was merely a research project and where the subjects had no conceivable personal motive for giving false information, a number of them nevertheless falsified their age, and the general tendency was to exaggerate the length of their driving experience.)

In view of the satisfactory outcome of this research project, plus the practical results achieved in PUTCO, the South African Road Safety Council has officially recommended the use of the tests for the selection of professional drivers and is continuing to explore the possibilities of their wider application on convicted traffic offenders after the installation of a points system.

THE TESTING PROGRAMME

One of the objects of the study being to check on the reliability of the test predictions, each protocol was analysed by two people. The majority were analysed by two principle assessors, the writer being one of them. In very difficult cases, or cases which presented a language problem (the subjects being allowed to write in either of the two official South African languages), an additional assessor was used. The testers worked independently. Their findings were then compared and their numerical ratings of accident potential combined as follows: if the personality patterns recorded by the two assessors were fundamentally the same and there was at most a difference of only one point in the numerical ratings, then the final rating was taken as the average of the two, e.g. 2—*good* and 3—*fair* combined to make 2·5—*fairly good*. If, however, there was any greater difference between the ratings, the protocol was given to a third assessor, and the rating of the odd man out was excluded. These differences of opinion—none of them being very marked—occurred in 14 out of the 115 cases. In 67 cases the ratings were identical. (In the practical driver selection project reported on in the two PUTCO follow-up studies, only one assessor per protocol is used, except in difficult cases.)

An indication of the reliability of the tests is given by the high degree of correlation between the two principle raters. Here the reliability coefficient was $r = 0.83$ for 96 subjects.

A test report giving the numerical prediction for each subject was lodged with the South African Road Safety Council when the testing was completed and before the examination of the accident records had begun. In addition the test report included a short statement on each of the subjects, outlining the sort of accident pattern—past, current, and future—which could be expected in the light of his personality pattern. The main purpose of this report was to see whether the tests would once again be able to fulfil one of their most important functions, namely to provide information on which to base a decision as to what action should be taken in each individual case.

THE ACCIDENT CRITERION

The accident criterion was based on a study of the operating conditions of the whole transit authority and an analysis of the accident records of 395 currently employed drivers. The investigation revealed that most of the driving was done on double-decker electric trolley buses, just a few routes being manned by one-man-operators driving single-decker diesel buses. There were fifty-five major routes (all in the same city and operating from the same central depot), and although it was possible to establish on which route each accident had occurred it was not possible to establish the exposure of a driver to any particular route. The dates of each man's accidents were recorded, also any time off driving such as annual leave, sick leave, delegation to non-driving duties, and overtime. It was therefore possible to calculate the time-intervals of actual driving exposure between accidents. Two types of accidents were recorded against each of the drivers, collisions, and passenger injuries (PIs), the latter being cases where a passenger was injured either boarding or alighting, or falling in the bus.

The type of accident was investigated first. A study of the PI accidents showed that most of these occurred on the trolley buses but that they were far more prevalent among certain drivers than others; that they correlated significantly with the collisions ($N = 395$, $r = 0.53$); and that they occurred in recognizable patterns—many of the worse drivers having an early record of collisions, followed by a pattern which included fewer collisions and more PIs. All the evidence pointed to the fact that these PIs were characteristic of the person's style of driving and of his general accident pattern. As they involved injury they were regarded as "accidents" by the transit company, and it was decided to include them in the accident criterion. (The supposition put forward by the investigators is that the PIs are largely caused by the driver starting before the passengers have fully boarded or alighted, or by his suddenly applying the exceptionally powerful brakes of the trolley buses in order to avoid a collision—i.e. near-miss-collisions involving injury.) Even a cursory examination of the individual records of the 395 drivers showed how very greatly they differed in their degree of accident involvement. It appeared therefore that the same sort of accident criterion used in the earlier studies, namely the mean of the time-intervals between successive accidents, would be a good discriminating measure.

But here again, in order to use these mean time-intervals ($\hat{t}$s) as an accident criterion it was necessary to ensure that any difference between the $\hat{t}$s of the individual subjects did, in fact, represent *fundamental* differences between individuals, not factors such as insufficient driving experience or exposure to different traffic hazards. It was also necessary to ensure that any unit of driving exposure, such as driving "days", on which the $\hat{t}$s were based, represented an equal number of driving hours, i.e. a standard driving "shift" of $7\frac{1}{2}$ hours. This was particularly necessary in view of the fact that an exceptionally severe driver shortage had resulted in the subjects doing appreciable amounts of overtime— amounts that varied significantly between individuals. Adjustments were therefore made for all these factors.

Adjustments for overtime were made by loading exposure proportionately to the actual amount of overtime worked by each subject. (In some cases this meant loading exposure by a factor as great as 1.45.)

The effects of insufficient driving experience were equalized by omitting from the calculation of the $\hat{t}$ any early "learning period" (such a learning period being characterized by an initial run of short time-intervals between accidents, followed by a very different stable pattern of longer time-intervals).

Making an adjustment to equalize exposure to different traffic hazards was more complicated. A study of the corporate accident statistics revealed that there were significant differences in the accident rates of the fifty-five routes operated—fifty of them TV bus routes and five being single-decker diesel routes manned by one-man-operators (OMO routes). The accident rates of the various routes varied between:

TV routes. Collisions 1·0–2·4 (With two central city routes at 3·0 and 6·9)
         Passenger injuries 0·4 to 0·8 (With two central city routes at 2·0 and 2·7)
OMO routes. Collisions 0·7–1·1
         Passenger injuries 0·1–0·2

This was obviously going to form a serious problem, but examination of the TV routes showed that there was probably sufficient interchange of drivers between routes to more or less neutralize the effects of these very different traffic hazards.

Examples of the findings were:

Route A   108 accidents in one year involving 91 different drivers.
Route B   57 accidents involving 55 different drivers.

Driver A   49 accidents over five years on 27 different routes.
Driver B   18 accidents over three years on 16 different routes.
Driver C   8 accidents over four years on 8 different routes.

The same interchange of drivers occurred on the OMO routes. But, as the accident rate of these routes was considerably lower than the TV routes, and as drivers were allocated to OMO duties for long periods of time, an adjustment would obviously have to be made to equalize the TV and OMO risks. This was achieved by analysing the records of twenty-six drivers with mixed exposure, finding the ratio of their TV time-intervals to their OMO time-intervals, and using the median of these twenty-six ratios to obtain the correction factor. This factor (0·74) was then used to reduce the relatively longer OMO time-intervals and equalize them with the shorter TV intervals.

Having established suitable correction factors, a check was made to see how well the differences in exposure risk had been equalized. Individual control charts were drawn up for 196 drivers using the logarithms of the successive time-intervals between accidents (with suitable corrections made for overtime). With the PIs included and the OMO intervals adjusted, these control charts showed very stable patterns of accident involvement—each man's pattern being consistent within itself, but at the same time different from that of the other drivers. This confirmed the conclusion that the environmental factors had been at least satisfactorily equalized, and that most of the obvious differences in the degree of accident involvement displayed by the individual drivers were due to personal factors inherent in the drivers themselves. For these personal factors were apparently influencing their records irrespective of the traffic conditions in which they drove, as every one of the drivers had had his accidents on a number of different routes.

It is interesting to note that in this project the inclusion of PI accidents (some of which could be interpreted as "near-miss" incidents) improved the reliability of the accident criterion. In the PUTCO study, where operating conditions were different, PI accidents were not included. These two dissimilar procedures for establishing an "accident" criterion naturally produced different overall accident rates, and a special standard had to be set for the five categories of the accident criterion. A statistical analysis of the $\hat{\imath}s$ of the 395 drivers gave a conversion table of:

Criterion category	Range of $\hat{\imath}s$ expressed in driving "days"
A—*Excellent*	250 and over
B—*Good*	150–249
C—*Satisfactory*	100–149
D—*Poor*	50– 99
E—*Bad*	0– 49

As the follow-up period was only $2\frac{1}{2}$ years and therefore did not allow for many long time-intervals, the A and B categories were again combined for statistical reliability.

THE VALIDATION STUDY

The validation of the tests took place $2\frac{1}{2}$ years after the test ratings had been lodged with the South African Road Safety Council—each man's accident record being assessed as from the day of his test.

Before the project had commenced it had been presumed that the subjects, who were professional bus drivers employed by an organization with its own medical services and training school, would meet the necessary minimum standards of health, vision, and driving ability. But a check on the men's personal files showed that these presumptions were not altogether justified. The transit authority was obviously so short of drivers that every available man was being used to prevent the service from being disrupted. At least one subject apparently had very defective eyesight, and at least three were apparently medically unfit, having been under treatment for severe hypertension over long periods. These men had to be excluded from the validation, as their records were obviously being affected by factors which no personality test could ever predict. Three of the group were found to have undergone psychiatric treatment at some time or another. But these were not excluded as the tests should be able to pick up any psychiatric condition. (The actual accident records of these physically and mentally unfit people are very interesting and are illustrated in later chapters.)

In addition, the records of several of the men indicated that they were either very inept drivers or that the training scheme was rather inadequate. But none were excluded on these grounds although we appreciated that leaving these men in the group, like leaving in a number of very doubtful health cases, would reduce any validity coefficient. However, we did not want to make the group any smaller than it was as, of the original 115 subjects tested, only 76 could be used for the validation. This loss was mainly due to a high turnover among the drivers resulting in too short an exposure after the test.

CORRELATION OF THE TEST RATINGS WITH THE ACCIDENT CRITERION

The bivariate distribution for this correlation is given in Table 16.11 (with the ratings grouped because of the small numbers in the cells). The resulting coefficient is $r = 0.53$ (significant at the 0.001 level).

TABLE 16.11. THE SOUTH AFRICAN ROAD SAFETY
COUNCIL RESEARCH PROJECT
*Correlation between the Projective Test Prediction
Ratings and the Accident Criterion*

Test Ratings

	Good	Fair	Poor	Bad	
Good	7	3	2	1	13
Fair	4	9	2	5	20
Poor	0	2	15	9	26
Bad	1	0	10	6	17
	12	14	29	21	76

(row labels: Criterion Ratings)

THE EXAMINATION OF ACHIEVED PERCENTAGES OF SUCCESS
AT EACH LEVEL OF THE TEST

The results are given in Table 16.12 below, which again shows the marked difference in the success rate of the test passes and the test failures.

TABLE 16.12. THE PERCENTAGES OF DRIVERS IN EACH
TEST CATEGORY WHO WERE SUCCESSES ON THE ACCI-
DENT CRITERION

Test ratings	No. of passes on the accident criterion	Percentage of passes on the accident criterion
Test passes Good	11/12	92 ⎫ 89
Satisfactory	12/14	86 ⎭
Test failures Poor	4/29	14 ⎫ 20
Bad	6/21	29 ⎭

The only significant discrepancy in this expectancy chart is the fact that the *bad* test ratings had a higher pass rate that the *poor* test ratings. With such small numbers this was mainly due to a couple of intelligent youngsters who were considered to be bad risks because of their delinquent outlook, and whose accident records were actually very bad at the time they were tested but improved later to a pass rating on the criterion as a result of severe disciplinary action.

The satisfactory distribution of each test rating on the criterion can be seen from Table 16.11 each level of the test showing a pattern very much in conformity with expectation. (The subject who was rated *bad* on the tests and turned out *good* was known to be a very heavy drinker—so the test rating was justified even if the accident record was still unaffected. The subject who was rated *good* on the test and turned out to be just plain *bad* was the inevitable Jonah of any research project—his code number was 13!)

THE TESTS AS INDICATORS OF IMPROVEMENT OR DETERIORATION

In the test report lodged with the South African Road Safety Council it was stated that in a number of cases the information revealed by the tests indicated that the subjects' accident records were likely to improve or deteriorate within the next few years.

The "improvers" were three cases who looked as though they were outgrowing their current irresponsible immaturity. Unfortunately in two of the three cases the report also said that these men were unlikely to stick to bus driving and they did in fact resign shortly after the test. The remaining case did improve during the follow-up period. The "deteriorators" were twenty cases described as poor risks because the tests had indicated that their records would be likely to get worse (mostly due to marked anxiety and/or drink). By the end of the $2\frac{1}{2}$-year follow-up period, the accident records of seventeen of these men were already showing marked deterioration. In certain cases (which will be illustrated in later case studies) the predicted deterioration was so marked that their $\hat{t}s$ shifted from *good* to the *poor/bad* area of the criterion.

This is another indication of the sensitivity of the tests and their ability to predict changes in accident potential.

THE ANALYSIS OF HOW ACCURATELY THE TESTS HAD CLASSIFIED THE SUBJECTS AS SAFE OR UNSAFE RISKS

Again taking the pass/fail cut-off on both the test and criterion as a definition of *safe* or *unsafe*, it can be seen that in 63 out of 76 (83%) the test predictions were correct. The significance of this result can be tested by a χ-square test on a dichotomous safe/unsafe split for both test and criterion.

	Test	
	Safe	Unsafe
Safe on criterion	23	10
Unsafe on criterion	3	40

The χ-square test (which included Yates' correction for small frequencies) yielded a result of:

$$\chi^2 = 29{\cdot}907 \qquad (N = 76)$$

This result is significant at the 0·001 level of probability.

The results of this particular statistical follow-up validation of the test, though very satisfactory, are naturally not quite as startling as the PUTCO follow-up study. This is no doubt partly due to the shorter duration ($2\frac{1}{2}$ years) of the follow-up period, and the impossibility of controlling the factor of exposure to different traffic conditions in the rigid way it was done in the PUTCO study. Although there was obviously a great deal of interchange of drivers between routes, no doubt some of the more senior men were allowed to pick the easier routes and stay on them whenever possible. (On the whole the predictions of accident potential were not as accurate with these long-service drivers which seems to confirm this.) However, despite any weaknesses in the accident criterion, the results of the study are nevertheless statistically highly significant. They are also of particular interest for two reasons:

(1) Because a satisfactory result was achieved using this time rather a different criterion, namely one which included the passenger injury accidents. The inclusion of these injury-producing incidents with the collision accidents adds another element of driving behaviour which can apparently be predicted by these tests, namely the sort of erratic and inconsiderate driving which is not only a little hard on one's passengers, but also leads to the all-too-familiar squeal of brakes of the "near-miss".

(2) Because they show the testing system to be effective with a different cultural group. The results of the PUTCO study were therefore not achieved merely because some racial characteristic such as extremism makes it easier to detect accident offenders among African subjects.

It would be strange indeed if the latter were not possible since all one is doing with these tests is using a logical process to move from a mental picture of a personality, to how such a person would behave in ordinary life, to how he would react to the driving situation, and to what sort of an accident risk this would produce. The most difficult part of this whole process is the first part, namely forming a concept of the personality dynamics of the individual from his projective test material. And we have always found this more difficult to do with Negro subjects than with Europeans because of their relatively lower standard of education, their more unfamiliar social background, and because they are in a state of cultural transition.*

---

* A fifth validation has recently been carried out. Trained by the PUTCO unit to use the African TAT and SRT, Spangenberg (1968) independently carried out a validation study on a group of Coloured bus drivers employed by a transport company in Cape Town. Using a time-interval criterion of *current* accident involvement over a period which straddled the testing date, he obtained a correlation between the test ratings and the accident criterion of $r = 0{\cdot}53$ for 75 subjects—a result which is also significant beyond the 0·001 level.

The Factor Analysis

Arising out of the SARSC research project came a development which indicates that it might be possible to assess accident potential, still in terms of personality, but by means of a very different battery of tests from the projective ones.

At the time the TAT analysts made their predictions of accident potential they also filled in an itemized marking sheet for each of the subjects. These sheets included thirty different items ranging from personality characteristics like immaturity or aggressiveness, to intelligence, or a tendency to alcoholism—all characteristics which had been found in the practical PUTCO project to have a bearing on accident potential. This itemized information was obtained solely from the projective test material, the method being to first assess the protocol as a whole, make the predictions of accident potential on the basis of the composite personality pattern revealed by this analysis, and *then* fill in the marking sheet, i.e. the sheets were not used as a means of analysing the TAT and SRT and making the predictions, they were merely a systematic listing of the total findings *on which the predictions had already been made.* As such they were found to serve no immediate useful purpose except to confirm yet again the importance of many of the characteristics listed. For interesting as this itemized information on individual traits was, it seemed to have no great potential for accident prediction. Research from all over the world had indicated that attempting to predict accidents by means of individual characteristics had proved to be a less reliable method than the composite personality method devised for the selection of the PUTCO drivers and now in its eighth year of practical operation. But the sheets were preserved in the hope that this detailed information on subjects with known accident records could some day serve a useful research purpose. Years later Eysenck's work on the assessment of personality in terms of two main factors, introversion/extroversion and emotional stability/neuroticism, provided the first indication of how this material could be used.

His extensive work in this field is too well known to need any detailed explanation, having been described in a number of books (*The Structure of Human Personality*, 1960, being a good example). But, briefly, the aspects which concern us here are his findings on the examination of personality structure by means of factor analysis. Time and again he and other workers in this field of experimental psychology have shown that if, say, a personality questionnaire is designed in such a way that each item (or sub-section) measures a different trait, this questionnaire is given to a group of people, and the scores on the individual items are subjected to a factor analysis, the following is typical of the results which emerge. The item scores (representing the various traits) will form two main clusters, the scores in one cluster correlating highly with one another, but not with the scores in the other cluster. These clusters of inter-correlated traits are therefore felt to represent two higher-order organizations of personality which he has called the factors of extroversion E and neuroticism or emotional instability N, these definitions being a good working description of the sort of traits they represent.

Because of the high intercorrelation between these traits it is possible to use Varimax rotation to establish what contribution each test item has made to the two factors, and to give that item of the questionnaire an appropriate E and N loading. This loading can then be used for each subject to obtain his E and N factor score, a score which determines his position on two lines each representing the continuum from extreme introversion to extreme extroversion or extreme emotional stability to extreme neuroticism. As these factors do not correlate with one another these lines can be drawn in the form of orthogonal axes (at right angles to one another) and one can plot the factor scores for each person on an E by N grid.

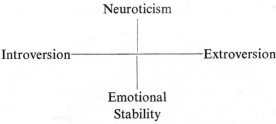

This has in fact been done many times using different groups of people and has repeatedly come up with findings which show that the ordinary, "average" person, being neither very high nor very low on either factor, has a point in the central area close to the intersection of the axes; whereas, for instance, convicted criminals or dysthymics have factor scores which place them nearer to the periphery. In addition, the scores of groups of such people are inclined to form constellations in well-defined areas of the chart, some of these areas being obvious indicators of severe maladjustment (Fig. 16.3).

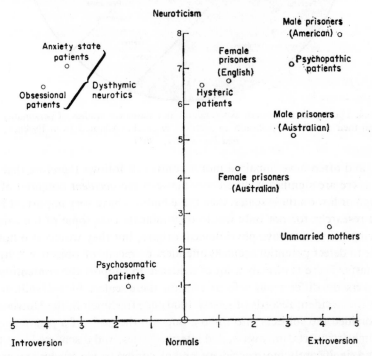

FIG. 16.3. Extroversion–introversion and neuroticism scores of various criminal, deviant and neurotic groups. (Eysenck, *Crime and Personality*, 1964)

However these findings, interesting as they are, might be of little more than academic interest were it not for the fact that considerable experimentation has shown that there are significant *physiological* differences between people who rank high or low on both the extroversion and the neuroticism scales. Extroverts, for example, are more difficult to condition than introverts and the effects of this conditioning wear off more quickly; they recover less quickly from glare; and they cannot maintain concentrated effort without repeated involuntary rest pauses. Neurotics, for example, tire more easily, suffer more

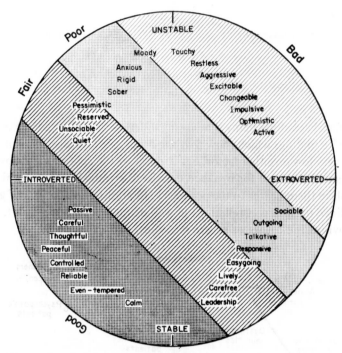

FIG. 16.4. The results of modern experimental and statistical studies of personality structure and their possible application to accident research. (Adapted from Eysenck, *Crime and Personality*, 1964)

from strain, and often have impaired motor control. It follows therefore that if it can be shown that there are significant differences between the *accident* potential of the people who rank high or low on these scales, then these findings have very important implications for accident research; for not only would they indicate that some of the causes of accident-producing behaviour have physiological origins, but they would also hold out hope of being able to detect potential accident offenders by means of objective "physiological" personality tests. There is already a lot of evidence to support the contention that high-accident drivers do differ from safe drivers on these scales. Fine (1963), for instance, investigated the accident records of nearly 1000 male freshmen in the University of Minnesota. He divided the subjects into three groups on the basis of a personality questionnaire—extreme extroverts, introverts, and intermediaries, and discovered that the extreme extroverts had significantly more accidents and also more traffic offences recorded against them than the other groups. Hakkinen (1958) found higher accident rates associated with people whose performance on his psychomotor personality tests indicated that certain over-emotional and neurotic tendencies were exerting impairing and paralysing influences on their test performance in stress situations (and therefore presumably in the driving situation as well). And throughout the practical PUTCO project and the SARSC research project, people rated down on the projective personality tests because they displayed very extrovert or neurotic tendencies, or more importantly *both*, were found to later develop bad accident records. Numerous other studies have come up with findings which fit into this general pattern.

It was the consideration of these findings which suggested a possible use for the SARSC data on individual personality traits. One day, looking speculatively at one of Eysenck's *E/N* diagrams (Fig. 16.4), I tentatively sketched in the area on the grid where I felt the *bad, poor, fair, good* accident risks would fall.

Then, remembering the marking sheets for the SARSC project, I began to wonder what would happen if one treated the scores on the different personality traits in the same manner as the items of a questionnaire to give composite *E* and *N* scores. I tentatively grouped the various items on the marking sheet according to Eysenck's definition of the traits which correlate highly with the *E* and *N* factors. The loading was a purely arbitrary one in which I gave a double loading to certain of the characteristics which I considered to be the more important accident predictors, so as to ensure that the *E* and *N* scale's would have the same range, i.e. from -10 to $+10$.

I then plotted each subject's composite *E* and *N* score on the two axes, giving him a dot *coloured according to his rating on the accident criterion*, i.e. the category of the accident criterion to which he had been allocated according to the mean of the time-intervals between his accidents subsequent to the test. The men with *bad* criterion ratings were given red dots, the *poor* orange dots, the *fair* blue, and the *good* green. And I found that most of the dots fell in the appropriate areas of the grid which I had roughly outlined. Encouraged by this I sent the sketch to Professor Eysenck, who wrote back saying that this confirmed his own ideas as to where, on his grid, the various shades of accident risk would lie, and offered to carry out a proper factor analysis of the itemized test scores. This was duly done, using 71 of the 76 cases from the follow-up validation study. The other 5 were omitted as there was a possibility that their personality assessment was incorrect. (After the statistical analysis was completed, the TAT analysts, out of pure interest, had talked to the drivers' supervisors just to see whether their description of the various men would tally with the personality pattern derived from the projective tests alone. On the whole they had tallied very well indeed for all except five cases.) These men were therefore omitted from the factor analysis, even if their accident predictions had been correct. This was felt to be necessary as the purpose of the factor analysis was to explore the relationship between accidents and various personality traits, not to validate the tests as this had already been done. It was therefore wiser to omit these five men, for if there was anything wrong with the personality diagnosis, this would merely confuse the issue.

The factor analysis of the seventy-one itemized marking sheets again showed that the scores representing the various traits formed themselves into two highly intercorrelated groups, i.e. in the language of factor analysis, two significant latent roots were present, easily identifiable from the nature of the traits as the *E* and *N* factors. It was then possible to give each "trait" a proper loading, to derive for each subject his proper factor score, and to replace the experimental diagram based on the common-sense approach with one based now on scientific evidence. The results were very similar—the dots moving a bit this way and a bit that way but the moves making no very important difference to the general pattern. (Which all goes to show that common-sense psychology does not deserve the condemnation which is heaped on it in some quarters!)

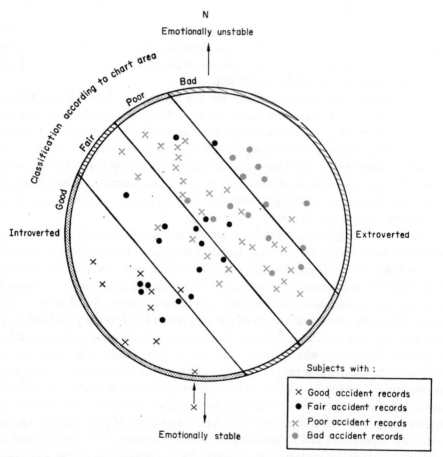

FIG. 16.5. The relationship between extroversion, emotional instability, and accidents in a group of South African bus drivers

This properly attested scientific background does, however, justify the publication of these results which are given in Fig. 16.5 above, which shows how most of the coloured dots, representing people whose actual accident records were *good, fair, poor* or *bad*, fall in the expected area of the *E* by *N* grid.

It will be noticed that one subject falls outside the circle. This was a case whose generally stable personality was in such contrast to the rest of the group that he had obviously been marked too favourably on all the *N* items. (A four point scale apparently does not allow for much celebration when you come across an exceptionally stable personality pattern among a rather unimpressive group of drivers!)

It will be noticed that the lines which divide the various accident categories are tilted slightly towards the vertical position. This was done because the analysis showed that the E factor correlated more highly with the accident criterion than the N factor. It will take many experiments with different groups to determine just what the tilt should be and how the demarcating lines should be drawn. But in this particular experiment the sub-division produces a distribution which is significantly different from chance.

The two-by-two safe/unsafe distribution yields:

$$\chi^2 = 29 \cdot 73 \qquad \text{(Significant at the } 0 \cdot 01 \text{ level).}$$

Confirmation that similar results are likely to be obtained with other groups has already come from the work of the British Road Research Laboratory (Quenault, RRL Report LR70, 1967). Here the criterion was traffic offences and the subjects consisted of two groups:

Group C   Fifty drivers, whose licences had been endorsed within the last three years for Careless Driving. (These drivers were found to have three times as many accidents as the R group, and each had had at least one accident—usually associated with the licence endorsement.)

Group R   Fifty drivers selected at random from the same geographical area and period of time with no convictions for Careless Driving, and most of them with no recorded accidents.

The purpose of this particular study was to see whether these groups would show up differently on various measures such as: the Maudesley Personality Inventory; an intelligence test; a test where the subject was asked to rank pictures of traffic situations according to whether he considered the situations represented danger, frustration, etc.; and a specially designed driving test, the Systematic Observation of Driving Behaviour. (This latter test is showing very promising results and will be described further in a later chapter.) According to the published results the only measure which distinguished between the two groups was the actual driving test. But the significance test on the MPI had been made using the number of C or R cases whose scores fell in the four *quadrants* of the Eysenck grid. These results are given below:

	C group		R group	
	Introverted	Extroverted	Introverted	Extroverted
Unstable	3	3	2	4
Stable	18	26	25	19

According to this grouping the MPI did not differentiate significantly between the C and R groups.

Fortunately the report also gave the exact position of each subject on the *E* by *N* grid, and, superimposing diagonal cut-offs similar to those used in the South African project, immediately showed that this would produce a more realistic division, with the majority of the R (Random) group falling in the *good/fair* side and the majority of the C (Careless) group on the poor/bad side. With the collaboration of Mr. Quenault and the permission of the Road Research Laboratory, Quenault's original diagram is reproduced in Fig.

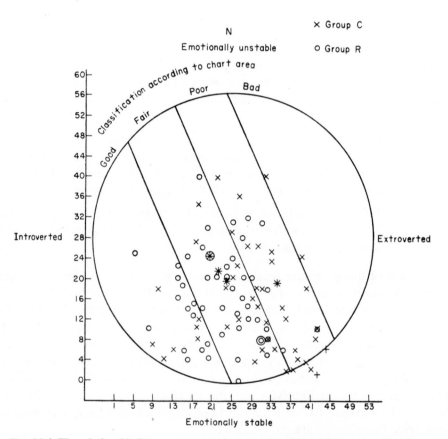

FIG. 16.6. The relationship between extroversion, emotional instability and traffic offences. (Quenault, British Road Research Laboratory, 1967)

16.6 with the new demarcation lines superimposed (some of the original points having been moved to correct for draughtsman and printing errors). The spacing of the sub-dividing lines is the same as that used for the South African study but they are tentatively tilted nearer to the vertical as the *E* factor would probably play an even greater part in traffic offences than in accidents.

Sub-dividing the grid areas in this manner produces a distribution which is significantly different from chance.

	R	C
Good	14	7
Fair	28	19
Poor	8	22
Bad	0	2

A dichotomous split into safe/unsafe yields:

	R	C
Safe	42	26
Unsafe	8	24

$\chi^2 = 11 \cdot 76$ (significant at the 0·01 level).

Naturally these results are not as clear-cut as in the South African project. The criterion is much weaker and the questionnaire method is apparently not as effective for assessing personality as the projective tests—one of the main reasons being the fact that it can be faked, whereas it is very hard to fake projective tests. It seems very likely, for instance, that several members of the C (Careless) group did not answer the questions on the MPI truthfully. This is particularly the case with the Dissociated Active types (see p. 364) among the C group, nearly all of whom passed the MPI with glowing colours—and all of whom had at least two accidents, one of them having four. It seems that they were probably doing a spectacular bit of whitewashing and presenting themselves as jet-propelled angels rather than similarly airborne motorists!

The fact that personality questionnaires are relatively easy to fake is known to be one of their great disadvantages. For even if you include a few catch questions which will indicate that the person is presenting himself in too good a light to be true, this does not achieve very much, particularly in a practical situation. In a pure research situation you can exclude the subjects with a high "lie score", thus preventing your results from being clouded by false information. But in a practical situation this means that the test is often invalid for the very people in whom you are most interested. One can hardly visualize an intelligent traffic offender whose driving licence is in jeopardy truthfully answering questions about himself if the truth is likely to place him in an unfavourable light.

But personality questionnaires are only one way of assessing personality in terms of broad factors like extroversion or emotional instability, factors which appear to have a very important bearing on accident potential. It appears that these factors can be determined by objective "biological" tests (a subject I will deal with in more detail in the next chapter).* If this is so—and there is considerable evidence building up to indicate that it is—then the possible application of Eysenck's E and N theory to the detection of traffic and accident offenders looks most encouraging, as the sort of tests which are currently

* See H. J. Eysenck, *The Biological Basis of Personality* (1967).

being used to measure extroversion or neuroticism include tests which measure functions like variability in reaction time, poor vigilance, and disorganization of psychomotor functioning. As such, they might be considered to have a good deal of practical "face validity", their connection with unsafe driving, let alone defective driving, being far more obvious to the layman than, for instance, a projective personality test. And, most important of all, the findings of such tests might stand up quite well in a court of law—a situation in which the projective tests would fare very badly.

For, good as the projective tests have proved to be, there is no doubt that their practical usefulness is limited—especially their usefulness with the general public. This may seem a strange way of ending a chapter which has been devoted almost entirely to demonstrating their value as accident predictors. But one must face the realities of the accident situation. Driving is so much a part of our everyday life that holding a licence is regarded as a right and not a privilege. Any restriction of this "right" invariably meets with stiff and vociferous opposition from the public—opposition which, in many cases, runs to employing the smartest lawyer available to defend that right. It would take much more than a projective test, where a person is judged by his apperceptive fantasy, to stand up to this sort of opposition. It is one thing to use such a test for the selection of professional drivers where the right to allow a person to drive is synonymous with the right to choose one's employees. It is quite another to refuse to allow a person to drive in a private capacity.

I therefore have to be quite honest and admit that on the broad question of accident prevention among the general public the only practical situation in which I can visualize these projective tests being used is clinically, i.e. as a means of determining what sort of treatment should be given to certain apparently incorrigible accident offenders. Their principal use will probably have to be restricted to research. But here I feel they could prove to be very valuable aids.

Because they are such reliable predictors and because they can produce so much information they could be used as "back-stops" for both the development and cross-checking of other testing methods, methods which for various reasons might be more practicable and more socially acceptable. In the meantime, however, an indication of their usefulness as research aids has already been given by Nau's study (1966) described in the section on "Age" in Chapter 18. Here they were used to investigate the personality dynamics of German juvenile traffic offenders and produced some remarkable information.

CHAPTER 17

ACCIDENTS AND PERSONALITY

THE validation studies reported in the last chapter provide very strong quantitative confirmation of the close relationship which exists between accidents and personality. But they are only one more link in the chain of evidence provided by research from all parts of the world which has shown only too clearly that an individual's personality exerts such a powerful and overriding effect on his accident potential that it can make a bad risk out of someone with all the necessary attributes of skill and physical fitness, and a good risk out of someone whose qualifications for driving are anything but ideal. Even experience cannot always compensate for personality defects, and some of the worst and most dangerous accident risks are to be found among people who have been driving for most of their adult lives.

Who then are the good risks or the bad ones? What sort of people are they? What characteristics do they display? And just how is their personality reflected in their driving behaviour?

The first questions are obviously far easier to answer than the last, as the descriptive evidence from all research sectors fits together in a very logical manner. A composite picture of the sort of people who constitute the various types of risks would read something like this:

The Bad Accident Risk

The mental defective or psychotic.

The person who is extremely unintelligent, unobservant, and unadaptable.

The disorganized or disorientated or badly disturbed person.

The badly integrated or maladjusted person.

The person with a distorted apperception of life and a distorted sense of values.

The person who is emotionally unstable and extremistic.

The person who lacks control, and particularly the person who exhibits uncontrolled aggression.

The person with pronounced anti-social attitudes or criminal tendencies.

The selfish, self-centred, or id-directed person.

The highly competitive person.

The over-confident, self-assertive person.

The irritable and cantankerous person.

The person who harbours grudges, grievances, and resentments.

The blame-avoidant person who is always ready with excuses.

335

The intolerant and impatient person.

The person with a marked antagonism to and resistance against authority.

The frustrated and discontented person.

The inadequate person with a driving need to prove himself.

The extremely anxious, tension-ridden, and panicky person.

The person who is unduly sensitive to criticism.

The helpless and inadequate person who is constantly in need of guidance and support.

The chronically indecisive person.

The person who has difficulty in concentrating.

The person who is easily influenced or intimidated.

The careless and frivolous person.

The person who is very lacking in personal insight and an appreciation of his own limitations.

The fatalistic person who makes no attempt to control his own destiny; the person who is prone to mysticism, superstition or primitive, unreasoning beliefs.

The person who already gives evidence of addiction to alcohol or drugs.

The person who has the sort of personality pattern that predisposes him to drink or drugs.

The person who has suicidal tendencies or who indulges in suicide fantasies.

The person who exhibits undue signs of ageing.

The person who exhibits the personality characteristics commonly associated with immaturity, such as: foolhardy impetuosity, irresponsibility, exhibitionism, inability to appreciate the consequences of his actions, hypersensitivity, easily aroused emotionalism, unrealistic goals, and a general lack of self-discipline, personal insight, worldly wisdom and common sense.

The Poor Accident Risk

The person who exhibits the personality faults of the bad accident risk, but in a less pronounced manner.

The person who displays little energy, stamina, or interest.

Also included in this group are the people whose faults or weaknesses are such that they could possibly improve with time; but the learning process is likely to be so expensive that such a person can only be considered a poor risk.

The Borderline Risk

There will always be a number of people whose accident potential will depend to an unusual degree on the influences and the stresses they encounter in the future. Examples of these cases are:

The young person whose prognosis looks good but whose character structure is relatively unformed.

The weak person who could easily be influenced.

The person who is nervous and lacking in self-confidence.

The person who has unresolved conflicts, but who gives evidence of a constructive, but as yet unsuccessful effort to make adequate adjustments to these conflicts.

The person with a not-too-pronounced anxiety neurosis. (This may make him ultra-cautious at the moment but he must be regarded as a doubtful risk, as he may deteriorate.)

The Fair Accident Risk

The person who has his good points and his bad points, with the bias in favour of the good.

The person who has certain weaknesses or unresolved conflicts which, although they will not unduly upset the balance of his personality, will nevertheless always impose certain strains on him and slightly impair his efficiency.

The highly intelligent person with a tendency to abstract thought and mental preoccupation. (This is more particularly the case with full-time professional drivers.)

Also included in this group is the person whose minor faults and weaknesses are such that he will probably improve in time but who, at the moment, cannot rise above them, and who is currently therefore only a fair risk.

The Good Accident Risk

The balanced and mature and well-controlled person with a healthy and realistic outlook, satisfactory interpersonal relations, a kindly and tolerant attitude to others, a well-developed social and civic conscience, and an ingrained sense of responsibility.

The person who is essentially a moderate individual, able to exercise adequate control over his impulses and his emotions.

The positive person who is able to assess a situation as a whole and make decisions—provided he is not too aggressive. (This is what one might call the "executive" class of good accident risk, namely the people who, though they may be dominant and forceful in their business lives, are realistic enough to carry only a moderate amount of this through into the traffic situation.)

The person who, as yet, cannot be said to be quite mature, but whose motivations are sound and who demonstrates an ability to learn quickly by experience and profit by his mistakes. (This sort of person will undoubtedly have a learning period before his record stabilizes itself at a good level.)

The contented person who is in no way outstanding but who is friendly, cheerful, adaptable, and accepting—provided he is reasonably intelligent, realistic, and mature.

The person who has his weaknesses and limitations but is realistically aware of them and who is careful and cautious and moderates his behaviour according to his limitations.

The rather withdrawn introvert—provided he is not too maladjusted.

The person who, though reasonably well integrated, is nevertheless unimpressively negative; the passive, somewhat compliant, subservient person, anxious to conform, not wishing to be in any way conspicuous, and with a strong need for acceptance and security.

Also included in this group are a few "oddities" such as (a) the person whose motivations (such as fear of authority or personal injury) are not necessarily sound, but which are so strong that they will result in an almost compulsive desire for social conformity or personal safety; (b) the person with an exaggerated concern for orderliness and system—the person who is almost an obsessive perfectionist.

This is a rather rough and ready way of classifying the various accident risks, but at least it enables us to cover the whole continuum of accident proneness.

It also serves to illustrate how certain characteristics can be an asset in one person and a liability in another, and why it is so important to know just how they are integrated into the personality as a whole. However, it would appear that there are other characteristics which are such obvious accident indicators that it is unlikely that any good qualities the person may possess would be able to compensate for them. In fact with many of these traits (using the term "trait" in a very general sense) it is unlikely that they will be found alone; also present will be a number of interrelated traits, the overwhelming weight of which will make that person a very bad risk indeed.

These very dangerous accident indicators figure prominently in the accident literature. Time and again when high and low accident groups have been compared, significant group differences have been found on a number of personal characteristics such as impulsiveness or carelessness or aggressiveness. And although it has often been difficult to quantify their importance by means of correlation techniques (the correlations between specific personality traits and accident criteria being usually low), it seems that this is largely due to methodological weaknesses, either in the tests used or in the criteria. For in two of the validation studies reported in the last chapter, where item scores derived from the projective tests were correlated with a sensitive time-interval accident criterion, high correlations were obtained for a number of individual characteristics.

These particular correlation studies are worth a little attention as they brought to light some very interesting information. The two studies covered rather different ground. The one involved the seventy-one White bus drivers used for the factor analysis described in Chapter 16, where the criterion was based on the men's accident records *subsequent* to the test. This was a very comprehensive study (using the Murray TAT and PUTCO SRT) where all seventy-one subjects were marked on thirty different items (the rating being on a five-point scale ranging from -2 to $+2$ to include the undesirable as well as the desirable aspects of the various characteristics. In the other correlation study the subjects were all African (Negro) bus drivers and the criterion was based on their past accident records. This study was carried out in the early stages of the PUTCO project, when the first experimental model of the PUTCO African TAT still did not yield enough information for all the subjects to be marked on each item. As a result some of the correlations are based on very small groups and the number of subjects is therefore given in each case. This rather

TABLE 17.1. THE RELATIONSHIP BETWEEN ACCIDENTS AND INDIVIDUAL PERSONALITY CHARACTERISTICS IN TWO GROUPS OF SOUTH AFRICAN BUS DRIVERS

Factor group	Group A (N = 71)		Group B (Different N's)	
	Characteristic	r	Characteristic	r
E	Irresponsibility	0·61***	Irresponsibility (57)	0·54***
E	Psychopathic tendencies (including dishonesty)	0·60***	Antisocial attitudes (11)	0·68**
			Dishonesty (47)	0·47***
E	Immaturity	0·60***	Immaturity (29)	0·56***
E	Lack of self-control and self-discipline	0·59***		
E	Carelessness and impulsiveness	0·56***		
			Carelessness (23)	0·69***
E and N	Lack of common-sense and self-insight	0·56***		
N	Imbalance (psychotic or severely neurotic or suicidal tendencies)	0·52***	Imbalance (including maladjustment and emotional instability) (31)	0·61***
N	Maladjustment (poor personality integration, evidence of conflicts)	0·52***		
N	Emotional instability	0·51***		
N and E	Distorted apperception of life	0·51***		
N and E	Discontentedness	0·45***	Discontentedness (26)	0·55**
E	Aggression (uncontrolled aggression, hostile interpersonal relations)	0·49***	Aggression (30) (including antagonism to authority and impatience)	0·60***
E	Antagonism to authority	0·44***		
E	Overconfidence and competitiveness	0·43***		
E and N	Selfishness (and disregard for the rights of others)	0·45***		
E and N	Low frustration tolerance and bad temperedness	0·41***		
E	Evidence of undue drinking (or drug taking)	0·45***	Drinking (Only 4 subjects rated so no correlation but all had bad accident records)	—
E and N	Lack of perseverance	0·44***		
N and E	Superstition and mysticism	0·41***		
N and E	Social rebellion (sees no need to conform)	0·33**		
E	Social extraversion (likes parties, gregarious, unduly interested in the opposite sex)	0·39**		
E	Crudeness and uncouthness	0·25*		
N	Anxiety	0·32**	Anxiety (55)	0·41**
N	Dysphoria	0·32**		
N	Lack of confidence	0·28*	Lack of confidence (13)	0·54*
N	Mental deterioration due to ageing	0·27*		

TABLE 17.1 (*cont.*)

| Factor group | Group A (N=71) | | Group B (different N's) | |
	Characteristic	r	Characteristic	r
N	Inadequacy	0·26*		
N	Laziness and lethargy	0·26*	Intelligence (66)	0·24*
—	Intelligence	0·18		
—	Chronological age	0·04		

*** Significant at the 0·001 level.
　** Significant at the 0·01 level.
　　* Significant at the 0·05 level.

outdated study is really only included to show how, despite its limitations, it came up with very similar results to the major study reported here.

Table 17.1 shows how, for the bigger group, 22 out of 30 items produced correlation coefficients which were significant beyond the 0·01 level, 19 of them being actually significant beyond the 0·001 level. In fact the only items on the marking sheet where there was no correlation were intelligence and age.

Looking down the list of the very significant coefficients, the reader might well be tempted to ask whether this does not show that certain of the items are sufficiently important *in themselves* to be considered reliable accident indicators. Would it not be more *practicable*, therefore, to use a simple personality test (which would, for instance, reveal specific characteristics like irresponsibility or carelessness) or a simple attitude test which would reveal for instance immature or antisocial attitudes, rather than a very complex test like the TAT—especially as the latter obviously requires specialized training? I am afraid the answer to that question lies in the difficulty of obtaining this sort of information by means of simple tests—in the unreliability of such tests as revealed by the much smaller coefficients obtained in many other studies. Most of the simple tests available are questionnaires of some kind, and not only *can* be quite easily faked but it seems that they usually *are* faked by the very people in whom one is most interested.

In addition, Table 17.1 illustrates another reason for the unreliability of trying to predict anything as complex as accident proneness on the basis of individual characteristics. For although the table clearly demonstrates the good predicting power of certain individual items on the marking sheet—like irresponsibility or immaturity—these items certainly do not represent *single traits*: they are really concepts and quite involved ones at that. This is in fact the first indication that better results can be obtained by using higher-order combinations of traits than by using individual traits. The second indication is that the items are inclined to form themselves into clusters, the similarity of their correlation with the criterion indicating that in many cases they must have been found in the same person. And in addition to forming clusters it would appear that most of the items seem to belong to two main classes, one connected with a tendency to impulsive, acting-out behaviour, and the other with a high emotional content. It is not surprising therefore that the actual factor analysis carried out on the item scores revealed the presence of the two strong latent roots of extroversion and emotional instability. (Column 1 shows which of the items were found to have a predominantly E or predominantly N loading.) Nor is it surprising to find that when one combines these apparently interrelated items into two separate test "batteries" (or factors) by means of varimax rotation, the correlation of these "batteries" is higher than the average for the individual items which they represent. This is shown by the following correlation coefficients:

E factor vs. the accident criterion   0·61

N factor vs. the accident criterion   0·47

This is encouraging because extroversion and emotional instability are aspects of personality which can be determined by means of instrumented tests which would be more objective than the TAT, and could prove more reliable than questionnaires.

But as the E and N factors are virtually unrelated, it is obviously necessary to form them into a single test battery which will test for both these factors. (For instance, a person could be both responsible and careful but could still be a bad risk because of pronounced anxiety.) This can be done experimentally by the method illustrated in Fig. 16.5 (p. 330).

Here each subject was allocated a position according to his E and N scores on two orthogonal axes; and the *areas* of the resulting chart representing the people with the *bad*, *poor*, *fair*, and *good* accident records (criterion ratings) were marked off. This presentation gives one a good idea of the part played by the E and N factors in determining accident potential, and also illustrates very clearly why a *combination* of higher-order factors is a very much more efficient all-round accident predictor than either factor alone. For although Fig. 16.5 shows that a high degree of extroversion or neuroticism is in itself sufficient to make a person a bad risk, it also shows that the *combination* of quite moderate amounts of both can be equally dangerous. Just why this could be so is something we can deal with later. For the moment the main point of interest is that this simple method of combining the E and N factor scores appears to increase the correlation. For the distribution of the coloured dots in the various areas of the chart representing the *good*, *fair*, *poor*, *bad* areas of the accident criterion is as Table 17.2 shows.

TABLE 17.2

Criterion rating	Placing on the chart according to E and N score			
	Good	Fair	Poor	Bad
Good	8	5	0	0
Fair	1	8	7	0
Poor	0	3	21	8
Bad	0	1	1	8

This tentative bivariate distribution yields a correlation coefficient of: $r = 0.79$.

Naturally one of the reasons why the coefficient is so high is that some of the lines of demarcation were drawn *to suit the actual material*, for although the slope of the centre line was largely dictated by the actual size of the coefficients ($r = 0.61$ for the E factor and $r = 0.47$ for the N factor), the demarcation lines on either side were arbitrarily drawn. Nevertheless, there must be some merit to this sort of simple demarcation system as a similar one was found to work quite well with Quenault's material also (Fig. 16.6, p. 332). It seems therefore that one should not overlook the somewhat artificial high coefficient which it has produced, especially as the χ-square test on the dichotomous safe/unsafe split based on the centre line only is highly significant at the 0.01 level. Further experimentation may yet reveal that a combination of E and N scores, derived this time from *objective* personality tests, will prove to be a reliable way of assessing accident potential.

For the moment, however, this pictorial representation is only an interesting indication of what one *hopes* is the shape of things to come—namely the sort of accident-predicting results which could be achieved if one could find tests as reliable and unfakeable as the projective tests on which this factor analysis was based (and where the ratings of future accident potential—made purely subjectively on the basis of the test protocol as a whole—produced a genuine "unmanipulated" coefficient of correlation with the accident criterion of $r = 0.73$). But the possibility of finding such tests does not seem in any way a vain hope. The considerable amount of experimental work which is currently being carried out on assessing factors such as extroversion and neuroticism by means of objective tests has not as yet been applied to the field of road accident research. Let us hope that the interest and the research capital will be forthcoming to pursue this line of research, for later in this chapter I will attempt to demonstrate further just how pertinent it could be.

Certainly, one thing which this particular factor analysis indicates very clearly is how necessary it is to assess personality on a broad front—in other words to use some sort of *battery* of personality tests which will reveal more than just isolated characteristics. Here again one cannot help regretting the many practical difficulties which are likely to prevent the use of projective tests on the general public. For this is exactly why a combination like the TAT–SRT is so effective, as *in itself* it constitutes a small, compact, and effective test battery—the reason being that although each person receives exactly the same test (i.e. the same TAT cards and comic strips) each person apperceives the pictures in such an individual way that the same card or comic strip can produce evidence of manic aggression in one person and neurotic anxiety in another. It would take a very long and subtle questionnaire, or a very comprehensive and no doubt expensive battery of performance tests, to reveal anything approaching the amount of information which can be obtained from the stories written in response to six TAT cards and eight comic strips.

However, as I said before, there is no point in dwelling on the might-have-beens. At least these tests can be used for selecting professional drivers and as supplementary aids for the development of more socially acceptable tests for use on the public. Just how useful they could be is best illustrated by giving some actual case studies which show the wealth of information which they can produce. At the same time these case studies will also serve as good illustrations of the complex relationship which obviously does exist between personality and accidents—and the need to take heed of this complexity.

The following examples have been taken from various follow-up studies on subjects tested by means of the TAT–SRT combination. They therefore include people belonging to different ethnic groups—it does not matter which as it is the relationship between a particular personality pattern and his accident potential which counts. In some cases the information about the subject's accident record relates to his record both before and after the test. In other cases where this was a prospective new driver being tested for employment, only the subsequent accident record is given (many of the bad cases being men taken on despite the test findings during an acute driver shortage). Because of the interesting relationship between accidents and everyday behaviour, some comments on the employee records of the subjects, who were all bus drivers, have also been included. The personality assessments are condensations of the actual "pen pictures" of the various personalities from which the predictions of future accident liability were made—and it will be noticed that they are very often written in most unpsychological language! But the reader should find them interesting as they represent authenticated examples of the way in which a man's accident potential can be determined from his personality alone.

The Good Accident Risk

Personality as revealed by the tests. Aged 46. A very ordinary person, not very intelligent or imaginative, but solid, responsible and reliable. He is well balanced and well adjusted to his own particular environment and he has no big problems. A very good risk.

His actual record. For the whole period of his exposure—nineteen years before the test and $2\frac{1}{2}$ years thereafter—his accident record was excellent. His disciplinary record was also excellent.

Personality. Aged 35. Staid and conventional. Over-cautious. Depressive; expects the worst. Lacks confidence. A rather panicky person, but law-abiding, peace-loving, and kindly. A good risk.

Actual record. He only started driving after the test. He had a learning period with one accident after ten days, and his record was then good for over six years. Disciplinary record good.

Personality. Aged 55. Very intelligent; has a disciplined and orderly mind. Has foresight and can act quickly in emergencies. Though he has only a post-elementary education he is exceptionally knowledgeable and well-read and it is surprising that he has remained a bus driver. However, although he has apparently had his setbacks and disappointments and is obviously rather bored and dissatisfied with the job, he has not become sour or unduly frustrated—possibly because he accepts his responsibilities and sets a high value on security. He has good family relationships. He worries about accidents—they have a morbid fascination for him and he is afraid of personal injury. A complex person but a good accident risk.

Actual record. For twenty-five years prior to the test and $2\frac{1}{2}$ years after the test, his accident and disciplinary record were good.

Personality. Aged 39. A person who has probably had a rather slummy youth, but who has now established himself in a reasonable home life where, though he does not get on well with his wife, he at least lives for his children. He is quick tempered but hasn't the courage to express his aggression openly, and has to dissipate it in sadistic fantasies. However, he seems to manage this pretty well and to operate on a fairly even keel. No doubt drinks a bit on occasion, but is a mature person with an adult outlook. Not a very likeable person but currently quite a good accident risk—though his early record was probably poor.

Actual record. He started driving at the age of 27 and his early record was indeed poor. His record subsequent to the test was good, but he drove trolley buses and his record contained a rather high proportion of passenger injury accidents.

The Currently Fair Risk who Should Improve to Good

Personality. Aged 28. Quite intelligent but not very imaginative. A pleasant person who enjoys life. Good interpersonal relations. Positive but not aggressive. A little immature still, but good material. Currently a fair risk and likely to improve later.

Actual record. Improved slowly from fair to good to excellent over four years and then remained so for a further five. His disciplinary record showed two warnings for reckless driving during his first year, after which he settled down.

Personality. Aged 32. Anxious and self-pitying and fearful and easily intimidated, but avoids trouble and relies on authority for help and support. A fair risk who should improve later.

Actual record. He had a short but expensive learning period (three accidents in fifty-one days) then improved from fair to ood over a period of two years. During his first year he was twice warned for speeding. (This is an African subject and the African passengers are inclined to bait the drivers who go too slowly, with the result that many of the more timid drivers are inclined to speed.)

Personality. Aged 28. (This is also an African subject.) Fairly intelligent but has a country background and has only recently come to town. He is vastly impressed with city life. His outlook is still immature, but he is a kindly, friendly person with a well-integrated personality. A fair risk who should improve to good; but will probably have a learning period.

Actual record. He had a most expensive learning period with five accidents in the first five months. Then he settled down and his record remained good over the following four years. It took him longer to outgrow his disciplinary offences and he was still speeding at the end of his first year. Later he settled down. During his first year he was described as "a real glamour-boy, very prone to fancy shirts and socks".

The Person who Is Likely to Remain only a Fair Risk

These cases are never straightforward because, for a driver to remain only a middling sort of risk year in and year out, never really benefiting by experience, means that although he must have a number of good qualities, at the same time there must be certain factors in his make-up which constantly impair his efficiency. The personality patterns of these cases therefore usually display a certain ambivalence and a number of conflicting traits.

Personality. Aged 39. Very introspective, but lacks self-insight. Frustrated by his own fears and limitations, but blames his failures on circumstances and tries to avoid his responsibilities. Lazy and lethargic; he would simply love to sit and do nothing. Only interested in himself and his own pleasures. Moody and temperamental but at the same time very passive. His efficiency will always be impaired by all the introspective daydreaming, the frustration, and the moodiness. Only a fair risk.

Actual record. He started bus driving at 28 and was exposed for twelve years before and $2\frac{1}{2}$ years after the test. His record was fair throughout. His disciplinary record was good (and his hobby was found to be fishing!).

Personality. Aged 35. Intelligent and imaginative. Given to creative thinking and possibly daydreaming. Easy-going, calm and reserved, sophisticated and mature. Basically a good type but possibly too imaginative for bus driving. A fair risk.

Actual record. Remained in the fair category for over eight years of exposure. His disciplinary record was also fair. A few reports of speeding but also several special reports from the public for competent and courteous driving.

The Person who Is Currently a Poor Risk but Could Improve Later

Personality. Aged 26. Immature and still rather silly and unrealistic, but alert, active, and reasonably intelligent, and has potential as his faults are not very exaggerated. Friendly and contented. Needs firm handling as he will show off. May drink. Currently a poor risk but should improve.

Actual record. Had a major accident due to reckless driving during his first year. Took nine months to settle down. After that his accident record was good for four years. His employee record showed a couple of serious offences during his first year, including disobeying instructions and one liquor offence. He then settled down and had a good disciplinary record.

Personality. Aged 34. Very pleasant and amenable and co-operative. Reliable and conscientious. Has no very undesirable qualities and has the best of intentions, but is a very simple-minded person with limited intelligence and little adaptability. A poor risk now but should improve later.

Actual record. His learning period took a whole year during which he had seven accidents. After that he improved tremendously and did very well until transferred to a more difficult route, where he immediately had three accidents within thirteen days. Transferred back to his old route, he settled down again and his record remained good for six years. His disciplinary record contained only petty dishonesty offences.

The Poor Accident Risk

Personality. Aged 38. An indecisive, slow-thinking person, inefficient and with very limited intelligence. He cannot sort out his life and is full of conflicts. He is an inadequate, confused person who is out of his depth and who needs to be led, but who resents authority and who is stupidly stubborn and aggressive. He would panic in an emergency and is obviously conditioned to trouble on the job. His record will have started badly and he is still a poor risk.

Actual record. He was exposed for two years before the test and two years thereafter. He started bus driving at the age of 36 and his early record was bad, with nine accidents in the first year, including an accident where he underestimated the height of his double-decker bus and hit an overhanging balcony. After that his standard improved from bad to poor, with fewer collisions but passenger injuries instead. His record subsequent to the test was poor.

His employee record was mediocre: not keeping to schedule and repeated dewirements, which he usually could not rectify, having left the bus garage without his bamboo pole.

Personality. Aged 30. Disorganized and confused in his thinking. Lazy and easily fatigued. Lacking in drive; an aimless person without direction or guts. A dreamer who solves his problems in fantasy. Colourless and negative, he lives in a world of unresolved fears. Possibly a drinker. A poor risk.

Actual record. A chronically poor accident record over five years. A consistently poor employee record—mostly careless offences such as reversing without a guide or damaging a bus by careless driving. Also a lot of lateness and absenteeism.

Personality. Aged 30. A disgruntled person. Very blame-avoidant. Depressive and fatalistic. Convinced that everything will go wrong. He will be accident-prone as his attitude is: "There you are, I told you it would happen." A poor risk.

Actual record. A poor record over five years of exposure. A poor disciplinary record which started with two dangerous driving offences in his first year, but later changed to chronic dishonesty. Was known to drink.

The Person who Is Currently a Bad Accident Risk but who Could Improve Later

Personality. Aged 22. Immature and egotistical with great self-confidence. Critical and superior. Isolated and withdrawn—but very intelligent. Currently a bad risk, but should improve later.

Actual record. His record started with a most expensive learning period but improved gradually from bad to fair to good over a period of four years. His disciplinary record took much longer to improve and he was still speeding at the end of three years.

Personality. Aged 22. Just a "crazy mixed-up kid", who still does not know what he is doing or where he is going. Still a juvenile delinquent, mixing with all the wrong people; scared of his associates but easily intimidated. (He hates this but is unable to stand up to them.) An unhappy delinquent, too, who feels sorry for himself and blames everyone else for his failures. However, there are a few factors which might save him. He is not viciously bad; he has a conscience; and there is evidence of hopeful conflicts (drink vs. religion, and sex vs. fear of the consequences); he dislikes his associates; he is afraid of social condemnation; and he has some education and wants to be an academic success. At the moment he is a bad risk and should not have a licence, but he may improve if he can break away from his delinquent companions.

Actual record. He was taken off driving shortly after the test because of his bad accident record, so there was no chance for him to demonstrate any possible improvement.

The Bad Accident Risk

These people can be roughly divided into two groups—the chronic minor accident-repeater and the more dangerous accident risk. However, it must be remembered that the inability of the chronic minor accident-repeater to cope with the driving situation means that if a dangerous situation develops he may not be able to cope with it, and must therefore be considered a potential serious accident risk.

The Chronic Minor Accident Risk

Personality. Aged 48. Rather old-womanish, but a decent and honourable person with a very ethical outlook. Stubborn and unadaptable. Too rigid for bus driving and should be in another kind of job. He will do his best but is nevertheless a bad risk.

Actual record. Fourteen minor accidents in eighteen months. His employee record showed no absenteeism or insubordination. But his driving record showed that he was always behind schedule and finally took to speeding. He was taken off driving.

Personality. Aged 37. An emotional person who lacks moderation and emotional control. He has a deep-seated sense of inferiority and is always moralizing and making excuses to himself, and to others, to explain away and justify his failures. He is not at all a manly person and always has to have someone to help him fight his battles and face the music for him; but does not admit this to himself. In his own eyes he is a person who works like a slave, struggles against insuperable odds, and makes stupendous sacrifices for everyone else. It would appear, however, that only in his favourite pipe-dreams are these noble efforts really appreciated. In reality he is henpecked and permanently trouble-prone. Although he is a kindly person who wants to get on with others and fawns on authority, he is too emotionally unstable to be anything but a bad accident risk as he is obsessed with a need to disprove the realities of his life, namely that he is not much good. A bad risk, especially with regard to minor accidents.

Actual record. He had been employed for two years before the test and $2\frac{1}{2}$ years thereafter. His record was consistently bad—twenty-eight minor collisions and passenger injuries before the test and twenty-two after the test! He was a chronic headache to the transit authority's personnel department. He was always in debt, always going to break up his marriage and then staging another reconciliation, and always in trouble of some sort.

Personality. Aged 28. Pleasant, sociable, and well meaning but extremistic and an impulsive extravert. The type who goes his own way rather than obey instructions. Dangerously stupid and unreliable, and so immature still that he seems to be a chronic Peter Pan. He is a bad accident risk, and though he is likely to be involved mostly in minor accidents he must also be regarded as a potentially dangerous accident risk.

Actual record. The control chart of this driver is given in Fig. 8.5 (p. 128) and shows 45 minor accidents over a period of ten years. Each time he was severely disciplined his record improved, only to go off again. He started driving at the age of 22, but ten years later his record was still blatantly unsatisfactory and he was finally discharged as being irredeemable, after he had been involved in a major accident. His disciplinary record was poor. He had no insubordination offences but repeated warnings for speeding and careless driving despite pay cuts and demotions.

The People who Are Dangerous Accident Risks

Personality. Aged 25. Immature, uncontrolled, and emotionally disturbed. Unbalanced and out of touch with reality. A dangerous accident risk.

Actual record. Ten accidents in eight months, including three major accidents (i.e. damage in excess of £100). His disciplinary record was also bad: ticket offences, insolence, disobeying instructions. He finally took a bus off route without permission and was involved in a major accident and discharged.

Personality. Aged 27. Pathologically anxious. A personality in a state of panic. A dangerous accident risk.

Actual record. Seven accidents in $5\frac{1}{2}$ months. His employee record started well, but then he started to drink and assault people. He was discharged.

Personality. Aged 35. Hopelessly inadequate and chronically afraid. He reacts to fear with hostility and aggression. Very maladjusted and unable to accept adult responsibility. A dangerous accident risk.

Actual record. Seven accidents in ten months. Employee record bad. There were several reports of reckless driving and finally his licence was suspended and he was discharged.

Personality. Aged 42. Heading for an anxiety neurosis and obviously functioning under very great strain. Very emotional and rather unbalanced. His self-involvement and his morbid preoccupation with thoughts of accidents and death distort his whole perspective.

Lost and unhappy and badly in need of support. Expects the worst to happen. He is strongly motivated to avoid accidents, but is too disturbed and fatalistic to be able to cope much longer. He finds driving a tremendous strain and probably drinks. A bad risk and should not be driving, the strain is too much for him.

Actual record. His record was very bad on trolley buses and he was transferred to single deckers on an easier route where it improved slightly, but he then resigned.

Personality. Aged 34. Unintelligent. Intolerant. Has a low frustration tolerance. Unduly agressive and quick-tempered. Very self-assured and over-confident. Resents authority. A bad risk.

Actual record. Chronically and dangerously accident-prone: thirty-four accidents in four years. His disciplinary record showed repeated traffic offences and reports for reckless driving, and two reports of assault. Discharged.

Personality. Aged 37. Temperamentally unstable. Has outbursts of temper and very bad interpersonal relations, especially with women. Unrealistic and impractical. He drinks. A dangerous accident risk.

Actual record. Five accidents in five months. Employee record bad. Several drinking offences and failed to report a fatal accident. Discharged.

Personality. Aged 28. Very immature and still has the attitudes of a juvenile delinquent. His is the show-off, bragging type of immaturity where he has to act the handsome, conquering hero to hide the fact that only in a gang has he any real courage and that on his own he is the farm boy who finds city life a bit too much for him. The sort of person who has not yet been able to integrate into society and should not have a driver's licence. A bad accident risk in a bus and a very bad risk in a private car.

Actual record. He was exposed for four years before the test (during which his record was very poor) and six months thereafter, when he was taken off driving because of his bad accident record. His disciplinary record was poor: operating ahead of schedule, smoking while driving, continuous absenteeism; making excuses about being in bad health, although on each occasion the doctor found him to be medically fit.

Personality. Aged 28. Quick-witted but ignorant and lacking in common sense. Very immature in his outlook. Irresponsible and unreliable. Hates having to accept responsibility and is still longing for the good old delinquent, spoon-fed days. Deceitful and blame-avoidant. Selfish and self-centred. His interpersonal relations are bad. He wants social approval but feels rejected and will turn nasty if he feels that he is being snubbed or belittled. Emotional, immoderate, unpredictable, and uncontrolled, and has a low frustration tolerance. His only saving graces as an accident risk are his cowardice and his need for approval, but he is nevertheless a bad risk as he is the type who has to learn his lessons the hard way. A bad risk in a bus and a worse risk in a private car.

Actual record. He had only been driving for eight months when he was tested and his previous record showed eight accidents during that time. His record subsequent to the test continued to be bad and he was discharged. His disciplinary record was also bad: general slackness; incivility to passengers; and a severe reprimand for turning off the passenger bell in the bus "because it made him mad"!

Personality. Aged 26. Defiant, aggressive, impulsive, and poorly controlled. Irresponsible, unreliable, and cannot be believed or trusted. A very bad risk.

Actual record. Eighteen accidents in three years, five of them involving injury. Had a disciplinary record to match: insubordination, dishonesty, lateness, and absenteeism, and a report from the accident bureau to his section manager that he was obviously lying about not being to blame for his accidents.

Personality. Aged 48. Quite intelligent and can make quick decisions, but unrealistic in his thinking. Bitter, cynical, and disgruntled. Frustrated (mostly by his own failures) but lacking in self-insight. Aggressive and has a low frustration tolerance, but bottles up his aggressions so that they seethe inside him because he is afraid to show them openly. Antagonistic to authority. Probably drinks to get even with life. No doubt competent as a driver, but too impatient and embittered and should be watched for drink. A dangerous accident risk as he is the type who could be involved in a serious accident.

Actual record. From the frequency angle his record was mediocre, but he had been involved in a fatal accident involving a pedestrian and also a major multiple-injury accident where he overturned a double decker bus, apparently due to speeding and having to take last-minute action to avoid a rear-end collision.

Personality. Aged 40. Intelligent and quite well educated, but very maladjusted. He feels frustrated by the circumstances of his life, but does nothing to help himself as he is an ineffectual day-dreamer who takes refuge from his problems and anxieties in drink. Almost an alcoholic. A weak person who cannot stand up to temptation. He probably gambles as well, and is usually in debt. A very poor risk and likely to deteriorate further. Should not be driving.

Actual record. His record before the test was poor, but subsequent to the test deteriorated to bad. His disciplinary record was also bad: he was known to drink but resigned before action could be taken against him.

Personality. Aged 34. A useless no-good who drinks. He has no strength of character. A weak, vacillating person with very little integrity, no drive, no energy, and no self-respect. He is always going to pull up his socks tomorrow, but tomorrow never comes. A dangerous accident risk. Should not be driving.

Actual record. Accident record bad and he was discharged six months after the test for drunken driving. (He was driving a bus with the steering wheel in one hand and a bottle of brandy in the other, and was taking the odd swig as he drove!)

The Good Risk who Is Likely to Deteriorate

Personality. Aged 39. A person who suffers from a great deal of inner turmoil and who makes excessive use of defence mechanisms to allay his anxiety. He is riddled with guilts which he internalizes—he is masochistic to the point of occasionally contemplating suicide. But he also has strong paranoid feelings of being victimized by society. Intelligent and well read. When he thinks on abstract subjects he thinks clearly and systematically—but when he thinks emotionally his thoughts run round like rats in a cage. He covers his inner turmoil with a pose of supercilious cynicism. So far he has probably managed to maintain a precarious balance. He is strongly motivated to be careful, but a great deal of energy and concentration goes into his introspective worrying. He is currently a borderline risk, but he should be watched as his mental balance is very precarious and he may easily deteriorate.

Actual record. For twelve years before the test and four months thereafter his accident record was excellent, then rapid deterioration set in and he had ten accidents in the next two years. His employee record was good.

Personality. Aged 52. Underneath an acute anxiety neurosis is a decent person, responsible, mature, with good intentions and no desire to get involved in trouble or arguments. But the anxiety is overwhelming and appears to be centred round a morbid preoccupation with accidents—much of which is tinged with guilt. (He may have already been involved in an accident due to drunken driving.) He is nostalgic about the past, which indicates that his past record was good, which one could expect with his good personality traits. Currently, however, he is too neurotic to be a good risk, and there is a definite danger of drink. He is currently a borderline risk. He was no doubt a good risk in the past but is at the moment very disturbed and must be watched for a deterioration which has already begun, and for drink.

Actual record. For seventeen years before the test and eight months thereafter his accident record was excellent. Then rapid deterioration set in and he had eight accidents in the space of fifteen months. There was no evidence of drunken driving in his professional record and unfortunately his record as a private motorist was not available. His disciplinary record was very good throughout.

Drivers who Had Received Psychiatric Treatment

In the last chapter I mentioned that during the SARSC research project we encountered three cases of professional drivers who had already undergone psychiatric treatment. Their test predictions, and also their accident records both before and after the tests, are very interesting. Their personal histories were unknown to the testers, but all had been rated as bad accident risks.

Personality. Aged 53. A very neurotic person, emotionally unstable and suffering from acute anxiety and depression. He is completely introverted and is obsessed with his own problems—problems which he is quite unable to solve. He tries to escape from the anxiety into self-centred fantasy and would like to escape into regression and complete withdrawal from reality. He feels discriminated against, misunderstood, and frustrated. He also feels rejected and longs passionately for acceptance and recognition and to be the centre of love and attention. He has strong feelings of inferiority and strong resentments against his wife. He is a matriculant and can write fluently (but "over-writes" with much lush sentiment and many florid phrases). He strung the whole TAT together as one story, but in doing so never managed to evade himself at all—in fact he is deeply emotionally involved in the whole story. He tried to use the test as a chance to show off his literary prowess but it turned into a complete catharsis. He probably drinks—or is certainly a sitting duck for drink or drugs. Unstable, badly integrated and emotionally disturbed. His only redeeming feature is his fear, but he is too self-involved and too unstable to be able to cope much longer. Despite his long driving experience he is currently a bad risk as he is likely to deteriorate dangerously.

Actual record. Amazingly enough he was found to have maintained a good record for six months before and one year after the test. But it then deteriorated very badly, with three accidents in short succession, and he resigned. It was later found that he was a codeine addict and had received several courses of treatment for depression and hallucinations. (In fact he confessed to stopping his bus on several occasions for elephants to cross the road—but was not very sure whether there had actually been any elephants at all!)

Personality. Aged 27. A spoilt child who wants to have everything his own way and who bitches like anything if he doesn't get it. He is essentially a fair-weather hero who is full of bravado when things are going well, but who collapses into whining excuses as soon as they go wrong. He is as selfish as they are made and thinks of nothing but his own interests. He is far more intelligent than the average bus driver, and is alert and imaginative, but is thoroughly immature and lacking in common sense. He harbours delusions of grandeur and likes to rule the roost and dictate to other people, but he overestimates his own capabilities. He has no sense of responsibility—just does what he wants to do and then expects to be helped out of the resultant mess. He has psychopathic tendencies. He likes to show off and admires speed, and fancies himself (in fantasy) as a hero.

He is a bad risk (especially in a private car) as he has to show off to prove himself.

Actual record. He had only just started to drive when he was tested and his subsequent record showed six accidents in eight months, followed by discharge. It was later found that he had been hospitalized in a clinic for nervous diseases after an attempted suicide.

Personality. Aged 27. A psychopathic personality. An immature delinquent with a rotten home background who hasn't outgrown his delinquency and his general delinquent outlook. A coward who runs from trouble but exhibits a mean, sadistic streak towards people who cannot hit back. Utterly selfish and has no regard for the feelings or rights of others. Drinks and probably takes drugs as well. His life has been one long failure. He has not made a success of anything, but he does not accept the responsibility for this; he finds extenuating circumstances or attributes it to circumstances beyond his control. Rather disgruntled and hard-done-by. He has no sense of values and a most anti-social outlook—and no integrity. Careless, slipshod, and evasive. He has no internalized sense of right or wrong. He is most unemotional about everything. He has no personal involvement in anything—he remains emotionally divorced from the most ghastly situations. A classic psychopath and a very bad accident risk.

Actual record. He had been discharged previously because he was always staying away from work and pleading an "anxiety state". But he kept on writing to the transit authority and was finally told he could have his job back if he got a certificate from a psychiatrist. He apparently told a very sad and completely inaccurate tale of woe to the psychiatrist, who asked that he be given another chance. He had just been taken on again when he was tested, and his subsequent accident record showed nineteen minor accidents in two years, starting with repeated collisions, changing after a severe warning to a pattern of passenger injury accidents, and later reverting again to a series of collisions which led to his second discharge.

The fact that three men out of a small group of professional drivers had required psychiatric treatment is alarming enough. But there is another aspect which is possibly more alarming still—namely the fact that the psychiatrists who treated these men did not inquire into their accident records and insist that they be taken off full-time professional driving. On the contrary, they went out of their way to see that these men did not lose their jobs, and appeared to be far more concerned with the mental health of their patients than with the bus-loads of passengers whom they advocated should be placed in these men's hands. It would appear, therefore, that there is a certain lack of awareness on the part of psychiatry of the relationship between mental health and accident involvement.

The examples given here clearly illustrate the value of these projective tests. They also illustrate how it is possible to assess a driver's accident potential from the apperceptive fantasies produced by a series of pictures and comic strips which have *nothing to do with the driving situation as such.* The SRT being a new projective test, one of the comic strips used is illustrated in Fig. 17.1. The Murray TAT cards used were: 1, 2, 3BM, 4, 6BM, 7BM, 9BM, 13 MF and 20—though 9BM and 20 can be omitted.

Naturally, when assessing this potential in terms of a general personality pattern, the assessor tries to visualize how this sort of person would react to the driving situation—to the demands it makes, the strains it imposes, the frustrations it engenders, and the opportunities it offers for people to behave in a way which they would not dare to do in everyday life. This system of deductive reasoning must be a fair approximation to the truth, judging by the accuracy of the predictions in terms of actual accident involvement. But it is nevertheless very important to have some definite information about the intervening processes—to know how various kinds of people really do drive, to know what their attitudes are to traffic rules and regulations and to other drivers—and for that matter how they view their own road behaviour.

In the course of the PUTCO project we have been able to get a good deal of information on the question of the general driving behaviour of various personality types—as illustrated by the following examples of reports given by the driving inspectors while checking up on men with bad accident records. (These inspectors are not aware of the contents of the confidential personality test reports.)

STORY:1

WHAT HAPPENS NOW ?

..... write a story of about ten lines to finish this comic strip, and tell what you think will happen now.

FIG. 17.1. One of the comic stips used in the Social Relations Test (SRT)

Personality patterns as revealed by the tests	*The cause of the drivers' unsatisfactory accident records as given by the driving inspectors*

Age 31.

So unintelligent that it takes him ages to think anything out.

Nice enough, kindly and well meaning, but so muddled in his reasoning that he would be bound to get things wrong. His reaction to his own mistakes is always to feel very hard-done-by.

Carelessness: due to his not having any interest. Does not want to improve himself and resents being reprimanded.

Recklessness: due to lack of judgement. Cannot assess a situation, and does not learn from experience.

Sixteen accidents in thirty-one months.

Age 34.

A hopelessly inadequate person with no intelligence, no energy, no stamina, no guts, and no initiative.

Carelessness: due largely to his inability to absorb instruction and put it into practice. Is not intelligent, has poor skills, and cannot help himself. Fails to concentrate, and has not got enough sense to help himself out of trouble. Is nervous and inclined to get all mixed up.

Four accidents in five months.

Age 27.

Unintelligent, slow-thinking and unadaptable. Very literal-minded. Very immature and lacking in common sense. Feels he ought to be acting "big and tough" but is actually chronically inadequate and afraid. Indecisive and very badly integrated; far too many conflicts, especially between his ambitions and his fears.

Neglect: forgets far too quickly; it's too much trouble to remember.

Carelessness: due to his inability to carry out the correct procedures. Pulls off in the wrong gear, delays his gear changes, forgets to double-declutch and does not worry about his mirrors.

Recklessness: due to his being impatient and wanting to be ahead of the other fellow.

Incompetence: cannot make decisions and messes around with unnecessary things.

Ten accidents in twelve months.

Age 25.

Very intelligent; an exceptionally well-written protocol; but immature, irresponsible, ambitious, exhibitionistic, and has grandiose ideas. Not driving material. Would be much better in another job.

Carelessness: immature, lacks sense of responsibility and is very erratic, moody and insolent. Is quite intelligent but a show-off who takes foolish chances.

Recklessness: has no judgement in regard to speed and distance.

Speeding: due chiefly to his showing off and wanting to get the job over as quickly as possible.

Five accidents in seven months.

Personality patterns as revealed by the tests	*The cause of the drivers' unsatisfactory accident records as given by the driving inspectors*
Age 28. Immature and unrealistic. Indulges in fantasies in which he acts the heroic role.	Recklessness: due to his being immature, a show-off and overconfident. Errors of judgement: due to not being able to judge distances in relation to speed. Carelessness: due to his lack of concentration and daydreaming. Has been christened "Stirling Moss" by the other drivers because of his speeding, and feels he must live up to it. Nine accidents in thirteen months.

The reports on the driving behaviour of the more unintelligent, introverted types are very interesting. The behaviour of the young extraverts is much as one would expect. But it must be remembered that these are *bus drivers*, driving on prescribed routes and under fairly constant supervision. Also they know that they are in a company vehicle and can therefore be identified, and that there will be an immediate come-back if there are complaints from the public. Without these restraints—as in a private car, and especially at night—it is not difficult to imagine just how some of these young extroverts would drive.

But although in the course of this project we have been able to obtain a good deal of information on the general driving behaviour of the PUTCO drivers and even about the specific accidents in which they are involved, we usually have to infer their actual "road" attitudes from their behaviour and from their personality tests. We cannot get the drivers to tell us, direct, just how they really view their own driving, and particularly how they feel about traffic rules and regulations. Ask a PUTCO driver this and he immediately assumes an angelic expression and produces a dissertation which would keep a safety organization in propaganda for the next three months! For this sort of information one apparently needs to go to the public, who seem to be far less inhibited when it comes to discussing their personal attitudes and behaviour.

A most interesting study along these lines has recently been carried out in Scotland by Parry, and in describing it in his *Aggression on the Road* (1968) he has achieved what to my mind is the near-impossible—he has produced a book which is of equal interest to scientist and layman alike. Parry's account of the generally illogical and "bloody-minded" attitudes and actions of some drivers will come as no surprise to many a lay reader—even if said reader fails to recognize himself therein! In fact one of Parry's most revealing—and most frightening—findings is the way in which so many drivers either do not know that there is anything wrong with the way they drive; or if they do know they certainly do not care, feeling that the provocation they receive more than justifies any of their own actions.

As Parry says, the reasons for these attitudes and this sort of behaviour are manifold, but his study was confined to the part played by aggression and anxiety. He obtained his information by giving to members of the general public a specially designed questionnaire where the Aggression (AG) and the Anxiety (AN) questions were nicely camouflaged among a number of others, all related to driving. The questions were derived from the opinions expressed by a sample of actual drivers on what they considered to be aggressive or anxious road behaviour. They were then vetted by police officers, driving instructors, and psychologists, and in a number of "brainstorming sessions" reduced to a workable and unambiguous questionnaire. This questionnaire was supplemented by a list of unfinished sentences which not only produced additional information, but also served as a useful way of triggering off some very open talking in the course of interviews with certain selected subjects.

The samples were obtained by calling on a random sample of houses in certain districts, stopping every tenth car and asking the driver to co-operate, and leaving piles of questionnaires at libraries, factories, etc.—a process which worked very well as 382 people, 279 males and 103 females, responded. (It seems that questionnaires of this kind do work very well indeed with volunteers from the public; whereas they are unfortunately almost useless for driver selection, and would no doubt be equally so with traffic offenders coming up for punitive action.) As Parry says, the public seem to be more than willing to discuss driving—especially other people's driving. This was particularly evident in the second part of the study where he interviewed 76 of the subjects whose responses had indicated extremes of aggression and/or anxiety, and also some whose responses showed no extremes but who still admitted to having been involved in an undue number of accidents.

In scoring the questionnaires Parry developed a special loading system for the AG and AN questions, based on the prevalence or rareness of certain types of response. This had the effect of giving a lower loading to the more common and innocuous attitudes and modes of behaviour and a higher loading to the extremes. For example, the item-AG score given to a person who gave a positive reply to these questions was as follows:*

I swear under my breath at other drivers	1·190
I swear out loud at other drivers	1·528
I make rude signs at other motorists when I am provoked	1·696
If another driver makes a rude sign at me I do something about it	1·696
On occasion I have come near to blows with another driver	1·908
I have been in a fight with another driver	1·924
I have driven at another vehicle in anger	1·942

And with the anxiety scores:

I persistently look at the fuel-gauge when driving	1·342
I feel a little apprehensive when I notice a police car about or following behind me	1·434
I worry about doing the wrong thing when driving	1·565
I use the brakes more than necessary	1·756
I get quite tense when driving	1·859

* From Parry, M. H., *Aggression on the Road*, 1968, published by Tavistock Publications. By courtesy of the publisher and the author.

To equalize the total AG and AN scores they were graded by splitting the range from 0 to maximum score into ten groups.

The age groups used and the number of subjects in each group given in Table 17.3.

TABLE 17.3

Group	Age limit	No. of subjects in each group	
		Males	Females
1	$17–24\frac{1}{2}$	77	36
2	$24\frac{1}{2}–34\frac{1}{2}$	92	25
3	$34\frac{1}{2}–44\frac{1}{2}$	41	30
4	$44\frac{1}{2}–54\frac{1}{2}$	40	7
5	$54\frac{1}{2}–64\frac{1}{2}$	27	4
6	$64\frac{1}{2}–74\frac{1}{2}$	2	1

A number of very interesting findings emerged from the analysis of the scores, especially in relation to age and sex. One of the most intriguing of these is illustrated in Figs. 17.2 and 17.3 which show the mean AG and AN scores for both males and females in the

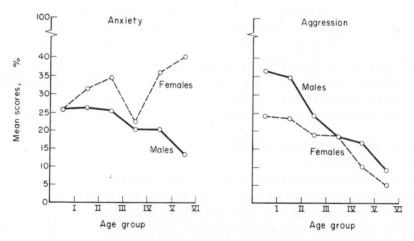

FIG. 17.2. The comparison of male and female scores on anxiety and aggression. (From Parry, 1968)

different age groups. Figure 17.2 gives a comparison of the sexes in terms of the separate traits of aggression and anxiety. Figure 17.3 shows the inter-relationship between the two traits. (Figure 17.2 was obtained by rearranging Parry's original fig. 13.)

It seems that when it comes to driving attitudes, aggression and anxiety go hand in hand for the males—but definitely not for the females. In fact the correlation between each subject's AG and AN scores was:

$$\text{Males} \quad +0·58$$
$$\text{Females} \quad -0·87$$

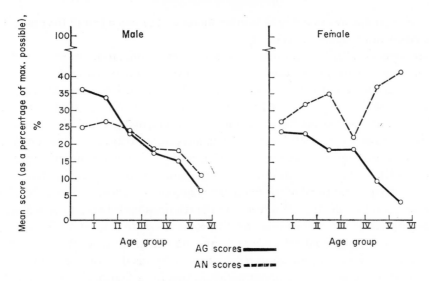

FIG. 17.3. The comparison between anxiety and aggression scores for different age groups. (From Parry, 1968)

It will be noticed that the aggression scores are very high for the 17–24 males, are not much lower for the 24–34 group, and then decrease steadily with age. The female aggression scores are generally lower than the males, but strangely enough closely resemble the male scores for the 44–54 group. The anxiety scores for the females are generally much higher than the males throughout, but the age trends are very different for the two sexes. Whereas they start together, there is a much more marked increase in the female scores up to the 34–44 age group (women with youngish children?); the scores then closely resemble the males for the 44–54 group (women whose children are now a bit older and women with increased driving experience?), and then climb rapidly again for the older groups (women with teenage children and/or at the menopausal ages?)—whereas with the males signs of anxiety continue to wane. (The suppositions of possible causes given in brackets are mine, to which I might add another. Perhaps some of the increased anxiety in the older women may be the accumulative effect of years spent, not only driving themselves, but sitting in the "suicide seat" while the *men* drive—as illustrated by Porterfield's American study (1960) where a high correlation was found between suicide–homicide rates for *males* and fatality rates for *women killed in motor accidents*!)

Figure 17.3 shows the way in which in males the aggression and anxiety decline with age, with the anxiety tending to slightly predominate in the later years. With the females the anxiety always predominates over the aggression, but overwhelmingly so at the older ages. Discussing the very similar scores obtained by the males and females in the 44–54 age group, Parry says that one is entitled to wonder whether there is a coming-together at this age in life of the sexes with regard to their motoring behaviour and attitudes. Closer scrutiny of the individual responses confirmed this, showing a startling similarity in their choice of items. Though extreme aggression and anxiety was not common in either group at this age, there was a tendency for both sexes to admit that they flashed their car lights at others in anger and swore out loud at other motorists; or had a fear of the brakes failing and had frequent thoughts of accidents.

As Parry remarks: "All very strange!" And very interesting, too.

In his chapter "Who causes accidents", Parry says that he has had to rely here on the number of accidents admitted to by the subjects themselves. Unfortunately he does not appear to have set any retrospective time limit, which might mean in effect that an honest 60–70-year-old motorist could have had a lot more accidents, particularly minor ones, to confess to—though it is doubtful whether such a creature exists as an honest motorist of any age (or one without a "windscreen wiper" memory as far as his motoring pecadilloes are concerned!). Parry's accident criterion must, however, be regarded as too weak for anything but the general trend of the findings to have any significance. Nevertheless, some very interesting trends do appear in regard to the relationship between these self-admitted accidents (especially the serious ones which people are hardly likely to forget anyway) and the equally self-admitted evidence of aggression and anxiety. As Parry was particularly interested in the more dangerous risks, he evaluated his data on accidents by using a point score with one point for a minor accident, two for a "serious" accident and three for a "very serious" one and came up with the findings shown in Table 17.4 (to which I have added a section using the serious accidents only and the same point loading).

TABLE 17.4. THE ACCIDENT POINT SCORE FOR GROUPS
DISPLAYING VARIOUS COMBINATIONS OF AGGRESSION
AND ANXIETY (PARRY, 1968)

Combination of traits	Point score per person using all accidents		Point score per person using serious and very serious accidents only	
	Males	Females	Males	Females
High AG and high AN	1·19	0·71	0·59	0·57
High AG and low AN	0·97	0·60	0·41	0·13
Low AG and high AN	0·73	0·58	0·33	0·10
Low AG and low AN	0·62	0·41	0·13	0·06

Parry's remarks with regard to his original figures are:

"It certainly appears that in both male and female samples combinations of High Aggression and High Anxiety are to be taken seriously. ... High Aggression, whether it is combined with High Anxiety or not, is still effective enough in making people more prone to accidents. High Anxiety on the other hand—whether combined with even Low Aggression—is not far behind in its influence on accident liability, so it follows naturally that a combination of Low Aggression and Low Anxiety is the safest in its consequences for contributing to accidents."

In the male groups, Parry's contentions with regard to the *total* accident points are upheld for the *serious* accidents also—except that the low AG and low AN groups show up even better. But some very interesting trends appear to be developing in the female groups. Here, however, the number of serious accidents reported is so small that one cannot take the results at face value—but it certainly looks as though some factors other than chance are operating (one of which could of course be a little judicious "forgetting"). But it is nevertheless interesting to observe that a high AG/high AN combination may be as lethal in females as it is in males! There were, in fact, two very serious accidents in the fourteen high AG/high AN females, whereas there were only four in the similar group of sixty-four males. One could speculate till the cows came home about the possible causes, but the trends look so interesting that this whole question of the diehards among the women offenders is obviously something that should be investigated further. (I remember one day while attending a driver improvement programme in one of the big Motor Vehicle Departments in America, commenting to one of the officials on the hard-bitten look of the women offenders. His reply was: "Yes, we don't get very many women here, but when we do, goddamit, they're worse than the men!")

Certainly Parry's findings do seem to bear out his original hypothesis, which was that people who display aggressive behaviour while driving, or drivers in a state of anxiety, are more liable to have accidents; and that certain combinations of aggression and anxiety are dangerous in motoring, presumably because anxiety to some extent precipitates aggressive behaviour and vice versa. This latter hypothesis about anxiety precipitating aggressive behaviour and vice versa would seem a very reasonable assumption, as people exhibiting high aggression or high anxiety would tend to over-react to any situation created either by their own actions or the actions of others. Certainly the importance of these traits is well substantiated by his findings. And, interestingly enough, although his study is limited to these particular traits, his findings are very much in conformity with those on Eysenck's higher-order personality factors of extraversion and neuroticism.

Space, unfortunately, does not permit of the inclusion here of any of the reports which Parry gives on the actual interviews with drivers who displayed extreme AG or AN scores or an undue number of accidents. These interviews, he said, show only too clearly the way people seem to change when they get behind the wheel of a car, and how behaviour not generally tolerated in everyday life is accepted unquestioningly as being part of motoring. But is the change a fundamental one? Is not this very often the would-be and suppressed self coming out? Parry seems to think so, too, for he quotes a conclusion which we in South Africa reached as a result of analysing the TATs of thousands of drivers (Shaw, 1965)—that as driving apparently offers unique opportunities for delusions of grandeur and anti-social behaviour, many accidents occur not only because people *drive as they live* but because they drive *as they would like to live*. In fact it would be psychologically unsound to expect that people could have two discrete personalities, a "driving" one and an "ordinary" one. What it really amounts to is that a well-integrated person would not change much behind the wheel of a car; it is the poorly integrated person who would find in driving an outlet for his frustrations, his conflicts, and his latent aggressions—and a compensation for his inadequacies.

The interviews which Parry records make spine-chilling reading. He describes the way in which some of the subjects, well spoken and quiet in their mannerisms, neat and tidy in appearance, and to all intents and purposes respectable and law-abiding citizens, casually admitted to having indulged in overtly aggressive driving, like trying to ram another car, or edge a car off the road at high speed. And all with no apparent feelings of guilt—in fact with feelings of complete justification that "some drivers are so dangerous that they have to be taught a lesson". ("The only way people learn is the hard way—you've got to frighten them into changing their ways. Reasoning alone is not much use.")

Just about every one of the offenders interveiwed felt that the fault lay with the other drivers and not with themselves. In fact, as Parry says, they considered themselves to be "the self-appointed judge and jury of motoring behaviour". Some of them were quite prepared to try and take the law into their own hands with acts of open aggression, others resorted to less dangerous behaviour such as swearing at other drivers and making rude signs (though they were highly disapproving of anyone who did the same to them): and both the older and the younger age groups were very prone to blaming the other. The chief offenders causing annoyance to the older drivers appeared to be the younger road-users:

"... no consideration shown."
"... always cutting in and out of traffic."
"... no regard for traffic regulations."
"... always racing," etc.

However, as Parry says, "This lack of affection seems to be mutual", for the opinions expressed by the younger group on the older drivers ran to:

"... creeping along the road."
"... always holding up traffic."
"... never know what they are about to do next."

The middle group, apparently not wishing to identify with either the young or the old group, spread the blame around pretty generally—on everyone but themselves. Whatever they had done was fully justified and they were quite prepared to say that they would do the same again under the same circumstances. As Parry remarks: "Bravado, perhaps, but one does not expect men of thirty or so to indulge in what is, after all, a juvenile show of strength."

Altogether a fascinating book and one well worth reading. Parry says that in his study he has only "scratched" the surface of the whole question of accident-producing attitudes and behaviour. But if so, then it is a very revealing "scratch". And the down-to-earth way in which he presents the whole accident problem will evoke much heartfelt agreement from the layman, who views the antics of what the theorists call the "normal" driver, not from the safe vantage point of some ivory tower of theoretical thinking, but strictly from road level, and who has to contend with the accident problem in all its grisly reality.

Another excellent recent British research study, this time carried out literally at road level (and often at considerable peril to the investigators) is the British Road Research Laboratory's study on the Systematic Observation of Driving Behaviour. This study is still in progress, and the indications are that it may be extended to include several European countries. If this does come about it will be most intriguing, for it will no doubt reveal the presence of rather different attitudes and different patterns of driving behaviour in the various countries. But, in the meantime, the British RRL study is coming to light with some very interesting findings. As yet not much work has been done on the actual personality traits associated with the various types of driving behaviour observed, but the possibility of using projective tests, purely for research purposes, is being explored.

The Systematic Observation of Driving Behaviour developed by the RRL is described in several of their reports (Quenault, RRL Reports 25, 70, 93, 146, 166, 167, 212, 213: 1966–8). The subjects for the research programme are motorists from the British public who voluntarily drive their own cars on a twelve-mile course under normal traffic conditions. They are accompanied by two observers, one seated at the back observing every time the subject uses his (or her) mirror, and one in the front marking off a number of "drive indices" on a check sheet. Although the drivers are told that this is in no way a test, it is felt that most, if not all, do drive as if under test conditions. Any tendency to take risks or indulge in unnecessary manoeuvres is therefore considered to be very significant.

In successive projects a number of drive indices have been used to subdivide the subjects into four categories which Quenault has called Safe (S), Injudicious (I), Dissociated Active (DA), and Dissociated Passive (DP).

The drive indices most often used are:

NA   Near-accidents incurred on the test run.

Ri.   Risks—any action which could lead to an accident or a near-accident.

UM   Unnecessary manoeuvres—any repeated item of behaviour not called for by the situation such as wide passing, following too close, driving too far out or too close to the kerb, or slowing at the approach of oncoming traffic.

L   Lapses—an occasional departure from the subject's usual pattern of driving, such as injudicious practices amounting almost to risks, e.g. taking corners too wide or too fast, or pulling out of stop streets ahead of oncoming traffic; or leaving the signal indicator on after a manoeuvre.

Ag/M   Mirror usage—ratio of mirror usage per manoeuvre.

O/T   Overtaking ratio—ratio of the number of times the subject overtook mechanically propelled vehicles to the number of times he was overtaken.

Quenault describes his four categories as follows:

Safe drivers are described as people who take all the necessary precautions; are well aware of what is going on around them; and who drive with anticipation.

Injudicious drivers are people who indulge in unusual manoeuvres such as wide passing, or a one-handed grip on the steering wheel; with a high incidence of near-accidents (mainly connected with overtaking and passing); and who do not always use their mirrors when needed. Their speeds tend to vary unnecessarily.

Dissociated active drivers are people who tend to be unpredictable and impatient. They indulge in various unusual manoeuvres; have a high incidence of near-accidents (mainly concerned with overtaking); have a low mirror usage; and overtake far more often than they are overtaken. Their speeds tend to be unnecessarily high, both in the restricted and de-restricted zones.

Dissociated passive drivers tend to be patient and stolid and to show a set pattern of driving behaviour, to some extent irrespective of the demands of the situation. They indulge in unusual manoeuvres, this time mostly slowing at the approach of oncoming traffic, or following behind other cars unnecessarily for long periods, positioning themselves incorrectly and often blocking other traffic. They are overtaken far more often than they overtake.

A study of the ages (given in RRL 70) of the subjects in these categories shows that:

The dissociated active (DA) category is predominately a young group with the median age in the 20's. (And, incidentally, nearly all the people in this group admit to at least two accidents.)

The safe (S) group are fairly evenly spread, with the median age in the 30's.

The Injudicious (I) group are also fairly evenly spread, with the median age in the 40's.

The Dissociated Passive (DP) group are predominately an older group with the median age in the 50's.

Quenault (RRL 212) has some very interesting comments to make on this quality of "dissociation" which has been so apparent in these driving tests.

"The word 'dissociated' is used to identify those drivers who appear to drive with a degree of awareness of the relevant presented information which is below that necessary for safe driving. Their mirror usage is either very low or non-existent, they do not appear to notice junctions (to the right and left as they drive up main roads) and they tend to look steadily and rigidly to the front.

"There is some evidence to suggest that these drivers do not see as differentiated an environment as do S drivers. For example, a high proportion of dissociated drivers will treat a roundabout as though it were a piece of straight road and go straight through, looking neither to right nor left.

"To some degree, these drivers lack anticipation and show poor judgement of traffic situations. They may pull out to pass parked vehicles in the face of oncoming traffic, overtake on blind bends and attempt to overtake on a three-lane highway in apparent disregard of the presence of two lanes of oncoming traffic.

"Their lack of full awareness of the situation and of the consequences of their own actions often lead them into near-accident or accident situations from which they are extricated on many occasions by the skill and anticipation of other drivers. When near-accidents do occur, the dissociated driver appears to be far less emotionally affected by the event than the observers (assessed as S drivers)."

The way in which the drive indices are used to sort people into these categories is being constantly refined, but the last detailed account (RRL 146) gives the method illustrated in Fig. 17.4.

This method was used to categorize 100 subjects, 50 of them with convictions for Careless Driving (C) over a previous three-year period, and 50 with no convictions over a

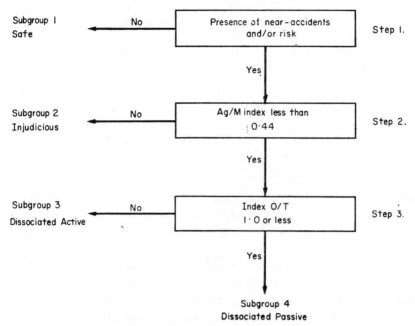

FIG. 17.4. A system for allocating drivers to different categories on the basis of "drive indices". (Quenault RRL 146, 1968)

TABLE 17.5
(From Quenault RRL 146)

Category	C group	R group		C	R
S	18	33	Safe	18	33
I	6	1			
DA	12	4	Unsafe	32	17
DP	14	12			

similar period (R). The report shows the distribution of subjects in the various categories to be as in Table 17.5.

This presentation cannot, however, be accepted as an indication of how well the various categories were able to distinguish between the C (conviction) and R (non-conviction) groups. From other portions of the report it appears that the Ag/M index (mirror usage) was also used to discriminate between the Safe category and the other categories, *and that different cut-off levels were used on the C and R groups* (0·44 for the C Group and 0·31 for the R Group). As this procedure requires preknowledge of whether the subjects have convictions or not before they can still be classified into the various driving categories, it naturally precludes the practical use of this sort of classification system for detecting future offenders.

Had the 0·44 cut-off been used *for both groups* the result would have been as in Table 17.6.

TABLE 17.6
(Derived from Quenault, RRL 146)

Category	C group	R group			C	R
S	18	23		Safe	18	23
I	6	1				
DA	12	9		Unsafe	32	27
DP	14	17				

These results are not nearly so clear-cut as the ones given in the report, so it would appear that this particular method of allocating people to sub-groups has not proved very successful in differentiating the C and R groups, and that the system will need to be further refined.

This does, however, appear to be happening. Now that itemized score sheets are available for large numbers of drivers, the RRL is carrying out a factor analysis which should produce very interesting results. Even a cursory examination of the index scores given in the reports shows that under the present system a good deal of valuable information is being neglected or incorrectly used. The scores show that many people display quite clearly defined *patterns* of driving—such as, for example, a pattern with risks, near accidents, and high and variable speeds coupled with poor mirror usage and poor signalling. This is obviously what Quenault would call a Dissociated Active (DA) driving pattern, but under the present system it can happen that if the overtaking ratio is low (which could be due to the particular traffic conditions encountered) this subject would have to be classified as Dissociated Passive (DP). In addition to overcoming anomalies like this, it seems probable that the factor analysis will show that the present Injudicious (I) category needs to be subdivided. From a brief experiment with personality tests it seems that the I category contains a number of rather different driving types: such as

The competent but immature and reckless type.

The competent but aggressive type.

The temperamental or highly strung type.

A more sophisticated scoring system will therefore probably improve the delineation of the various categories and, at the same time, improve their power to discriminate between the safe and the unsafe risks.

But these are no doubt merely the teething problems of a project which has very considerable potential. For an encouraging aspect of this study is the fact that a systematic driving test like this can be so revealing, *even when the subject knows he is on test*. (A not so encouraging aspect is the fact that Quenault says that some 25% of the people whom the RRL has tested can be considered basically unsafe drivers!)

Another very good study along the same lines, but using very sophisticated equipment (the Ford Drivometer) is Greenshields and Platt's study (1967) on the different driving patterns displayed by beginner drivers, experienced low-accident drivers, and high-accident and high-violator offenders. Here, using an equally sophisticated scoring system based on Multivariate Discrimination Analysis, they have been able to differentiate not only between groups, but between individuals, using drive indices such as accelerator reversals and "macro" and "micro" steering changes. Although the study does not deal with the personality element as such, it illustrates yet again that certain actions performed by a driver, often unnecessary and many of them possibly involuntary, are reliable indicators of his accident potential. As such, the study, like Quenault's, may have a closer tie-up with functions of personality than is immediately apparent.

Hakkinen, for instance, found the same sort of psychomotor malfunctioning in the high-accident offenders among his bus drivers—this time in a laboratory situation. He found that they displayed a noticeable lack of control of motor functions, in the form of hastiness and motor restlessness; they were easily distractable; they had difficulty in choosing the right responses; they were unable to maintain a steady level of performance; and in many of them tension produced a narrowing of perception and sometimes a complete unawareness of certain stimuli. And Hakkinen was sure that many of these impairments of functioning were related to personality defects.

Confirmation of this hypothesis is beginning to appear in our work in South Africa where we are now experimenting with Hakkinen's Ambiguous Situation Test in conjunction with the projective tests. Our findings are still too tentative to warrant any detailed description, but it is already emerging very clearly that nearly all of those whom we fail on the projective tests also put up a very poor performance on the AST, displaying many of the signs of motor disorganization described by Hakkinen. And here the connection with accident involvement is again obvious, as there is now ample evidence to connect failure on the projective tests with a high accident potential.

Still further confirmation comes from the work of Eysenck and many others who have found motor disturbances like these to be accentuated in very emotional or very extroverted people (and particularly in people who are both)—again factors associated with a high accident potential. The highly extroverted people show poor vigilance and concentration; there is much evidence of motor restlessness and their reactions are impulsive and improperly thought out. And, given any repetitive task they cannot keep up a steady performance; instead it is constantly interrupted by involuntary rest pauses, i.e. momentary blackouts. Highly emotional people, on the other hand, tire more easily, display considerable tension, and often show panic reactions under stress. Either they react impulsively, and often irrationally, or they become rigid and unadaptable even to the extent of "freezing" so that they appear incapable of taking any action at all.

But Eysenck's findings (backed by a growing amount of evidence from our own recent work) have a deeper and much more serious connotation as far as accidents are concerned. For they mean that there is a *double* reason why the people who display these sort of psychomotor impairments are bad accident risks. For these are also the people who display the sort of personality traits like carelessness, aggressiveness, and low frustration tolerance which *are likely to involve them in accident-producing situations*. In other words, they are not only the people who are likely to create these situations, *but having created them, they may be even less well equipped than others to handle them.*

This is a very alarming and depressing thought. It is even more so in view of Eysenck's theory (and it can hardly be called a theory any more as supporting evidence for it has come from so many different sources) that both the motor disturbances and the dangerous personality traits *are largely physiological in origin*, which means that they are going to be very hard to eradicate.

There is conclusive evidence, for instance, that emotional instability is associated with an imbalance between the sympathetic and parasympathetic components of the autonomic nervous system.

This portion of the nervous system is, in a sense, part of our heritage from our more primitive ancestors—the part which in animals is designed to gear them up in an emergency for flight or fight, and then restore the *status quo* and later keep the body functioning normally. The sympathetic system is the component which goes into action as soon as an emergency occurs. Aided by adrenalin, which is poured into the bloodstream, it accelerates the heartbeat to make more blood available to the brain and the muscles, and increases the sugar content of the blood to give more energy. It steps up the rate of breathing to provide more oxygen. It dilates the pupils of the eyes to enable the person to see better, and causes sweating of the hands, presumably to enable him to grasp his opponent more easily. However, useful as this sort of reaction may be in the jungle—or even in a bar-room brawl—it is singularly inappropriate in the traffic situation where the fight reaction is only asking for more trouble and flight is almost impossible.

The parasympathetic system is the one which puts a brake on the emergency reactions, sees that they do not become so extreme that they upset the whole bodily equilibrium, and tries to get everything back to normal as soon as possible. If there is an imbalance between the two systems and the emotional reaction is too strong, then the parasympathetic "brakes" will be ineffective, or they will fail altogether, or the measures which the parasympathetic system has to adopt to cope with this over-reaction will, themselves, be deleterious to performance (such as the overproduction of cortisone and allied products to offset the adrenalin which, in themselves, can have side effects like inducing muscle tremor). In the traffic situation this is further complicated by the fact that the dangerous situation *precipitated* by an overactive sympathetic system can develop so quickly and so disastrously that the parasympathetic system has little time to do anything about it.

Whereas the part played by the autonomic nervous system in high emotionality is now very well authenticated, it is still not very clear exactly what part of the nervous system is responsible for extroversion. It is obviously part of the central nervous system, and is thought to be the reticular formation at the base of the brain which processes external stimuli and distributes them to the cortex. In a very extroverted person, instead of this reticular system transmitting the stimuli freely, a sort of resistance is built up (like the resistance in a wire which is too small or thin to take an electrical charge) and the stimuli do not go through at full strength. Extroverts therefore suffer from a sort of "stimulus starvation", which in turn results in a "stimulus hunger"—they want louder noises, more light, more action, more excitement.

This is obviously a most inadequate description of a very complex theory, but the interested reader is referred to any of Eysenck's books on the structure of personality and the biological basis of personality (1960, 1967) and the layman will find a simple and very readable account in Eysenck's Pelican book, *Fact and Fiction in Psychology*, 1964.*

But although the biological basis of personality is still, to a certain extent, a theory, it is nevertheless a very plausible one, and it will be surprising indeed if further research invalidates any of its basic tenets. For there can be little doubt that a personality factor like extroversion, which is so largely an inherited one, must have some form of physiological origin. No one can inherit anything as vague as a "temperament". All one can inherit is a particular form of bodily structure, and it must be this physiological structure which at least *predisposes* the individual toward the particular temperament. What a person becomes in the end will therefore be the result of his environment working on this basic material.

And certainly the idea that extroverts suffer from "stimulus hunger", fits in very well with the traits which these people usually display. As Eysenck (1965) says:

"The typical extrovert is sociable, likes parties, has many friends, needs to have people to talk to, and does not like reading or studying by himself. He craves excitement, takes chances, acts on the spur of the moment, and is generally an impulsive individual. He is fond of practical jokes, always has a ready answer and generally likes change; he is carefree, easy going, optimistic, likes to 'laugh and be merry'. He prefers to keep moving and doing things, tends to be aggressive and loses his temper quickly; his feelings are not kept under tight control and he is not always a reliable person."

When it comes to driving, therefore, the implications of the stimulus hunger of the extrovert are obvious—more irresponsible behaviour, more speed, more courting of danger and disaster.

But to add to these implications there is another aspect of extroversion which can be equally dangerous in the driving situation. Because of the partial blocking of external stimuli, extroverts do not condition so easily and such conditioning as does occur is more easily extinguished. In other words, they do not learn readily by experience and are apt to soon "forget" what they have learned, unless they are constantly re-conditioned (i.e. reminded) by the unpleasant consequences of their actions. They are, in fact, the people who have to "learn their lessons the hard way".

Add to all this, for good measure, the implications of a combination of extroversion and the sort of high emotionality which would trigger off the extroverted behaviour and it is no wonder that this combination is so lethal—especially when it comes to driving.

* A very interesting new development in the work of Eysenck and his wife (1968a) suggests the existence of a third main dimension of personality representing a predisposition to psychotic breakdown. This predisposition appears to be a continuous variable in the normal population, to be quite independent of extroversion, and to be virtually independent of the factor of neuroticism. If these findings are confirmed by further investigation (and confirmation for them appears to be building up) they, too, could have a very important implication for accident work. As yet the research on this factor has been confined to questionnaires. But there can be little doubt that such a tendency to psychotic breakdown must demonstrate itself in observable and measurable psychomotor disturbances. A factor such as this new *P* factor would definitely fill a gap in accident causation not covered by the *E* and *N* factors, and I personally feel very confident that some day a battery of psychomotor tests specifically designed to bring out these three factors, plus an element of intelligence, will prove to be a reliable accident predictor. Certainly the more one studies the research findings of the world and sees how these findings do dovetail into this conceptualization, the more feasible the whole idea becomes.

Here you have all the ingredients for an explosive situation; the irritations to produce the emotionalism; the frustrations to increase the stimulus hunger; the wish to *do* something about it and the lack of self-control to modify or restrain this wish; the tremendous feeling of power and release engendered by the fact that it only requires a little pressure on the accelerator to bring a powerful engine into action. Is it any wonder that such people are accident-prone—particularly as (and this is yet *another* dangerous implication of this very plausible theory) these people *are the very ones who are most likely to drink and on whom drink will have the most dangerous effect as it will make them even more extroverted?**

Fortunately the whole picture is not as black as I have painted it. People are not all highly emotional extroverts—but it would seem from the behaviour of many drivers that there are quite enough of such people on the road to constitute a very real danger. And if both extroversion and emotional instability have a physiological basis, then the difficulties of modifying their behaviour are very fundamental ones.

It appears that there is possibly one way in which this might be achieved, but it seems extremely unlikely that society would ever countenance it—for it involves the use of certain drugs.

Experiments on delinquent children have shown that a drug such as benzedrine has the effect of making these children less psychopathic, i.e. less boisterous and excitable, less argumentative, and apparently better able to exert conscious control over their emotions and activities. But then, on the other hand, many of these particular kinds of drugs are also known to have side effects such as affecting night vision, which preclude their use on drivers without further thorough investigation. In any case one cannot really visualize a state of affairs where society would condone this apparently drastic measure, entailing as it does the whole question of human rights—though, ironically enough, one of the "rights" it would be protecting is the right to use a weapon of destruction which is as lethal as a gun. But even if further research and experimentation can produce drugs with no deleterious side effects *and* establish their value as long-term moderators of behaviour, there seems very little possibility that society would condone their use on traffic offenders —however dangerous the activities of these offenders may be. As far as accident prevention is concerned, this is an approach which is likely, for the moment at least, to remain a purely theoretical one; but is nevertheless a very interesting one, and Eysenck's *Crime and Personality* (1964), in which he applies his theory to the question of criminal behaviour, should provide any curious reader with much food for thought.

For the moment, no doubt, such drastic measures are not within our reach, and it seems that the most we can do with the very bad accident risks is to try and identify them as soon as possible and then try to prevent them from driving by withdrawing their licences. But as many of the personality traits which would bring about their dangerous behaviour are obviously deep-seated ones, in the case of the worst offenders it seems to be purely wishful thinking to continue to pursue a policy where licences are withdrawn for only a short period of time in the hope that something miraculous will take place

---

* Buikhuisen (1968) has recently confirmed that two successive groups of people convicted for drunken driving in Holland have displayed more extreme extroversion and neuroticism than is found in the general Dutch public.

during that period to change this pattern of road behaviour. As Tillmann and Hobbs said way back in 1949, it is not a matter of learning a lesson but rather it is a matter that basic inherent personality characteristics must change before such a person can be considered a safe driver.

The chronic accident offenders therefore present very much the same problem in the driving situation as the unfit, the inept, the handicapped, and the recidivist criminals do in society in general—and to remedy their defects would be just as difficult. But at least it seems very clear that the worst cases should be permanently debarred from driving. It seems equally clear that the driving privileges of many of the lesser but still dangerous offenders should be curtailed to a much greater degree than is at present being done in many parts of the world. Further down the scale of the traffic offenders the picture looks a lot brighter, for, judging only by the effect which even one traffic policeman seems to have on every driver in the vicinity, it appears that the people who display many of the less-pronounced personality faults can be "persuaded" to keep them under control—at least while they are driving—and give vent to them in less dangerous ways.

CHAPTER 18

THE NETWORK OF ACCIDENT CAUSATION (1)

THE prominence given to the personality of the driver in accident research in no way negates the importance of the many other factors which can affect accident potential. In fact every one of the major researchers has stressed the multiplicity of accident causes. The reason why the personality element has received so much attention and has proved to be the best accident predictor is no doubt because of the way in which it can influence or even override so many of the other factors. This is hardly surprising when one considers the wide range of human attributes and functions which the word "personality" covers. According to the definition given by Allport (1952): "Personality is the dynamic organization within the individual of those psychophysical systems that determine his unique adjustments to the environment."

Or, as Eysenck (1965) defined it: "Personality, if it means anything at all, means the relatively permanent, firmly-set patterns of behaviour, habits and tendencies which a person has developed throughout his life on the basis of his heredity and in response to the rewards and punishments which he has received throughout his life."

It is no wonder, therefore, that when one comes to examine the many other factors related to accidents one finds that the effects which they exert on a person's accident potential are so often accentuated or alleviated by his personality.

But the relationship between personality and these other factors works both ways. The personality factor can, in turn, be overridden. For a person to be a safe risk it is usually necessary that he meets certain basic minimum standards on a number of equally important factors such as ability, health, and vision. The reason why it was possible to obtain such a high correlation between personality and accidents, both in Hakkinen's study and the PUTCO study, was because so many of these basic standards were already met. In both studies the subjects were professional drivers, neither very young nor very old, all of them with sufficient ability to pass a training course, all required to meet high standards of physical fitness, and all exposed to the same or equalized traffic conditions. In such controlled groups the effect of many of the non-personality factors would naturally be much more muted than in the general driving public.

The most important of these are considered to be exposure in terms of time and hazard, experience, age, sex, intelligence, driving skill, psychomotor functioning, health, physique, vision, alcohol and drugs, temporary factors—and another factor seldom mentioned in the research literature and virtually never in the theoretical writings—discipline.

Many of these factors are interrelated with one another—and all with the personality factor—so much so that there appears to be little point in discussing them *in vacuo*. As it is, the progress and usefulness of accident research already seems to have been handicapped by a tendency to overlook (or dispute) the necessity for this approach, and to adopt instead a fragmented approach—as can be seen from the many rather sterile attempts which have been made to relate accidents to isolated characteristics. The discussion which follows will therefore be a very general one in which research findings on all the different factors which can affect accident potential are considered in terms of their interrelationship—and in terms of their practical implications.

Exposure

Dealing first with the question of exposure. The effects of different amounts and kinds of exposure on accident potential have been discussed in earlier chapters, especially in connection with the studies of Hakkinen and Coppin and the PUTCO one. But as the latter is one of the few major research projects where strict controls have made it possible to examine the effects of the same exposure on different people, and different exposure on the same people, it might be worth while to re-examine some of the findings here.

Many of these findings, such as the increased accident rates associated with greater exposure and with more difficult and hazardous driving conditions, are merely empirical confirmation of common sense. But the study has supplied evidence on other more controversial aspects of the exposure problem. The first of these is the wide and lasting difference in accident potential displayed by people *exposed to the same conditions*. The study has demonstrated how drivers exposed to the same conditions for periods of six years can display very different individual patterns of accident involvement, ranging all the way from chronic accident repeating to remaining virtually accident-free. It has also shown that many of the chronic repeaters had more accidents *per annum* than the good ones did over the whole six years. Nor were these differences by any means merely due to differences in driving skill or experience—as was shown by the fact that it was possible to predict differential accident rates by means of personality tests alone. It would appear that people react to the same driving conditions in very different ways.

The study has also shown that the *same* people can make radical changes in their way of reacting to the *same* conditions. Figure 15.3 (p. 288) showed how, in groups of drivers exposed for periods of six years to the same driving conditions, the introduction of a new disciplinary measure brought about a sudden and lasting decrease in the number of accidents—in each case some 40% of the group being responsible for the decrease. The skills and the environment remained the same; it was apparently the driving behaviour which changed. But here again the differences between the reactions of one driver and another were apparent. It seems from this and other evidence from many aspects of the PUTCO study that the attitude which a driver adopts to rules and regulations can be more important than the conditions under which he drives—a finding familiar to many traffic officers and transport operators, but nevertheless one which is in sharp contrast to the views of many of the theoretical thinkers on accident causation who maintain that it is the environment which produces the accidents and not the man.

Not that I am suggesting for one moment that the environment is blameless: dangerous road conditions result in Black Spots on any accident map—and there were many such spots on the routes which these PUTCO drivers covered. My contention is that the evidence points to the fact that some people adjust spontaneously to these difficult and dangerous conditions, some can be "persuaded" to do so, some are incapable of doing so, and some will create dangerous conditions *wherever* they drive. Accident rates are undoubtedly influence by exposure factors, but it seems that they are not necessarily dictated by these factors—except in those people who, for some personal reason, are unable to stand the strain of long exposure or unable to adjust to more demanding conditions. (This latter phenomenon has been found in quite a number of the PUTCO drivers, especially the older ones, and an example of this inability to adjust to different conditions was given in Fig. 8.8, p. 130.)

However, interesting as such findings may be, all they really add up to is some research support for the existing accident-prevention policy of the practical officials—the engineers and traffic controllers who are trying to improve driving conditions for the many, and the enforcement officers who are trying to ensure that such improved conditions are not exploited by the few (or the not-so-few, depending on which country one is talking about!).

Nevertheless, it would seem from both Parry (1968) and Willett, in his *Criminal on the Road* (1964), that before the enforcement officers get the degree of support they ask it is not only some of the researchers who will have to be persuaded that the environment is not the cause of most of the trouble. The offending motorist appears only too keen to "pass the buck" whenever he gets a chance. And in doing so he has the backing of many of the motoring associations, who are usually very keen to defend the rights of the poor, maligned motorist: and also someone like the County Surveyor of Dorset who, as Willett says, "considers that the chaotic and unfair road traffic laws combine with archaic and bad highway systems to encourage and even compel drivers to commit offences" (Leeming, 1960). However, Willett's own study on 653 British motorists convicted of serious traffic offences indicates that some of this compulsion might be coming from within the driver himself.

"However, a review of all the cases in this study does not suggest that any one of them should have been dropped or dismissed for the reasons put forward by Leeming. This is not, of course, to say that the offence might not have happened had the road been of a different design, especially if the danger was caused by overtaking in such a way as to imperil oncoming traffic, since incidents of this kind could not occur on a proper dual carriageway. But in every case there was evidence that the offender failed to take precautions that should have been obvious to any motorist, and that he more or less ignored the danger at the time."

No, important as the exposure element is in determining accident and citation rates it appears that it, too, can be overridden by other factors.

Experience

Lack of experience is another factor which is regarded as being responsible for a large proportion of the accidents—especially the accidents of youth. But as it is virtually impossible to determine which comes first, the youth or the inexperience, this chicken-or-the-egg controversy is guaranteed to be with us forever more. As things stand at the moment, it seems that the theorists are inclined to blame the inexperience, while the practical officials tend to blame the youth (and the permissive attitude to youth encouraged by the theorists!). No doubt, as usual, the truth lies somewhere in between; but it seems that any attempt to find out just *where* requires a very detailed analysis, for not only are the age-experience factors inextricably interwoven, but the problem is further complicated by a dozen and one other factors, one of which is that the "where" would be different for each individual. For even the *rate* at which people of any age acquire experience—whether in terms of proficiency or wisdom—will differ from person to person. Individual differences in intelligence and ability will influence the rate of learning even the pure mechanics of driving; individual differences in intelligence and personality will influence the degree to which people will benefit by experience—or even appreciate the need to do so. The matter will be still further complicated by the age at which people start to drive—with the quicker adaptability of the younger beginner-drivers being offset by immaturity of outlook, and the slower adaptability of the older beginner-drivers being compensated for by their more mature judgement. The matter will be even further complicated by the fact that women of all ages are reputed to take longer to acquire proficiency, but are said to acquire discretion quicker. (Whether they are less prone to accidents as a result of these conflicting trends is another question which we can leave for later discussion!)

Some of the many complications of the experience factor are illustrated by a recent British Road Research Laboratory study (Skelly, 1968). In this study questionnaires were sent after one year to all the motorists of Great Britain who had passed their driving licence tests at the first attempt, on one particular day in 1965. (Only 40% of the candidates did pass at the first attempt and one wonders what further complications might have resulted if the second- or third-attempters had also been used.) Of the 1128 drivers who replied, 17% admitted to having been involved in at least one accident during their first year of driving—3% having two or more accidents. As nearly half of these accidents had been reported to the police, Skelly deduces that they were probably quite serious ones involving injury. It would seem from this figure of 17% that the inexperienced driver presents a sizeable problem. But on examining the study one finds that it is extremely difficult to establish, even from the detailed report, just to what extent the inexperience factor was being affected by other factors such as sex or age. For instance, Skelly gives an age analysis of the accident group, which at first sight looks extremely interesting as it shows a U-shaped distribution, with the young age groups, then the older age groups, having the greatest proportion of accident-involved drivers, and the 31–44 group being the best of all. A finding like this would not be surprising, as this age group of beginner drivers should be able to display both adaptability and maturity. But even this seemingly logical explanation becomes *statistically* suspect in view of the fact that there was no sex-split in this analysis, and that the greatest proportion of the female drivers, who by and large had much better accident records than the males, were in this particular age group and could therefore have been largely responsible for its relatively good showing. And even the *logic* would become suspect if the findings of Skelly's study were to be unanalytically compared with a German study on newly qualified drivers where the results were quite different; where the 25–44 age group showed up very badly indeed, and where the younger drivers put up by far the best performance. For not only did the young German drivers start with better records but they remained better over five years. In fact this whole study comes up with results which are often in such conflict with the usual finding that the highest accident rates are associated with youth, that it is well worth investigating in some detail.

Actually it was the totally uncritical acceptance of this concept by so many German officials which first prompted Munsch to undertake the study. Figure 18.1 shows the results of two preliminary investigations carried out by the Medical-Psychological In-

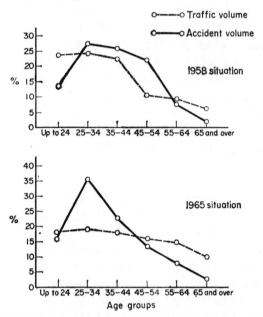

FIG. 18.1. The accident rates, and rates of participation in traffic, for various age groups of German drivers. (From Munsch, 1966)

stitute of Bavaria in 1958 and 1965, where the accident rates of various age groups (irrespective of experience) were compared with their estimated mileage. Munsch says that when the first German study was carried out, the discrepancies between the age trends in Germany and the commonly accepted American accident statistics were at first disregarded.

> "At first, we did not pay much attention to such findings, and considered them only as the occasional exception which, as it is said, only proves the rule. After all, it was not up to us in Germany, where the complete motorisation of traffic came very late, to doubt the findings which our American colleagues had obtained from extensive statistics."

But the second study, carried out in 1965, caused some of the German scientists, at least, to doubt whether the American findings on the preponderance of youthful accidents really did apply to German conditions. In fact, as Munsch says, this strengthened their suspicion "that there must be an important difference in the structure of the totals investigated by us and by the Americans".

This second study also caused them to doubt whether another generally held belief was applicable, namely that "the lesser the degree of maturity in life, the greater the liability to accidents". Munsch felt that probably one of the reasons why the German studies had come up with such different findings was that post-war conditions in Germany were different from those in the United States and had resulted in German middle and higher age groups containing a larger proportion of newly qualified drivers. But he nevertheless felt that a closer study of these abnormal conditions might provide findings which could be of interest to all. He therefore carried out a special study to investigate the *progressive* effects of experience on different age categories, "young persons" up to 24 years of age, "adults" between 25 and 44, and "elderly adults" of 45 and over. The index used was an "incidence" index consisting of accidents and traffic offences, i.e. the number of culpable accidents of all types, plus breaches of traffic regulations (per 100 people). The investigation involved the records up to 1965 of three groups who started

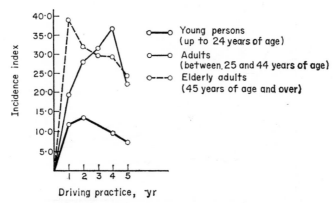

FIG. 18.2. The effects of progressive experience on the index rates (accidents plus traffic offences) for various age groups of German drivers. (From Munsch, 1966)

to drive in 1954, 1957, and 1960; but comment is restricted here to the 1960 group because changes in traffic conditions and in police reporting make the comparison with earlier groups rather confusing. Figure 18.2 shows the progressive "incidence" rates over five years for the 1960 group. All the drivers had driven approximately the same mileage, under very similar conditions, since acquiring their licences. The samples consisted of people sent to the Institute for a variety of reasons; 12% being drivers applying for reinstatement of licence after annulment; 12% being drivers for commercial firms; and 76% being people wanting permits to drive taxis or buses.

The remarkable feature about Fig. 18.2 is the tremendous difference of the trends in the three age groups and the markedly better performance of the young drivers. Munsch feels that this indicates that ability is possibly much more important than maturity and:

"... that only young people and young people alone are the ones who have the possibility of meeting the increasingly exacting demands of traffic today. Everyone who has to deal with the problem of young people and traffic should realise this—not in order to vindicate young people, but in order to avoid drawing wrong conclusions and working on the wrong track."

Unfortunately it seems possible that Munsch does not appreciate that an index based on accidents *plus* traffic offences does not necessarily justify this conclusion regarding the ability element. The index he uses is nearer to a point count on a points enforcement system, and as such represents a factor more like "risk to the community". For this reason it would be interesting to compare his findings with some based on an American points system. Figure 18.3 is derived from some of Coppin's figures (*The California Driver*

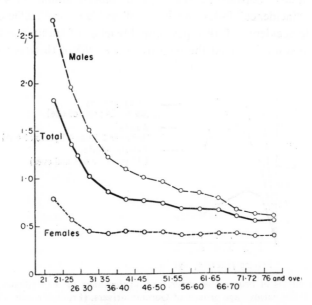

FIG. 18.3. Average number of negligent operator points (+ moving FTAs) by age and sex. (From *The California Driver Record Study*, Part 5, Table 34, June 1965)

Record Study, Part 5, June 1965) and shows the average point count for various age groups for the three-year period 1961–3. It is based on "negligent operator" points plus FTAs (failing to appear at a negligent operator hearing).

    Although the California points count is compiled in a different manner from Munsch's "incidence" index (for instance it allows two points for serious offences), this is hardly likely to account for the dramatic reversal in the order of the "risk to the community" factor in the age groups. As the American graph covers a three-year period, it can be compared with the first three years depicted in Munsch's graph, where the young people showed up so much better than the older ones, and where the average incidence index for these years (calculated from his actual figures) and compared with a rough average for Coppin's point count is:

	Bavaria index per person (over 3 years)	California point count per person (over 3 years)
Young persons	0·38	2·23
Adults	0·81	1·22
Elderly adults	1·04	0·78

There must be some very interesting reasons, both cultural and sociological, to account for these conflicting findings.

Munsch draws several conclusions from the trends shown in his study. One is that there is a special sort of maturity in driving which he calls "traffic maturity", which is akin to a traffic sense. This, he says, is something which develops with growing experience and is obviously independent of physical maturity ("else why should people who are physically mature have such a high incidence rate?"). People of any age apparently need a number of years, and probably about 100,000 km of driving to acquire this traffic sense. (The graphs of the other years showed that it had taken up to seven years for all the age groups to reach a low level of incidence.) Young people, Munsch feels, though they might not be so mature in their attitudes and might be inclined to take risks, are nevertheless able to acquire this traffic sense quicker than older people—which no doubt accounts for their better records. In fact he feels "that the degree of accident proneness of a person to a determining extent is dependent on the degree of experience in the special kind of traffic (years of practice)". However, although prolonged experience usually does bring about a decrease in accident proneness, I think Munsch is getting a little confused on this point as his "incidence" index contains traffic offences as well as accidents. Also, even if the accident element were largely responsible for creating the trends displayed, his contentions are not borne out by his "adult" group, which get progressively *worse* over the first four years despite increasing experience. However, the principle underlying his arguments is a very valid one.

No doubt the very strong emphasis Munsch placed on this question of traffic maturity and traffic sense (which he defines as "no mystical supernatural power but only a special quality of ordinary sense—in the case of trained drivers the sense of sight and feeling") was largely a rather strong reaction on his part against the impact which American accident statistics appear to be having on German policy decisions regarding the education of the driver (an impact apparently very different from that in the United States itself!). Munsch says that as long as everyone in Germany uncritically accepts American findings that the accident problem is largely caused by the young drivers, then everyone will just sit back and say the problem is insoluble.

"As long as this opinion is held, then it is after all the duty of traffic training to give the young people the necessary adult qualities as quickly as possible. However, as it is realized that this is not possible, it is hardly surprising that traffic training finds itself in the cul-de-sac of resignation."

He feels that this emphasis on the immaturity factor is incorrect, and that the emphasis should be on developing ability and traffic sense. He feels that beginner drivers of all ages should be trained *to drive*; that this training should be continued at intervals during the first four years of driving practice; and that this should if necessary be made a legal requirement. The latter is probably a rather Utopian suggestion, but nevertheless one which many driving instructors would, I am sure, support, having had ample experience of the way in which a newly qualified driver can leave a training school a shining example of good driving behaviour, and degenerate unrecognizably in the space of a few short years.

His paper is interesting for a number of reasons. It illustrates once again the difficulties which are created for researchers when findings which are applicable to one country are uncritically imported into another, thus obscuring the need for local research to assess local priorities. But the paper is also interesting because of the stress it places on the need for the type of driver training which is aimed at developing a real traffic sense—the sort of training which is such a prominent feature of the famous American Smith–Cummings Defensive Driving Training System (although it is possible that the originators of this scheme do not appreciate the sheer necessity for this defensive element if one is going to stay alive in the traffic conditions created by Germany's rather aggressive and competitive driving!).

Nevertheless, this whole question of driving experience, and its effect on accident potential, is so essentially a practical issue that it seems the common-sense approach is the one which is likely to get the quickest results. It seems, therefore, that Munsch is quite right in insisting that thorough *training* for beginners should be compulsory. But such training must be flexible enough to allow for individual rates of acquiring driving proficiency, and comprehensive enough to ensure that a new driver knows how to drive in all kinds of traffic and by night as well as by day, and that he, and particularly she, does acquire a traffic sense. There are also many writers who suggest that licence tests should include high-speed driving and the ability to control a skid. (Although I wonder sometimes whether by the time we scientists have finished "improving" the licensing tests, the mortality rate of the licensing examiners will not be so high that no further applicants for the job will be forthcoming—thus defeating the object of the whole scientific exercise!)

The contentious question of whether driver training should be given in the schools, and whether so much emphasis should be placed on driver *education*, is still, it seems, a hot debating point. But as yet the evidence that good driving attitudes can be taught in the classroom is so inconclusive that it would seem preferable for the many countries who cannot afford this very expensive experiment to adopt the policy of first-things-first and concentrate on providing, instead, centralized and properly controlled training centres. (In fact there is still so much controversy on this subject that, rather than accept the findings of any of the studies carried out to date, it might be as well to await the outcome of the major investigations currently being sponsored by the United States National Highway Safety Bureau.)

But despite the importance of competence in traffic there are ample research findings to show that this is not enough to ensure safe driving. It seems that the need is not only for providing experience by means of thorough training, but for some sort of licensing test which will make it possible to pinpoint at least some of the more blatant cases of people whose personality defects and incorrect attitudes are obviously going to make them a potential danger. Parry (1968), in his *Aggression on the Road*, quotes the views of a number of British MOT licensing examiners of which this is one example:

"You will find it extremely difficult to get anyone [i.e. an examiner] to commit himself, but there are many who feel it's time that something was attempted in making the Test a bit more sophisticated. We are aware that many drivers whom we pass as being capable of handling a vehicle are, in fact, unworthy of the licence given them. But it is not our job to assess any undesirable personality characteristics the examinee possesses. Our suspicions are confined to, and remain, personal beliefs and do not enter into the assessment of driving. People you almost know for certain will misuse the driving licence when given it, come here all dressed up, polite, and on their best driving behaviour. You can only assess them as you see them. If you feel very strongly about their manner you may fail them, but you cannot do such a thing indefinitely... the law provides that their 'driving ability' be fairly assessed, and that is all.... I would certainly encourage any modernization of the prescribed test."

Age

From the foregoing section alone, it is obvious that the age factor and its effect on accident rates is another case where it is rather dangerous to attempt to generalize from research findings—especially those applying to different periods of time and different countries. This is particularly so when it comes to assessing the contribution which the various age groups make to the total accident picture. For instance, the proportion of young drivers is now much greater than it used to be and is not necessarily the same in different countries. Even the accident *potential* of the various age groups is not necessarily the same the world over. Munsch's figures alone, compared with those of the United States, show how a combination of different traffic conditions and a different social and economic structure can change the picture from one country to another. For example, the role of the young driver in the American traffic and accident pattern is probably unique. In the first place the minimum licensing age in many other countries is round the 18 mark, whereas in the United States it is usually 16 and can be as low as 14. This means that many young American drivers acquire their driving experience at a relatively young age. Secondly, far more young Americans not only learn to drive early but also have their own cars. (I doubt if there is another country in the world where high schools have a parking problem!) And, by and large, America's attitude to youth is more permissive than elsewhere, which in itself is bound to have its effect on youthful behaviour. On the other hand, however, because the driving behaviour of the American public as a whole is so much more disciplined and controlled than in many other parts of the world, the young American driver is possibly set a better example on the road by his elders. Like chameleons, young people are very quick to adopt the local colour, and there is no denying that the example set by the adult drivers in many of the high-accident-rate countries must make the young drivers feel that they, too, are quite entitled to indulge in a little unbridled self-expression.

It would seem, therefore, that the sort of research findings which would be applicable to the consideration of minimum licensing ages definitely need to be based on local conditions. (Like Coppin's very good study, *The Teen-aged Driver*, which came up with the finding that there was no statistical justification in the California records for raising the minimum age from 16 to 18—a very important finding for the United States, but possibly not exportable to other countries.)

With regard to the relative contribution of the various age groups, Germany is probably by no means the only country where the youthful drivers are not the main offenders. In fact it would appear that the higher a country's accident rate, the greater the contribution of the other age groups—of which the main culprits seem to be the males in the 25–34 range. And here again it is not just a question of lack of training or experience, it appears to be a matter of locally accepted and as yet tolerated standards of driving behaviour (countries like Zambia and South Africa, with two of the highest accident rates in the world, being very good examples). But although these shifts in emphasis definitely do occur, it would appear that the most common trend throughout the world is for the young drivers under 25, and again particularly the young males, to be involved in a very disproportionate number of accidents—particularly fatal accidents and single-car accidents. Apparently, however, even this common finding is *interpreted* in different ways by different people. On the whole, the traffic officials seem to feel that there is no real excuse for this, and that one certainly cannot put all the blame on the inexperience factor. They say that an inexperienced driver should have more sense than to go dicing with death at high speeds. The sociologists, on the other hand, particularly the American sociologists, seem to hold a far more benign view. In a couple of recent papers read at psychological meetings (papers which for some reason have remained unpublished), it has been suggested that: (a) the teenage accident problem in America probably does not exist at all, being largely a statistical mirage, or: (b) even if it does it is because the attitudes of the teenagers are being aggravated by discrimination on the part of the police, the insurance companies, and the "majority group" in general. Why, for instance, argue the sociologists, has no one investigated the effect on the teenage driving behaviour of their being constantly denigrated as dangerous and irresponsible drivers—or what the effect would be on the teenage accident rate if they were relieved of some of their boredom and frustration by being allowed to have private apartments. (One is tempted to ask, *which* accident rate?) However, popular as such views might be with the teenagers themselves, it would appear that they are not shared by a number of people, besides the traffic officials, who are in closer contact with the realities of the accident situation, and who seem to think that sterner measures are called for. In fact the views expressed by Hansson (1966), Director of the Road Safety Research Council of Sweden, at a recent international congress seem to be representative of accident prevention officials in many countries. Summing up a very good paper on the problem of the young driver both in Europe and in the United States, he says that whatever the causes of the problem, measures must be promptly taken to curb it.

"What sort of measures are appropriate? I do not claim to have found the magic formula that will forever eliminate all accidents involving young drivers. But if results are to be achieved, I think it inevitable that at least some of the measures must be made *compulsory*. In other words, it will not suffice merely to offer wider opportunities for traffic education. If such education is to have a lasting effect, it will be necessary in certain cases to require young people to take courses of instruction. For example, those who fail to pass the driving test after a course in an ordinary school of motoring, but who still want to continue their efforts to obtain a driving licence, should be required to attend such a course. This kind of intensified training especially recommends itself for the pupil who shows such poor aptitude for driving that he cannot meet the normal criteria for a licence. In addition—and here I have American examples in mind—a court or other authority should be empowered to enjoin traffic offenders to submit to instruction under penalty of a suspended licence.

"In this connection I suggest that *all* kinds of traffic education stress the importance of a high standard of road ethics. The need for unconditional compliance with traffic rules and the culpability of unprincipled traffic behaviour must be impressed on children in their years at school, and repeated thereafter in schools of motoring and other forms of traffic education. The consequences of traffic violations, such as different kinds of punishment, revocation or suspension of licences, and financial loss, must be hammered home.

"Under the heading of financial consequences, consideration should be given to the substantial raising of insurance premiums. Another is to make provision for payment of accident damages where gross negligence is proved, along the lines of the criminal compensation laws in force in some countries. Traffic accidents are often caused by gross negligence on the part of the driver. Just as often, however, the young driver is unable to pay any share of the damages when the insurance company claims indemnity. In such cases, the young driver should be given the chance to meet his obligation, at least in part. Why not let him earn his way, for instance by requiring him to mend or build roads?

"Some of the surveys I have cited indicate excessive speed to be a common cause of accidents among young drivers. Why not stipulate a maximum speed limit for drivers in the age group who have shown themselves to be most sadly at fault in this respect? France took this step quite recently. For instance, a speed limit of 80 or 90 kilometres per hour could be fixed for drivers up to the age of 21 and for drivers who have held their licences for less than one or two years. Obviously, the enforcement of these rules cannot be 100% effective, yet they should be effective enough to promote greater traffic safety. In any event, a measure along the lines of that taken by France could be worth a trial in other countries.

"A method tried out in the United States is to grade traffic offences according to degrees of gravity. The grading is by points according to a scale. If the points add up to a certain score, the offender is either warned or his licence is suspended for varying lengths of time. Having regard to the kinds of offences that young drivers are prone to commit, we could consider the introduction of a similar scoring system, preferably one that would apply to all licensed drivers regardless of age. If the system were rigidly enforced, it would certainly make drivers more solicitous about their licences and thereby improve self discipline in traffic."

The last paragraph might come as a surprise to many Americans who are probably unaware of the fact that the United States is one of the few countries in the world where such systems operate—and the only one where they have operated for as long as thirty years (a point worth considering in view of America's very low accident rate).

The findings of another continental speaker at the same international congress, Elizabeth Nau (1966) from the Freie Universität of Berlin,* fully endorse the stronger line recommended by Hansson. Nau says that an intensive study of the personality dynamics of German juvenile traffic offenders (made by means of projective tests) had revealed significant psychological, psychiatric, social, and criminological connections.

31% were found to have "trauma of the brain";

22% showed physical retardment;

42% showed retardment in character;

and, "contrary to other publications" (on the intelligence level of juvenile delinquents),

46% had an intellectual capacity below the average.

The examination also revealed that:

43% displayed neurotic behaviour;

68% showed disturbance of character, appearing as defects in "contact" (interpersonal relations);

50% showed a strong desire to show off;

53% displayed a tendency to violence;

37% were inclined to chronic alcoholism.

Nau says that the importance of the subjects' prehistory in relation to future development was revealed by the fact that:

86% had experienced grave educational difficulties;

89% had been involved in a previous criminal trial;

72% had been involved in previous traffic offence cases.

Her contention is that judging the degree of delinquency of juvenile offenders in traffic requires a "specially thorough diagnosis of the personality" and that a psychiatric examination of the individual is, in her experience, "more essential than the exclusive analysis of unlawful behaviour in traffic". And she concludes by saying that measures for the "re-integration" of these juvenile offenders would only prove successful if applied in time, and adapted to the individual.

The need for an imaginative and constructive approach to the problem of young traffic and accident offenders is illustrated by the success of a very interesting experiment which is being carried out in Denver, Colorado. This is a Driver Improvement Clinic with a difference, which was originated by Judge Finesilver. Talking to him about this scheme, which is well known throughout the United States, he told me how it had originated. He said that during a spell as judge in a traffic court, he was very disturbed at the lack of parental control over the young offenders who were constantly appearing before him. Finally, one day, on questioning a teenager had up yet again for speeding, he found that his parents were away, and on asking him how, then, he was going to pay the fine,

* Taken from a short English summary of Nau's original paper.

was told: "Oh, that's OK—when my parents are away they always leave me money for my traffic fines." At that stage the judge decided that something had better be done and founded his driver clinic. Being a hard-headed realist, he made attendance compulsory (either attend or pay a really heavy fine). But instead of preaching "safety"—which, he says, does not even go in one ear and out the other, it never penetrates at all because it creates so much antagonism—he made the whole theme of the course, "driving is a *man's* job and therefore worth doing well". His lecturers and group leaders were people like traffic officials who discussed the technical problems of handling traffic, engineers who discussed power steering and braking distances, and doctors who discussed optical illusions occurring during night driving. He said it was very interesting to see the way in which a teenager's attitude would change as the course progressed. At first he would act patently bored and don't-care, but gradually he would get interested, till finally he could be found in the thick of the discussion disputing some tricky technical point with the lecturer. As Judge Finesilver said to me: "I have some figures on the results of this system, but I am no statistician and no doubt somebody will pick holes in them; but I *can* tell you that these kids very seldom come up before me again in court"—an assessment of practical results vouched for by many other citizens of Denver.

As a constructive idea for combating the accidents of youth, this one seems to me definitely worth thinking about, not only for itself but from the angle of designing safety propaganda. It has always struck me that the conventional DRIVE SAFELY, or KEEP DEATH OFF THE ROADS sort of propaganda is only meaningful to those who probably do not need it anyway. It is preaching to the converted. The ones who need converting will just be antagonized. Here some very different approach is needed. Judge Finesilver's method of creating an image of driving as a highly technical operation requiring not only skill but maturity of judgement is one way. Another apparently effective way is the one described in Barmack and Payne's study on young airmen (1961b) where the approach was to imply that getting involved in accidents was "sick" behaviour, the kind that should be referred to a psychiatrist. Yet another, which seemed to have worked very well, was the one adopted by the RAF during the last war, where a comic strip on the antics of "Pilot Officer Prune", with his low-flying jaunts and aerial acrobatics, was specifically designed to give the impression that, incidentally, Prune was the world's biggest "clot". The market research people are very shrewd in their approach to advertising. Could we not be a little more subtle in our safety propaganda—particularly that directed at the young driver?

The question of the "old" driver (usually taken to represent 65, or even 70 and over) presents a very different problem, and a most enlightening survey is given in the March 1965 issue of *Traffic Digest and Review* published by Northwestern University. The issue is called *The Senior Driver* and contains, for instance, excerpts from the Denver symposium on the same subject (1964); an article by Baker giving a very good overall picture of the problem; one by Judge Finesilver describing a Denver course for older drivers (yes, there is one in Denver for the non-delinquent "senior citizens" too!); one by McFarland and Welford of Cambridge, England (whose study, 1962, on age and skills is so good that it has been magnanimously described by one of today's breed of super-critics as being "very difficult to fault"); a comprehensive article by Kuhlen on the psychological aspect of ageing; and an unusual and very thought-provoking article by Mrs. Benjamin

Borchardt on the humanitarian aspect of discriminatory measures against the older driver. The whole issue is well worth reading as it provides a very balanced assessment and one which, with allowances for different traffic conditions, is applicable anywhere in the world.

Briefly the problem of the older driver seems to come down to the following considerations.

Older drivers do appear to have a disproportionate number of accidents relative to their numbers or their mileage. But their absolute contribution to total accident figures is not anything like that of the younger age groups, and their accidents are different from the accidents of youth. They may have serious consequences, especially for the driver himself, as older people are less resistant to injury—but they are accidents of omission rather than commission e.g. incorrect turning or failing to keep a proper lookout, rather than speeding or following too close.

The causes of these accidents seem to be very much a question of mental, physical, and psychophysical deterioration. Reactions become slower; movements are slower and less well co-ordinated; health and vision deteriorate—particularly night vision and the ability to see while exposed to the glare of oncoming headlights, or to readjust afterwards. Older drivers have difficulty in assessing and computerizing a complex traffic situation, and are inclined to concentrate on certain aspects only. Their short-term memory can let them down, for although they have registered some pertinent factor, this can later slip their minds. In other words the older driver is really not one hundred per cent fit to cope with the demands of driving in heavy traffic, especially freeway driving.

But then in most cases the older drivers fully realize this and limit their driving accordingly—and their whole approach to driving is far more cautious and realistic than many of the younger people. This very caution is, however, often claimed to be a source of great irritation to other drivers, and many times the older people are blamed for causing accidents ("they *will* dither along in the middle of the road", etc.). Personally I feel that this line of argument is rather overplayed. The keenest propounders of this philosophy are usually those whose personality make-up is such that they themselves are inherently doubtful accident risks (as we know by experience from the TATs written by such people *and* their actual accident records—a finding substantiated by Parry's study). The older driver does sometimes constitute a danger, but apparently this danger is not anything like as great as it is made out to be by them as "do'th protest too much".

Ageing is, in any case, a very individual matter, and all the suggestions put forward by experienced authorities in *The Senior Driver* stress the importance of this. They say it would be very unwise to lay down any stipulated maximum age limits. (For acquiring new licences, yes—but for retaining them, no.) The personal record of each individual is a far better indication of need for action than any prescribed age standard. Kerrick, Director of the Driver Licence Program for the AAMVA (the body which advises the various American States on co-ordinating driver policy) relates his experience with the introduction in one State of a law requiring re-examination every two years of all drivers 70 years of age or over.

"Very often such re-examinations resulted in issuance of special licences restricting the licensee to daylight driving for example, or to limited areas of operation.

"However, in many cases, we found that such restrictions represented the only type of driving the licensee wanted to do in the first place. In other words, he had begun to limit his own driving long before it was done officially. The law was repealed, and we returned to requiring re-examination in individual cases on a 'for cause' basis.

"About 20 states now operate on this basis. This means that if the licensing agency is notified that a licensee appears to be failing to a point affecting his ability to drive safely and he is not voluntarily making the necessary adjustments, that licensee may be called in for re-examination. In other states such re-examinations are requested only on a basis of questionable driving records."

The general feeling of the various writers seems to be that it is both unfair and unwise to discriminate against the older drivers. Though their records should be very carefully watched in view of the age factor, they should be called up for re-examination only as often as is customary for *all* drivers to be called up and, like the other drivers, only when the record warrants it—but here medical evidence might be necessary which, wherever possible, should be obtained through the driver himself and from his or her personal doctor. The very deleterious effect on the older driver of a policy such as demanding frequent licence renewal can be illustrated by a brief extract from Mrs. Borchardt's very interesting contribution.

"The mobility of the older person is essential for now he has time on his hands. His isolation is a waste of human resources and a cost in human suffering.

"Urban life makes living more difficult for the aged. The corner grocer, the butcher, the family doctor, and even the family itself are disappearing or out of reach. The psychological effects of driving an automobile are potent and far-reaching. It is no wonder that the older person feels his independence is gone and that his very life is over when his license is not renewed.

"Failure to pass the test for a renewal of a driver's license is one of the most traumatic of experiences. The injury to the ego is so deep that many do not recover. One can observe a physical and mental deterioration take place. Depression and pessimism are obvious. Men seem to be more affected than women for various reasons.

"With the senior citizens, the renewal of a driver's license is a very big issue. The entire business is fraught with and accompanied by mental anguish. From renewal to renewal, it occupies the mind consciously and unconsciously. The individual loses confidence with so much at stake, and with the departure of assurance often will not even try to take the test. This should not be!"

This is an important point and one which could be overlooked in framing legislation regarding driving licences. Withdrawing or withholding driving privileges from the young is usually only a temporary measure. And although the sociologists might argue that the young also have egos which might be damaged by such a measure, I think most people would maintain that these young egos can stand up to quite a bit of hammering, and often benefit considerably thereby. In any case, either time or effort on the part of the young driver can restore his driving privileges. But with the older driver the decision is permanent. Once a licence is taken away, it is taken away for good. The necessity for such a radical destruction of morale should, wherever possible, be avoided.

The Sex Factor

The question of whether men or women are the better accident risks is really of academic interest only. There is so much speculation on the subject, and so many contrary views are held, that no sweeping decisions regarding licensing regulations, or for that matter insurance premiums, are ever likely to be based on the sex factor alone.* Even decisions on the advisability of employing women as professional drivers are more likely to be made on the basis of practical considerations than on any "global" statistics. However, since the subject of women drivers is such a perennial talking point, it might be interesting to see what the scientific literature has to offer on the subject (which in view of the number of women drivers on the roads today is singularly little).

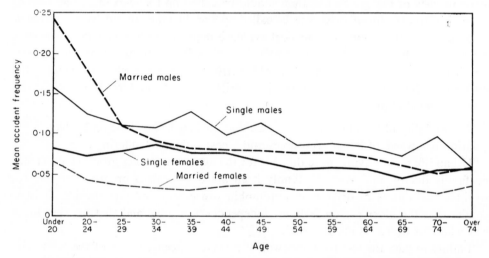

Fig. 18.4. Mean accident frequency by age, sex, and marital status, among Californian drivers for 1962. (From *The California Driver Record Study*, Part 5, Chart 2, 1965)

Statistically speaking, the findings from all over the world seem to follow very much the same pattern, with the absolute accident rate of the men—especially for serious accidents—very much higher than that of the women. Figure 18.4, for instance, shows one of Coppin's very interesting findings on the relative accident rates per driver population in California for males and females, both married and single. (And here the discrepancy between the male/female rate is not the only point which invites speculation. What, for example, accounts for the highest accident rate of all being that of the *married* teenage males? Are these the shotgun-marriage types, perhaps?)

Opinions on the reasons for the generally higher accident rates of males seem to be sharply divided. One school of thought maintains that they are merely a reflection of the much higher mileage that the men cover—often estimated as being from three to five times that of the women, and undertaken under much more difficult traffic conditions. But the other school maintains that this is not just a matter of exposure, and that there

* Though it is interesting to note that the Royal Automobile Association of Britain is currently granting a 10% reduction in premiums to women drivers.

are fundamental differences in the accident potential of the two sexes; that as far as trivial accidents of the scratch and scrape type are concerned, the relative rates of the women would probably be as high if not higher than those of the men; but that women are better risks with regard to the serious, fatal and injury-producing accidents; and that they are less inclined to commit serious traffic offences.

Neither school of thought has the backing of very much experimental evidence. There is, for instance, very little experimental evidence available of what would happen if males and females were exposed to exactly the same driving conditions. This is mainly because exposure can only be controlled amongst professional drivers. But one study, carried out by Viteles (1932), though rather outdated as far as traffic conditions are concerned, does appear to support the second school. This study involved men and women taxi drivers whose conditions of work were very much the same, except that the women, though driving equal hours, were not employed on night shift—a reservation which would hardly account for the marked differences in accident history. A comparison of the number of accidents of all kinds per $1000 revenue showed that the women had nearly *three times as many* accidents as the men. On the other hand, their accident repair cost index was less, the proportion of accidents followed by claims was less, and the cost of these claims was roughly *one-third* of that of the men. It would be interesting to see what findings are emerging in cities like Los Angeles where there are a number of women bus drivers.

Other figures from Coppin's studies on the general driving public (CDRS, Reports 2 and 5) although with no control over exposure, do seem to follow the same sort of trend. Coppin gives the following male/female ratios for his sample of 148,000 California drivers for the three-year period 1961–3. The accidents he refers to are the more serious "reportable" ones involving death, injury, or property damage in excess of $100. (In California the ratio of male to female licensed drivers is as low as 1·4 to 1.)

Total reportable accidents—Ratio 2:1.

Accidents not reported to the California Highway Patrol (presumably mostly property damage accidents)—Ratio rather less than 2:1.

CHP accidents (usually those involving death or injury)—Ratio rather more than 2:1.

Total moving violations—Ratio ±3:1.

Double count violations (reckless driving, driving under suspension)—Ratio ±6·5:1.

People called in for re-examination after an accident involving a fatality—Ratio ±5·4:1.

Proportion of the respective driving population classified as Negligent Operators—±13:1.

Willett (1964) reports that in Britain the male/female ratio for motoring offences for 1959 was 21 to 1; and that in a random sample of 653 motoring offences less than 9% were women—the proportion being from 0% to 2% for the more serious categories (causing death, driving dangerously, and driving while disqualified). The category with the highest representation of women was "failing to stop or report an accident" (usually not a serious one) which, Willett says, may be a panic reaction, possibly not unrelated to what their husbands would have to say on the matter!

Findings similar to these can be found in many parts of the world, and Van der Burgh (1966) gives a very interesting résumé of findings from a number of different countries, all of which follow much the same trends as those of Coppin and Willett.

On psychological grounds alone, women should really be less dangerous accident risks than men as the personality characteristics which are regarded as being the essentially "male" ones are also those commonly found in accident offenders. In fact Willett suggests that to a man the car itself may be a symbol of masculinity and power, and that many male drivers identify driving cautiously and at a moderate pace with feminity. He mentions a remark made to him by a senior police officer that "most men think that criticism of their driving is criticism of their manliness".

Van der Burgh, from his personal experience of psychological tests and road tests on drivers in Holland, goes even further and maintains that the unfair opinion which men usually hold of women drivers is often based on the behaviour of those women drivers who are still inexperienced, and that with equal experience they are actually better and safer drivers. No doubt the epithet "better" would be bitterly disputed, but in view at least of women's lesser accident involvement, Van der Burgh's description of the characteristics on which he classes them as "safer" drivers is very interesting. The following is a translation of some of his findings (1966).

"1. *Consideration*. The woman is always concerned with saving the life and the health of others. This for example prevents her from driving hard and from breaking traffic regulations. In general women obey traffic rules not because, like men, they are afraid that breaking the rules will result in a fine, but because they have the insight to realize that by these means their own lives and those of fellow road users are made safe. Men are fonder of speeding than women, they are more enterprising, more energetic, more daring by nature, and these characteristics contribute to making men fanatical and sometimes irresponsible motorists. Often men will deliberately look for obstacles in traffic when there are none, simply because they would like to be conquerors. The man is more careless, not so concerned about running into danger, and is inclined to overestimate himself (especially if he is still unmarried) with regard to his ability to control traffic situations. Men have a far lesser degree of self-criticism than women.

"2. *Outlook*. Whereas men are inclined to regard a fellow road user impersonally as just another motor car, women are more realistic and more inclined to see the person. In situations where contact with people is important, e.g. in traffic, the women are more aware of drivers as people, and adjust more easily than the men.

"3. *Maturity*. The female motorist at every age and in all respects is more mature than the man; she is more balanced, more self-controlled and more considerate than the man. Consequently she shows a greater sense of responsibility, especially between the age of 18–24 years. This is the age when male motorists are especially characterized by lack of consideration, exhibitionism, speeding, and a general tendency to behave in an immature and delinquent fashion."

On behalf of all women drivers, everywhere, I would like to say, "Thank you, Dr. Van der Burgh. It is not very often that we get any kind words bestowed on us!"

Other writers have mentioned other characteristics which could make women safer risks, such as the fact that they are much more conforming, they are less extroverted, and on the whole they drink less. In my opinion they are also much more impressionable and far more affected by the accidents they have witnessed. In other words, as a result of the present accident situation, many of them are just plain scared. The younger ones are often very loath to say so and put up a brave front (while their parents sit up half the night worrying more about the driving of their daughter's "date" than his evil intentions). But the older married ones have less reason to hide their true feelings and are possibly the motive force behind much of the growing demand for more action and less talk.

However, sufficient unto the day of this eternal controversy on men versus women drivers. In any case it is not a question where personal opinions or even scientific findings are likely to be of much practical help. It is even doubtful whether anything which science can come up with in the way of an erudite exposition on the differences between men and women with regard to innate driving skill will be news to any experienced driving instructor. He has probably learned all there is to know on the subject long ago—the hard way!

Medical Factors

The medical aspect of accident involvement is a subject which is beyond the scope of a book of this nature, except to say that most countries seem to feel that there is a lot of hit-and-miss about the medical aspects of licensing policies, and that there is an urgent need for more research into the effects which various diseases have on accident potential. As witness of this are the number of recent national and international conferences on the subject; and a study of the proceedings of these conferences would probably be the easiest way for any interested reader to obtain up-to-date knowledge. Proceedings of meetings like this are usually available from the body which organized the conference on payment of quite a small fee. In addition, bodies like the World Health Organization are also able to supply information. A few suggestions along these lines are:

U.S.A., 1964. *The Proceedings of the National Conference on Medical Aspects of Driver Safety and Driver Licensing.* (Information: U.S. Public Health Dept.)

Europe, 1965. Report on a Symposium on Epilepsy. *Epilepsy and Driving Licences*; obtainable from the British Epilepsy Association, 3–6 Alfred Place, London, WC 1. (Price 2s. 6d.)

WHO, 1956. *Guiding Principles in the Medical Examination of Applicants for Motor Vehicle Driving Permits,* WHO/Accid. Prevent./56/1. REV. 2.

Europe, 1966. *The Proceedings of the Second Congress of the International Association for Accident and Traffic Medicine.* Information RESO Congress Service, Klara N Kyrkogata 31, Fack, Stockholm, Sweden.

U.S.A., 1959. *Medical Guide to Physicians in Determining Fitness to Drive a Motor Vehicle,* published by the American Medical Association.

WHO, 1962. *Road Traffic Accidents* by L. G. NORMAN, Public Health Papers, No. 12, WHO, Geneva.

On the question of the practical application of medical findings it would seem that there is no real indication of what proportion of accidents are caused by severe illness. However, the fact that those few figures which are available only seem to point to about 1 in 1000 accidents being caused by the onset of severe illness, seems unimportant, as the many side effects of ill health must, of necessity, lower a person's driving efficiency. Most big transport operators insist on routine medical examinations for their drivers, looking, *inter alia*, for the following conditions: loss of weight, obesity, hypertension, cardiac conditions, diabetes, neurological conditions, epilepsy, enlarged liver or liver damage. Where there is good driver management the driver's medical record and accident record are always viewed together. Any pronounced medical symptoms call for an investigation of his accident record; or, vice versa, any deterioration in the accident record calls for a special medical examination. Figure 18.5 is an illustration of what can happen when this sort of liaison does not exist. It shows the progressive days between the accidents of a bus driver whose medical file revealed that he had suffered from hypertension for many

FIG. 18.5. The time-intervals between the accidents of a driver suffering from hypertension

years and whose accident record showed repeated bouts of accident involvement, both before and during periods of treatment.

With regard to the general public it seems that although opinions appear to be changing on some issues (as, for instance, a much more lenient view being taken these days about the licensing of controlled epileptics), nevertheless, there is a feeling that the medical aspect of accident involvement is very much overlooked in many countries. There seems to be a good deal of support for the policy of a medical examination being made obligatory for certain classes of driver such as:

For all new applicants for a driver's licence (and particularly those over 50).

Before the licensee resumes driving after an accident where he was hospitalized for injuries received, or where a medical condition was thought to be a factor in the accident itself.

After treatment in a mental hospital, or conviction for being under the influence of drink or drugs, or for being a narcotics addict.

When someone has declared the driver to be very incompetent (presumably with good substantiating evidence).

The medical and psychiatric aspects of accident involvement are obviously fields of research which require urgent attention. And here one of the questions which will have to be thrashed out is the ethical one of whether the confidential nature of the doctor–patient relationship is more important than the question of risk to the community.

Vision

Defective vision is possibly one of the most important—and neglected—of all the factors contributing to accident potential, if only for the reason that so many people are affected by it. Many different studies have shown that as much as 20% of a driving population have visual defects which would affect driving efficiency. (When a thorough system of eye-testing was first introduced in PUTCO, we found that 25% of the currently employed drivers needed corrective spectacles and 3% were irredeemable. A number of the 25% had quite good accident records, but all admitted that before they got their spectacles driving had been a tremendous strain.) For although it is possible to compensate to a certain degree for poor vision by more careful driving, or by manoeuvres like screwing up one's eyes to get a better focus, the danger is obvious and the fatigue inevitable. And yet, despite the obvious implications of defective vision, the licensing eye-tests are often primitive in the extreme. There is even a good deal of pseudo-scientific talk about the poor accident-predicting powers of vision tests because of the low correlation coefficients obtained between such tests and various accident criteria.

It is up to the eye specialists to say exactly what form sight-screening tests for licensing examinations should take; but ideally, it seems, they should really cover not only visual acuity but muscular balance, stereopsis, colour vision, field of vision, night vision, and recovery from glare. There is still a good deal of discussion on the question of stereopsis (depth perception), as it is felt that defects in static stereopsis can be overcome in the driving situation because the driver has a number of other means by which to judge depth relations (such as perspective diminution). But, nevertheless, if better stereoscopic vision can be achieved by improving focusing difficulties, this will obviously help matters all round. Colour vision is another disputed point, and it certainly does seem that colour-blind drivers manage very well. But here again it appears that a common-sense precaution would be to insist that any indication of colour blindness should be investigated to see just how bad it is—an investigation which should include a thorough road test. Hulbert's work (1958) on dynamic vision has also brought up some very interesting points; but despite the importance of dynamic vision the problem seems to be a practical one of the elaborate and expensive equipment needed for the examination. The other aspects can be quickly covered by using an instrument such as the Bausch and Lomb Ortho-Rater (1944). (Over fifteen years, and involving thousands of eye tests, we have found that the Ortho-Rater gives a very reliable indication of whether a person needs to be referred to an optician.)

Restricted range of vision can be tested with a number of simple instruments, but I personally doubt its importance (unless accompanied by other defects) as most drivers are constantly moving their heads. It seems possible that some of Quenault's Dissociated Passive Drivers (see p. 364), with their unnaturally rigid posture, would be more tunnel-visioned than a normal driver with this particular visual defect.

The problem of night vision is one which I feel might be more effectively dealt with by spot-checks on accident offenders and some much-needed public propaganda than by licensing tests. Undoubtedly failing a licence test on this score would bring this deficiency to the driver's attention; but the practical difficulties of providing every licensing office with a darkroom might be insurmountable. In any case it is something which can develop insidiously with age, or over a matter of months from a deficiency of vitamin A. But as people are often unaware of the causes of night-driving difficulties and their remedies, I think this subject is worth a brief discussion. (Here I am relying for most of my facts on Jayle *et al.*'s excellent book *Night Vision*, 1950.)

To understand what happens in night vision one needs to appreciate that the retina of the eye contains two kinds of structures known as rods and cones. The cones react to daylight and "see" in colour; the rods to night light and "see" in greys and blacks. Because the rods are centred at the back of the eye there is a gap where the optic nerve enters, resulting in a blind spot straight ahead (and consequent difficulties for one-eyed people). Night vision is measured in terms of a "threshold", i.e. the amount of illumination necessary before objects can be discerned. As far as the driver with defective night vision is concerned, this means that he might have difficulty in seeing an objec at a distance and only faintly lit up by his headlights—an important consideration when driving at speed. The danger increases if the driver also suffers from an impaired rate of recovery from glare. (The two are not strictly synonymous, but often go together.) We all know that if we are dazzled by a bright light it takes a little while before we can see again. What happens here is that the light decomposes a photosensitive pigment in the retina of the eye, the visual purple. This chemical decomposes in light and regenerates again in darkness. Two of the substances necessary for this regeneration are oxygen and vitamin A, and therefore conditions which result in a deficiency of either will result in slower adaptation (e.g. high altitudes or smoking or alcohol for oxygen, and dietary deficiencies or liver complaints for vitamin A). The rate of the decomposition depends on the duration of the light and its intensity, and it depends also on the amount of exposure to light which the subject has undergone during the previous day. For instance, someone who has been exposed to brilliant sunlight on a beach for $4\frac{1}{2}$ hours (with no sun-glasses) will need $1\frac{1}{2}$ times the time to adapt to darkness as the ordinary person would.

Vitamin A, which is one of the necessities for regenerating the visual purple, is stored in the liver. Any condition which retards this storage means that the reserves in the liver are soon used up. Examples of conditions which retard this storage are:

> An imbalanced diet.
> Pregnancy, especially in the later months.
> Chronic liver diseases, such as cirrhosis or chronic jaundice.
> Menopause in women, especially in cases with severe disturbances.
> Tuberculosis.
> Diabetes (which can also result in blind spots on the eye).
> Concussion.
> Certain psychiatric conditions such as hysteria.

A deficiency of vitamin A can produce, if it is bad enough, permanent damage to the eyes.

In connection with dietary deficiency, Jayle mentions some very interesting findings, and says that during the last war, prisoners of war and inmates of concentration camps often suffered from acute night blindness. But the civilian population was also affected.

Table 18.1 shows the mean level of vitamin A in the blood serum, and the night vision threshold, for groups of subjects in France during the war years.

TABLE 18.1. A COMPARATIVE STUDY OF THE MEAN VALUES OF DARK ADAPTATION THRESHOLD AND THE LEVEL OF VITAMIN A IN THE BLOOD SERUM DURING THE COURSE OF THE WAR YEARS (EXTRACTED FROM TABLE VIII FROM JAYLE, 1950. DERIVED FROM CHEVALLIER)

Years	Mean threshold level	Level of vitamin A in the blood serum
1939–40	13	90
1941	31	40
1942	43	39
1943	39	44
1945	63	25
1946	52	30

In this connection it is interesting to note that among Negro subjects (in whom the transition to urban living often results in faulty dietary habits) we have, in the PUTCO unit, found a 20% failure rate on the glare-adaptation tests. This has been rectified, for as long as the men are in the driving school, by administering vitamin A; but we have difficulty in following this up because the drivers are scattered in different areas. The actual dosage and duration of treatment needs further investigation. Jayle says you can administer large doses of vitamin A without deleterious effects, but other authorities seem to disagree.

Jayle also has a number of suggestions to make regarding night driving, of which these are some of the most important:

Wear dark glasses during the day, especially when exposed to very bright illumination.

Do not wear tinted glasses or dark glasses at night, as these impair acuity.

Cut down on smoking during night driving.

Avoid too much alcohol. A little alcohol appears to improve night vision but too much definitely impairs it.

Do not fast, and if necessary suck glucose sweets.

Remember that fatigue impairs both night vision and adaptation.

Never look directly at the headlights of oncoming cars—watch the side of the road instead (or shut one eye).

Keep your eyes constantly moving. If you have any difficulty seeing something clearly, look a little to the side instead of directly at it. If there is only one light ahead, like a cycle light, it may seem to wander around in the most bewildering way. Give it a wide berth because you may not be able to place it correctly.

Remember that age impairs night vision as older people adapt more slowly, they need more illumination to see by, and they have a marked narrowing of their field of vision at night. (Depressing as it may be, Jayle says that these effects begin to appear in the 40's and become much more pronounced after 50.)

Remember that twilight is the most dangerous time for driving because (a) acuity falls so rapidly at this stage, and (b) the eye is not yet fully adapted to the lesser illumination.

CHAPTER 19

THE NETWORK OF ACCIDENT CAUSATION (2)

Intelligence

There seems to have been some rather circumscribed thinking on the relationship between accidents and intelligence, most of it once again fostered by the low coefficients obtained when intelligence scores are correlated with accident rates. However, this relationship cannot be expected to be a linear one, and need not obscure what is essentially a logical issue. A moron or an imbecile is obviously incapable of handling a vehicle in modern traffic, and the sooner he is spotted the better. Here the German approach has a great deal to recommend it. Anyone suspected of being a dangerous risk on account of intellectual impairment (among other things) can be referred to one of the Federal Medical Psychological Institutes for further examination. He can be referred by a medical officer as the result of an accident injury, or by the judiciary, or the traffic police, or the licensing officials. This seems to be an advance on even most American States which operate driver clinics, for as far as my personal knowledge goes I think these clinics are usually only entitled to deal with convicted traffic offenders or drivers injured in accidents. But even the German procedure is far from ideal, as the sieve is not anything like fine enough. Very often a person has to exhibit gross intellectual impairment before he can be prohibited from driving. But at least it is very much a step in the right direction, and one which could no doubt be improved upon when the judiciary, for instance, can be persuaded to take a more realistic view of the accident situation.

The effect which superior intelligence, on the other hand, can exert on accident potential, has seldom really been examined except in connection with bus drivers. Here it is only to be expected that superior intelligence is not necessarily an asset and may even be a liability. Someone with a very active mind would find full-time driving rather monotonous, which could easily result in inattention or even frustration, depending on the individual personality make-up. But on this question it would be most unwise to generalize from full-time drivers to the general public as there is little reason to suspect that superior intelligence, in itself, would affect the accident potential of the ordinary motorist one way or another—except perhaps in the case of the traditional absent-minded professor!

With regard to the wide intermediate range it is very apparent that adequate intelligence is not anything like sufficient to ensure safe driving, as personality defects can provide the impetus for the most irrational driving behaviour. But, on the other hand, there can be equally little doubt that a lower than average level of intelligence would accentuate these defects. It is dangerous enough for a driver's behaviour to be motivated by selfishness, or exhibitionism, or irritability; it is doubly dangerous when he lacks the intelligence to assess the possible consequences of his actions or is unable to think quickly and decisively in a crisis. Undoubtedly one of the reasons for the good predicting power of Hakkinen's psychomotor personality tests was because they contained an appreciable element of intelligence. And in the equally successful PUTCO project intelligence was one of the factors assessed by means of the projective tests; and the effect which intelligence (or lack thereof) would exert on a person's driving behaviour was always taken into consideration when predicting his accident potential. Even in the diagram of the coloured dots given in Fig. 16.5 (p. 330), arbitrarily shifting the dots at right angles to the diagonal axis on the basis of a five-point intelligence rating was found to slightly improve the accuracy of the classification. However, as the factor analysis, based on correlation coefficients, provided no *empirical* justification for this action, this method of obtaining a better correlation remains a speculative one. But no doubt ways and means can be found for overcoming what seems at this stage to be purely a technical difficulty in presenting the evidence. The same applies to the whole question of furnishing empirical evidence of the degree to which varying levels of intelligence do affect accident potential. For here again the problem is further complicated by the fact that much would depend on the personality make-up of the individual—which is no doubt why the best results achieved to date have been where each person was assessed on his individual merits and as a functioning whole.

Nevertheless, such experimental difficulties should not debar the inclusion, in the meantime, of some element of intelligence testing in any practical measure designed to pick out the really sub-standard driver. But here it would possibly be desirable to use tests which incorporated a strong performance element, and which did not correlate too highly with formal educational standards. A certain degree of literacy is essential for reading traffic signs and understanding the basic requirements of the various highway codes, but many of the standard IQ tests are thought to penalize those people who have not had the benefit of formal school education. Again, a thorny question and one which I prefer to leave to the specialists in this field. But at least I can confidently say that over many years of selecting drivers with widely divergent standards of education, our South African unit has found that covering the intelligence angle by means of psychomotor tests does, in fact, sift the *trainable* from the *untrainable* driver very satisfactorily. And the question of detecting sub-standard proficiency is, after all, one of the basic steps for the prevention of accidents.

Driving Ability and Psychomotor Functions

The relationship between accidents, driving ability, and psychomotor functions, embracing as it does all the psychophysical aspects of driving, is obviously a very complex one, and here again there is an urgent need for further research. However, this is definitely no field for the tyro accident researcher, as this sort of research needs to be carried out by people with specialized training and experience, and should be carried out in collaboration with the engineers. No doubt one of the reasons why Hakkinen's contribution in this field has been so outstanding is because he was a qualified engineer before he took up psychology. The work of Cumming (1964) in Melbourne, Australia, on the capabilities of the driver, is another example of this dual qualification. But although such a combination in one researcher is rare, much can still be achieved by collaboration between the two professions.

As far as many aspects of this sort of work are concerned I must candidly admit that I am completely out of my depth, and can therefore give only a very sketchy and inadequate account of it. In any case it would require a book all of its own. But the importance of its implications for determining accident potential are so apparent that one hopes that such a book will soon be written. For this is no question of interesting but possibly inapplicable theory. A person driving a modern high-powered car under the sort of conditions so often found on the world's not-so-modern streets and highways, is very often being taxed to the limit of his capabilities, if not beyond them. Science must come to his rescue before he, too, becomes yet another accident statistic. It is essential that more be known about the capabilities of the average driver, and particularly the limits of his capabilities. Then perhaps both the highway and the vehicle can be further adapted to suit the driver, thereby relieving some of the strain engendered by the fact that at the moment he is the one who is expected to make so many of the adjustments.

But there are other ways in which a greater knowledge of psychomotor functions (and malfunctions) can be put to practical use. Research has already shown that certain kinds of psychomotor malfunctioning are attributable to innate characteristics within the individual which, in turn, are closely related to his accident potential. In the last chapter I discussed some of these in relation to various aspects of personality. The more we can learn about these malfunctionings the better, for we could then apply this knowledge not only to devising instrumented tests for selecting professional drivers or examining traffic offenders, but we could possibly apply this knowledge to the development of standardized road driving tests both for the issue and renewal of driving licences. One of the weaknesses of any ordinary road test has always been that the person under test is naturally on his best behaviour. Unless he is very stupid or mentally disturbed he is hardly likely to indulge in blatantly reckless or aggressive driving—even if this is exactly what he will do the moment he is out of the examiner's sight. But research has already indicated that many potentially dangerous drivers display certain *involuntary* psychomotor malfunctions which can be spotted by a trained observer in a systematic driving test—or by means of certain equipment fitted to the vehicle. The work of Quenault, and Greenshields and Platt, described in the last chapter, are excellent illustrations. If driving examiners could not only be trained to use these or similar methods, but also be *permitted* to use them, then it might be possible to detect many a dangerous accident risk before he becomes involved in his almost inevitable accident. I say "permitted" because there are a great many experienced driving examiners who are already fully aware of many of these danger signals but are not permitted to use this awareness as justification for failing a prospective driver. What science is now slowly revealing in the laboratory, they have long ago encountered in actual practice. And even if they know very little of the scientific intricacies of psychomotor malfunctioning they can spot many of the related danger signals a mile off—but without official backing there is nothing they can do about it, as was illustrated by the views of one of the British MOT testers quoted in the section on experience.

Temporary Factors

How important are the temporary factors, the transient ones like fatigue, or one drink too many, or momentary irritability or frustration or inattention? How big a role do they play in the accident situation? The answer to that question would, it seems, be very dependent on the psychological orientation of the respondent. A behaviourist-specifist would say the temporary factors are all-important, and that accidents are largely the result of one of these temporary states coinciding with some hazardous situation in the environment. The generalist psychologist, on the other hand, would say, no, he disagrees: undoubtedly a number of accidents are due to temporary factors but not as many as one might think—for the reason that many of the factors are not all that temporary. Very often what could be taken as the mood of the moment, so to speak, is actually more a reflection of the individual's make-up, e.g. the drinking, the irritability or inattention, and sometimes even the fatigue.

The generalist way of thinking seems to be more in line with research findings. In fact it would appear that what we, in our South African unit, have been predicting all along by means of projective personality tests is the repeated emergence of many seemingly temporary states, and their influence in determining differential accident rates. Here, when a potential driver is considered to be a bad risk because, for example, we consider him to be sour and frustrated and bad-tempered, we do not expect him to act (or drive) like this all the time. He would very soon be dead if he did. But what we do expect (and what apparently does happen, judging by the accuracy of the forecasts) is that these temperamental failings are very near the surface and that it takes very little encouragement from the environment (traffic conditions or other people's driving behaviour for instance) to trigger them off. The same applies to a "temporary" factor like drink. The reasons which make some people drink more than others, and react very differently to alcohol, are by no means fortuitous. Even fatigue can be a very individual matter.

All in all it would seem that a number of these so-called temporary factors (which are also often included in the so-called chance factors) are really neither. Man is, on the whole, master of his own destiny—in traffic and elsewhere. Not completely so, unfortunately, but sufficiently so to account for the pronounced differences between one driver and another.

Malfetti (1960) expressed this very well on a paper on youth:

"Adolescent or not, *no driver is immune to accident-producing behavior*. Driving is a highly complex task, and driver behavior at any moment is a point on a continuum, with safe driving at one end and unsafe driving at the other.

"The initial position and stability of this point are determined largely by the characteristics of the individual; physical characteristics such as age, size and sex; physiological characteristics such as perceptual abilities and response capacities; intellectual characteristics; personality characteristics; social characteristics like role in society; and educational characteristics like appreciation of the traffic problem.

"In constant interaction with these characteristics are hundreds of forces, usually transient, which relate to a particular driving episode. Examples, to name a few, are the behavior of the other drivers, presence of police, signals, flow of traffic, condition of highway and the vehicle. Also where the driver is going, how much time he has, how he is feeling, what he is thinking about, looking at, and listening to.

"As these forces interact with one another, and with the characteristics of the individual, they may move the behavior point toward one end of the continuum. The position of the point differs markedly among individuals. For some drivers it is so close to unsafe that a minimum of negative forces make for danger. For others, the point is far enough from the unsafe end that even considerable negative forces might not be harmful.

"The position of the point may also vary markedly in a person from day to day (he may be unusually fatigued or emotionally upset), or even from moment to moment when strong forces like alcohol or drugs are operative.

"*But most important is the understanding that for each driver, the unsafe end of the continuum can be reached. When sufficient negative forces are in play no one is immune.*"

As Malfetti said, his theory parallels a phenomenon in chemistry. Elements and compounds have different melting points. From element to element and compound to compound the range of melting points is great, yet there is not a known substance that will not melt or decompose under sufficient heat. A very nice simile. It is only a pity that so many drivers seem to regard their accidents as the result of somebody else putting this kind of heat on *them*!

Two of the factors usually classed as temporary ones which deserve special attention are alcohol and fatigue. The latter is rather beyond the scope of this book, but two good sources of information are McFarland and Moseley's *Human Factors* (1954) and a more recent paper by Brown (1967) of the Medical Research Council, England, "Car driving and fatigue". In this paper Brown summarizes the findings of his own considerable work on the subject and also those of other studies.

He says that there are a number of studies where continuous driving of from six to ten hours' duration has been accompanied by impaired performance on a variety of *laboratory* tests. But, in contrast, there are a number of other studies involving actual road tests where the skill of the driver appears to have remained unimpaired and where, for instance, as in one Harvard study, the number of near-miss incidents was at its greatest during the *first* two hours of a continuous driving test. Also in one of his own studies, where a police driver assessed the subject's actual driving before and after seven hours at the wheel, and found that there was a decrease in perceptual ability and courtesy to other road users rather than in skill involving the use of the vehicle controls. He feels that there are a number of reasons for these somewhat conflicting results, one of which is that laboratory tests are measuring fatigue associated with bodily rhythms as apart from *driver* fatigue. In the actual driving task the standard of performance can be maintained because driving demands the handling of information which is usually within the total capacity of most people, so that they can maintain a satisfactory level of performance even under the stress of natural fatigue. However, as he points out, natural fatigue must not be overlooked as this imposes strains which will evidence themselves in a number of ways, such as a slowing of reaction time, impaired recovery from glare, and the narrowing of the span of attention. Drivers should be on the lookout for these signs, and professional drivers should not be asked to cope beyond regular hours and beyond their individual capacity.

Another possible explanation is given by Bena, Hoskovec and Stikar (1968), from Czechoslovakia, who suggest that as the motivation of fear of accidents is missing in laboratory tests, a subject, tired after a long journey, might adopt a more relaxed attitude to these tests than he would on the road. Bena also stresses the dangers of prolonged driving and gives a graph showing that accident rates increase gradually from eight up to twelve hours' continuous driving, but increase rapidly after that. Interviews with a number of long-service truck drivers revealed that 42% of them had had at least one near-accident due to falling asleep; 20% had experienced visual delusions, 13% amnesia, 7% visual delusions and amnesia, and 5% had experienced all the phenomena.

Brown also mentions that the fatigue associated with bodily rhythms differs in different people, as is shown by the work of Colquhoun and Corcoran (1964) which suggests that introverts are more alert in the morning and extroverts in the afternoon (i.e. to paraphrase this finding, introverts are inclined to start the day at peak performance and go off, while extroverts warm up as the day—and often the night—progresses). Personally I feel here that temperament affects the issue to a considerable degree, and in a number of different ways. Nervous people, for instance, are often very tense at the beginning of a journey and their performance improves after a while as, with familiarity of the situation, their tension wears off. On the other hand, neurotic or highly emotional people are inclined to tire more easily because of the strains which they impose upon themselves.

Brown also offers an interesting physiological explanation, derived from the work of a number of researchers, for a phenomenon often mentioned in the accident literature, namely that driver fatigue can be increased as the result of monotonous as well as over-demanding driving conditions.

"...arousal, or alertness, is maintained by impulses sent to the cortex via the brain stem reticular formation. The assumption is that these impulses depolarize the cells of the cortex so that they are more readily fired by sensory stimulation. Frequent sensory stimulation maintains a high level of arousal, thus facilitating perception, coordination and other higher brain mechanisms, which are inhibited when sensory input is lacking."

A finding like this would mean that extroverts would tire more easily under conditions of monotonous driving and introverts under demanding conditions. Bena et al. also report that most of the near accidents and the visual delusions and amnesia experienced by their truck drivers occurred on straight highways rather than winding roads; and also occurred more often among people who under normal circumstances tired quickly, especially when doing mental work (again an extrovert characteristic).

Fatigue, therefore, is likely to be a very individual matter—but nevertheless an important factor which should not be overlooked. No doubt it is one of the "iceberg" factors where its contribution to the accident problem is probably greater than it would appear from the statistical findings alone. Brown, for instance, gives figures which show that less than 1% of the fatal accidents recorded in Britain in 1965 were attributed to driver fatigue. But this must be a gross underestimate of the manner in which it contributes to other causes.

Alcohol and Drugs

The importance of alcohol in road accidents has long been recognized, but it is only recently that it has begun to receive the attention it warrants. Irrespective of all the underlying origins of the problem, alcohol by itself is probably one of the most, if not the most important single factor in precipitating accidents. In the United States nearly half of the fatal accidents are reputed to involve drinking drivers. No doubt the contribution which it makes to total accident rates will vary from one country to another. Drinking habits vary among different nationalities; and, in addition, the contribution of alcohol-related accidents is likely to be relatively less in those countries where poor driving skills or more undisciplined driving behaviour result in a higher accident rate for the population as a whole. But this is no criterion by which to gauge its importance. It merely means that in those countries alcohol is only one of many unsolved problems!

Anyone concerned with accident research and prevention would wish to study the subject in detail, and some good sources of information would be:

1968, U.S.A. *Alcohol and Highway Safety*. The recent comprehensive report to Congress from the US Dept. of Transport. Available from the Superintendent of Documents, US Govt. Printing Office, Washington, DC 20402. Current price 50 cents.

1962, England. *The Proceedings of the Third International Conference on Alcohol and Road Traffic*, possibly still available from the British Medical Association, Tavistock Square, London, WC 1.

1965, U.S.A. *Alcohol and Traffic Accidents*. Proceedings of the 4th International Conference on Alcohol and Road Traffic, Dec. 1965. Available from Indiana University, Bloomington, USA. Price approximately $7.

1964, U.S.A. *Accident Research*, Haddon, Suchman & Klein.

Here I am only going to present some of the research findings which could be of interest to the general reader and which are pertinent to the question of identifying and controlling the drinking driver.

The effects of alcohol are determined chiefly by the concentration of alcohol in the brain, which in turn is determined directly by the concentration in the blood. Several factors influence the rate at which it enters the blood—the rate at which it is ingested, the amount, whether it is taken neat or diluted, and whether accompanied or preceded by food. Food taken beforehand has the effect of markedly holding down the rate of absorption, as do, to a lesser extent, drinks such as beer and sweet wines which contain carbohydrates. Blood–alcohol concentration can be measured by sampling a person's blood, breath, or urine. It is measured for scientific purposes in terms of the weight of alcohol in a given volume of blood—or, more precisely, as milligrams per 100 millilitres (mg/100 ml). The public are more used to seeing alcohol concentrations described in terms of % per weight, which is the same thing said in a different way. The three measurements most often encountered are 50, 100, or 150 ml—or 0·05, 0·10, or 0·15%.

The particular blood–alcohol level which is regarded as grounds for action varies tremendously from one country to another. For example:

0·05 % is the level at which action can be taken in countries like Sweden and Norway, where the penalties for the first offence are licence revocation for $1\frac{1}{2}$ years and a mandatory jail sentence of 20 days. (A third offence leads to a substantial sentence and lifetime revocation.)

0·08 % is Britain's level for action under the new breathalyser legislation. People can be pulled up for traffic offences and suspected drunkenness, and 0·08 % earns at least a fine and a year's licence suspension.

0·10 % and 0·15 % are the usual levels needed in the U.S.A; but a conviction for drunken driving can be so difficult to get that often only the obvious cases are arrested—and 0·15 % is way above the level at which people become affected.*

In many countries there is no accepted standard for measuring the blood–alcohol concentration, and a driver has to be patently drunk and incapable before a conviction will hold.

Because of its effect on the brain, alcohol brings about marked personality changes and therefore marked changes in behaviour. Contrary to general belief it is not a stimulant. It is (most confusingly) classified as a depressant because one of its main effects is to act as a depressant on the stimulus-conveying reticular formation of the central nervous system. As a result it makes people more extroverted—more boisterous, restless, and impulsive, more confident, and often more aggressive and more emotionally uncontrolled, i.e. more psychopathic. (As Eysenck (1965) says, the classic definition of conscience is "that which is soluble in alcohol".) And this whole shift of personality is towards the accident-producing characteristics.

In a mature, well-controlled, well-balanced and integrated person, and someone who is in any case rather an introvert, this sort of personality change will not matter very much as he has a long way to go before, personality-wise, he will become a bad accident risk. But with an immature or poorly controlled extrovert (who in addition is just the sort of person who is likely to drink) the danger limit is very close. And the behaviour of a number of the in-betweens will be shifted by alcohol into the more dangerous sphere. From the point of view of personality alone, alcohol makes more people liable to behave in an accident-producing fashion, and makes those who were liable in the first instance even more so.

But in addition to making people more likely to precipitate dangerous situations, it makes them far less capable of handling them. Alcohol brings about a progressive deterioration in the faculties and skills needed for driving. Up to blood concentrations of 0·04 or 0·05 %, most people seem to have enough reserve ability to be able to compensate. But beyond this "threshold" (which varies among individuals) the deleterious effects increase very quickly indeed—more or less on a logarithmic progression. There is a rapidly progressive deterioration in judgement, co-ordination, comprehension, span of attention, and particularly vision (where apart from blurring or double vision there is a marked deterioration in night vision and recovery from glare). And, in addition, alcohol

* 1969. Three very interesting articles on drinking–driving legislation in Britain, the U.S.A. and Scandinavia (by Dempster, Hricko and Wagner respectively) have recently appeared in the Aug. and Dec. 1969 issues of *Traffic Digest and Review*.

will also induce involuntary rest pauses, i.e. uncontrollable momentary black-outs of which the person is probably not even aware. Cohen and Hensel (1958) also demonstrated with a group of experienced bus drivers that after a few drinks they were far less capable of carrying out a manoeuvre although they were progressively more sure that it could be done.

And just to add to the complexities and dangers is the question of the hitherto almost unexplored perils of combining alcohol with any of the drugs and patent medicines which are injected or swallowed in such quantities today. By themselves many of these medicaments are known to have side effects which could impair driving, and combined as they so often are with alcohol, the effects must often be disastrous. In fact Steyn (1967), at a meeting of the South African Association for the Advancement of Science, said that it was his considered opinion that the combined effects of alcohol and the many hundreds of drugs on the market today are the greatest single cause of traffic accidents. He mentions that certain *depressant* drugs such as sleeping pills and sedatives have an accentuating effect on alcohol symptoms; and even without the alcohol, *stimulants* of the nervous system such as pep-pills, benzedrine, drinamyl, dexedrine, etc., can be dangerous, as the stimulation only lasts two or three hours, and is usually followed by drowsiness. (In any case, many of these drugs are often used as "boosters" to cope with a hangover.) These drugs, he says, are widely used as stimulants, and many of them, such as the amphetamines and closely related drugs like preludin, are extensively used as appetite-suppressants for losing weight.

It appears from various authors that even the caffeine in coffee can have undesirable side effects and is reputed to impair motor functioning. The proverbial sobering-up effect of black coffee apparently has its snags. It does somewhat slow down the rate of absorption of alcohol into the blood stream and, being a CNS–stimulant, will possibly offset the CNS–depressant effect of the alcohol to a certain degree; but it apparently also delays its excretion. So drinking black coffee is not going to beat the breathalyser—especially as 5 oz of vodka, for instance, taken on an empty stomach, will produce a blood–alcohol level which can remain above the danger level for up to *five hours*. Smoking will also tend to maintain a high alcohol content as it impedes the supply of oxygen to the blood—plus having side effects of its own like narrowing and blurring of vision.

Steyn, in his paper, goes on to mention a number of medicaments which even by themselves, could have dangerous side effects, such as impaired vision, or dizziness, or shock. He instances chloromycetin, neomycin, streptomycin, atropine, penicillin, cortisone, the sulphonamides, and pain-or fever-reducing drugs. He also feels that even "the pill" in its various versions could affect driving, some of the side effects being nervous exhaustion, headaches, spasm, emotional reactions, and various types and degrees of personality disturbance, e.g. depressive states or a sense of irresponsibility. He says that very highly intelligent females are susceptible to such disturbances induced by "the pill".

And then there are the addictive drugs like morphine, heroin, marijuana (dagga), cocaine, pethadine, methadon, whose dangers are blatantly obvious. He mentions that the use of addictive drugs, and also nutmeg, convolvulus (morning glory), mescaline, LSD, benzedrine, as well as the sniffing of petrol, glue, benzene, chloroform, ether, and other volatile liquids, are being increasingly used at social gatherings, especially those of youth. And here one wonders just how many of the terrible accidents which happen, where whole carloads of young people are killed, occur while the driver is in a state of doped euphoria.*

In fact when one seriously considers the effects which drink, or drugs (even the mild ones), or worse a combination of both, can have on driving behaviour and driving skills, there can be little doubt that these effects must permeate the accident situation to a degree which extends far beyond that revealed by the usual accident statistics, where in only the more obvious cases are these factors listed as even contributory causes.

To my mind, however, this consideration, vitally important as it is, should not be allowed to distract attention from other sources of accident-producing behaviour—as it appears to be doing to a certain extent in America. Undoubtedly alcohol alone accentuates many personal defects, particularly psychomotor and personality defects, thus increasing the danger; but it must not be overlooked that very often it is acting on people who, even when stone cold sober, are already bad accident risks. This has been very clearly demonstrated in studies like Hakkinen's and the South African studies, where the subjects were all bus drivers, i.e. groups where signs of drink are carefully watched for, and where the penalty for drunken driving is usually instant dismissal. These groups, even without the influence of alcohol, displayed every shade of accident potential, and included many people who were, inherently, very bad risks indeed.

Nor should it be overlooked that certain personality defects *predispose* people to drink, especially to excess; just as certain personality attributes predispose people to refrain from drinking or moderate their drinking—especially when they have to drive afterwards—or even to take extra care when they know they have had one more than is safe. The sort of people who drink to excess are very often the sociopathic people. Many of them have histories of social problems, often aggravated by drink but also indicative of deeper social and personal maladjustment—psychopathic tendencies, criminality, violence, sex offences, drugs, marital problems, and psychiatric problems. Many of them display a lack of balance and control. And many of them are the sort of inadequate people who would look for a way of bolstering their egos and escaping from an underlying sense of failure; from the anxiety, the frustrations, the hostilities, and the paranoid feelings created by their personal inadequacies. As such, many of them could be detected before they ever became involved in a serious or fatal drink-related accident. They could be detected by a good personality test, or on the basis of their socially deviant, if not criminal histories. And many of them, in any case, have a history of previous accidents and traffic offences.

Nor should preoccupation with the dangerous effects of drink blind us to the fact that there are different kinds of drinkers who need to be approached in very different ways. There is not much point in haranguing the public in general with the sort of propaganda which is directed at the excessive drinker—who would in any case be impervious to it. The effect of this on the more moderate (even if still dangerous) social drinker could be a negative one. Alcohol is so much a part of our present-day social life that too much of this sort of anti-drink propaganda is more likely to make people deaf to such appeals,

* Note, 1969. Some very interesting work on drugs and driving is currently being carried out by Crancer and his associates in the Department of Motor Vehicles of the State of Washington.

or even actively antagonistic to them. They do not want to be branded as drunken drivers—nor for that matter do they want to be preached at.

Borkenstein, who is not only an experienced researcher on all aspects of alcohol and accidents (his big study, 1964, is one of the best known and he is still very active in this research field) but also has the practical background of twenty years of driver law enforcement, deals with this whole question in quite one of the best papers I have ever encountered on this subject—"A realistic approach to drinking and driving" (*Traffic Safety*, 1967). He classifies the vast population who not only drink but also drive into five categories, and outlines the sort of differential approach needed to get through to them and to influence them in the right direction.

(1) The responsible, moderate social drinkers who seldom if ever reach their impairment threshold. These people should not only be left alone, but should be given public recognition for their moderation and not antagonized.

(2) The social drinkers who usually display moderation but can occasionally slip up. They constitute a definite problem but not by any means the entire problem; and here enforcement is likely to have a possibly unseen but nevertheless potent effect.

(3) The compulsive sociopathic drinkers. These are not just the people who drive immediately after they have had too much to drink, but the people who drink too much all the time. "They drink in the morning. They drink at noon. They drink all day long. And these people drive. When they drive they are the high-risk drivers all the time they are driving because of the alcohol they have in their systems most of the time." These people, he says, are the most dangerous group of offenders. "They are identifiable ahead of time because of the medical implications. In addition, if we have the right kind of driver licensing examinations or investigations, after drivers have been convicted twice for driving under the influence, they can be grounded and their driver licenses policed pending therapy. These people are not going to be stopped by public relations. They are not going to be stopped by enforcement. They are compulsive repeaters." These, he says, are the sort of people who, under the present system, come up time and again before the enforcement officers.

(4) The people who have just learnt to drive and who have not yet reached an adequate level of skill, and in whom even small amounts of alcohol can break down their driving ability very rapidly. This group should be tackled by admonition during driver training and enforcement if they refuse to comply.

(5) The group of drivers who are extremely sensitive to alcohol. They should never drink. These people are comparatively rare but identifying them by their behaviour is not too difficult. This group includes many aged drivers.

These five groups, Borkenstein says, require differential handling and also differential propaganda. Would not it be better, he says, to inform rather than evangelize?

"If every driver were to know that a blood reading below ·04 or ·05 per cent is relatively harmless, we might have as many people drinking, but fewer people exceeding the critical level when driving. In this way we would accomplish our goal. We're not after the drinking driver, *per se*. We're after the *driver who drinks too much*, and in this way increases his likelihood of becoming involved in an accident."

Borkenstein goes on to say:

"We know through our own studies, socio-economic, ethnic and others, that the more responsible an individual he is, the less likely he is to become involved in an arrest for driving under the influence. His sense of responsibility—to his family, to his community, to his church, to his business—has an inhibiting effect. He doesn't want the shame, the reputation tear-down. It is the irresponsible individual who has nothing to lose who has the greatest tendency to take chances."

He suggests that in our approach to the problem of alcohol and accidents we are inclined to get our perspective rather distorted. In measuring the size of the problem we are looking at the fatal and serious accident offenders only, which are the tail-end of a distribution of people who are potential offenders but have not yet met to the point of friction that will precipitate accidents. He compares this with considering the safety regulations at Kennedy Airport in terms of the very few crashes which have actually occurred there, thereby neglecting all the information which can be obtained from other phenomena such as near misses.

But he also makes another point, namely that we can easily underestimate the effects of our control measures if we measure them only by the negligible effect which they appear to have on the recidivist drinker and the recidivist accident offender. This sort of thinking and the arguments based on this sort of thinking create a defeatist attitude which is as harmful as it is misleading.

In fact this sort of defeatist thinking seems to aggravate Borkenstein beyond words. In the discussion which followed this paper (which was delivered at one of the United States National Safety Council's conferences) one speaker from the floor remarked that suspending or revoking licences does not appear to prevent people from driving. "This is perfectly clear from the records of driver registry services. People will go on driving whether or not their licences have been lifted." Borkenstein's reply to this was:

"This argument makes me explode, because I think that this is a great blind spot in law enforcement manpower allocation. Here you have an identified high-accident group. Controlling this group is hitting at the very heart of our problem. In my opinion a significant part of traffic-policing manpower should be allocated to supervising suspended and revoked driver licenses. This should be one of the most rewarding parts of law enforcement—to see to it that people who have identified themselves by their actions and by their problems as accident drivers be considered a target group. And yet there is very little of this being done. I agree with you, but at the same time it indicates surrender to remark resignedly, 'Well, people go ahead and drive anyhow'. I think it's an indictment of our traffic law-enforcement process."

Asked whether alcoholism, which must be considered a disease, could be got at by punishment, Borkenstein replied: "But this is not punishment. I don't think of this as punishment. If therapy is successful for these drivers, then restore their licenses, just as in many places epileptics who are under medication are licensed as long as they stick to their medication. It's the same type of situation."

Altogether a very good paper, forthright, constructive and very down to earth—and, what is more, containing arguments which are applicable to not only the drinking driver but to the accident problem as a whole, particularly the interpretation of accident statistics.

Social Factors and Discipline

"Social" is such an all-embracing—and vague—psychological term that a discussion on the effects which social factors would have on accidents could range all the way from considering driving as a form of social interaction, to examining the accident rates of different socio-economic classes or races, to trying to assess the broad effects from country to country of different social mores and socially accepted modes of driving behaviour. In the course of this book a number of these aspects have been discussed in connection with various studies. Here I think the need is to examine their practical implications. These, I feel, fall under two main headings—the individual and the community as a whole.

That driving is a form of social interaction is something no one disputes, but the role which the individual plays in this interaction is a more contentious matter and one which again seems to boil down to the perennial psychological and sociological controversy of which comes first in importance—the man (and his heredity) or the environment. Are the higher accident rates associated with socio-economic groups or racial groups the result of the conditions in which these people live, or of the people themselves? To my way of thinking (and here I am not thinking from any psychological orientation but purely in terms of the practical implications) the continuation of this sort of controversy is merely going to impede the whole progress of accident prevention. I do not mean that either side of the controversy should stage an unconditional surrender. They can continue to hammer out their differences of opinion in academic journals till either one side or the other wins, or until (we hope) they reach some form of compromise. What I mean is that from the purely practical angle of accident prevention, *does it matter?* Does it matter that numerous studies have shown that higher accident rates are associated with "deprived" areas? And though "race" is almost a forbidden word in modern parlance— so much so that studies on racial differences are virtually taboo—such studies would inevitably show that certain races would, on the whole, have higher accident rates than others because different races exhibit different personality characteristics. But, again, the question remains, *does this matter?* In every country in the world driving is part of the social interaction of various socio-economic groups—and in most countries of various racial groups as well. Whether these socio-economic or racial factors result in deprivation of any kind for any section of the community is neither here nor there as far *as the accident problem is concerned.* The old plea, "I'm depraved because I'm deprived" does not alter the fact that any resultant dangerous or inept driving is going to lead to accidents—in many of which it is the "deprived" themselves, or their fellows, who are going to be the main victims. Here I think one must consider priorities in terms of the accident situation alone. No doubt removing social discrimination or slums would have beneficial effects, but the progress on either front is not exactly conspicuous—and not for the lack of trying either. But in the meantime, from the point of view of driver control it is the *individual* who counts. *Can* he drive and *how does he drive?* Does he, as an individual, need more training and/or does he need more discipline? These are the questions we need to worry about—the others, accident-wise, are side issues, their greatest contribution being to highlight areas in which attention to the training or the disciplinary factor is needed.

As far as the community as a whole is concerned, the social element of accident prevention has several important practical implications. The first is that different social conditions in different countries will produce different driving conditions, which means in turn that each country needs to determine its own priorities and not blindly follow the thinking or the policy of any other country. But there is another aspect which in a sense is international, and that is the attitude which the community—any community—adopts towards driving offences and the treatment of the driving offender. Although this attitude does vary to a certain extent from one country to another, the tendency throughout the world is to adopt a very much more lenient attitude toward driving offenders than towards the petty criminal or even the more dangerous criminal. Killing someone with a gun is regarded as murder, or at best manslaughter, and it takes a good lawyer to produce acceptable evidence of extenuating circumstances or to obtain any mitigation of sentence. Killing someone with a car is very often something else altogether—it is bad luck—it isn't intentional—it could happen to anyone. Extenuating circumstances are the rule rather than the exception, and the sentences imposed are ridiculously light by comparison. Willett (1964) quotes a case of a man who was *convicted* of causing death by dangerous driving and fined exactly £1. And Preston (Cohen and Preston, 1968) who says that every traffic offence is made to sound like a hard-luck story, describes a case where the fine for two civic "crimes" (receiving 5 gallons of petrol) was £20; whereas the same person's fine for *fifteen* previous traffic offences, many of them serious ones, added up to £19. 10s. And another case where a young man was fined £10 for stealing chocolates, but 10s. for driving without lights. "The £10 fine must have been effective as he was never caught stealing chocolates again, but he later had an accident and once more he was without lights."

It seems that the treatment meted out to the "criminal" offender is partly inspired by an attitude of, "What a reprehensible thing to do—I would never do a thing like that!"; whereas the treatment meted out to a traffic offender is largely inspired by an attitude of: "After all, to err is human—and there but for the grace of God go I." This whole question of the attitude of the judiciary—and the support it receives from the public— has been most interestingly dealt with in a number of recent books such as Willett's *Criminal on the Road* (1964), Barbara Preston's section of Cohen and Preston's *Causes and Prevention of Road Accidents* (1968), and Parry's *Aggression on the Road* (1968)—all of them eminently worth reading. They deal with this subject (among many other practical aspects of the road situation) far more adequately than I can do here. The purpose of this present volume is to deal with accident proneness, which is essentially concerned with the accident potential of the individual. But the corporate accident rate of a community, or a nation, is the sum total of the accident performance of the individuals who comprise that particular entity. And there can be little doubt that the accident potential of the active driving offender is greatly increased when he feels that neither society nor the law is going to condemn him for his activities.

For it is certainly not only the law which refrains from condemning the active traffic offender out of hand; society is often only too keen to adopt the same attitude. Possibly because most people do stupid and foolish things on the road from time to time, most people seem to have a vaguely guilty feeling about traffic offences—a feeling which has probably encouraged the belief that the majority of traffic offenders are by no means criminals and should not be treated as such. But in protecting himself against the long-odds chance of being arraigned in the traffic dock, the ordinary lawabiding citizen is-unwittingly protecting a great many unlawful ones. What he does not realize is the high proportion of the dangerous traffic offenders who are not law-abiding citizens at all; they are people with records of crime, or petty crime, in other spheres of life as well. This is a finding which has emerged very clearly from recent research in different parts of the world. It is really only Tillmann's finding all over again, but whereas the tendency has often been to regard his finding as being applicable to only a few extreme cases, recent research has shown that these cases are by no means few and far between, and that the concept of the average traffic offender as an otherwise good citizen is a very false one.

This is very clearly illustrated by preliminary reports (Buikhuisen, 1968) on a big research project being undertaken by the Criminological Institute of the State University of Groningen on behalf of the Dutch Minister of Justice. Buikhuisen says that a follow-up study of all subjects convicted during 1955 and 1956 for drunken driving has shown that 65% of them had criminal records, and that 17% had previous convictions for the same offence. This finding seems to be in sharp contrast to the line of thinking which has prompted the Dutch Government (like that of Belgium and West Germany) to establish a special prison for the detention of traffic offenders—90% of whom are convicted for drunken driving. This line of thinking, Buikhuisen says, was prompted by "the generally accepted idea that traffic offenders are not criminals", and that "it is therefore considered to be important to separate them from common delinquents in order to prevent them from being negatively influenced by these people".

Willett's study (1964) has also shown that in a sample of 653 traffic offenders the proportion with criminal records was about *three times* that of the average for the public. Here the proportions of people in each category of *motoring* offence who were found to have previous convictions for one or more *non-motoring* offences were as follows (the offences being those which could be regarded as being intentional, harmful or dishonest):

Causing death	80·0%
Driving while disqualified	77·0%
Driving under the influence	18·3%
Driving dangerously	13·4%
Failing to stop after or report an accident (not necessarily a serious one)	5·1%
Failing to insure	24·5%

Willett says that if one adds to these figures the people who had been convicted of offences such as failing to comply with maintenance orders, pavilion-breaking, exposing the person, etc.—offences which could indicate anti-social or sociopathic attitudes—plus some sixty offenders with no actual convictions but nevertheless known to the police as notorious or suspected persons, this would bring the proportion of people in whom the police had cause to be interested for reasons unconnected with motoring up to one-third of the total sample of traffic offenders examined.

In fact one of the main findings of Willett's study was that "the contention that the serious motoring offender, unlike the majority of other offenders found guilty of criminal offences, is a respectable citizen whose behaviour apart from his motoring offences is reasonably in accord with the requirements of law and order", is so questionable that the stereotype should be changed. The fact that he also found considerable evidence that this sort of serious traffic offender does not regard himself as a criminal, nor does he think that society should regard him as such, is an indication of one very probable source of such mistaken ideas. Indeed, it makes one all the more suspicious that among the more vociferous protesters against stricter traffic law enforcement—especially in the columns of the Press—are a great many people who definitely do "protest too much"; and that these people are enlisting the support of the ordinary motorist for the cause of freedom from bureaucratic interference purely for their own self-interest.

Undoubtedly the exact proportion of traffic offenders with criminal records would vary from country to country, being in all probability *greater* in those countries where enforcement policy is strict and where the public either wish (or have been "persuaded") to co-operate with such a policy. Here the traffic offenders are more likely to be the sort of people who are prepared to defy not only the law but public opinion. (Both Holland and England have relatively low accident rates, and Buikhuisen's findings follow the same trends revealed in the studies of American investigators like Canty (1956) and Selzer *et al.* (1963, 1968).)

In the higher-accident-rate countries the proportion of traffic offenders with actual criminal records is likely to be less. My personal opinion is that in these countries, among the traffic and accident offenders there will probably be many more people who, though they may have developed a hearty respect for the well-enforced criminal laws, still have very little respect for the poorly enforced traffic laws. At the moment this must remain merely an opinion, for these are usually the countries where as yet no adequate statistical evidence is available—a fact which to my mind is significant in itself. But it is, nevertheless, an opinion which is borne out by the incredible improvement in fatality rates which occurs in these countries during intermittent periods of strict driver supervision. South Africa, for instance, with its very high accident rate, recently mounted intensive campaigns over holiday periods, including a 70 mph speed limit, the threat of alchotester examinations, and the patrolling of all main highways by police cars and helicopters, and the accident rate on these highways has decreased markedly— while on the other roads the carnage has merely continued. It is also an opinion which has received confirmation from long experience with professional drivers, and the effects which varying degrees of discipline have exerted on these drivers. My feeling is that many of the traffic offenders in these high-accident countries are the sort of people who might hesitate before committing a civil offence, knowing that they stand a good chance of being caught—and penalized. But they would display a very different attitude in the driving situation, where lax discipline would produce safety in numbers, and where they would feel (or at any rate hope) that they could get away with any amount of lawlessness, aggression, and compensatory bravado. These, to my mind, are the people on whom disciplinary measures have the greatest effect; and it is *this* effect, the curb which is placed on *these* sort of people, by which the efficacy of these measures should be judged—not by their failure to control the activities of the incorrigible recidivists on whom no amount of law enforcement in any sphere shows appreciable results. This type of recidivist—who is usually an incorrigible social as well as a traffic and accident offender—presents a different problem, and one for which society has yet to find the answer.

FIG. 19.1. Road deaths in Britain, 1926–66. (From Cohen and Preston, 1968)

The effects which discipline in the form of road safety legislation can have on nation-wide accident rates is vividly illustrated by Barbara Preston; and the fact that we do not know exactly *why* such legislation works does not detract in any way from the telling evidence she has produced that it *does* work. Presenting a graph (Fig. 19.1) of Britain's road fatality totals from 1926 to 1966 she says: "One of the few cheering things about road accidents is that there has always been a reduction in the number killed on the roads whenever new road safety legislation has been introduced. Part of the reduction may be due to the safety measures, part to the attendant publicity perhaps, but, however deviously, road safety measures work."

Describing the various factors which could have affected these figures, she mentions, *inter alia*:*

1926–30 The fatality rate rose steadily.
1931–2 The decrease (8%) could have been partly due to the depression, but it also followed the 1930 Road Traffic Act which provided for minimum licensing ages, penalties of disqualification and endorsement, arrest without warrant for "driving under the influence", and making "careless driving" an offence.

* From Cohen, J. and Preston, B., *Causes and Prevention of Road Accidents*, Faber and Faber, London. With permission.

1934–9   This marked decrease (11%) followed the 1934 Road Traffic Act which made provision for driver licensing tests, 30 mph speed limits in built-up areas, and pedestrian crossings with Belisha beacons.

1940–5   A tremendous increase in road fatalities occurred during the war years (even 1939's increase occurred in the last four months). Part of the increase could have been due to black-out difficulties, but most of it seems to have been caused by some change in outlook due to the war. As Preston says, similar increases occurred in 1914 and 1915, and a possible explanation might be: "In times of war killing becomes a virtue, and too great consideration for life, one's own or others, a vice, cowardice. Does this spill over even to civilian drivers? Even in times of peace army personnel have worse accident records than civilians and often have to pay higher insurance premiums."

1945–50   Petrol rationing kept the fatality rate down until 1948 when, as petrol became more plentiful, the fatality rate increased again.

1952   The introduction of zebra crossings in 1952 brought about a 10% decrease in pedestrian deaths. (Though the effect of this appears to have worn off later: as Preston says; "The maximum fine for contravening pedestrian crossing regulations is £50; the average imposed in 1965 was £4. 4. 0.")

1956   The small decrease here could have been due to the shortage of petrol after Suez, but it also coincided with the 1956 Road Traffic Act which provided for increased penalties for dangerous driving.

1960–2   This decrease followed the 1960 Road Traffic Act. This was largely a consolidating Act, though it also made provision for the compulsory roadworthy testing of older vehicles. However the Act and its passage through Parliament was extensively reported in the Press, accompanied by much discussion on road safety—a fact which Preston thinks may have had a very salutary effect.

1966   This year saw the introduction of the 70 mph speed limit, and over the first eleven months there was a noticeable decrease in road deaths, unfortunately offset by a disastrous December when 192 people were killed on the five days of Christmas. As Preston says: "There was very little propaganda against drinking and driving that Christmas, and it is even possible that some people may have thought that they would have a 'last fling' before the new drink legislation was introduced."

Unfortunately, the graph does not include the introduction of the breathalyser legislation in October 1967, but the effects of this are very well known. The immediate effects were amazing. The first Christmas saw a reduction of 36% in fatalities over the previous year. Some of the effects appear to be wearing off as the scare value lessens and as legal quibbles weaken its effectiveness, but, nevertheless, in its first year of operation there was a reduction of some 15%—which is a fantastic reduction.

Barbara Preston's account of developments in Britain over a forty-year period should be studied in the original. It is extremely interesting, and all the more convincing because it is so conservatively presented. She makes no extravagant claims that the various Road

Traffic Acts were indeed wholly responsible for the periodic observed decreases in fatality rates. But, nevetheless, the coincidences are too coincidental, and there seems to be ample justification for her assumption that each time such legislation was introduced it played a significant part in reducing road accidents. As an illustration of the immediate effects of discipline and better driver control it is a very impressive one.

The Network of Accident Causes

There is no denying the fact that accidents have many causes, or that the detailed investigation of any particular accident would reveal that it had been precipitated by a number of different factors, some environmental and some person-centred, and all helping to precipitate it.

But in the light of research findings from all over the world there can be equally little doubt that the person-centred factors play an extremely important role. Only too often it is the driver himself who, by his own driving behaviour, creates or accentuates the hazards in that environment. And there can be equally little doubt that whatever the cause or causes of this driving behaviour, whether they stem from inexperience, poor health, poor vision, poor intelligence, poor driving ability, alcoholism, personality defects, the pressures of an unsatisfactory environment, or poorly controlled anti-social attitudes, they represent a potential for accidents which is anything but equal from one driver to another.

CHAPTER 20

WHAT OF THE FUTURE?

To SUM up, then, on the whole question of accident proneness.

It would be very gratifying to be able to end this section of the book by giving clear-cut answers to two basic questions: "Is accident proneness a myth or a reality?" and "If it is a reality, how much does it matter in the accident situation as a whole?"

But even to attempt to make a statement on these lines without hedging it in with all the necessary reservations would defeat one of the main purposes of this book, which has been to try and clear up some of the confusion which surrounds the whole subject and not add to it. For how can one supply a definitive answer to any question about accident proneness when there is no accepted standard definition of the term and when the answer could be differently interpreted by every person who reads it?

For instance, if writer A ended a book or a paper on accident proneness by giving a clear-cut statement in reply to these questions, he could only do so in terms of what the term itself meant to him (or of what he believed was the usual interpretation). This could be:

> Accident proneness means an undue propensity for accidents, an undue accident *potential*. An accident-prone person is therefore not a good accident *risk*. But the actual *number* of accidents he has will be influenced by the degree to which his accident potential is encouraged to manifest itself or the degree to which it is damped down (by factors such as exposure, or traffic conditions, or discipline).

His answers to the two questions might then easily be:

> *Is it a myth or a reality?* It is very much a reality.
>
> *How much does proneness matter in the accident situation as a whole?* It matters a great deal as there are a lot of people who could be called accident-prone, and its dangers should never be overlooked or ignored.

Now let us presume that the same basic questions were answered by writer B, whose ideas on the meaning of the term were quite different, namely:

> Accident proneness is a term which is applicable only to people who are involved in multiple serious accidents.

B's answers to the two questions might then easily be:

> (1) It could possibly be regarded as a reality inasmuch as there are a few people who could, perhaps, be called "accident-prone" —but it is really more of a myth than a reality.
>
> (2) It matters very little as such people have been shown to account for only a small proportion of the total number of recorded accidents.

Now if these two "clear-cut" statements were quoted out of context it could so easily be assumed that because A "supported" the idea of accident proneness, whereas B "opposed" it, there must be fundamental differences in the thinking of the two writers.

In reality, however, this might not be the case at all: writers A and B could actually have a very similar outlook on the whole accident problem and its causes. Both of them could believe that drivers differed very much in their potential for accidents and that these differences represented a continuum of risk from the very bad to the very good: the chronic accident-repeaters were therefore by no means the only people who should be receiving attention, they were just the relatively small tip of the iceberg and the real danger lay in the less discernible but much bigger portion just beneath the surface. A and B could really be in agreement about all this: the reason for their different statements on "accident proneness" *as such* was that A, with his wider definition of the term, was referring to quite a sizeable portion of the berg, while B with his narrower definition was talking about only the tip.

It is not difficult to see how much confusion this could lead to, and one of the aims of this book has been to show how often this has actually happened. The puzzled note which runs through so much of the continental research writing is a very good case in point. Very often these writers do not seem to be aware that their definition of proneness is quite different from that of many American writers, and they tie themselves in logical knots trying to reconcile their belief in unequal susceptibility (which to them means proneness) with the currently popular American pronouncements that proneness is of so little importance. Nor are the continentals by any means the only people who do this; even some of the American writers quoted in this book, who believe in personal differences, have landed themselves in a similar predicament. It seems, therefore, that before taking at its face value any bald statement for or against accident proneness, as such, it is essential to find out just *what* it is that is being supported or condemned.

But something which I have also tried to point out in this book is the existence of another factor which has caused endless confusion. Reverting back again to our hypothetical writers A and B. Their very different statements on the validity and the usefulness of accident proneness could have been, as we have seen, just a semantic difference. In reality they had very similar views and they were merely talking at cross-purposes. But, on the other hand, these statements could have represented radically different views and beliefs. The first writer could have "supported" the whole *concept* of proneness (i.e. the existence of differential accident susceptibility) because it was a natural corollary of his particular psychological beliefs, and because the evidence on proneness, as he interpreted it, confirmed those beliefs. The second writer could have "opposed" the whole *concept* because it was contrary to his particular psychological beliefs, and because the evidence, again as he interpreted it, either belied the concept or at best was very inconclusive. It is even possible, in the case of either of the writers, that his particular psychological orientation could have biased his assessment of the evidence one way or another.

This is now a very different state of affairs; for here we have a fundamental difference of opinion, which could lead to fundamentally different ways of thinking on the whole accident problem. The "supporter" of accident proneness (on these grounds) would believe that a great many accidents were anything but accidental, and would no doubt be in favour of driver control measures like points systems. The "opposer" of accident proneness, on the other hand, would believe that most accidents were random occurrences, and would no doubt consider such enforcement systems as a waste of money as they would have only a very limited target (just the "abnormal" people, such as the psychiatric cases or the confirmed alcoholics—and these probably not amenable to discipline anyway).

For this reason it is very important indeed that anyone assessing a statement for or against accident proneness should be able to ascertain not only WHAT the writer is talking about but WHY he is talking as he does. As long as the reader knows this he can make his own decisions. But he needs enough information to go on. In other words, he needs to know the psychological as well as the statistical grounds on which writer A or writer B is basing his contentions. Judging by the confusion which still exists on this issue it appears that this seldom happens. In fact, in most of the theoretical *psychological* discussions on proneness it is so difficult to see the psychological wood for the statistical trees that the reader has to make his own deductions—which need not necessarily be the right ones. For instance, I may be quite wrong in the interpretation which I have put on the writings of the theoretical opponents of accident proneness. But then the psychological justification for the contention that one driver must be very like another driver was anything but clear; the arguments were nearly all based on statistical data. If I am wrong, then I am open to correction; but for the sake of general clarity all round I feel that the psychological issues must be fully discussed too.

However, the main point that I wish to make here, and the reason why I have discussed the accident proneness controversy at such length in this book, is that I feel that anyone who is concerned with the role of the driver in the accident situation should be alerted to the fact that these controversial issues do exist—and that they have important practical implications.

But another aim of this book has been to put forward a plea for moderation. Accidents have many causes and the only realistic way to attack the problem is to attack it on a broad front, with no undue emphasis being placed on any particular aspect. If too much or too little blame is put on the driver because the pendulum of theoretical scientific thinking has swung too far in either direction, it could upset the whole balance of any accident-prevention programme. And if, in this book, I have come out rather strongly on the side of the supporters of the proneness concept, and been rather critical of its opponents, it was because I felt that whereas in the thirties and the forties the pendulum had swung too far to the "pro" side, now, in the sixties, it was showing strong signs of swinging too far to the "anti" side. I felt that a little weight was necessary to help to bring it back once more to the middle path—especially as this present swing could have some unfortunate repercussions.

The most vehement of today's critics of accident proneness say that even the principle underlying the idea itself has no validity, and that there is no proof that individual drivers differ in their innate potential for accidents. A view like this, which runs contrary to virtually every research finding, must, I feel, be contradicted.

The slightly less extreme critics say that this concept of unequal liability may have a limited validity, but too little to have any appreciable effect on the accident situation—

a statement which again is extremely doubtful even as applied to conditions where accident rates are low, and apparently quite untrue of conditions where accident rates are high.

They also say that it is very necessary to play down the role played by accident proneness—even if it does exist—because (a) the public must be disillusioned of the idea that a minority of accident-prone people are responsible for the majority of the accidents, and (b) overemphasis on "proneness" has greatly impeded research on other aspects of the accident problem. These are again statements which I feel are very unjustified. An exaggerated emphasis may have been put on proneness during the thirties and forties—although I find it very hard to believe that the man-in-the-car-on-the-street, who has eyes in his head, and who knows all about the many risks associated with driving, would ever have really swallowed a theory like this. But to say that the whole progress of research has been impeded is patently untrue. Even in the psychological and statistical fields alone, the early days produced some very good work; and over the last twenty years there have been a great number of studies which have added immeasurably to our knowledge on the causes of accidents. To try and repress this sort of research on the grounds that it is unproductive or misleading could be very dangerous indeed, and could do far more harm than was ever done by earlier over-enthusiasm. For, beside a number of little fruitless studies where the dilettante quality of the research was probably more to blame than the subject matter, what harm has research on the accident potential of the driver done? If it has resulted in the introduction of enforcement programmes like points systems, then it seems that the results have been rather more beneficial than harmful. And even this is a very big IF. In reality it seems more likely that these programmes were based on practical experience with traffic and accident offenders, rather than any theoretical thinking, and that the better and sounder research projects have merely resulted in confirming the need for these programmes, and indicated ways in which they can be improved. But the current strong antagonism to the idea of accident proneness *could* affect the practical accident programmes. It could influence bureaucratic attitudes and consequently the allocation of funds for these programmes. It could also undermine the authority of the traffic officials with the public and, through them, the judiciary. For it must not be overlooked that publicity given to the sort of extreme thinking which exonerates the driver will be very quickly taken up by a certain section of the public, the section which is inherently opposed to restrictions like speed limits and disciplinary measures of any kind—in fact the section which research has shown to contain many of the most dangerous accident offenders!

These are some of the reasons why I feel that the present rather exaggerated swing of the pendulum of the thinking on accident proneness could have serious repercussions, and why I have tried in this book to restore the equilibrium.

One of the ways I have tried to do this has been to show that the actual research findings do not support extreme thinking *in either direction*: in fact the only policy they support is a truly moderate one which conceives of accidents as having many causes—all of them needing urgent attention; which allows for environment-caused as well as driver-caused accidents; and which, even in the driver-caused accidents, allows for behavioural patterns which are consistent with seemingly different psychological beliefs, e.g. habits as well as personality traits.

In this book the main emphasis has been on the driver because this is the sphere in which psychological research—especially scientifically controlled experimental research—can make its greatest contribution. Quite obviously this contribution would be expedited if somehow we could manage to delete that controversial and so often ill-defined term "accident proneness" from the scientific and lay vocabulary, thereby eliminating much of the confusion which is caused by the vagueness of the term itself. But much as one would like to see this happen, it seems that it never will. The term "accident proneness" has now become part of the English language—for better or for worse. This is why my co-author and I chose it for the title of this book. Our feeling was that if we are all going to be saddled with it, let us at least try to ensure that the result will be "for better".

For in the light of the major research findings from all over the world it appears that "accident proneness" as a *concept*, if fully explained and interpreted in a flexible and realistic manner, can indeed contribute a great deal to our knowledge of the driver and how to handle him. Expressed in the light of these research findings this *concept* can be interpreted as follows.

"Accident proneness"—or differential liability to accidents—or whatever one cares to call it—is merely a human function. It represents the relative ability or inability of human beings to cope with and adjust to the demands of the driving situation, whether these demands are made on their capabilities, or their physical or psychological or sociological fitness for the task. The degree to which they cope with the situation, and the adequacy of the adjustments they make, are therefore going to depend on the interplay of a whole complex of factors within the individual, many of which will change over the course of his or her "driving" life—a span of development which can encompass everything from inexperience to experience, and from adolescence to senility. During this process of development some of the factors will change in one direction, thus helping the adjustment, and some will change in another, thus hampering it. The accident susceptibility of the individual *at any one time* will therefore be very much a reflection of his ability or inability to maintain a balance between these factors; of how he uses his abilities or adjusts to his limitations; and of how able *and* willing he is to be integrated into the "driving" society.

At various stages of a person's life the balance is likely to be swayed in one direction or the other, with the result that his potential as an accident risk, his innate "proneness", is likely to go through various phases. To some extent there will be a degree of generality about these phases. On the whole, young people, despite their greater physical fitness and better brain–muscle co-ordination, will be doubtful risks because of their lesser experience and their psychological and sociological immaturity. On the whole, the middle age groups will be better risks. And on the whole the older people, despite their experience and their psychological and sociological maturity, will again become doubtful risks because of the relentless deterioration of their physical and even mental functions.

But there will also be a great deal of individuality. Many an irresponsible youth can become in his twenties a responsible road-user. Many a diffident, well-behaved youngster can blossom forth in his thirties into an arrogant man who owns not only the world but the road as well—sometimes remaining that way until well into his fifties. Many a frivolous teenage girl can mature into a conscientious and careful woman. Many a docile daughter can grow into a domineering matron. Some people will strike it rough in life, but will manage to retain their balance and their equanimity; others will become nervous wrecks, or sour and cantankerous, even at an early age. And some people will drink to excess while they are young, and then reform; others will take to drink when they grow older. The complexities are endless, and so, too, are all the factors which will dictate from time to time the accident potential of the individual.

Accident proneness cannot therefore be expected to be a static function which remains unchanged throughout very long periods of time; and to expect it to do so is to expect human beings to function in this one respect as they function in no other. But, nevertheless, it can remain operative for quite long enough to matter.

Nor can it be split into a dichotomy—either a person is "prone" or he is not—any more than any other human function can be split in this way. There are different *degrees* of accident proneness, ranging all the way from the multiple accident offender to the totally accident-free. There are also different *kinds* of accident proneness, as in the person who is liable to a specific type of accident, or the person who could easily cause a serious accident, or the person who is more likely to be involved in only very minor ones (though there is obviously going to be an overlap between the various classes).

An undue proneness to accidents can be caused by many factors as it represents a variety of human maladjustments. It is therefore similar to other complex human maladjustments, like incompetence or criminality, and has as many causes. But these causes can be determined and remedial action can be taken.

And, lastly, the amount of damage which could be prevented by curtailing the activities of the unduly "accident-prone" depends on how far down the scale of proneness it is both feasible and permissible for action to be taken.

In other words, for accident proneness to have any real meaning the concept must, of necessity, be a flexible one which allows for proneness to manifest itself in different ways in different people and for different reasons, to be liable to change over time, and, in its less deeply ingrained forms, to be amenable to remedial measures such as training or discipline, or to the pressures exerted by the climate of social opinion.

However, the fact that accident proneness can be conceived in such a flexible manner does not detract from its usefulness. On the contrary it is this very flexibility which makes it more realistic and more applicable to the accident problem. Nor does this flexibility mean that it cannot be studied—and predicted—by scientific means. In fact one of the principal aims of this book has been to show just how much the scientific study of accident proneness, as conceived in this flexible manner, has contributed to our knowledge of why accidents happen and to whom—and to show how the practical application of this knowledge can help to reduce these accidents. Admittedly there are still technical difficulties in applying some of the knowledge we have gained and the techniques we have so far devised for sifting the bad risks from the good. But many of these difficulties can no doubt be overcome by further systematic research; and we have come such a long way already that this research does not present any overwhelming difficulties.

But something which I have also tried to do is to show how research on accident proneness has done rather more than uncover many of the reasons why *individual* people have accidents. It has shown that one of the potent reasons why accidents happen at all, is that they are encouraged rather than prevented by the prevalent attitude of the *commu-*

nity to the whole accident problem—especially in those countries where accident rates are still unnecessarily high. For research has clearly demonstrated that neither the accident researchers, nor the car designers, nor the highway engineers, nor the driving instructors, nor the licensing officials, nor the law-enforcement officers, can prevent many of the accidents which occur unless they get the co-operation of the public as a whole. It is the attitude of the public, and particularly the "driving" public, which is going to dictate the pace of progress in accident prevention. In the last resort it is the driver, and his willingness to forego some of his freedom to drive as and how he likes, which will be the deciding factor.

And by "the driver" I do not mean "him"—"the other fellow"—the eternal scapegoat. I mean *us*. We are all in this together. Driving is a form of social and technical interaction in which most of us participate today; and as Sam Levenson so pertinently said with regard to modern living: "Either our ethics keep up with our physics or we shall all be cremated equal." In other words, whether driving is to retain any of its pleasures, or whether it is to become a sort of motorized form of jungle warfare in which we ourselves stand a good chance of becoming war casualties, is very much over to *us* to decide.

SECTION II

NEW STATISTICAL TECHNIQUES FOR THE EVALUATION OF THE CONCEPT OF ACCIDENT PRONENESS

by

HERBERT S. SICHEL, D.Sc.

CHAPTER 21

NEW STATISTICAL TECHNIQUES FOR THE EVALUATION OF THE CONCEPT OF ACCIDENT PRONENESS

1. Statistical Models Used in the Past—A Critical Appraisal

Historically the concept of accident proneness was born when Greenwood *et al.* (1919) and Greenwood and Yule (1920) published their now famous papers. In essence they stipulated that each person, if exposed to the same environmental hazard, possesses a potential inclination to accidents as measured by the parameter λ in a Poisson distribution. The number of observed accidents in equal time periods would fluctuate around λ in accordance with this particular law. By postulating that λ would vary from person to person and that the λ's themselves, among a large number of persons exposed to equal risks, were following a Pearson Type III probability function, Greenwood and Yule derived the negative binomial distribution law. Greenwood and Yule, and subsequently scores of other investigators, fitted the negative binomial to many observed accident frequencies. Invariably this distribution represented the observations much better than the Poisson law which is based on the concept of equal liability. The idea of accident proneness was immediately hailed as a milestone in accident research. After all, it made psychological sense and the statisticians had "proved" it. All that remained to be done was to construct some battery of psychological tests with predictive validity, and one could expect to eliminate those persons possessing a high accident potential *before* they could do harm to themselves and others.

Alas, these early hopes were not realized. The psychologist produced selection tests which never came up to expectation when tried out under rigorous experimental conditions. The statisticians themselves were quick to point out that the negative binomial distribution could be derived from initial assumptions diametrically opposed to the theory of constant liability *within* a person and varying liability *between* individuals.

Furthermore, who really could be sure that the environmental hazards were the same to all and sundry? If they were not, a good negative binomial fit to observed accident frequencies meant pretty little in practice. Alternatively, if the risks to which individuals were exposed were the same, could a negative binomial distribution not be the outcome of "transitory states" within a person although the overall mean for each subject was the same?

The doubts that a good negative binomial fit did not necessarily establish a proof of accident proneness led investigators to the more direct approach of correlating the number of accidents incurred by individuals in two or more non-overlapping periods. The resulting correlation coefficients were used as a yardstick of accident proneness. If the coefficient in a group of persons was significantly different from zero, then it was argued that the hypothesis of equal liability was rejected. The higher the coefficient found, the stronger the proneness factor in a particular group of subjects.

Not much heed was taken of the fact that a correlation coefficient from a bivariate negative binomial distribution means something completely different than one of equal numerical magnitude derived from a bivariate normal population. The reader is invited to construct a bivariate negative binomial distribution with a correlation coefficient of, say, $\varrho = 0.9$. He will no doubt be impressed with the large scatter in the array distributions around the regression lines. Similar large variations are totally absent when dealing with a bivariate normal distribution whose $\varrho = 0.9$.

By using the bivariate approach to accident statistics one has by no means overcome the difficulties raised and discussed in connection with the interpretation of univariate distributions: For example, if some persons drive long distances on average, and others short distances, the resulting correlation coefficient will be substantial. Yet this does not establish accident proneness.

Let us now assume for a moment that environmental risks are identical for every person and that each individual has constant liability within himself but that these liabilities vary among members of the group under investigation.

Not infrequently we shall find that the results of such bivariate tabulation of accidents during two adjacent time periods, even if the initial assumptions as given in the foregoing paragraph are met, will have a handful of pairs of observations with high numbers of accidents in both time periods. The vast majority of data, however, will lie in the quadrant 0–2 accidents on both variables. Under such circumstances the correlation will be high if the few outlying pairs of observations are included and will be practically zero if they are excluded. In the former case one would conclude high proneness in the group and the verdict in the latter case would be "no proneness".

Furthermore, the slope of the customary regression line which is used for the prediction of an individual's number of accidents in the second period, given the number of accidents which he incurred in the first period, is radically changed by the inclusion or exclusion of the few outliers. Similar changes will take place with respect to probability and confidence limits associated with the bivariate negative binomial distribution.

This raises the fundamental question why the assessment of an *individual's* accident liability and the prediction of his future accident performance should be so much influenced by the accident records of other members in the group, let alone by a few "outliers".

In practical life we wish to make inferences with respect to *individuals* and not *groups* of persons and hence it appears that, in the light of the foregoing, the bivariate approach will lead us no further than the univariate attempts.

We now turn to the most critical shortcomings of the Greenwood–Yule model which apply to the univariate distribution as well as to its bivariate form. Whilst these objections are essentially of a non-statistical nature they are, nevertheless, based on common sense and they expose the limitations of applying this particular mathematical model in a practical situation.

Before one can make use of the negative binomial distribution law one must have collected accident data from a group of persons who all were exposed to risk for exactly the same time span. As accidents to individuals are fortunately "rare" events in the statistical sense, the duration of this exposure must be relatively long as otherwise we would not obtain any meaningful statistical distribution for subsequent analysis. In addition, it is required that individual exposures are obtained from identical calendar periods as otherwise one would have strong doubts as to the constancy of environmental hazards. These severe limitations on data collection will result in the drawing of non-representative samples from a given population at risk as they invariably will include all the stayers, who are the survivors of the fittest. Those, for whom attention is most required, that is the potentially high accident risks—the young, the inexperienced, the irresponsibles— they are automatically excluded from the group under study.

As an example we refer to an investigation by Adelstein (1952) which dealt with the accident histories of shunters in a given five-year period. He found that 1442 persons were involved in the analysis of whom only 182 were exposed during the entire five-year span. Consequently only 12·6% of the population at risk could be included in the Greenwood–Yule model. In addition, Adelstein showed conclusively that the accident *rate* of the 182 stayers was very much lower than that for the other groups who had shorter exposures. In fact, by analysing accident rates in terms of time elapsed since the start of exposure to risk, a perfect hyperbolic learning curve was obtained. This same type of learning was established in the authors' study of PUTCO bus drivers. There just cannot be any doubt that some, *but not all*, persons adjust themselves to dangerous situations during the passage of time. Some may call this phenomenon experience, others may talk of self-preservation or maturity.

Unfortunately, the negative binomial distribution makes no allowance for this important learning factor.

The foregoing remarks are not intended to detract from the pioneering efforts of Greenwood, Yule, Woods, and Newbold. They were the first to draw attention to the phenomenon now called accident proneness, and they were the first to point out that mathematical statistical methods should and must be employed in analysing accidents incurred by individuals among a group of persons who were exposed to the same environmental risk.

That their model proved rather indecisive is due to the complexity of any Poisson mixture distribution where the observed events could have been generated by a multiplicity of causes and where one just cannot unravel what has gone before.

Enough has been said about the disadvantages of the Greenwood–Yule model if applied to the analysis of real-life accident statistics. The reader who would like to know more about mathematical accident models used in the past is referred to the excellent critical review by Arbous and Kerrich (1951).

2. A New Statistical Approach to Accident Research

To make progress in the study of the personal factor in accidents it is necessary to devise statistical methods which:

(a) are person-centred, the accident history of one individual should have no influence on the statistical analysis of another person's accidents;

(b) make use of *all* available data, thus ensuring that no accident risk group is automatically excluded from the analysis;

(c) are capable of testing the hypothesis of constant liability within the individual, although not necessarily related to the personal component alone;

(d) permit of reliability estimates in the statistical sense, such as confidence intervals.

With these criteria in mind one immediately must think of time, mileage, or other exposure intervals between recurrent events.

Valuable theoretical mathematical studies in this direction were carried out by Maguire *et al.* (1952), Bates and Neyman (1952a, b), and Bates (1955).

In the subsequent sections the development of the underlying theory follows closely the study of one of the authors (Sichel, 1965), specifically designed to cope with data collected in the PUTCO company which runs a large fleet of buses.

The researcher should have at his disposal, for each individual person studied:

(1) the length of exposure to risk L, measured in exposure units such as actual driving days or mileage;

(2) the number of accidents r during exposure period L;

(3) the date or mileage when accidents occurred.

Whilst it is possible to break up the entire exposure period L into *equal* time units and analyse statistically the number of accidents within these sub-periods, this approach would lead us straight back to the Greenwood–Yule model. It would be insensitive as the vast majority of observations would fall into the zero (non-accident) class and, furthermore, our statistical variable would be discrete. Such a procedure would sacrifice a lot of information because it does not take account of the exact point in time when an accident occurred. For example, if a particular person had ten accidents in L, it would be difficult to test whether this discrete observation originated from a specified distribution law such as the Poisson or negative binomial. On the other hand, if we took the ten time or mileage intervals between successive accidents (where the first interval is defined as the time elapsed between the start of the exposure and the first accident) we would obtain ten *continuous* measurements which could be tested against a variety of distribution laws. Furthermore, we could plot the ten intervals between the accidents as a time series and test whether any trend had developed within exposure period L.

Such trends could be associated, for example, with "learning", with the deterioration in an individual's capability to cope with a hazardous occupation, or with changes in the environment itself.

Whereas the number of accidents r is meaningless without the dimension L (which in any case will vary from person to person), the time or mileage interval t_i, between successive accidents of the same individual is completely independent of the observed exposure length L, provided that the latter is reasonably long.

We start with the assumption (as Greenwood and Yule did) that the number of accidents of an individual in repeated periods of length L is distributed according to Poisson's law of rare events and that the environmental risk is constant throughout.

If this is the case it is easy to show (and well known), that the intervals between successive accidents in an unlimited exposure period ($L \rightarrow \infty$) are distributed according to the negative exponential law

$$\phi(t) = \frac{1}{\theta} e^{-t/\theta} \quad (0 \leqslant t \leqslant \infty). \tag{1}$$

Here $\phi(t)$ gives the probability density for individual time or mileage intervals t and θ is the *average* interval between accidents provided the person is exposed to risk for an infinite period of time or length of mileage. θ is a parameter characterizing an individual's *overall* liability to accidents. A large θ would indicate a long average time interval associated with a person having few accidents and vice versa.

Of course, no person is exposed to risk forever, and our observations are confined to a limited finite exposure period L.

Consequently we deal here with a typical statistical estimation problem where the parameter θ in the negative exponential distribution law (1) is estimated from a sample drawn from this universe. The sample consists of r accident intervals incurred by one and the same person during an exposure period of length L. We shall return to this estimation problem later on.

3. Statistical Control Charts for Intervals between Successive Accidents

In the negative exponential distribution law of eq. (1) the population mean and standard deviation are identical as

$$E(t) = \sigma(t) = \theta. \tag{2}$$

This will make the comparison of time graphs of successive accident intervals generated by *different* persons, cumbersome and insensitive as the probability limits (on a conventional statistical control chart) are dependent on σ, and σ is identical to the mean θ. We expect θ to vary from person to person.

By making the transformation

$$x = \ln t, \tag{3}$$

all the above difficulties are overcome as the transformed distribution

$$f(x) = \frac{1}{\theta} e^{x-(1/\theta)e^{x}} \quad (-\infty < x < +\infty) \tag{4}$$

has constant variance

$$\text{var}(x) = \text{var}(\ln t) = \frac{\pi^2}{6}, \tag{5}$$

which is independent of parameter θ.

The expected mean value of eqn. (4) is

$$E(x) = E(\ln t) = \ln \theta - \gamma, \tag{6}$$

where γ is Euler's constant $= 0.5772$.

While the original distribution (1) is J-shaped, its log-transformation gives rise to a negatively skew, unimodal frequency distribution. The shape of this particular probability function (4) is also independent of parameter θ.

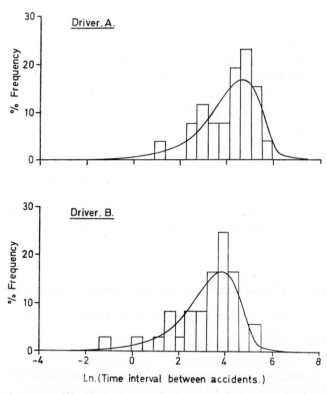

FIG. 21.1. Histograms of log-time-intervals between accidents and expected distributions for driver A, with $\bar{t} = 103$ days based on 26 accidents, and for driver B, with $\bar{t} = 46$ days from 36 accidents. Both men were exposed to the same environmental risk

If two distributions $f(x)$ with different parameters θ are plotted, they will look exactly alike except that they are displaced against each other.

The shift will depend on the magnitude of the two θ parameters as may be seen from eqn. (6).

As an example, the observed histograms for drivers A and B, both of whom were exposed to the same environmental risk, are plotted against the natural logarithms of their time intervals between successive accidents in Fig. 21.1. The theoretical density distributions, defined in eqn. (4), have been superimposed over the histograms as smooth curves. The shift of the distributions against each other is clearly discernible. Driver A is obviously the safer of the two as he has longer time-intervals between his accidents.

Parameter θ in the log-time-interval distribution of eqn. (4) is estimated by the arithmetic mean of the actual time intervals, i.e. by

$$\bar{t}_r = \frac{1}{r} \sum_{i=1}^{r} t_i,$$ (7)

which is the maximum likelihood solution of eqn. (4). Estimator $\bar{t}_r$ will be biased low if the exposure length L is short, a difficulty which will be dealt with at a later stage.

Whilst the observed frequency distributions may be tested against the log-time-interval model with the help of the conventional χ^2-test, it is preferable to plot successive log-time-intervals on a statistical control chart because:

(i) for small numbers of observations the χ^2-test is insensitive, it has little "power" in the statistical sense,
(ii) the χ^2-test does not take account of possible time trends in the observations unless these are substantial or unless the number of observations is large. This, fortunately, is never the case for an individual person exposed to risk of accidents.

The cumulative distribution function of eqn. (4) is given by

$$F(x) = \int_{-\infty}^{x} f(x) \, dx = 1 - e^{-(1/\theta)e^x}$$ (8)

from which we obtain the control chart limits, for the *population* of log-time-intervals, as

$$x_p = \ln \theta + \ln \left[-\ln (1-p) \right],$$ (9)

where $p = 0.001, 0.025, 0.500, 0.975,$ and 0.999, as is customary in statistical quality control. From eqn. (9) it follows that the population median of log-time-intervals is

$$Me(x) = x_{0.5} = \ln \theta + \ln (\ln 2).$$ (10)

If we wish to establish the control chart limits for an individual person we must take cognizance of the small number of observations at our disposal. Provided that the exposure period L is reasonably long, an unbiased maximum likelihood estimator for parameter $\ln \theta$ in eqn. (9) is

$$u = \ln \bar{t}_r + \ln r - \psi(r-1),$$ (11)

where $\bar{t}_r = \dfrac{1}{r} \sum_{i=1}^{r} t_i,$

$$\psi(r-1) = \frac{d \ln \Gamma(r)}{dr} \quad \text{(digamma function)},$$

and $r =$ number of accidents.

Substitution of u for $\ln \theta$ into eqn. (9) gives the control limit *estimates*:

$$\hat{x}_p = \ln \bar{t}_r + \ln r - \psi(r-1) + \ln \left[-\ln (1-p) \right].$$ (12)

The above limits are, of course, subject to wide statistical variations due to the paucity of data available for an individual person.

A much more practical and statistically more meaningful approach is to set a *standard* of an acceptable average time-interval between successive accidents θ_s. This may be the mean of all time-intervals from all persons at the same risk, or their median or any other rational level. In such a case the control limits are obtained from eqn. (9) where the numerical value of θ_s is substituted for θ. Actual control charts for individual PUTCO drivers have been given in previous sections of this book and further ones were published by Shaw and Sichel (1961) and Shaw (1965).

Statistical accident control charts of log-time-intervals for people who are exposed to essentially the same environmental risk have proved of considerable value in analysing the personal component of an individual's overall liability.

The control charts lend themselves easily to statistical tests involving run-up and down tests, runs above or below the median level, number of observations above and below the median and out-of-control points at the 0·025 or 0·001 level of probability.

Perhaps the most important aspect is the ease with which the charts are kept up to date and the fact that this particular graphical display is well understood by "laymen". A few salient points may help in the interpretation of the log-time interval control charts:

(1) The significant factor is not the number of accidents (for this may be dependent on short or long total exposures) but the time interval $\ln t_i$, i.e. the height of each plotted point on the ordinate.

(2) A good record (better than standard) is one where the plotted points are mostly above the median line.

(3) A bad record (worse than standard) is one where the points are mostly below the median line.

(4) An upward trend of plotted points indicates a lengthening of the time intervals, i.e. an improvement.

(5) Conversely, a downward trend indicates a shortening in time intervals which signifies a deterioration in the individual's accident potential.

Accident control charts of individuals at risk are kept for hundreds of drivers at PUTCO. Each driving division has its own standard control limits. In addition to reflecting the past accident performance of an individual it also indicates his current liability which may or may not be the same as his past record.

A study of accident graphs of these drivers produced the following valuable information:

(a) In many of the subjects, particularly the inexperienced ones, a definite "learning period" was clearly in evidence. During this period, a new driver usually had several accidents at relatively short intervals.

(b) At the end of the learning period a pronounced improvement was noticeable for many but not all drivers. For them the time intervals became longer and each person developed his own individual accident "pattern".

(c) For a majority of drivers this pattern was remarkably stable. The average level was different for each individual indicating the presence of a personal factor, bearing in mind that the environmental risk was essentially the same within a particular driving division.

(d) Significant learning periods were only found among the men who had turned out later to be good accident risks.

(e) In the case of the bad risks, "accident proneness" was definitely exhibited. These drivers had started with short time-intervals between accidents and even after the period when learning should have ceased, had continued to show no real improvement.

(f) Only in a moderate number of cases was there evidence of a slow, gradual improvement over a period of years.

(g) Where a sudden deterioration did occur in the pattern, it could usually be traced back to such factors as ill health, domestic or other worries, or the individual taking to drink.

(h) A very interesting phenomenon was demonstrated in the control charts of men who had been transferred from one division to another. They showed up the change in the environmental risk and the reaction of the driver to his new driving conditions.

(i) For a minority of drivers the charts showed no pattern and fluctuated in a seemingly unpredictable manner. Later experiences proved, however, that the very fact that these people did fluctuate meant that they were not good risks. In many cases it was found that these men were drinkers.

(j) The effects of age were clearly demonstrated by factors such as the greater incidence of bad records and unduly expensive learning periods amongst the young drivers. Obvious deterioration among certain of the older drivers after the age of 50 was also in evidence.

The most significant aspect of the whole investigation was the proof it provided of the individuality of each driver's accident liability. For a majority of men at risk it was possible to predict—at least roughly—their future behaviour using their past performance as a predictor.

If the above conclusions were essentially correct it should be possible to verify them globally in terms of the mathematical model of eqn. (4). We wish to test whether the distribution of *observed* log-time-intervals between successive accidents conforms, at least broadly, to our model. We have to bear in mind that different drivers may have different accident liabilities characterized by parameter θ, or even better by its transformation $\ln \theta$. These differences stem partly from the variations in liabilities among drivers within the same division and partly from the differences in environmental risk between divisions. Furthermore, it is necessary for the purpose of this test to eliminate learning periods of individuals, where they exist, as these constitute a transitory stage. In addition, the remaining number of accidents for an individual should be at least ten as otherwise a bias towards the low side would result in the estimation of a driver's parameter $\ln \theta$. This bias is due to the limited exposure period L *vis-à-vis* the number of accidents r incurred in L, a statistical topic which we have not yet discussed. Estimator u, given in eqn. (11), is only unbiased if L is reasonably long as stated before.

In the light of the above remarks we eliminated the initial time-intervals constituting a learning period, using the control charts as a guide. Any driver who then was still left with ten or more further accident-intervals was included in the subsequent analysis.

An important practical point to remember when dealing with log-time-interval observations is the sensitivity of the variable at the lower end of the scale.

In our studies time-intervals were expressed in driving days between successive accidents. Some bus drivers had two accidents on the same day. In such cases it is vital to
convert the hours which elapsed between these two accidents into *fractions* of days.

To eliminate possible differences between parameters $\ln \theta$ caused by variations in
drivers' liabilities or by changes in environmental risk from division to division, we proceed as follows:

The log-time-interval distribution $f(x)$ given in eqn. (4) is *standardized* by making the
transformation

$$y = x - [\ln \theta + \ln (\ln 2)]. \tag{13}$$

The standardized distribution then becomes

$$\Lambda(y) = (\ln 2)e^{y-(\ln 2)e^y}, \quad (-\infty < y < \infty). \tag{14}$$

The median, mean, and variance of distribution (14) is now

$$Me(y) = 0, \tag{15}$$

$$E(y) = -\ln (\ln 2) - \gamma, \tag{16}$$

$$var\,(y) = \frac{\pi^2}{6} \quad (as \ before). \tag{17}$$

The obvious advantage of this standardized form lies in the fact that 50% of the
observed (and transformed) variables will lie above the zero point and the other 50%
below it. Furthermore, it no longer contains parameter θ.

To reduce observed variables $x = \ln t$ to the required standardized form, we write

$$\hat{y} = \sqrt{\frac{r}{r-1}} (x - \bar{x}) - \ln (\ln 2) - \gamma, \tag{18}$$

where r is the number of accidents of a person, $x = \ln t$ is the individual time-interval
between successive accidents relating to this person, $\bar{x} = \frac{1}{r} \sum_{i=1}^{r} x_i$ is the arithmetic mean
of this person's log-time-intervals, and γ is Euler's constant.

$\hat{y}$, of eqn. (18), is a statistical estimate of y in eqns. (13) and (14). The expectation and
variance of the estimate $\hat{y}$ are

$$E(\hat{y}) = -\ln (\ln 2) - \gamma, \tag{19}$$

$$var\,(\hat{y}) = \frac{\pi^2}{6}, \tag{20}$$

which are the same as those given for y in eqns. (16) and (17).

For each of 323 drivers the reduced variables $\hat{y}$ were calculated from eqn. (18) giving
a total of 4864 reduced log-time-intervals. The observed histogram of these could now
be compared with the theoretical distribution $\Lambda(y)$ of eqn. (14).

The time-interval distributions $\phi(t)$ of eqn. (1), the log-time-interval distribution $f(x)$
of eqn. (4) and its standard form $\Lambda(y)$ in eqn. (14) are theoretically speaking applicable
only if exposure lengths L tend to infinity. In practice, however, this restriction only
applies to unreasonably short exposure lengths L. When L is short, the exact log-time-

interval distribution in its standardized form is given by

$$\Lambda_0(y) = \frac{r}{L} e^y \left(1 - \frac{1}{L} e^y\right)^{r-1} \quad (-\infty \leqslant y \leqslant \ln L), \tag{21}$$

where r = number of accidents and

$$L = \left[1 - \left(\frac{1}{2}\right)^{1/r}\right]^{-1}. \tag{22}$$

Provided that $r \geqslant 10$, the standardized distribution $\Lambda_0(y)$ of eqn. (21) looks very similar to $\Lambda(y)$ of eqn. (14) when plotted.

From eqn. (22) one sees that, for r reasonably large, L also becomes large. By substituting eqn. (22) for L into eqn. (21) and then going over to the limit for $r \to \infty$, one can easily show that

$$\lim_{r \to \infty} \Lambda_0(y) = \Lambda(y).$$

In our data the average number of accidents per driver was

$$r = \frac{4864}{323} \sim 15.$$

By virtue of eqns. (21) and (22) the standardized log-time-interval distribution becomes numerically

$$\Lambda_0(y) = 0 \cdot 67737 e^y (1 - 0 \cdot 045158 e^y)^{14}.$$

It is this density function which was superimposed on the histogram of the 4864 "reduced" observations in Fig. 21.2. The agreement between theory and observations is excellent. Had we used the standardized log-time-interval distribution for unlimited exposure L, as given in eqn. (14) instead of the theoretically more correct eqn. (21), the difference would hardly have been noticeable to the eye. The χ^2-test for 17 degrees of freedom yield-

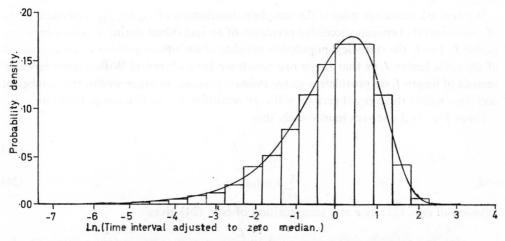

FIG. 21.2. Standardized log-time-interval histogram and theoretical distribution for 4864 accidents incurred by 323 bus drivers. Each individual had at least 10 accidents after the exclusion of the learning period

ed an associated probability of 0·77. However, this test is questionable due to the rather unconventional way in which we eliminated the variations in the θ's by making use of 323 sample means, one for each driver.

4. Statistical Point Estimation of Individual Liability with the Help of $\bar{t}_L$

In the previous section we had pointed out that parameter θ in the negative exponential time-interval distribution of eqn. (1) characterized a person's overall liability provided his accidents followed a stable or nearly stable Poisson process. For each individual at risk, parameter θ must be estimated from a few time-intervals during a limited exposure of length L. One possible estimator is the arithmetic mean of successive time-intervals $\bar{t}_r$ suggested in eqn. (7). Due to the limit L being superimposed on the time continuum, as shown hereunder in Fig. 21.3, certain statistical difficulties arise.

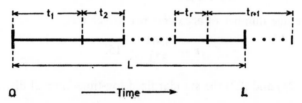

FIG. 21.3. Diagrammatic representation of time-intervals between successive accidents during a limited exposure period of length L

The r time-intervals in L *do not* constitute a random sample of r items drawn from a negative exponential distribution as the finite exposure length L excludes automatically the larger time-intervals of t.

5. The Sampling Distribution of Estimator $\bar{t}_L$

We now ask ourselves what is the sampling distribution of $\bar{t}_L$, i.e. the arithmetic mean of time-intervals between successive accidents of an individual during a *limited* exposure period L. For $\bar{t}_L$ the statistical population consists of an infinite number of exposures, all of the same length L as that single one which we have observed. Within these repeated periods of length L we postulate a stable Poisson process. In other words, the number of accidents within these equal periods will vary according to the Poisson distribution.

From Fig. 21.3 one sees immediately that

$$\sum_{i=1}^{r} t_i \leq L \tag{23}$$

and

$$\sum_{i=1}^{r} t_i + t_{r+1} > L. \tag{24}$$

Division of eqn. (23) by r and transposition of eqn. (24) gives

$$\bar{t}_r \leq \frac{L}{r}, \tag{25}$$

$$t_{r+1} > L - r\bar{t}_r. \tag{26}$$

The sampling distribution of arithmetic means of r items drawn randomly from a negative exponential population without any limit L superimposed is given by

$$\omega(\bar{i}_r) = \frac{1}{\Gamma(r)} \left(\frac{r}{\theta}\right)^r \bar{i}_r^{r-1} e^{-\frac{r}{\theta}\bar{i}_r}. \tag{27}$$

Furthermore, due to the independence of $\bar{i}_r$ and t_{r+1} we have as the bivariate distribution for variables $\bar{i}_r$ and t_{r+1},

$$p(\bar{i}_r, t_{r+1}) = \omega(\bar{i}_r)\phi(t_{r+1}) = \left[\frac{1}{\Gamma(r)} \left(\frac{r}{\theta}\right)^r \bar{i}_r^{r-1} e^{-\frac{r}{\theta}\bar{i}_r}\right]\left[\frac{1}{\theta} e^{-\frac{t_{r+1}}{\theta}}\right]. \tag{28}$$

From eqns. (28), (25), and (26) we obtain the conditional sampling distribution of the arithmetic mean $\bar{i}_L$, for r fixed as

$$g(\bar{i}_L \mid r) = \frac{\displaystyle\int_{L-r\bar{i}_r}^{\infty} p(\bar{i}_r, t_{r+1})\, dt_{r+1}}{\displaystyle\int_0^{L/r}\int_{L-r\bar{i}_r}^{\infty} p(\bar{i}_r, t_{r+1})\, d\bar{i}_r\, dt_{r+1}} = r\left(\frac{r}{L}\right)^r \bar{i}_L^{r-1} \quad \left(0 < \bar{i}_L \leqslant \frac{L}{r}\right) \tag{29}$$

the mean of which is

$$E(\bar{i}_L \mid r) = \frac{L}{r+1} \tag{30}$$

with a variance of

$$\operatorname{var}(\bar{i}_L \mid r) = \frac{L^2}{r(r+1)^2(r+2)}. \tag{31}$$

Equations (30) and (31) are familiar results in connection with a random division of a line of length L by r points, except that the derivation here was achieved in a different way and that in the random division problem we are interested in the distribution of $r+1$ *individual* line segments. In our work we deal with the *mean* of the first r segments.

The probability of exactly r accidents during exposure L is obtained from eqn. (28) in two steps:

$$I(r) = \int_0^{L/r}\int_{L-r\bar{i}_r}^{\infty} p(\bar{i}_r, t_{r+1})\, d\bar{i}_r\, dt_{r+1} = \frac{1}{r!}\left(\frac{L}{\theta}\right)^r e^{-L/\theta}. \tag{32}$$

Substitution of $\lambda = L/\theta$ yields

$$I(r) = e^{-\lambda}\frac{\lambda^r}{r!}, \tag{33}$$

where $r = 1, 2, 3, \ldots, \infty$. $r = 0$ has been excluded automatically as we must have at least one accident in L before we can make use of estimator $\bar{i}_r$ in the above formulae.

As

$$\sum_{r=1}^{\infty} I(r) = 1 - e^{-\lambda},$$

the probability of $r = 1, 2, 3, \ldots, \infty$ accidents in L becomes

$$\pi_1(r) = \frac{1}{e^{\lambda}-1}\frac{\lambda^r}{r!}, \tag{34}$$

which is the Poisson distribution truncated at 0.

To obtain the unconditional sampling distribution of estimator $\bar{\imath}_L$, we have to find the expectation of the conditional sampling distribution in eqn. (29), i.e.

$$E[g(\bar{\imath}_L \mid r)] = \sum \pi_1(r) g(\bar{\imath}_L \mid r) \quad \text{(for } r = 1, 2, \ldots, \infty)$$

$$= \frac{1}{\theta(e^\lambda - 1)} \sum \frac{r^r}{(r-1)!} \left(\frac{\bar{\imath}_L}{\theta}\right)^{r-1}, \tag{35}$$

where

$$L = \lambda\theta.$$

In the summation, care must be taken at the discontinuities at the terminal points of the distribution in eqn. (29), i.e. at L/r.

Finally, we find for the sampling distribution of estimator $\bar{\imath}_L$,

$$g\left(\bar{\imath}_L \mid \frac{L}{i+1} < \bar{\imath}_L \le \frac{L}{i}\right) = \frac{1}{\theta(e^{L/\theta} - 1)} \sum_{r=1}^{i} \frac{r^r}{(r-1)!} \left(\frac{\bar{\imath}_L}{\theta}\right)^{r-1}, \tag{36}$$

where

$$i = 1, 2, 3, \ldots, \infty \quad \text{and} \quad 0 < \bar{\imath}_L \le L.$$

From eqn. (36) one sees that the sampling distribution of $\bar{\imath}_L$ consists of a series of parabolic arcs with discontinuities at points L/i.

Due to its peculiar shape we have called it the *porcupine distribution*. In Fig. 21.4 we have plotted an example for $\theta = 100$ and $L = 1000$ corresponding to $\lambda = 10$.

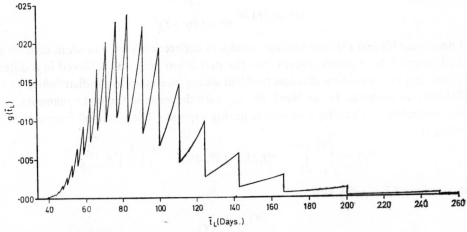

FIG. 21.4. "Porcupine" sampling distribution of estimator $\bar{\imath}_L$ for $\theta = 100$ and $L = 1000$ days

The jth moment about the origin of the porcupine distribution is

$$\mu_j' = \frac{\theta^{j-1}}{e^\lambda - 1} \sum_{i=1}^{\infty} \int_{L/(i+1)}^{L/i} \left\{ \sum_{r=1}^{i} \frac{r^r}{(r-1)!} \left(\frac{\bar{\imath}_L}{\theta}\right)^{r+j-1} \right\} d\bar{\imath}_L = \frac{\theta^j}{e^\lambda - 1} \sum_{r=0}^{\infty} \frac{\lambda^{r+j+1}}{r!(r+1)^j(r+j+1)} \tag{37}$$

from which we obtain the mean and variance of estimator $\bar{\imath}_L$ as

$$E(\bar{\imath}_L) = \left(1 - \frac{\lambda}{e^\lambda - 1}\right)\theta, \tag{38}$$

$$\text{var}(\bar{\imath}_L) = \frac{\theta^2}{2(e^\lambda - 1)}\left[\lambda^2\left\{Ei(\lambda) - \ln\lambda - \gamma + \frac{1}{2}\right\} - (1+\lambda)e^\lambda + 4\lambda + 1 - \frac{2\lambda^2}{e^\lambda - 1}\right], \quad (39)$$

where $Ei(\lambda)$ is the exponential integral and $\gamma =$ Euler's constant.

Equation (38) shows that estimator $\bar{\imath}_L$ is biased low.

In Table 21.1 we have calculated this bias, expressed as a percentage of the true θ, for a few values of λ.

TABLE 21.1. PERCENTAGE BIAS OF
ESTIMATOR $\bar{\imath}_L$

$\lambda = L/\theta$	% bias
0·5	− 77·1
1·0	− 58·2
2·0	− 31·3
3·0	− 15·7
4·0	− 7·5
5·0	− 3·4
10·0	− 0·04
20·0	− 0·00

As long as $\lambda \geqslant 5$ the bias becomes unimportant. Hence, for $\theta = 100$ days, it would be desirable to have an exposure period of $L = 500$ days or more.

In Table 21.2 the standard error of estimator $\bar{\imath}_L$ has been evaluated for $\theta = 100$ days from eqn. (39) at three different levels of L.

TABLE 21.2. STANDARD ERROR
$\sigma(\bar{\imath}_L)$ AS A FUNCTION OF EXPOSURE
LENGTH L FOR $\theta = 100$ DAYS

L (days)	$\sigma(\bar{\imath}_L)$ (days)
500	56
1000	39
5000	15

From eqn. (39) it can be shown that for large values of λ

$$\sigma(\bar{\imath}_L) \doteqdot \frac{\theta}{\sqrt{\lambda}} = \frac{\theta^{3/2}}{\sqrt{L}}. \quad (40)$$

Hence it follows that, if θ is estimated by $\bar{\imath}_L$, the error of estimation is directly proportional to $\theta^{3/2}$ and inversely proportional to $L^{1/2}$. Consequently we can estimate the liabilities of bad drivers, with low θ's, far better than those of good drivers with larger θ's if we hold exposure period L constant. Common sense dictates that a larger exposure period L should reduce the error of estimation. However, a law of diminishing return is reached, as in all statistical sampling because L is appearing under a square root.

6. Confidence Limits if Parameter θ is Estimated from $\bar{\imath}_L$

For a specified confidence level α we have

$$\alpha = \int_{\bar{\imath}_{L,\alpha}}^{L} g\left(\bar{\imath}_L \mid \frac{L}{i+1} < \bar{\imath}_L \leqslant \frac{L}{i}\right) d\bar{\imath}_L, \tag{41}$$

where $i = 1, 2, 3, \ldots, \infty$.

If we define

$$s = \frac{L}{\bar{\imath}_{L,\alpha}}, \tag{42}$$

where s is now a continuous variable in the range $r \leqslant s \leqslant \infty$ and k is the nearest integer below s, we may write eqn. (41) as

$$\alpha = \frac{1}{\theta(e^{\lambda}-1)}\left[\sum_{i=1}^{k-1}\int_{L/(i+1)}^{L/i}\left\{\sum_{r=1}^{i}\frac{r^r}{(r-1)!}\left(\frac{\bar{\imath}_L}{\theta}\right)^{r-1}\right\}d\bar{\imath}_L + \int_{L/s}^{L/k}\left\{\sum_{r=1}^{k}\frac{r^r}{(r-1)!}\left(\frac{\bar{\imath}_L}{\theta}\right)^{r-1}\right\}d\bar{\imath}_L\right]. \tag{43}$$

After integration, summation and substitution of $\lambda = L/\theta$, we find for the upper limit of λ,

$$\alpha = \frac{1}{e^{\lambda_U}-1}\sum_{i=1}^{k}\left[1-\left(\frac{i}{s}\right)^i\right]\frac{\lambda_U^i}{i!}. \tag{44}$$

From the observed mean time-interval $\bar{\imath}_L \equiv \bar{\imath}_{L,\alpha}$ and the given exposure length L, we obtain s from eqn. (42).

We then solve eqn. (44) for λ_U and finally, for the lower limit of θ,

$$\theta_L = \frac{L}{\lambda_U}.$$

Replacing α by $1-\alpha$ in equation (44) will permit us to calculate λ_L and hence the upper limit of θ becomes

$$\theta_U = \frac{L}{\lambda_L}.$$

Consequently,

$$\text{prob.}\ (\theta_L \leqslant \theta \leqslant \theta_U) = 1 - 2\alpha$$

gives the exact probability that the true unknown parameter θ will be within the limits θ_L and θ_U in repeated confidence estimates of the same kind.

Although $\bar{\imath}_L$ is a biased estimator of θ if λ is small, as previously discussed, the above confidence limits are unbiased and exact for any level of λ.

In Table 21.3 the upper and lower limits for 80% confidence intervals are given for ten PUTCO drivers of the Wynberg division whose environmental risk was virtually identical during their respective periods of driving.

The upper and lower limits θ_U and θ_L were calculated from eqn. (44). The rank order in Table 21.3 is based on the magnitude of the estimates $\bar{\imath}_L$. The width of the confidence intervals in the final column is perfectly rank-correlated with the average time-interval

TABLE 21.3. ESTIMATES $\bar{t}_L$ AND ASSOCIATED 80% CONFIDENCE INTERVALS FOR TEN DRIVERS
IN THE WYNBERG DIVISION OF PUTCO

Driver	Number of accidents	Exposure (days)	Mean time-interval between accidents (days)	Lower 10% limit (days)	Upper 10% limit (days)	80% Confidence interval for θ (days)
	r	L	$\bar{t}_L$	θ_L	θ_U	$\theta_U-\theta_L$
I	14	492	34	26	54	28
H	15	809	42	33	62	29
J	11	723	54	41	89	48
K	32	2041	59	50	74	24
L	20	1943	85	68	119	51
M	16	1843	108	84	164	80
D	12	2260	188	141	328	187
N	8	2004	227	164	505	341
O	1	600	319	233	NS*	—
E	5	2104	363	248	NS*	—

* No solution.

estimates $\bar{t}_L$ in the fourth column, with the only exception of driver K. As the confidence-interval width is a function of $\sigma(\bar{t}_L)$ we would have expected this correlation in terms of eqn. (40). The exception, driver K, also follows from eqn. (40) as he had a much longer exposure L than the other three drivers preceding him in Table 21.3. If the estimate of the mean time-interval between accidents is large and is based on a few accidents only, it may happen that eqn. (44) will not yield a mathematical solution for the *upper* confidence limit, as was the case for drivers O and E in Table 21.3.

In Fig. 21.5 the mean time-interval estimates $\bar{t}_L$ for the same ten drivers have been plotted as circlets and the associated 80% confidence intervals as vertical lines. A pre-set divisional standard for the Wynberg section of $\theta_s = 100$ days is indicated as a horizontal line. It will be seen that four of the drivers are worse than the standard required as their upper limits lie below the line of $\theta_s = 100$, whereas another four are better because their lower limits are above this line. The remaining two drivers could not be fitted into the dichotomy "above-or-below standard", as their confidence interval straddles the line of $\theta_s = 100$.

Although the confidence intervals are unhelpfully large for drivers with few accidents and high $\bar{t}_L$, it is still possible to infer that they are significantly better than a pre-set standard even if $\bar{t}_L$ is based on a single accident as was the case for driver O. This worthwhile statistical property stems from the fact that the chances are practically nil that a bad driver will have a single, very long time-interval between two successive accidents, or from the start of the exposure to the first accident. This may be seen from the area of a negative exponential distribution with low parameter θ which has been cut off at a fairly high point in the tail. Conversely, if a single long time-interval has been achieved, it must come from a negative exponential distribution with a relatively large value for parameter θ. Of course, this argument only holds if successive time intervals follow a stable negative

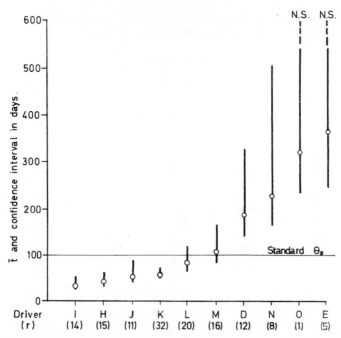

FIG. 21.5. Average time-interval estimates $\bar{t}_L$ and associated 80% confidence belts for ten Wynberg bus drivers who were exposed to the same environmental risk. The divisional standard was $\theta_S = 100$ days

exponential law. Evidence to this effect must be sought in the control charts previously described.

Bad drivers are more easily classified as "below standard" because they have frequent accidents during relatively short time exposures. As the confidence intervals are short for these cases, no real statistical problem exists.

Estimator $\bar{t}_L$ was used throughout the early periods of the authors' investigation to classify drivers into various categories. It has, however, two major shortcomings:

(1) It cannot cope with zero accidents in L. Yet a long exposure L, with not a single accident incurred in it, certainly indicates a safe driving performance.

(2) It does not make use of the time elapsed between the last accident and the end of the observational period L. This is seen from that part of time-interval t_{r+1} in Fig. 21.3 which falls inside L. It does sometimes happen that there is one accident during exposure L which occurred shortly after the start of driving and that the remaining time to the end of the observational period was long and accident-free. Such a pattern again indicates safe driving.

From a statistical point of view $\bar{t}_L$ does not make use of all the information contained in the original observations.

Nevertheless, $\bar{t}_L$ is still a most useful estimator where the end of the exposure period coincides with an observed accident which, for example, is often the case with discharged persons whose dismissals may have been precipitated by their last mishap.

Again in "split-half" studies, where the division is undertaken on a basis of equal numbers of accidents during the first and second periods, $\bar{\imath}_L$ is the most appropriate statistic.

7. Statistical Point Estimation of Individual Liability with the Help of $\hat{\imath}_L$

To overcome the difficulties inherent in the $\bar{\imath}_L$ estimator we have a fresh look at eqn. (30) which gave the expectation of the $g(\bar{\imath}\,|\,r)$ distribution under the condition that r was held constant, i.e.

$$E(\bar{\imath}_L\,|\,r) = \frac{L}{r+1}.$$

As we *do* know the number of accidents incurred in exposure period L, it suggests itself that we could use this mean value as an estimator, say

$$\check{\imath}_L = \frac{L}{r+1}, \tag{45}$$

which would allow an estimate for θ even if we had no accidents in L.

In fact $\check{\imath}_L$ is well known and is used in engineering applications dealing with the reliability of industrial equipment or weaponry. [See, for example, Epstein (1960).] The expectation of this estimator is

$$E(\check{\imath}_L) = \sum_{r=0}^{\infty} \frac{L}{r+1}\; \frac{e^{-\lambda}\lambda^r}{r!} = (1-e^{-\lambda})\theta. \tag{46}$$

The bias is still negative as the zero accident drivers have a longer time spell to their first accident than the duration of the exposure period L. However, as we have included zero accidents, the bias is much smaller than that for estimator $\bar{\imath}_L$ given in eqn. (38).

Lower and upper confidence limits for parameter θ, if we use $\check{\imath}_L$ of eqn. (45), are given by

$$\theta_L = \frac{2L}{\chi_\alpha^2(2r+2)} \tag{47}$$

and

$$\theta_U = \frac{2L}{\chi_{1-\alpha}^2(2r)}, \tag{48}$$

where $\chi_\alpha^2(v)$ is the χ^2 variable with v degrees of freedom at confidence level α which may be obtained from published statistical tables.

$$\text{prob.}\,(\theta_L \leqslant \theta \leqslant \theta_U) \geqslant 1 - 2\alpha \tag{49}$$

is the probability that the unknown parameter θ will be straddled by the confidence interval calculated from eqns. (47) and (48) in repeated estimations of a similar kind. Unfortunately, it involves an inequality which is due to the discrete nature of estimator $\check{\imath}_L$ involving $r = 0, 1, 2, \ldots, \infty$.

Narrower, *exact* confidence intervals may be obtained by adding to the observed number of accidents a rectangular random deviate $z(0 \leqslant z \leqslant 1)$, taken from a random number table. This ingenious device is due to Stevens (1957) and has not been applied a great deal because some statisticians feel that one should not introduce another statistical variable when we have already enough variation in the original observations.

This criticism of Stevens's work is completely unfounded as was pointed out by Kendall and Stuart (1961). The introduction of z does yield narrower limits because we get rid of the inequality in eqn. (49). Here is really a case where one loses *less* on the swings than what one makes on the roundabouts.

The author has used Stevens's method extensively and has shown theoretically that the average reduction of the confidence interval width is substantial, ranging from 20% to 50% for $r = 0, 1, 2, 3, 4$.

The new estimator is defined most generally as

$$\hat{t}_L = \frac{L}{r+z+c},$$

(50)

where z is the rectangular random deviate, $0 \leqslant z \leqslant 1$, and c is a constant which will reduce the negative bias of estimator $\check{t}_L$.

The expected mean of this estimator is

$$E(\hat{t}_L) = \theta\lambda e^{-\lambda} \sum_{i=0}^{\infty} \frac{\lambda^i}{i!} \ln\left(1+\frac{1}{c+i}\right).$$

(51)

Numerical tests for different values of c led to the use of $c = \frac{3}{8}$, a constant which is known in connection with a transformation of the Poisson variate to normality and which stabilizes its variance.

Our specific estimator then becomes

$$\hat{t}_L = \frac{L}{r+z+\frac{3}{8}}.$$

(52)

In Table 21.4 the biases arising from the use of three estimators of parameter θ are compared with each other for selected values of λ.

TABLE 21.4. PERCENTAGE BIAS OF ESTIMATORS $\bar{t}_L$, $\check{t}_L$, AND $\hat{t}_L$

$\lambda = \dfrac{L}{\theta}$	$\bar{t}_L$	$\check{t}_L$	$\hat{t}_L$
0·5	− 77·1	− 60·7	− 50·8
1·0	− 58·2	− 36·8	− 23·7
2·0	− 31·3	− 13·5	− 1·4
3·0	− 15·7	− 5·0	+ 3·9
4·0	− 7·5	− 1·8	+ 4·4
5·0	− 3·4	− 0·7	+ 3·8

For $\lambda > 5$ all biases gradually disappear. For the wide range $1·8 \leqslant \lambda \leqslant \infty$, the maximum absolute bias is 4·4% for estimator $\hat{t}_L$. This performance cannot be matched by the other two estimators.

8. Confidence Limits if Parameter θ Is Estimated from $\hat{t}_L$

The exact upper and lower confidence limits are found in the following way: First we invert eqn. (50) to give us

$$x = \frac{L}{\hat{t}_L} = r + z + c.$$

By virtue of $0 \leqslant z \leqslant 1$ we have $r + c \leqslant x \leqslant r + c + 1$. x is now a continuous step function with probability density

$$f(x)\, dx = e^{-\lambda} \frac{\lambda^r}{r!}\, dx \quad (r = 0, 1, 2, \ldots, \infty).$$

The cumulative probability function is then

$$F(x) = F(r + z + c) = e^{-\lambda} \sum_{i=0}^{r-1} \frac{\lambda^i}{i!} \int_{i+c}^{i+c+1} dx + \frac{e^{-\lambda}\lambda^r}{r!} \int_{r+c}^{r+c+z} dx.$$

If $r = 0$, the sum on the right-hand side of the equation is taken as 0. After integration and substitution of r for i,

$$F(r + z + c) = e^{-\lambda} \sum_{r=0}^{r-1} \frac{\lambda^r}{r!} + z e^{-\lambda} \frac{\lambda^r}{r!}.$$

But

$$e^{-\lambda} \frac{\lambda^r}{r!} = e^{-\lambda} \sum_{r=0}^{r} \frac{\lambda^r}{r!} - e^{-\lambda} \sum_{r=0}^{r-1} \frac{\lambda^r}{r!}.$$

Substitution of this last equation into the previous one yields

$$F(r + z + c) = z e^{-\lambda} \sum_{r=0}^{r} \frac{\lambda^r}{r!} + (1 - z) e^{-\lambda} \sum_{r=0}^{r-1} \frac{\lambda^r}{r!} = zQ(2\lambda \,|\, 2r + 2) + (1 - z)Q(2\lambda \,|\, 2r).$$

Hence the upper confidence limit for parameter λ is obtained from a solution of

$$\alpha = zQ(2\lambda_U \,|\, 2r + 2) + (1 - z)Q(2\lambda_U \,|\, 2r). \tag{53}$$

Replacement of α by $1 - \alpha$ and of λ_U by λ_L gives the lower limit. In eqn. (53) α is the confidence level and $Q(\chi^2 \,|\, \nu)$ the cumulative χ^2-distribution with ν degrees of freedom as listed in statistical tables.

Finally, we find for the upper and lower confidence limits of parameter θ

$$\theta_U = \frac{L}{\lambda_L} \tag{54}$$

and

$$\theta_L = \frac{L}{\lambda_U}. \tag{55}$$

It is interesting to note that constant c has been eliminated in formula (53). This means that the confidence limits are the same irrespective of the magnitude of c in eqn (50). The bias of $\hat{t}_L$, however, is dependent on the numerical choice of constant c.

As an example we take driver O (in Table 21.3). For him we had $r = 1$ accident, $L = 600$ days exposure of driving, and $z = 0 \cdot 9905$ (drawn from a 4-digit random number table and dividing by 10^4).

The point estimate for his average time interval between accidents is from eqn. (52).

$$\hat{t}_{600} = \frac{600}{1+0\cdot9905+0\cdot375} = 254 \text{ days.}$$

The upper limit λ_U for an 80% confidence interval is calculated from equation (53) as

$$0\cdot1 = 0\cdot9905Q(2\lambda_U|4)+0\cdot0095Q(2\lambda_U|2),$$

where $2\lambda_U = \chi^2$.

The solution of this equation,

$$\lambda_U = 3\cdot8803,$$

is obtained from the tabulated values of the cumulative χ^2-distribution. Special graphs may be constructed to simplify the calculation process.

The lower limit λ_L is found by solving

$$0\cdot9 = 0\cdot9905Q(2\lambda_L|4)+0\cdot0095Q(2\lambda_L|2),$$

which gives

$$\lambda_L = 0\cdot5224.$$

From eqns. (54) and (55)

$$\theta_U = \frac{600}{0\cdot5224} = 1149 \text{ days,}$$

$$\theta_L = \frac{600}{3\cdot8803} = 155 \text{ days.}$$

The lower confidence limit is well above the divisional standard of $\theta_s = 100$ days. This driver then is safer than average, a result we had previously arrived at with the $\tilde{t}_L$ technique as given in Table 21.3.

It is of interest to see what point estimate and 80% confidence interval we would have obtained, if we had used the conventional estimation method. From formula (45)

$$\tilde{t}_{600} = \frac{600}{1+1} = 300 \text{ days.}$$

From eqn. (48)

$$\theta_U = \frac{1200}{\chi^2_{0\cdot9}(2)} = \frac{1200}{0\cdot2107} = 5695 \text{ days,}$$

and from eqn. (47)

$$\theta_L = \frac{1200}{\chi^2_{0\cdot1}(4)} = \frac{1200}{7\cdot7794} = 154 \text{ days.}$$

The above results are summarized in Table 21.5.

This example shows that it is feasible to calculate confidence limits for the mean time-interval between successive accidents even if we have observed only one accident in L. The limits are, understandably, very wide, but it is still possible in many such cases to classify an individual as *above* a pre-set standard.

TABLE 21.5. CALCULATION OF 80% CONFIDENCE
INTERVALS AND POINT ESTIMATES BY TWO
METHODS RELATING TO DRIVER O, WITH $r = 1$,
$L = 600$, AND $z = 0.9905$

	$\hat{t}_L$ (days)	$\check{t}_L$ (days)
Average time interval	254	300
Lower limit	155	154
Upper limit	1149	5695
Width of confidence interval	994	5541

As will be seen from Table 21.5, the width of the confidence interval for this driver was about 80% shorter if one compares the $\hat{t}_L$ method with the more conventional $\check{t}_L$ technique. *On average*, the reduction in confidence interval width for $r = 1$ will be of the order of 40–50%.

9. Statistical Criteria for the Classification of Individuals and a Test for Differential Accident-liability Among a Group of Persons

Two very important questions arise in practice:

(a) How does one classify a person into "above-or-below-standard" given his entire accident record? Such classification is necessary not only for the purpose of eliminating high accident risks from a driving population but it is also vital if psychological selection procedures have to be validated against a reliable criterion.

(b) Is there available any statistical measure to assess whether a proneness factor is existent among a group of persons all of whom are exposed to the same environmental risk?

We had previously discussed the historical approach which was largely based on the negative binomial distribution in both its uni- and bivariate forms. We had pointed out the shortcomings of comparing observed accident frequencies in a group of persons with those expected theoretically from the negative binomial and Poisson probability laws. Perhaps the most important of all criticism was the wastage of available data if one followed in the steps of Greenwood and Yule. We have tried to overcome this difficulty by estimating the accident liability of an individual. This train of thought freed us from the shackles of the requirement that all persons had to be exposed to risk for the identical length of time.

What remains to be done is to find a statistical test which will tell us whether, among a group of individuals similarly exposed to risk, there exists a phenomenon of accident proneness, given that exposure lengths L differ widely from person to person.

Equation (53) shows how to obtain the upper confidence limit of λ for a fixed level of α. We now calculate for each driver his own probability level α under the hypothesis that for each and every person in the group parameter θ, the true average interval between successive accidents, was the same. In addition it is postulated that estimates $\hat{t}_L$ only differed because of chance variations introduced by dealing with a statistical sample drawn from an individual's accident population.

In such a situation

$$\alpha_i = z_i Q \left(\frac{2L_i}{\theta} \mid 2r_i + 2 \right) + (1 - z_i) Q \left(\frac{2L_i}{\theta} \mid 2r_i \right). \tag{56}$$

Here z_i is the rectangular random deviate for the ith person in the group, to be looked up from random number tables for each person separately $(0 \leqslant z_i \leqslant 1)$; L_i is the observed length of exposure to risk for the ith person in the group (in days or miles); θ is the unknown true average time or mileage interval between successive accidents, to be estimated from the entire group of persons at risk; $r_i =$ observed number of accidents for the ith person in the group during his own exposure period L_i; and $\frac{2L_i}{\theta} = \chi^2$.

θ is estimated from

$$\hat{\theta} = \frac{\sum\limits_{i=1}^{N} L_i}{\sum\limits_{i=1}^{N} r_i}, \tag{57}$$

where L_i and r_i as defined above and N is the number of persons in the group at risk.

What we really do in formula (56) is to carry out a statistical significance test for *each* individual to establish that his observed r_i in L_i does not reject the hypothesis of equal liability, among a group of persons, all of whom are assumed to have a common parameter θ. For the purpose of this exercise, θ is estimated by $\hat{\theta}$ in eqn. (57).

If a particular person's $\alpha_i \geqslant 0.975$, we reject the hypothesis that his true unknown mean time between accidents was the postulated common $\hat{\theta}$. If we look at it as a single tail significance test, our rejection probability level is 0.025 and we may conclude that this particular individual was significantly *worse* than the average.

Conversely, an $\alpha_i \leqslant 0.025$ would indicate a person with a significantly *better* than average accident performance.

Here, then, is a way to classify individuals into risk categories offering a solution to the problem posed under question (a) at the beginning of this section.

It is, of course, permissible to substitute into equation (56) θ_s, a pre-set standard, for θ instead of $\hat{\theta}$ of formula (57).

In such a case our significance test is against the standard and the results may therefore be different.

Whilst in practice the ranking of individual persons at risk is frequently undertaken in terms of $\hat{t}_L$, this may be misleading as will be shown in the following example.

Suppose two drivers A and B are exposed to the same environmental risk. A had 200 driving days, after exclusion of a learning period, with one accident during this period. B, on the other hand, drove for 1000 days after his initial "learning" and incurred nine accidents.

According to formula (52) we have for A:

$$_A\hat{t}_{200} = \frac{200}{1 + z + \frac{3}{8}}.$$

Without loss of generality let us assume that A's random number was $z = \frac{5}{8}$, giving

$$_A\hat{t}_{200} = 100 \text{ days.}$$

If B's random number is also taken as $\frac{5}{8}$ we have

$$_B\hat{t}_{1000} = \frac{1000}{9+\frac{5}{8}+\frac{3}{8}} = 100 \text{ days, as well.}$$

If the standard for the division was $\theta_s = 200$ days, ordinary ranking would result in both drivers being classified as "below standard".

From eqn. (56) we calculate for A

$$\alpha_A = \frac{5}{8}Q(2\,|\,4)+\frac{3}{8}Q(2\,|\,2)$$
$$= (\frac{5}{8})(0\cdot736)+(\frac{3}{8})(0\cdot368)$$
$$= 0\cdot60.$$

This magnitude of α does *not* reject the hypothesis of A being a "standard" driver in spite of his observed $\hat{t}_L = 100$ falling appreciably short of the standard $\theta_s = 200$.

For driver B we find from eqn. (56).

$$\alpha_B = \frac{5}{8}Q(10\,|\,20)+\frac{3}{8}Q(10\,|\,18)$$
$$= (\frac{5}{8})(0\cdot968)+(\frac{3}{8})(0\cdot932)$$
$$= 0\cdot95.$$

Hence driver B's performance is significantly *worse* than the pre-set standard, at the 5% level of probability.

The lesson from this example, where the *estimates* of parameter θ for two drivers were exactly the same, is to take the significance level α into account when classifying people into above-average, average, or below-average categories.

Returning now to the problem referred to under (b) at the beginning of this section, it follows from eqn. (56) that the frequency distribution of individual probability levels α_i should follow a continuous rectangular distribution law $(0 \leqslant \alpha_i \leqslant 1)$ *if* parameter θ is identical for all persons in the same group.

Conversely, if θ differs from individual to individual, the resulting observed frequency distribution of α_i will depart from the equal-liability hypothesis embodied in the rectangular model. This departure is tested with the conventional χ^2-test.

The observed frequency distribution of α_i will display a U-shape if there are some very good and some very bad accident performers in the group. The large frequencies for $\alpha_i \geqslant 0\cdot95$ will relate to the bad drivers whilst those for $\alpha_i \leqslant 0\cdot05$ will indicate good accident risks.

A significant departure of the observed frequencies of α_i from the rectangular model, as measured by the χ^2-test, affords strong statistical evidence that the true unknown accident liabilities of individuals in the group differed significantly from each other.

In the Wynberg Division of PUTCO we had 296 men with varying exposures L_i at risk.

The environmental conditions for all drivers were virtually homogeneous. The buses were all the same and each man drove for eight hours a day. By far the greatest portion of the driving was done on the *one* major route, on a split shift embracing the morning and evening peak periods. There were, however, two minor routes, and a part of the bus fleet operated during the interim period. The exposure of the drivers was, nevertheless, equalized by the operating conditions of the company, which were such that there was a constant interchange of duties—a driver being allocated a bus, shift or route according to the immediate demands of the operating requirements. Thus, over a short space of time, the drivers were exposed to a very similar range of hazards with regard to vehicle, traffic conditions, time of day and mileage. Over the period covered by our investigation, which entailed exposures of up to nine years, any remaining residual environmental differences were effectively eliminated.

For each of these 296 Wynberg drivers individual probability levels α_i were calculated after exclusion of learning periods from their total exposure. To decide who displayed initial learning, if any, and for what length of time, the 296 individual control charts were consulted. Parameter θ was estimated from formula (57) as $\hat{\theta} = 113.5$ days.

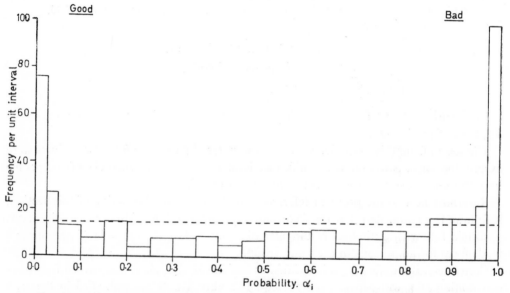

FIG. 21.6. Histogram of α_i probabilities based on the actual accidents of 296 Wynberg bus drivers who were exposed to the same environmental risk. The observed U-shape deviates from the rectangular distribution, shown as the dotted line, and thus strongly indicates differential accident liability

The histogram of the 296 α_i probabilities is shown in Fig. 21.6 displaying the typical U-shape which indicates differences in individual liabilities. The dotted horizontal line in the same Fig. 21.6 gives the expected rectangular distribution based on the equal-liability hypothesis. The χ^2-test, for 21 degrees of freedom, yielded an associated probability of $P < 0.00001$ with a total χ^2 of 416.5. Consequently, the equal-liability theory is decisively rejected in our set of data.

Just to demonstrate what happens if the equal-liability hypothesis holds, we carried out a *sampling experiment* in the following manner.

For each of the 296 drivers $\lambda_i = (L_i/\theta)$ was calculated. Note that the same exposure periods L_i were used for each subject as actually observed and that these periods differed substantially from each other. For the common parameter θ we took $\hat{\theta} = 113\cdot5$ days. With the help of random number and cumulative Poisson distribution tables, random occurrences of accidents r_i were generated, one for each driver based on his own parameter λ_i.

Subsequently 296 probabilities α_i were calculated and the resulting histogram of these is shown in Fig. 21.7. As will be seen, this observed histogram does *not* deviate significantly from the rectangular distribution which was postulated by the equal-liability theory. The χ^2-test yielded an associated probability of $P = 0\cdot35$ for 21 degrees of freedom with a total χ^2 of $22\cdot9$.

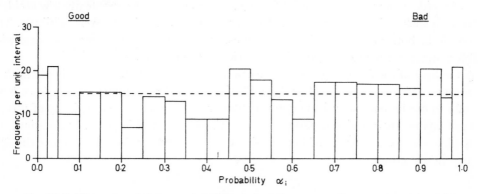

FIG. 21.7. Histogram of 296 α_i probabilities derived from a sampling experiment in which all individual parameters θ were kept constant at $113\cdot5$ days. The departure from the rectangular distribution, shown as the dotted line, is not significant

Returning to the histogram of α_i based on the actual data and shown in Fig. 21.6, there were 61 high accident risk drivers whose $\alpha_i \geqslant 0\cdot95$, whereas we had 52 low accident performers with $\alpha_i \leqslant 0\cdot05$. By chance we should expect $296\times0\cdot05 \doteqdot 15$ persons in each category provided the equal-liability model was applicable. As at least some of the 113 drivers may have appeared in the extreme class intervals of the distribution by pure chance, we have no other practical option than to look at all of the 113 men as either potentially dangerous or relatively safe depending on which extreme side of the distribution they fell.

Does the rejection of the equal-liability hypothesis by means of the α-test support the concept of *accident proneness* in our set of observations?

Before answering this question we first have to define more clearly what we mean by the term "accident proneness". The writers consider the *total accident liability* of an individual as the sum of two components.

The first one is dependent on the *environmental risk* to which persons are exposed. For example, a bus driver in heavy city traffic may be expected to incur more accidents per unit time or mileage, in the long run, than his counterpart in a small provincial town. Again, two bus drivers on the same route may have different accident rates because one of them completes a much larger mileage per unit time than the other.

The second component is *person-centred*. If environmental risks are held constant and individuals have significantly different accident rates, we speak of *accident proneness*. Here we should distinguish carefully between accident proneness which is *temporary* and proneness which is *stable in time*. Some individuals in a group of persons may have a high accident rate for a certain lengthy period. They may have personal trouble, they may be sick and strained, or they may be under the influence of alcohol. In a subsequent lengthy period these personal difficulties may have been resolved, being manifest in a low accident rate. This clearly establishes temporary proneness which is *not* predictable from one period to another.

Conversely, we may have persons whose accident rates are consistently high during the passage of time which, by itself, does neither exclude spells of short duration relatively free of accidents nor certain trending in time. Others may have consistently low accident rates with spells of short duration and trends at somewhat higher levels admitted. The emphasis in both cases is on long exposures. Under these circumstances we deal with stable proneness which *is* predictable for periods of long duration.

In the light of the foregoing the α-test carried out on our data has definitely established temporary accident proneness. For "proof" of stable and predictable proneness we have to refer to our individual accident control charts which showed that a majority of drivers did not change their accident patterns over periods measured in years. In addition, the control chart average levels of log-time-intervals differed significantly among the 296 drivers in our group.

10. The Reliability of the Accident Interval Criterion

Reliability in the statistical sense is not the same as the psychometrician's definition of it.

To the statistician an estimate is the more reliable, the narrower the confidence interval at a given probability level. The confidence interval is, however, very wide in the case of estimating accident liability θ, as was shown in Table 21.3. The main concern of the statistician is to demonstrate that different individuals have significantly different liabilities θ. To this end he uses accepted statistical tests of some kind or other.

On the other hand, the psychometrician's main interest lies in the *validation* of predictor variables against the dependent criterion variable. If the predictor or criterion variables cannot be reproduced, no correlation can be expected between them. Hence the psychometrician's definition of reliability consists of a correlation coefficient between split-halves of tests or criteria, or the test or criterion administered at different times (test–retest). The higher these correlation coefficients, the better the psychometrician's reliability. The old approach of correlating the number of accidents incurred by a group of individuals in one exposure period, of constant duration for everyone, with the corresponding number incurred by the same individuals in another non-overlapping period constitutes, therefore, a reliability coefficient.

In the present investigation estimators $\bar{\imath}_L$ and $\hat{\imath}_L$, which supply statistical estimates of parameter θ, are proposed as accident criteria.

It was previously shown that the standard errors of estimates $\bar{\imath}_L$ and $\hat{\imath}_L$ were large, especially for persons with high θ's, or for persons with short exposure periods L. It is fairly evident that a high reliability correlation coefficient could only be secured from very long, virtually infinite exposure periods for each individual. This, of course, is a very unrealistic condition.

To show that—in spite of the foregoing—there still exists a fair correlation between split-half $\bar{t}_L$ and $\hat{t}_L$ estimates, two examples will be given.

The first refers to the 296 Wynberg drivers. The split was achieved in the following manner.

If a driver had incurred r accidents in total exposure period L, the first $\frac{1}{2}r$ accidents gave rise to an average time interval $\bar{t}_1$ and the second $\frac{1}{2}r$ accidents to a second average time interval $\bar{t}_2$. Where r was an odd figure, $\bar{t}_1$ was based on $\frac{1}{2}(r+1)$ and $\bar{t}_2$ on $\frac{1}{2}(r-1)$ accidents—alternating to $\frac{1}{2}(r-1)$ and $\frac{1}{2}(r+1)$ for every second person with an odd number of accidents in L.

Due to the excessive standard errors of $\bar{t}_1$ and $\bar{t}_2$ when r_1 and $r_2 = 1$, drivers who had two or three accidents in the *total* exposure period L were excluded from this analysis.

In the original publication by Sichel (1965) 62 drivers were lost due to this particular elimination rule. Subsequently, however, with more data having come to hand, it was possible to reduce the number of drivers who had r_1 or $r_2 = 1$. Consequently only 40 drivers out of the 296 were "lost" from this analysis. As none of the remaining 40 drivers were any longer at risk—as their services had been terminated—no further follow-up studies could be undertaken.

A scattergram for $\bar{t}_1$ and $\bar{t}_2$ showed that the resulting bivariate distribution was very skew, fanning out considerably towards higher $\bar{t}$'s. This is to be expected as we deal here with a *mixture* of bivariate parent distributions due to different parameters θ and different sample sizes r coming into play when comparing $\bar{t}_1$ with $\bar{t}_2$.

Correlation coefficients based on skew surfaces are difficult to interpret. In such cases it is wise to transform the variates in order to obtain a distribution nearer to that of a bivariate normal probability function. This was achieved by correlating $\log \bar{t}_1$ with $\log \bar{t}_2$. It can be shown that such a transformation has the added advantage of a higher precision of estimating the product-moment coefficient of the untransformed variables.

The bivariate distribution of $\log \bar{t}_1$ and $\log \bar{t}_2$ for the 256 Wynberg drivers is shown in Fig. 21.8. The class interval boundaries are following a geometric scale with a common ratio of 1·3. This is equivalent to first looking up the logarithms of $\bar{t}_1$ and $\bar{t}_2$ and then correlating these logarithms with each other.

The correlation coefficient was $\hat{\varrho} = 0·62$. The reliability coefficient is calculated from the Spearman–Brown formula as

$$\hat{\varrho}_{SB} = \frac{2\hat{\varrho}}{1+\hat{\varrho}} = 0·77.$$

The second example refers to PUTCO's Umlazi Division in Durban, in particular the men with company numbers 6000 who were described in some detail in a previous chapter. This group of drivers was signed on without any test selection although a TAT was administered to them. Of the 193 drivers *all* could be taken into the split-half correlation analysis as the number of accidents incurred by each of them was equal to or in excess of $r = 4$. Whilst driving conditions in this division were difficult it is also apparent that this

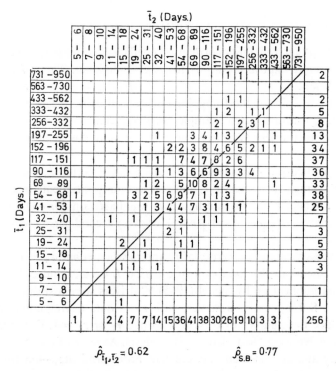

$$\hat{P}_{\bar{t}_1,\bar{t}_2} = 0.62 \qquad \hat{P}_{S.B.} = 0.77$$

Fig. 21.8. Bivariate table for 256 Wynberg bus drivers giving pairs of $\bar{t}$ estimates for two consecutive exposure periods. The class intervals follow a 1.3 geometric scale which is equivalent to a logarithmic transformation. All men were exposed to the same environmental risk

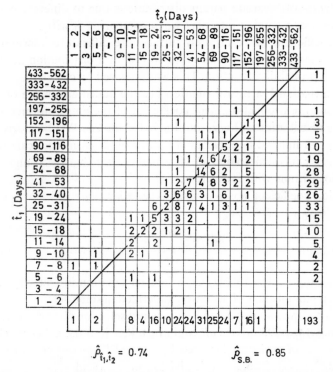

$$\hat{P}_{\bar{t}_1,\bar{t}_2} = 0.74 \qquad \hat{P}_{S.B.} = 0.85$$

Fig. 21.9. Bivariate table for 193 Umlazi bus drivers giving pairs of $\hat{t}$ estimates for two consecutive exposure periods. All men were exposed to the same environmental risk

group had an unusually short mean time-interval between accidents. As these men had no other option than to "learn" fast or face instant dismissal, the influence of learning is more strongly in evidence than for the Wynberg drivers as may be seen by comparing the bivariate distributions in Figs. 21.8 and 21.9. In Fig. 21.9 the bivariate observations are markedly displaced to the right of the diagonal indicating an improvement in the second period. Even so, 110 of the total number of 193 drivers did not change significantly in the second period whereas 83 bettered their performances strongly. Of interest is the fact that, when correlation coefficients were worked out separately for these two groups, *both* coefficients were in excess of 0·70.* The coefficient for the two groups combined, as shown in Fig. 21.9, was $\hat{\varrho} = 0·74$ and after the Spearman–Brown correction the reliability coefficient became

$$\hat{\varrho}_{SB} = \frac{2 \times 0·74}{1 + 0·74} = 0·85.$$

There are two further points to be mentioned in connection with the observed bivariate distribution in Fig. 21.9:

(1) All 193 men were exposed to exactly the same environmental conditions as they drove identical buses on the same and only route.

(2) The split of the total exposure periods was carried out in a different way than previously employed for the Wynberg division. Exposure length L, for each driver, was subdivided into equal periods $\frac{1}{2}L$ and, from the number of accidents incurred in $\frac{1}{2}L$ the estimates $\hat{t}_1$ and $\hat{t}_2$ were obtained. We consider this splitting method slightly superior as $\hat{t}_L$ is a better estimator of θ than estimator $\bar{t}_L$ for reasons previously discussed.

11. Final Comments

Although split-half correlations have their usefulness, the authors do not share the enthusiasm of employing them indiscriminately, especially in the context of accident research. The criticism of correlation coefficients arising from bivariate observed frequency distributions, which was made in the first section of this chapter, applies to the psychometrician's reliability coefficients as well. No matter how high or low a coefficient one has obtained, it is most important to know how a given bivariate distribution has been built up. Furthermore, one should not throw away valuable information contained in a time-series which gives much insight into the behaviour of an individual exposed to risk. To this end we introduced the accident time-interval control charts.

The statistical estimation of an individual's accident-liability, together with the associated confidence limits, will put into focus the element of chance as well as real differences between persons who are exposed to the same environmental hazards. The new approach, which is centered around the individual and not a group, should make it possible to identify the high and low accident risks which are both deserving attention albeit in different and dissimilar ways. For the purpose of test validation, a reliable criterion is an axiomatic precondition. The methods given in the foregoing will enable the research worker to

* The split into a "non-improver" and an "improver" group was based on TAT predictions. This test distinguished successfully between these two categories.

gauge how trustworthy—or unreliable—this criterion is when it comes to ranking individuals on an accident performance scale.

No doubt, the sophisticated statistical reader will have noticed several times over that estimates for θ, given r, t_1, t_2, ..., t_r and L, are "sufficient" if they contain only the number of accidents r and the exposure L in the case of a stable Poisson process, or—put into another form—if time intervals follow the negative exponential distribution function. However, we know that this model does not hold for everyone and that trends in time are possible. Consequently, a great deal of additional information is gained by bringing in the actual intervals between accidents.

The practical usage of the statistical techniques described in this chapter have proved of value in analysing the accident records of bus drivers. Admittedly, the problems are slightly different when dealing with motor-car accidents in general. Yet the authors feel that these same methods, if used intelligently and with minor modifications, should also be of considerable help when applied to the road accident records of the driving public.

REFERENCES

ADELSTEIN, A. M. (1952) Accident proneness: a criticism of the concept based upon an analysis of shunters' accidents, *JR Statist. Soc.* A, **115**, 354–410.

ADLER, A. (1941) The psychology of repeated accidents in industry, *Am. J. Psychiat.* **98**, 99–101.

Alcohol and Highway Safety (1968) The Report to Congress from the US Dept. of Transport, US Govt. Printing Office, Washington, DC.

Alcohol and Road Traffic (1963) Proceedings of the 3rd International Conference on Alcohol and Road Traffic, British Medical Association, London.

Alcohol and Traffic Safety (1966) Proceedings of the 4th International Conference on Alcohol and Traffic Safety, December 1965, Department of Police Administration, Indiana Univ., Bloomington.

ALLPORT, G. W. (1952) *Personality*, Constable, London.

ALLSTATE INSURANCE CO. (1960) *A Teenage Pattern*, Allstate Insurance Co., USA.

AMERICAN MEDICAL ASSOCIATION (1959) *Medical Guide for Physicians in Determining Fitness to Drive a Motor Vehicle*, Chicago. Summary in *J. Am. Med. Ass.* **169**, 1195–7.

ARBOUS, A. G. and KERRICH, J. E. (1951) Accident statistics and the concept of accident proneness, *Biometrics* **7**, 340–432.

ASSOCIATION FOR THE AID OF CRIPPLED CHILDREN (1961) *Behavioral Approaches to Accident Research*, New York.

BAKER, J. S. (1961) Case studies of traffic accidents, *Traff. Saf. Res. Rev.* **5** (4), 15–17.

BAKER, J. S. (1965) Evaluating the senior driver, *Traff. Dig. Rev.* **13** (3), 23–25.

BARMACK, J. E. and PAYNE, D. E. (1961a) Injury-producing private motor vehicle accidents among airmen, *Highway Res. Bd. Bull.* 285. Also *Traff. Saf. Res. Rev.* **6** (3), 24–32.

BARMACK, J. E. and PAYNE, D. E. (1961b) The Lackland accident countermeasure experiment, *Highway Res. Board Proceedings* **40**, 513–22.

BATES, G. E. (1955) Joint distributions of time intervals for the occurrence of successive accidents in a generalized Polyá scheme *Ann. Math. Stat.* **26**, 705–20.

BATES, G. E. and NEYMAN, J. (1952a) Contributions to the theory of accident proneness. I. An optimistic model of the correlation between light and severe accidents, *Univ. Calif. Publ. Stat.* **1**, 215–54.

BATES, G. E. and NEYMAN, J. (1952b) Contribution to the theory of accident proneness, II. True or false contagion, *Univ. Calif. Publ. Stat.* **1**, 255–76.

BAUSCH and LOMB (1944) *Standard Practice in the Administration of the Bausch and Lomb Occupational Vision Tests with the Ortho Rater*, Bausch & Lomb, Rochester, NY.

BEAMISH, J. J. and MALFETTI, J. L. (1962) A psychological comparison of violator and non-violator automobile drivers in the 16 to 19 year age group, *Traff. Saf. Res. Rev.* **6** (1), 12–15.

BENA, E., HOSKOVEC, J., and ŠTIKAR, J. (1968) *Psychologic a Fyziologie Řidiče*, 2nd edn., Nakladatelsvi Dopravy a Spoju, Prague.

BÖCHER, W. (1962) Die charakterlichen Eignungvoraussetzungen des Kraftfahrzeugführes, *Zentralblatt für Verkehrsmedizin, Verkehrspsychologie und Angrenzende Gebiete*, **4**, 215–25.

BÖCHER, W. (1968a) *Verkehrsmedizin und Psychologie*, Sonderdruck aus *Handbuch der Verkehrsmedizin*, Ministry of Health, Bonn, West Germany.

BÖCHER, W. (1968b) Die Psychiatrie in der Verkehrsmedizin, *Die Heil Kunst*, 4, München.

BÖCHER, W. (1968c) *Die prognostische Beurterlung der wegen Trunkenheit am steuer aufgefallenen Kraftfahrer unter besonderer Berücksichtigung kriminal-sociologischer Erhebungen*, Gericht-medizinischen Institut der Universität zu Köln.

BORCHARDT, MRS. BENJAMIN (1965) Licencing the senior driver, *Traff. Dig. Rev.* **13** (3), 7–8.

BORKENSTEIN, R. F. (1967) A realistic approach to drinking and driving, *Traff. Saf.* **67** (10), 9.

BORKENSTEIN, R. F., CROWTHER, R. F., SHUMATE, R. P., ZIEL, W. B., and ZYLMAN, R. (1964) (Ed. A. Dale), *The Role of the Drinking Driver in Traffic Accidents*, Department of Police Administration, Indiana Univ., Bloomington.

BRITISH EPILEPSY ASSOCIATION (1965) *Epilepsy and Driving Licences*, London.

BROWN, I. D. (1967) Car driving and fatigue, *Triangle* **8**, 131–7.

BUIKHUISEN, W. (1968) *A Research Programme on Drunken Driving*, preliminary report from the Criminologisch Instituut, Rijksuniversiteig, Groningen, Holland.

BURG, A. (1967) *The Relationship Between Vision Test Scores and Driving Record: General Findings*, Department of Engineering (ITTE), UCLA: Los Angeles (final report monograph, USPHS).

Bÿdragen voor de Nota Verkeersveiligheid (1965) SWOV, The Hague, Holland. (See also *Nota Verkeersveiligheid*.)

CAMPBELL, B. J. (1958) *The Point System*, AAMVA, Washington, DC.

CANTY, A. (1956) Problem drivers and criminal offenders, *Canadian Services Med. J.* **7**, 136–43.

CASE, H. W. and STEWART, R. G. (1956) Driving attitudes, *Traff. Quart.*, July, 364–76.

CHAMBERS, E. G. (1952) Discussion on Dr. Adelstein's paper, *JR Statist. Soc.* A, **115**, 408.

CHARTERS, W. W. (1927) *The Teaching of Ideals*, McMillan, New York.

COBB, P. W. (1938) *The Accident-prone Driver*, report to the Secretary of Agriculture, US Govt. Printing Office, Washington, House Document No. 462, No. 6.

COBB, P. W. (1939) *Automobile Driver Tests Administered to 3663 Persons in Connecticut, 1936–1937, and the Relation of the Test Scores to the Accidents Sustained*, report to the Highway Research Board, Washington, DC, unpublished.

COHEN, J. and HENSEL, M. (1956) *Risk and Gambling*, Philosophical Library, New York.

COHEN, J. and PRESTON, BARBARA (1968) *Causes and Prevention of Road Accidents*, Faber & Faber, London.

COLQUHOUN, W. P. and CORCORAN, D. W. J. (1964) *Brit. J. Soc. Clin. Psychol.* **3**, 226.

COMMISSION ON JUVENILE DELINQUENCY, ADULT CRIME AND CORRECTION (1959) Report to the 1959 Legislative State of Minnesota.

CONGER, J. J. (1960) Personality factors in motor vehicle accidents, *Medical Times* **88**, 202–84.

CONGER, J. J., GASKILL, H. S., GLAD, D. D., RAINEY, R. V., SAWREY, W. L., and TURRELL, E. S. (1957) Personal and interpersonal factors in motor vehicle accidents, *Am. J. Psychiat.* **113**, 1069–74.

CONGER, J. J., GASKILL, H. S., GLAD, D. D., HASSELL, LINDA, RAINEY, R. V., and SAWREY, W. L. (1959) Psychological and psychophysical factors in motor vehicle accidents, *J. Am. Med. Ass.* **169** (14), 1581–7.

COPPIN, R. S. (*See* DEPARTMENT OF MOTOR VEHICLES, STATE OF CALIFORNIA).

CORCORAN, D. W. J. (1965) Personality and the inverted-U relation, *Brit. J. Psychol.* **56**, 267–73.

CRESSWELL, W. L. and FROGGATT, P. (1963) *The Causation of Bus Driver Accidents: An Epidemiological Study*, Oxford Univ. Press, London.

CUMMING, R. W. (1964) The analysis of skills in driving, *J. Australian Rd. Res. Bd.* **1**, 4–14.

DARNTON, R. (1964) Accidents called a major disease (Editorial), *The New York Times*, New York.

DENVER SYMPOSIUM (1964) *On the Senior Driver and Pedestrians*, Denver, Colorado.

DEPARTMENT OF MOTOR VEHICLES, STATE OF CALIFORNIA, *Control of the Negligent Driver.*

    Part 1 (Feb. 1961) COPPIN, R. S. and SAMUELS, I., *Characteristics of Negligent Drivers.*

    Part 2 (Oct. 1962) COPPIN, R. S. and VAN OLDENBEEK, G., *Driving Performance of Negligent Drivers.*

    Part 3 (June 1966) COPPIN, R. S. and VAN OLDENBEEK, G., *Six Years After Action Driving Record.*

DEPARTMENT OF MOTOR VEHICLES, STATE OF CALIFORNIA, *The 1964 Driver Record Study.*

    Part 1 (Dec. 1964) COPPIN, R. S., LEW, A., and PECK, R. C., *An Introduction and Methodological Description.*

    Part 2 (March 1965) COPPIN, R. S., LEW, A., and PECK, R. C., *Accidents, Traffic Citations and Negligent Operator Count by Sex.*

    Part 3 (April 1965) COPPIN, R. S., LEW, A., and PECK, R. C., *Drivers by Age, Sex and Area of Residence.*

    Part 4 (May 1965) COPPIN, R. S., LEW, A., and PECK, R. C., *The Relationship Between Concurrent Accidents and Citations.*

    Part 5 (June 1965) PECK, R. C., COPPIN, R. S., and MARSH, W. C., *Driver Record by Age, Sex and Marital Status.*

    Part 6 (Nov. 1965) MCBRIDE, R. S., PECK, R. C., and COPPIN, R. S., *The Stability of Reported Accidents and Citations.*

    Part 7 (March 1966) LEW, A., COPPIN, R. S., and PECK, R. C., *The Relationship Between Types of Convictions and Accidents.*

Part 8 (Jan. 1967) PECK, R. C. and COPPIN, R. S., *The Prediction of Accident Involvement using Concurrent Driver Record Data.*

Part 9 (March 1967) MCBRIDE, R. S., PECK, R. C., and COPPIN, R. S., *The Prediction of Accident Involvement from Driver Record and Biographical Data.*

DEPARTMENT OF MOTOR VEHICLES, STATE OF CALIFORNIA (Jan. 1965) COPPIN, R. S. and VAN OLDENBEEK, G., *Driving under Suspension and Revocation.*

DEPARTMENT OF MOTOR VEHICLES, STATE OF CALIFORNIA (Feb. 1965) COPPIN, R. S., FERDUN, G. S., and PECK, R. C., *The Teen-aged Driver.*

DEPARTMENT OF MOTOR VEHICLES, STATE OF CALIFORNIA (Jan. 1966) COPPIN, R. S. and VAN OLDENBEEK, G. *The Fatal Accident Re-examination Program in California.*

DE RIDDER, J. C. (1961) *The Personality of the Urban African in South Africa,* Routledge and Kegan Paul, London; Humanities Press, New York.

DE SILVA, H. R. (1942) *Why we have Automobile Accidents,* John Wiley, New York.

DUNBAR, H. FLORENCE, WOLFE, T. P., TAUBER, E. S., and BRUSH, A. L. (1939) The psychic component of the disease process in cardiac, diabetic and fracture patients, *Am. J. Psychiat.* **95**, 1319, 1342.

Epilepsy and Driving Licences (1965) Report of a symposium in Vienna, Social Studies in Epilepsy, No. 4, Brit. Epilepsy Association.

EPSTEIN, B. (1960) Tolerance limits based on life test data taken from an experimental distribution. *J. Ind. Quality Control,* Aug. p. 10.

EYSENCK, H. J. (1960) *The Structure of Human Personality,* 2nd edn., Methuen, London; John Wiley, New York.

EYSENCK, H. J. (1964) *Crime and Personality,* Routledge and Kegan Paul, London.

EYSENCK, H. J. (1965) *Fact and Fiction in Psychology,* Harmondsworth, Penguin, Pelican Edn.

EYSENCK, H. J. (1968) *The Biological Basis of Personality,* C. C. Thomas, Springfield, Ill.

EYSENCK, H. J. and EYSENCK, SYBIL B. J (1968a) A factorial study of psychoticism as a dimension of personality, *Multivariate Behavioural Research,* Special Issue, pp. 15–32.

FARMER, E. and CHAMBERS, E. G. (1939) *A Study of Accident Proneness amongst Motor Drivers,* Industrial Health Research Board, London, Report No. 84.

FINE, B. J. (1963) Introversion–extraversion and motor vehicle driver behaviour, *Percept. Mot. Skills* **16**, 95–100.

FINESILVER, S. G. (1965) Let's keep older drivers on the road. *Traff. Dig. Rev.* **13** (3), 4–6.

FORBES, T. W. (1939) The normal automobile driver as a traffic problem, *J. Gen. Psychol.* **20**, 471–4.

FORBES, T. W. (1950) *Street and Highway Traffic; Handbook of Applied Psychology,* New York.

FORBES, T. W. (1954) Contribution by psychologists to the reduction of highway traffic accidents in the United States of America, *Bull. Ass. Int. Psychotechnique (Psych. Appl.),* pp. 43–58.

FROGGATT, P. and SMILEY, J. A. (1964) The concept of accident proneness: a review, *Brit. J. Ind. Med.* **21** (1).

GARWOOD, F. and JEFFCOATE, G. O. (1955) *The Influence of the Age of Drivers on Various Human Factors Contributing to Accidents and on the Severity of Injury,* Road Research Laboratory, Note RN/2522/F.G.

GOEN, R. L. (1968) Is the driver "traffic's forgotten man"? *Traff. Saf.* **68** (7).

GOLDSTEIN, L. G. (1961a) *Research on Human Variables in Safe Motor Vehicle Operation: A Correlation Summary of Predictor Variables and Criterion Measures,* the Driver Behavior Research Project, George Washington University.

GOLDSTEIN, L. G. (1961b) Where we are in accident research, paper read at the meeting of the Accident Prevention Study Section of the United States Public Health Service, United States Public Health Service, Washington, DC.

GOLDSTEIN, L. G. (1963) Whither accident research?, *Traff. Saf. Res. Rev.* **7** (1).

GOLDSTEIN, L. G. and MOSELLE, J. N. (1958) A factor study of drivers' attitudes with further study on driver aggression, *High Res. Bd. Bull.* **172**, 9–29.

GOODMAN, L. A. and KRUSKAL, W. H. (1954) Measures of association for cross classification, *J. Am. Statis.* **49**, 732.

GREENSHIELDS, B. D. and PLATT, F. N. (1967) Development of a method of predicting high-accident and high-violation drivers, *J. Appl. Psychol.* **51** (3), 205–10.

GREENWOOD, M. (1949) Discussion on Dr. Smeed's paper, *JR Statis. Soc.* A, **112**, 25.

GREENWOOD, M., WOODS, HILDA M., and YULE, G. U. (1919) *A Report on the Incidence of Industrial*

Accidents upon Individuals with Special Reference to Multiple Accidents, Report 4. Industrial Fatigue Research Board, London.

GREENWOOD, M. and YULE, G. U. (1920) An enquiry into the nature of frequency distributions representative of multiple happenings, with particular reference to the occurrence of multiple attacks of disease or repeated accidents, *JR Statis. Soc.* **83**, 255–79.

GROSSJOHANN, A. (1953) Das Medizinisch-psychologische Institut für Verkehrssicherheit in Stuttgart, *Int. Arch. J. Verk. Wesen*, **8**.

GRUNERT, J. (1961a) Strukturspezifische Unfallkeime des Kraftfahrers, *Z. Exp. Angew. Psychol.* **8**, 42–53.

GRUNERT, J. (1961b) Unfallkeim—Unfalldisposition—Unfall, *Z. Exp. Angew. Psychol.* **8**, 519–39.

HADDON, W., Jnr. and BRADES, V. A. (1959) Alcohol in the single vehicle fatal accident, *J. Am. Med. Assoc.* **169**, 1587–93.

HADDON, W., SUCHMAN, E. A., and KLEIN, D. (1964) *Accident Research*, Harper & Row, New York.

HAIGHT, F. A. (1964) Accident proneness, the history of an idea, *Automobilismo e Automobilismo Industriale* **4**, 3–15.

HAKKINEN, S. (1958) *Traffic Accidents and Driver Characteristics: A Statistical and Psychological Study.* Finland's Institute of Technology, Scientific Researches, No. 13, Helsinki.

HALD, A. and KOUSGAARDE, E. (1967) *A Table for Solving the Binomial Equation, B (c, n, p) = P*, Munksgaard, Copenhagen.

HANSSON, H. (1966) The problem of the young driver, *Proceedings of the 1966 International Road Safety Congress Barcelona*. Also summary in *Int. Rd. Saf. Traff. Rev.* **15** (2), 39–43.

HOFFMAN, H. (1967) *Ausgewählte Internationale Bibliographie 1965–63 zur Verkehrsmedizin*, Lehmanns, München.

HOYOS, Graf C. (Ed.) (1965) Verkehrsverhalten und Persönlichkeit, In: *Psychologie des Strassenverkehrs.*

HULBERT, S. F. *et al.* (1958) A preliminary study of dynamic acuity and its effects in motorists' vision, *J. Amer. optom. Ass.* **29**, 359–64.

IMHOFF, C. (1963) In Letters to the Editor, *Traff. Saf. Res. Rev.* **7** (3).

IRWIN, J. O. (1941) Comments on the paper "Theory and observation in the investigation of accident causation", Chambers, E. G. and Yule, G. U., *JR Statis. Soc.* (supplement), **7**, 89–109.

IRWIN, J. O. (1964) The personal factor in accidents—a review article, *JR Statis. Soc.*, A, **127**, 438–51.

JACOBS, H. H. (1961) Conceptual and methodological problems in accident research, *Behavioral Approaches to Accident Research*, Association for the Aid of Crippled Children, New York, pp. 3–25.

JAYLE, C. E., OURGAUD, A. G., BARSINGER, L. F., and HOLMES, W. J. (1950) *Night Vision*, C. C. Thomas, Springfield, Ill., 1950; English edn., 1959.

JOHNSON, H. M. (1946) The detection and treatment of accident-prone drivers, *Psych. Bull.* **43** (6), 489–532.

Journal of American Insurance (1967) Editorial, Let's stop pampering deadly drivers, May–June, pp. 4–6.

KAESTNER, N. F. (1964) The similarity of traffic involvement records of young drivers and drivers in fatal traffic accidents, *Traff. Saf. Res. Rev.* **8** (2), 34–39.

KAPLAN, A. (1964) *Conduct of Inquiry*, Chandler Publications, San Francisco.

KENDALL, M. G. and STUART, A. (1961) *The Advanced Theory of Statistics*, vol. 11, Charles Griffin & Co. Ltd., London.

KERR, W. (1957) Complementary theories of safety psychology, *J. Soc. Psychol.* **45**, 3–9.

KERRICK, J. C. (1965) In: Extracts from the Driver Symposium on Senior Drivers, *Traff. Dig. Rev.* **13** (3).

KLOPFER, B. and KELLY, D. (1942) *The Rorschach Technique*, Yonkers on Hudson, New York.

KRALL, VITA (1953) Personality characteristics of accident repeating children, *J. Abnorm. Soc. Psychol.* **48** (1) 99–107.

KUHLEN, R. G. (1965) A look at aging, *Traff. Dig. Rev.* **13** (3), 9–12.

LAHY, J. M. (1927) *La Sélection Psychophysiologique des Travailleurs: Conducteurs de Tramways et d'Autobus*, Dunod, Paris.

LAHY, J. M. and KORNGOLD, S. (1936) Recherches expérimentales sur les causes psychologiques des accidents du travail, *Trav. Humain*, B, No. 1, Paris.

LAUER, A. R. (1960) *The Psychology of Driving*, C. C. Thomas, Springfield, Ill.

LEEMING, J. J. (1960) Approaches to road accidents, *Traff. Eng. Control* **2**, 100.

LEVENSON, S. (1968) *Everything but Money*, McDonald, London.

MacIver, J. (1961) Safety and human behavior, *Behavioral Approaches to Accident Research*, Association for the Aid of Crippled Children, New York, pp. 59–76.

Maguire, B. A., Pearson, E. S., and Wynn, A. H. A. (1952) The time intervals between industrial accidents, *Biometrika* **39**, 168–80.

Malfetti, J. L. (1960) Traffic Safety and the Adolescent Driver. Read before School Health Section, American Public Health Association, *Journal of School Health*, **30** (6), 228–34.

Malfetti, J. L. and Fine, B. (1962) *Characteristics of Safe Drivers: A Pilot Study*, Safety Research and Education Project, Progress Report, New York, Columbia University. Also in *Traff. Saf. Res. Rev.* **6** (3), 3–9.

McFarland, R. A. (1961) The accident-prone driver, extract reported in *Traff. Saf.* May 1961.

McFarland, R. A. (1962) The epidemiology of motor vehicle accidents, *J. Am. Med. Ass.* **180** (4), 289–300.

McFarland, R. A. and Moore, R. C. (1960) Youth and the automobile, in *Values and Ideals of American Youth* (E. Ginsberg, Ed.), Columbia Univ. Press, New York.

McFarland, R. A., Moore, R. C., and Warren, A. B. (1955) *Human Variables in Motor Vehicle Accidents: A Review of the Literature*, Harvard School of Public Health.

McFarland, R. A. and Moseley, L. A. (1954) *Human Factors in Highway Transport*, Harvard School of Public Health.

McFarland, R. A., Tune, G. S., and Welford, A. T. (1965) On the driving of automobiles by older drivers, *Traff. Dig. Rev.* **13** (3), 13–16. Originally published (1964) in *J. Gerontol.* **19**, 190–7.

McGuire, F. L. (1956) Psychological comparison of automobile drivers, *US Armed Forces Med. J.* **7**, 1741, 1748.

Mittenecker, E. (1962) *Methoden und Ergebnisse der psychologischen Unfallforschung*, Deuticke-Verlag, Wien, 1962.

Morton, J. (1968) The suicide driver, *Traff. Saf.* **68** (8), 12.

Moynihan, D. P. (1962) The legal regulation of automobile design, *Passenger Car Design and Highway Safety*, Association for the Aid of Crippled Children, New York and Consumers Union, Mount Vernon.

Munsch, G. (1966) Physical maturity and mature driving, *Proceedings of the 2nd Congress of the International Association of Accident and Traffic Medicine*, 2, Stockholm (H. B. Wolf and E. Forsberg, Eds.), Kirurgiska Universitetskliniken, Malmo, Sweden.

Murray, H. A. (1938) *Exploration in Personality*, Oxford Univ. Press, London.

National Safety Council, *Accident Facts*, 1968 edn., Chicago.

Nau, E. (1966) The personality of the juvenile traffic offender, *Proceedings of the 1966 International Road Safety Congress, Barcelona*.

Neavles, J. C. and Winokur, J. (1957) The hot-rod driver, *Bull. Menninger Clinic* **21** (1), 28–35.

New York Times (1964) "Accidents called a major disease", leading article by Robert Darnton, 20 December 1964.

Newbold, E. M. (1926) *A Contribution to the Study of the Human Factor in the Causation of Accidents*, Report Industrial Health Research Board, London, No. 34.

Norman, L. G. (1962) *Road Traffic Accidents: Epidemiology, Control and Prevention*, Public Health Papers No. 12, World Health Organization, Geneva.

Nota Verkeersveiligheid (1967) SWOV, The Hague, Holland.

Parry, M. H. (1968) *Aggression on the Road*, Tavistock Publications, London, New York, Sydney, Toronto, Wellington.

Payne, E. J. (1919) *Education in Accident Prevention*, Lyons & Carnaham, Chicago.

Porterfield, A. L. (1960) Traffic fatalities, suicide and homicide, *Am. Sociol. Rev.* **25**, 897–901.

Quenault, S. W. (1966) *Some Methods of Obtaining Information on Driver Behaviour*, Road Research Laboratory Report LR 25.

Quenault, S. W. (1967) *Driver Behaviour—Safe and Unsafe Drivers*, I, Road Research Laboratory Report LR 70.

Quenault, S. W. (1968) *Driver Behaviour—Safe and Unsafe Drivers*, II, Road Research Laboratory Report LR 146.

Quenault, S. W., Goldby, C.W., and Pryer, P. M. (1968) *Age Group and Accident Rate—Driving Behaviour and Attitudes*, Road Research Laboratory Report LR 167.

REITER, R. (1953) Verkehrsunfallziffern aus dem Raum Mitteleuropa und ihre Bezeichungen zu bioklimatologischen Indikatoren, *Munsch. Med. Wschr.* **2.**

ROMMEL, R. C. S. (1959) Personality characteristics and attitudes of youthful accident repeating drivers, *Traff. Saf. Res. Rev.* **3** (1), 13–14.

ROSS, H. L. (1960) Traffic law violation: a folk crime, *Social Problems* **8** (3), 231–41.

SCHNEIDER, W. and SCHUBERT, G. (1967) Die Begutachtung der Fahrereignung, *Handbuch der Psychologie in 12 Bänden*; Sonderdruck aus Band 11, *Forenische Psychologie* (Ed. Undeutsch, U.), Göttingen.

SCHUBERT, G. (1965) Zusammenstellung von bisherigen wissenschaftlichen Untersuchungen über Prädiktoren und Kriterien des sicheren Kraftfahrens, *Die Auswirkung von Konstitution und Persönlichkeit auf die Unfallgefährdung im Verkehr*, Ministry of Health, Bonn, West Germany.

SCHUBERT, G. (1967) Untersuchung der verkehrsspezifischen Haltungen und Meinungen von Kraftfahrern durch Fragebogen, *Die Auswirkung von Konstitution und Persönlichkeit auf die Unfallgefährdung im Verkehr* (Gevielfältigtes Manuskript.)

SCHUBERT, G. and SPOERER, E. (1967) Untersuchungsverfahren zur Begutachtung von Kraftfahrern, *Die Auswirkung von Konstitution und Persönlichkeit auf die Unfallgefährdung im Verkehr*, Ministry of Health, Bonn, West Germany.

SCHULZINGER, M. S. (1956) *The Accident Syndrome*, C. C. Thomas, Springfield, Ill.

SCHUSTER, D. H. (1968) Prediction of Follow-up driving accidents, *Traff. Saf. Res. Rev.* **12,** 17–21.

SCHUSTER, D. H. and GUILFORD, J. P. (1962) The Psychometric Prediction of Problem Drivers, *Traff. Saf. Res. Rev.* **6,** 16–20.

SELZER, M. L. (1961) Personality versus intoxication as a critical factor in accidents caused by alcoholic drivers, *J. Nerv. Men. Dis.* **132,** 298–303.

SELZER, M. L. (1965) *Alcoholism, Mental Illness and Stress in 96 Drivers Causing Fatal Accidents*, Univ. of Michigan Medical School and Highway Safety Research Institute.

SELZER, M. L., PAYNE, C. E., GIFFORD, J. D., and KELLY, W. L. (1963) Alcoholism, mental illness, and the drunk driver, *Am. J. Psychiat.* **120,** 326–31.

SELZER, M. L., ROGERS, J. E., and KERN, S. (1968) Fatal accidents: the role of psychopathology, social stress, and acute disturbance, *Am. J. Psychiat.* **124,** 8.

SHAW, LYNETTE (1965) The practical use of projective personality tests as accident predictors, *Traff. Saf. Res. Rev.* **9** (2), 34–72. Also condensation in *Int. Rd. Saf. Traff. Rev.* (Winter 1966), World Touring and Automobile Association, London **14** (1), 30–37.

SHAW, LYNETTE and SICHEL, H. S. (1961) The reduction of accidents in a transport company by the determination of the accident liability of individual drivers, *Traff. Saf. Res. Rev.* **5** (4), 2–12.

SICHEL, H. S. (1965) The statistical estimation of individual accident liability. *Traff. Saf. Res. Rev.* **9** (1), 8–15.

SKELLY, G. B. (1968) *Aspects of Driving Experience in the First Year as a Qualified Driver*, Road Research Laboratory Report LR 149

SLOCOMBE, C. S. and BINGHAM, W. V. (1927) Men who have accidents, *Personnel J.* **6,** 251–7.

SLOCOMBE, C. S. and BRAKEMAN, E. E. (1930) Psychological tests and accident proneness, *Brit. J. Psychol.* **21,** 29–38.

SMEED, R. J. (1949) Some statistical aspects of road safety research, *JR Statis. Soc.* A, **112,** 1949.

SMEED, R. J. (1960) Proneness of drivers to road accidents, *Nature, London* **186,** 273–5.

SOUTH AFRICAN ROAD SAFETY COUNCIL (1965) Research project on personality tests, unpublished report by SHAW, L. and SICHEL, H. S.

SPANGENBERG, H. H. (1968) The use of projective tests in the selection of bus drivers, *Traff. Saf. Res. Rev.* **12,** 118–21.

STEVENS, W. L. (1957) Shorter intervals for the parameter of the binomial and Poisson distributions, *Biometrika* **44,** 436–40.

STEYN, D. G. (1967) How to make our traffic ways safer, with special reference to ethyl alcohol, drugs, disease and diet, read at the Annual Congress of the South African Association for the Advancement of Science.

SUCHMAN, E. A. (1961) A conceptual analysis of the accident phenomenon, *Behavioral Approaches to Accident Research*, Association for the Aid of Crippled Children, New York, pp. 26–47.

SUCHMAN, E. A. and SCHERZER, A. L. (1960) *Current Research in Childhood Accidents*, Association for the Aid of Crippled Children, New York.

SYMONDS, P. M. (1928) *The Nature of Conduct*, Macmillan, New York.

TENNEY, E. A. (1962) *The Highway Jungle. The Story of the Public Safety Movement and the Failure of "Driver Education" in the Public Schools*, Exposition Press, New York.

THORNDIKE, E. L. (1903) *Educational Psychology*, Teacher's College, New York.

THORNDIKE, R. L. (1951) *The Human Factors in Accidents with Special Reference to Aircraft Accidents*, Project 21–30–001, Report 1, US Air Force, School of Aviation Medicine, Randolph Field, Texas.

TILLMANN, W. A. and HOBBS, G. E. (1949) The accident-prone automobile driver, *Am. J. Psychiat.* **106** (5), 321–31.

TILLMANN, W. A., HARRIS, L. H., PHIPPS, MARGARET A., and HOWE, J. L. (1965) *Group Therapy Amongst Persons Involved in Frequent Automobile Accidents*, Report of the US Army Medical Research and Development Command, Washington, DC.

Traffic Digest and Review (1965) *The Senior Driver*, Northwestern Univ. Evanston, Ill., March, 1963.

UNDEUTSCH, U. (1963) *Persönlichkeit und Vorkommens-häufigheit der "Unfäller" unter den Kraftfahren*, Kirschbaum Verlag, Bad Godesberg.

UNITED STATES DEPARTMENT OF TRANSPORTATION (1968) *Alcohol and Highway Safety*, Washington, DC.

VAN DER BURGH, A. (1966) Het verschil tussen man en vrouw in het wegverkeer, *Verkeerstijdschrift*, Aug.–Sept., The Hague, Holland.

VAN DER BURGH, A. (1968) Het gewicht van de menselijke factor in het wegverkeer (as yet unpublished).

VAN DER BURGH, A. (1969) Beschouwingen met betrekking tot de Nota Verkeersveiligheid, *Psychologie* **12** (7), 437–59.

VILARDO, F. (1967) *Historical Development of the Concept of Accident Proneness*, National Safety Council publication, Chicago.

VITELES, M. S. (1932) *Industrial Psychology*, W. W. Norton, New York.

WALBEEHM, T. B. (1960) *The Accident-Prone Driver*, World Touring and Automobile Organization, London.

WALLIS, W. A. and ROBERTS, H. V. (1960) *Statistics: A New Approach*, 8th edn., Methuen, London.

WATSON, J. B. (1930) *Behaviourism*, Kegan Paul, London.

WELFORD, A. T. (1951) *Skill and Age*, Nuffield Foundation, London.

WELFORD, A. T. (1958) *Ageing and Human Skill*, Nuffield Foundation, London.

WELFORD, A. T. (1962) On changes of performance with age, *Lancet* **1**, 335–9.

WHITFIELD, J. W. (1954) *A Preliminary Enquiry into the Evidence for Individual Differences in Accident Liability among Coal Miners*, Applied Psychology Unit No. 71.

WILLETT, T. C. (1964) *Criminal on the Road*, Tavistock Publications, London.

WONG, W. A. and HOBBS, G. E. (1949) Personal factors in industrial accidents: A study of accident proneness in an industrial group, *Industr. Med. Surg.* **18**, 291–4.

WORLD HEALTH ORGANIZATION (1956) *Guiding Principles in the Medical Examination of Applicants for Motor Vehicle Permits*, WHO/Accid. Prevent./1, Rev. 2, Geneva.

WORLD HEALTH ORGANIZATION (1962) *Road Traffic Accidents* by L. G. NORMAN, Public Health Papers No. 12, Geneva.

WORLD HEALTH ORGANIZATION (1966) *Report of the Inter-regional Seminar on the Epidemiology, Control and Prevention of Road Accidents*, WHO/Accid. Prevent. 66/6, Geneva.

AUTHOR INDEX

SUBJECT INDEX